Microsoft Office Access Complete 2013

A SKILLS APPROACH

Cheri Manning

Catherine Manning Swinson

Triad Interactive, Inc

MICROSOFT OFFICE ACCESS 2013: A SKILLS APPROACH
Published by McGraw-Hill Education, 2 Penn Plaza, New York, NY 10121. Copyright © 2014 by McGraw-Hill Education. All rights reserved. Printed in the United States of America. No part of this publication may be reproduced or distributed in any form or by any means, or stored in a database or retrieval system, without the prior written consent of McGraw-Hill Education, including, but not limited to, in any network or other electronic storage or transmission, or broadcast for distance learning.

Some ancillaries, including electronic and print components, may not be available to customers outside the United States.

This book is printed on acid-free paper.

1 2 3 4 5 6 7 8 9 0 RMN/RMN 1 0 9 8 7 6 5

ISBN   978-0-07-739423-3
MHID   0-07-739423-2

Senior Vice President, Products & Markets: *Kurt L. Strand*
Vice President, Content Production & Technology Services: *Kimberly Meriwether David*
Director: *Scott Davidson*
Senior Brand Manager: *Wyatt Morris*
Executive Director of Development: *Ann Torbert*
Development Editor: *Alan Palmer*
Development Editor: *Allison McCabe*
Digital Development Editor: *Kevin White*
Marketing Manager: *Tiffany Russell*
Content Project Manager: *Rick Hecker*
Content Project Manager: *Brent dela Cruz*
Buyer: *Nichole Birkenholz*
Design: *Lisa King*
Cover Image: © *Burazin/Photographer's Choice/Getty Images*
Content Licensing Specialist: *Joanne Mennemeier*
Typeface: *10.5/13 Garamond Premier Pro Regular*
Compositor: *Laserwords Private Limited*
Printer: *R. R. Donnelley*

All credits appearing on page or at the end of the book are considered to be an extension of the copyright page.

Library of Congress Cataloging-in-Publication Data

Manning, Cheri.
    Microsoft Office Access complete 2013 : a skills approach / Cheri Manning, Catherine Manning Swinson.
        pages cm
    ISBN 978-0-07-739423-3 (alk. paper)
    1. Database management. 2. Microsoft Access. I. Swinson, Catherine Manning. II. Title.
    QA76.9.D3M337443 2014
005.75'85—dc23   2014040123

The Internet addresses listed in the text were accurate at the time of publication. The inclusion of a website does not indicate an endorsement by the authors or McGraw-Hill Education, and McGraw-Hill Education does not guarantee the accuracy of the information presented at these sites.

www.mhhe.com

brief contents

office 2013

1	Essential Skills for Office 2013	OF-2

access 2013

1	Getting Started with Access 2013	AC-2
2	Working with Tables	AC-50
3	Working with Forms and Reports	AC-100
4	Using Queries and Organizing Information	AC-150
5	Exploring Advanced Tables	AC-196
6	Exploring Advanced Forms	AC-248
7	Exploring Advanced Reports	AC-298
8	Exploring Advanced Queries and Macros	AC-336
9	Finalizing the Database	AC-374
	Appendix A	ACA-1
	Glossary	ACG-1
	Office Index	OFI-1
	Access Index	ACI-1
	Photo Credits	ACCR-1

contents

office 2013

chapter 1
Essential Skills for Office 2013 — OF-2

- Skill 1.1 Introduction to Microsoft Office 2013 — OF-3
- Skill 1.2 Opening Files — OF-6
- Skill 1.3 Closing Files — OF-8
- Skill 1.4 Getting to Know the Office 2013 User Interface — OF-9
- Skill 1.5 Using the Start Page — OF-14
- Skill 1.6 Changing Account Information — OF-15
- Skill 1.7 Changing the Look of Office — OF-17
- Skill 1.8 Working in Protected View — OF-18
- Skill 1.9 Picking Up Where You Left Off — OF-19
- Skill 1.10 Creating a New Blank File — OF-20
- Skill 1.11 Using Help — OF-21
- Skill 1.12 Working with File Properties — OF-22
- Skill 1.13 Saving Files to a Local Drive — OF-23
- Skill 1.14 Saving Files to a OneDrive — OF-25
- Skill 1.15 Saving Files with a New Name — OF-26
- Skill 1.16 Closing the Application — OF-27

access 2013

chapter 1
Getting Started with Access 2013 — AC-2

- Skill 1.1 Introduction to Access 2013 — AC-3
- Skill 1.2 Working with Security Warnings — AC-6
- Skill 1.3 Understanding and Viewing Table Relationships — AC-7
- Skill 1.4 Organizing Objects in the Navigation Pane — AC-10
- Skill 1.5 Switching between Database Object Views — AC-12
- Skill 1.6 Navigating Records — AC-14
- Skill 1.7 Creating a New Record in a Table — AC-16
- Skill 1.8 Creating a New Record in a Form — AC-18
- Skill 1.9 Finding and Replacing Data — AC-20
- Skill 1.10 Cutting, Copying, and Pasting Data — AC-22
- Skill 1.11 Using Undo and Redo — AC-23
- Skill 1.12 Deleting Records — AC-24
- Skill 1.13 Checking Spelling — AC-25
- Skill 1.14 Deleting and Renaming Database Objects — AC-26
- Skill 1.15 Exporting Data to Excel or Word — AC-27
- Skill 1.16 Exporting Data to a PDF File — AC-29
- Skill 1.17 Previewing and Printing Database Objects — AC-30
- Skill 1.18 Using Compact and Repair — AC-32
- Skill 1.19 Backing Up a Database — AC-33

chapter 2
Working with Tables — AC-50

- Skill 2.1 Designing a Table — AC-51
- Skill 2.2 Creating and Saving a Table in Datasheet View — AC-53

Skill 2.3	Renaming Fields	AC-54
Skill 2.4	Adding Fields in Datasheet View	AC-55
Skill 2.5	Using Quick Start to Add Related Fields	AC-56
Skill 2.6	Adjusting Table Column Widths	AC-57
Skill 2.7	Creating a Table in Design View	AC-58
Skill 2.8	Inserting Fields in Design View	AC-59
Skill 2.9	Setting the Primary Key	AC-60
Skill 2.10	Deleting Fields	AC-61
Skill 2.11	Changing Data Type	AC-62
Skill 2.12	Formatting Fields	AC-64
Skill 2.13	Modifying Field Properties	AC-66
Skill 2.14	Applying an Input Mask from Design View	AC-68
Skill 2.15	Working with Attachment Fields	AC-70
Skill 2.16	Adding a Total Row to a Table	AC-72
Skill 2.17	Adding a Lookup Field from Another Table	AC-73
Skill 2.18	Adding a Lookup Field from a List	AC-78
Skill 2.19	Creating Relationships	AC-80

chapter 3
Working with Forms and Reports — AC-100

Skill 3.1	Creating a Single Record Form Based on a Table or Query	AC-101
Skill 3.2	Creating a Multiple Items Form	AC-102
Skill 3.3	Creating a Split Form	AC-103
Skill 3.4	Creating a Form Using the Form Wizard	AC-104
Skill 3.5	Creating a New Blank Form	AC-107
Skill 3.6	Adding Fields to a Form in Layout View	AC-108
Skill 3.7	Creating a Basic Report Based on a Table or Query	AC-111
Skill 3.8	Creating a Report Using the Report Wizard	AC-112
Skill 3.9	Creating a New Blank Report	AC-116
Skill 3.10	Adding Fields to a Report in Layout View	AC-117
Skill 3.11	Formatting Controls	AC-118
Skill 3.12	Applying a Theme	AC-120
Skill 3.13	Resizing Controls	AC-121
Skill 3.14	Moving and Arranging Controls	AC-122
Skill 3.15	Adding Design Elements to Form and Report Headers	AC-124
Skill 3.16	Adding Page Numbers to Reports	AC-126
Skill 3.17	Grouping Records in a Report	AC-127
Skill 3.18	Adding Totals to a Report	AC-129
Skill 3.19	Previewing and Printing a Report	AC-130
Skill 3.20	Controlling the Page Setup of a Report for Printing	AC-132

chapter 4
Using Queries and Organizing Information — AC-150

Skill 4.1	Using the Simple Query Wizard	AC-151
Skill 4.2	Creating a Query in Design View	AC-154
Skill 4.3	Adding Text Criteria to a Query	AC-157
Skill 4.4	Adding Numeric and Date Criteria to a Query	AC-160
Skill 4.5	Using AND and OR in a Query	AC-162
Skill 4.6	Specifying the Sort Order in a Query	AC-166

Skill	4.7	Hiding and Showing Fields in a Query	AC-167
Skill	4.8	Adding a Calculated Field to a Query	AC-168
Skill	4.9	Finding Unmatched Data Using a Query	AC-170
Skill	4.10	Finding Duplicate Data Using a Query	AC-173
Skill	4.11	Using a Parameter Query	AC-176
Skill	4.12	Filtering Data Using AutoFilter	AC-178
Skill	4.13	Filtering Data Using Filter by Selection	AC-180
Skill	4.14	Sorting Records in a Datasheet	AC-182

Chapter 5
Exploring Advanced Tables — AC-196

Skill	5.1	Creating a Desktop Database from a Template	AC-197
Skill	5.2	Creating a New Blank Database	AC-200
Skill	5.3	Using Quick Start Application Parts	AC-202
Skill	5.4	Importing Data from Excel	AC-204
Skill	5.5	Importing Data from a Text File	AC-209
Skill	5.6	Adding Records to a Table by Importing	AC-214
Skill	5.7	Linking to a Table in Another Access Database	AC-217
Skill	5.8	Adding a Calculated Field to a Table	AC-220
Skill	5.9	Creating a Custom Text Field Format	AC-222
Skill	5.10	Creating a Custom Input Mask	AC-224
Skill	5.11	Modifying Lookup Field Properties	AC-226
Skill	5.12	Creating Field Validation Rules	AC-228
Skill	5.13	Creating Record Validation Rules	AC-230
Skill	5.14	Enforcing Deletions and Updates in Relationships	AC-232

Chapter 6
Exploring Advanced Forms — AC-248

Skill	6.1	Creating a Blank Form from an Application Part	AC-249
Skill	6.2	Working with a New Form in Design View	AC-250
Skill	6.3	Setting the Sort Order in a Form	AC-252
Skill	6.4	Controlling Data Entry in a Form	AC-253
Skill	6.5	Controlling Data Entry for a Field in a Form	AC-255
Skill	6.6	Disabling User Interface Elements in a Form	AC-256
Skill	6.7	Adding a List Box Control to a Form	AC-257
Skill	6.8	Adding a Command Button Control to a Form	AC-260
Skill	6.9	Adding a Combo Box Control to a Form	AC-263
Skill	6.10	Adding a Subform Based on a Table or Query	AC-266
Skill	6.11	Adding a Subform Based on a Form	AC-269
Skill	6.12	Modifying the Subform Properties	AC-272
Skill	6.13	Displaying the Form Header and Footer	AC-274
Skill	6.14	Adding Images to Forms	AC-275
Skill	6.15	Creating a Navigation Form with Tabs	AC-277
Skill	6.16	Defining the Tab Order of Controls	AC-280

Chapter 7
Exploring Advanced Reports — AC-298

- Skill 7.1 Working with a Report in Design View — AC-299
- Skill 7.2 Understanding Report Sections — AC-301
- Skill 7.3 Arranging Controls in a Report — AC-303
- Skill 7.4 Adding Calculated Controls to a Report — AC-304
- Skill 7.5 Adding Report Grouping in Design View — AC-306
- Skill 7.6 Working with Group Headers and Footers — AC-307
- Skill 7.7 Hiding Repeated Values in a Report — AC-309
- Skill 7.8 Adding a Subreport Based on a Report — AC-310
- Skill 7.9 Displaying the Subreport Page Header — AC-313
- Skill 7.10 Adding a Subreport Based on a Table or Query — AC-314
- Skill 7.11 Applying Conditional Formatting to a Report — AC-317

Chapter 8
Exploring Advanced Queries and Macros — AC-336

- Skill 8.1 Understanding Action Queries — AC-337
- Skill 8.2 Updating Records through a Query — AC-338
- Skill 8.3 Creating a New Table through a Query — AC-340
- Skill 8.4 Deleting Records through a Query — AC-342
- Skill 8.5 Moving Records through a Query — AC-344
- Skill 8.6 Setting Join Properties in a Query — AC-346
- Skill 8.7 Adding Totals to a Query — AC-348
- Skill 8.8 Creating a Crosstab Query — AC-351
- Skill 8.9 Modifying a Query in SQL View — AC-354
- Skill 8.10 Creating a Stand-Alone Macro — AC-358

Chapter 9
Finalizing the Database — AC-374

- Skill 9.1 Using the Table Analyzer — AC-375
- Skill 9.2 Using the Performance Analyzer — AC-379
- Skill 9.3 Viewing Dependencies — AC-380
- Skill 9.4 Customizing the Navigation Pane — AC-381
- Skill 9.5 Configuring Database Startup Options — AC-383
- Skill 9.6 Limiting Views and Design Options — AC-385
- Skill 9.7 Splitting a Database — AC-386
- Skill 9.8 Creating a Locked ACCDE File — AC-388
- Skill 9.9 Encrypting a Database with a Password — AC-389
- Skill 9.10 Using the Database Documenter — AC-391
- Skill 9.11 Printing the Relationship Report — AC-392

Appendix A — ACA-1
Glossary — ACG-1
Office Index — OFI-1
Access Index — ACI-1
Photo Credits — ACCR-1

preface

How well do you know Microsoft Office? Many students can follow specific step-by-step directions to re-create a document, spreadsheet, presentation, or database, but do they truly understand the skills it takes to create these on their own? Just as simply following a recipe does not make you a professional chef, re-creating a project step by step does not make you an Office expert.

The purpose of this book is to teach you the skills to master Microsoft Office 2013 in a straightforward and easy-to-follow manner. But *Microsoft® Office 2013 Access Complete: A Skills Approach* goes beyond the **how** and equips you with a deeper understanding of the **what** and the **why**. Too many times books have little value beyond the classroom. The *Skills Approach* series has been designed to be not only a complete textbook but also a reference tool for you to use as you move beyond academics and into the workplace.

WHAT'S NEW IN THIS EDITION

This edition of the *Skills Approach* text includes a *Let Me Try* exercise and student data file for each skill. These exercises are the same as the simulated *Let Me Try* exercises in SIMnet 2013. We included the student data files to give students the opportunity to explore the skill in the live application in addition to practicing it in a simulated environment (SIMnet).

The *Let Me Try* exercises are not intended as a running project or case study. Each *Let Me Try* data file is independent of the others, so the skills may be taught in any order.

ABOUT TRIAD INTERACTIVE

Triad Interactive specializes in online education and training products. Our flagship program is SIMnet—a simulated Microsoft Office learning and assessment application developed for the McGraw-Hill Companies. Triad has been writing, programming, and managing the SIMnet system since 1999.

Triad is also actively involved in online health education and in research projects to assess the usefulness of technology for helping high-risk populations make decisions about managing their cancer risk and treatment.

about the authors

CHERI MANNING

Cheri Manning is the president and co-owner of Triad Interactive. She is the author of the Microsoft Excel and Access content for the *Skills Approach* series and SIMnet. She has been authoring instructional content for these applications for more than 12 years.

Cheri began her career as an Aerospace Education Specialist with the Education Division of the National Aeronautics and Space Administration (NASA), where she produced materials for K–12 instructors and students. Prior to founding Triad, Cheri was a project manager with Compact Publishing, where she managed the development of McGraw-Hill's Multimedia MBA CD-ROM series.

CATHERINE MANNING SWINSON

Catherine Manning Swinson is the vice president and co-owner of Triad Interactive. She is the author of the Microsoft Word and PowerPoint content for the *Skills Approach* series and SIMnet. She also authors SIMnet content for Microsoft Outlook, Windows, and Internet Explorer. She has been authoring instructional content for these applications for more than 12 years.

Catherine began her career at Compact Publishing, one of the pioneers in educational CD-ROM-based software. She was the lead designer at Compact and designed every edition of the *TIME Magazine Compact Almanac* from 1992 through 1996. In addition, she designed a number of other products with Compact, including the *TIME Man of the Year* program and the *TIME 20th Century Almanac*.

acknowledgments

CONTRIBUTORS

Kelly Morber, *Saints Philip and James School, English teacher and Malone University*, M.A.Ed.
Timothy T. Morber, MEd, LPCC-S, *Malone University*

TECHNICAL EDITORS

Menka Brown
Piedmont Technical College

Sylvia Brown
Midland College

Mary Locke
Greenville Technical College

Daniela Marghitu
Auburn University

Judy Settle
Central Georgia Technical College

Pamela Silvers
Asheville-Buncombe Technical College

Candace Spangler
Columbus State Community College

Debbie Zaidi
Seneca College

REVIEWERS

Our thanks go to all who participated in the development of *Microsoft Office 2013: A Skills Approach*.

Sven Aelterman
Troy University

Nick Agrawal
Calhoun Community College

Laura Anderson
Weber State University

Viola Bain
Scott Community College

Greg Ballinger
Miami Dade College

Bill Barzen
Saint Petersburg College

Julia Bell
Walters State Community College

Don Belle
Central Piedmont Community College

Judy Boozer
Lane Community College

Ben Brah
Auburn University

Sheryl Starkey Bulloch
Columbia Southern University

Kate Burkes
Northwest Arkansas Community College

Michael Callahan
Lone Star College

Patricia Casey
Trident Technical College

Wally Cates
Central New Mexico Community College

Jimmy Chen
Salt Lake Community College

Sharon Cotman
Thomas Nelson Community College

Susan Cully
Long Beach City College

Jennifer Day
Sinclair Community College

Ralph De Arazoza
Miami Dade College

Bruce Elliot
Tarrant County College

Bernice Eng
Brookdale Community College

Penny Fanzone
Community College of Baltimore County

Valerie Farmer
Community College of Baltimore County

Jean Finley
Asheville-Buncombe Technical Community College

George Fiori
Tri-County Technical College

Deborah Godwin
Lake-Sumter Community College

Cathy Grant-Churchwell
Lane Community College

Diana Green
Weber State University

Joseph Greer
Midlands Technical College

Debra Gross
Ohio State University

Rachelle Hall
Glendale Community College

Dexter Harlee
York Technical College

Marilyn Hibbert
Salt Lake Community College

Judy Irvine
Seneca College

Sherry E. Jacob
Jefferson Community & Technical College

Linda Johnsonius
Murray State University

Rich Klein
Clemson University

Kevin Lee
Guilford Technical Community College

Mohamed Lotfy
Regis University

Carol Martin
Central Pennsylvania Community College

Sue McCrory
Missouri State University

Ken Moak
Tarrant County College

Cecil Morris
American Intercontinental University

Kathleen Morris
University of Alabama

Patrick J. Nedry
Monroe County Community College

Mitchell Ober
Tulsa Community College

Ashlee Pieris
Raritan Valley Community College

Pamela Silvers
Asheville–Buncombe Technical Community College

Bonnie Smith
Fresno City College

Randy Smith
Monterey Peninsula College

W. Randy Somsen
Brigham Young University–Idaho

Nathan Stout
University of Oklahoma

Carl Struck
Suffolk Community College

Song Su
East Los Angeles College

Kathleen Tamerlano
Cuyahoga Community College

Margaret Taylor
College of Southern Nevada

Debby Telfer
Colorado Technical University

David Trimble
Park University

Georgia Vanderark
Stark State College

Philip Vavalides
Guilford Technical Community College

Dennis Walpole
University of South Florida

Michael Walton
Miami Dade College

Paul Weaver
Bossier Parish Community College

Nima Zahadat
Northern Virginia Community College

Debbie Zaidi
Seneca College

Matthew Zullo
Wake Tech Community College

Instructor Walkthrough

Microsoft Office Access Complete 2013: A Skills Approach

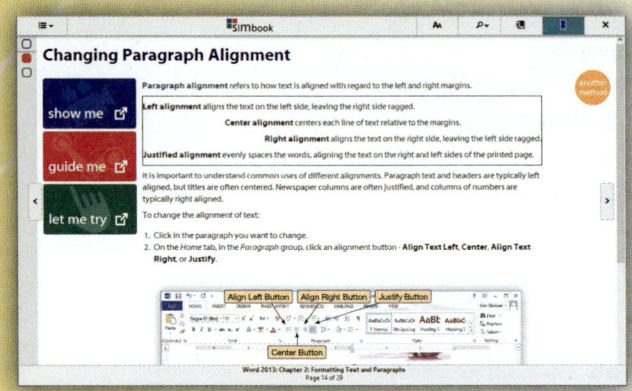

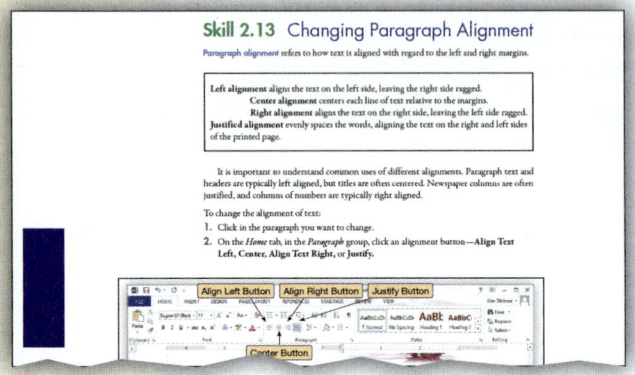

> 1-1 Content in SIMnet for Office 2013

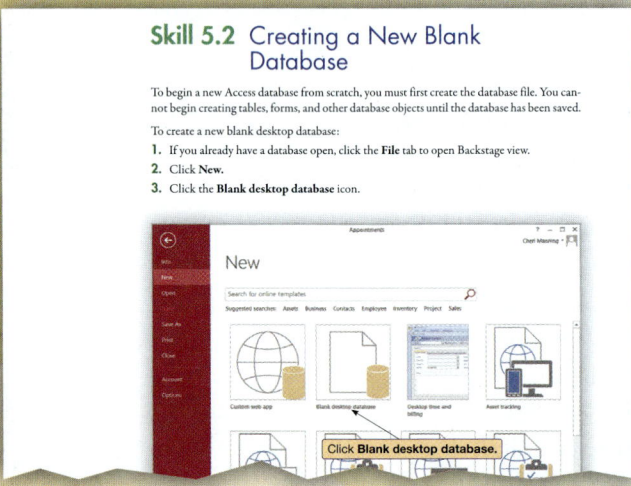

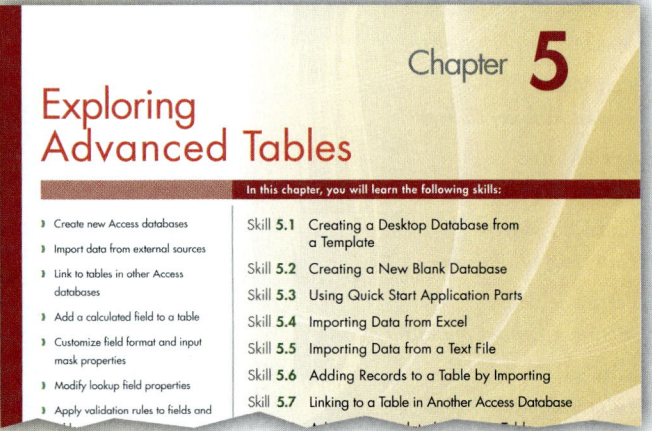

> At-a-glance Office 2013 skills

Quick, easy-to-scan pages, for efficient learning

> Introduction—Learning Outcomes are clearly listed.

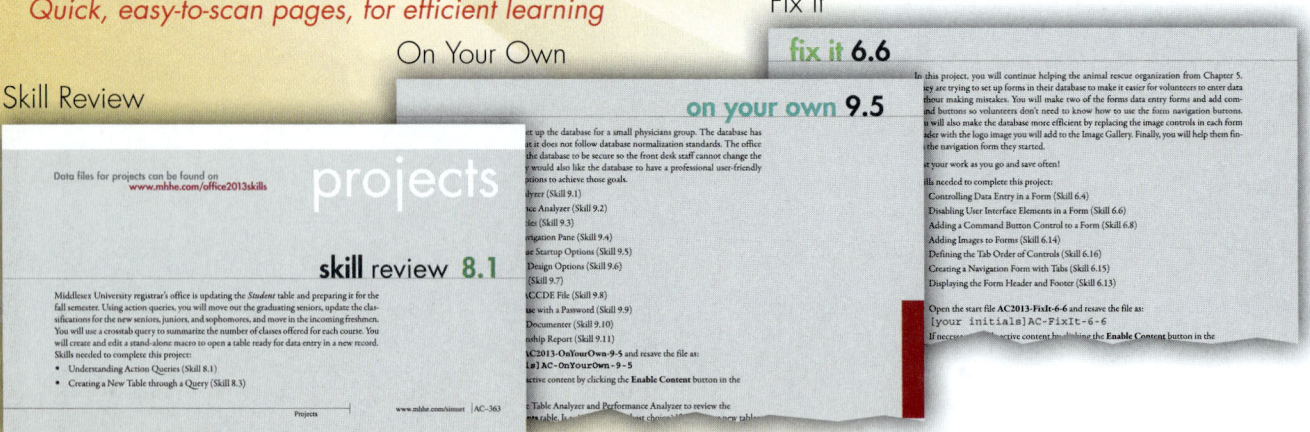

> Diverse end-of-chapter projects

Projects that relate to a broad range of careers and perspectives, from nursing, education, business, and everyday personal uses

Features

From the Perspective of…

SPORTING GOODS STORE PURCHASING MANAGER

Our store keeps inventory, purchasing, and sales in separate databases. We use a series of linked tables to keep tables up-to-date between database files. When I receive a shipment of goods from a purchase order, I import the information from the shipper (usually provided in a CSV file) into a linked table in my database. The original table in the inventory database is then updated automatically. A similar process happens with sales. When a sale is recorded in the sales database, the inventory database is updated automatically through the linked tables, which then updates the linked table in my database so I know when it's time to submit another purchase order. Without these links between databases, it would be a nightmare to keep track of inventory and to know when to order more.

Tips and Tricks

tips & tricks

Some of the database templates can be complicated, with many related tables. Before entering data, take some time to review the tables and table relationships. You should remove any unnecessary fields, but be careful not to remove a field that is part of a relationship.

another method

If you are opening the Access application directly, you begin at the Start page. Templates are listed at the right side of the page just as they are in the New page.

Tell Me More

tell me more

You can add totals to the group through the *Group, Sort, and Total* pane. In the orange bar for the group level, click the **More** button [More ▶] to view all the group options. Click **with no totals** to add totals. If totals have been added already, this button will display a brief description of the totals. You can click it to change the field or function and other totaling options.

let me try

If the database is not already open, open the data file **AC7-Sales** and try this skill on your own:
1. If it is not already open, open the **POsbyVendorReport** report in Design view.
2. Hide the group header.
3. Display the group footer.

Another Method

another method

› From Datasheet view, on the *Table Tools Fields* tab, in the *Add & Delete* group, click the **More Fields** button, point to **Calculated Field** at the bottom of the list, and click the field type you want to add.
› From Design view, add a new field, expand the **Data Type** list, and select **Calculated**. After you've created the expression in the Expression Builder, select the format for the calculated field through the Format property in the Field Properties pane.

let me try

If the database is not already open, open the data file **AC5-Sales** and try this skill on your own:
1. Open the **Inventory** table and add a new **Currency calculated field** to the far right of the table to calculate the retail value of the inventory stock for each item.

Let Me Try

let me try

If the database is not already open, open the data file **AC6-Sales** and try this skill on your own:
1. Open the **InventoryForm** form in Design view.
2. Set the **Inventory** table as the form's record source.
3. Add the **ItemID** field to the right of the **Field1:** label. Add the bound text control without the label control.
4. Save and close the form.

› **Instructor materials available on the online learning center, www.mhhe.com/office2013skills**

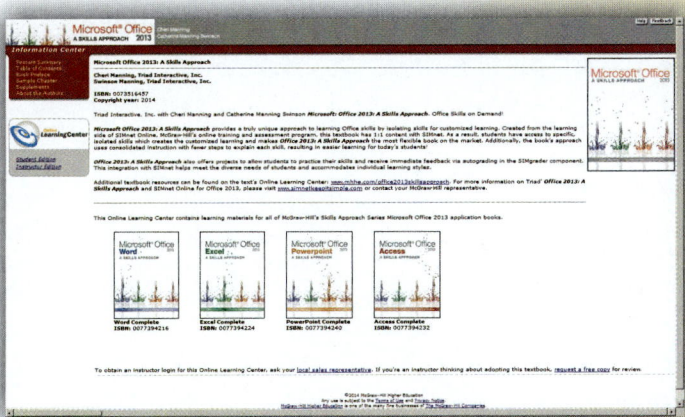

- Instructor Manual
- Instructor PowerPoints
- Test Bank

Instructor Walkthrough

SIMnet for Office 2013 Online Training & Assessment

❯ Includes:
- Microsoft® Office Suite
- Computer Concepts
- Windows 7
- Windows 8
- Browsers
- File Management

EASY TO USE

SIMnet is McGraw-Hill's leading solution for training and assessment of Microsoft Office skills and beyond. Completely online with no downloads for installation (besides requiring Adobe Flash Player), SIMnet is accessible for today's students through multiple browsers and is easy to use for all. Now, SIMnet offers SIMbook and allows students to go mobile for their student learning. Available with videos and interactive "Guide Me" pages to allow students to study MS Office skills on any device. Its consistent, clean user interface and functionality will help save you time and help students be more successful in their course.

LIFELONG LEARNING

SIMnet offers lifelong learning. SIMnet is designed with features to help students immediately learn isolated Microsoft Office skills on demand. Students can use SIMSearch and the Library to learn skills both in and beyond the course. It's more than a resource; it's a tool they can use throughout their entire time at your institution.

MEASURABLE RESULTS

SIMnet provides powerful, measureable results for you and your students. See results immediately in our various reports and customizable gradebook. Students can also see measurable results by generating a custom training lesson after an exam to help determine exactly which content areas they still need to study. Instructors can use the dashboard to see detailed results of student activity, assignment completion, and more. SIMnet Online is your solution for helping students master today's Microsoft Office Skills.

SIMNET FOR OFFICE 2013

...Keep IT SIMple! To learn more, visit www.simnetkeepitsimple.com and also contact your McGraw-Hill representative.

office 2013

chapter 1

Essential Skills for Office 2013

In this chapter, you will learn the following skills:

- Learn about Microsoft Office 2013 and its applications Word, Excel, PowerPoint, and Access
- Demonstrate how to open, save, and close files
- Recognize Office 2013 common features and navigation elements
- Modify account information and the look of Office
- Create new files
- Use Microsoft Help

Skill **1.1** Introduction to Microsoft Office 2013
Skill **1.2** Opening Files
Skill **1.3** Closing Files
Skill **1.4** Getting to Know the Office 2013 User Interface
Skill **1.5** Using the Start Page
Skill **1.6** Changing Account Information
Skill **1.7** Changing the Look of Office
Skill **1.8** Working in Protected View
Skill **1.9** Picking Up Where You Left Off
Skill **1.10** Creating a New Blank File
Skill **1.11** Using Help
Skill **1.12** Working with File Properties
Skill **1.13** Saving Files to a Local Drive
Skill **1.14** Saving Files to a OneDrive
Skill **1.15** Saving Files with a New Name
Skill **1.16** Closing the Application

introduction

This chapter introduces you to Microsoft Office 2013. You will learn about the shared features across the Office 2013 applications and how to navigate common interface elements such as the Ribbon and Quick Access Toolbar. You will learn how to open and close files as well as learn how to work with messages that appear when you first open files. You will become familiar with the Office account and learn how to modify the account as well as the look of Office 2013. Introductory features such as creating and closing files and using Office Help are explained.

Skill 1.1 Introduction to Microsoft Office 2013

Microsoft Office 2013 is a collection of business "productivity" applications (computer programs designed to make you more productive at work, school, and home). The most popular Office applications are:

Microsoft Word—A word processing program. Word processing software allows you to create text-based documents, similar to how you would type a document on a typewriter. However, word processing software offers more powerful formatting and design tools, allowing you to create complex documents, including reports, résumés, brochures, and newsletters.

FIGURE OF 1.1
Microsoft Word 2013

Microsoft Excel—A spreadsheet program. Originally, spreadsheet applications were viewed as electronic versions of an accountant's ledger. Today's spreadsheet applications can do much more than just calculate numbers—they include powerful charting and data analysis features. Spreadsheet programs can be used for everything from personal budgets to calculating loan payments.

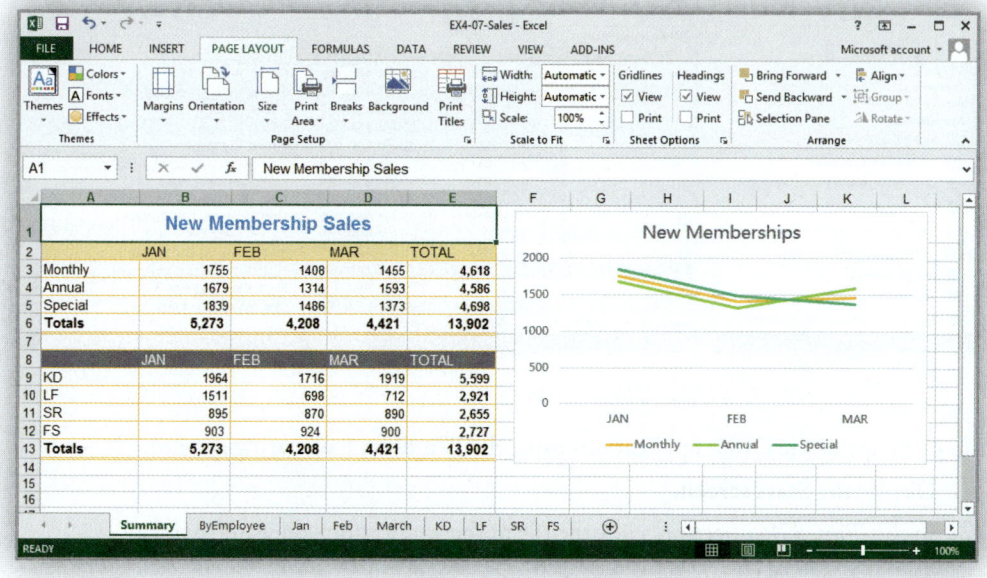

FIGURE OF 1.2
Microsoft Excel 2013

skill 1.1   Introduction to Microsoft Office 2013

Microsoft PowerPoint—A presentation program. Such applications enable you to create robust, multimedia presentations. A presentation consists of a series of electronic slides. Each slide contains content, including text, images, charts, and other objects. You can add multimedia elements to slides, including animations, audio, and video.

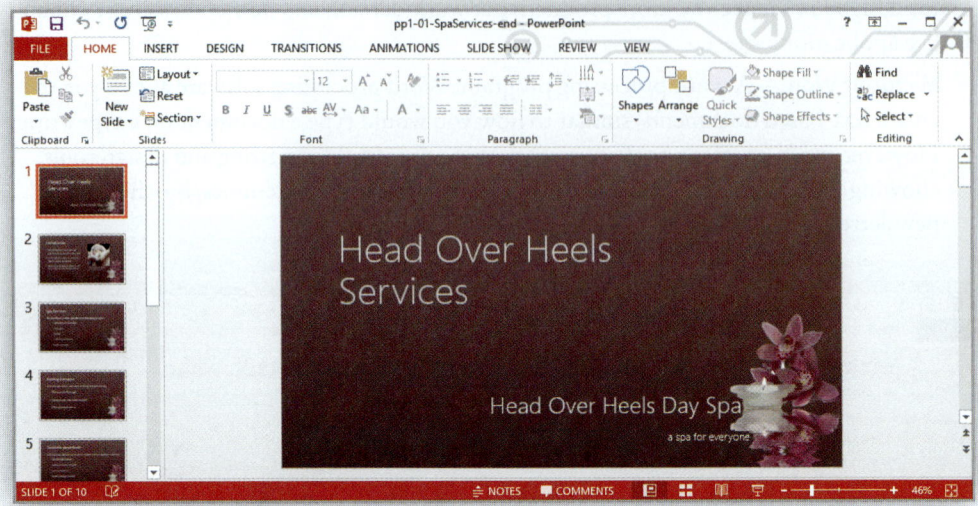

FIGURE OF 1.3
Microsoft PowerPoint 2013

Microsoft Access—A database program. Database applications allow you to organize and manipulate large amounts of data. Databases that allow you to relate tables and databases to one another are referred to as *relational* databases. As a database user, you usually see only one aspect of the database—a *form*. Database forms use a graphical interface to allow a user to enter record data. For example, when you fill out an order form online, you are probably interacting with a database. The information you enter becomes a record in a database *table*. Your order is matched with information in an inventory table (keeping track of which items are in stock) through a *query*. When your order is filled, a database *report* can be generated for use as an invoice or a bill of lading.

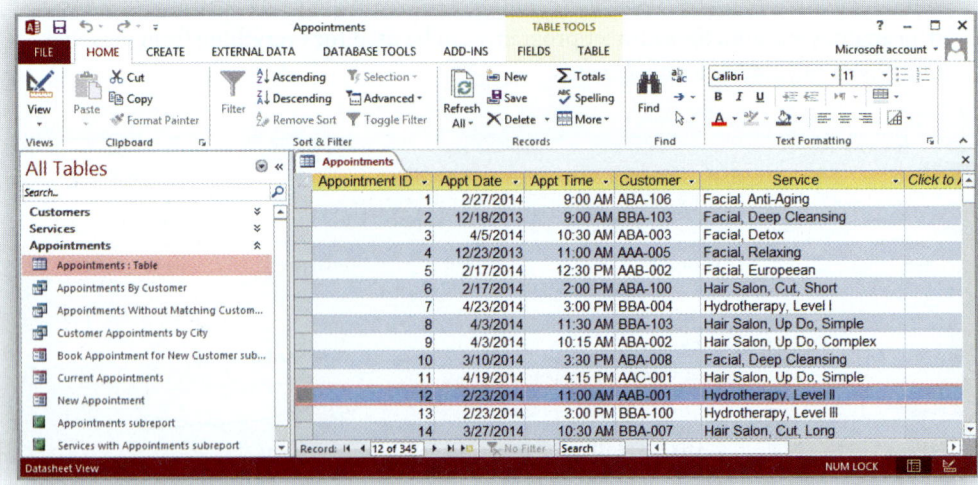

FIGURE OF 1.4
Microsoft Access 2013

To open one of the Office applications using the Windows 8 operating system:

1. Display the **Start screen.**
2. In the *Pinned Apps* section, click the tile of the application you want to open.

To open one of the Office applications using the Windows 7 operating system:

1. Click the Windows **Start** button (located in the lower left corner of your computer screen).
2. Click **All Programs.**
3. Click the **Microsoft Office** folder.
4. Click the application you want to open.

tips & tricks

You can download a free trial version of Microsoft Office from Microsoft's Web site (http://office.microsoft.com). The trial allows you to try the applications before buying them. When your trial period ends, if you haven't purchased the full software license yet, you will no longer be able to use the applications (although you will continue to be able to open and view any files you previously created with the trial version).

tell me more

There are two main versions of Microsoft Office, each offering a different way to pay for the program:

Office 365—This version allows you to download and install Office and pay for it on a yearly or monthly subscription basis. It includes full versions of the different Office applications along with online storage services for your files. When the next version of Office is released, the subscription can be transferred to the new version. If you do not want to install the full version of Office on your computer, you can access limited versions of each application online with an Office 365 subscription.

Office 2013—This version allows you to install Office and pay for it once, giving you a perpetual license for the programs. This means that when the next version of Office is released, you will need to purchase the application suite again. You can associate a Windows Live account with Office 2013, giving you access to online storage for your files.

If you are a home user, business, or a student, there are different purchasing options for both Office 365 and Office 2013. Both versions require that you are running the Windows 7 or Windows 8 operating system.

Skill 1.2 Opening Files

Opening a file retrieves it from storage and displays it on your computer screen. The steps for opening a file are the same for Word documents, Excel spreadsheets, PowerPoint presentations, and Access databases.

To open an existing file from your computer:

1. Click the **File** tab to open Backstage view.
2. Click **Open**.
3. The *Open* page displays listing the recently opened files by default.
4. Click **Computer**.
5. A list of folders you have recently opened files from appears on the right. Click a folder to open the **Open** dialog with that folder displayed.

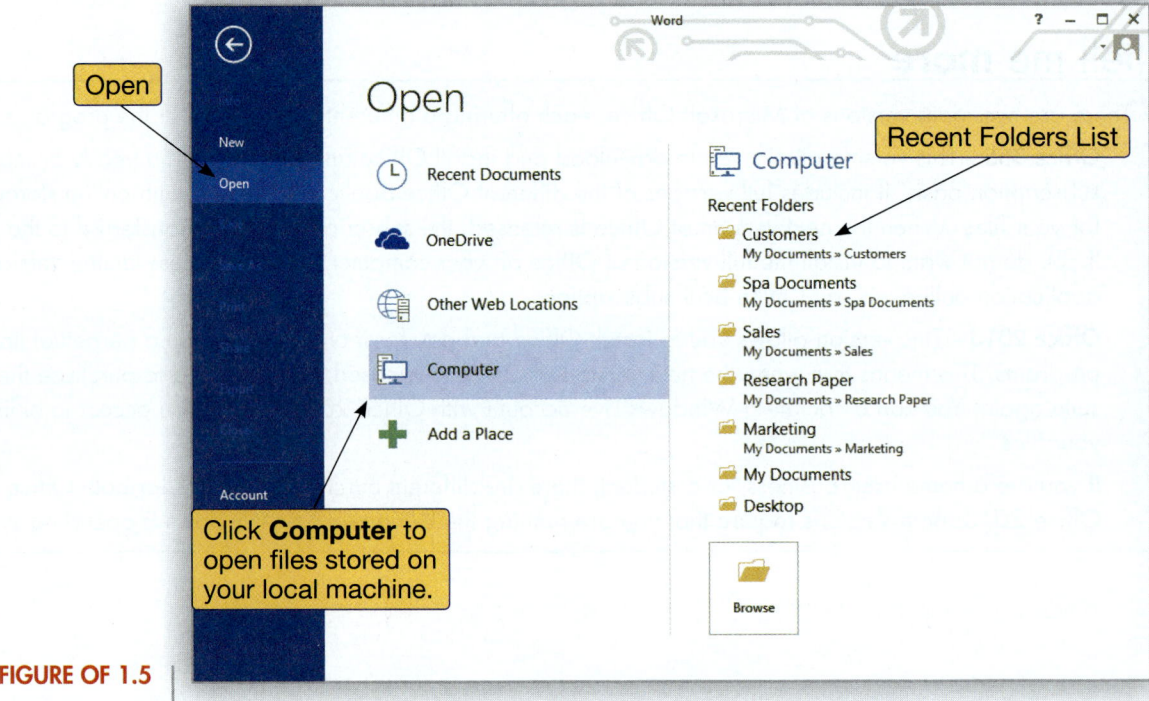

FIGURE OF 1.5

6. Select the file name you want to open in the large list box.
7. Click the **Open** button in the dialog.

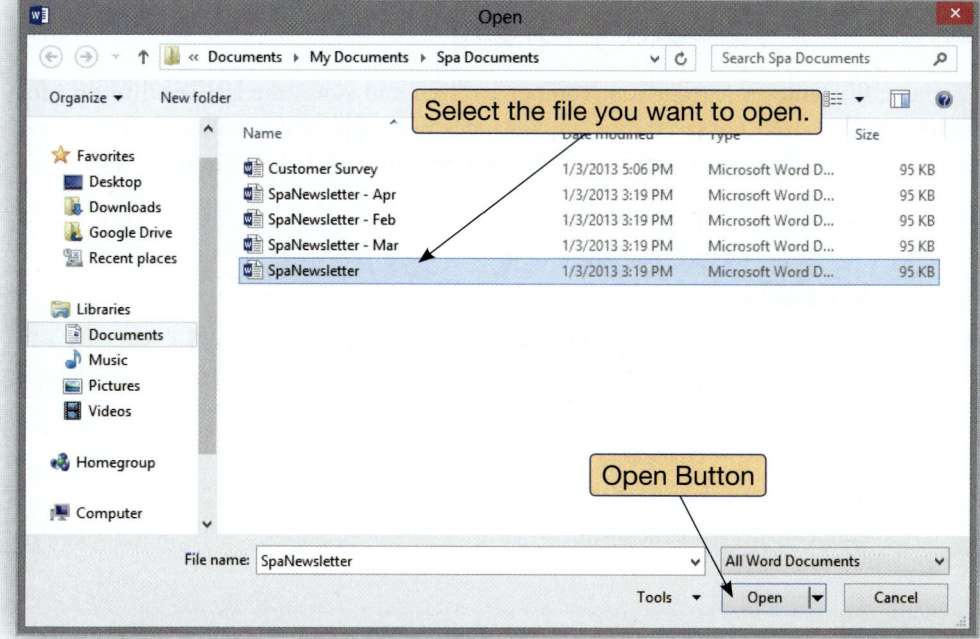

FIGURE OF 1.6

tips & tricks

If you do not see the folder containing the file you want to open, click the **Browse** button. The *Open* dialog will open to your *Documents* folder. Navigate to the location where the file you want to open is located, select the file, and click **Open.**

tell me more

The screen shot shown here is from Word 2013 running on the Microsoft Windows 8 operating system. Depending on the operating system you are using, the *Open* dialog will appear somewhat different. However, the basic steps for opening a file are the same regardless of which operating system you are using.

another method

To display the *Open* page in Backstage view, you can also press Ctrl + O on the keyboard.

To open the file from within the *Open* dialog, you can also:

- Press the Enter key once you have typed or selected a file name.
- Double-click the file name.

let me try

Try this skill on your own:
1. Open the student data file **of1-SpaNewsletter.**
   NOTE: You may see a yellow security message at the top of the window. See the skill *Working in Protected View* to learn more about security warning messages.
2. Keep the file open to work on the next skill.

skill 1.2   Opening Files

Skill 1.3 Closing Files

Closing a file removes it from your computer screen and stores the last-saved version for future use. If you have not saved your latest changes, most applications will prevent you from losing work by asking if you want to save the changes you made before closing.

To close a file and save your latest changes:

1. Click the **File** tab to open Backstage view.
2. Click the **Close** button.
3. If you have made no changes since the last time you saved the file, it will close immediately. If changes have been made, the application displays a message box asking if you want to save the changes you made before closing.

    Click **Save** to save the changes.

    Click **Don't Save** to close the file without saving your latest changes.

    Click **Cancel** to keep the file open.

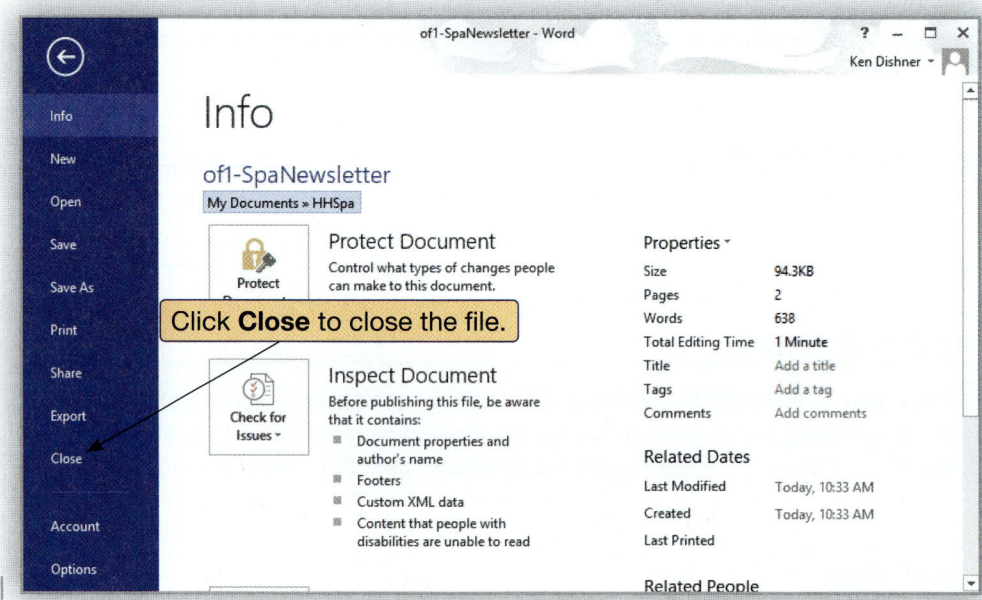

FIGURE OF 1.7

another method

To close a file, you can also press Ctrl + W on the keyboard.

let me try

If necessary, open the student data file **of1-SpaNewsletter** and try this skill on your own:
　　Close the file.

Skill 1.4 Getting to Know the Office 2013 User Interface

THE RIBBON

If you have used a word processing or spreadsheet program in the past, you may be surprised when you open one of the Microsoft Office 2013 applications for the first time. Beginning with Office 2007, Microsoft redesigned the user experience—replacing the familiar menu bar/toolbar interface with a new Ribbon interface that makes it easier to find application functions and commands.

The Ribbon is located across the top of the application window and organizes common features and commands into tabs. Each tab organizes commands further into related groups.

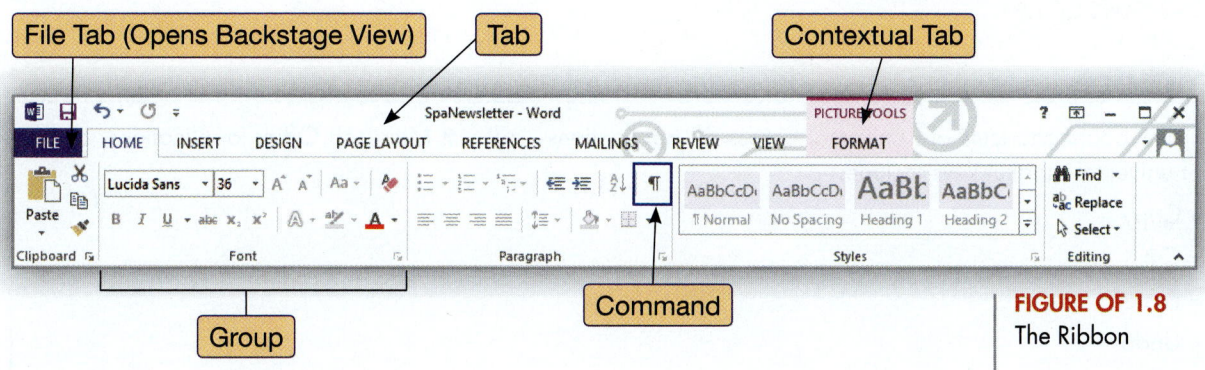

FIGURE OF 1.8
The Ribbon

When a specific type of object is selected (such as a picture, table, or chart), a contextual tab will appear. Contextual tabs contain commands specific to the type of object selected and are only visible when the commands might be useful.

Each application includes a Home tab that contains the most commonly used commands for that application. For example, in Word, the *Home* tab includes the following groups: *Clipboard, Font, Paragraph, Styles,* and *Editing,* while the Excel *Home* tab includes groups more appropriate for a spreadsheet program: *Clipboard, Font, Alignment, Number, Styles, Cells,* and *Editing.*

tips & tricks

If you need more space for your file, you can minimize the Ribbon by clicking the **Collapse the Ribbon** button in the upper-right corner of the Ribbon (or press Ctrl + F1). When the Ribbon is minimized, the tab names appear along the top of the window (similar to a menu bar). When you click a tab name, the Ribbon appears. After you select a command or click away from the Ribbon, the Ribbon hides again. To redisplay the Ribbon permanently, click the **Ribbon Display Options** button in the upper-right corner of the window and select **Show Tabs and Commands.** You can also double-click the active tab to hide or display the Ribbon.

BACKSTAGE

Notice that each application also includes a File tab at the far left side of the Ribbon. Clicking the *File* tab opens the Microsoft Office Backstage view, where you can access the commands for managing and protecting your files, including *Save, Open, Close, New,* and *Print.* Backstage replaces the Office Button menu from Office 2007 and the *File* menu from previous versions of Office.

To return to you file from Backstage view, click the **Back** button located in the upper left corner of the window.

KEYBOARD SHORTCUTS

Many commands available through the Ribbon and Backstage view are also accessible through keyboard shortcuts and shortcut menus.

Keyboard shortcuts are keys or combinations of keys that you press to execute a command. Some keyboard shortcuts refer to F keys or function keys. These are the keys that run across the top of the keyboard. Pressing these keys will execute specific commands. For example, pressing the F1 key will open Help in any of the Microsoft Office applications. Keyboard shortcuts typically use a combination of two keys, although some commands use a combination of three keys and others only one key. When a keyboard shortcut calls for a combination of key presses, such as Ctrl + V to paste an item from the *Clipboard,* you must first press the modifier key Ctrl, holding it down while you press the V key on the keyboard.

Press and hold **Ctrl** and then press **V** to paste text or item in a file.

FIGURE OF 1.9

tell me more

Many of the keyboard shortcuts are universal across all applications—not just Microsoft Office applications. Some examples of universal shortcut keys include:

- Ctrl + C = Copy
- Ctrl + X = Cut
- Ctrl + V = Paste
- Ctrl + Z = Undo
- Ctrl + O = Open
- Ctrl + S = Save

SHORTCUT MENUS

Shortcut menus are menus of commands that display when you right-click an area of the application window. The area or object you right-click determines which menu appears. For example, if you right-click in a paragraph, you will see a shortcut menu of commands for working with text; however, if you right-click an image, you will see a shortcut menu of commands for working with images.

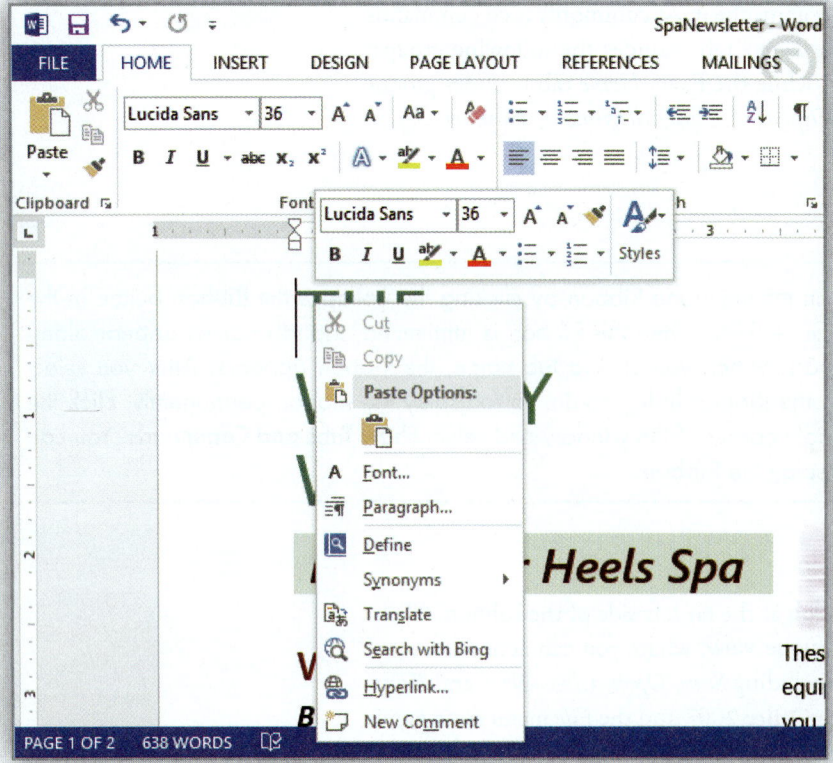

FIGURE OF 1.10
Right-Click Shortcut Menu

THE MINI TOOLBAR

The **Mini toolbar** gives you access to common tools for working with text. When you select text and then rest your mouse over the text, the Mini toolbar fades in. You can then click a button to change the selected text just as you would on the Ribbon.

another method

To display the Mini toolbar, you can also right-click the text. The Mini toolbar appears above the shortcut menu.

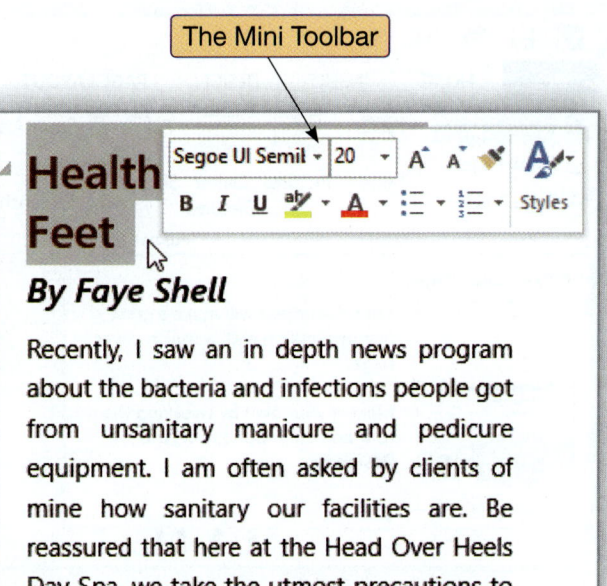

FIGURE OF 1.11

QUICK ACCESS TOOLBAR

The **Quick Access Toolbar** is located at the top of the application window above the *File* tab. The Quick Access Toolbar, as its name implies, gives you quick one-click access to common commands. You can add commands to and remove commands from the Quick Access Toolbar.

To modify the Quick Access Toolbar:

1. Click the **Customize Quick Access Toolbar** button located on the right side of the Quick Access Toolbar.
2. Options with checkmarks next to them are already displayed on the toolbar. Options with no checkmarks are not currently displayed.
3. Click an option to add it to or remove it from the Quick Access Toolbar.

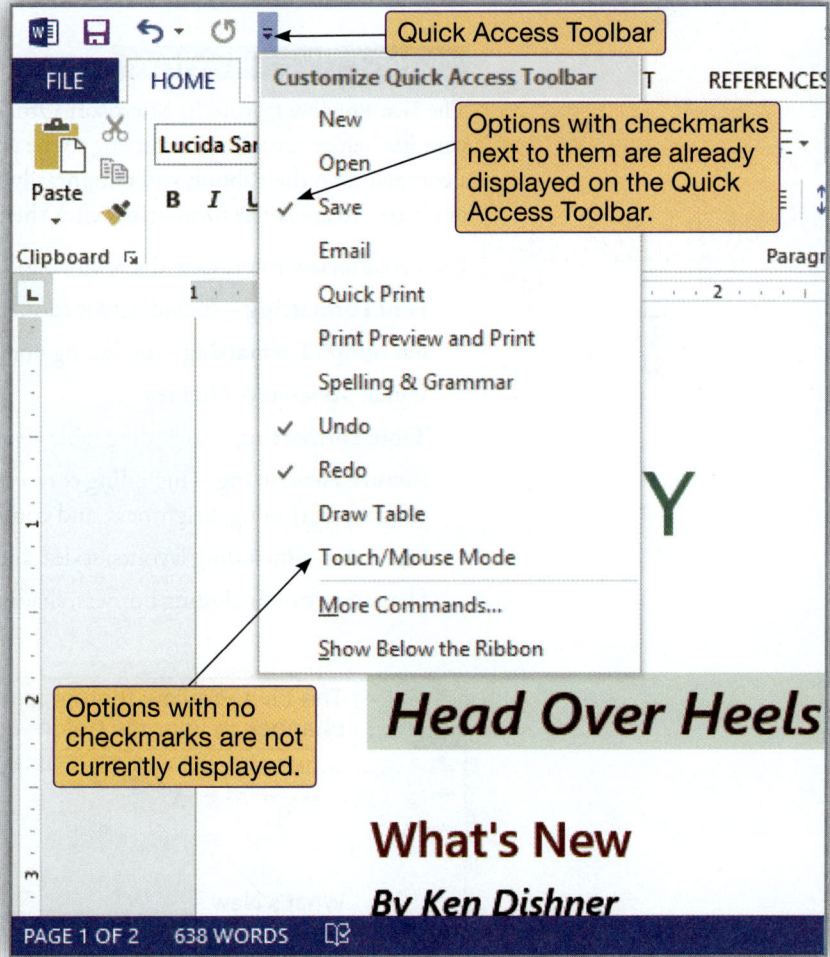

FIGURE OF 1.12

tips & tricks

If you want to be able to print with a single mouse click, add the *Quick Print* button to the Quick Access Toolbar. If you do not need to change any print settings, this is by far the easiest method to print a file because it doesn't require opening Backstage view first.

skill 1.4 Getting to Know the Office 2013 User Interface

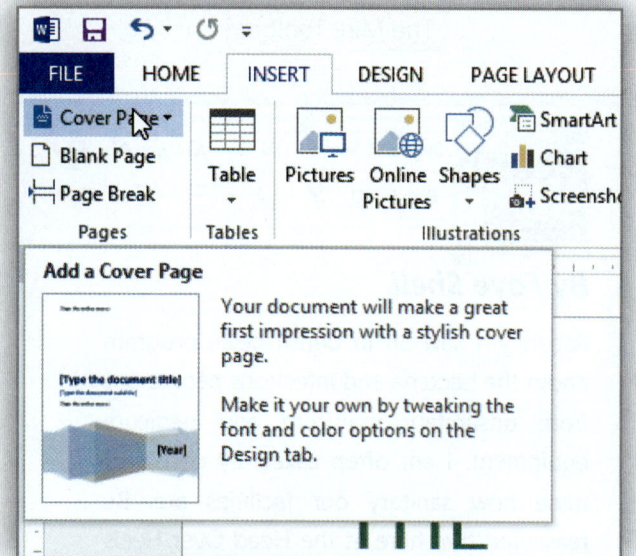

ENHANCED SCREENTIP

A **ScreenTip** is a small information box that displays the name of the command when you rest your mouse over a button on the Ribbon. An **Enhanced ScreenTip** displays not only the name of the command, but also the keyboard shortcut (if there is one) and a short description of what the button does and when it is used. Certain Enhanced ScreenTips also include an image along with a description of the command.

FIGURE OF 1.13
Cover Page Enhanced ScreenTip

USING LIVE PREVIEW

The **Live Preview** feature in Microsoft Office 2013 allows you to see formatting changes in your file before actually committing to the change. When Live Preview is active, rolling over a command on the Ribbon will temporarily apply the formatting to the currently active text or object. To apply the formatting, click the formatting option.

Use Live Preview to preview the following:

Font Formatting—Including the font, font size, text highlight color, and font color

Paragraph Formatting—Including numbering, bullets, and shading

Quick Styles and Themes

Table Formatting—Including table styles and shading

Picture Formatting—Including correction and color options, picture styles, borders, effects, positioning, brightness, and contrast

SmartArt—Including layouts, styles, and colors

Shape Styles—Including borders, shading, and effects

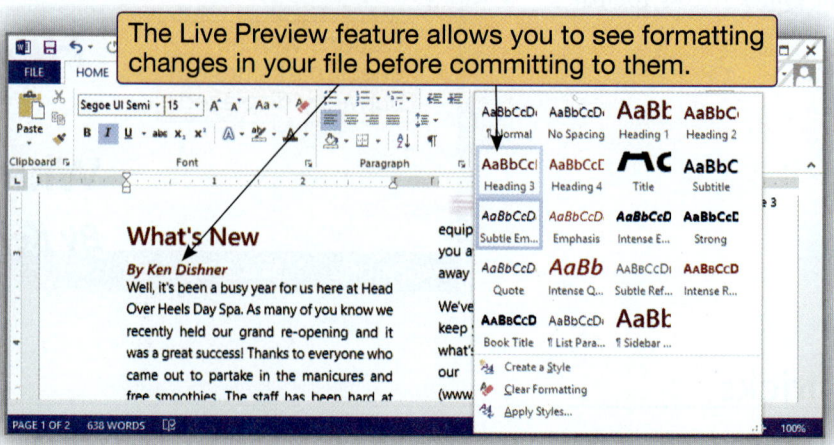

FIGURE OF 1.14

THE OPTIONS DIALOG

You can enable and disable some of the user interface features through the *Options* dialog.

1. Click the **File** tab to open Backstage view.
2. Click **Options.**
3. Make the changes you want, and then click **OK** to save your changes.

- Check or uncheck **Show Mini toolbar on selection** to control whether or not the Mini toolbar appears when you hover over selected text. (This does not affect the appearance of the Mini toolbar when you right-click.)
- Check or uncheck **Enable Live Preview** to turn the live preview feature on or off.
- Make a selection from the *ScreenTip style* list:
  - **Show feature descriptions in ScreenTips** displays Enhanced ScreenTips when they are available.
  - **Don't show feature descriptions in ScreenTips** hides Enhanced ScreenTips. The ScreenTip will still include the keyboard shortcut if there is one available.
  - **Don't show ScreenTips** hides ScreenTips altogether, so if you hold your mouse over a button on the Ribbon, nothing will appear.

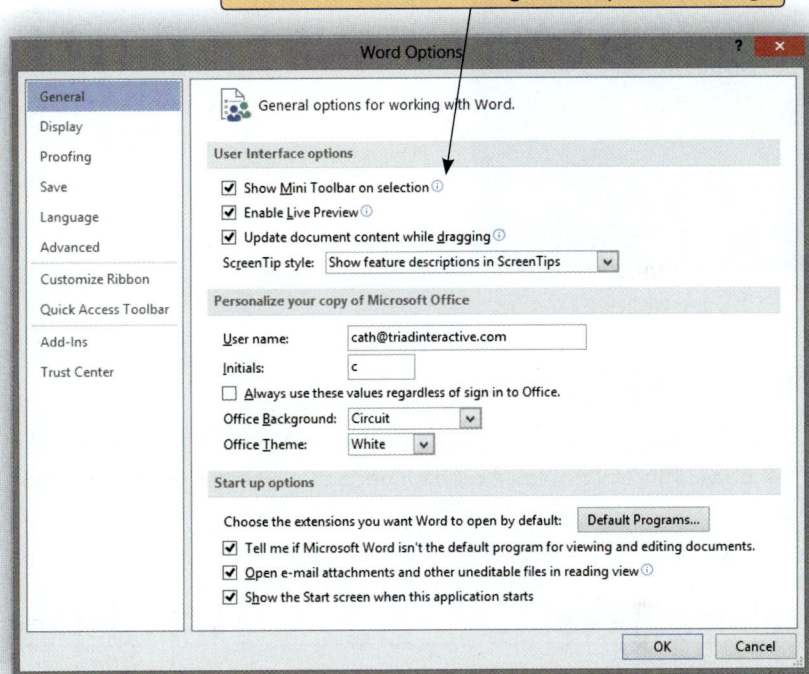

FIGURE OF 1.15

let me try

Open the student data file **of1-SpaNewsletter** and try this skill on your own:

1. Explore the Ribbon. Click on different tabs and note how commands are arranged together in groups.
2. Click the picture to display the *Picture Tools* contextual tab.
3. Click the **File** tab to display Backstage view. Click the **Back** button to return to the file.
4. Right-click an area of the file to display the shortcut menu.
5. Explore the Mini Toolbar at the top of the shortcut menu. Click away from the menu to hide it.
6. Click the **Customize Quick Access Toolbar** arrow to display the menu of items that can be displayed on the Quick Access Toolbar. Note the ones with checkmarks are the items currently displayed.
7. Click the **Insert** tab. In the *Pages* group, roll your mouse over the **Cover Page** button to display the Enhanced ScreenTip.
8. Click the **File** tab.
9. Click **Options** to open the *Options* dialog.
10. Disable **Live Preview.**
11. Change the ScreenTips so they don't show feature descriptions.
12. Close the file.

skill 1.4   Getting to Know the Office 2013 User Interface

Skill 1.5 Using the Start Page

When you launch an Office 2013 application you are first taken to the **Start page**. The *Start* page gives you quick access to recently opened files and templates for creating new files in each of the applications.

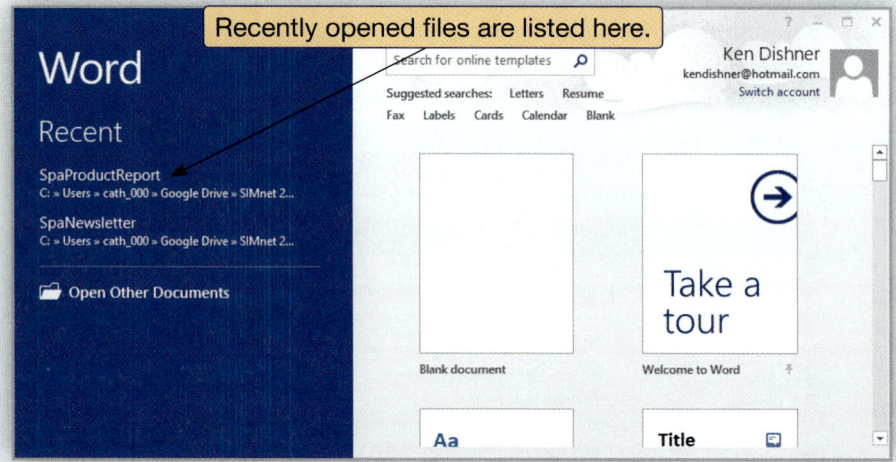

To open a recent file from the *Start* page:

1. Launch the application.
2. The *Start* page displays.
3. Click a file in the left pane to open the file.

FIGURE OF 1.16

tips & tricks

If you do not see the file you want to open in the list of recent files, click **Open Other Documents** at the bottom of the left pane. This will display the *Open* page that includes buttons for finding and opening files from other locations such as your computer or your OneDrive.

tell me more

In previous versions of Office when you launched an application, a blank file opened ready for you to begin working. If you want to start a new blank file, click the blank file template in the list of templates. It is always listed as the first option.

let me try

To try this skill on your own:
1. Launch **Microsoft Word.**
2. If you have files listed under *Recent,* click a file to open it.
3. Close the file.

from the perspective of . . .

A BUSY PARENT

Learning Microsoft Office was one of the best things I did to help manage my family's busy lifestyle. I use Word to write up and print a calendar of everyone's activities for the week. I keep a handle on the family finances with a budget of all expenses in an Excel spreadsheet. I've even learned how to use Excel to calculate loan payments and found the best offer when I had to buy a new family car. I used PowerPoint to create a presentation for my family of our summer vacation pictures. Once I became more familiar with Access, I used it to help organize my family's busy schedule. I created a database with one table for activities, another for parent contact information, another one for carpooling, and another one for the schedule. Being able to organize all the information in a database has been invaluable. I always thought Office was only for businesses, but now I can't imagine running my household without it!

Skill 1.6 Changing Account Information

Office 2013 includes an **Account page** that lists information for the user currently logged into Office. This account information comes from the Microsoft account you used when installing Office. From the *Account* page, you can update your user profile, including contact and work information. You can also change the picture associated with the user account.

To change the user information

1. Click the **File** tab.
2. Click **Account.**
3. The current user profile is listed under *User Information*.
4. Click the **Change photo** link.

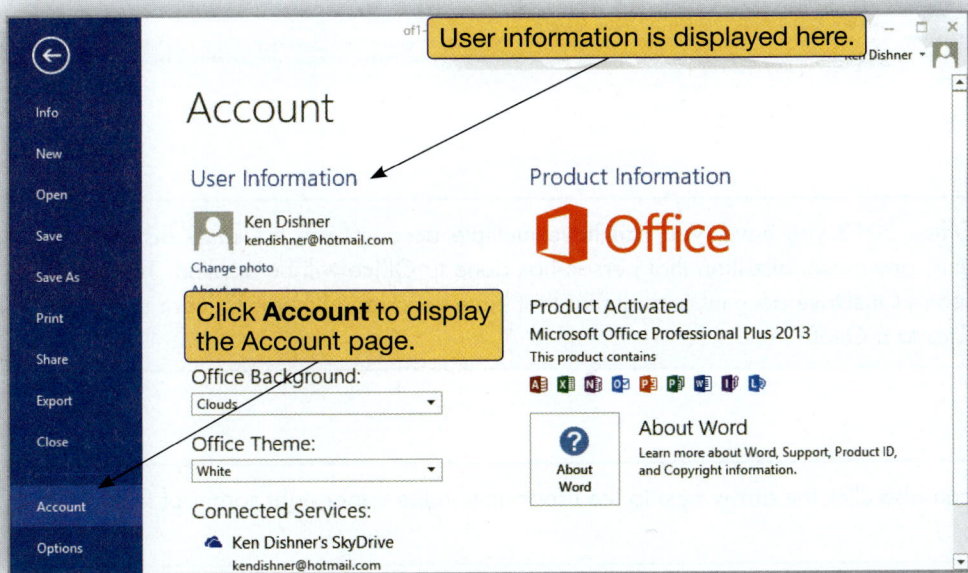

FIGURE OF 1.17

5. The *Profile* page on *live.com* is displayed in the browser window.
6. Click the **Change Picture** link.
7. On the *Picture* page, click the **Browse** button.
8. Navigate to the location of the picture you want to use for you profile and select it.
9. Click the **Open** button.
10. The picture appears on the page. Click the **Save** button to save the profile change.

From the *Profile* page, you can also edit your contact information and work information. Click the **Edit** link under each section to display the edit page. Fill in the form with your information and click the **Save** button.

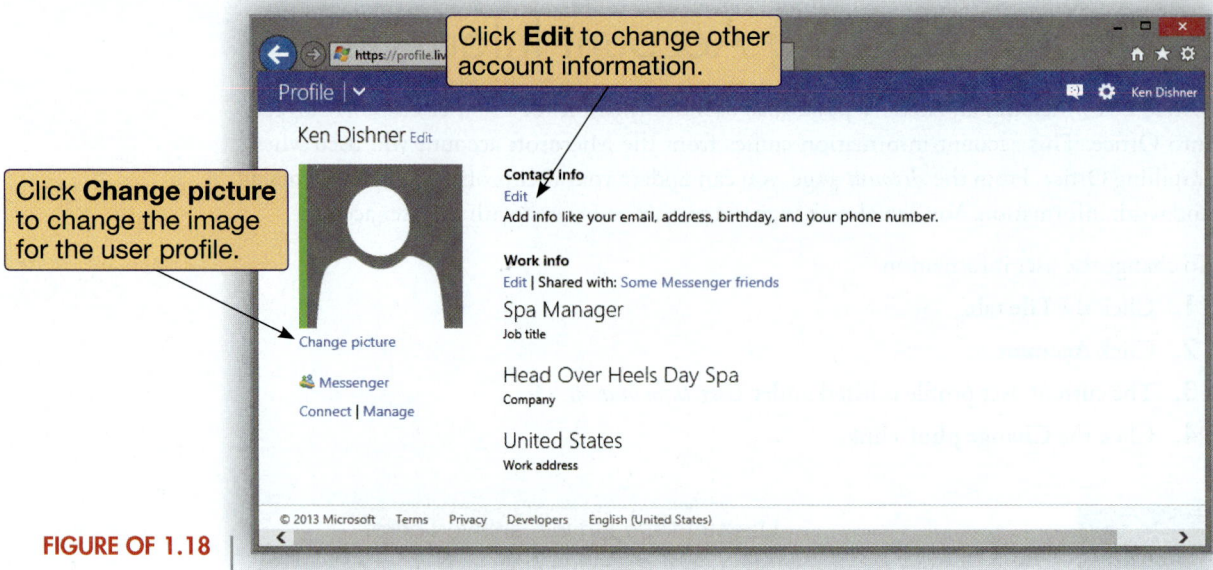

FIGURE OF 1.18

tell me more

Depending on the version of Office 2013 you have, you can have multiple accounts use the same installation of Office. When you switch accounts, any personalization that person has done to Office will be applied. The account will also have access to that person's OneDrive account and all files that have been saved there. To learn more about OneDrive, see the skill *Saving Files to a OneDrive*.

another method

To change the user photo, you can also click the arrow next to the user name in the upper right corner of the window and click the **Change photo** link.

let me try

Open the student data file **of1-SpaNewsletter** and try this skill on your own:
1. Open the **Account** page in Backstage view.
   NOTE: If you are using this in class or in your school's computer lab, check with your instructor about permissions before completing the following steps.
2. Change the photo for the user account.
3. Change the picture using a photo of your choice.
4. Save the changes to the picture.
5. Close the browser window.
6. Keep this file open for working on the next skill.

Skill 1.7 Changing the Look of Office

In addition to managing the Office account, you can also control the look of Office from the *Account* page. Changing the Office background changes the background image that displays in the upper right corner of the window near the user profile. Changing the Office theme changes the color scheme for Office, affecting the look of the Ribbon and dialogs.

To change the look of Office:

1. Click the **File** tab to open Backstage view.
2. Click **Account**.
3. Click the **Office Background** drop-down list and select an option to display as the background.
4. Click the **Office Theme** drop-down list and select a color option for your applications.

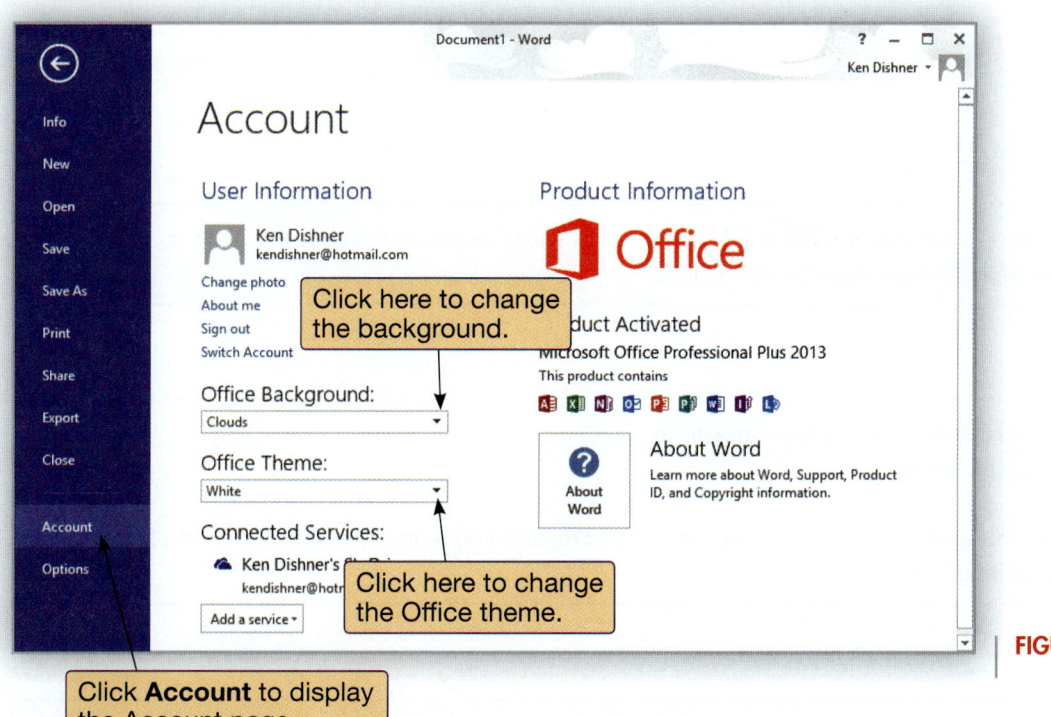

FIGURE OF 1.19

let me try

If necessary, open the student data file **of1-SpaNewsletter** and try this skill on your own:

1. Open the **Account** page in Backstage view.
   NOTE: If you are using this in class or in your school's computer lab, check with your instructor about permissions before completing the following steps.
2. Change the Office background to the **Circuit** background.
3. Change the Office color to **Light Gray.**
4. Close the file.

Skill 1.8 Working in Protected View

When you download a file from a location that Office considers potentially unsafe, it opens automatically in **Protected View**. Protected View provides a read-only format that protects your computer from becoming infected by a virus or other malware. Potentially unsafe locations include the Internet, e-mail messages, or a network location. Files that are opened in Protected View display a warning in the Message Bar at the top of the window, below the Ribbon.

To disable Protected View, click the **Enable Editing** button in the Message Bar.

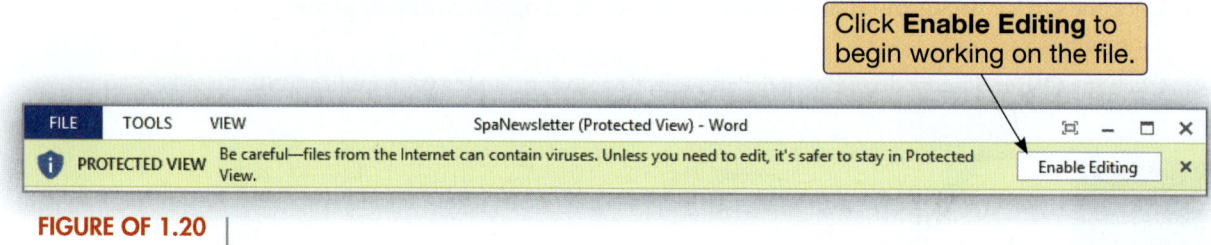

FIGURE OF 1.20

tips & tricks

To learn more about the security settings in Office 2013, open the Trust Center and review the options. We do not recommend changing any of the default Trust Center settings.

another method

You can also enable editing from the Info page in Backstage.
1. Click the **File** tab to open Backstage.
2. Click **Info**.
3. The Info page provides more information about the file. If you are sure you want to remove it from Protected View, click the **Enable Editing** button.

let me try

Open the student data file **of1-SpaNewsletter** and try this skill on your own:
1. If you downloaded the file from the Internet, the file will open in Protected View.
2. Click the **Enable Editing** button to begin working with the file.
3. Close the file.

Skill 1.9 Picking Up Where You Left Off

When you are working in a long document or a presentation and reopen it to work on it, you may not remember where you were last working. Office 2013 includes a new feature that automatically bookmarks the last location that was worked on when the file was closed.

To pick up where you left off in a document or presentation:

1. Open the document or presentation.
2. A message displays on the right side of the screen welcoming you back and asking if you want to pick up where you left off. The message then minimizes to a bookmark tag.
3. Click the **bookmark tag** to navigate to the location.

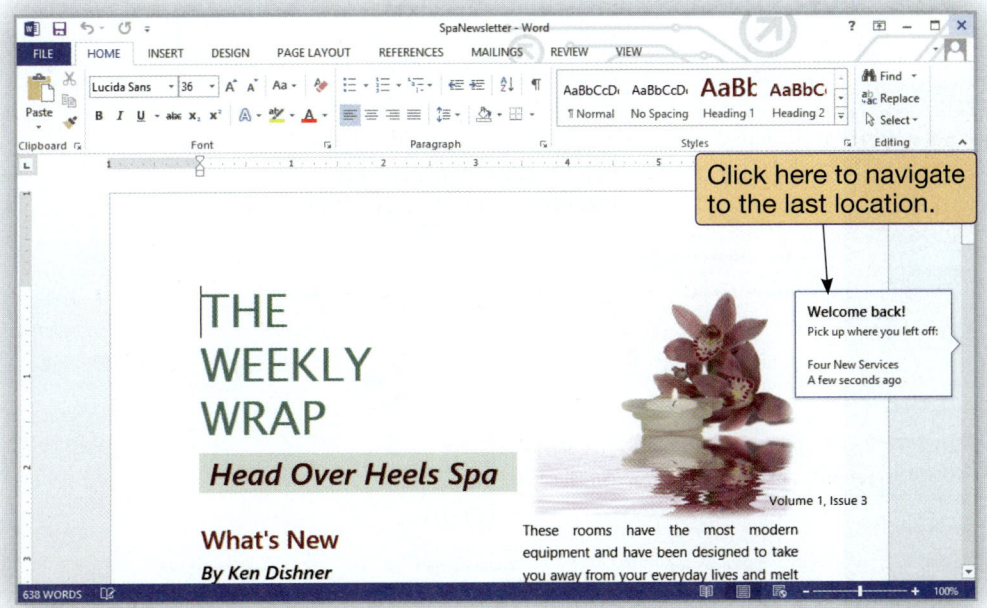

FIGURE OF 1.21

tips & tricks

The bookmark tag only displays until you navigate to another part of the document. If you scroll the document, the bookmark tag disappears.

tell me more

This feature is only available in Word and PowerPoint. Excel and Access do not give you the option of picking up where you left off when you open a file.

let me try

Open the student data file **of1-09-SpaNewsletter** and try this skill on your own:
1. Navigate to the location where the last location the file was at when last closed.
2. Close the file.

Skill 1.10 Creating a New Blank File

When you first open an Office application, the *Start* page displays giving you the opportunity to open an existing file or create a new blank file or one based on a template. But what if you have a file open and want to create another new file? Will you need to close the application and then launch it again? The **New command** allows you to create new files without exiting and reopening the program.

To create a new blank file:

1. Click the **File** tab to open Backstage view.
2. Click **New.**
3. The first option on the *New* page is a blank file. Click the **Blank document** thumbnail to create the new blank file.

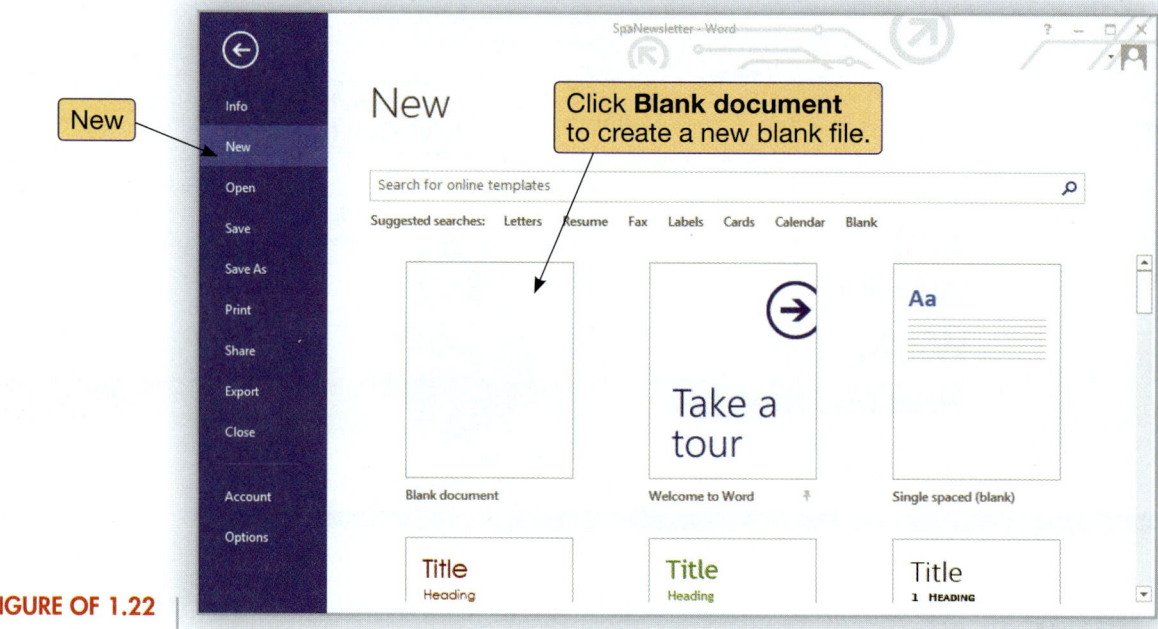

FIGURE OF 1.22

tell me more

In addition to a blank file, you can create new files from templates from the *New* page.

another method

To bypass the Backstage view and create a new blank file, press Ctrl + N on the keyboard.

let me try

Open the student data file **of1-SpaNewsletter** and try this skill on your own:
1. Create a new blank file.
2. Close the file but do not save it.

Skill 1.11 Using Help

If you don't know how to perform a task, you can look it up in the **Office Help** system. Each application comes with its own Help system with topics specifically tailored for working with that application.

To look up a topic using the Microsoft Office Help system:

1. Click the **Microsoft Office Help** button. It is located at the far right of the Ribbon.
2. Click in the **Search online help** box and type a word or phrase describing the topic you want help with.
3. Click the **Search** button.
4. A list of results appears.
5. Click a result to display the help topic.

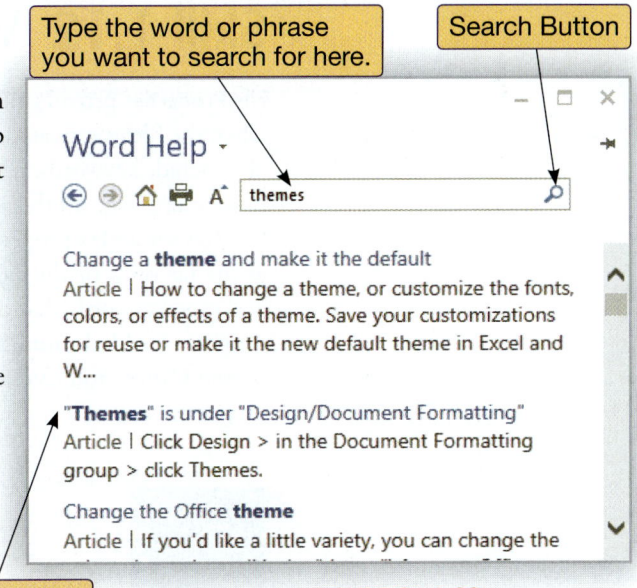

FIGURE OF 1.23

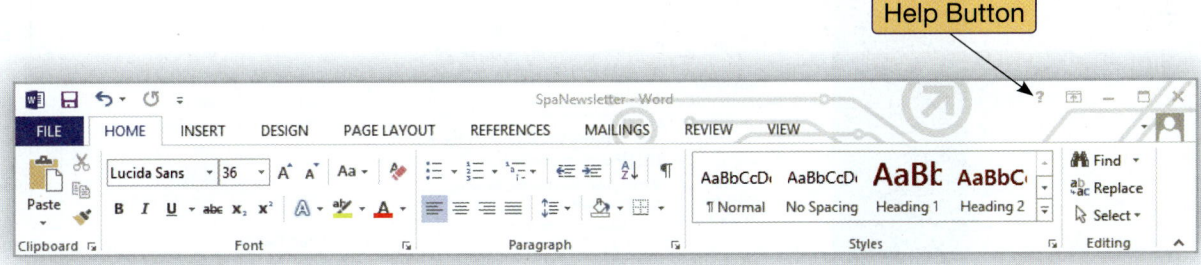

FIGURE OF 1.24

tips & tricks

To search for topics in Microsoft Office Help, you must have an active Internet connection. If you are working offline (not connected to *Office.com*), Help is still available, but it is limited to information about finding buttons of the Ribbon.

tell me more

The Help toolbar is located at the top of the Help window. This toolbar includes buttons for navigating between screens, changing the size of text, and returning to the *Help Home* page. Click the **printer icon** on the toolbar to print the current topic. Click the **pushpin icon** to keep the Help window always on top of the Microsoft Office application.

another method

To open the Help window, you can also press F1 on the keyboard.

let me try

Open the student data file **of1-SpaNewsletter** and try this skill on your own:

1. Click the **Microsoft Office Help** button.
2. Search for topics about **themes.**
3. Click a link of your choice.
4. Close the **Help** window.
5. Keep this file open for working on the next skill.

Skill 1.12 Working with File Properties

File Properties provide information about a file such as the location of the file, the size of file, when the file was created and when it was last modified, the title, and the author. Properties also include keywords, referred to as **tags**, that are useful for grouping common files together or for searching. All this information about a file is referred to as **metadata**.

To view a file's properties, click the **File** tab to open Backstage view. Properties are listed at the far right of the *Info* tab. To add keywords to a file, click the text box next to *Tags* and type keywords that describe the file, separating each word with a comma. The Author property is added automatically using the account name entered when you installed and registered Office. You can change the author name or add more names by editing the Author property.

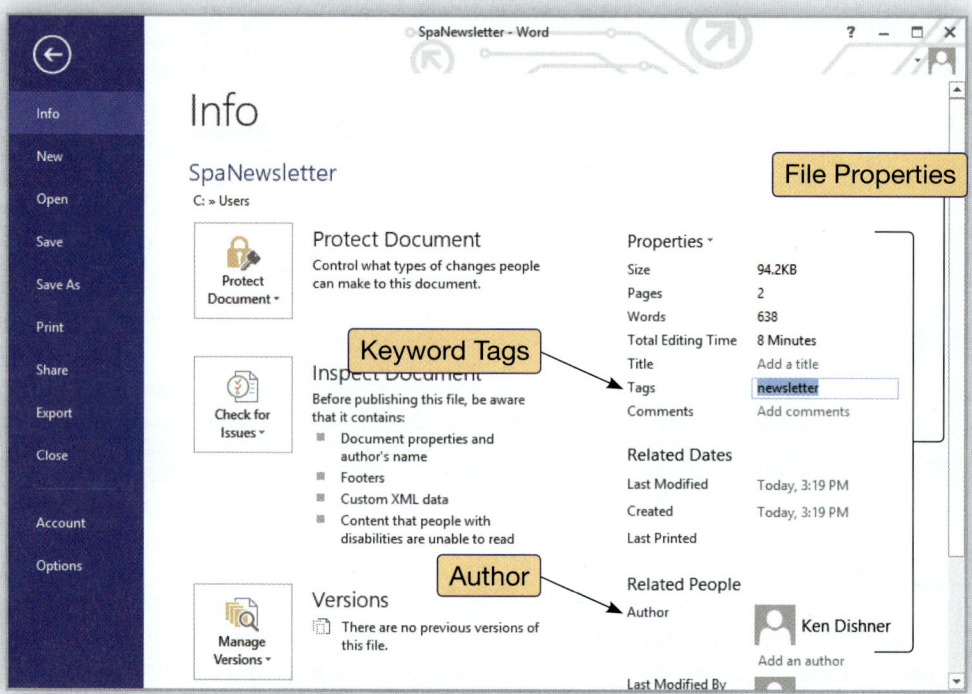

FIGURE OF 1.25

tips & tricks

Some file properties are generated automatically by Windows and cannot be edited by the user, such as the date the file was created and the size of the file.

let me try

If necessary, open the student data file **of1-SpaNewsletter** and try this skill on your own:
1. Add a tag to the document that reads **newsletter.**
2. Keep this file open for working on the next skill.

Skill 1.13 Saving Files to a Local Drive

As you work on a new file, it is displayed on-screen and stored in your computer's memory. However, it is not permanently stored until you save it as a file to a specific location. The first time you save a file, the *Save As* page in Backstage view will display. Here you can choose to save the file to your OneDrive, your local computer, or another location.

To save a file to a local drive:

1. Click the **Save** button on the Quick Access Toolbar.
2. The *Save As* page in Backstage view appears.
3. On the left side of the page, click **Computer** to save the file to a local drive.
4. Word displays a list of recent folders; select a folder where you want to save the file.

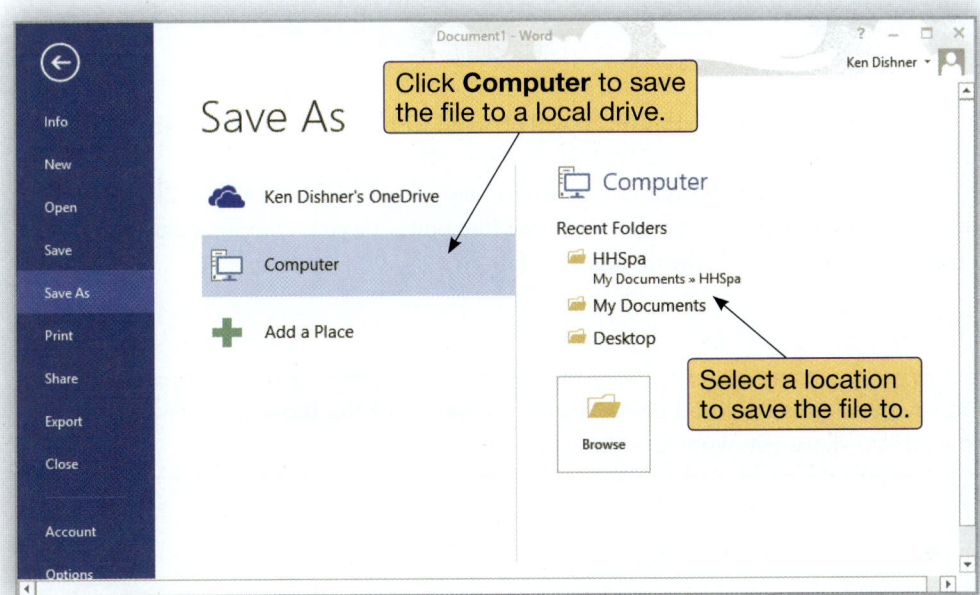

FIGURE OF 1.26

5. The *Save As* dialog opens.
6. If you want to create a new folder, click the **New Folder** button near the top of the file list. The new folder is created with the temporary name *New Folder*. Type the new name for the folder and press **Enter**.
7. Click in the **File name** box and type a file name.
8. Click the **Save** button.

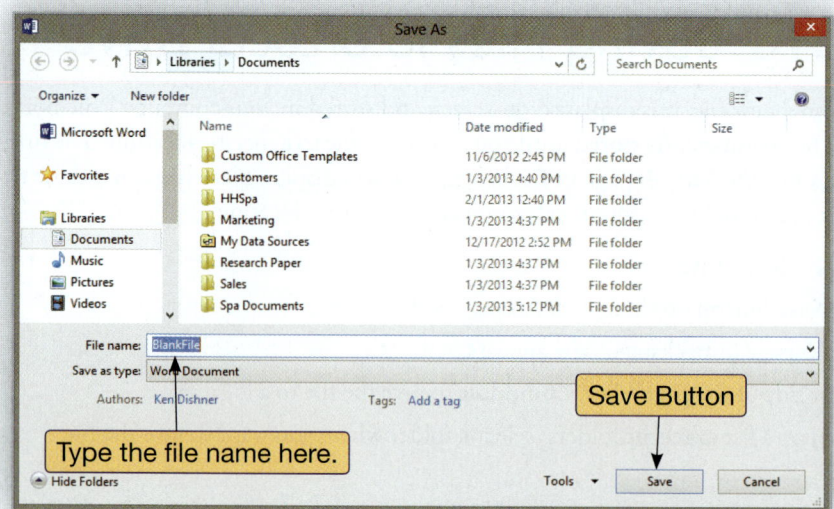

FIGURE OF 1.27

The next time you save this file, it will be saved with the same file name and to the same location automatically.

As you are working with files, be sure to **save often!** Although Office 2013 includes a recovery function, it is not foolproof. If you lose power or your computer crashes, you may lose all the work done on the file since the last save.

tips & tricks

If the location where you want to save the file is not listed under *Recent Folders*, click the **Browse** button to open the *Save As* dialog. Navigate to the location where you want to save the file.

another method

To save a file, you can also:
- Press Ctrl + S on the keyboard.
- Click the **File** tab, and then select **Save.**
- Click the **File** tab, and then select **Save As.**

let me try

Try this skill on your own:
1. Create a new blank file.
2. Save the file to the **My Documents** folder on your computer. Name the file **BlankFile.**
3. Close the file.

Skill 1.14 Saving Files to a OneDrive

NOTE: When Microsoft Office 2013 first published, this feature was named **SkyDrive**. It has since been renamed **OneDrive**.

OneDrive is Microsoft's free cloud storage where you can save documents, workbooks, presentations, videos, pictures, and other files and access those files from any computer or share the files with others. When you save files to your OneDrive, they are stored locally on your computer and then "synched" with your OneDrive account and stored in the "cloud" where you can then access the files from another computer or device that has OneDrive capability.

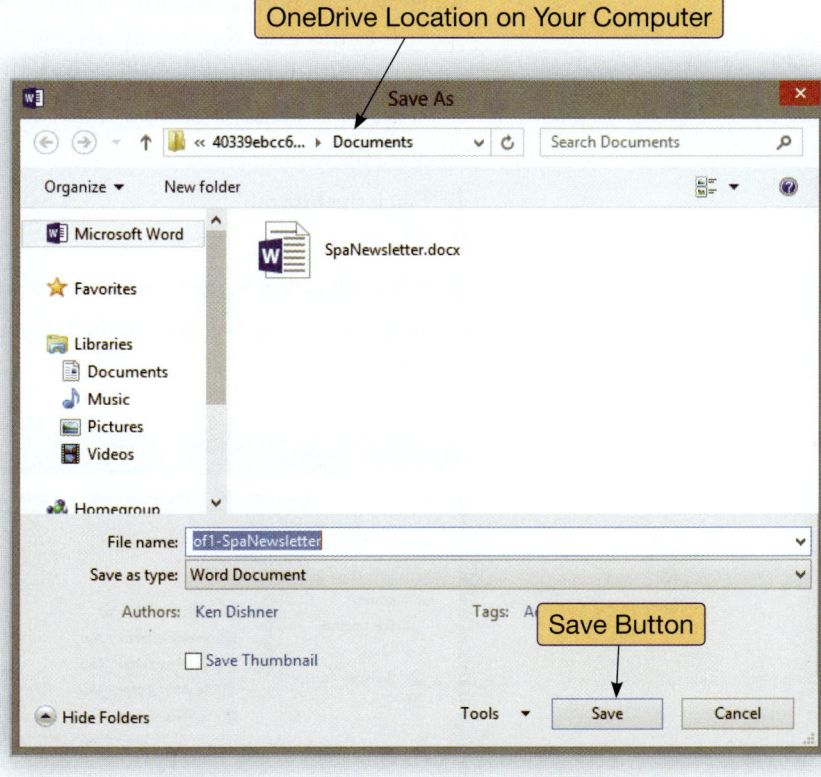

FIGURE OF 1.28

To save a file to your OneDrive:

1. Click the **File** tab.
2. Click **Save As.**
3. Verify the OneDrive account is selected on the left side of the page.
4. Under *Recent Folders*, click the **OneDrive** account you want to save to.
5. The *Save As* dialog opens to your OneDrive folder location on your computer.
6. Click in the **File name** box and type a file name.
7. Click the **Save** button.

tips & tricks

By default, your OneDrive includes folders for documents, pictures, and files you want to make public. You can save your files in any of these folders or create your own. To create a new folder in your OneDrive, click the **New Folder** button near the top of the file list. The new folder is created with the temporary name *New Folder*. Type the new name for the folder and press `Enter`.

tell me more

When you are working on an Excel or Word file that has been saved to your OneDrive, others can work on the file at the same time you are working the file. The application will mark the area being worked on as read only so others cannot modify the same information you are working on. However, if you are sharing a PowerPoint presentation, only one user at a time can work on the presentation.

let me try

If necessary, open the student data file **of1-SpaNewsletter** and try this skill on your own:

1. Save the file to the **Documents** folder on your OneDrive. **NOTE:** If you are using this in class or in your school's computer lab, check with your instructor before completing this step.
2. Keep this file open for working on the next skill.

skill 1.14 Saving Files to a OneDrive

Skill 1.15 Saving Files with a New Name

When working on files you may want to save a file but not overwrite the original file you opened. In this case, you should save the file with a new name. When you save a file with a new name, the original file still exists in its last saved state and the new file you save will include all the changes you made.

To save a file with a new name:

1. Click the **File** tab.
2. Click **Save As.**
3. Select a location to save the file, either your OneDrive or your local drive.
4. In the *Save As* dialog, click in the **File name** box, type a new name for the file, and click **Save.**

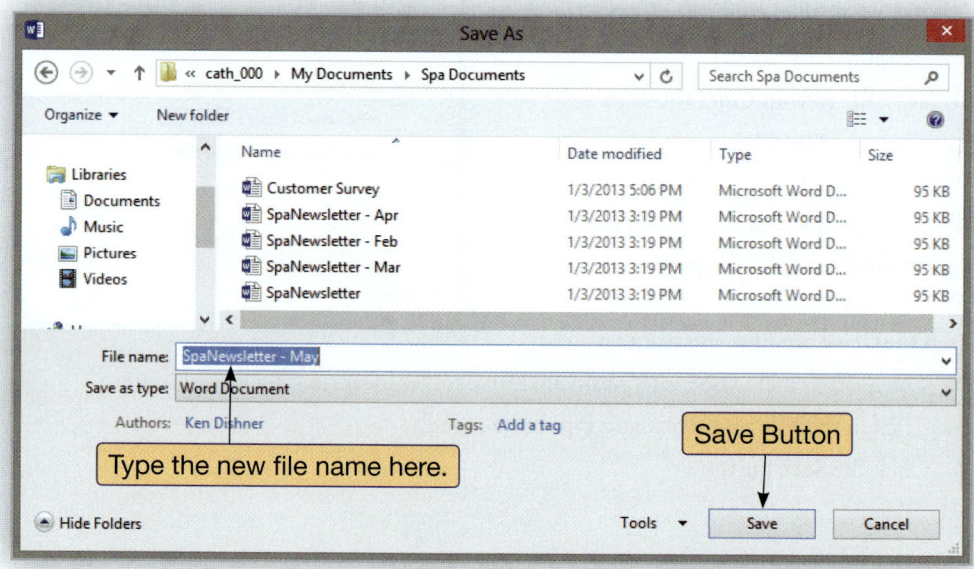

FIGURE OF 1.29

tell me more

Beginning with Office 2007, Microsoft changed the file format for Office files. If you want to share your files with people who are using Office 2003 or older, you should save the files in a different file format.

1. In the *Save As* dialog, click the arrow at the end of the *Save as type* box to expand the list of available file types.
2. To ensure compatibility with older versions of Office, select the file type that includes 97-2003 (for example, Word 97-2003 Document or Excel 97-2003 Workbook).

let me try

If necessary, open the student data file **of1-SpaNewsletter** and try this skill on your own:
1. Save the file to the **Documents** folder on your computer with the name **SpaNewsletter.**
2. Keep this file open for working on the next skill.

Skill 1.16 Closing the Application

When you close a file, the application stays open so you can open another file to edit or begin a new file. Often, when you are finished working on a file, you want to close the file and exit the application at the same time. In this case, you will want to close the application.

To close an application:

1. Click the **Close** button in the upper-right corner of the application.
2. If you have made no changes since the last time you saved the file, it will close immediately. If changes have been made, the application displays a message box asking if you want to save the changes you made before closing.
   Click **Save** to save the changes.
   Click **Don't Save** to close the file without saving your latest changes.
   Click **Cancel** to keep the file open.

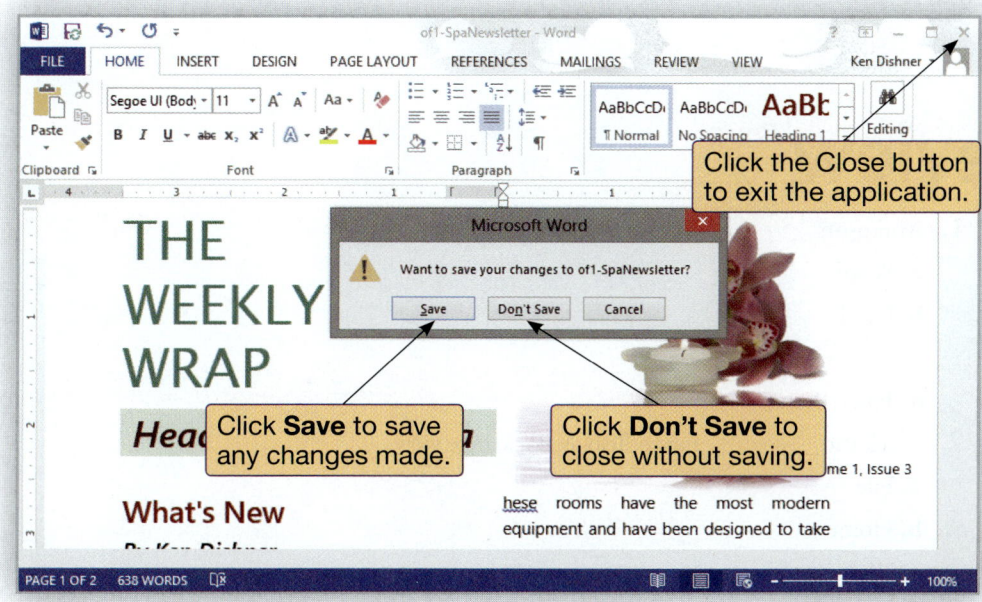

FIGURE OF 1.30

another method

To close the application, you can also:
- Right-click the title bar and select **Close.**
- Click the application icon in the upper-left corner of the application and select **Close.**

let me try

If necessary, open the student data file **of1-SpaNewsletter** and try this skill on your own:
   Close the application.

key terms

Microsoft Word
Microsoft Excel
Microsoft PowerPoint
Microsoft Access
Ribbon
Tab
Groups
Contextual tabs
Home tab
File tab
Backstage
Keyboard shortcuts
Shortcut menus
Mini toolbar

Quick Access Toolbar
ScreenTip
Enhanced ScreenTip
Live Preview
Start page
Account page
Protected View
New command
Office Help
File Properties
Tags
Metadata
OneDrive

concepts review

1. Microsoft _____ is a spreadsheet program.
   a. Word
   b. Excel
   c. Access
   d. PowerPoint

2. Click the _____ tab to display Backstage view.
   a. File
   b. Home
   c. View
   d. Contextual

3. To display a shortcut menu _____ an area of the file.
   a. left-click
   b. right-click
   c. double-click
   d. None of the above

4. If you have downloaded a file from the Internet and it opens in Protected View, you should never open the file.
   a. True
   b. False

5. The _____ is located across the top of the application window and organizes common features and commands into tabs.
   a. menu bar
   b. toolbar
   c. title bar
   d. Ribbon

6. The _____ provide(s) information about a file such as the location of the file, the size of file, when the file was created and when it was last modified, the title, and the author.
   a. file properties
   b. user profile
   c. account information
   d. Options dialog
7. When you save files to your OneDrive, they are available to access from other computers that have OneDrive capability. If you are working on an Excel or Word file, others can be working on the same file at the same time you are working on the file.
   a. True
   b. False
8. You can change user information from the _____ page in Backstage view.
   a. Account
   b. Options
   c. Share
   d. Info
9. To paste an item from the *Clipboard*, use the keyboard shortcut _____.
   a. Ctrl + C
   b. Ctrl + X
   c. Ctrl + V
   d. Ctrl + P
10. The _____ gives you quick one-click access to common commands and is located at the top of the application window above the *File* tab.
    a. Ribbon
    b. Quick Access Toolbar
    c. Options dialog
    d. Backstage view

access 2013

Chapter 1: Getting Started with Access 2013

Chapter 2: Working with Tables

Chapter 3: Working with Forms and Reports

Chapter 4: Using Queries and Organizing Information

Chapter 5: Exploring Advanced Tables

Chapter 6: Exploring Advanced Forms

Chapter 7: Exploring Advanced Reports

Chapter 8: Exploring Advanced Queries and Macros

Chapter 9: Finalizing the Database

chapter 1

Getting Started with Access 2013

In this chapter, you will learn the following skills:

- Identify the elements of a Microsoft Access 2013 database
- Use the Navigation Pane to open, organize, and view database objects
- Understand and view table relationships
- Understand database object views
- Navigate records in tables and forms
- Create new records, enter, edit, find, and move data in tables and forms
- Delete records in tables and forms
- Rename and delete database objects
- Preview and print database objects
- Export data to other formats
- Use the Compact & Repair tool
- Perform a backup

Skill 1.1 Introduction to Access 2013
Skill 1.2 Working with Security Warnings
Skill 1.3 Understanding and Viewing Table Relationships
Skill 1.4 Organizing Objects in the Navigation Pane
Skill 1.5 Switching between Database Object Views
Skill 1.6 Navigating Records
Skill 1.7 Creating a New Record in a Table
Skill 1.8 Creating a New Record in a Form
Skill 1.9 Finding and Replacing Data
Skill 1.10 Cutting, Copying, and Pasting Data
Skill 1.11 Using Undo and Redo
Skill 1.12 Deleting Records
Skill 1.13 Checking Spelling
Skill 1.14 Deleting and Renaming Database Objects
Skill 1.15 Exporting Data to Excel or Word
Skill 1.16 Exporting Data to a PDF File
Skill 1.17 Previewing and Printing Database Objects
Skill 1.18 Using Compact and Repair
Skill 1.19 Backing Up a Database

skills

introduction

This chapter is an introduction to the concepts necessary for understanding and working with relational databases. You will learn about the database objects that make up an Access database and how they relate to one another. You will learn to navigate, create, edit, and delete records in tables and forms. You also will learn the importance of database maintenance duties such as compact and repair and creating a backup.

Skill 1.1 Introduction to Access 2013

In the simplest terms, a *database* is a collection of data. An effective database allows you to enter, store, organize, and retrieve large amounts of related data. Access is different from other Microsoft Office applications you may have used. Although you create and work with a single Access database file, inside the file, there are multiple objects. Within each Access database, you create, edit, and save (and delete) objects. The types of objects in an Access database are:

> *Tables*—Store all the database data. They are the essential building blocks of the database. A table looks similar to a spreadsheet. Each row in the table contains all the data for a single *record*. Each column in the table represents a specific data value called a *field*. All records in a table have the same fields.

Figure AC 1.1 shows the *Appointments* table, which stores the data for each customer appointment.

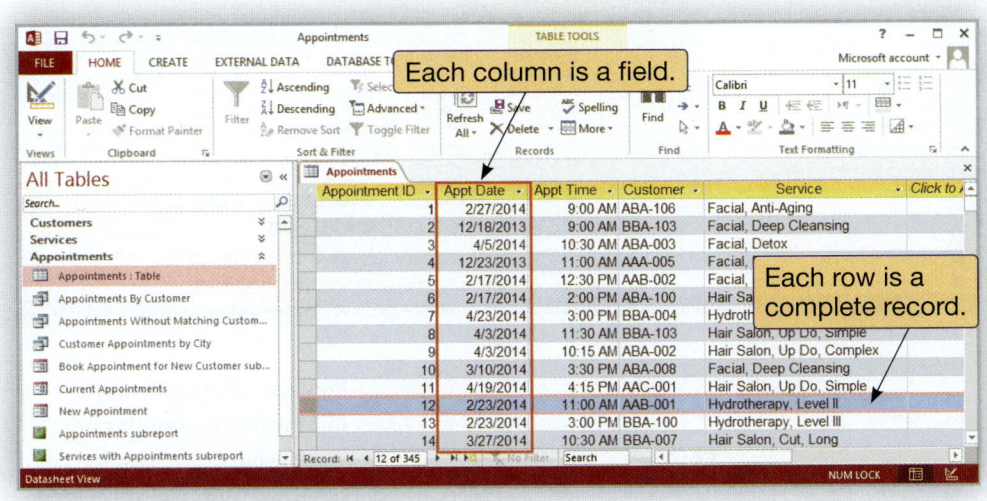

FIGURE AC 1.1

Because Access allows you to relate tables to one another, it is often referred to as a relational database. A *relational database* is a group of tables related to one another by common fields.

> *Forms*—Allow users to input data through a friendly interface. Entering data through a form is easier than entering it directly into a table. All the data entered into a form are stored in the underlying database table(s).

Figure AC 1.2 shows the *New Appointment* form, which allows a data-entry operator to enter new appointments. When a new appointment is created using this form, a new record is added to the *Appointments* table.

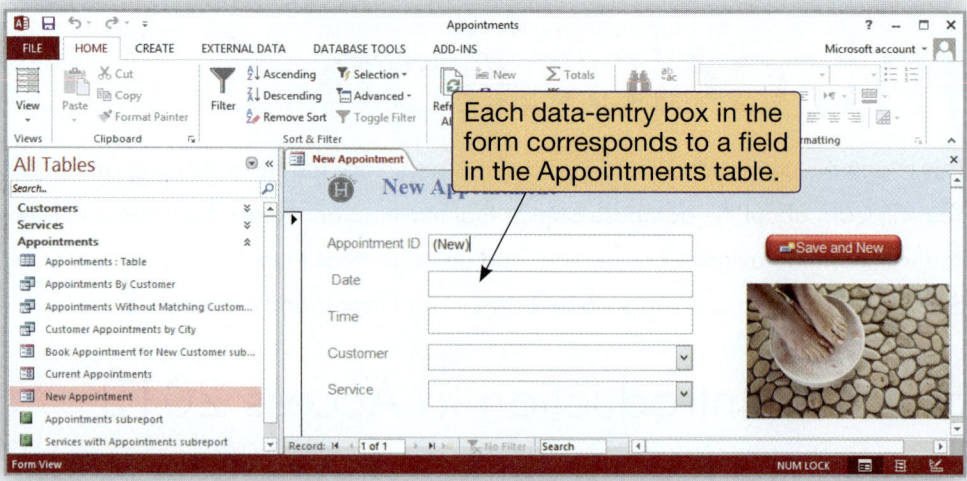

FIGURE AC 1.2

Queries—Extract data from a table or related tables. Queries can also perform actions on tables such as updating data values or deleting data. Query results may look like a table, but they do not store data permanently. The query results are updated dynamically each time the query is run—retrieving data fresh from the table(s) upon which the query is based.

The query in Figure AC 1.3 returns a list of all the appointments for customers who live in a specific city. The query combines data from two tables: *Appointments* and *Customers*.

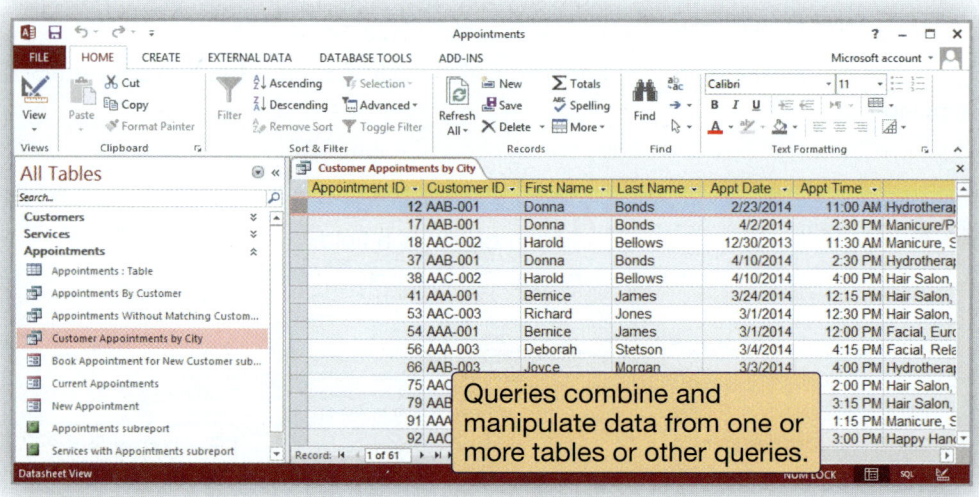

FIGURE AC 1.3

Reports—Display database information for printing or viewing on-screen. Reports do not allow data entry; they are read-only.

The report in Figure AC 1.4, *Services with Appointments subreport,* displays a printable summary of each service and a list of the current appointments for that service (the *subreport*). This report combines data from multiple tables and queries in a format suitable for printing.

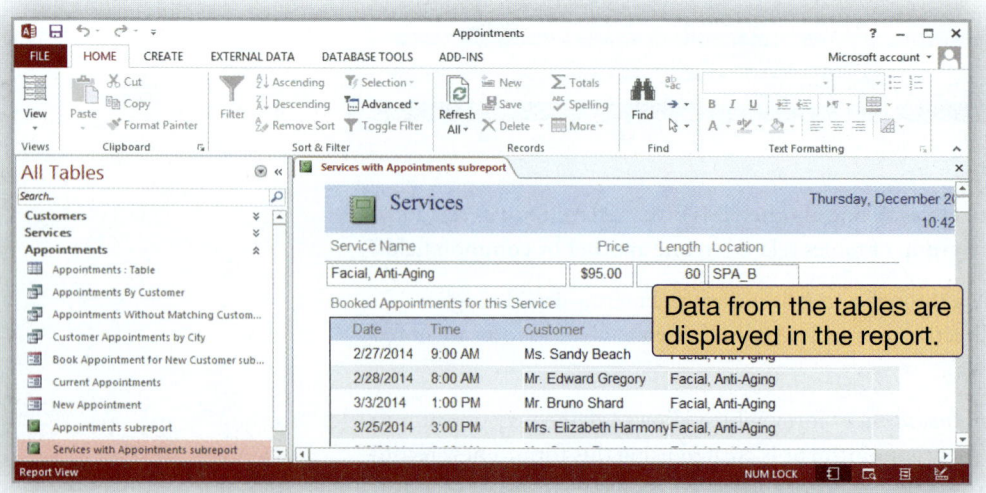

FIGURE AC 1.4

All the database objects are organized in the **Navigation Pane,** which is docked at the left side of the screen. Each database object in the Navigation Pane has a name and an icon representing the type of object.

The Navigation Pane is usually expanded when you open an Access database. If you need more room to work, you can collapse the Navigation Pane by clicking the **Shutter Bar Open/Close** button. To expand the Navigation Pane again, click the **Shutter Bar Open/Close** button.

To open a database object, double-click the object name in the Navigation Pane. The object will appear as a new tab within the Access work area unless it is specifically designed to open in a window format. You can have multiple database objects open at the same time. To navigate from one object to another, click the object tab.

To close an object, click the **X** at the far right side of the object. Be careful not to click the X in the upper right corner of the database window—that will close the database!

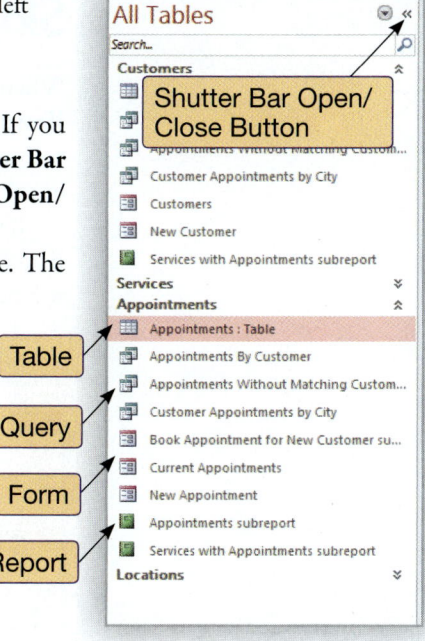

FIGURE AC 1.5

tell me more

A fourth type of database object called a *Macro* is a collection of programming code usually used within forms and reports to create buttons and other user interface elements. You will not work with macros until you are a more experienced Access user.

another method

You can also close an open database object by right-clicking the object tab and selecting **Close**.

let me try

If the database is not already open, open the data file **AC1-Appointments** and try this skill on your own:
1. Open the *Appointments* table. (If the Navigation Pane is not open, open it.)
2. Open the *New Customer* form.
3. Close the Navigation Pane.
4. Click the tabs to move back and forth between the *Appointments* table and the *New Customer* form.
5. Close the *New Customer* form.
6. Close the *Appointments* table.
7. Open the Navigation Pane.

Skill 1.2 Working with Security Warnings

When you open a database for the first time, Access may display a security warning in the **Message Bar** at the top of the window, below the Ribbon. Access disables active content such as ActiveX controls and VBA macros to protect your computer from becoming infected by a virus or other malware.

If you trust the source of the database, click the **Enable Content** button in the Message Bar. When you enable active content for a database, Access remembers the setting and you will not see the security warning message the next time you open the database.

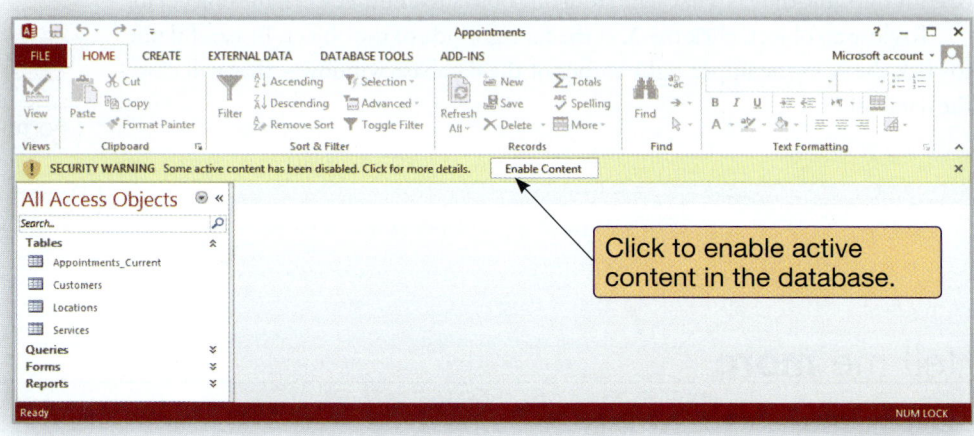

FIGURE AC 1.6

tips & tricks

To learn more about the security settings in Access 2013, open the Trust Center and review the options. We do not recommend changing any of the default Trust Center settings.

another method

You can also enable active content from the Info page in Backstage.
1. Click the **File** tab to open Backstage.
2. Click **Info.**
3. The Info page provides more information about the database. If you are sure you want allow active content, click the **Enable Editing** button.

let me try

If the database is not already open, open the data file **AC1-Appointments** and try this skill on your own:
1. Open the database and enable active content. Once you have done this for the database, you will not see the warning again. If you do not see the warning, you may have enabled active content previously.
2. Close the database and reopen it to confirm that the warning does not appear again.

Skill 1.3 Understanding and Viewing Table Relationships

Remember that Access is a relational database. Objects in your database are related to one another through relationships defined by common fields between tables. Before working with a database, you should understand the underlying database structure—how the tables are related.

For example, a table of customer data might include fields for customer ID, title, first name, last name, and address information. Another table for tracking customer appointments might have fields for appointment ID, appointment date, appointment time, customer, and service. The two tables are related by the data in the *Customer ID* and *Customer* fields, so the database can generate reports combining information from the two tables.

There are three types of relationships: one-to-many, one-to-one, and many-to-many. One-to-many relationships are the most common. In a **one-to-many relationship**, the main table contains a **primary key** field that is included as a field (the **foreign key**) in the secondary table. Thus, one record in the first table can relate to many records in the second table. In Figure AC 1.7, the *Customer ID* field in the *Customers* table is the primary key. Records in the *Appointments* table are related to the *Customers* table through the *Customer* field (the foreign key in the relationship).

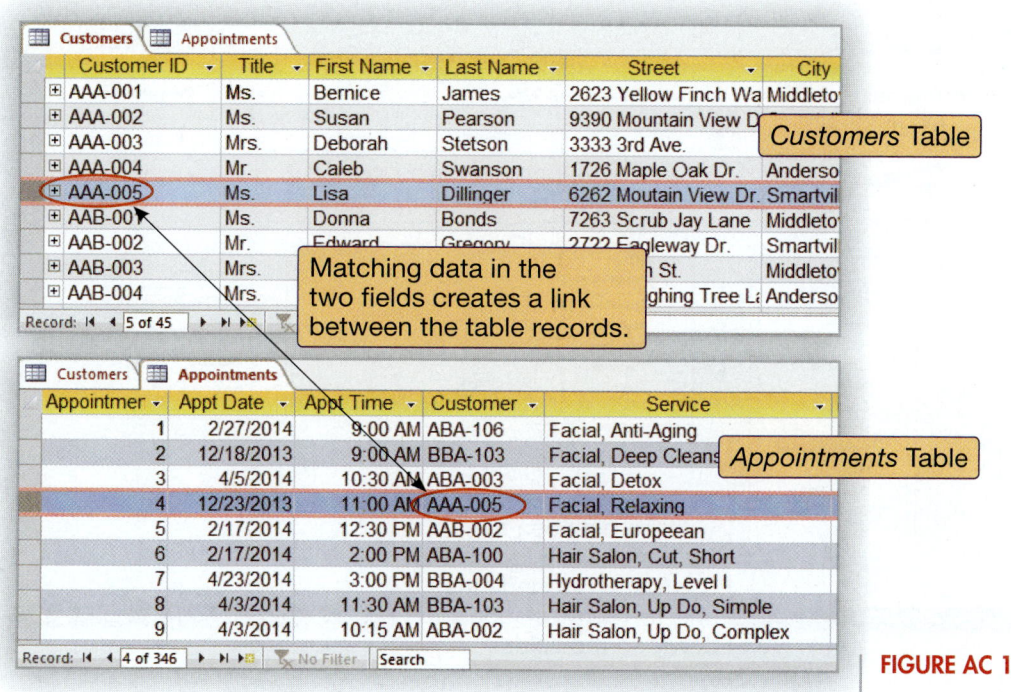

FIGURE AC 1.7

The relationships between primary and foreign key fields are fundamental to understanding and working with any relational database. You will learn more about primary key fields in other skills.

The **Relationships window** provides a visual representation of the relationships in your database.

To open the Relationships window, on the *Database Tools* tab, in the *Relationships* group, click the **Relationships** button.

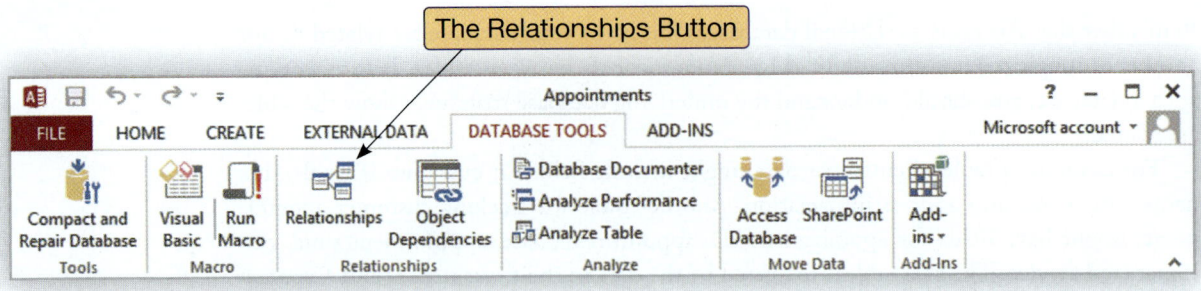

FIGURE AC 1.8

In the Relationships window, each table is represented by a box listing all the fields in the table. Primary key fields are identified with a key icon next to the field name. Lines representing the type of relationship connect related fields. In a one-to-many relationship, the one field in the main table that relates to many records in the secondary table is represented by a 1. The corresponding field in the secondary table is represented by an infinity symbol.

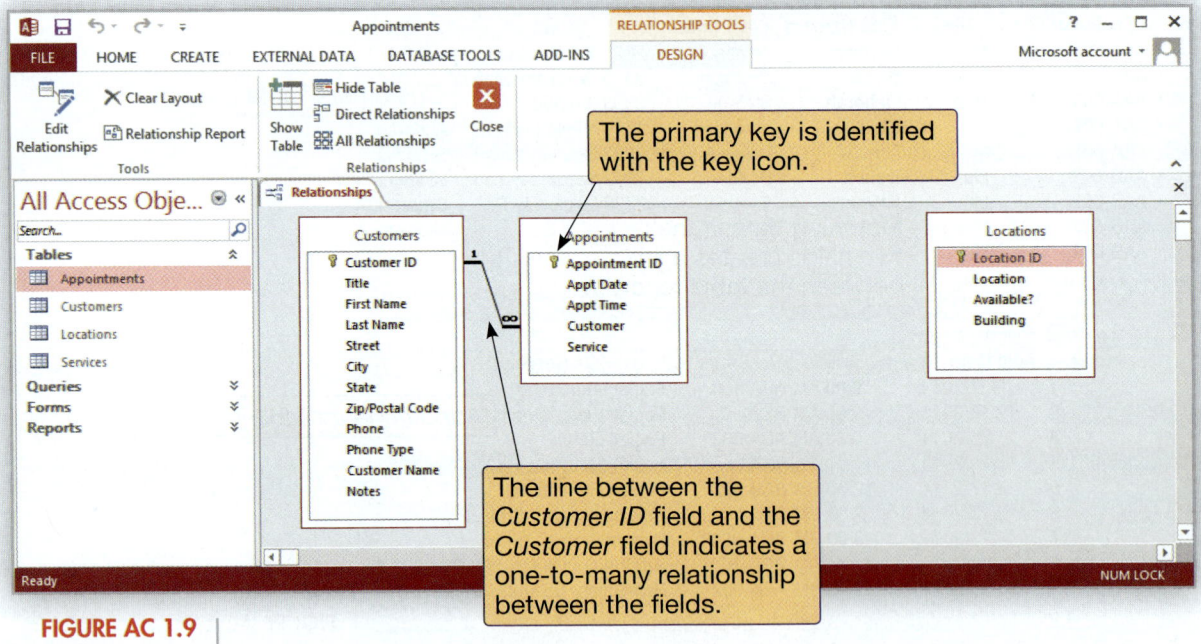

FIGURE AC 1.9

To display a table that isn't already showing in the Relationships window:

1. On the *Relationship Tools Design* tab, in the *Relationships* group, click the **Show Table** button to open the *Show Table* dialog.

2. Double-click the table you want to add to the Relationships window. You can also select the table name and then click the **Add** button in the *Show Table* dialog.

3. When you are finished adding tables to the Relationships window, click the **Close** button to close the *Show Table* dialog.

Figure AC 1.10 shows the effect of adding the *Services* table to the Relationships window. Notice the new lines representing the relationships between the *Appointments* table and the *Services* table and between the *Services* table and the *Locations* table.

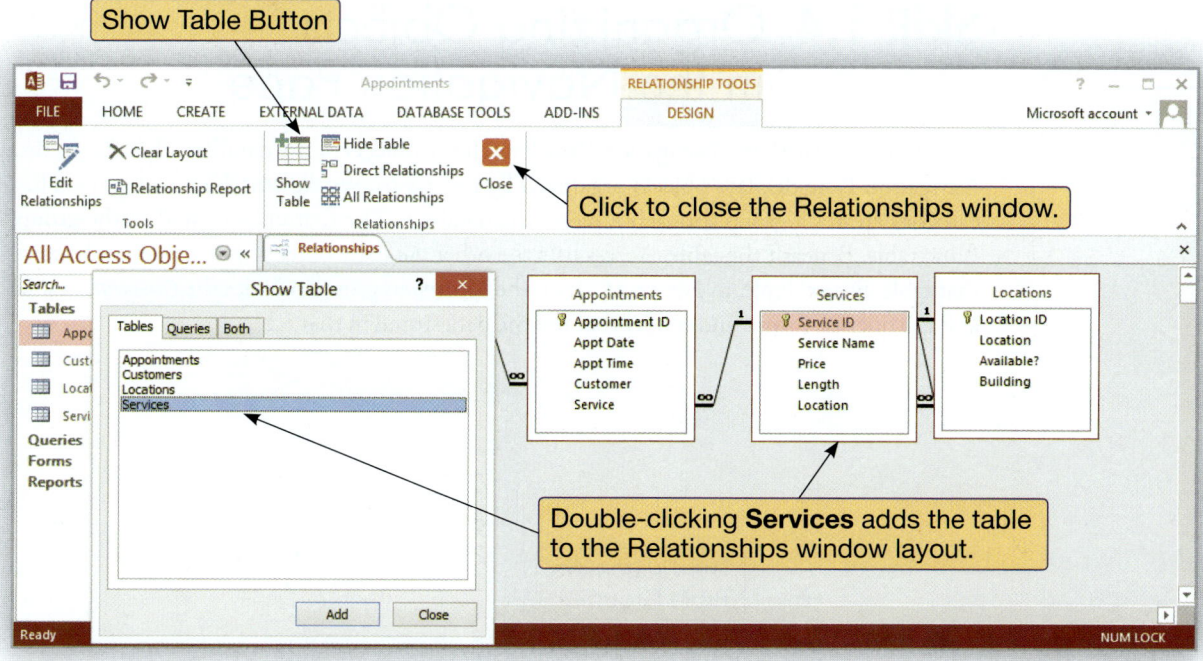

FIGURE AC 1.10

On the *Relationship Tools Design* tab, in the *Relationships* group, click the **Close** button to close the Relationships window.

If you have made changes to the layout of the Relationships window, Access will ask if you want to save the changes. Click **Yes.**

tips & tricks

You can display all the database relationships at once by clicking the **All Relationships** button on the *Relationship Tools Design* tab.

tell me more

To hide a table in the Relationships window:

1. Select the table by clicking it in the Relationships window.
2. On the *Relationship Tools Design* tab, in the *Relationships* group, click the **Hide Table** button.
3. Select the table by clicking it in the Relationships window.

another method

To open the *Show Table* dialog, right-click anywhere in the Relationships window and select **Show Table...** from the shortcut menu.

let me try

If the database is not already open, open the data file **AC1-Appointments** and try this skill on your own:

1. Open the Relationships window.
2. Open the *Show Table* dialog.
3. Show the *Services* table.
4. Close the *Show Table* dialog.
5. Close the Relationships window, saving the layout changes.

skill 1.3 Understanding and Viewing Table Relationships

Skill 1.4 Organizing Objects in the Navigation Pane

As you have learned, the Navigation Pane lists all the objects in the database. By default, the Navigation Pane displays objects organized by the *Tables and Related Views* category. This category creates a group for each table in the database. The first object listed in the group is the table. Beneath the table, Access lists the other database objects that are dependent on that table. For example, in Figure AC 1.11, the *Customers* group includes the *Customers* table and the queries, forms, and report that use the data stored in that table.

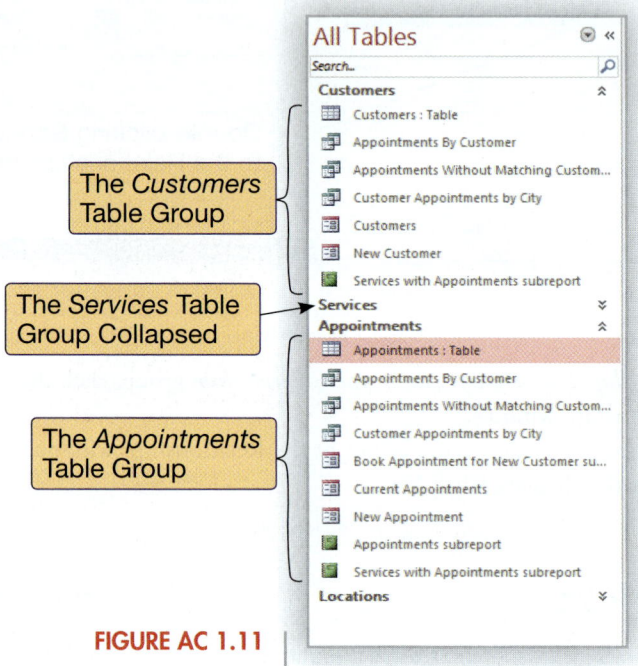

FIGURE AC 1.11

If you are working with the database objects in a single group, it may be helpful to collapse the other groups:

- To collapse a group in the Navigation Pane so only the group name is visible, click the **Collapse Group** button ⌃ located at the right side of the group name.
- To expand a group, click the **Expand Group** button ⌄.

If you would rather group the database objects by object type, you can change the category by which the Navigation Pane is grouped:

1. Click the top of the Navigation Pane to display the category and group list.
2. In the *Navigate to Category* section, select **Object Type.**

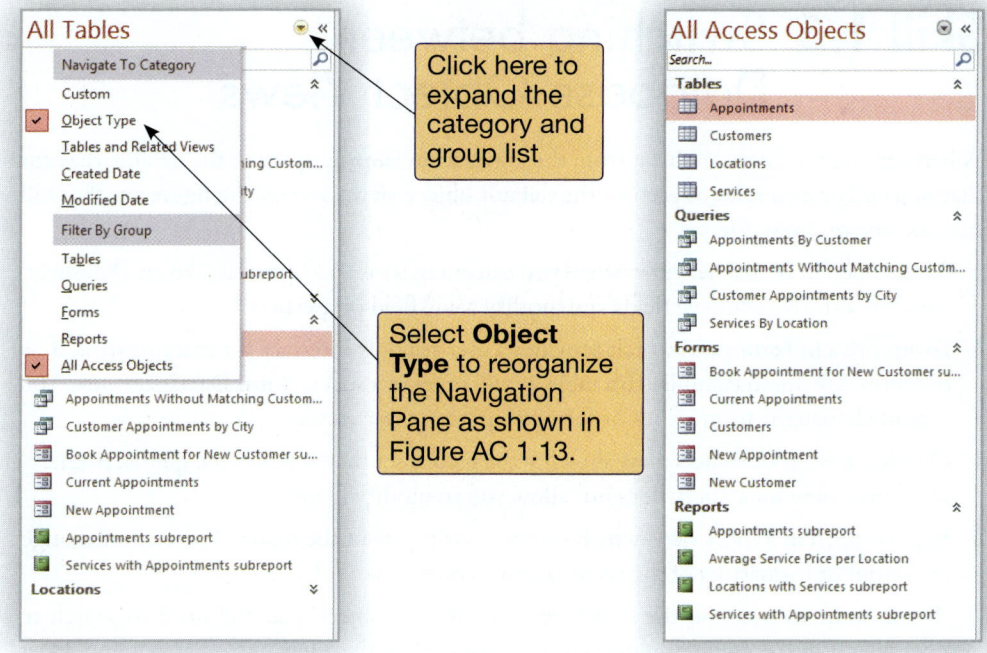

FIGURE AC 1.12

FIGURE AC 1.13

Now the Navigation Pane groups all the tables together in one group, all the queries together in another, all the forms together in another, and all the reports together in the final group.

You can also apply a filter to the Navigation Pane to display only a specific group within the category. Click the top of the Navigation Pane, and click an option in the *Filter by Group* section. The groups available vary, depending on the category and the actual objects in your database.

To remove the group filter, click the top of the Navigation Pane again, and select **All Access Objects** in the *Filter by Group* section.

tell me more

In addition to grouping the Navigation Pane by the *Tables and Related Views* group and the *Object Type* group, there are three other grouping options:

- **Custom**—Groups objects into those you have assigned to the custom group and those that are unassigned.
- **Created Date**—Groups database objects by the date they were created.
- **Modified Date**—Groups database objects by the date they were last changed.

let me try

If the database is not already open, open the data file **AC1-Appointments** and try this skill on your own:
1. Change the Navigation Pane grouping option to **Object Type.**
2. Change the Navigation Pane grouping option to **Tables and Related Views.**

skill 1.4 Organizing Objects in the Navigation Pane

Skill 1.5 Switching between Database Object Views

When you open a database object from the Navigation Pane, it opens in the default view for that object. For examples of each of the default object views, review the figures in the skill *Introduction to Access 2013*.

- Tables open in **Datasheet view** where you can enter, sort, and filter data. From Datasheet view you can also add new fields and modify some field properties.
- Forms open in **Form view**, which provides a user-friendly interface for entering data. If the form is formatted similar to a table, it will open in a special form Datasheet view. You cannot change the form layout or formatting from these views.
- Queries open in **Datasheet view** showing the record set that matches the query criteria. Datasheet view for a query does not allow you to modify fields.
- Reports open in **Report view**, which shows a static view of the report. You cannot change the layout or formatting of the report from Report view.

If you want to work on the structure of a database object, you will need to switch to another view. On the *Home* tab, in the *Views* group, click the **View** button arrow, and select the view you want.

You can also switch views from the buttons at the far right side of the status bar. The button representing the current view appears highlighted. The name of the current view appears at the left side of the status bar.

Design view is used to modify the structure of the database object. When you are working with an object in Design view, you see only the structural elements of the object, not the data.

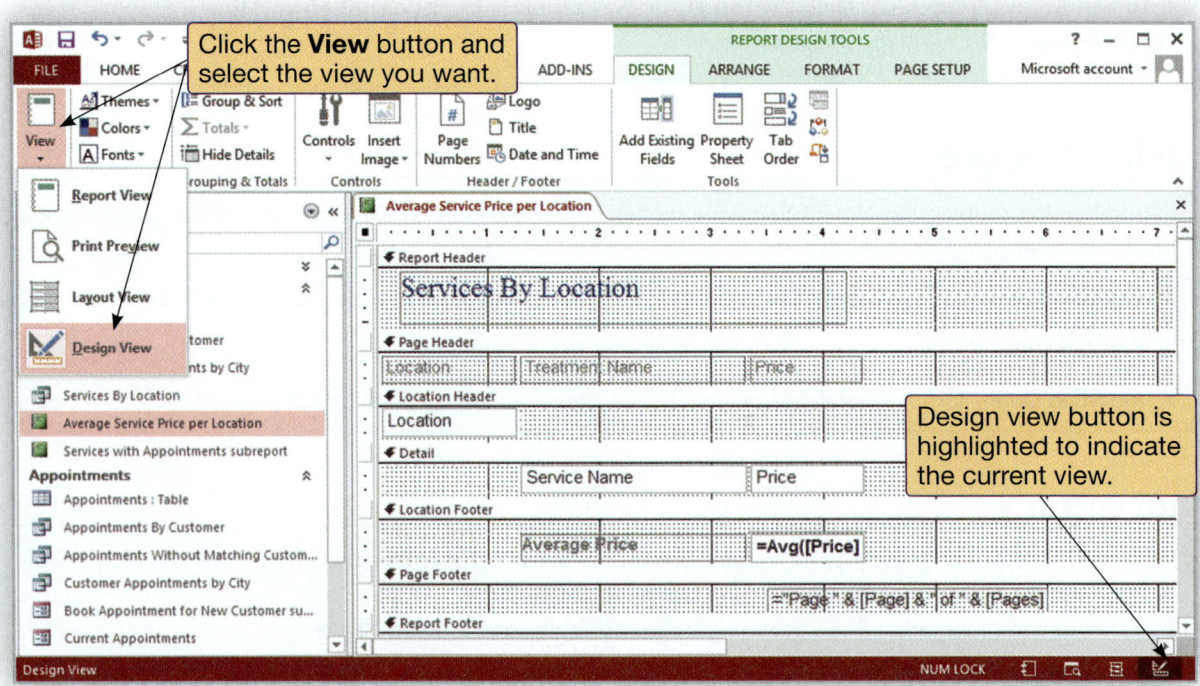

FIGURE AC 1.14
A report in Design view

For queries, Design view gives you a visual grid to create the underlying programming code that defines the parameters and criteria used to generate the resulting dataset. Queries also offer **SQL view** where advanced users can write code directly to build the query.

Forms and reports also offer **Layout view** where you can modify some (but not all) structural elements. The benefit of Layout view is that you can see live data in the object while you work on the object layout.

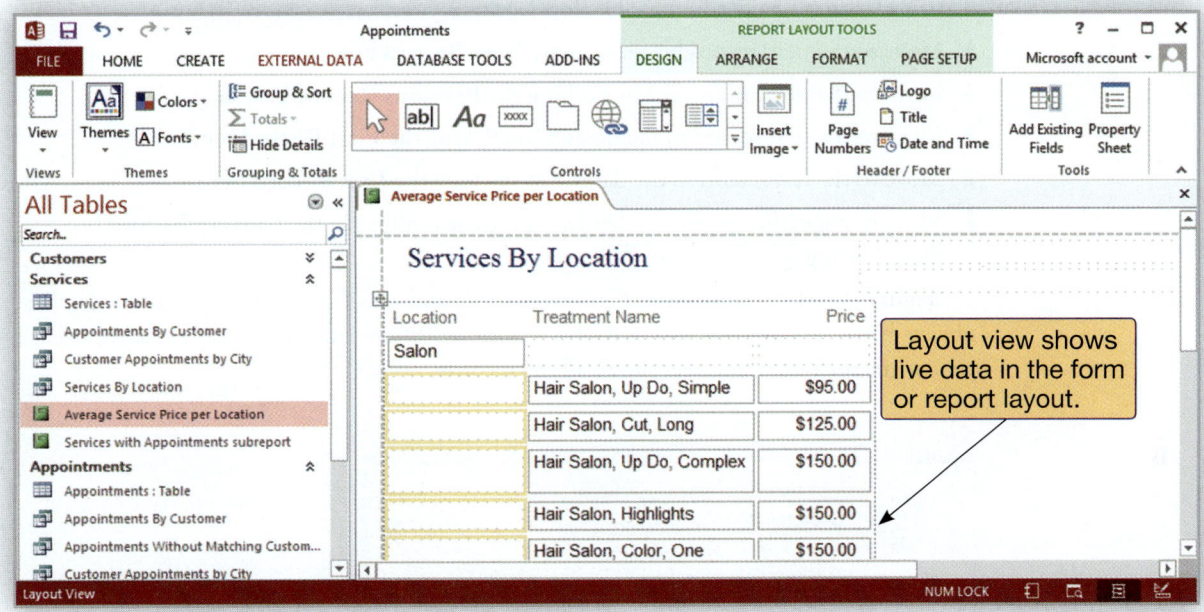

FIGURE AC 1.15
A report in Layout view

Reports include **Print Preview**, which shows how the report will look when printed. When you are in Print Preview view, only the *Print Preview* tab is available. From this tab, you can adjust print settings and export the report to another file format.

tips & tricks

Table data and query results in Datasheet view are sometimes referred to as **datasheets**.

another method

To switch views you can also right-click the object tab and select the view you want.

let me try

If the database is not already open, open the data file **AC1-Appointments** and try this skill on your own:
1. Open the *Average Price per Location* report from the Navigation Pane. You may need to expand the *Locations* group or the *Reports* group to find the report. It will open in Report view.
2. Switch to Design view.
3. Switch to Layout view.
4. Close the report.

skill 1.5 Switching between Database Object Views

Skill 1.6 Navigating Records

Tables, forms, and query results often contain many records and can be difficult to navigate. At the bottom of the datasheet or form window, you'll find navigation buttons to help you move quickly to the beginning or end of the dataset. You can jump to a specific record number or advance through records one at a time.

To navigate among records in a table, form, or query results:

- Move to the next record by clicking the **Next Record** button.
- Move to the previous record by clicking the **Previous Record** button.
- Move to the first record in the dataset by clicking the **First Record** button.
- Move to the last record in the dataset by clicking the **Last Record** button.
- Move to a specific record number by typing the number in the **Current Record** box, then pressing ⏎ Enter or Tab ⇥.

Figure AC 1.16 shows the *Customers* form and the *Customers* table. Both database objects have the same navigation tools even though the form displays only one record at a time while the table datasheet shows all the records.

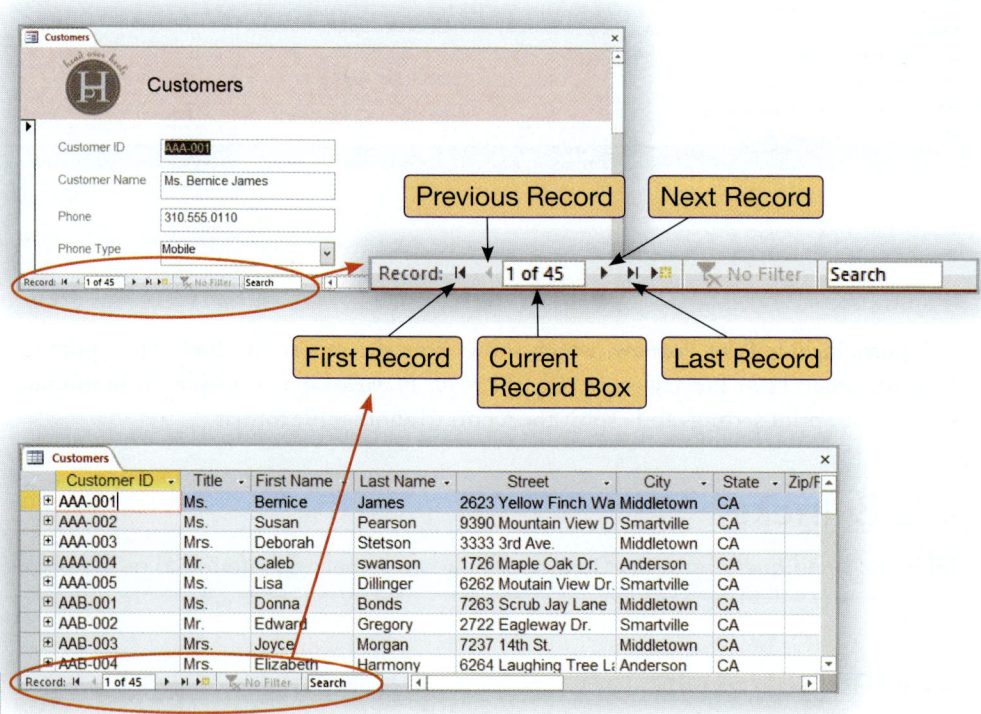

FIGURE AC 1.16

You can use the arrow keys on your keyboard to navigate through fields in a record or between records.

- Press → to go to the next field in the record.
- Press ← to go to the previous field in the record.
- Press ↓ to go to the next record.
- Press ↑ to go to the previous record.
- Press Ctrl + ↑ to go to the first record.
- Press Ctrl + ↓ to go to the last record.

You can use Tab to navigate from field to field and from record to record:

- Pressing Tab moves you from field to field within a record.
- Pressing Tab from the last field in the record will move you to the first field in the next record.
- If you are on the last record in the dataset, pressing Tab will create a new blank record (if creating a new record is allowed).

another **method**

The record navigation commands are also available from the *Home* tab, in the *Find* group. Click the **Go To** button, and then click one of the navigation options from the menu.

let me **try**

If the database is not already open, open the data file **AC1-Appointments** and try this skill on your own:
1. If necessary, open the *Customers* table in Datasheet view.
2. Go to the **last** record.
3. Go to the **previous** record.
4. Go to the **first** record.
5. Go to the **next** record.
6. Go to record number **20**.
7. Close the table.

from the perspective of . . .

PROJECT MANAGER

I inherited a database from the person who had my job before me. I am not a database expert, so before I attempted any data entry, I made sure I understood the structure of the database. I used the Relationships window to see how the tables relate to one another. I also switched the Navigation Pane organization to show the tables and related views, so I could see which forms and reports go with which tables. After spending some time exploring the database objects, I felt much more comfortable about using the database. I'm really glad I didn't jump in and start making changes right away.

Skill 1.7 Creating a New Record in a Table

Data are entered in records—through tables or forms. When entering records in a table, you must use Datasheet view. When you enter data in a table, Access commits the data (saves them) each time you move to a new field or begin a new record.

To enter data in a new record in a table:

1. Open the table in Datasheet view.
2. If the last row of the table is visible, you can enter data by typing in the first field in the next row available for data entry indicated by * in the row selector.
3. If the last row of the table is not visible, insert a new record by clicking the **New (blank) record** button at the bottom of the table, or on the *Home* tab, in the *Records* group, click the **New** button.

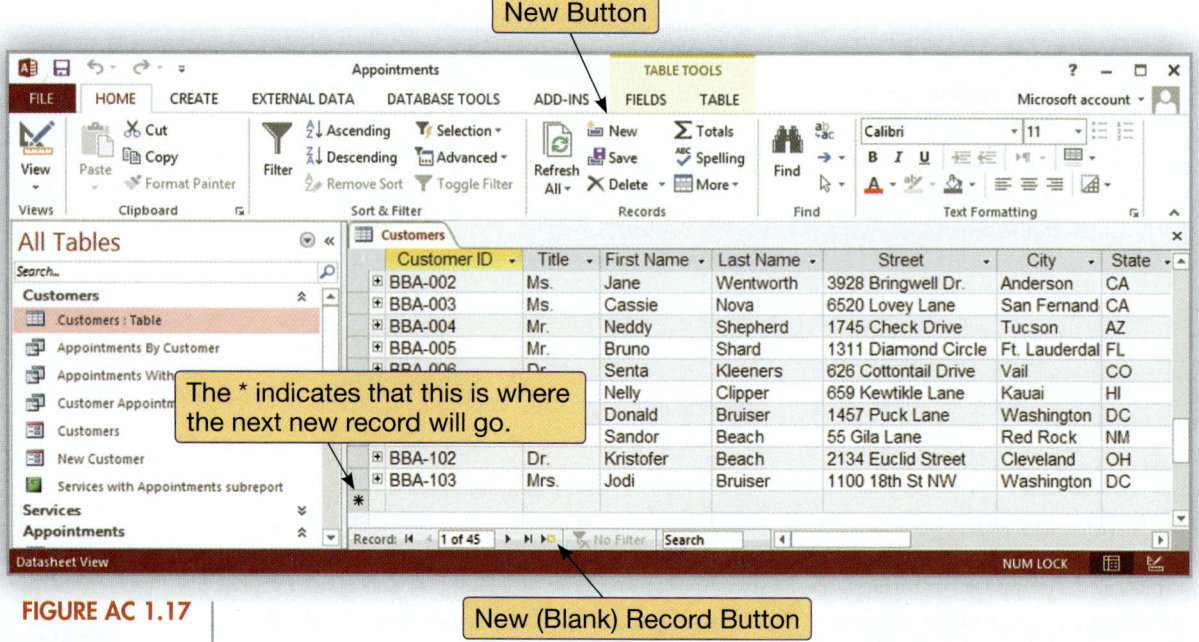

FIGURE AC 1.17

4. Enter the data in the first field of the record. Notice that when you begin entering data, the * changes to a pencil icon to indicate you are writing data to the record.
5. Press Tab or Enter to move to the next field.
6. When you've entered all the data for the new record, press Tab or Enter to start another new record.

Not all fields allow you to enter data by typing.

- If a field uses the AutoNumber format, you will not be able to type in that cell of the datasheet. Instead, move to the next cell to begin entering data. Access will populate the AutoNumber field automatically with the next number in sequence.
- Some fields require a specific input format (called an input mask). When you enter data in a field that has an input mask, Access will display placeholder characters such as underscores to guide you as you enter data. Access will not let you enter characters that

violate the input mask rules (for example, entering a number when a letter is required). The input mask may also include characters that are displayed automatically such as the hyphen in the Customer ID in Figure AC 1.18 or the parentheses around the area code in a phone number.

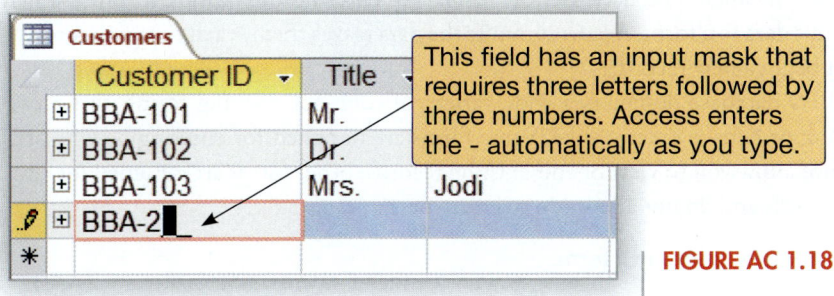

FIGURE AC 1.18

- Some fields (called lookup fields) have lists from which you choose values. Click the arrow in the field to display the list of available values and click the value you want.

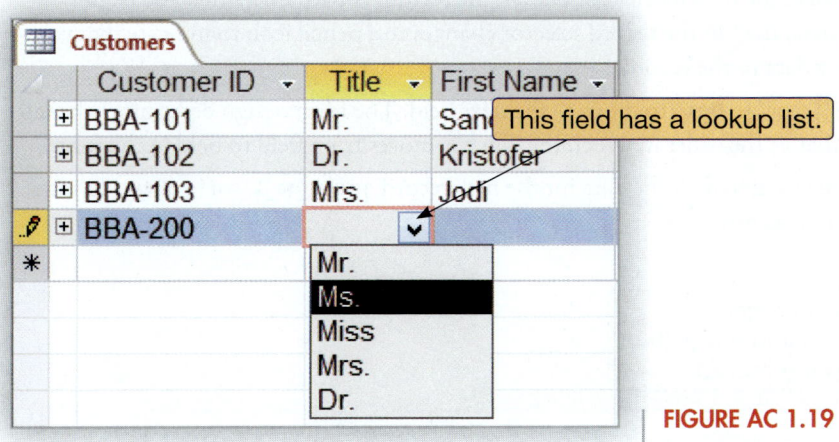

FIGURE AC 1.19

another method

Here are other ways to add a new blank record to the table:
- On the *Home* tab, in the *Find* group, click the **Go To** button, and select **New**.
- Right-click any of the row selector buttons and select **New Record** from the menu.
- Use the keyboard shortcut Ctrl + +.

let me try

If the database is not already open, open the data file **AC1-Appointments** and try this skill on your own:
1. Open the *Customers* table in Datasheet view.
2. Begin a new record.
3. Enter the customer ID: **BBA-200**. Notice that this field requires a specific format.
4. Select **Ms.** as the title from the lookup list in the next field.
5. Enter data for the remaining fields in the table using a name, address, and phone number of your choice.

skill 1.7   Creating a New Record in a Table

Skill 1.8 Creating a New Record in a Form

When you use a form to enter data, you are actually adding data to the underlying table. The form is a more convenient and user-friendly format for entering and editing records. When you enter or edit data in a form, Access commits the data (saves them) each time you move to a new field or begin a new record.

Access offers database designers a wide variety of tools for creating forms, so no two forms may look or behave exactly alike. Some forms are designed for entering new records only and do not allow you to view or edit existing records; other forms are designed for editing existing records and do not allow you to create new ones.

To enter data in a new record in a form:

1. Open the form in Form view.
2. Some forms are designed to automatically open to a new record where you can immediately begin entering data. If necessary, you can start a new blank record by clicking the **New (blank) record** button at the bottom of the form window. Or, on the *Home* tab, in the *Records* group, click the **New** button.
3. Type or select the data in the first field of the record. Notice that when you begin entering data, the * in the record selector changes to a pencil icon to indicate that you are writing data to the record.
4. Press Tab or Enter to move to the next field. The form design determines the tab order— that is, the order in which the Tab key moves from field to field in the form.
5. When you've entered all the data for the new record, press Tab or Enter to start another new record.

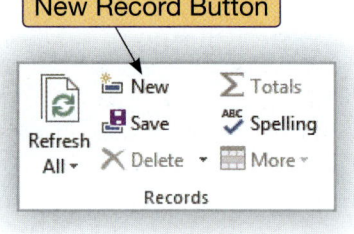

FIGURE AC 1.20

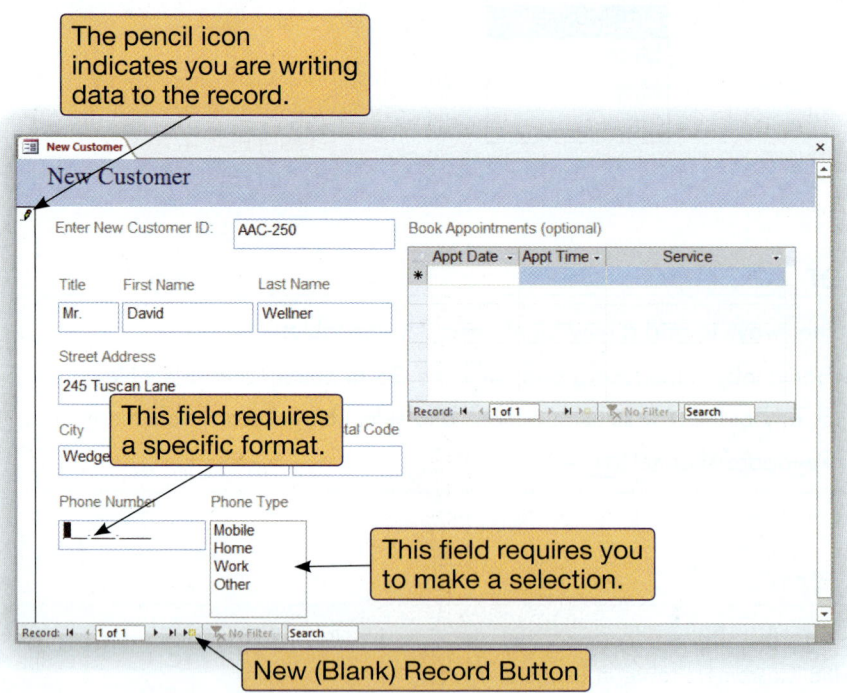

FIGURE AC 1.21

If the field in the underlying table requires a specific number or format, the form will require that same format. Other fields may present a list of values to choose from, rather than allowing you to enter your own values. For more information about data entry restrictions controlled by the underlying table, refer to the skill *Creating a New Record in a Table*.

Some forms may include interface elements to make it easier for users unfamiliar with Access. The form in Figure AC 1.22 includes a *Save and New* button to help users who may be unfamiliar with Access and think they need to save the record before moving on. You know better. Access saves the data as you enter it in each field in the form.

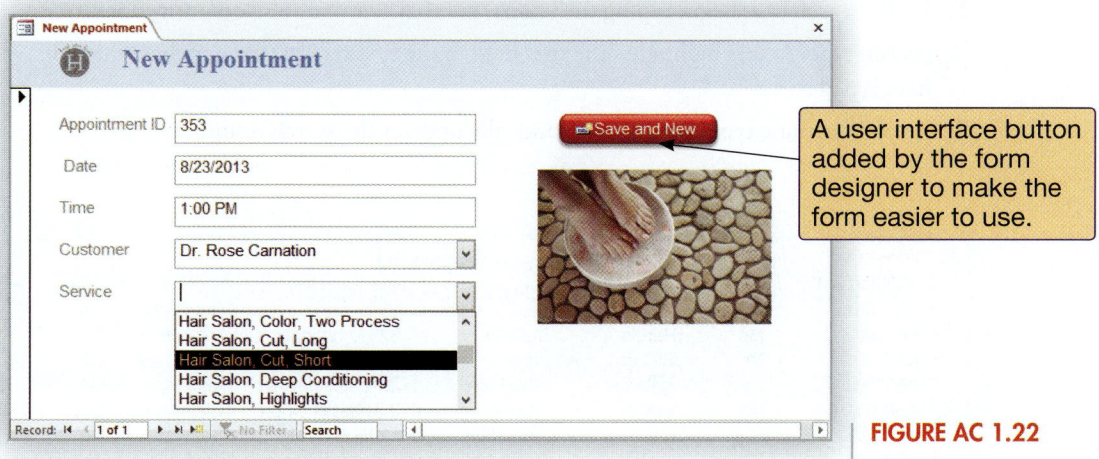

FIGURE AC 1.22

tips & tricks

If one of the fields is a *Long Text* field, you won't be able to use ←Enter to move to the next field. Pressing ←Enter will just keep adding blank lines to the text. Use Tab or the mouse to move to the next field.

another method

Here are other ways to enter a new blank record in a form:
- On the *Home* tab, in the *Find* group, click the **Go To** button, and select **New.**
- Right-click any of the row selector buttons and select **New Record** from the menu.
- Use the keyboard shortcut Ctrl + +.

let me try

If the database is not already open, open the data file **AC1-Appointments** and try this skill on your own:
1. Open the *New Appointment* form. Notice that this form automatically opens to a new record.
2. Notice that you cannot enter data in the Appointment ID field. When you begin entering data in the next field in the form, Access will add the next sequential appointment number to this field automatically.
3. Enter the date `8/23/14` and time `1:00 PM` for the appointment. Notice that the form requires specific formats for these fields.
4. Select the customer **Dr. Rose Carnation** and the service **Hair Salon, Cut, Short** from the lists for those fields.
5. Click the **Save and New** button in the form to save the data and start a new record.
6. Close the form.

skill 1.8 Creating a New Record in a Form

Skill 1.9 Finding and Replacing Data

Access provides a number of ways to search for information in your database. For a simple search in a table, form, or query, you can use the Search box next to the navigation buttons at the bottom of the datasheet or form.

1. In the Search box, begin typing the letters, numbers, or symbols you want to find.
2. As you type, Access highlights the first field in the first record that matches what you have typed so far.
3. As you continue typing, Access dynamically updates the search result.

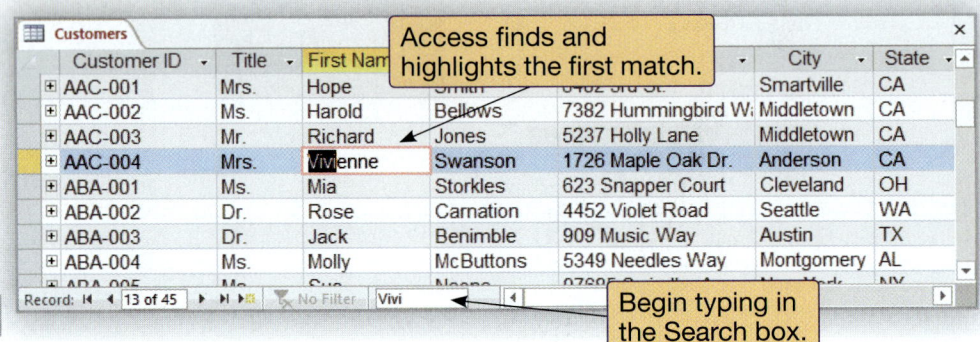

FIGURE AC 1.23

If you need to find multiple records that match your search parameters, not just the first one, use the *Find* command. If you have used other Microsoft Office applications, the *Find and Replace* dialog will be familiar to you.

To search for specific records using the *Find* command:

1. Open the database object you want to search. The *Find* command is available for any object in Datasheet view, Form view, Report view, or Layout view.
2. On the *Home* tab, in the *Find* group, click the **Find** button to open the *Find and Replace* dialog.
3. Type the data you want to search for in the *Find What* box.
4. Click **Find Next** to go to the first record that matches the search criteria. Continue clicking **Find Next** until Access displays a message that there are no more records that meet your search criteria.
5. Click the red **X** in the upper right corner of the dialog to close it.

To narrow the search parameters in the *Find and Replace* dialog:

- Use the *Look In* list to specify whether to search only in the currently selected field or throughout the entire document (the open database object).
- Use the *Match* list to specify a match for the any part of the field, the whole field, or only the beginning of the field.
- Use the *Search* list to search only up or down from the current record or to search all the records.
- Use the *Match Case* check box to find only records that match the case of your find text. This check box is available even if you are searching for numerical data.

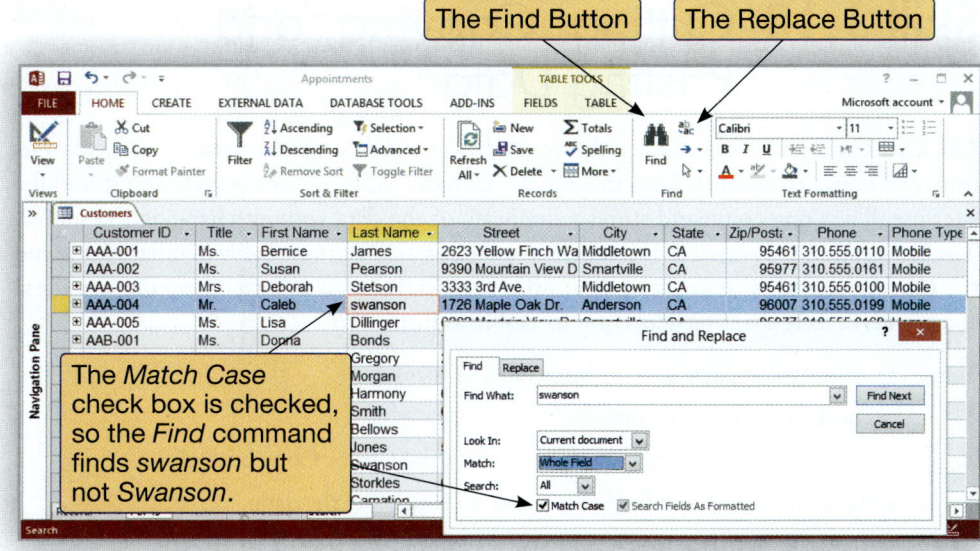

FIGURE AC 1.24

To find and replace data:
1. On the *Home* tab, in the *Find* group, click the **Replace** button. If the *Find and Replace* dialog is already open, click the **Replace** tab.
2. Enter the data to find in the *Find What* box.
3. Enter the data to replace it with in the *Replace With* box.
4. Click the **Replace** button to find and replace just the first instance, or click the **Replace All** button to replace all instances at once.
5. Access warns you that you will not be able to undo this operation. Click **Yes** to continue.
6. Click the red **X** in the upper right corner of the dialog to close it.

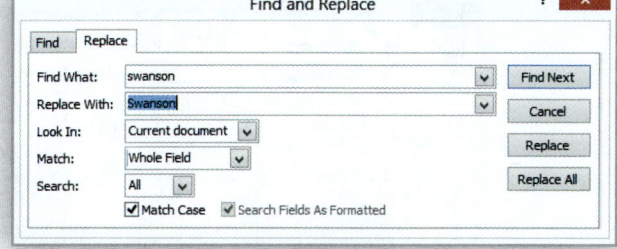

FIGURE AC 1.25

tips & tricks

Use wildcards in the *Find and Replace* dialog if you are not sure of the exact data you want to find.
- Use an asterisk * when you know the beginning of the search word or phrase, but not the end. For example, B* will find records for Ben, Bob, and Betty.
- Use question marks ? in place of specific letters or numbers. For example, B?? will find records for Ben and Bob but not Betty.

let me try

If the database is not already open, open the data file **AC1-Appointments** and try this skill on your own:
1. Open the *Customers* table in Datasheet view.
2. Use the Search box to begin searching for a customer with the first name beginning with *Vivi*. Notice that as you type `v` and then `i`, Access first highlights a record with the word *View* in the *Street* field. Once you finish entering `viv` in the Search box, Access finds the record with *Vivienne* in the *First Name* field.
3. Use the *Find and Replace* dialog to find the record with the text `swanson`, matching the case exactly.
4. Replace all instances of `swanson` with `Swanson`. Be sure to match the case exactly.
5. Close the table.

skill 1.9 Finding and Replacing Data

Skill 1.10 Cutting, Copying, and Pasting Data

The *Cut, Copy,* and *Paste* commands are used to move data within a database object and from one object to another. Data that are **cut** are removed from the database and stored for later use. The **Copy** command stores a duplicate of the data without changing the source. The **Paste** command is used to insert copied or cut data. You are probably familiar with using the *Cut, Copy,* and *Paste* commands in other applications. As expected, you can use these commands in Access during data entry in a table or form.

To use cut or copy and paste data within a table or form:

1. Select the data to be cut or copied.
2. On the *Home* tab, in the *Clipboard* group, click the **Cut** or **Copy** button.
3. Navigate to the record and field where you want to paste the data.
4. Click the **Paste** button.

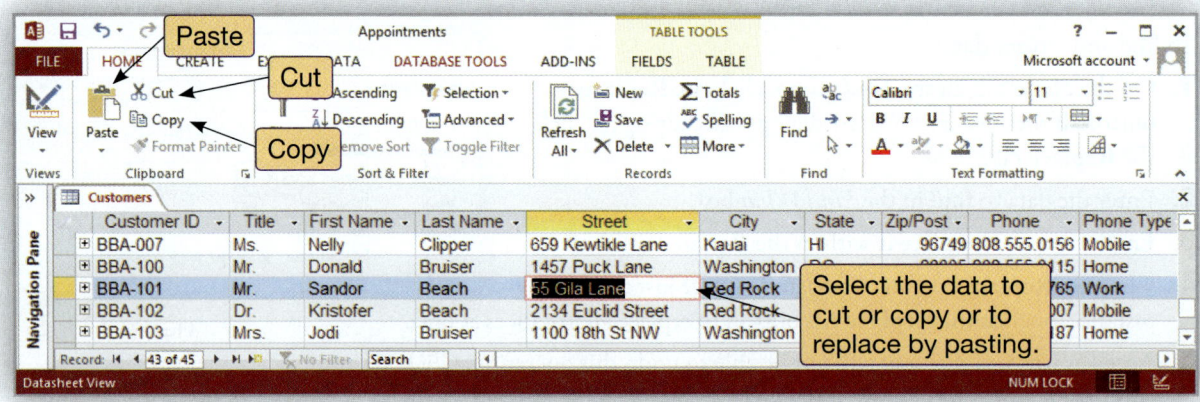

FIGURE AC 1.26

another method

Use the keyboard shortcuts for the *Cut, Copy,* and *Paste* commands:

- Cut = Ctrl + X
- Copy = Ctrl + C
- Paste = Ctrl + V

Use the command from the right-click menu:

- The *Cut* and *Copy* commands are available from the menu when you select data then right-click.
- To paste, you can right-click within a field and select **Paste.**

let me try

If the database is not already open, open the data file **AC1-Appointments** and try this skill on your own:

1. Open the *Customers* table in Datasheet view.
2. Find the record with the Customer ID **BBA-101**.
3. Copy the data in the *Street* field.
4. Move to the next record (Customer **BBA-102**).
5. Paste into the *Street* field, replacing the existing data.
6. Close the table.

Skill 1.11 Using Undo and Redo

If you make a mistake when working, the **Undo** command allows you to reverse the last action you performed. The **Redo** command allows you to reverse the Undo command and restore the file to its previous state. The Quick Access Toolbar gives you immediate access to both these commands.

To undo the last action taken, click the **Undo** button on the Quick Access Toolbar, or click the **Undo** button arrow and select the action to undo.

If you are working on data entry in Datasheet view or Form view, the *Undo* command is applied to the entire record, not each individual field within the record. If you made multiple changes to the record at the same time, the *Undo* command will reverse all the changes at once. In addition, the *Undo* command can be applied only to the last modified record. If you made changes to multiple records, you are out of luck.

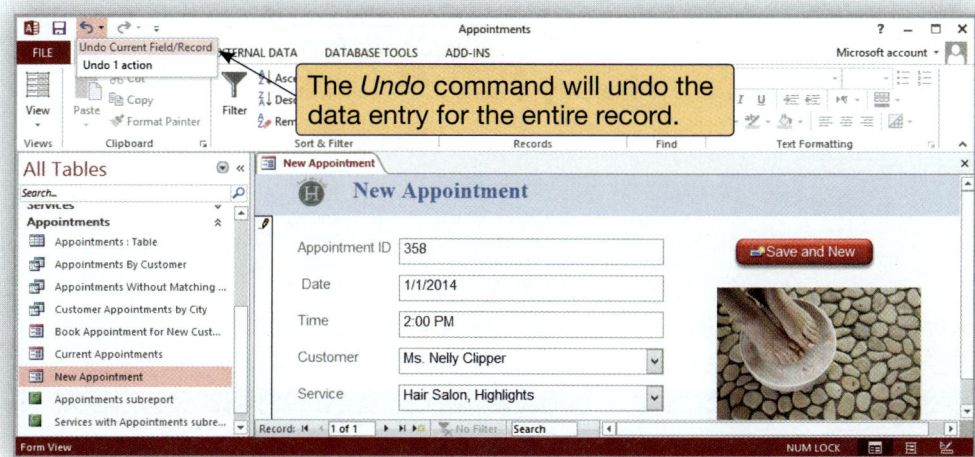

FIGURE AC 1.27

To redo the last action taken, click the **Redo** button on the Quick Access Toolbar.

The *Redo* command is useful mostly when you are working with formatting design elements in forms and reports. It is not available for data entry tasks.

tips & tricks

If you are familiar with using *Undo* and *Redo* in other Office applications, be very careful in Access. There are many actions that cannot be undone. Usually, but not always, Access will warn you before you do something that can't be undone.

another method

Use the keyboard shortcuts:
- Undo = Ctrl + Z
- Redo = Ctrl + Y

let me try

If the database is not already open, open the data file **AC1-Appointments** and try this skill on your own:
1. Open the *New Appointment* form in Form view.
2. Enter data for a new appointment. Do not continue to another new record.
3. Undo the data entry. Notice that the data entry for the entire record is undone at once.
4. Close the form.

Skill 1.12 Deleting Records

You can delete records. However, if your database has a complex structure, deleting records may not be as simple as the procedures listed below because records in one table may be linked to records in another table. Access will prevent you from deleting records if the deletion would violate the integrity of the database. *You cannot undo a record deletion.*

To delete a record in Datasheet view:

1. Click the record selector so the record you want to delete is selected.
2. On the *Home* tab, in the *Records* group, click the **Delete** button.
3. Access warns you that you cannot undo the deletion. Click **Yes** to continue.

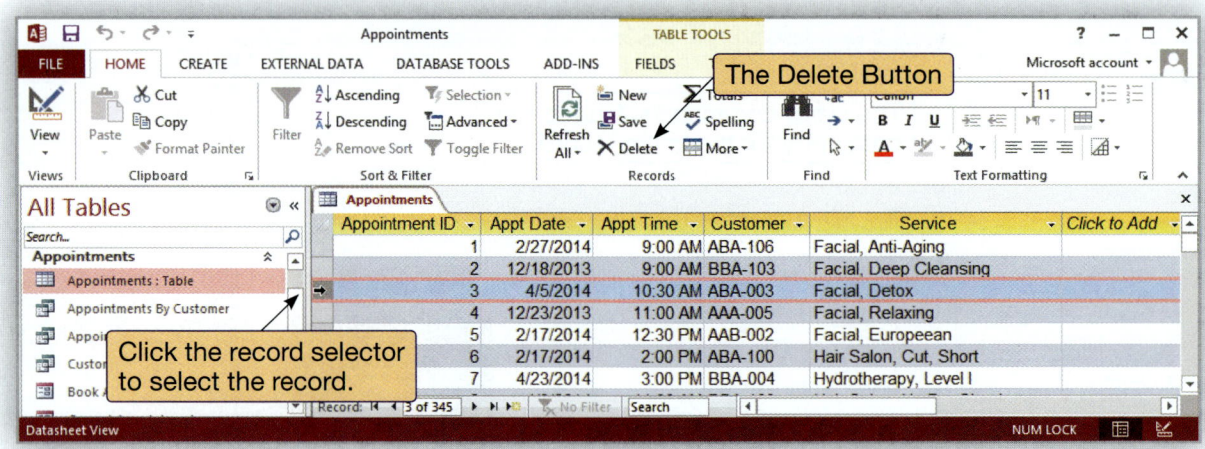

FIGURE AC 1.28

Deleting a record in a form will delete the record in the underlying table.

To delete a record in Form view:

1. Navigate to the record you want to delete.
2. On the *Home* tab, in the *Records* group, click the **Delete** button arrow, and select **Delete Record.**
3. Access warns you that you cannot undo the deletion. Click **Yes** to continue.

another method

- Right-click the record selector and select **Delete Record.**
- Select the record, and press (Delete).
- Select the record and use the keyboard shortcut (Ctrl) + (-).

let me try

If the database is not already open, open the data file **AC1-Appointments** and try this skill on your own:

1. Open the *Appointment* table in Datasheet view.
2. Delete the appointment with the Appointment ID **3**. It should be the third record in the table.
3. Close the table.

Skill 1.13 Checking Spelling

Like other Office applications, Access includes a built-in spelling checker. In Access, the *Spelling* command analyzes the current database object for spelling errors, not the entire database.

To check for spelling errors:

1. On the *Home* tab, in the *Records* group, click the **Spelling** button.
2. The first spelling error appears in the *Spelling* dialog.
3. If you want Access to skip checking spelling for the current field, click the **Ignore '[field name here]' Field** button.
4. Review the spelling suggestions and then select an action:
   - Click **Ignore** to make no changes to this instance of the word or click **Ignore All** to make no changes to all instances of the word.
   - Click the correct spelling in the *Suggestions* list, and click **Change** to correct just this instance of the misspelling or click **Change All** to correct all instances of the misspelling in the current database object or record.
   - Click **Add** to make no changes to this instance of the word and add it to the spelling checker dictionary, so future uses of this word will not show up as misspellings. When you add a word to the dictionary, it is available for all the Office applications.
   - Click **AutoCorrect** to update the AutoCorrect list to automatically autocorrect the misspelling with the selected suggestion when you enter data.
5. After you select an action, the spelling checker automatically advances to the next suspected spelling error.
6. When the spelling checker finds no more errors, it displays a message telling you the check is complete. Click **OK** to close the dialog and return to your worksheet.

FIGURE AC 1.29

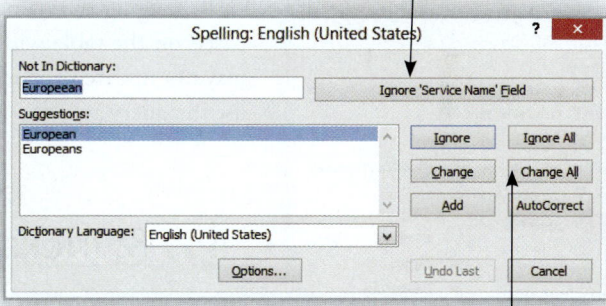

FIGURE AC 1.30

tips & tricks

If you are working with a form that shows one record at a time, the spelling checker checks only the current, active record.

another method

To open the *Spelling* dialog, you can use the keyboard shortcut F7.

let me try

If the database is not already open, open the data file **AC1-Appointments** and try this skill on your own:
1. Open the *Services* table in Datasheet view.
2. Check for spelling errors, correcting any errors that Access finds.
3. Close the table.

Skill 1.14 Deleting and Renaming Database Objects

When you are in the process of designing your database, you may find that you have database objects you no longer need or that you want to use different names for objects. Access allows you to delete and rename forms, reports, and other database objects.

To delete a database object:

1. Right-click the object name in the Navigation Pane and select **Delete.**
2. Access displays a confirmation message, asking if you want to delete the object. Click **Yes** to delete it or **No** to cancel the delete command.

Be careful! Once you delete a database object, you cannot undo the deletion.

To rename a database object:

1. Right-click the object name in the Navigation Pane and select **Rename.**
2. Type the new object name, and press Enter.

Changing the name of a table may have unexpected consequences. Forms and reports based on the table will update automatically to use the new table name. However, queries may not update properly, causing errors not only in the query, but in forms and reports that use the query as well.

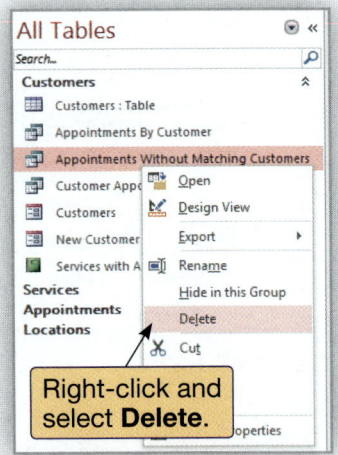

FIGURE AC 1.31

FIGURE AC 1.32

tips & tricks

Access will warn you if you try to delete a table that would invalidate relationships. If you are sure you want to delete the table, Access will automatically delete the relationships, and then delete the table. If you do not allow Access to delete the relationships, Access will not delete the table.

another method

You can delete a table or other database object by selecting it in the Navigation Pane, and then on the *Home* tab, in the *Records* group, click the **Delete** button.

let me try

If the database is not already open, open the data file **AC1-Appointments** and try this skill on your own:

1. If necessary, open the Navigation Pane.
2. If necessary, change the Navigation Pane category to **Tables and Related Views.**
3. If there are open database objects, close them all.
4. In the *Customers* group, delete the query *Appointments Without Matching Customers.*
5. In the *Customers* group, rename the form *Customers* to: `Master Customer Form`

Skill 1.15 Exporting Data to Excel or Word

You can export Access data to a variety of other applications, including Microsoft Excel and Microsoft Word. This is helpful if you want to share the data with someone who may not have Access or may not need to see the entire database.

When you export Access data to Word, you are actually exporting to a text format called **Rich Text Format** (or **RTF**). This format can be used with any word processing program, not just Microsoft Word.

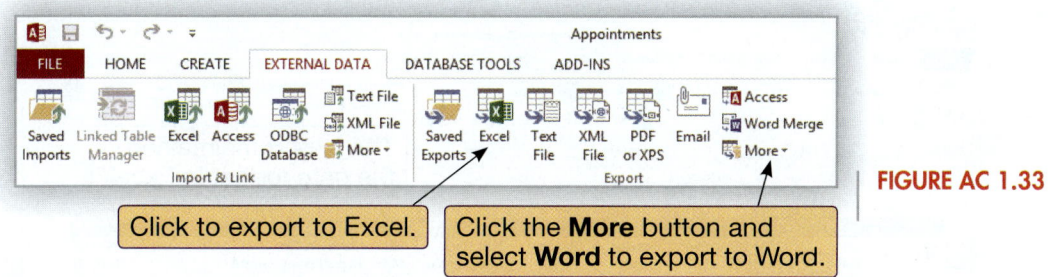

FIGURE AC 1.33

To export data to Excel or Word:

1. In the Navigation Pane, click the object you want to export.
2. On the *External Data* tab, in the *Export* group, click the **Excel** button to export to Excel. To export to Word, click the **More** button and select **Word**.
3. Access automatically suggests a file name based on the name of the object you selected. If you want to change the file name or the location of the saved file, click the **Browse...** button and make your changes in the *File Save* dialog.
4. If you are exporting to Word, or if you are exporting a report, the *Export data with formatting and layout.* check box is checked automatically. You do not have the option to uncheck it. If you are exporting to Excel, the box is not checked by default. Be sure to check it if you want to maintain data formats such as dates and currency styles.

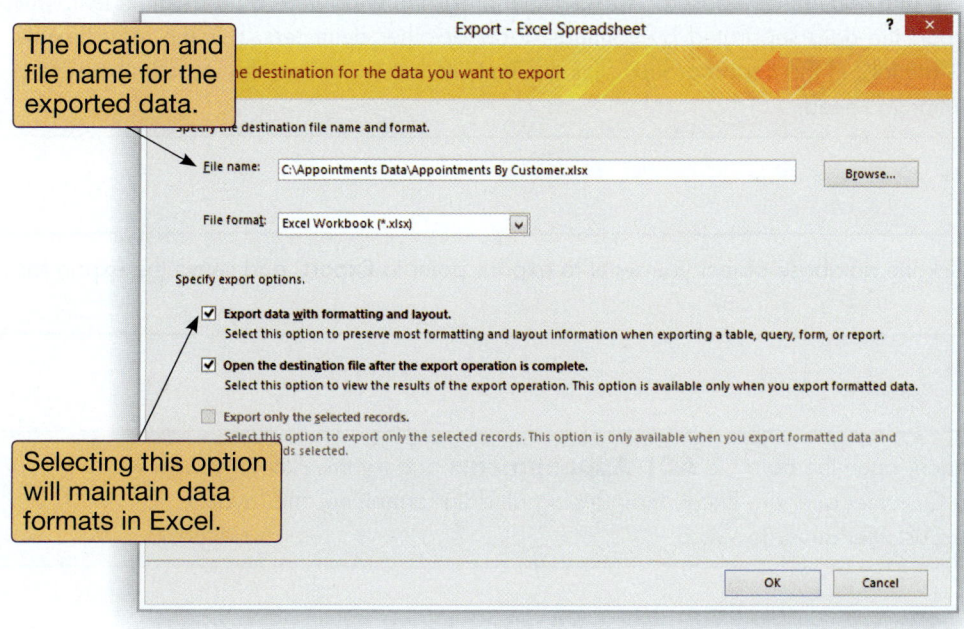

FIGURE AC 1.34

skill 1.15 Exporting Data to Excel or Word

5. When the *Export data with formatting and layout.* option is checked, you also have the option to check the box to **Open the destination file after the export operation is complete.**
6. If you have a table, query, or form open with specific records selected, you can elect to export only those records. Click the **Export only the selected records.** check box.
7. Click **OK** to begin the export process.
8. After the export is complete, you have the option to save the export steps so you can easily run the same export again later. Check the **Save export steps** check box.
9. Click the **Close** button.

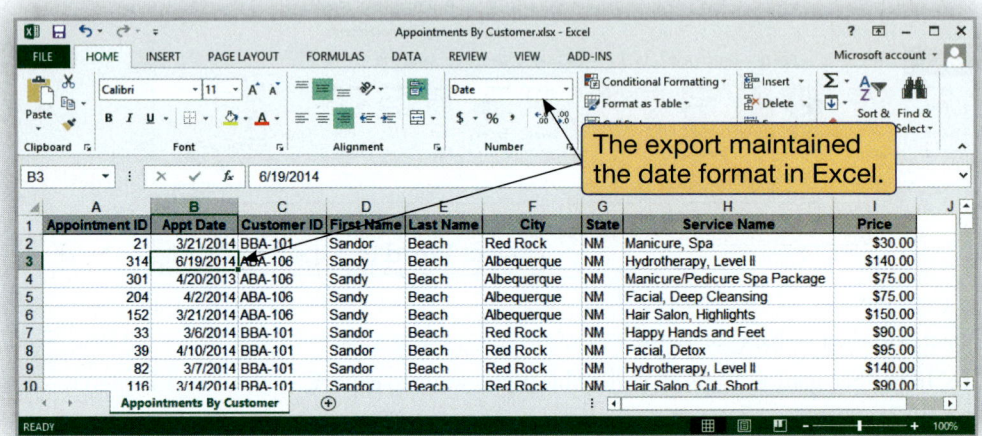

FIGURE AC 1.35

tips & tricks

If you save your export specifications, you can run the export again later by clicking the **Saved Exports** button on the *External Data* tab, *Export* group.

tell me more

If you need to import Access data into another database or spreadsheet program, export the data as plain text. This export option allows you to export the data separated by commas, tabs, or other delimiters. It is the most flexible export option. On the *External Data* tab, in the *Export* group, click the **Text File** button. Follow the steps in the wizard to export the data in the text format you need.

another method

In the Navigation Pane, right-click the database object you want to export, point to **Export,** and select the export format you want to use.

let me try

If the database is not already open, open the data file **AC1-Appointments** and try this skill on your own:
1. Export the *Appointments by Customer* query to Excel, maintaining all data formatting and layouts.
2. Export the *Appointments by Customer* query to Word.

Skill 1.16 Exporting Data to a PDF File

You are probably familiar with **PDF** (**Portable Document Format**) files. This type of file can be read by anyone who has the Adobe Reader software installed (which is almost everyone with a computer nowadays). If you need a version of one of your database objects, particularly reports, to look exactly like it would when printed from Access, consider exporting the object to a PDF file.

To export a database object to a PDF file:

1. In the Navigation Pane, click the object you want to export.
2. On the *External Data* tab, in the *Export* group, click the **PDF or XPS** button.
3. In the *Publish as PDF or XPS* dialog, Access automatically suggests a file name based on the name of the object you selected. If necessary, make the location and file name changes in the dialog.
4. Click **Publish.**
5. When you return to Access, the *Export-PDF* window will be open. If you want to save the export steps to repeat again later, check the **Save export steps** check box.
6. Click the **Close** button to close the window.

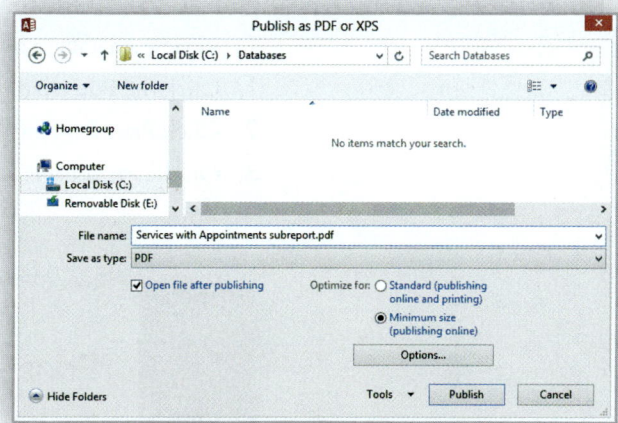

FIGURE AC 1.36

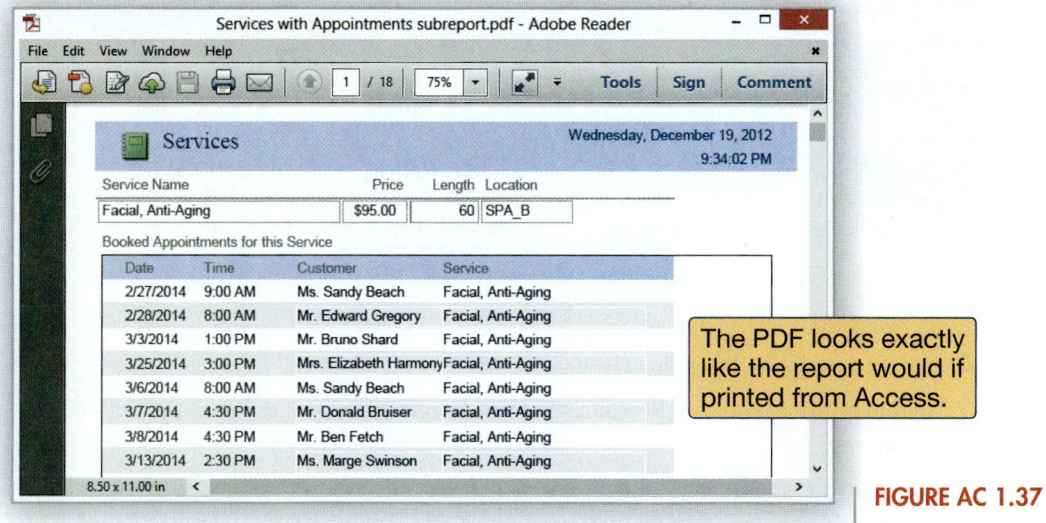

FIGURE AC 1.37

The PDF looks exactly like the report would if printed from Access.

another method

In the Navigation Pane, right-click the database object you want to export, point to **Export,** and select **PDF or XPS.**

let me try

If the database is not already open, open the data file **AC1-Appointments** and try this skill on your own:

Export the *Services with Appointments subreport* report as a PDF file.

Skill 1.17 Previewing and Printing Database Objects

Normally in Access, reports are the only database objects printed. However, there may be times when you want to print a table, form, or the results of a query. Although these database objects do not have a Print Preview view like reports do, you can still print and preview them from Backstage. From Backstage, Print Preview shows you a reduced version of the active database object as it will appear when printed. Save time and paper by always checking your page layout in Print Preview view before you print.

To preview a database object for printing:

1. Click the **File** tab to open Backstage.
2. Click **Print.**
3. On the *Print* page, click the **Print Preview** button.

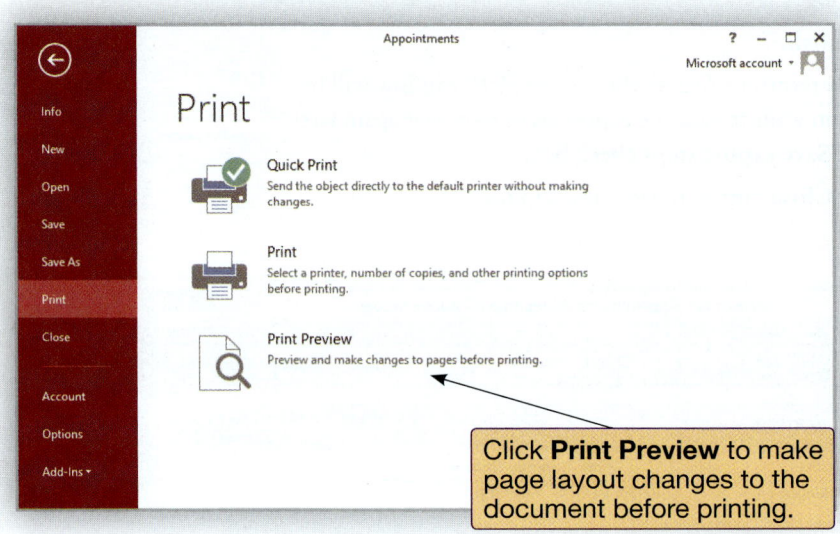

FIGURE AC 1.38

4. Access switches to Print Preview view.
5. Before printing, you should ensure that the data fit on the printed page the way you want.
   a. On the *Print Preview* tab, in the *Zoom* group, click the **Two Pages** button or click the **More Pages** button and select **Four Pages, Eight Pages,** or **Twelve Pages.** This lets you preview how the printed data will break across pages.
   b. If the object you are printing has many columns or is wider than 8.5 inches, switch the page orientation from portrait to landscape. On the *Print Preview* tab, in the *Page Layout* group, click the **Landscape** button.
6. To print, click the **Print** button located at the far left side of the *Print Preview* tab.
7. The *Print* dialog opens. From the *Print* dialog, you can set a range of pages to print, enter the number of copies to print, and choose to print to any printer connected to your computer.
8. Click **OK** in the dialog to print the database object.
9. Click the **Close Print Preview** button at the far right side of the Ribbon to return to your regular Access view.

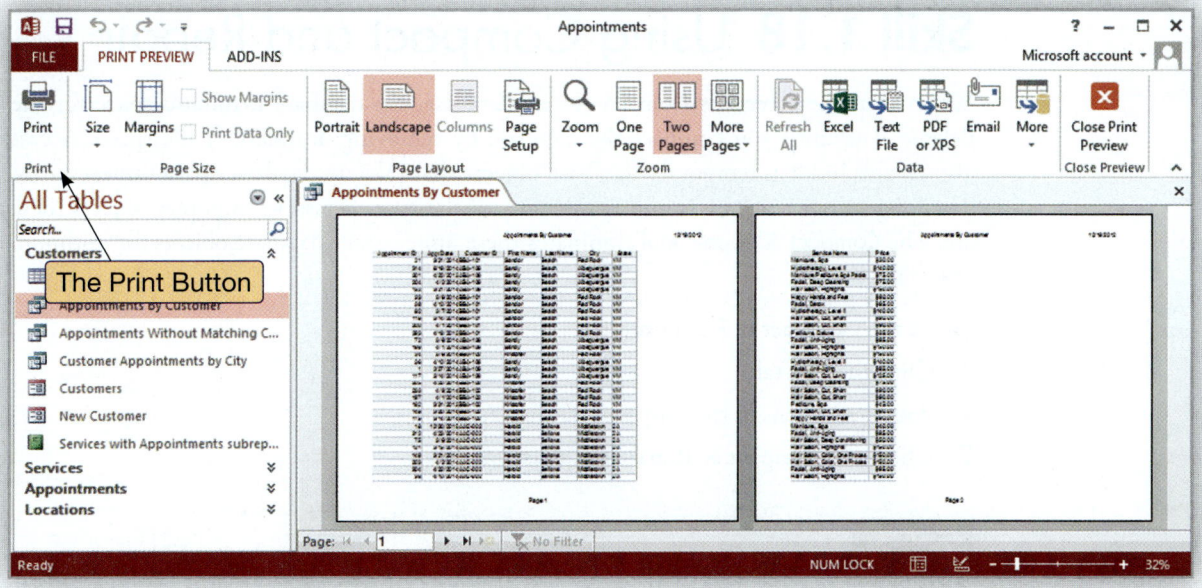

FIGURE AC 1.39

Two-page preview of how the object will look when printed with landscape orientation.

tips & tricks

Access is the only Office application that uses a dedicated Print Preview page. Word, Excel, and PowerPoint incorporate a Print Preview directly into Backstage.

tell me more

The Quick Print command prints database objects using all the default print settings.

1. Click the **File** tab.
2. Click **Print.**
3. On the *Print* page, click the **Quick Print** button.

another method

To print the current database object using the default print settings, you can also press Ctrl + P. The *Print* dialog will open. Click **OK** to print the database object.

let me try

If the database is not already open, open the data file **AC1-Appointments** and try this skill on your own:
1. Preview how the *Appointments by Customer* query would look if it were printed.
2. Change the orientation to **Landscape.**
3. Change the view to show two pages at once.
4. Close Print Preview.

skill 1.17   Previewing and Printing Database Objects

Skill 1.18 Using Compact and Repair

When you delete records from an Access database, the database maintains space for the deleted data until you compact the database by removing unnecessary file space. Access also creates hidden, temporary database objects that take up database space unnecessarily. The longer your database is in use, the more of these unnecessary temporary objects there are. The **Compact & Repair tool** eliminates these unnecessary database objects for optimum efficiency.

To use the Compact & Repair tool:

1. Click the **File** tab.
2. Backstage opens to the Info page automatically.
3. Click the **Compact & Repair Database** button.

FIGURE AC 1.40

If you need to interrupt the compact and repair process for any reason, press and hold Esc.

tips & tricks

To help your database run as efficiently as possible, it is a good practice to run the Compact & Repair tool on a regular basis.

tell me more

You can set your database to compact automatically when you close it by changing the database options:

1. Click the **File** tab.
2. Click the **Options** button.
3. Click **Current Database** at the left side of the *Access Options* dialog.
4. Click the check box in front of **Compact on Close.**
5. Click **OK.**

let me try

If the database is not already open, open the data file **AC1-Appointments** and try this skill on your own:
- Run the **Compact & Repair** tool.

Skill 1.19 Backing Up a Database

Remember that the *Undo* function is very limited in Access. If you are about to add a significant amount of data that you may not want to keep, or if you are experimenting with the design of the database, you should create a backup first. By backing up your database, you create a copy of it and preserve the data at a certain point. At any time you can open the backup and restore your data from an earlier stage. Be sure to create a backup of your database before making any major changes to the database structure.

To create a backup of your database:

1. Close and save any open objects.
2. Click the **File** tab.
3. Click **Save As.**
4. Click **Backup Database** in the *Save Database As* section at the right side of the screen.
5. Click the **Save As** button.

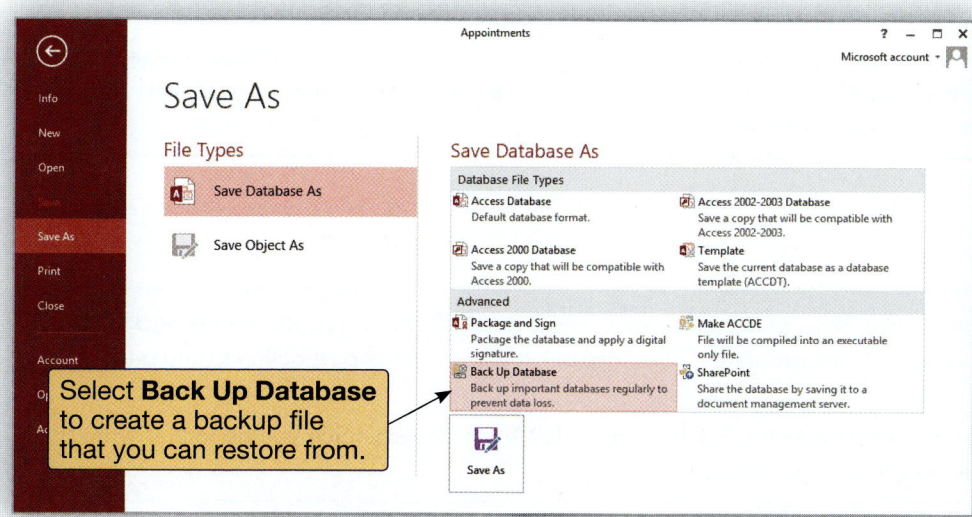

FIGURE AC 1.41

6. The *Save As* dialog box opens.

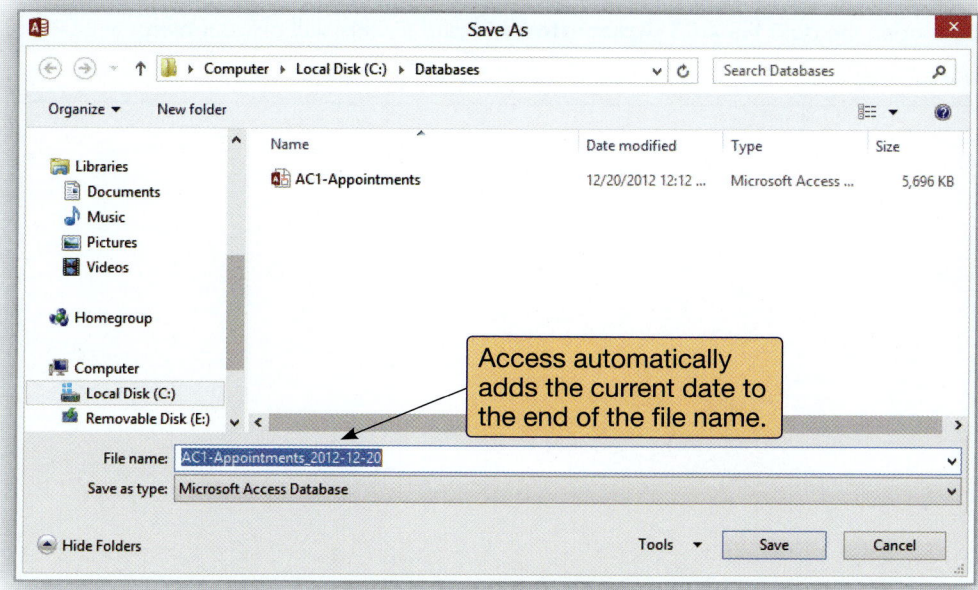

FIGURE AC 1.42

7. If necessary, navigate to the location where you want to save the backup file. Access automatically creates a new file name for the backup using the original file name with the current date.
8. Click **Save** to create the backup file.

To make a copy of the database to experiment with, but not necessarily keep as a backup:

1. Follow the same steps as you would to create a backup, but in the *Save As* page, select **Access Database** in the *Save Database As* section.
2. If necessary, navigate to the location where you want to save the copy. In the *File name* box, enter a name for the database copy.
3. Click **Save** to create the copy.

    You are now working on a copy of the database, and any further changes you make will not affect the original.

tips & tricks

To save a copy of the database, you must close all open database objects. If you have any database objects open when you invoke the *Save As* command, Access will offer to close them for you. If any of the open objects have not been saved, Access will also offer to save them for you.

tell me more

If you find that you need to restore a database object (such as a table, query, form, or report) from a backup copy, click the *External Data* tab. In the *Import & Link* group, click the **Import Access Database** button to find and restore the database object you want.

If you want to completely replace a database with a backup copy, delete the database file you no longer want and then rename the backup so it has the original file name.

let me try

If the database is not already open, open the data file **AC1-Appointments** and try this skill on your own:
  Create a backup of the database.

key terms

Database
Table
Record
Field
Relational database
Form
Query
Report
Navigation Pane
Macro
Message Bar
One-to-many relationship
Primary key
Foreign key
Relationships window
Datasheet view
Form view
Report view
Design view
SQL view
Layout view
Print Preview
Datasheets
Cut
Copy
Paste
Undo
Redo
Rich Text Format (RTF)
PDF (Portable Document Format)
Compact & Repair tool

concepts review

1. _____ are the basic building blocks of a database.
   a. Tables
   b. Forms
   c. Queries
   d. Reports

2. Each row in a table contains all the data for a single _____.
   a. field
   b. form
   c. record
   d. query

3. Each column in a table represents a specific data value called a _____.
   a. field
   b. form
   c. record
   d. query

4. All data entered into a form are stored in the underlying _____.
   a. form
   b. table
   c. All of the above
   d. None of the above

5. You must manually save the record each time you enter data in a table or form.
   a. True
   b. False

6. When you are entering data in a new record in a form, the *Undo* command will _____.
   a. undo only the most recently entered field
   b. undo the entire record at once
   c. undo only formatting and layout changes to the record
   d. do nothing. The *Undo* command does not work in forms.
7. You can undo a record deletion.
   a. True
   b. False
8. To rename a database object, double-click the name in the Navigation Pane and type the new name.
   a. True
   b. False
9. You can export Access data to which of the following file formats?
   a. PDF
   b. PowerPoint
   c. Adobe
   d. All of the above
10. Creating a backup of the database removes unnecessary file space and hidden, temporary objects from your database.
    a. True
    b. False

Data files for projects can be found on www.mhhe.com/office2013skills

projects

skill review 1.1

In this project, you will review a database created for the Computer Science department of a local college. They would like your assistance in using Access to keep track of which employees have borrowed items from the department. Become comfortable with the department's database by completing the steps below.

Skills needed to complete this project:
- Introduction to Access 2013 (Skill 1.1)
- Working with Security Warnings (Skill 1.2)
- Backing Up a Database (Skill 1.19)
- Organizing Objects in the Navigation Pane (Skill 1.4)
- Switching between Database Object Views (Skill 1.5)
- Navigating Records (Skill 1.6)
- Creating a New Record in a Table (Skill 1.7)
- Finding and Replacing Data (Skill 1.9)
- Deleting Records (Skill 1.12)
- Creating a New Record in a Form (Skill 1.8)
- Understanding and Viewing Table Relationships (Skill 1.3)
- Exporting Data to Excel or Word (Skill 1.15)
- Deleting and Renaming Database Objects (Skill 1.14)
- Using Compact and Repair (Skill 1.18)

1. Open the start file **AC2013-SkillReview-1-1**.
2. If necessary, enable active content by clicking the **Enable Content** button in the Message Bar.
3. Save a copy of the file to work on.
   a. Click the **File** tab.
   b. Click **Save Database As**.
   c. Verify that *Access Database* is selected in the *Save Database As* section.
   d. Click **Save As**.
   e. If necessary, navigate to the location where you save your personal project files.
   f. In the *File name* box, change the file name to:
      `[your initials]AC-SkillReview-1-1`
   g. Click **Save**.
   h. Enable active content in the new database by clicking the **Enable Content** button in the Message Bar.
4. Use the Navigation Pane.
   a. By default, the Navigation Pane displays the *Tables and Related Views* category. All tables and related objects are visible.

b. Click the top of the Navigation Pane and under the *Filter By Group* section, select **Items.**

c. Observe that the Navigation Pane now displays the title *Items* at the top and only objects related to the *Items* table are visible.

d. Click the top of the Navigation Pane and select the **Object Type** category.

e. Observe that now all database objects are visible in the Navigation Pane, grouped by object type.

5. Open the *Items* table.

    a. In the Navigation Pane, double-click the table object named **Items.**

    b. Review the fields in this table: *Item ID, ItemName, Description, Category,* and *Cost.*

    c. If necessary, use the horizontal scroll bar to view all the fields.

6. Switch views for the *Items* table.

    a. Note the state of the *View* button (on the *Home* tab, in the *Views* group). When you are in Datasheet view, the *Views* button displays Design view.

    b. On the *Home* tab, in the *Views* group, click the **View** button.

    c. Observe that the *View* button has switched to **Datasheet** view to indicate that clicking the button will return you to Datasheet view.

    d. Review the field names in Design view.

    e. Go back to Datasheet view by clicking the **View** button again.

7. Navigate records in a table.

    a. Observe the record navigation buttons at the bottom of the table. Move your mouse over the different arrow buttons and observe the ScreenTips.

    b. Observe which record in the table becomes highlighted as you click the following record navigation buttons: **Last record, First record, Next record, Previous record.**

    c. Find the *Current Record* box, which indicates the current record number and the total number of records. Click to select the number in the *Current Record* box. Type the number **5** in this box and press ⎯Enter. The *Current Record* box should now display **5 of 21** and the fifth record in the table should be highlighted.

    d. Use the following shortcut keys on your keyboard and observe which field/record becomes highlighted: **Tab, up arrow, down arrow, left arrow, right arrow.** In addition, try holding Ctrl while pressing the **up arrow** or **down arrow.**

8. Enter a new record in the *Items* table.

    a. Click the **New (blank) record** button at the bottom of the table.

    b. Enter the following record into your table, using Tab to move from one field to the next. When you reach the *Category* field, observe that it is a lookup field. Use the **drop-down arrow** to view and select from the available values.

ItemID	ItemName	Description	Category	Cost
ACC1	Accounting 2.0	Accounting software for small businesses	Software	$149.00

9. Find the record with an item ID of **GRA1** and edit the content.

    a. Type **GRA1** in the Search box at the bottom of the table.

    b. Edit the content in the *ItemName* field to: `Graphics Studio 10.1`

10. Delete the *SPH1* item record.

    a. Type **SPH1** in the Search box at the bottom of the table.

    b. Click the record selector box at the left side of that row to highlight the entire record.

    c. On the *Home* tab, in the *Records* group, click the **Delete** button.

    d. Click **Yes** to verify that you want to delete the record.

11. Close the *Items* table by clicking the **X** at the upper right corner of the table. Be careful not to close the Access database instead.

12. Enter a new record in a form.

    a. In the Navigation Pane, double-click the form object named **Items Form.**

    b. Observe the record navigation buttons at the bottom of the form and note that they are the same as those in the table.

    c. Click the **New (blank)** record button at the bottom of the form.

    d. Enter the following record into your form, using Tab to move from one field to the next.

ItemID	ItemName	Description	Category	Cost
CAM1	Digital Camera	10 megapixel SLR digital camera	Equipment	$499.00

13. Find and edit the record with the item ID **LAP1.**

    a. On the *Home* tab, in the *Find* group, click the **Find** button.

    b. Type **LAP1** in the *Find What* box.

    c. Click the **Find Next** button.

    d. Close the *Find and Replace* dialog by clicking the **X** in the upper right corner of the dialog.

    e. The form should now display the *Laptop 1000* item.

    f. Click in the *Cost* field and change the value from **$550** to **$450.**

14. Find and delete the record with the item ID **PB03.**

    a. On the *Home* tab, in the *Find* group, click the **Find** button.

    b. Type **PB03** in the *Find What* box.

    c. Click the **Find Next** button.

    d. Close the *Find and Replace* dialog by clicking the **X** in the upper right corner of the dialog.

    e. The form should now display the *Presentation Basics* item.

    f. On the *Home* tab, in the *Records* group, click the **Delete** button arrow, and select **Delete Record.**

    g. Click **Yes.**

15. Close the *Items Form* form.

16. Open the *Items* table again.

    a. In the Navigation Pane, double-click the table object named **Items.**

    b. Observe that the *CAM1* item record you entered in the form was added to the table. It should be listed as the fifth item in the table.

    c. Click the **Last record** button at the bottom of the table.

    d. Close the *Items* table.

17. Review the table relationships.

    a. On the *Database Tools* tab, in the *Relationships* group, click the **Relationships** button.

    b. Verify that all table relationships are shown. On the *Relationship Tools Design* tab, in the *Relationships* group, click the **All Relationships** button.

c. Save the changes to the relationship window layout by clicking the **Save** button on the Quick Access Toolbar.

d. Close the Relationships window. On the *Relationship Tools Design* tab, in the *Relationships* group, click the **Close** button.

18. Export the *Items* table to Excel.

    a. In the Navigation Pane, if necessary, click the *Items* table once to select it.

    b. On the *External Data* tab, in the *Export* group, click the **Excel** button.

    c. Click the **Browse** button.

    d. If necessary, navigate to the location where you save your personal project files.

    e. In the *File name* box, type:

       `[your initials]AC-SkillReview-1-1-Items`

    f. Click **Save**.

    g. In the *Export–Excel Spreadsheet* window, click **OK**.

    h. Click the **Close** button to finish without saving the export steps.

19. Rename the *Employees* table.

    a. In the Navigation Pane, right-click *Employees* and select **Rename**.

    b. Type: `Staff`

    c. Press `Enter`.

20. Use Compact & Repair.

    a. Minimize the Access 2013 window and navigate to the folder where you saved this database. Observe the file size.

    b. Return to Access and click the **File** tab.

    c. Click the **Compact & Repair Database** button.

    d. Minimize Access 2013 and look at your database file again. How much did the file size decrease?

21. Back up the database.

    a. If necessary, maximize Access 2013 and click the **File** tab.

    b. Click **Save As**.

    c. In the *Save Database As* section, under *Advanced,* click **Back Up Database,** and click the **Save As** button.

    d. If necessary, navigate to the location where you save your personal project files. Click the **Save** button.

22. Close the database and exit Access.

skill review 1.2

You have just been hired by a small health insurance company in the south Florida area. One of your duties is using Access 2013 to manage the company's list of in-network doctors and covered procedures. Become comfortable with the company's database by completing the steps below.

Skills needed to complete this project:

- Introduction to Access 2013 (Skill 1.1)
- Working with Security Warnings (Skill 1.2)
- Backing Up a Database (Skill 1.19)
- Organizing Objects in the Navigation Pane (Skill 1.4)

- Understanding and Viewing Table Relationships (Skill 1.3)
- Navigating Records (Skill 1.6)
- Deleting Records (Skill 1.12)
- Creating a New Record in a Table (Skill 1.7)
- Cutting, Copying, and Pasting Data (Skill 1.10)
- Using Undo and Redo (Skill 1.11)
- Previewing and Printing Database Objects (Skill 1.17)
- Exporting Data to Excel or Word (Skill 1.15)
- Switching between Database Object Views (Skill 1.5)
- Creating a New Record in a Form (Skill 1.8)
- Finding and Replacing Data (Skill 1.9)
- Checking Spelling (Skill 1.13)
- Exporting Data to a PDF File (Skill 1.16)
- Using Compact and Repair (Skill 1.18)

1. Open the start file **AC2013-SkillReview-1-2.**
2. If necessary, enable active content by clicking the **Enable Content** button in the Message Bar.
3. Save a copy of the file to work on.
   a. Click the **File** tab.
   b. Click **Save Database As.**
   c. Verify that *Access Database* is selected in the *Save Database As* list.
   d. Click **Save As.**
   e. If necessary, navigate to the location where you save your personal project files.
   f. In the *File name* box, change the file name to:
      `[your initials]AC-SkillReview-1-2`
   g. Click **Save.**
   h. If necessary, enable active content in the new database by clicking the **Enable Content** button in the Message Bar.
4. The Navigation Pane is organized using the *Object Type* category. Switch to use the *Tables and Related Views* category instead.
   a. Observe the organization of objects in the Navigation Pane.
   b. Click the top of the Navigation Pane and select the **Tables and Related Views** category.
   c. Observe the changes in the Navigation Pane.
5. Review the table relationships.
   a. On the *Database Tools* tab, in the *Relationships* group, click the **Relationships** button.
   b. Add the *Orders* table to the Relationships window. On the *Relationship Tools Design* tab, in the *Relationships* group, click the **Show Table** button.
   c. In the *Show Table* dialog, double-click **Orders.**
   d. Click the **Close** button to close the *Show Table* dialog.
   e. Save the changes to the relationship window layout by clicking the **Save** button on the Quick Access Toolbar.
   f. Close the Relationships window. On the *Relationship Tools Design* tab, in the *Relationships* group, click the **Close** button.

6. Navigate records in a table.
   a. In the Navigation Pane, double-click the object labeled **Physicians : Table.**
   b. Go to the last record in the table. Click the **Last Record** navigation button at the bottom of the table.
7. Delete the record.
   a. Click the record selector box on the left side of that row to highlight the entire record. Verify that you have selected the record with the physician ID **TW01.**
   b. On the *Home* tab, in the *Records* group, click the **Delete** button.
   c. Click **Yes** to verify that you want to delete the record.
8. Enter a new record in the *Physicians* table.
   a. Click the **New (blank) record** button at the bottom of the table.
   b. Enter the following record into your table, using Tab or → to move from one field to the next. When you reach the *City* field, observe that it is a lookup field. Use the **drop-down arrow** to view and select from the available values.

PhysicianID	FirstName	LastName	StreetAddress	City	ZipCode	Phone	MemberCount
JB02	James	Bryant	3091 Main Street	Miami	33143	(305) 555-2122	16

9. Copy the street address from the record with the last name Hartzell to the record with the last name Diggs.
   a. Type **Hartzell** in the Search box at the bottom of the table. Confirm that you have located the record for Heidi Hartzell.
   b. Select the data in the *StreetAddress* field.
   c. On the *Home* tab, in the *Clipboard* group, click the **Copy** button.
   d. Type **Diggs** in the Search box at the bottom of the table. Confirm that you have located the record for Steve Diggs.
   e. Select the data in the *StreetAddress* field.
   f. On the *Home* tab, in the *Clipboard* group, click the **Paste** button.
   g. Confirm that the address for Steve Diggs is now 2204 Plainfield Avenue.
10. Undo the change.
    a. On the Quick Access Toolbar, click the **Undo** button.
    b. Confirm that the address for Steve Diggs is 2860 Godfrey Road again.
11. Preview how the *Physicians* table would look if it were printed from Access.
    a. Click the **File** tab.
    b. Click **Print.**
    c. Click **Print Preview.**
    d. Change the zoom to two pages. On the *Print Preview* tab, in the *Zoom* group, click the **Two Pages** button.
    e. Observe that in portrait orientation, the last column prints on a second page.
    f. Change the orientation to landscape. On the *Print Preview* tab, in the *Page Layout* group, click the **Landscape** button.
    g. Observe that the printed table would now fit on a single page.
    h. Close the print preview by clicking the **Close Print Preview** button at the far right side of the Ribbon.

12. Export the *Physicians* table to Excel. Be sure to include formatting and layout. Open the destination file when the export is complete.
    a. If necessary, select the *Physicians* table by clicking the **Physicians** tab.
    b. On the *External Data* tab, in the *Export* group, click the **Excel** button.
    c. Click the **Browse** button.
    d. If necessary, navigate to the location where you save your personal project files.
    e. In the *File name* box, type:
       `[your initials]AC-SkillReview-1-2-Physicians`
    f. Click **Save**.
    g. Click the **Export data with formatting and layout.** check box.
    h. Click the **Open the destination file after the export operation is complete.** check box.
    i. In the *Export–Excel Spreadsheet* dialog, click **OK**.
    j. Review the exported data in Excel, and then exit Excel and return to Access.
    k. Click the **Close** button to finish without saving the export steps.
13. Close the *Physicians* table by clicking the **X** at the upper right corner of the table. Be careful not to close the Access database instead.
14. Switch views for a form.
    a. In the Navigation Pane, double-click the **PhysiciansForm** form.
    b. Note the state of the *View* button (on the *Home* tab, in the *Views* group). When you are in Form view, the *View* button displays Layout view.
    c. Switch to Layout view. On the *Home* tab, in the *Views* group, click the **View** button.
    d. Observe that the *View* button has switched to Form view to indicate that clicking the button will return you to Form view.
    e. Review the form design in Layout view. Observe that while you can see live data, you cannot edit data in the record. Review the features available on the *Form Layout Tools* tabs.
    f. Switch back to Form view by clicking the **View** button again.
15. Add a new record in a form
    a. Observe the record navigation buttons at the bottom of the form and note that they are the same as those in the table.
    b. Click the **New (blank) record** button at the bottom of the form.
    c. Enter the following record into your form, using Tab or → to move from one field to the next.

PhysicianID	FirstName	LastName	StreetAddress	City	ZipCode	Phone	MemberCount
KS01	Karen	Singer	850 Tyler Street	Miami	33155	(305) 555-2490	21

16. Edit a record in a form
    a. Find the record with a physician ID of **SD01**. Type `SD01` in the Search box at the bottom of the form.
    b. Click inside the *ZipCode* field and change the number from **33304** to **33309**.
    c. Close *PhysiciansForm* by clicking the **X** at the top right of the form.

17. Spell check the *Procedures* table.
    a. In the Navigation Pane, double-click the object labeled **Procedures : Table**.
    b. On the *Home* tab, in the *Records* group, click the **Spelling** button.
    c. The first misspelling found is *Vacine*. Click the **Change** button to accept the suggestion *Vaccine*.
    d. The next misspelling found is *Cardac*. Click the **Change** button to accept the suggestion *Cardiac*.
    e. Click **OK** in the message box telling you that the spelling check is complete.
18. Export the table as a PDF file.
    a. The *Procedures* table should still be open. Confirm that it is the active database object by clicking the **Procedures** tab.
    b. On the *External Data* tab, in the *Export* group, click the **PDF or XPS** button.
    c. If necessary, navigate to the location where you save your personal project files.
    d. In the *File name* box, type:
       `[your initials]AC-SkillReview-1-2-Procedures`
    e. If necessary, click **Open file after publishing** check box so you can review the PDF file.
    f. Click **Publish**.
    g. Observe that the PDF maintains the look of the Access table exactly.
    h. Close the PDF and return to Access.
    i. Click the **Close** button to close the window without saving the export steps.
    j. Close the *Procedures* table by clicking the **X** in the upper right corner of the tab.
19. Use Compact & Repair.
    a. Minimize the Access 2013 window and navigate to the folder where you saved this database. Observe the file size.
    b. Return to Access and click the **File** tab.
    c. Click the **Compact & Repair Database** button.
    d. Minimize Access 2013 and look at your database file again. How much did the file size decrease?
20. Back up the database.
    a. If necessary, maximize Access 2013 and click the **File** tab.
    b. Click **Save As**.
    c. In the *Save Database As* area, under *Advanced,* click **Back Up Database,** and click the **Save As** button.
    d. If necessary, navigate to the location where you save your personal project files. Click the **Save** button.
21. Close the database and exit Access.

challenge yourself 1.3

In this project, you will work on a database for a small greenhouse. The database contains records of the plants in the greenhouse and the employees who assist with maintenance duties.

Skills needed to complete this project:
- Introduction to Access 2013 (Skill 1.1)
- Working with Security Warnings (Skill 1.2)
- Backing Up a Database (Skill 1.19)
- Switching between Database Object Views (Skill 1.5)

- Creating a New Record in a Table (Skill 1.7)
- Finding and Replacing Data (Skill 1.9)
- Using Undo and Redo (Skill 1.11)
- Deleting Records (Skill 1.12)
- Organizing Objects in the Navigation Pane (Skill 1.4)
- Creating a New Record in a Form (Skill 1.8)
- Understanding and Viewing Table Relationships (Skill 1.3)
- Exporting Data to Excel or Word (Skill 1.15)
- Checking Spelling (Skill 1.13)
- Previewing and Printing Database Objects (Skill 1.17)
- Deleting and Renaming Database Objects (Skill 1.14)
- Using Compact and Repair (Skill 1.18)

1. Open the start file **AC2013-ChallengeYourself-1-3**.
2. If necessary, enable active content by clicking the **Enable Content** button in the Message Bar.
3. Save a copy of the file to work on. Name the file: `[your initials]AC-ChallengeYourself-1-3`
4. If necessary, enable active content in the new database by clicking the **Enable Content** button in the Message Bar.
5. Enter and edit data in the *Employees* table.
    a. Open the *Employees* table.
    b. Switch to Design view. Note the field designated as the primary key.
    c. Switch to back to Datasheet view.
    d. Enter the following record into your table and note that the *Position* field is a lookup field.

EmployeeID	FirstName	LastName	Position	WeeklyHours
59267311	Tracy	Seidel	Greenhouse Tech 2	15

   e. Find the record with a *LastName* value of *Rojas*.
   f. Change the *WeeklyHours* value from 35 to **30**.
   g. Undo the change.
   h. Delete the record with an *EmployeeID* of 23605379.
   i. Close the *Employees* table.
6. Enter and edit data in the *EmployeesForm*.
    a. Open the *EmployeesForm*.
    b. Enter the following record into your form:
    c. Close the *EmployeesForm*.

EmployeeID	FirstName	LastName	Position	WeeklyHours
77913350	George	Phillips	Greenhouse Tech 2	20

7. Review table relationships.
    a. Open the Relationships window. Remember the primary key from the *Employees* table? Do you see how that field creates the connection between the *Employees* table and the *Maintenance Log* table?
    b. Close the Relationships window.

8. Export the *Employees* table to Excel. Include layout and formatting. You do not need to save the export steps. Name the file:
   `[your initials]AC-ChallengeYourself-1-3-Employees`
9. Open the *Plants* table and run the spelling checker on the *FlowerColor* field. Correct any spelling errors in the *FlowerColor* field. You can ignore data in the other fields in this table.
10. Preview how the *Plants* table will look when printed. Change the zoom view to see if all the columns will fit on one page when printed in portrait view. If they will not, change to layout orientation.
11. Close the *Plants* table.
12. Open the *Purchases* table, observe that there are no records, and then close the table.
13. Delete the *Purchases* table.
14. Observe the file size of your database. Use the *Compact & Repair Database* command and check the file again. How much did the file size decrease?
15. Create a backup of this database using the default name chosen by Access.
16. Close the database and exit Access.

challenge yourself 1.4

In this project, you will work with a database for a volunteer organization that ships and administers vaccines to various relief centers all over the world. The database must maintain a list of all approved vaccines and keep track of all shipments made to the relief centers.

Skills needed to complete this project:

- Introduction to Access 2013 (Skill 1.1)
- Working with Security Warnings (Skill 1.2)
- Backing Up a Database (Skill 1.19)
- Organizing Objects in the Navigation Pane (Skill 1.4)
- Understanding and Viewing Table Relationships (Skill 1.3)
- Navigating Records (Skill 1.6)
- Creating a New Record in a Table (Skill 1.7)
- Finding and Replacing Data (Skill 1.9)
- Deleting Records (Skill 1.12)
- Previewing and Printing Database Objects (Skill 1.17)
- Creating a New Record in a Form (Skill 1.8)
- Deleting and Renaming Database Objects (Skill 1.14)
- Exporting Data to Excel or Word (Skill 1.15)
- Using Compact and Repair (Skill 1.18)

1. Open the start file **AC2013-ChallengeYourself-1-4**.
2. If necessary, enable active content by clicking the **Enable Content** button in the Message Bar.
3. Save a copy of the file to work on. Name the file:
   `[your initials]AC-ChallengeYourself-1-4`
4. Change the organization of the Navigation Pane to use the **Tables and Related Views** category.

5. Open the Relationships window and study the table structure of the database.
6. Open the *Vaccines* table and browse the records using the record navigation buttons and keyboard shortcuts.
7. Enter the following record into the *Vaccines* table. Note that the *TargetAudience* field is a lookup field.

VaccineID	VaccineName	TargetAudience
MAL	Malaria	At-risk individuals

8. Find the record with the value **TD** in the *VACCINEID* field and change the value of the *TargetAudience* field from **Adults** to **Teenagers**.
9. Find and delete the record with a *VaccineID* of **LYD**.
10. Preview how the *Vaccines* table would look if it were printed. If necessary, change the orientation to landscape.
11. Close the *Vaccines* table.
12. Open the *VaccinesForm* form and enter the following as a new record:

VaccineID	VaccineName	TargetAudience
DF	Dengue Fever	At-risk individuals

13. Close the *VaccinesForm* form.
14. In the Navigation Pane, rename the **VaccinesForm** form to: **VaccineDetails**
15. Export the *Vaccines* table to Excel. Maintain all formatting and layout. You do not need to save the export steps. Save the exported file as: **[your initials]AC-ChallengeYourself-1-4-Vaccines**
16. Observe the file size of your database. Use the **Compact & Repair Database** feature and check the file again. How much did the file size decrease?
17. Create a backup of this database using the default name chosen by Access.

on your own 1.5

You have an extensive movie collection at home. You have realized that Access 2013 is a great tool to help you keep a list of all the movies you own and keep track of which friends and relatives have borrowed your movies. Demonstrate your basic understanding of Access by working with this database.

Skills needed to complete this project:
- Introduction to Access 2013 (Skill 1.1)
- Working with Security Warnings (Skill 1.2)
- Understanding and Viewing Table Relationships (Skill 1.3)
- Navigating Records (Skill 1.6)
- Creating a New Record in a Table (Skill 1.7)
- Creating a New Record in a Form (Skill 1.8)
- Finding and Replacing Data (Skill 1.9)
- Using Undo and Redo (Skill 1.11)
- Deleting Records (Skill 1.12)
- Checking Spelling (Skill 1.13)
- Using Compact and Repair (Skill 1.18)
- Backing Up a Database (Skill 1.19)

1. Open the start file **AC2013-OnYourOwn-1-5.**
2. If necessary, enable active content by clicking the **Enable Content** button in the Message Bar.
3. Save a copy of the file to work on. Name the file:
   `[your initials]AC-OnYourOwn-1-5`
4. Spend some time exploring the structure of the database. Identify the database objects and how they are related to one another. Open and explore the tables and forms without making any data changes.
5. Earlier this week, you acquired four new movies. Add these four movies to your database. You may use real or fake movies, but you must fill in all the fields and ensure your new data are consistent with the ones that are already there. You can enter the new records in a form or table—whichever you prefer.
    a. Use *Undo* if you make a mistake when entering the new records.
    b. Be sure to check your new records for spelling errors.
6. Find the movie with the word *Lincoln* in the title. Change the format to Blu-Ray.
7. You seem to have lost your solar system movie. Find and remove that movie from your database.
8. Make your database file size smaller and create a backup.

fix it 1.6

A local pet store has hired you to fix its database, which keeps track of inventory, customers, and store sales.

Skills needed to complete this project:
- Introduction to Access 2013 (Skill 1.1)
- Working with Security Warnings (Skill 1.2)
- Understanding and Viewing Table Relationships (Skill 1.3)
- Navigating Records (Skill 1.6)
- Finding and Replacing Data (Skill 1.9)
- Cutting, Copying, and Pasting Data (Skill 1.10)
- Deleting Records (Skill 1.12)
- Checking Spelling (Skill 1.13)
- Deleting and Renaming Database Objects (Skill 1.14)
- Exporting Data to Excel or Word (Skill 1.15)
- Exporting Data to a PDF File (Skill 1.16)
- Previewing and Printing Database Objects (Skill 1.17)
- Using Compact and Repair (Skill 1.18)
- Backing Up a Database (Skill 1.19)

1. Open the start file **AC2013-FixIt-1-6.**
2. If necessary, enable active content by clicking the **Enable Content** button in the Message Bar.
3. Save a copy of the file to work on. Name the file:
   `[your initials]AC-FixIt-1-6`

4. The employees can no longer see their forms and reports in the Navigation Pane. Can you help them?
5. Spend some time exploring the structure of the database. Identify the database objects and how they are related to one another. Open and explore the tables and forms without making any data changes.
6. The owner tells you that a former employee would often make data entry errors, and he wants your help in finding and correcting errors in the *Pets* table.
   a. The employee often misspelled the word *terrier*. Find his misspellings and fix them.
   b. The record for the Black Labrador Retriever is missing data in the *MainColor* field. (The color should be *Black*.)
   c. One of the records has the data in the *Breed* and the *MainColor* fields swapped. Find the record and fix it Hint: Find the record with *White* in the *Breed* field. It might be a good idea to cut and paste the breed data and then type the color.
   d. There is also a duplicate record for the Bengal breed. Delete the record with the pet ID **1446011**.
7. Once the data errors are fixed, export the tables to Excel and export the form to a PDF file. Use the following file names:
   a. `[your initials]AC-FixIt-1-6-Pets.xlsx`
   b. `[your initials]AC-FixIt-1-6-Customers.xlsx`
   c. `[your initials]AC-FixIt-1-6-Sales.xlsx`
   d. `[your initials]AC-FixIt-1-6-PetsForm.pdf`
8. The *CustomersReport* report is poorly formatted. Delete it for now. You will need to recreate it at another time.
9. The owner plans on printing the *Customers* table. Make sure it will fit on one page when printed.
10. The owner wonders why the database file size is so large. Help him reduce the file size.
11. Create a backup of the database so you can easily fix the data if these problems crop up again.

Working with Tables

chapter 2

- Create a new table in Datasheet view and Design view
- Establish the table primary key
- Add and delete fields in Datasheet view and Design view
- Format fields in Datasheet view and Design view
- Work with Attachment fields
- Modify field properties in Datasheet view and Design view
- Create lookup fields
- Create table relationships

In this chapter, you will learn the following skills:

Skill 2.1 Designing a Table
Skill 2.2 Creating and Saving a Table in Datasheet View
Skill 2.3 Renaming Fields
Skill 2.4 Adding Fields in Datasheet View
Skill 2.5 Using Quick Start to Add Related Fields
Skill 2.6 Adjusting Table Column Widths
Skill 2.7 Creating a Table in Design View
Skill 2.8 Inserting Fields in Design View
Skill 2.9 Setting the Primary Key
Skill 2.10 Deleting Fields
Skill 2.11 Changing Data Type
Skill 2.12 Formatting Fields
Skill 2.13 Modifying Field Properties
Skill 2.14 Applying an Input Mask from Design View
Skill 2.15 Working with Attachment Fields
Skill 2.16 Adding a Total Row to a Table
Skill 2.17 Adding a Lookup Field from Another Table
Skill 2.18 Adding a Lookup Field from a List
Skill 2.19 Creating Relationships

skills

introduction

In this chapter you will learn the skills essential for creating well-designed tables. You will learn to create tables from scratch in both Datasheet view and Design view. You will add and rename fields, set field formats, and modify field properties. In Design view, you will add primary keys and apply an input mask to control formatting. Finally, you will create lookup fields and enforce referential integrity in table relationships.

The *Let Me Try* exercises in this chapter use the AC2-Appointments database. You can keep the database open while you work in this chapter, opening and closing database objects as required for each *Let Me Try*.

Skill 2.1 Designing a Table

Remember that Access is a relational database—objects in your database are related to one another through relationships defined by common fields between tables. Take advantage of these relationships, and design your database so information is stored in one table only. For example, a database of customer appointments need not include every detail about each customer. The appointments table should include fields required for the appointment only. Details about customers, services, and staff should be kept in separate, related tables.

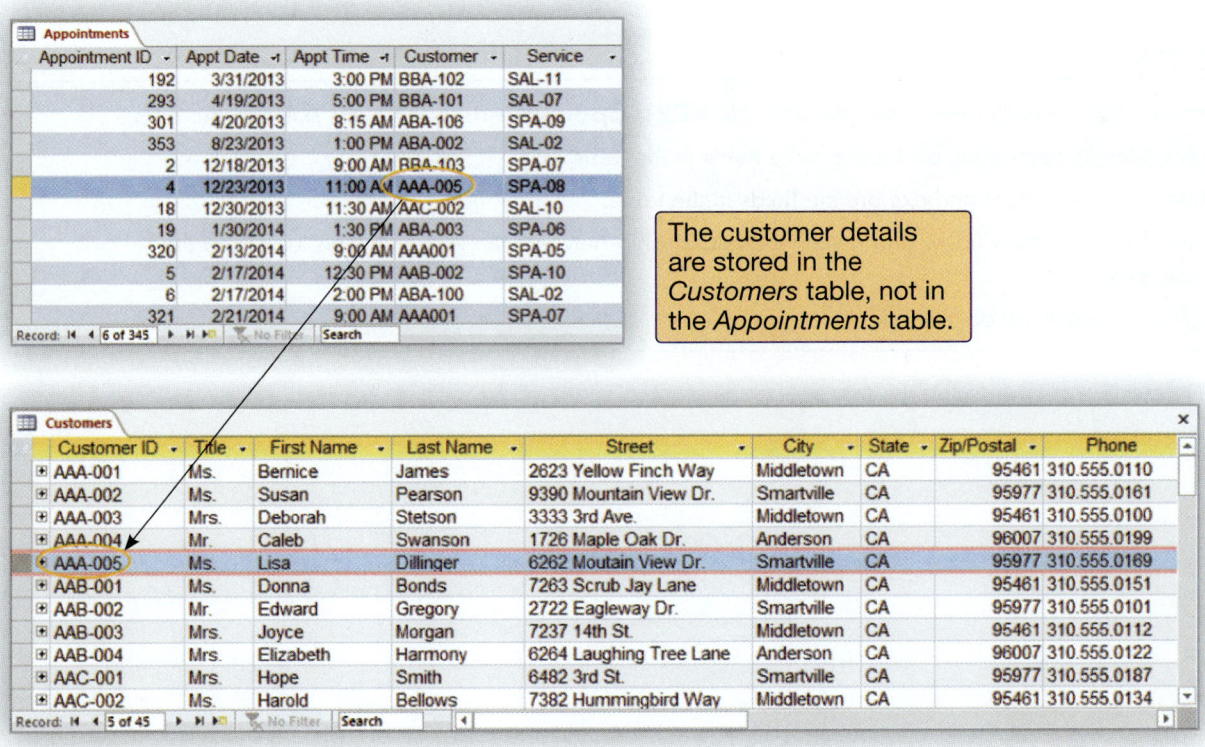

FIGURE AC 2.1

skill 2.1 Designing a Table

Storing each unique piece of data in a single table helps prevent data entry errors. There is only one record for each customer, so every time a new appointment record is created you only need to reference the related field (in this case the *Customer ID* field) rather than entering all the customer information again.

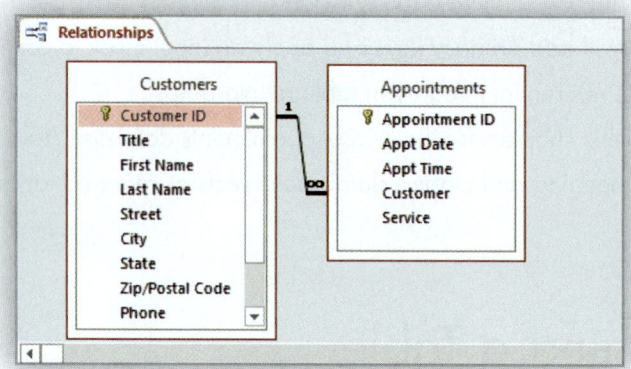

FIGURE AC 2.2
The Relationships window shows the one-to-many relationship between the *Customer ID* field in the *Customers* table and the *Customer* field in the *Appointments* table.

tips & tricks

Keeping repeated data in separate tables where they are stored only once keeps the database file size down, allowing the database to operate more efficiently.

let me try

If the database is not already open, open the data file **AC2-Appointments** and try this skill on your own:

1. Open the *Appointments* table and explore the fields in the table.
2. Open the *Customers* table and explore the fields in the table.
3. Open the Relationships window and review the relationship between the *Appointments* table and the *Customers* table.
4. Close all open database objects.

Skill 2.2 Creating and Saving a Table in Datasheet View

One way to create a new table is to add a blank table and add fields directly in Datasheet view.

1. On the *Create* tab, in the *Tables* group, click the **Table** button to insert a new table.
2. The new table opens in Datasheet view. The first field is automatically added as an AutoNumber field named *ID*.
3. To add a new field, begin typing data for the first record. Access names the first field *Field1*. Access will apply a data type based on what you type. For example, if you type a date, Access will automatically apply the Date/Time data type to the field.
4. Press Tab or Enter to enter data for the next field.
5. Repeat steps 3 and 4 to enter all the data for the first record.

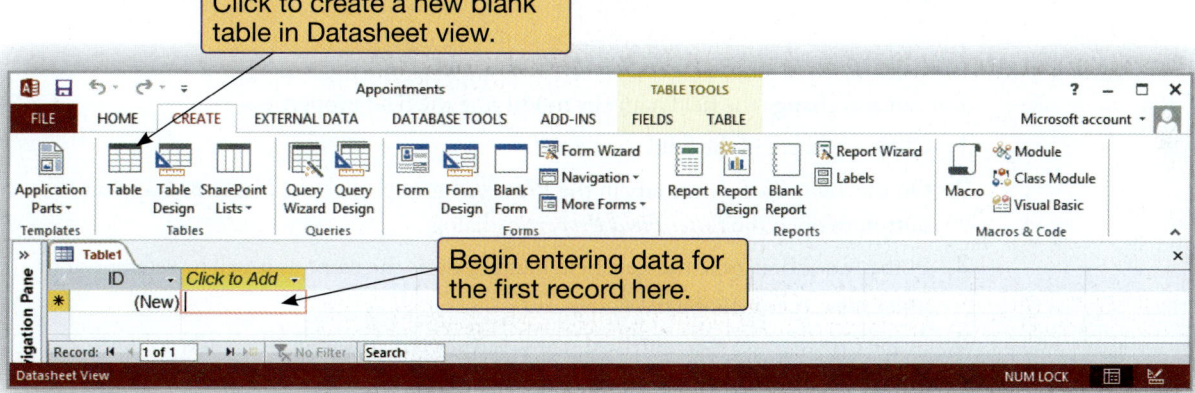

FIGURE AC 2.3

When you create a new database object, you must save the object for the changes to take effect. Access will warn you if you try to close an object that requires saving.

To save a table for the first time:

1. Click the **Save** button on the Quick Access Toolbar.
2. The *Save As* dialog opens.
3. Type a meaningful name in the *Table Name* box.
4. Click **OK**.

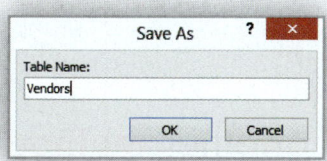

FIGURE AC 2.4

another method

To save a database object, you can use the keyboard shortcut Ctrl + S.

let me try

If the database is not already open, open the data file **AC2-Appointments** and try this skill on your own:

1. Create a new table in Datasheet view.
2. Allow Access to create the first AutoNumber field named *ID*.
3. Enter data for the second field: `Bob's Mud Supply`
4. Close the table, saving it with the name: `Vendors`

Skill 2.3 Renaming Fields

When you create a new, blank table in Datasheet view, Access names the fields *Field1*, *Field2*, and so forth by default.

To rename a field, double-click the column header and type the new field name.

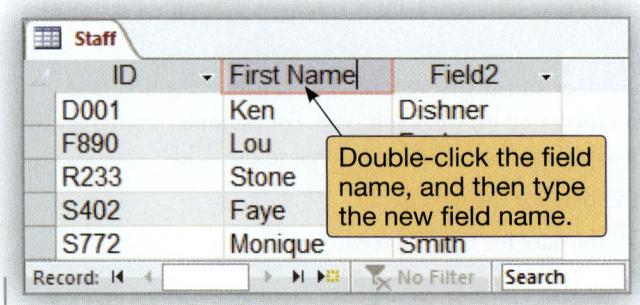

FIGURE AC 2.5

You can also change the field name by modifying the field properties:

1. Click anywhere in the field to select it.
2. On the *Table Tools Fields* tab, in the *Properties* group, click the **Name & Caption** button to open the *Enter Field Properties* dialog.
3. In the *Name* box, type the new field name. This is the name as it will be referenced by other objects in your database.
4. In the *Caption* box, type the field name as it should appear in labels and column headings. If you do not include a caption, Access will use the field name instead.
5. In the *Description* box, type additional information about the field (if necessary).
6. Click **OK**.
7. Save the table.

another method

To rename a field:
1. Right-click the field name at the top of the column in Datasheet view and select **Rename Field.**
2. The field name appears highlighted.
3. Type the new name, and press ← Enter.

let me try

If the database is not already open, open the data file **AC2-Appointments** and try this skill on your own:

1. Open the *Staff* table in Datasheet view.
2. Rename the *ID* field to: `Staff ID`
3. Rename the *Field1* field to: `First Name`
4. Rename the *Field2* field to: `Last Name`
5. Save the table.

Skill 2.4 Adding Fields in Datasheet View

You can always add a new field to a table by typing data in the blank cell at the end of a record, but what if you want to set up the table without entering data? Use the *Click to Add* heading at the far right side of the table.

To add a new field to a table:

1. At the far right side of the table, there is a column with the header *Click to Add*. Click the arrow to expand the list of available field types.
2. Click the field type you want to add.
3. Access creates a new field with the temporary name highlighted.
4. Type the new field name and then press ⏎ Enter.

You can also add a new field by clicking the field type you want from the *Table Tools Fields* tab, *Add & Delete* group. If there isn't a button for the data type you want, click the **More Fields** button to expand the *Data Type* gallery.

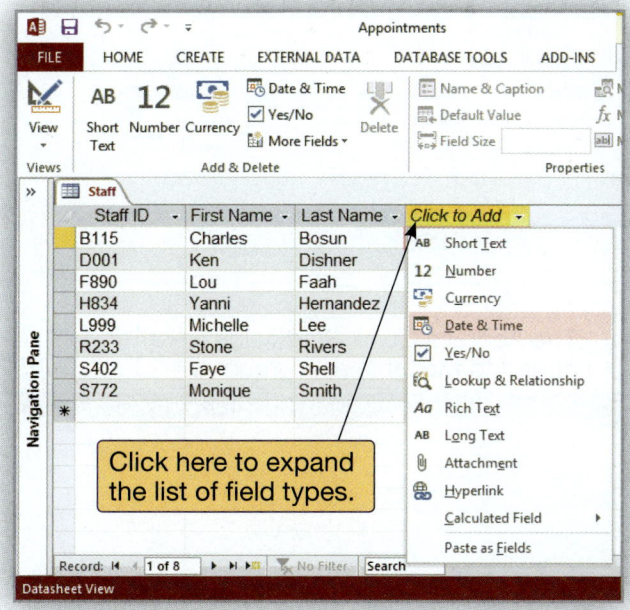

FIGURE AC 2.6

another method

You can also insert a new field by right-clicking any field name and selecting **Insert Field.** A new blank text field is inserted to the left of the field you selected.

let me try

If the database is not already open, open the data file **AC2-Appointments** and try this skill on your own:

1. If necessary, open the *Staff* table in Datasheet view.
2. Add a new *Date/Time* field to the far right side of the table.
3. Name the field: `Start Date`
4. Save the table.

skill 2.4   Adding Fields in Datasheet View

Skill 2.5 Using Quick Start to Add Related Fields

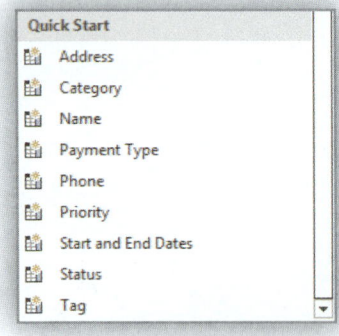

FIGURE AC 2.7
Quick Start Section of the *Fields Types* Gallery

Almost any table that keeps a list of people or businesses requires separate fields for street address, city, state, zip code, and country. Access makes it easy to insert these commonly used fields in a group. The last section in the *Field Types* gallery, **Quick Start field types**, provides an easy way to add address fields and other common field groups to your table.

To add a *Quick Start* group of fields:

1. The Quick Start fields will be inserted to the left of the selected field. To add them to the far right of the table, click anywhere in the *Click To Add* column.
2. On the *Table Tools Design* tab, in the *Add & Delete* group, click the **More Fields** button.
3. Scroll to the bottom of the *Field Types* gallery to the *Quick Start* section.
4. Click the *Quick Start* option you want.

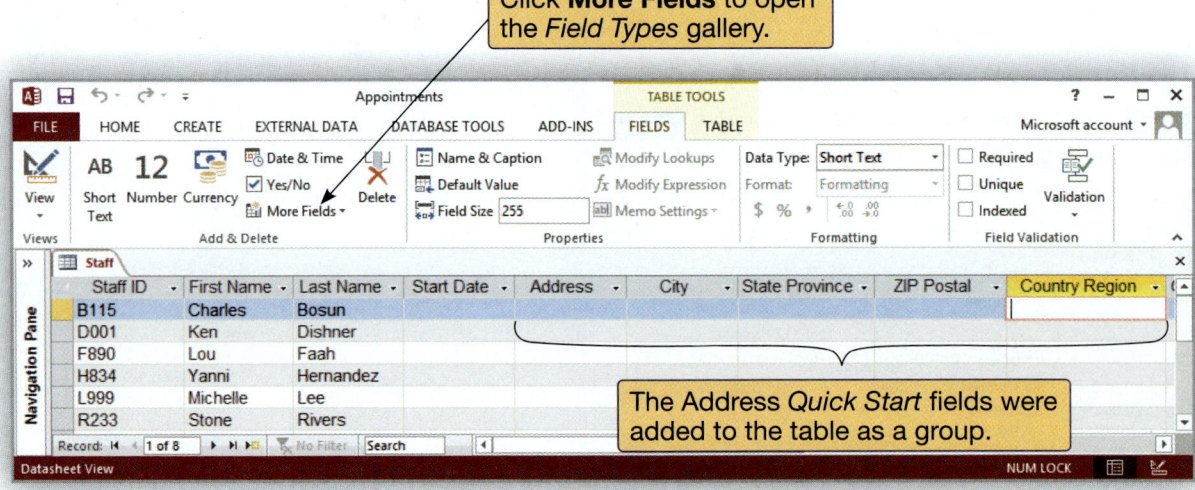

FIGURE AC 2.8

let me try

If the database is not already open, open the data file **AC2-Appointments** and try this skill on your own:

1. If necessary, open the *Staff* table in Datasheet view.
2. Add the **Address** *Quick Start* fields to the table to the right of the *Start Date* field.
3. Save and close the table.

Skill 2.6 Adjusting Table Column Widths

When you insert a new field, it is created with the standard width, which may not be wide enough to display all your data. Adjusting column widths in Datasheet view is similar to working with column widths in Excel.

To use the mouse to change the column size:

1. Move the mouse to the right border of the field header.
2. The cursor changes to a ↔ shape.
3. Click and drag to resize the column width, or double-click the right column border to automatically resize the column to best fit the data.

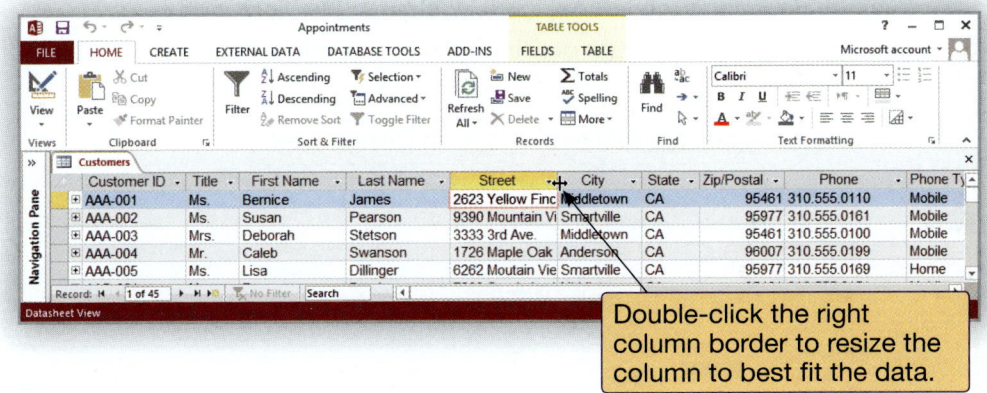

Double-click the right column border to resize the column to best fit the data.

FIGURE AC 2.9

To use the *Column Width* dialog to change the column size:

1. On the *Home* tab, in the *Records* group, click the **More** button, and select **Field Width** to open the *Column Width* dialog.
2. Type the width you want in the **Column Width** box, or click the **Best Fit** button.
3. Click **OK**.

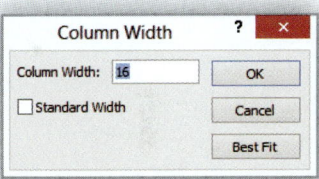

FIGURE AC 2.10

tips & tricks

Do not confuse field size with field width. **Field size** refers to the number of characters the field can hold in the database. **Field width** or column width refers to the number of characters that are visible on screen. This can be a little confusing because Access uses the terms *field width* and *column width* interchangeably.

Refer to the skill *Modifying Field Properties* for more information about working with the Field Size property.

another method

You can also open the *Column Width* dialog by right-clicking the field column header and selecting **Field Width**.

let me try

If the database is not already open, open the data file **AC2-Appointments** and try this skill on your own:

1. If necessary, open the *Customers* table in Datasheet view.
2. Modify the width of the *Street* column to best fit the data.
3. Save and close the table.

Skill 2.7 Creating a Table in Design View

Another way to create a new table is in Design view. In Design view, you create the fields without entering data. You must specify the field name and data type for each field. You also have the option of adding a description.

To create a table in Design view:

1. On the *Create* tab, in the *Tables* group, click the **Table Design** button.
2. Type the name of the first field. Press Tab.
3. Expand the list of data types, and select the data type you want. Press Tab again.
4. Type a useful description of the field. Press Tab to go to the next field.
5. Continue adding fields. When you are finished, save the table.

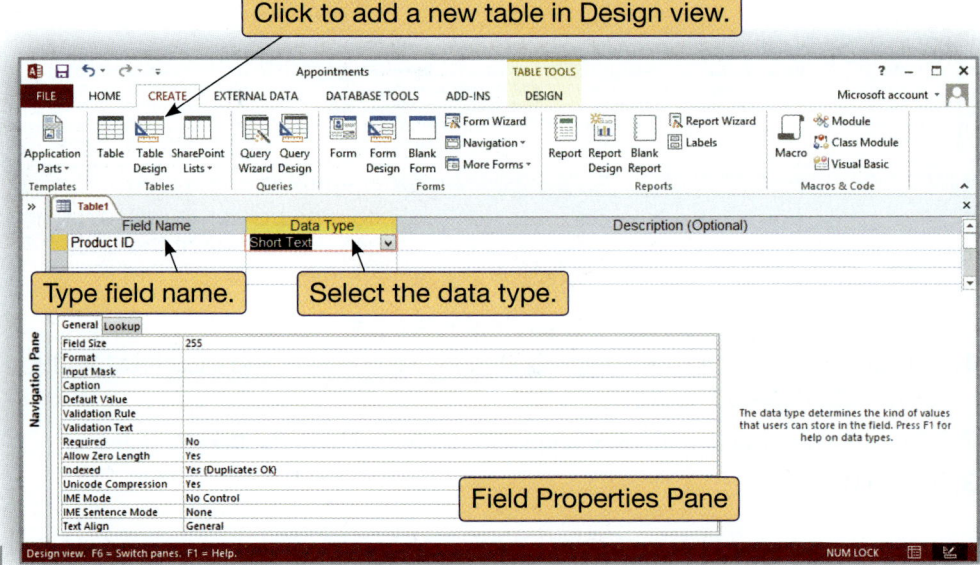

FIGURE AC 2.11

Notice that the Design view window is divided into two panes. The top pane lists the table fields. You may need to use the scroll bar at the right side of the pane to see all the fields. The bottom pane is the **Field Properties pane**. It displays details about the selected field. You will learn more about using the Field Properties pane in other skills.

let me try

If the database is not already open, open the data file **AC2-Appointments** and try this skill on your own:

1. Add a new table in Design view.
2. Name the first field: `Product ID`
3. Make the data type: `Short Text`
4. Add the description: `Internal product ID`
5. Close the table, saving it with the name: `Products`
6. Access asks if you want to designate a primary key. Click **No** to close the table without a primary key.

Skill 2.8 Inserting Fields in Design View

If you are working in Design view, you can always add new fields to the end of the field list by typing a new field name and selecting a data type. You can also insert fields between existing fields.

To insert a new field in Design view:

1. Click the field below where you want to insert the new field.
2. On the *Table Tools Design* tab, in the *Tools* group, click the **Insert Rows** button.
3. Enter the field name and select the data type. Enter a description if you want.
4. When you are finished, save the table.

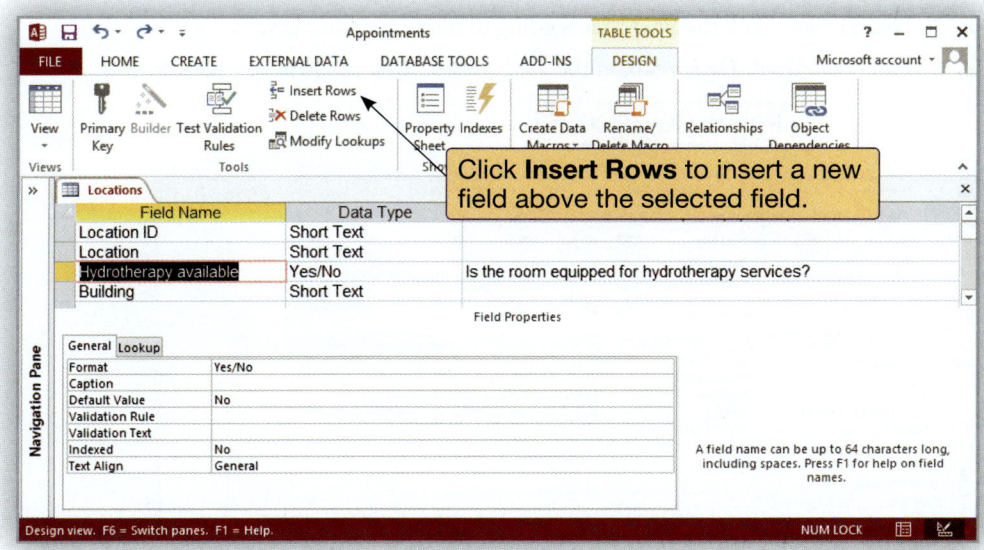

FIGURE AC 2.12

another method

You can also right-click the row selector at the left side of the field and select **Insert Rows** to insert a new field row above the selected field.

let me try

If the database is not already open, open the data file **AC2-Appointments** and try this skill on your own:

1. If necessary, open the *Locations* table in Design view.
2. Insert a new field above the *Hydrotherapy available* field.
3. Enter the field name: `Stations`
4. Select the data type **Number.**
5. Enter the description: `Number of therapy stations in room`
6. Save the table.

Skill 2.9 Setting the Primary Key

Every Access table should have a primary key defined. The **primary key field** contains data unique to that record. Primary keys are often IDs—product IDs, employee IDs, or record IDs. The primary key is the basis for relationships between tables.

> If your data do not already contain a field that is unique for each record, you can add a new field that uses the AutoNumber data type. Using an AutoNumber field ensures that each record has a unique numerical ID.

> If your table contains a field that you know is unique for each record (such as a previously established product ID, employee ID, or part number), you can set this field as the primary key.

To set the primary key in a table:

1. In Design view, click the field that is going to be the primary key.
2. On the *Table Tools Design* tab, in the *Tools* group, click the **Primary Key** button.

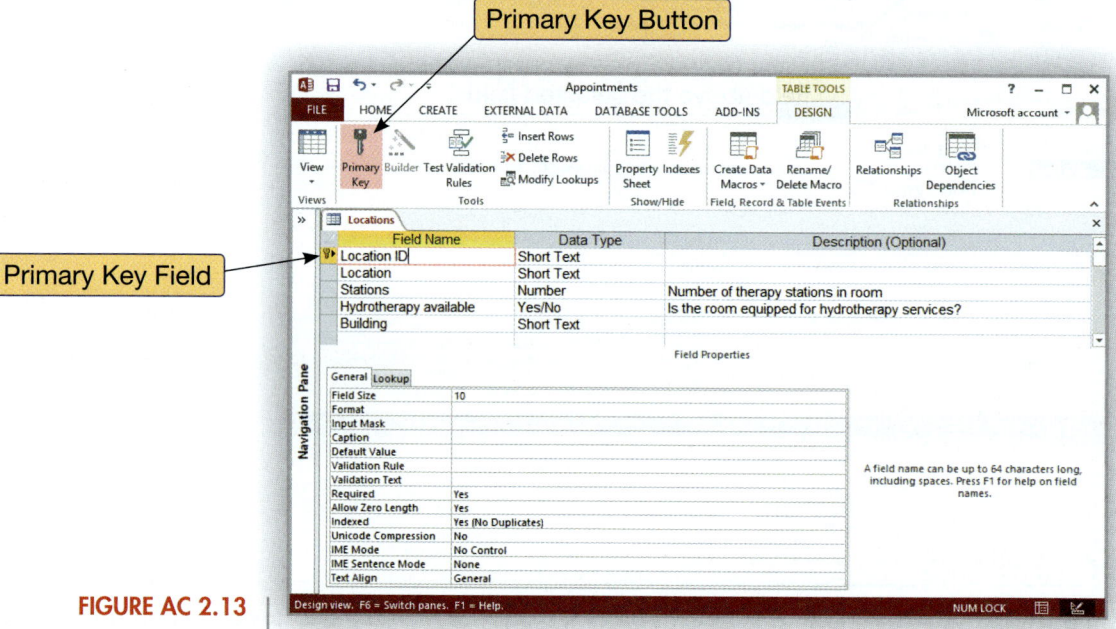

FIGURE AC 2.13

Notice that on the *Table Tools Design* tab, in the *Tools* group, the *Primary Key* button is highlighted to indicate that the selected field is the primary key and a key icon appears in the row selector at the left side of the field.

tips & tricks

Once you establish a field as the primary key, Access automatically sets the *Required* property to *yes* to ensure that each record has a unique primary key.

another method

In Design view, right-click the row selector and select **Primary Key.**

let me try

If the database is not already open, open the data file **AC2-Appointments** and try this skill on your own:

1. If necessary, open the *Locations* table in Design view.
2. Set the *Location ID* field as the primary key.
3. Save the table.

Skill 2.10 Deleting Fields

You can delete fields from both Datasheet view and Design view. When you delete a field, you delete all the data in that field, and the action cannot be undone.

To delete a field in Datasheet view:

1. Click anywhere in the field you want to delete.
2. On the *Table Tools Fields* tab, in the *Add & Delete* group, click the **Delete** button.
3. When Access asks if you if you want to permanently delete the field, click **Yes**.

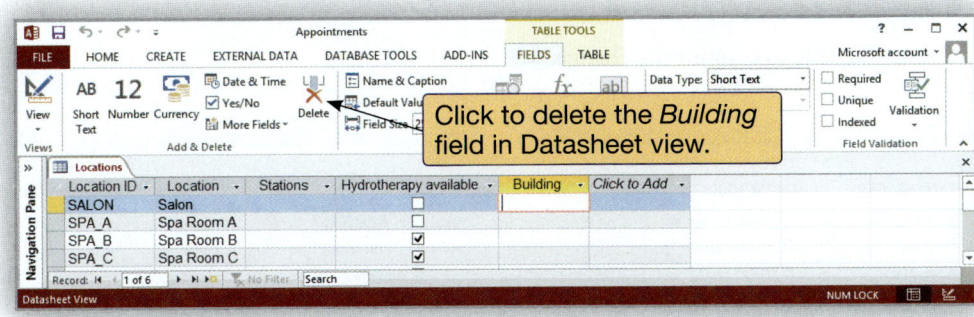

FIGURE AC 2.14

To delete a field in Design view:

1. Click anywhere in the field you want to delete.
2. On the *Table Tools Design* tab, in the *Tools* group, click the **Delete Rows** button.
3. When Access asks if you if you want to permanently delete the field, click **Yes**.

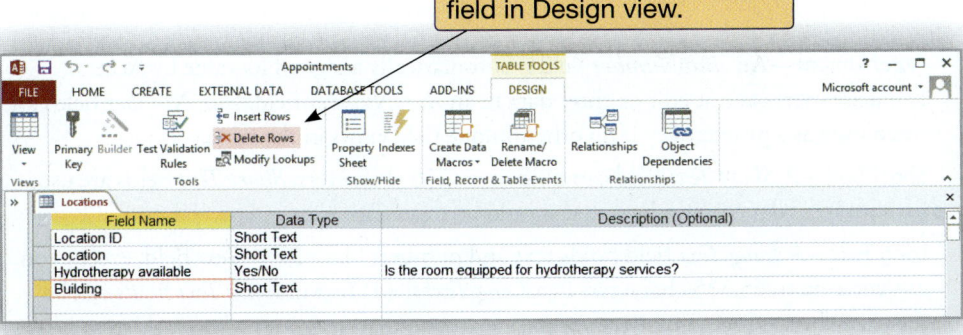

FIGURE AC 2.15

another method

- In Design view, right-click the row selector to the left of the field name, and select **Delete Rows**.
- In Datasheet view, right-click the field name at the top of the column and select **Delete Field**.
- In Datasheet view, select the field by clicking the column heading, and then on the *Home* tab, in the *Records* group, click the **Delete** button.

let me try

If the database is not already open, open the data file **AC2-Appointments** and try this skill on your own:

1. If necessary, open the *Locations* table in Datasheet view.
2. Delete the *Building* field.
3. Save the table.
4. If necessary, open the *Services* table in Design view.
5. Delete the *Building* field.
6. Save and close the table.

Skill 2.11 Changing Data Type

One key to database efficiency is ensuring that each field is assigned the appropriate data type. For example, you can't run calculations on a field with the Short Text field type, and you can't sort a date field efficiently unless you use the Date/Time field type. Carefully consider the type of data you will include in each field before you decide on the data type.

To change the data type for a field from Datasheet view:

1. Click anywhere in the field you want to change.
2. Click the **Table Tools Fields** tab, in the *Formatting* group, expand the **Data Type** list, and select the data type you want.
3. Save the table to commit the change.

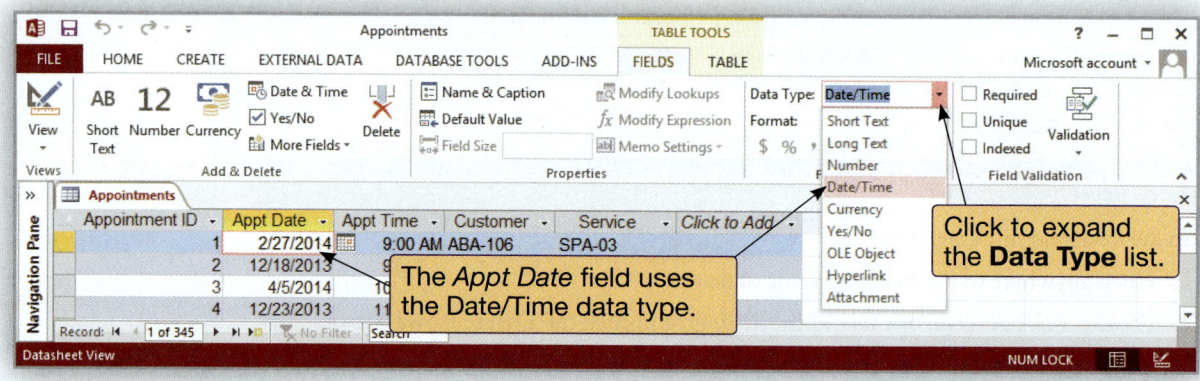

FIGURE AC 2.16

AutoNumber—An *AutoNumber* field is automatically assigned its value by Access. Database users cannot edit or enter data in an *AutoNumber* field. *AutoNumber* fields are often used as a primary key if no other unique field exists in the table.

Short Text—A *Short Text* field can hold up to 255 characters. *Short Text* fields are used for short text data or numbers that should be treated as text.

Long Text—A *Long Text* field holds text and numbers like a *Short Text* field, except you can enter up to 65,535 characters in a *Long Text* field. Text in *Long Text* fields can be formatted using Rich Text Formatting.

Number—A *Number* field holds a numerical value. The default number is described as a long integer, a number between −2,147,483,648 and 2,147,483,647.

Date/Time—A *Date/Time* field stores a numerical value that is displayed as a date and time. The format in which the date and/or time displays is controlled by the Format property. Using the Date/Time data type allows you to sort the field by date.

Currency—A *Currency* field stores a numerical value with a high degree of accuracy (up to four decimal places to the right of the decimal). Access will not round the values stored in currency fields, regardless of the format in which the value displays.

Yes/No—A *Yes/No* field stores a true/false value as a −1 for yes and 0 for no. Yes/No fields can display the words *Yes/No* or *True/False* or a checkbox as shown in Figure AC 2.17.

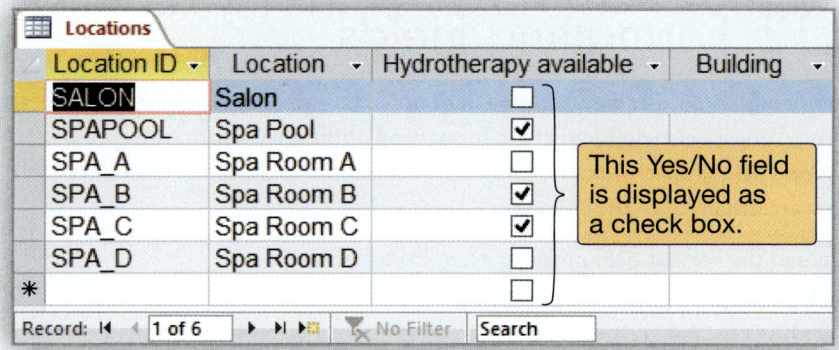

FIGURE AC 2.17

OLE Object—The *OLE Object* data type stores a graphic or file as part of the database. It is maintained in Access 2013 for backward compatibility with databases created prior to Access 2007. In general, you should use the newer Attachment data type instead.

Hyperlink—A *Hyperlink* field stores a Web address or e-mail address. Fields with the Hyperlink data type can be active and set to open the computer's default e-mail program or Web browser populated with the data from the *Hyperlink* field.

Attachment—An *Attachment* field stores files as attachments to records. Attachments can be images, Word documents, or almost any other type of data file.

Calculated Field—A *Calculated* field uses an expression (a formula) to calculate a value.

tips & tricks

In previous versions of Access, the *Short Text* data type was simply *Text* and the *Long Text* data type was *Memo*.

another method

You can also change the data type from Design view:
1. Click in the **Data Type** column for the field that you want to change.
2. Click the **drop-down arrow** to see the list of available data types.
3. Select the appropriate data type for your data.
4. Save the table to commit the change.

let me try

If the database is not already open, open the data file **AC2-Appointments** and try this skill on your own:
1. If it is not already open, open the *Appointments* table in Datasheet view.
2. Change the data type for the *Appt Date* field to **Date/Time.**
3. Save the table.

skill 2.11   Changing Data Type

Skill 2.12 Formatting Fields

When designing a table, you specify what type of data can be entered in each field by selecting the data type. You can also define specific formatting options to control the appearance of data. The **Format field property** does not affect the data stored in the table; it only controls the way the data are displayed to the end user.

To make changes to the Format field property from Datasheet view:

1. Click anywhere in the field you want to format.
2. On the *Table Tools Fields* tab, in the *Formatting* group, expand the **Format** list, and select the format you want. Not all properties are available for all field data types.

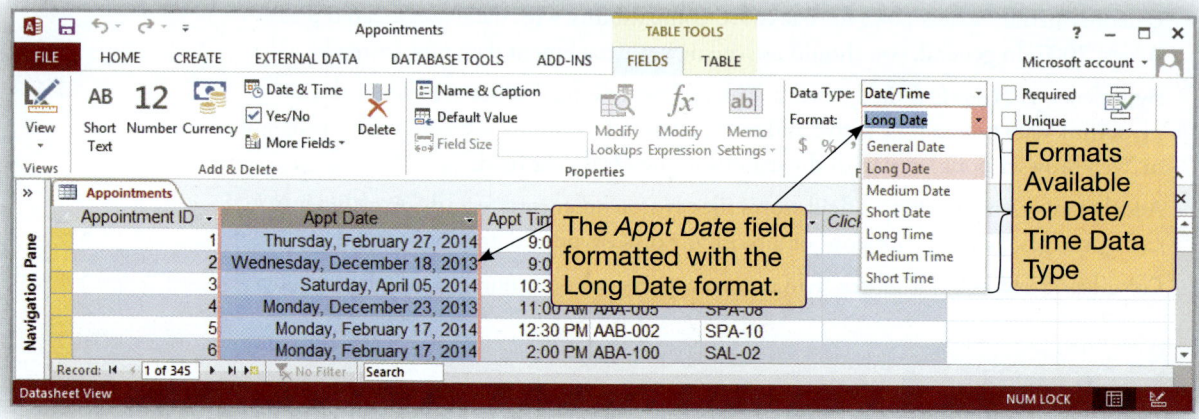

FIGURE AC 2.18

You can quickly apply the Currency, Percent, or Comma number formats by clicking the appropriate button in the *Formatting* group. These formats can be used with AutoNumber, Number, and Currency data types.

- The **Currency format** displays a $ symbol before the number and two digits to the right of the decimal place.
- The **Percent format** displays the number as a percentage, so .05 displays as 5, and 5 displays as 500. It does not display the % symbol in the table.
- The **Comma Style format** displays the , symbol within the number and two digits to the right of the decimal. This is the same as selecting **Standard** from the *Format* list.

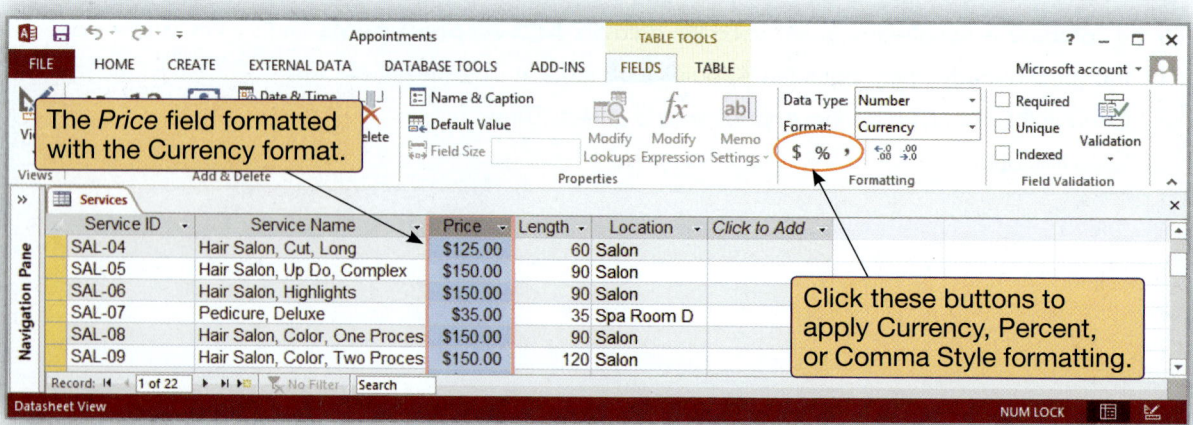

FIGURE AC 2.19

To modify the Format field property in Design view:

1. Click anywhere in the field you want to format.
2. In the Field Properties pane, click in the **Format** property box.
3. Click the arrow at the right end of the box to expand the list of available formats, and select the format you want.

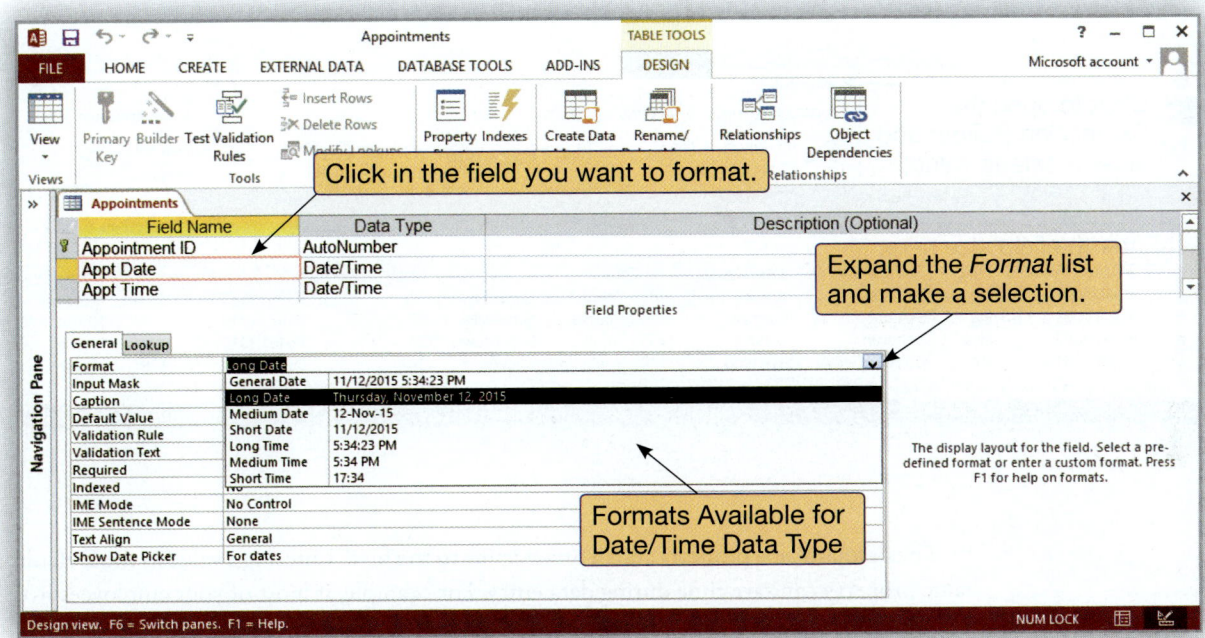

FIGURE AC 2.20

tell me more

To increase or decrease the number of digits that appear to the right of the decimal in your *AutoNumber, Number,* and *Currency* fields, on the *Table Tools Fields* tab, in the *Formatting* group, click the **Increase Decimals** or **Decrease Decimals** button.

let me try

If the database is not already open, open the data file **AC2-Appointments** and try this skill on your own:

1. If necessary, open the *Appointments* table in Datasheet view.
2. Apply the **Long Date** format to the *Appt Date* field. Hint: Verify that the data type is **Date/Time** before applying the format.
3. If necessary, expand the column width for the *Appt Date* field so you can see the full date in Datasheet view.
4. If necessary, open the *Services* table in Design view.
5. Apply the **Currency** format to the *Price* field. Change only the formatting, not the data type.
6. Save and close the tables.

skill 2.12 Formatting Fields

Skill 2.13 Modifying Field Properties

You can modify a variety of field properties to control data entry. The Format field property is discussed in detail in the skill *Formatting Fields*, and the Name and Caption properties are covered in the skill *Renaming Fields*. Two other useful properties are the Default Value property, and the Field Size property. Both of these field properties can be modified from either Datasheet view or Design view.

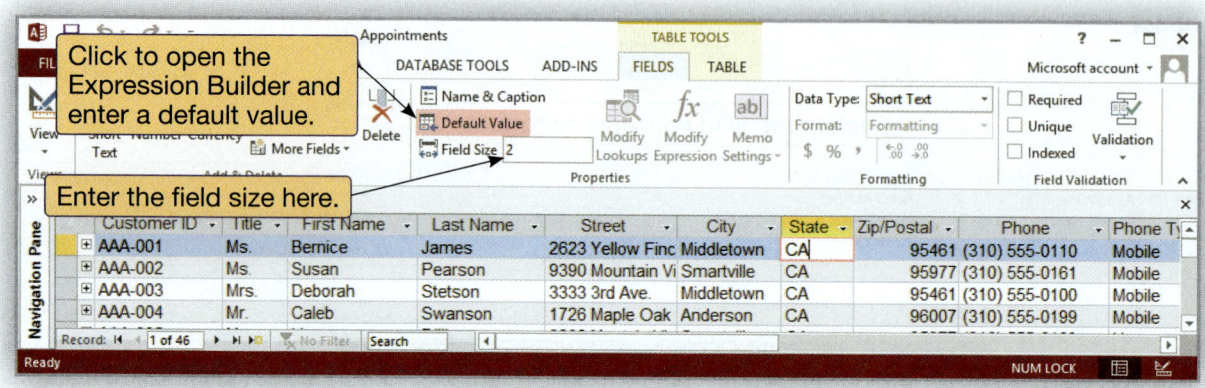

FIGURE AC 2.21

The **Default Value property** adds a preset value to the field. Entering a value in the Default Value property can save time during data entry. For example, if most of your employees live in California, use CA as the default value for the *State* field.

To add a default value in Datasheet view:

1. Select the field to which you want to add a default value.
2. On the *Table Tools Fields* tab, in the *Properties* group, click the **Default Value** button to open the *Expression Builder*.
3. In the *Expression Builder*, enter the numerical value, text, or formula you want to use as the default value for the field. The default value expression always begins with the = sign, which Access adds for you. If the default value is a text string with a space or other special character in it, you must enclose it in quotation marks. If the text is something simple, such as *CA*, you do not need to type the quotation marks. Access will add them for you.
4. Click **OK**.
5. Save the table.

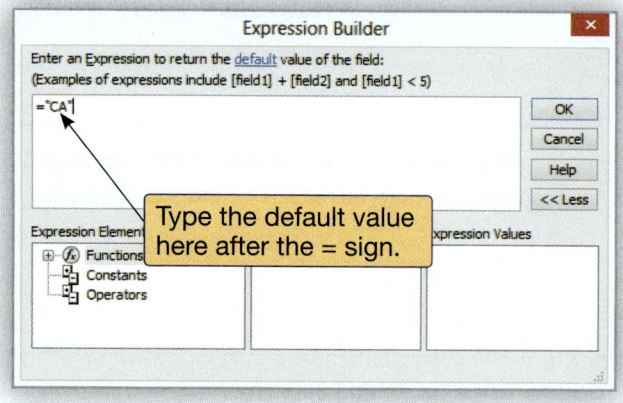

FIGURE AC 2.22

When a field has a default value set, the *Default Value* button appears highlighted. Whenever a new record is created, the default value is entered into this field automatically.

You can also set the default value from Design view:

1. Select the field.
2. In the Field Properties pane, click in the **Default Value** box and type the numerical value, text, or formula you want to use as the default value.
3. If you want to use the *Expression Builder,* click the **Build...** button at the right side of the *Default Value* box.
4. Save the table.

The **Field Size property** limits the number of characters that can be entered in a text field. The default size for a *Short Text* field is 255 (the maximum size for a *Short Text* field). Limiting the field size can ensure that data are entered properly. For example, if you want entries in the *State* field to always use the two-letter state abbreviation, limit the field size to 2.

To modify the Field Size property in Datasheet view:

1. Select the field.
2. On the *Table Tools Fields* tab, in the *Properties* group, type the new field size in the **Field Size** box and press ⏎ Enter.
3. If you are making the field size smaller, Access will warn you that the smaller size may result in data loss, as Access will delete any data in the field that exceeds the new field size limit. Click **Yes** to continue with the change.
4. Save the table.

To modify the Field Size property in Design view, follow the same steps, entering the new field size value in the **Field Size** box in the Field Properties pane.

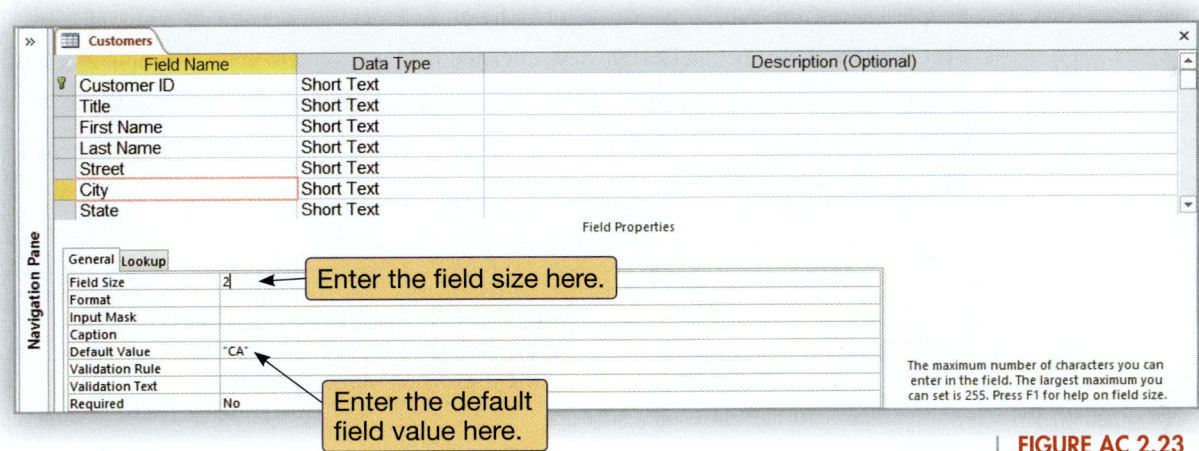

FIGURE AC 2.23
Modifying field properties in Design view

tips & tricks

You cannot limit the size of *Long Text* fields.

tell me more

If the selected field is a *Long Text* field, the *Memo Settings* button controls two properties exclusive to *Long Text* fields:

- Rich Text Formatting allows you to add text formatting.
- Append Only saves a history of changes made to the text in the field.

let me try

If the database is not already open, open the data file **AC2-Appointments** and try this skill on your own:

1. If necessary, open the *Customers* table in Datasheet view.
2. Set the **Default Value** property for the *State* field to **CA**.
3. Switch to Design view.
4. Change the **Field Size** property for the *State* field to **2**.
5. Save the table.

skill 2.13   Modifying Field Properties

Skill 2.14 Applying an Input Mask from Design View

One of the keys to an effective database is consistent data entry. An **input mask** forces users to enter data in a consistent format. Input masks are only available from the Design view Field Properties pane. The *Input Mask Wizard* offers a variety of common input masks including phone number and date and time formats.

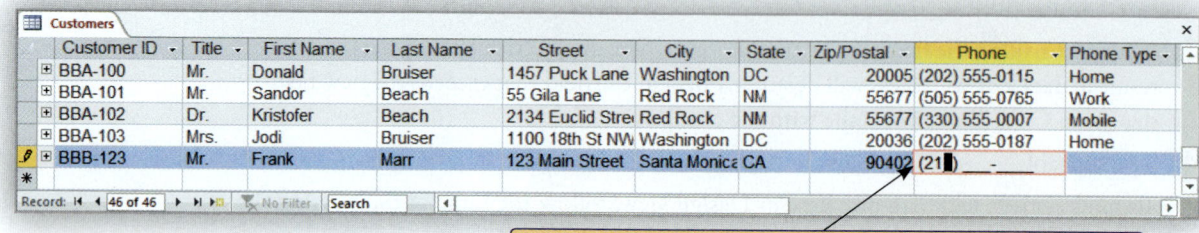

FIGURE AC 2.24

The *Phone* field has the Phone input mask applied.

To apply one of the sample input masks to a field:

1. With the table open in Design view, click the field you want to apply the input mask to.

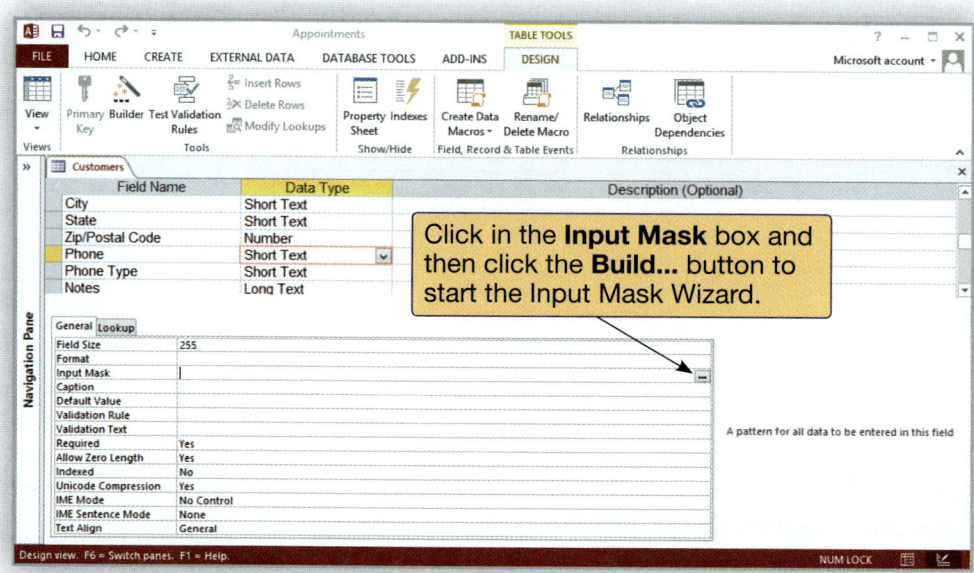

FIGURE AC 2.25

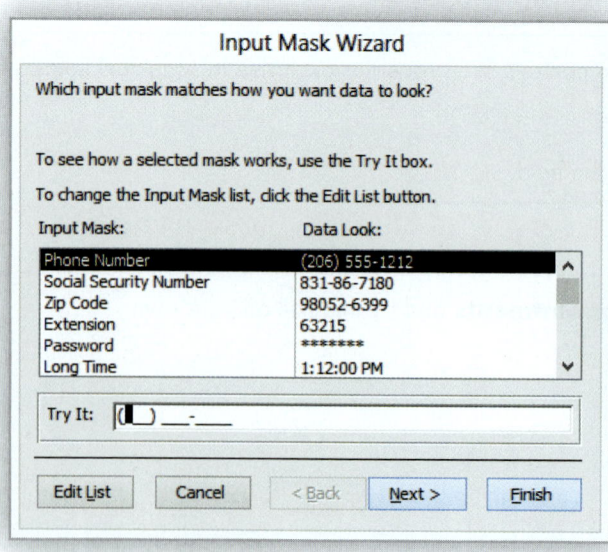

2. Click the **Input Mask** box in the Field Properties pane.
3. Click the **Build...** button to open the *Input Mask Wizard*.
4. Click **Yes** when Access prompts you to save the table.
5. Click the input mask format you want.
6. To test the format, click in the **Try It** box, and type a sample to see how the input mask will affect data entry as shown in Figure AC 2.26.
7. Click **Next**.
8. Click **Next** again to continue without making any customizations to the input mask as shown in Figure AC 2.27.

FIGURE AC 2.26

9. In the next step, you specify how Access will store the data—with or without the input mask symbols. Unless you truly need the symbols stored in the database, select the second option as shown in Figure AC 2.28. This will help reduce the size of the database. Click **Finish.** You can also click **Next** and then click **Finish** on the final step of the wizard.
10. Save the table.

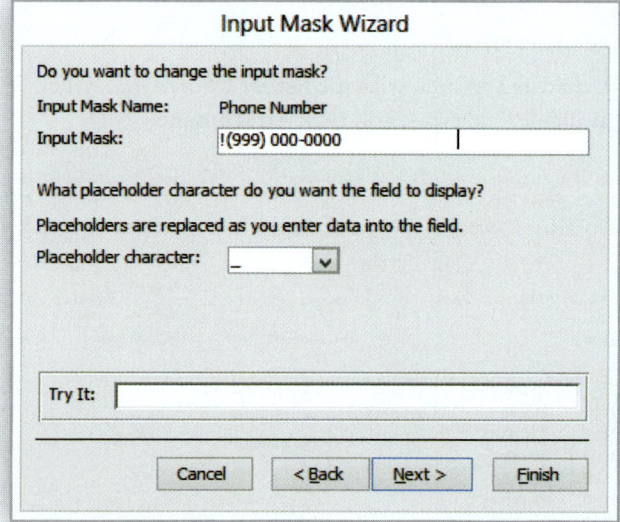

FIGURE AC 2.27

FIGURE AC 2.28

tips & tricks

- The Input Mask property is available for *Short Text* or *Date/Time* data type fields only. If you want to use the Social Security input mask, use the Short Text data type for the field that stores the social security numbers.
- If the field has a format specified through the Format property, the format takes precedence over the input mask format.

let me try

If the database is not already open, open the data file **AC2-Appointments** and try this skill on your own:

1. If necessary, open the *Customers* table.
2. Switch to Design view.
3. Apply the **Phone** input mask format to the *Phone* field. Do not change default format or placeholder characters. Store the data without the symbols.
4. Save the table.
5. Switch to Datasheet view and enter a new record in the *Customers* table, using any customer information you want. The *Customer ID* field has an input mask applied that requires three letters followed by three numbers. Input in the *Phone* field is controlled by the input mask you applied in step 3.

skill 2.14   Applying an Input Mask from Design View

Skill 2.15 Working with Attachment Fields

One of the most useful enhancements to recent versions of Access is the ability to create **Attachment fields** to store files as attachments to records. Attachments can be pictures, Word documents, or almost any other type of data file. For security reasons, Access will not allow program files (for example, .exe or .bat files) or any files greater than 256 MB as attachments.

To add an *Attachment* field from Datasheet view:

1. At the far right side of the table, there is a column with the header *Click to Add*. Click the arrow to expand the list of available field types, and click **Attachment**.

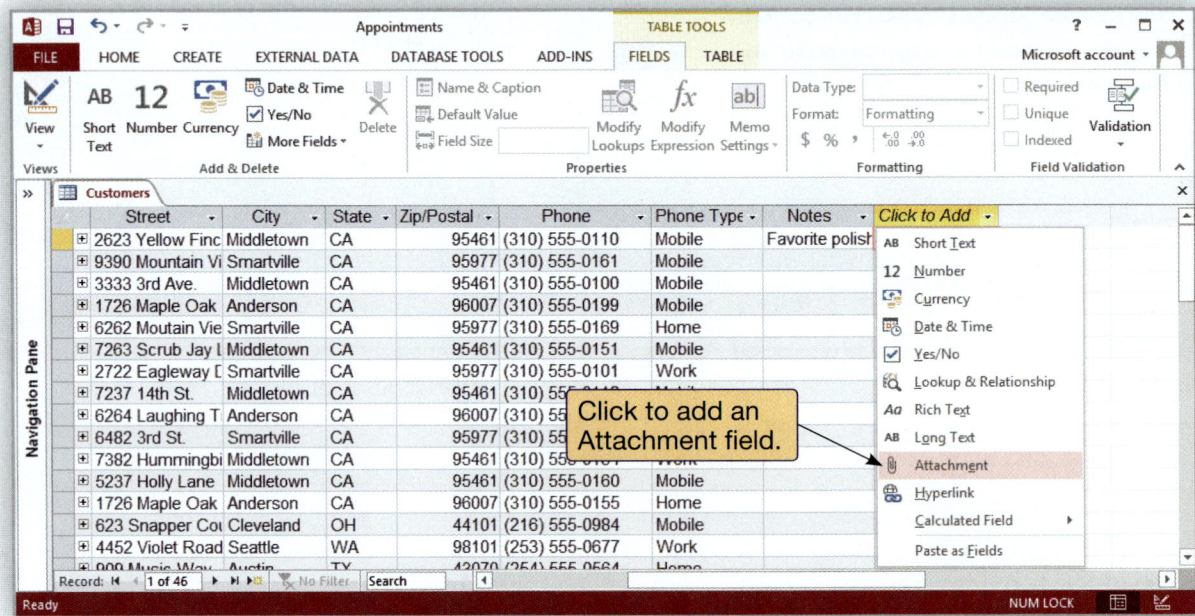

FIGURE AC 2.29

2. Notice that you cannot rename the *Attachment* field. It is designated by a paperclip icon. (You can, however, rename the field in Design view.)

FIGURE AC 2.30

To add an attachment:

1. Double-click the *Attachment* field in the record to which you want to add the attachment.
2. The *Attachments* dialog opens.
3. Click the **Add...** button and browse for the file you want to add.
4. Double-click the file to add it, or click the file once, and then click the **Open** button.
5. Click **OK** to save the attachment and close the *Attachments* dialog.

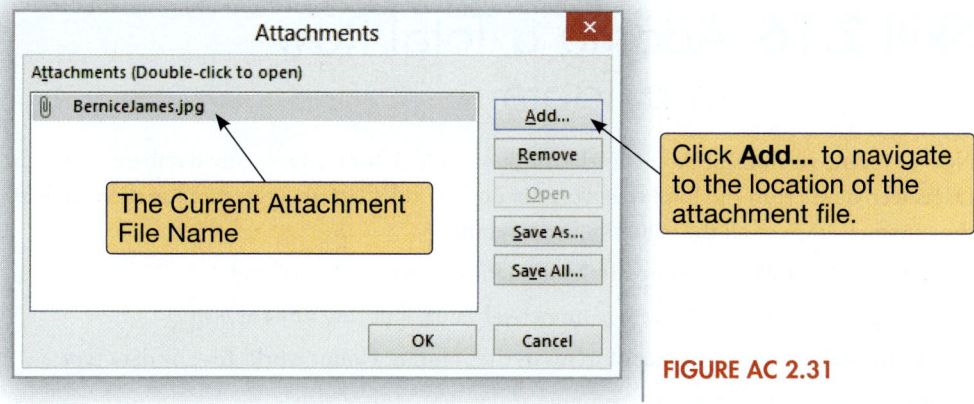

FIGURE AC 2.31

The number next to the attachment icon in each record tells you how many attachments there are. Records can have multiple attachments in a single *Attachment* field.

FIGURE AC 2.32

tips & tricks

Attachment fields cannot be changed to another data type.

tell me more

The attachment is not visible in the table. However, when you start working with forms and reports, the attachment is available for display in those database objects.

let me try

If the database is not already open, open the data file **AC2-Appointments** and try this skill on your own:

1. If necessary, open the *Customers* table in Datasheet view.
2. Add an *Attachment* field at the far right of the table.
3. Add the JPEG image file **BerniceJames** to the customer record for Bernice James. The image file is located with your student data files for this chapter.
4. Save the table.

skill 2.15 Working with Attachment Fields

Skill 2.16 Adding a Total Row to a Table

New to recent versions of Access is the ability to add a Total row to any database object in Datasheet view. From the **Total row**, you can quickly calculate an aggregate function such as the sum or average of all the values in the column.

Sum—Calculates the total of all the numerical values in the column.

Average—Calculates the average numerical value, ignoring null values.

Count—Counts the number of items in the column. Count works for any data type.

Maximum—Returns the largest numerical value.

Minimum—Returns the smallest numerical value.

Standard Deviation—Calculates the statistical standard deviation for numeric field types only.

Variance—Calculates the statistical variance for numeric field types only.

To add a Total row to a datasheet:

1. On the *Home* tab, in the *Records* group, click the **Totals** button.
2. In the Total row at the bottom of the datasheet, click the column where you want to add a total.
3. Click the arrow, and select the function you want to use.
4. Save the table.

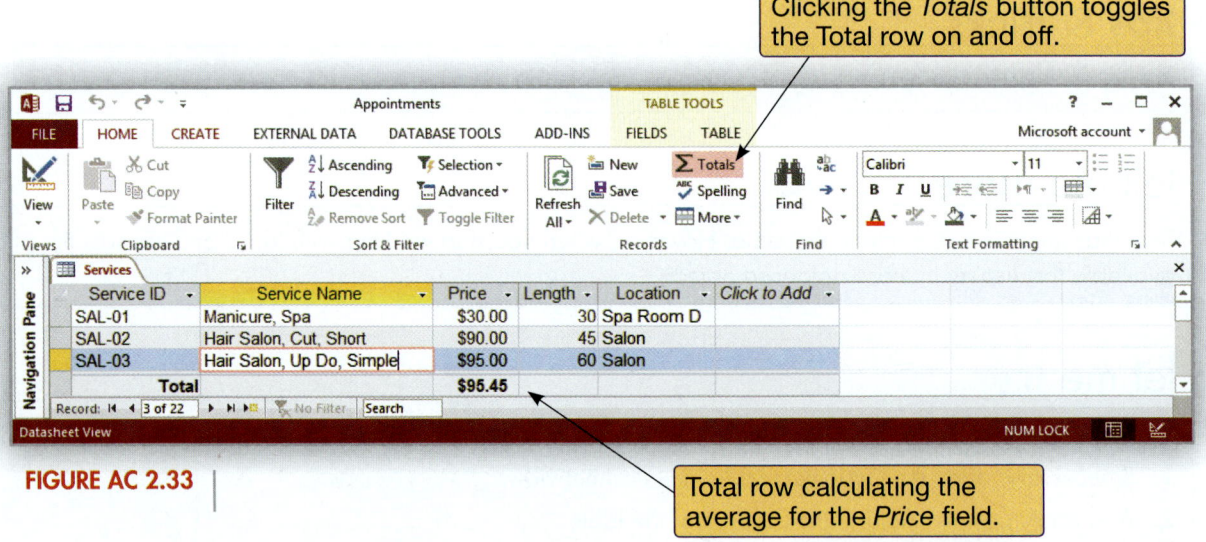

Clicking the *Totals* button toggles the Total row on and off.

Total row calculating the average for the *Price* field.

FIGURE AC 2.33

let me try

If the database is not already open, open the data file **AC2-Appointments** and try this skill on your own:

1. If necessary, open the *Services* table in Datasheet view.
2. Display the Total row.
3. Use the Total row to calculate the average of the values in the *Price* field.
4. Save the table.

Skill 2.17 Adding a Lookup Field from Another Table

A **lookup field** allows the user to select data from a list of items. One type of lookup list presents values from a field in another table or a query. Whether you begin with a new field or modify the data type for an existing field, the process using the *Lookup Wizard* is the same.

To create a new lookup field from Datasheet view:

1. On the *Table Tools Fields* tab, in the *Add & Delete* group, click the **More Fields** button.
2. From the *Basic Types* section of the *Field Types* gallery, click **Lookup & Relationship**.
3. The *Lookup Wizard* opens.

To create a new lookup field from Design view, type the name for the new field to expand the **Data Type** list, and select **Lookup Wizard...** to open the *Lookup Wizard*.

To modify an existing field to use a lookup list:

1. Open the table in Design view.
2. Select the field you want to change to use a lookup list.
3. Expand the **Data Type** list, and select **Lookup Wizard...** to open the *Lookup Wizard*.

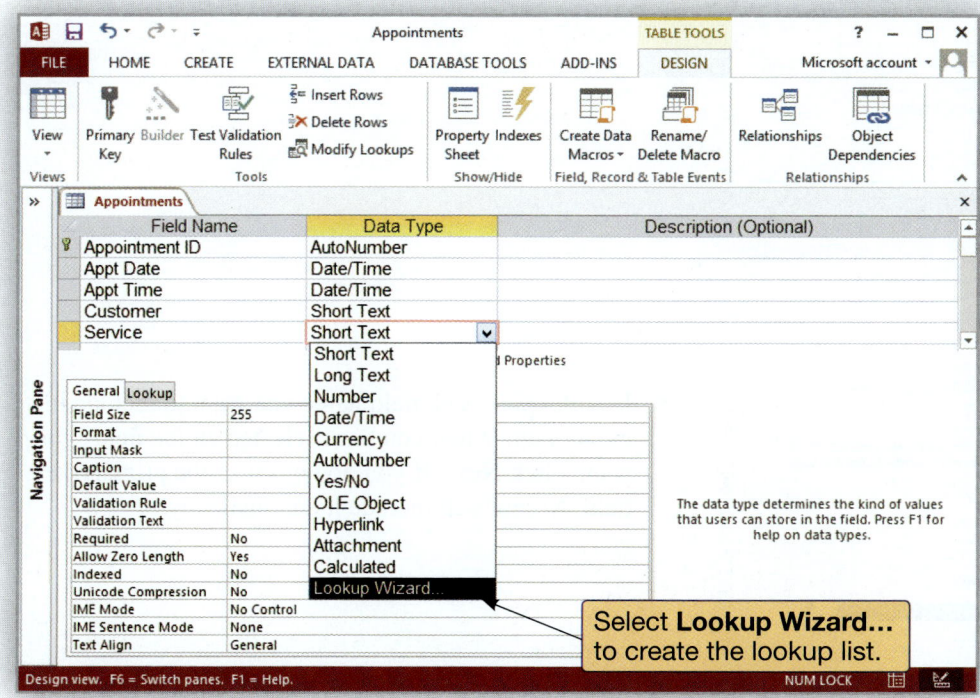

FIGURE AC 2.34

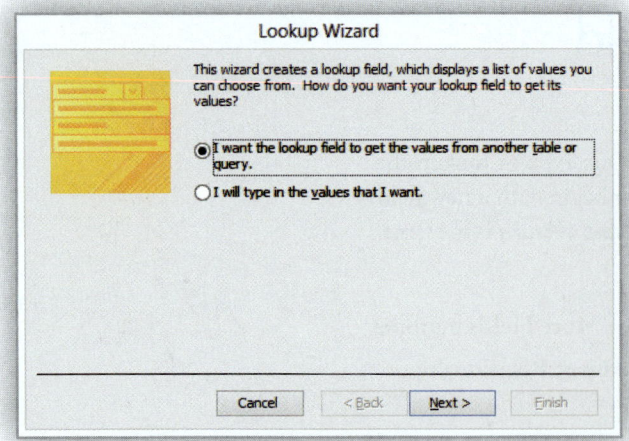

FIGURE AC 2.35

To add the lookup field using the *Lookup Wizard*:

1. The first step of the wizard asks you to determine where your lookup list data will come from. The **I want the lookup field to get the values from another table or query.** radio button is selected by default. Click **Next** to go to the next step.

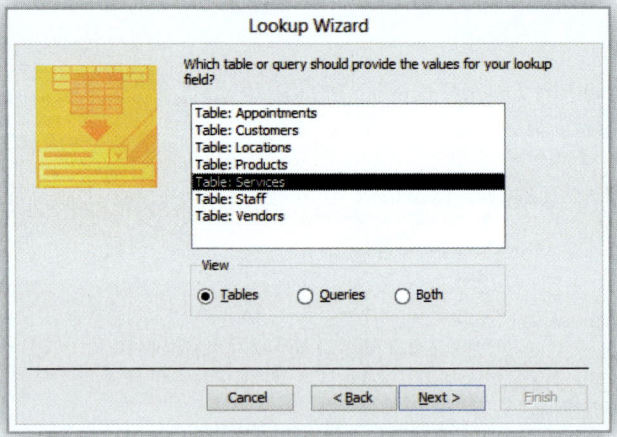

FIGURE AC 2.36

2. Click the name of the table or query that includes the field you want to use for your lookup field values. Click **Next.**

FIGURE AC 2.37

3. Double-click each field name you want to include in the lookup. When you have selected all the fields you want, click **Next.** If you do not select the primary key field, Access will include it automatically.

4. If you want items in the lookup list sorted in a particular order, select the field to sort by. The sort order is ascending by default. Click the **Ascending** button if you want to switch the sort order to descending. Click **Next**.

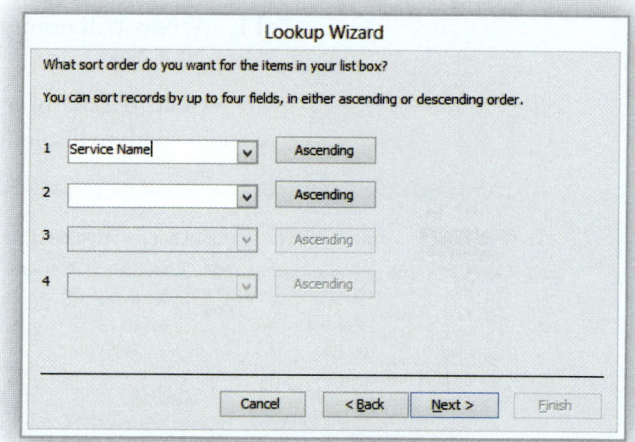

FIGURE AC 2.38

5. By default, the **Hide key column (recommended)** check box is checked. This hides the primary key in the lookup list.

6. Adjust the column width as necessary to display the values in the lookup list. Click and drag the right border of the column header to make the column wider or narrower. You can double-click the right column border to autofit the column to the data. Click **Next** to continue.

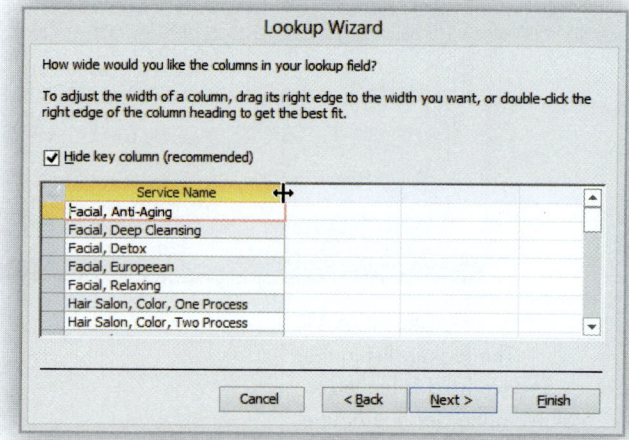

FIGURE AC 2.39

7. If you are modifying an existing field, Access keeps the original field name. If this is a new field, Access gives the field a generic field name such as *Field1*. You should change the name of the new field to something more meaningful.

8. Click the **Enable Data Integrity** check box to require that only values from the lookup list are allowed in the field.

9. Verify that the **Restrict Delete** radio button is selected to prevent any deletions in the table containing the lookup values that would invalidate data in the table containing the lookup field.

10. Click the **Finish** button to add the new lookup field to the table.

FIGURE AC 2.40

skill 2.17   Adding a Lookup Field from Another Table

11. Access will prompt you to save the table so table relationships can be created. Click **Yes**.

Switch to Datasheet view to test the new lookup field. You may need to adjust the column width to display the lookup data properly.

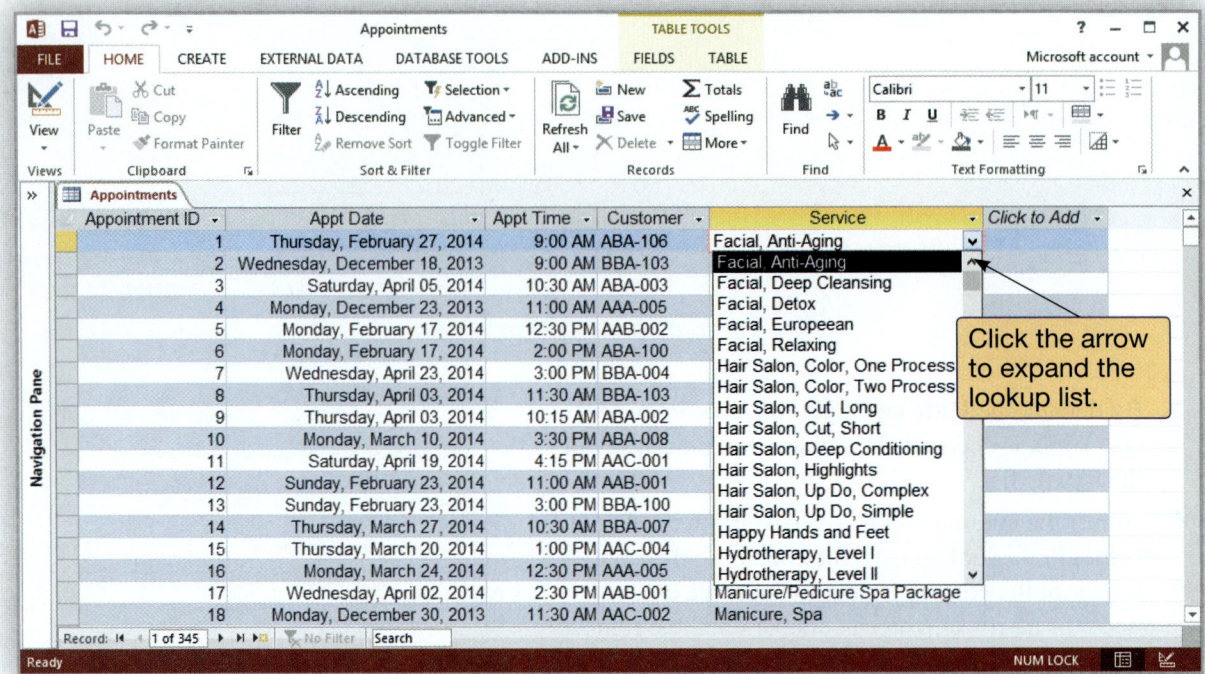

FIGURE AC 2.41
The lookup list in the *Service* field is limited to values in the *Service Name* field in the *Services* table. This prevents data entry errors and ensures data integrity between the two tables.

tell me more

When you create a lookup field that references data in another table, Access automatically creates a one-to-many relationship between the table that contains the list data (the "one") and the table that includes the lookup list (the "many"). This concept is discussed further in the skill *Creating Relationships*.

let me try

If the database is not already open, open the data file **AC2-Appointments** and try this skill on your own:

1. If necessary, open the *Appointments* table in Design view.
2. Modify the *Service* field to use a lookup list with the following parameters:
   a. The lookup data will come from the *Services* table.
   b. Include the *Service Name* field in the lookup list.
   c. Sort the lookup list by the *Service Name* field.
   d. Hide the key column and adjust the lookup column width as necessary to display the data.
   e. Enforce data integrity.
   f. Do not allow deletions in the *Services* table that would violate the integrity of records in the *Appointments* table.
3. Save the table.

from the perspective of . . .

SMALL BUSINESS OWNER

I use an Access database to keep track of business contacts, inventory, sales, and customers. When I first set up the database, I included all the customer information with every record in the sales table. Later, when I tried to analyze my sales records to find repeat customers, I realized my mistake. There were multiple records for the same customer, but with the customer information entered slightly differently in each. I know that Cindy Williams and Cynthia Williams are the same person, but Access doesn't. I had to bring in a temp to pull out the customer information into a separate table and make sure the sales records were referencing the correct customers. If I had designed the tables the right way in the first place, I could have saved a lot of time and money. Now my sales table uses a lookup field to add customer data. No more mistakes!

Skill 2.18 Adding a Lookup Field from a List

Lookup fields are useful for fields that reference a specific list of items. A lookup field does not need to reference data in another table or query. You can enter your own values to create a custom list.

To review the procedures for creating new lookup fields, refer to the skill *Adding a Lookup Field from another Table*.

To modify an existing field to use a lookup field with values you specify:

1. Open the table in Design view.
2. Click the field you want to modify to use a lookup list.
3. Click the **Data Type** drop-down arrow and select **Lookup Wizard...**
4. The first step of the wizard asks you to determine where your lookup list data will come from. Click the **I will type in the values that I want.** radio button. Click **Next** to go to the next step.

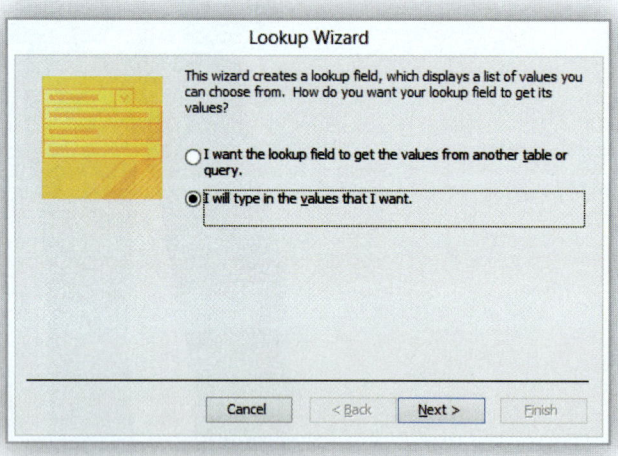

FIGURE AC 2.42

5. First, enter the number of columns you want in your lookup list.
6. Press Tab to go to the first cell in the first blank column.
7. Type the values in the table exactly as you want them to appear in the lookup field. Click and drag the right border of the column header to make the column wider or narrower. You can double-click the right column border to autofit the column to the data. Click **Next** to continue.

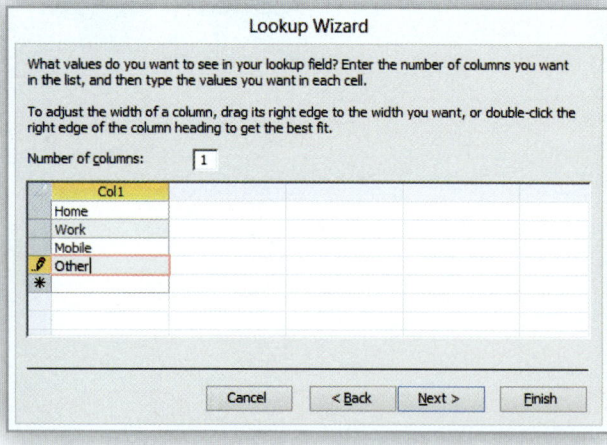

FIGURE AC 2.43

8. Access will keep the original field name. If you want to change it, type a new name.
9. If you want to restrict data entry to only items in the list, click the **Limit To List** check box.
10. Click the **Finish** button to complete the lookup list.

Switch to Datasheet view to test the new lookup field. You may need to adjust the column width to display the lookup data properly.

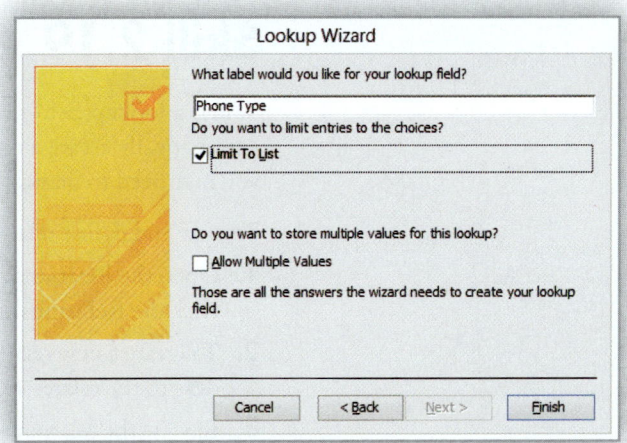

FIGURE AC 2.44

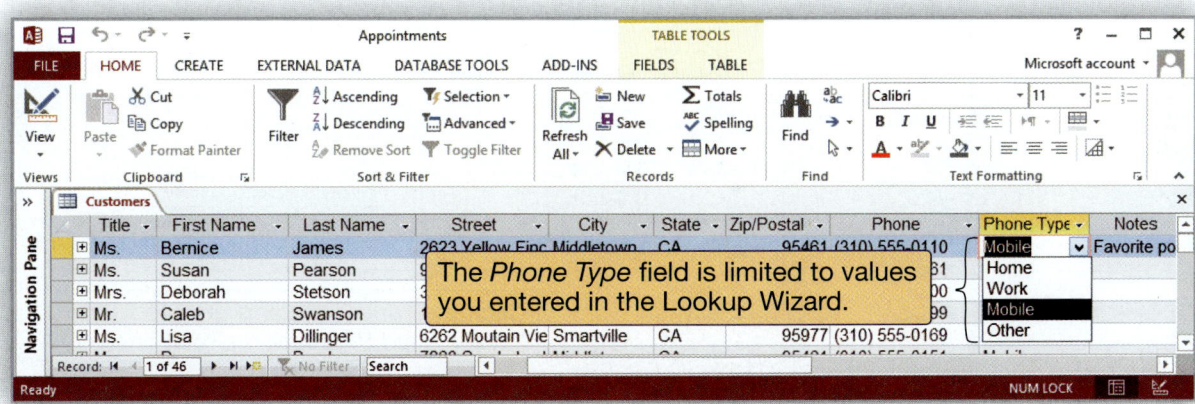

The *Phone Type* field is limited to values you entered in the Lookup Wizard.

FIGURE AC 2.45

tell me more

If the field you want to change to a lookup field uses the *Date/Time* or *Currency* data type, you will need to change the data type to *Number* before you can modify it to be a lookup field.

let me try

If the database is not already open, open the data file **AC2-Appointments** and try this skill on your own:

1. If necessary, open the *Customers* table.
2. Switch to Design view.
3. Modify the *Phone Type* field to use a lookup list with the following values: `Home, Work, Mobile, Other`.
4. Limit the lookup list to values in the list.
5. Save the table.

skill 2.18 Adding a Lookup Field from a List

Skill 2.19 Creating Relationships

When a lookup field in one table references values in a field in another table, Access will automatically create a one-to-many relationship between the tables for you. In other cases, you may need to manually create a relationship between two tables.

To view and define relationships between tables:

1. Open the Relationships window. On the *Database Tools* tab, in the *Relationships* group, click the **Relationships** button.
2. To create a new relationship, click the primary key field name in the primary table and drag to the related field name in the secondary table.
3. Review the relationship in the *Edit Relationships* dialog, and then click the **Create** button.

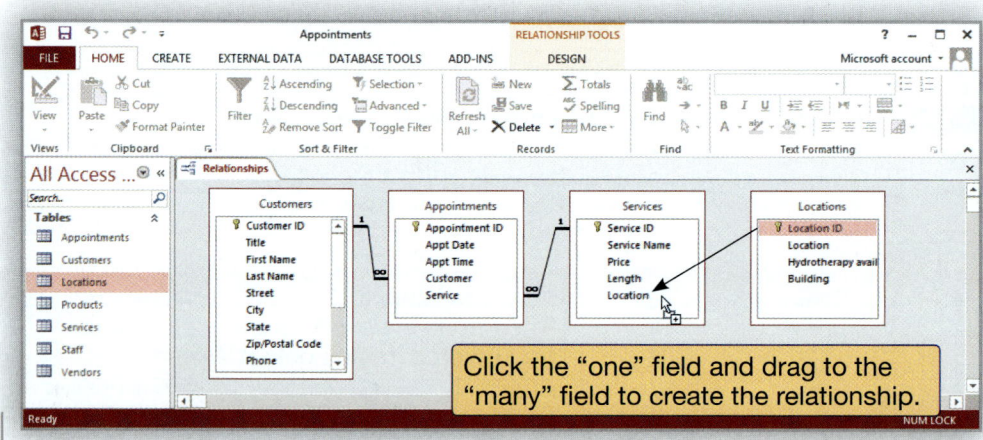

FIGURE AC 2.46

Enforcing **referential integrity** ensures that related database records remain accurate. If a relationship has *Enforce Referential Integrity* checked, then the tables will conform to the following rules:

- You cannot add a record to the secondary table without an associated record in the primary table.
- You cannot make changes to the primary table that would cause records in the secondary table to become unmatched.
- You cannot delete records from the primary table if there are related records in the secondary table.

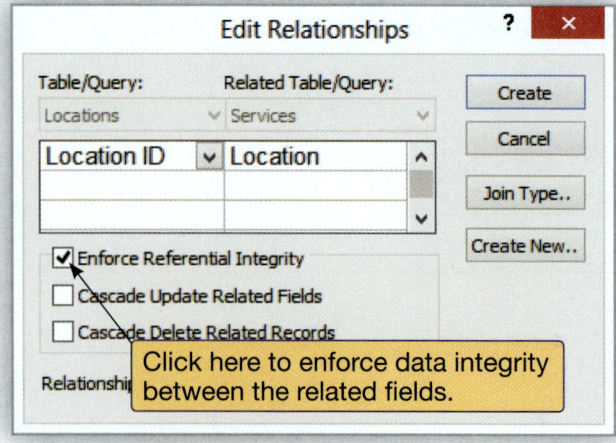

FIGURE AC 2.47

To enforce referential integrity in a relationship:

1. Double-click the relationship line to open the *Edit Relationships* dialog.
2. Click the **Enforce Referential Integrity** check box.
3. Click **OK**.

Notice the change to the relationship line. The 1 indicates the "one" table in the one-to-many relationship. The infinity symbol indicates the "many" table. When these symbols appear, you know that the relationship has referential integrity enforced.

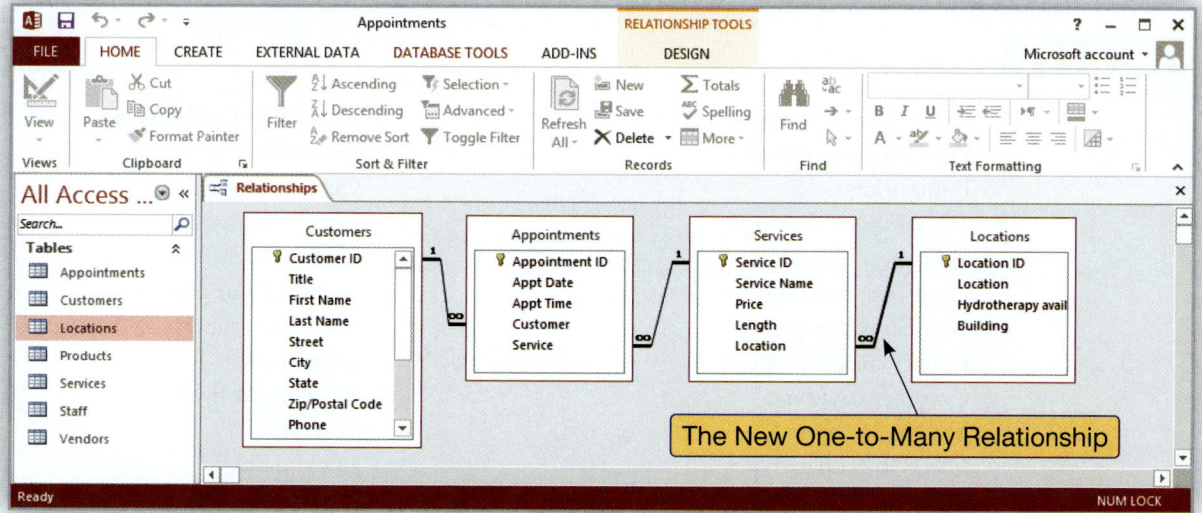

FIGURE AC 2.48

tell me more
To delete the relationship between two tables, right-click the relationship line, and select **Delete.**

another method
To open the *Edit Relationships* dialog, you can also:
- Double-click any field name showing in the Relationships window.
- Double-click any empty area of the Relationships window.

When you open the *Edit Relationships* dialog with either of these methods, you will need to select the primary table from the *Table/Query* list at the left side of the dialog. When you make a selection, Access will populate the dialog with the existing relationships.

let me try
If the database is not already open, open the data file **AC2-Appointments** and try this skill on your own:
1. If necessary, save and close all open database objects.
2. Open the Relationships window.
3. If necessary, show the *Locations* table and the *Services* table.
4. Create a new relationship between the *Location ID* field in the *Locations* table and the *Location* field in the *Services* table.
5. Enforce data integrity between the two fields.
6. Close the Relationships window, saving the layout changes.

skill 2.19 Creating Relationships

key terms

Quick Start field types
Field Properties pane
Primary key field
AutoNumber data type
Short Text data type
Long Text data type
Number data type
Date/Time data type
Currency data type
Yes/No data type
OLE Object data type
Hyperlink data type
Attachment data type

Calculated Field data type
Format field property
Currency format
Percent format
Comma Style format
Default Value property
Field Size property
Input mask
Attachment field
Total row
Lookup field
Referential integrity

concepts review

1. A well-designed database _____.
   a. repeats important data in multiple tables
   b. stores each unique piece of data in only one table
   c. uses the AutoNumber data type for primary key fields
   d. Both B and C

2. Users can enter and edit data in an AutoNumber field.
   a. True
   b. False

3. To rename a field, _____.
   a. click the column header, and type the new field name
   b. double-click the column header, and type the new field name
   c. right-click the column header, select **Rename Field,** and type the new field name
   d. Both B and C

4. A table's primary key must _____.
   a. use the AutoNumber data type
   b. be linked to other tables
   c. be unique for every field
   d. Be named *ID*

5. To include a photo image with each record in a table, use a field with this data type:
   a. Photo
   b. Attachment
   c. Hyperlink
   d. Memo

6. The Currency field format is the same as the Currency data type.
   a. True
   b. False
7. The Percent field format displays the % symbol in the data table.
   a. True
   b. False
8. To control the number of characters a user can enter into a table field, use _____.
   a. the Field Size property
   b. the Field Width property
   c. the Long Text data type
   d. Rich Text Formatting
9. An input mask _____.
   a. creates a relationship between two tables
   b. modifies the field Format property
   c. changes the field data type to Short Text
   d. forces users to input data in a consistent format
10. If two tables have referential integrity enforced, _____.
    a. you cannot add a record to the secondary table without an associated record in the primary table
    b. you cannot make changes to the primary table that would cause records in the secondary table to become unmatched
    c. Both A and B
    d. None of the above

projects

Data files for projects can be found on
www.mhhe.com/office2013skills

skill review 2.1

In this project, you will continue to work with the Computer Science department database from the *Chapter 1 Skill Review 1.1*. It uses Access to manage employees and various items that are loaned to students and faculty. You will create two new tables in this database: one for the companies that the department frequently purchases from and another with a list of classrooms.

Skills needed to complete this project:
- Designing a Table (Skill 2.1)
- Creating and Saving a Table in Datasheet View (Skill 2.2)
- Renaming Fields (Skill 2.3)
- Changing Data Type (Skill 2.11)
- Adding Fields in Datasheet View (Skill 2.4)
- Using Quick Start to Add Related Fields (Skill 2.5)
- Adjusting Table Column Widths (Skill 2.6)
- Applying an Input Mask from Design View (Skill 2.14)
- Adding a Lookup Field from Another Table (Skill 2.17)
- Formatting Fields (Skill 2.12)
- Modifying Field Properties (Skill 2.13)
- Adding a Total Row to a Table (Skill 2.16)
- Working with Attachment Fields (Skill 2.15)
- Deleting Fields (Skill 2.10)
- Creating a Table in Design View (Skill 2.7)
- Setting the Primary Key (Skill 2.9)
- Inserting Fields in Design View (Skill 2.8)
- Adding a Lookup Field from a List (Skill 2.18)
- Creating Relationships (Skill 2.19)

1. Open the start file **AC2013-SkillReview-2-1**.
2. If necessary, enable active content by clicking the **Enable Content** button in the Message Bar.
3. Save a copy of the file to work on named:
   `[your initials]AC-SkillReview-2-1`
4. Create a table in Datasheet view to store vendor company data.
   a. On the *Create* tab, in the *Tables* group, click the **Table** button.
   b. You are now in the Datasheet view of a new table. Notice that Access has created a new field named *ID* with the AutoNumber data type.
   c. Create the next field by typing `Greg's College Supplies` in the cell directly underneath the **Click to Add** heading.

d. Press Tab to go to the next field in this record.

e. Create another new field by typing: `www.gregscollegesupplies.com`

f. Press Tab again.

g. Go to the next row in the table and enter another record with the following:

   `Cindy's Business Supplies`
   `www.cindysbusinesssupplies.com`

5. Rename the fields.

   a. Right-click the **ID** field heading, and click **Rename Field**.

   b. Type `VendorID` and press Enter.

   c. Repeat the process for **Field1**, renaming it: `CompanyName`

   d. Repeat the process for **Field2**, renaming it: `WebSite`

6. The data type for the *WebSite* field is *Short Text*. Change it to **Hyperlink**.

   a. Click the **WebSite** column header to select the field.

   b. On the *Table Tools Fields* tab, in the *Formatting* group, expand the **Data Type** list, and select **Hyperlink**.

7. Add a new field to the table to store phone numbers.

   a. Click the arrow next to the **Click to Add** heading in the last available field, and select **Short Text**.

   b. Type `Phone` to overwrite the default field name *Field1*.

8. Add a group of related fields using *Quick Start*.

   a. Click the cell underneath the last **Click to Add** heading.

   b. On the *Table Tools Fields* tab, in the *Add & Delete* group, click the **More Fields** button.

   c. Scroll down and select **Address** from the *Quick Start* category.

   d. Observe the five new fields. Type the following data into these new fields:

Address	City	StateProvince	ZipPostal	CountryRegion
370 Pine St	Phoenix	Arizona	85018	USA
900 Finch Way	Phoenix	Arizona	85013	USA

9. Resize all of the columns in this table to the best fit possible by double-clicking the right edge of their field headings.

10. Save the table.

    a. On the Quick Access Toolbar, click the **Save** button.

    b. In the *Save As* dialog, type `Vendors` in the *Table Name* box.

    c. Click **OK**.

11. Switch to Design view.

    a. On the *Home* tab, in the *Views* group, click the **View** button to switch to Design view.

    b. Observe that when you created the new table, Access automatically assigned the *VendorID* field as the primary key.

12. Add an input mask to the new *Phone* field to force users to enter data in the (206) 555-1212 format.

    a. Select the **Phone** field by clicking anywhere in that row.

    b. In the Field Properties pane, click the **Input Mask** box, and then click the **Build...** button to start the *Input Mask Wizard*.

c. The first input mask sample is the phone number format you want. Test it by typing any sample phone number in the *Try It* box. Click **Next** to continue.

d. Click the **Next** button to continue without making any changes to the input mask or the placeholder character.

e. Verify that the radio button to store the data without the symbols is selected, and click **Next**.

f. Click **Finish**.

g. Observe that the Input Mask box now displays the input mask format:
!\(999") "000\-0000;;_

h. Switch back to Datasheet view by clicking the **Datasheet View** button at the lower right part of the status bar.

i. When Access prompts you to save the table, click **Yes**.

j. Under this field heading, enter the following phone numbers:
(623) 555-6810 for Greg's and **(623) 555-8200** for Cindy's. Notice how the input mask adds the correct characters to the phone number and will prevent you from typing any character other than a number.

13. Close the *Vendors* table. If Access prompts you to save the changes to the table, click **Yes**.

14. Create a *CompanyName* lookup field in the *Items* table using values from the *Vendors* table.

    a. Open the *Items* table in Datasheet view.

    b. Click the arrow next to the **Click to Add** heading in the last available field, and select **Lookup & Relationship**.

    c. In the *Lookup Wizard,* verify that the **I want the lookup field to get the values from another table or query.** radio button is selected, and click **Next**.

    d. Select **Table: Vendors** as the table that will provide the values for your lookup field, and click **Next**.

    e. From the *Available Fields* list, select the **CompanyName** field and click the single > button to add it to the right. Click **Next**.

    f. Click the arrow to expand the **1** list and choose **CompanyName** as the sort field. Observe that even though you added only the *CompanyName* field to the lookup list, Access included the *VendorID* field (the primary key) automatically. Click **Next**.

    g. Verify that the **Hide key column (recommended)** check box is checked and that the two companies you entered in the table earlier appear in the lookup field preview. Click **Next**.

    h. In the last screen, type **CompanyName** as the label for this new field.

    i. Limit data entry to the values in the list by clicking the **Enable Data Integrity** check box.

    j. Click **Finish**.

    k. Use this new lookup field to add *CompanyName* values for the first three records. Choose **Greg's** for the first two and **Cindy's** for the third.

15. Notice that many of the columns in the table are too narrow and the data are not fully visible.

    a. Resize the *ItemName* and *CompanyName* columns to the best fit possible by double-clicking the right edge of their field headings.

b. Resize the *Description* column to be exactly **45** wide.

  i. Click the **Description** column header to select the field.

  ii. On the *Home* tab, in the *Records* group, click the **More** button, and select **Field Width**.

  iii. In the *Column Width* dialog, type **45** in the *Column Width* box.

  iv. Click **OK**.

16. Modify the *Cost* field to use the **Currency** format.

  a. Click the **Cost** column header to select the field.

  b. On the *Table Tools Fields* tab, in the *Formatting* group, click the **Apply Currency Format** button.

  c. Notice that the *Format* box now displays *Currency*.

17. Modify the size of the *ItemID* field.

  a. Click the **ItemID** field heading.

  b. On the *Table Tools Fields* tab, in the *Properties* group, type **4** in the *Field Size* box. Press ⏎ Enter.

  c. Click **Yes** to continue.

  d. If Access shows additional messages, click **OK** to dismiss each one. Changing the field size to 4 will not delete any data or delete the field.

18. Add a Total row to the datasheet to display the sum of the values in the *Cost* field.

  a. On the *Home* tab, in the *Records* group, click the **Totals** button.

  b. In the new Total row, click the cell in the *Cost* column, expand the list, and select **Sum**.

  c. Observe that the *Totals* button appears highlighted. Click it again, and notice that the button is no longer highlighted and the Total row is hidden.

  d. Click the **Totals** button again. The Total row appears again, still displaying the sum of the values in the *Cost* field.

19. Add an *Attachment* field and an attachment.

  a. Click the arrow next to the **Click to Add** heading in the last available field. Select the **Attachment** option.

  b. Find the record with an ID of **LAS1**.

  c. Double-click the paperclip icon for this record, which is located in the new *Attachment* column you just created.

  d. Click **Add** in the *Attachments* dialog and then find the file named **laser_pointer.jpg** in your student data files folder.

  e. Double-click the file and then click **OK**. Note the **(1)** added to the paperclip icon to indicate that the record has one attachment.

20. Delete the *Location* field from the *Items* table.

  a. Click the **Location** field column heading to select the field.

  b. On the *Table Tools Fields* tab, in the *Add & Delete* group, click the **Delete** button.

  c. Click **Yes** to confirm the deletion.

21. Save and close the *Items* table.

22. Close any open tables. If Access prompts you to save changes, click **Yes**.

23. Create a table in Design view:

  a. On the *Create* tab, in the *Tables* group, click the **Table Design** button.

  b. Type **RoomNo** for the first field name. Press Tab.

  c. Accept the default data type, Short Text.

d. With the cursor still in this row, on the *Design* tab, in the *Tools* group, click the **Primary Key** button.

e. Create the following fields in Design view:

FieldName	DataType	Description
Capacity	Number	Maximum number of students
UpgradeDate	Date/Time	Date when the instructor's computer was last upgraded

24. Save the table.
    a. On the Quick Access Toolbar, click the **Save** button.
    b. In the *Save As* dialog, type **Classrooms** in the *Table Name* box.
    c. Click **OK**.

25. Modify field properties and formatting in Design view.
    a. Click anywhere in the **UpgradeDate** row. In the Field Properties pane, click in the **Format** box. Click the arrow to expand the selection list, and select **Medium Date**.
    b. Click anywhere in the **Capacity** field. In the Field Properties pane, click in the **Default Value** box. Type: **40**

26. Add a new lookup field to the *Classrooms* table to use values you enter yourself.
    a. Click in the first empty cell in the **Field Name** column and type: **Type**
    b. Press `Tab` or click in the **Data Type** cell. Expand the selection list, and select **Lookup Wizard...**
    c. In the *Lookup Wizard*, click the **I will type in the values I want.** radio button. Click **Next**.
    d. Use only 1 column and enter the following three values:

        Auditorium

        Computer Lab

        Lecture Room

    e. Click **Next**, and verify that **Type** is the label for the lookup field.
    f. Limit data entry to the values in the list by clicking the **Limit to List** check box.
    g. Click **Finish**.

27. Save and close the table.

28. Review the relationship between the *Vendors* table and the *Items* table.
    a. Open the Relationships window. On the *Database Tools* tab, in the *Relationships* group, click the **Relationships** button.
    b. Show all tables. On the *Relationship Tools Design* tab, in the *Relationships* group, click the **All Relationships** button.
    c. There is a relationship between the *VendorID* field in the *Vendors* table and the *CompanyName* field in the *Items* table. This relationship was created when you created the *CompanyName* lookup field in the *Items* table.
    d. Double-click the line connecting the two field names to open the *Edit Relationships* dialog.
    e. Look at the *Relationship Type* box near the bottom of the dialog and note that the relationship type is one-to-many.
    f. Verify that entries in the *CompanyName* field will have matching entries in the *VendorID* field by noting that the **Enforce Referential Integrity** check box is checked.
    g. Click **OK**.

29. Create a new relationship between the *EmployeeID* field in the *Employees* table and the *EmployeeID* field in the *Loans* table.
    a. Click the **EmployeeID** field in the *Employees* table and drag it to the **EmployeeID** field in the *Loans* table.
    b. The *Edit Relationships* dialog opens.
    c. Click the **Enforce Referential Integrity** check box.
    d. Click **Create**.
    e. Observe the new line connecting the *Employees* table and the *Loans* table.
30. Close the Relationships window. If Access prompts you to save changes to the layout, click **Yes**.
31. Close the database and exit Access.

skill review 2.2

In this project you will continue working with the health insurance database from *Chapter 1, Skill Review 1.2*. You will create two new tables in this database: one that contains a list of all the patients and another for the in-network hospitals that are affiliated with this insurance company.

Skills needed to complete this project:
- Designing a Table (Skill 2.1)
- Creating and Saving a Table in Datasheet View (Skill 2.2)
- Renaming Fields (Skill 2.3)
- Adding Fields in Datasheet View (Skill 2.4)
- Using Quick Start to Add Related Fields (Skill 2.5)
- Modifying Field Properties (Skill 2.13)
- Adding a Total Row to a Table (Skill 2.16)
- Applying an Input Mask from Design View (Skill 2.14)
- Adjusting Table Column Widths (Skill 2.6)
- Adding a Lookup Field from Another Table (Skill 2.17)
- Changing Data Type (Skill 2.11)
- Deleting Fields (Skill 2.10)
- Working with Attachment Fields (Skill 2.15)
- Creating a Table in Design View (Skill 2.7)
- Setting the Primary Key (Skill 2.9)
- Inserting Fields in Design View (Skill 2.8)
- Formatting Fields (Skill 2.12)
- Adding a Lookup Field from a List (Skill 2.18)
- Creating Relationships (Skill 2.19)

1. Open the start file **AC2013-SkillReview-2-2**.
2. If necessary, enable active content by clicking the **Enable Content** button in the Message Bar.
3. Save a copy of the file to work on named:
   `[your initials]AC-SkillReview-2-2`

4. Create a table in Datasheet view to store hospital data.
   a. On the *Create* tab, in the *Tables* group, click the **Table** button.
   b. You are now in the Datasheet view of a new table. Notice that Access has created a new field named *ID* with the AutoNumber data type.
   c. Create the next field by typing **Miami City Hospital** in the cell directly underneath the *Click to Add* heading.
   d. Press Tab to go to the next field in this record.
   e. Create another new field by typing: **87**
   f. Press Tab again.
   g. Enter two more records in the table with the following data:

   | Central Lauderdale Hospital | 59 |
   | West Palm Hospital | 61 |

5. Rename the fields.
   a. Right-click the **ID** field heading, and click **Rename Field**.
   b. Type **HospitalID** and press Enter.
   c. Repeat the process for **Field1**, renaming it: **HospitalName**
   d. Repeat the process for **Field2**, renaming it: **MemberVisits**
6. Add a new field to the table to store phone numbers.
   a. Click the arrow next to the **Click to Add** heading in the last available field, and select **Short Text**.
   b. Type **Phone** to overwrite the default field name *Field1*.
7. Add a group of related fields using *Quick Start*.
   a. Click the cell underneath the last *Click to Add* heading.
   b. On the *Table Tools Fields* tab, in the *Add & Delete* group, click the **More Fields** button.
   c. Scroll down and select **Address** from the *Quick Start* category.
   d. Observe the five new fields. Type the following data into these new fields:

Address	City	StateProvince	ZipPostal	CountryRegion
4500 Miami Blvd	Miami	FL	33126	USA
320 Palmer Rd	Ft. Lauderdale	FL	33301	USA
800 Jefferson St	West Palm Beach	FL	33403	USA

8. Modify the size of the *State Providence* field.
   a. Click the **State Providence** field heading.
   b. On the *Table Tools Fields* tab, in the *Properties* group, type **2** in the *Field Size* box. Press Enter.
   c. Click **Yes** to continue.
   d. If Access shows additional messages, click **OK** to dismiss each one. Changing the field size to 2 will not delete any data or delete the field.
9. Add a Total row to the datasheet to display the average of the values in the *MemberVisits* field.
   a. On the *Home* tab, in the *Records* group, click the **Totals** button.
   b. In the new Total row, click the cell in the *MemberVisits* column, expand the list, and select **Average**.

c. Observe that the *Totals* button appears highlighted. Click it again, and notice that the button is no longer highlighted and the Total row is hidden.

   d. Click the **Totals** button again. The Total row appears again, still displaying the average of the values in the *MemberVisits* field.

10. Save the table.

    a. On the Quick Access Toolbar, click the **Save** button.

    b. In the *Save As* dialog, type **Hospitals** in the *Table Name* box.

    c. Click **OK**.

11. Switch to Design view.

    a. On the *Home* tab, in the *Views* group, click the **View** button to switch to Design view.

    b. Observe that when you created the new table, Access automatically assigned the *HospitalID* field as the primary key.

12. Add an input mask to the new *Phone* field to force users to enter data in the (206) 555-1212 format.

    a. Select the **Phone** field by clicking anywhere in that row.

    b. In the Field Properties pane, click the **Input Mask** box, and then click the **Build...** button to start the *Input Mask Wizard*.

    c. The first input mask sample is the phone number format you want. Test it by typing any sample phone number in the *Try It* box. Click **Next** to continue.

    d. Click the **Next** button to continue without making any changes to the input mask or the placeholder character.

    e. Verify that the radio button to store the data without the symbols is selected, and click **Next**.

    f. Click **Finish**.

    g. Observe that the Input Mask box now displays the input mask format: **!\(999") "000\-0000;;_**

    h. Switch back to Datasheet view by clicking the **Datasheet View** button at the lower right part of the status bar.

    i. When Access prompts you to save the table, click **Yes**.

    j. Under this field heading, enter the following phone numbers:
    (305) 555-1100 for Miami; **(954) 555-2000** for Lauderdale; **(561) 555-6500** for West Palm. Notice how the input mask adds the correct characters to the phone number and will prevent you from typing any character other than a number.

13. Resize all of the columns in this table to the best fit possible by double-clicking the right edge of their field headings.

14. Close the *Hospitals* table. If Access prompts you to save the changes to the table, click **Yes**.

15. Create a *HospitalName* lookup field in the *Physicians* table using values from the *Hospitals* table.

    a. Open the *Physicians* table in Datasheet view.

    b. Click the arrow next to the **Click to Add** heading in the last available field, and select **Lookup & Relationship.**

    c. In the *Lookup Wizard,* verify that the **I want the lookup field to get the values from another table or query.** radio button is selected, and click **Next**.

    d. Select **Table: Hospitals** as the table that will provide the values for your lookup field, and click **Next**.

e. From the *Available Fields* list, select the **HospitalName** field and click the single > button to add it to the right. Click **Next.**

f. Click the arrow to expand the **1** list and choose **HospitalName** as the sort field. Observe that even though you added only the *HospitalName* field to the lookup list, Access included the *HospitalID* field (the primary key) automatically. Click **Next.**

g. Verify that the **Hide key column (recommended)** check box is checked and that the three hospitals you entered in the table earlier appear in the lookup field preview. Click **Next.**

h. In the last screen, type `HopitalName` as the label for this new field.

i. Limit data entry to the values in the list by clicking the **Enable Data Integrity** check box.

j. Click **Finish.**

k. Use this new lookup field to add *HospitalName* values for the first three records. Choose **West Palm Hospital** for the first two and **Central Lauderale Hospital** for the third.

l. Adjust the width of the *HospitalName* field to best fit the data by double-clicking the right edge of the field heading.

16. Modify the *MemberCount* field to use the **Number** data type instead of the *Currency* data type.

    a. Click the **MemberCount** column header to select the field.

    b. On the *Table Tools Fields* tab, in the *Formatting* group, expand the **Data Type** list, and select **Number.**

    c. Notice that the *Format* box no longer displays *Currency*. It is not necessary to specify a format for this field.

17. Delete the *YearsInPractice* field.

    a. Click the **YearsInPractice** field column heading to select the field.

    b. On the *Table Tools Fields* tab, in the *Add & Delete* group, click the **Delete** button.

    c. Click **Yes** to confirm the deletion.

18. Add an *Attachment* field and an attachment to the *Physicians* table.

    a. Click the arrow next to the **Click to Add** heading in the last available field. Select the **Attachment** option.

    b. Go to the record for **Antonio Gonzalez,** and double-click the paperclip icon, which is located in the new *Attachment* column you just created.

    c. Click **Add** in the *Attachments* dialog and then find the file named **Gonzalez.jpg** in your student data files folder.

    d. Double-click the file and then click **OK.** Note the **(1)** added to the paperclip icon to indicate that the record has one attachment.

19. Close any open tables. If Access prompts you to save changes, click **Yes.**

20. Create a table in Design view:

    a. On the *Create* tab, in the *Tables* group, click the **Table Design** button.

    b. Type `MemberID` for the first field name. Press `Tab`.

    c. Accept the default data type, *Short Text*. Press `Tab`.

    d. Enter the following in the Description: `First letter of last name followed by a randomly generated seven-digit number`

    e. With the cursor still in this row, on the *Design* tab, in the *Tools* group, click the **Primary Key** button.

f. Create the following fields in Design view. None of these fields require a description.

FieldName	DataType
FirstName	Short Text
LastName	Short Text
Address	Short Text
City	Short Text
State	Short Text
Zip	Number
DOB	Date/Time

21. Save the table.
    a. On the Quick Access Toolbar, click the **Save** button.
    b. In the *Save As* dialog, type **Patients** in the *Table Name* box.
    c. Click **OK**.
22. Modify field properties and formatting in Design view.
    a. Click anywhere in the **DOB** row. In the Field Properties pane, click in the **Format** box. Click the arrow to expand the selection list, and select **Short Date**.
    b. Click anywhere in the **State** field. In the Field Properties pane, click in the **Default Value** box. Type: **FL**
23. Add a new lookup field to the *Patients* table to use values you enter yourself.
    a. Click in the first empty cell in the **Field Name** column and type: **Gender**
    b. Press Tab or click in the **Data Type** cell. Expand the selection list, and select **Lookup Wizard...**
    c. In the *Lookup Wizard,* click the **I will type in the values I want.** radio button. Click **Next**.
    d. Use only 1 column and enter the following two values:
    Female
    Male
    e. Click **Next,** and verify that **Gender** is the label for the lookup field.
    f. Limit data entry to the values in the list by clicking the **Limit to List** check box.
    g. Click **Finish**.
    h. Save and close the table.
24. Review the relationship between the *Physicians* table and the *Hospitals* table.
    a. Open the Relationships window. On the *Database Tools* tab, in the *Relationships* group, click the **Relationships** button.
    b. Show all tables. On the *Relationship Tools Design* tab, in the *Relationships* group, click the **All Relationships** button.
    c. If necessary, click and drag the **Hospitals** table so you can see the line connecting the *Hospitals* table and the *Physicians* table.
    d. There is a relationship between the *HospitalID* field in the *Hospitals* table and the *HospitalName* field in the *Physicians* table. This relationship was created when you created the *HospitalName* lookup field in the *Physicians* table.
    e. Double-click the line connecting the two field names to open the *Edit Relationships* dialog.

- f. Look at the *Relationship Type* box near the bottom of the dialog and note that the relationship type is one-to-many.
- g. Verify that entries in the *CompanyName* field will have matching entries in the *VendorID* field by observing that the **Enforce Referential Integrity** check box is checked.
- h. Click **OK**.

25. Create a new relationship between the *ProcedureID* field in the *Procedures* table and the *ProcedureID* field in the *Orders* table.
    - a. Click the **ProcedureID** field in the *Procedures* table and drag it to the **ProcedureID** field in the *Orders* table.
    - b. The *Edit Relationships* dialog opens.
    - c. Click the **Enforce Referential Integrity** check box.
    - d. Click **Create**.
    - e. Observe the new line connecting the *Procedures* table and the *Orders* table.
26. Close the Relationships window. If Access prompts you to save changes to the layout, click **Yes**.
27. Close the database and exit Access.

challenge yourself 2.3

In this project you will continue working with the greenhouse database from *Chapter 1, Challenge Yourself 1.3*. You will add a table to keep track of the fertilizers used in the greenhouse and the plants that use them.

Skills needed to complete this project:

- Designing a Table (Skill 2.1)
- Creating and Saving a Table in Datasheet View (Skill 2.2)
- Renaming Fields (Skill 2.3)
- Adding Fields in Datasheet View (Skill 2.4)
- Changing Data Type (Skill 2.11)
- Deleting Fields (Skill 2.10)
- Inserting Fields in Design View (Skill 2.8)
- Setting the Primary Key (Skill 2.9)
- Adding a Lookup Field from a List (Skill 2.18)
- Adding a Total Row to a Table (Skill 2.16)
- Adding a Lookup Field from Another Table (Skill 2.17)
- Adjusting Table Column Widths (Skill 2.6)
- Using Quick Start to Add Related Fields (Skill 2.5)
- Working with Attachment Fields (Skill 2.15)
- Formatting Fields (Skill 2.12)
- Modifying Field Properties (Skill 2.13)
- Creating Relationships (Skill 2.19)

1. Open the start file **AC2013-ChallengeYourself-2-3**.
2. If necessary, enable active content by clicking the **Enable Content** button in the Message Bar.

3. Save a copy of the file to work on named:
   `[your initials]AC-ChallengeYourself-2-3`
4. Create a new table in Datasheet view using the following data. Allow Access to create the *AutoNumber ID* field for now. Name the table: **Fertilizers**

FertilizerName	NutrientRatio	Price
Monoammonium phosphate	11-52-0	$25
Polymer Coated Urea	44-0-0	$35
Nitrogen Solution	28-0-0	$12

5. If necessary, change the format of the *Price* field to use the **Currency** format.
6. Delete the *ID* field that Access created and add a new primary key field. Switch back and forth between Datasheet view and Design view as necessary, saving the table when prompted to do so by Access.

   a. Delete the **ID** field.

   b. Insert a new field at the beginning of the table. Name the field: **FertID**

   c. Set the Data Type to **Short Text.**

   d. Enter the following three values (in the appropriate record) under the **FertID** field: `MAP1, PCU1, NSO1`

   e. Make the **FertID** field the Primary Key.

7. Add a new lookup field. You can use Datasheet view or Design view, whichever you prefer.

   a. Name the new field: **Form**

   b. The lookup field should display the following four values: **Granule, Liquid, Slow-Release, Organic**

   c. Limit data entry to the values in the list.

   d. Save the changes to the table.

8. Add a Total row in Datasheet view that sums up all the fertilizer prices.

9. Save and close the *Fertilizers* table.

10. Open the *Plants* table and make the following changes:

    a. Add a lookup field named **PreferredFertilizer** to the *Plants* table to reference the *FertilizerName* field in the *Fertilizers* table. The lookup list should be sorted alphabetically by the FertilizerName data. It is not necessary to limit values to the list.

    b. Test this field by choosing any fertilizer for the first three plants.

    c. Resize all the columns in the table to best fit the data.

    d. Add an *Attachment* field. Add the image **geranium.jpg** to the record for the **spotted geranium.**

    e. Change the Format property of the *DatePlanted* field to **Medium Date.**

    f. Set the Default Value property for the *FlowerColor* field to **white** and add a Description for this field that reads: `Main color only. Do not enter multiple colors.`

    g. Save and close the table.

11. Review the table relationships and make the following changes.

    a. Show all the tables in the Relationships window.

    b. Create a one-to-many relationship between the **PlantID** field in the **Plants** table and the **PlantID** field in the **MaintenanceLog** table. Enforce referential integrity.

c. Modify the relationship between the **FertID** field in the **Fertilizers** table and the **PreferredFertilizer** field in the **Plants** table to enforce referential integrity.

d. Close the Relationships window, saving the layout changes.

12. Close the database and exit Access.

challenge yourself 2.4

In this project you will continue working with the vaccines database from *Chapter 1, Challenge Yourself 1.4*. You will add a table to the database to track volunteer information.

Skills needed to complete this project:

- Designing a Table (Skill 2.1)
- Creating and Saving a Table in Datasheet View (Skill 2.2)
- Renaming Fields (Skill 2.3)
- Adding Fields in Datasheet View (Skill 2.4)
- Using Quick Start to Add Related Fields (Skill 2.5)
- Setting the Primary Key (Skill 2.9)
- Formatting Fields (Skill 2.12)
- Adding a Lookup Field from a List (Skill 2.18)
- Modifying Field Properties (Skill 2.13)
- Working with Attachment Fields (Skill 2.15)
- Adding a Lookup Field from Another Table (Skill 2.17)
- Adjusting Table Column Widths (Skill 2.6)
- Adding a Total Row to a Table (Skill 2.16)
- Changing Data Type (Skill 2.11)
- Creating Relationships (Skill 2.19)

1. Open the start file **AC2013-ChallengeYourself-2-4**.
2. If necessary, enable active content by clicking the **Enable Content** button in the Message Bar.
3. Save a copy of the file to work on named:
   `[your initials]AC-ChallengeYourself-2-4`
4. Create a new table to keep track of volunteer information. Use Datasheet view and/or Design view as appropriate.

   a. Name the table: `Volunteers`

   b. Enter the following data and fields as shown below. If you use the **Name** *Quick Start* option to add the first name and last name fields be sure to rename them to match the format shown below.

VolunteerID	LastName	FirstName	DOB
R56623	Richardson	Tyra	5/9/80
G33390	Graham	Susan	3/28/72
H58892	Hernandez	Mario	5/11/67

   c. Set the **VolunteerID** field as the *Primary Key* field.

   d. Set the format of the **DOB** field to **Medium Date**.

e. Add a lookup field to display the following three values:

   `Clerical, Manager, Nurse`

f. Name the new lookup field: `Position`

g. Set the default value of the **Position** field to **Nurse.**

h. Add a new *Attachment* field. Attach the photo **sgraham.jpg** to the **Susan Graham** record.

5. Save and close the *Volunteers* table.
6. Add a new lookup field named `LeadVolunteer` to the *Locations* table to include both the **FirstName** and **LastName** fields from the *Volunteers* table. Sort the lookup list alphabetically by the **LastName** field. Test this field by choosing employee **Mario Hernandez** for the first location and employee **Susan Graham** for the second. Resize the datasheet column as necessary to best fit the data.
7. Save and close the *Locations* table.
8. Make the following modifications to the *Shipments* table. Work in Datasheet view or Design view as appropriate.

    a. Resize the **DateShipped** and **Cost** columns to best fit the data.

    b. Add a Total row that sums up all the amounts in the **Cost** field.

    c. Change the Data Type of the **Quantity** field from *Text* to **Number.** If Access warns about potential data loss, just click Yes to proceed.

9. Save and close the *Shipments* table.
10. If necessary, modify the table relationships to enforce referential integrity between the *Locations* table and *Volunteers* table relationship. Hint: Display all the tables in the Relationships window if the *Volunteers* table is not visible.
11. Close the Relationships window, saving any layout changes.
12. Close the database and exit Access.

on your own 2.5

In this project, you will continue working with the movie database from *Chapter 1, On Your Own 1.5.* You will create a new table to track and organize your home/vacation movies. These are the movies you recorded with your camcorder, such as your son's first birthday and your vacation in Hawaii.

Skills needed to complete this project:
- Designing a Table (Skill 2.1)
- Creating and Saving a Table in Datasheet View (Skill 2.2)
- Renaming Fields (Skill 2.3)
- Adding Fields in Datasheet View (Skill 2.4)
- Creating a Table in Design View (Skill 2.7)
- Inserting Fields in Design View (Skill 2.8)
- Setting the Primary Key (Skill 2.9)
- Adding a Lookup Field from a List (Skill 2.18)
- Adjusting Table Column Widths (Skill 2.6)
- Adding a Total Row to a Table (Skill 2.16)
- Modifying Field Properties (Skill 2.13)

1. Open the start file **AC2013-OnYourOwn-2-5.**
2. If necessary, enable active content by clicking the **Enable Content** button in the Message Bar.
3. Save a copy of the file to work on named:
   `[your initials] AC-OnYourOwn-2-5`
4. Create a **HomeMovies** table and add at least five fields that you believe are appropriate for this type of collection. At a minimum, you must have:
   a. An ID for each movie. This field will serve as the primary key.
   b. A name for each movie.
   c. The running time for each movie in minutes.
   d. The other two (or more) fields are your choice.
5. Demonstrate your knowledge of lookup fields by creating a value list in one of your fields.
6. Enter data for least four home/vacation movies. They can be real or fictional.
7. Resize columns in Datasheet view if necessary.
8. Calculate the total number of minutes in your home movie collection using a Total row.
9. Modify at least two Field Properties for one or more fields in your table.
10. Close the database and exit Access.

fix it 2.6

In this project, you will continue working with the pet store database from *Chapter 1, Fix It 1.6*. Once again, one of the employees has messed up the database, and it's up to you to fix it. This time, you'll implement a few changes to make it harder for employees to make data entry errors.

Skills needed to complete this project:
- Adding a Lookup Field from a List (Skill 2.18)
- Formatting Fields (Skill 2.12)
- Deleting Fields (Skill 2.10)
- Adding Fields in Datasheet View (Skill 2.4)
- Inserting Fields in Design View (Skill 2.8)
- Working with Attachment Fields (Skill 2.15)
- Adding a Total Row to a Table (Skill 2.16)
- Using Quick Start to Add Related Fields (Skill 2.5)
- Modifying Field Properties (Skill 2.13)

1. Open the start file **AC2013-FixIt-2-6.**
2. If necessary, enable active content by clicking the **Enable Content** button in the Message Bar.
3. Save a copy of the file to work on named: `[your initials] AC-FixIt-2-6`
4. Fix the *Pets* table as follows:
   a. In this store, there are only two types of pets sold: cats and dogs. Edit the **AnimalType** field so that these are the only two choices for this field. Do not allow any other type of animal to be entered.

    b. The **Price** field should display the numbers using $ and two decimal places.

    c. The store realizes it rarely types in the cage number for each animal it receives. Therefore, remove the **CageNum** field from the table.

    d. The store needs to keep vaccination information. Add a new field named **Vaccines** that only accepts a yes or no value.

    e. Add another new field that can store photographs and insert the **poodle.jpg** image for the record with the Poodle breed.

    f. The store needs to know the total price of its pet inventory. Enable the feature that displays a total row in Datasheet view and show the sum of the prices.

    g. Save and close the table.

5. Fix the *Sales* table as follows:

    a. The dates in the *Sales* table should look like this: **30-Jun-10**

    b. Add a new field in Datasheet view using the **Payment Type** *Quick Start* option.

    c. Save and close the table.

6. Fix the *Customers* table as follows:

    a. The default value for the *Newsletter* field should be **1** so that it appears checked every time you create a new record.

    b. The *CustomerID* field should never have a value with more than **4** characters and it should be the primary key.

    c. Save and close the table.

7. Open each table in Datasheet view and look at the columns closely. Two columns need to be larger. Find them and resize them.

8. Close the database and exit Access.

Working with Forms and Reports

chapter 3

- Create a variety of forms
- Create a variety of reports
- Add controls to forms and reports
- Resize and arrange controls
- Add formatting to forms and reports
- Add header and footer elements
- Group and total data in a report
- Modify the page settings and print a report

In this chapter, you will learn the following skills:

Skill **3.1** Creating a Single Record Form Based on a Table or Query
Skill **3.2** Creating a Multiple Items Form
Skill **3.3** Creating a Split Form
Skill **3.4** Creating a Form Using the Form Wizard
Skill **3.5** Creating a New Blank Form
Skill **3.6** Adding Fields to a Form in Layout View
Skill **3.7** Creating a Basic Report Based on a Table or Query
Skill **3.8** Creating a Report Using the Report Wizard
Skill **3.9** Creating a New Blank Report
Skill **3.10** Adding Fields to a Report in Layout View
Skill **3.11** Formatting Controls
Skill **3.12** Applying a Theme
Skill **3.13** Resizing Controls
Skill **3.14** Moving and Arranging Controls
Skill **3.15** Adding Design Elements to Form and Report Headers
Skill **3.16** Adding Page Numbers to Reports
Skill **3.17** Grouping Records in a Report
Skill **3.18** Adding Totals to a Report
Skill **3.19** Previewing and Printing a Report
Skill **3.20** Controlling the Page Setup of a Report for Printing

skills

introduction

In this chapter, you will learn to create a variety of forms and reports, including using the *Form Wizard* and the *Report Wizard*. You will also learn to create a form and a report from scratch in Layout view and add controls, formatting, and header and footer elements. You will work with grouping in reports and calculate totals using the automatic tools in Layout view. Finally, you will use Print Preview view to preview the printed report and make page layout adjustments before printing. The *Let Me Try* exercises in this chapter use the AC3-Appointments database. You can keep the database open while you work in this chapter, opening and closing database objects as required for each *Let Me Try*.

Skill 3.1 Creating a Single Record Form Based on a Table or Query

While you can enter data directly in a table in Datasheet view, a form provides a more user-friendly data entry format. Remember, a form displays data from an underlying table or query and allows database users to enter, edit, and delete data, but it does not contain records or data itself. It is only an interface to the underlying table or query (the **record source**). The easiest form to create is a simple Single Record form. A **Single Record form** displays one record at a time.

To create a Single Record form based on a table or query:

1. In the Navigation Pane, select the table or query record source for your form.
2. On the *Create* tab, in the *Forms* group, click the **Form** button.
3. When you save the form, notice that the default name in the *Form Name* box is the same as the name of the table or query that you based the form on. Type a new name if you want to use something else.

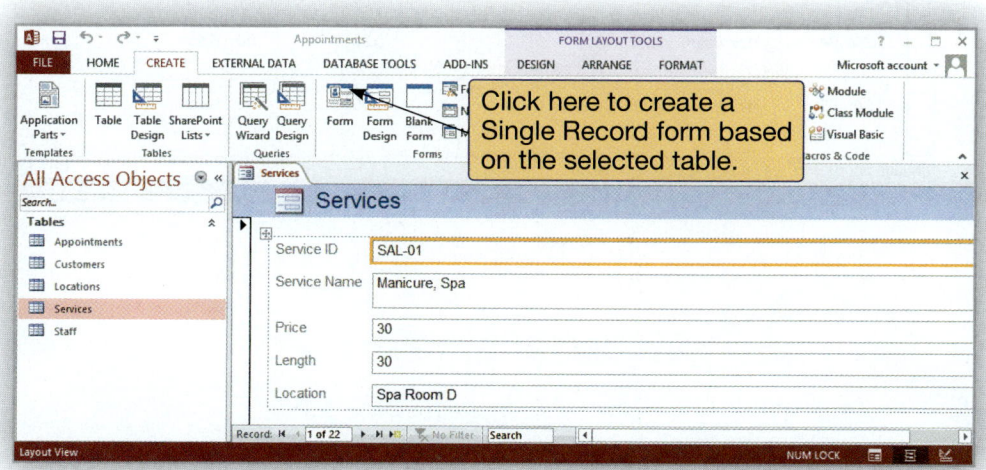

FIGURE AC 3.1
A Single Record form based on the selected table, *Services*

tips & tricks

If Access finds a one-to-many relationship between the table you are basing the form on and another table, Access automatically inserts a Datasheet subform at the bottom of the form. The Datasheet subform displays the records from the related table.

let me try

If the database is not already open, open the data file **AC3-Appointments** and try this skill on your own:

1. Create a Single Record form from the **Services** table.
2. Save the form as: `ServicesForm`
3. Close the form.

Skill 3.2 Creating a Multiple Items Form

Some form types display all the records at once. A **Datasheet form** reproduces the exact look and layout of the table datasheet as a form. A **Multiple Items form** has a similar layout displaying multiple records at once. However, a Multiple Items form is more flexible than a Datasheet form because you can modify the layout and design of a Multiple Items form. Use a Multiple Items form when you need to see multiple records at the same time.

To create a Multiple Items form:

1. In the Navigation Pane, select the table or query record source for your form.
2. On the *Create* tab, in the *Forms* group, click the **More Forms** button, and select **Multiple Items.**
3. When you save the form, notice that the default name in the *Form Name* box is the same as the name of the table or query that you based the form on. Type a new name if you want to use something else.

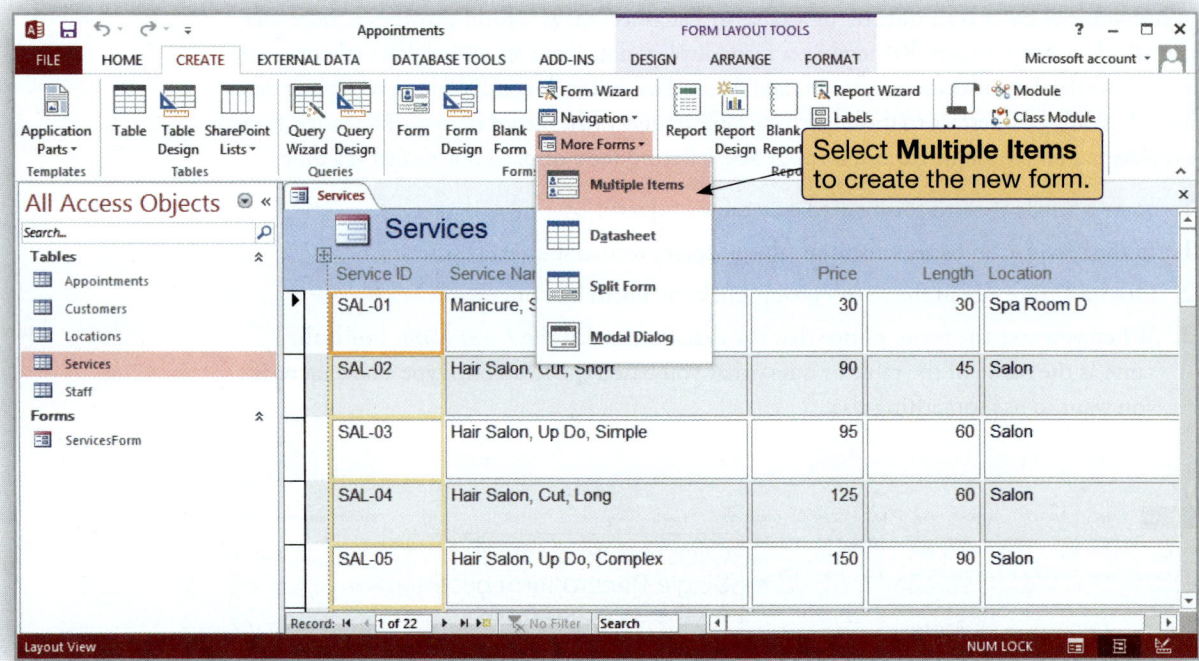

FIGURE AC 3.2
A Multiple Items form based on the selected table, *Services*

let me try

If the database is not already open, open the data file **AC3-Appointments** and try this skill on your own:
1. Create a Multiple Items form from the **Services** table.
2. Save the form as: `ServicesFormMulti`
3. Close the form.

Skill 3.3 Creating a Split Form

A **Split form** combines the convenience of a continuous Datasheet form with the usability of a Single Record form displaying one record at a time. In a Split form, both formats are displayed and work together, so when you navigate records in one section, the other section synchronizes. Use a Split form when you need to see a large group of records at one time while having quick access to an individual record's details.

To create a Split form:

1. In the Navigation Pane, select the table or query record source for your form.
2. On the *Create* tab, in the *Forms* group, click the **More Forms** button, and select **Split Form.**
3. When you save the form, notice that the default name in the *Form Name* box is the same as the name of the table or query that you based the form on. Type a new name if you want to use something else.

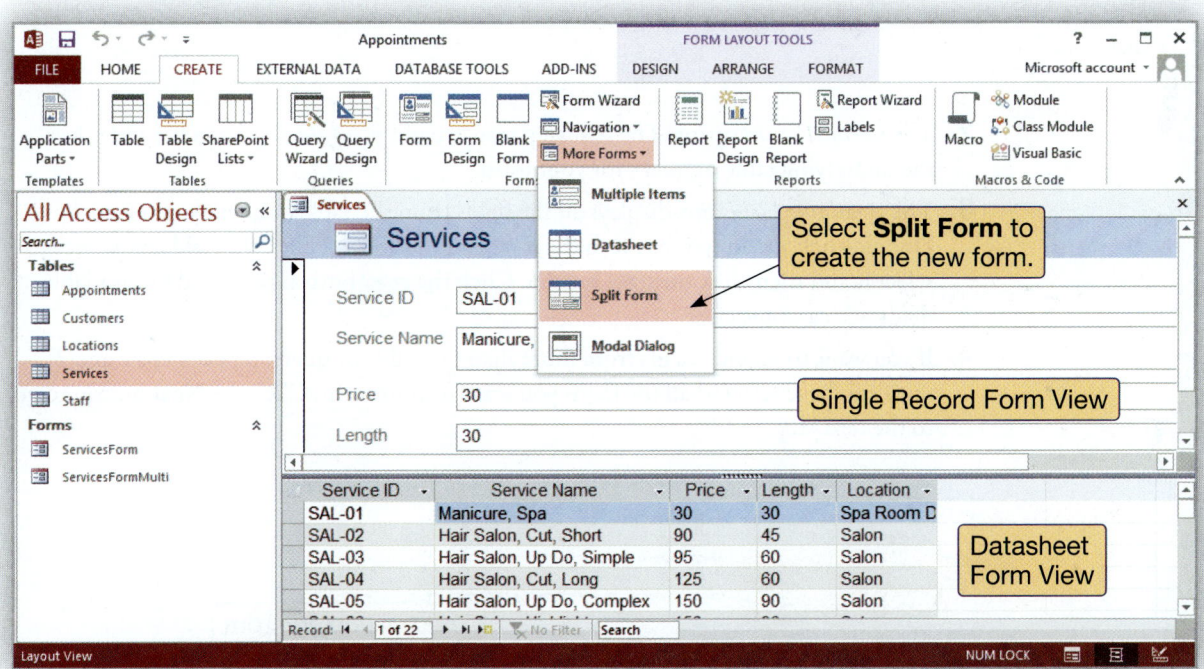

FIGURE AC 3.3
A Split form based on the selected table, *Services*

tips & tricks

The Datasheet form at the bottom of the Split form is not a subform; it is a special form view showing the same dataset.

let me try

If the database is not already open, open the data file **AC3-Appointments** and try this skill on your own:
1. Create a Split form from the **Services** table.
2. Save the form as: `ServicesFormSplit`
3. Close the form.

Skill 3.4 Creating a Form Using the Form Wizard

Another easy way to begin a new form is to use the **Form Wizard**. Instead of automatically creating a form that includes every field in the underlying table, the *Form Wizard* walks you through the steps of creating the form, including selecting fields and a layout. You can use the *Form Wizard* to create a form combining fields from multiple related tables.

To create a new form using the *Form Wizard*:

1. On the *Create* tab, in the *Forms* group, click the **Form Wizard** button.

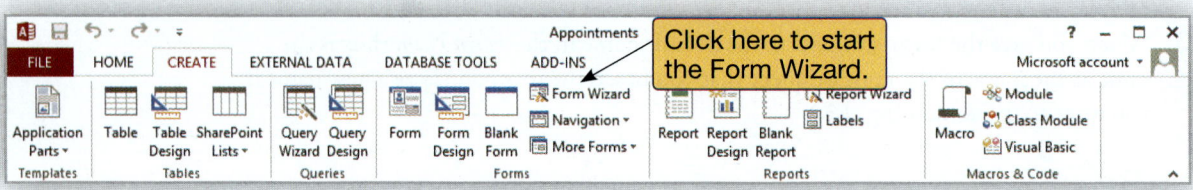

FIGURE AC 3.4

2. The *Form Wizard* opens. The first step is to expand the *Tables/Queries* list and select the underlying table or query for your form.

3. The *Available Fields* box displays all the fields from the table or query you selected. Double-click a field to move it to the *Selected Fields* box or click the field name once to select it and then click the > button. Click the >> button to add all the available fields with a single click.

4. If you want to include fields from more than one table or query, repeat steps 2 and 3 until you have selected all the fields you want in your form. Click the **Next** button to go to the next step.

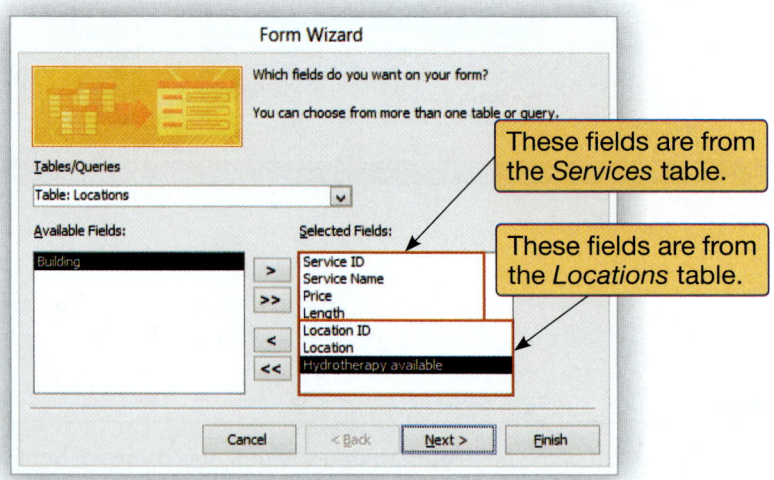

FIGURE AC 3.5

5. If you selected fields from related tables, the next step in the wizard asks how you want to organize the data in the form. To create a form with a subform, in the *How do you want to view your data?* box, select the table that is the "one" part of the one-to-many relationship. The wizard will create a **subform**—a form within the form—to display the related records from the "many" table. Verify that the **Form with subform(s)** radio button is selected, and then click **Next**.

In Figure AC 3.6, the records in the *Locations* table are related to records in the *Services* table in a one-to-many relationship where the record in the *Locations* table is the "one" part of the relationship. The *Form with subform(s)* option will create a Single Record form for each *Locations* record with a subform displaying all the related records from the *Services* table.

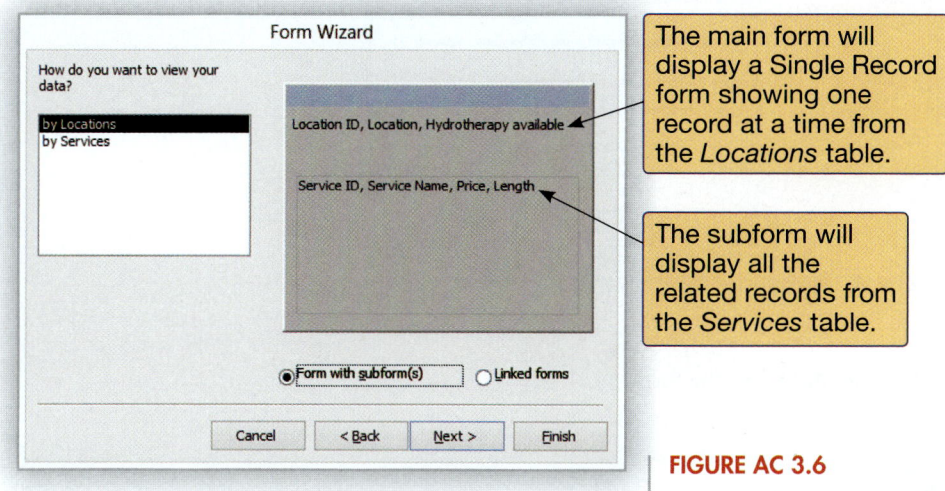

FIGURE AC 3.6

If you selected fields from only one table or query, you will not see this step.

6. The next step asks you to select layout options. If your form includes a subform, select a layout for the subform: **Tabular** or **Datasheet.** If the form does not include a subform, you can select from a list of layout options for the main form: **Columnar, Tabular, Datasheet,** or **Justified.** Click the radio button for the layout option you want, and then click **Next.**

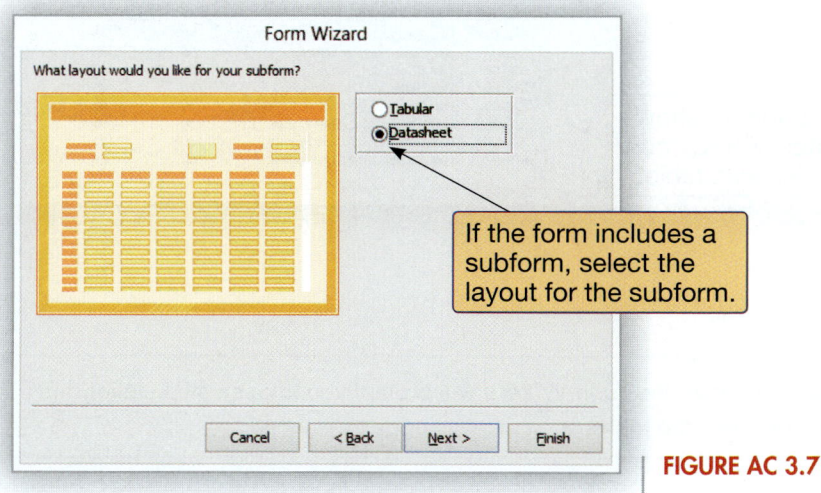

FIGURE AC 3.7

7. Enter a title for the form. If your form includes a subform, enter the title for the subform as well. The subform will be saved as a separate database object. Select whether you want to open the form to view and enter information (Form view) or modify the form's design (Design view).

skill 3.4 Creating a Form Using the Form Wizard

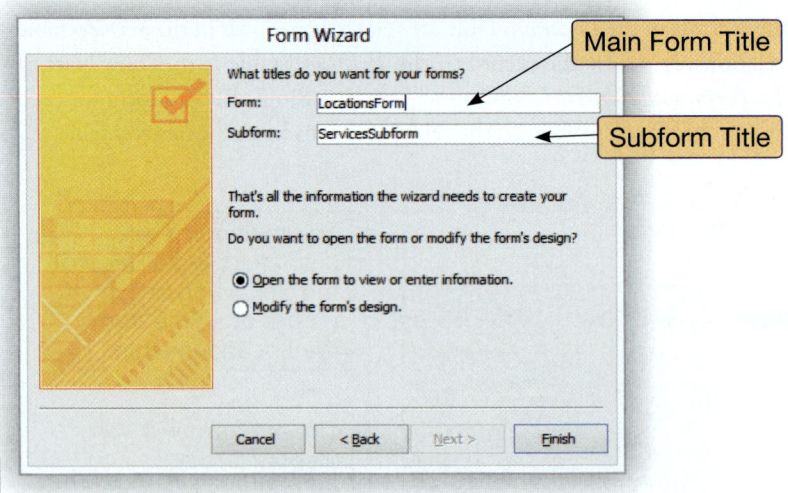

FIGURE AC 3.8

8. Click **Finish** to save the form.

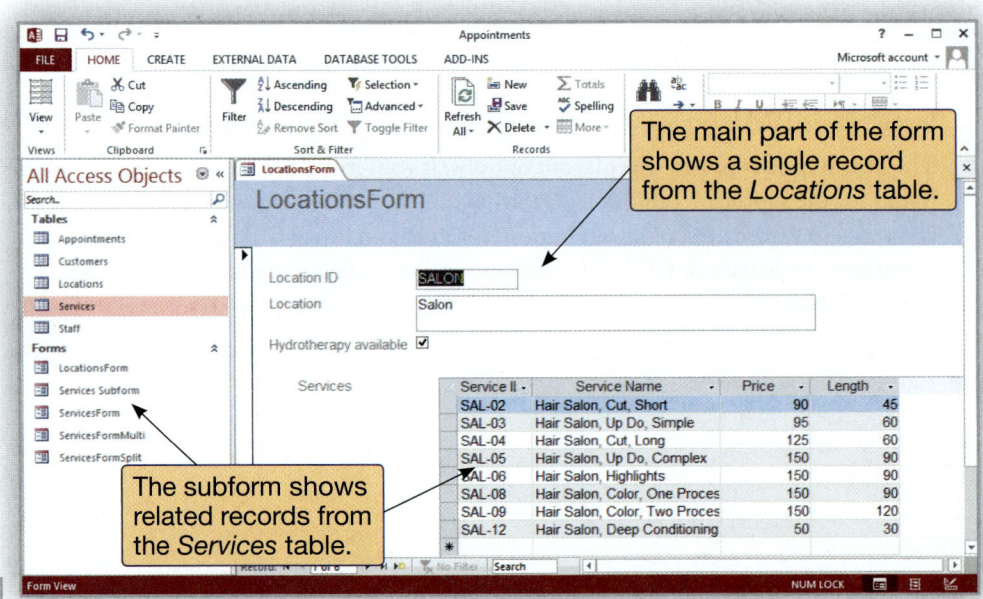

FIGURE AC 3.9

tips & tricks

If you try to combine fields from tables that are not related, the *Form Wizard* will prompt you to open the Relationships window to create the appropriate relationships between the tables.

let me try

If the database is not already open, open the data file **AC3-Appointments** and try this skill on your own:
1. Use the *Form Wizard* to create a new form. Include the **Service ID**, **Service Name**, **Price**, and **Length** fields from the *Services* table and the **Location ID**, **Location**, and **Hydrotherapy available** fields from the *Locations* table.
2. View the data by the *Locations* table, with related data from the *Services* table as a subform.
3. Use the **Datasheet** layout option for the subform.
4. Name the main form: `LocationsForm` and the subform: `ServicesSubform`
5. Close the form.

Skill 3.5 Creating a New Blank Form

One way to start a new form is to begin with a blank form and add fields from tables and queries manually. You can start a new blank form directly in either Layout view or Design view. Layout view may be easier to work with, but if you need to add advanced controls, you'll need to work in Design view instead.

To create a new blank form directly in Layout view, on the *Create* tab, in the *Forms* group, click the **Blank Form** button.

To create a new blank form directly in Design view, on the *Create* tab, in the *Forms* group, click the **Form Design** button.

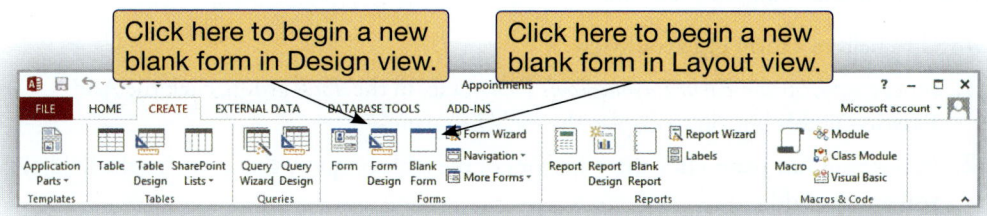

FIGURE AC 3.10

Notice that there are no records in the new form. The new blank form does not have a record source defined. The form is an empty layout until you add controls.

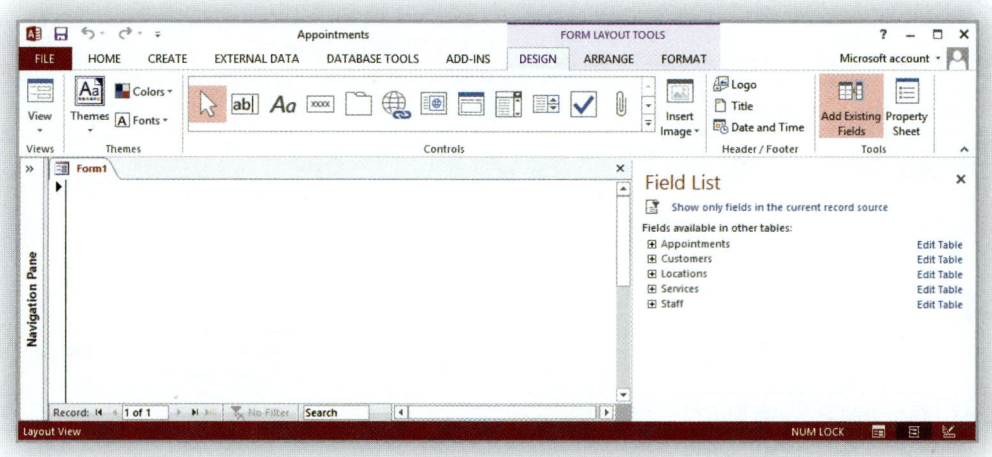

FIGURE AC 3.11
A new blank form in Layout view

tips & tricks

Access will sometimes select a table or query to use as the record source for the form based on the object selected in the Navigation Pane or based on the first table listed in the Navigation Pane. If this is not the record source you want to use for the form, don't worry. The record source will be updated as you add fields.

let me try

If the database is not already open, open the data file **AC3-Appointments** and try this skill on your own:
1. Create a new blank form so it opens directly in Design view.
2. Close the form without saving it.
3. Create a new blank form so it opens directly in Layout view.
4. Save the form as: `TestForm`

Skill 3.6 Adding Fields to a Form in Layout View

If you are starting with a blank form, you will need to add **controls** to display field data. The most common type of control is the **text box control**. Text box controls can display text, numbers, dates, and similar data. A text box control that displays data from a table or query field is called a **bound control** because it is connected (bound) to the field. **Unbound controls** are not connected to field data directly.

Adding a field to a blank form places two controls in a **stacked layout** where an unbound text control, called a **label control**, displays the name of the field to the left of a bound text box control displaying the field data.

To add a field to a form in Layout view:

1. If necessary, on the *Form Layout Tools Design* tab, in the *Tools* group, click the **Add Existing Fields** button to display the *Field List* pane.
2. In the *Field List* pane, click the + in front of the table or query that contains the field(s) you want to add.
3. Double-click a field name to add it to the form. A new bound control is automatically created at the top of the form, along with a label control.
4. To edit the text in a label control, double-click the control to place the cursor within the text. Edit the text normally.

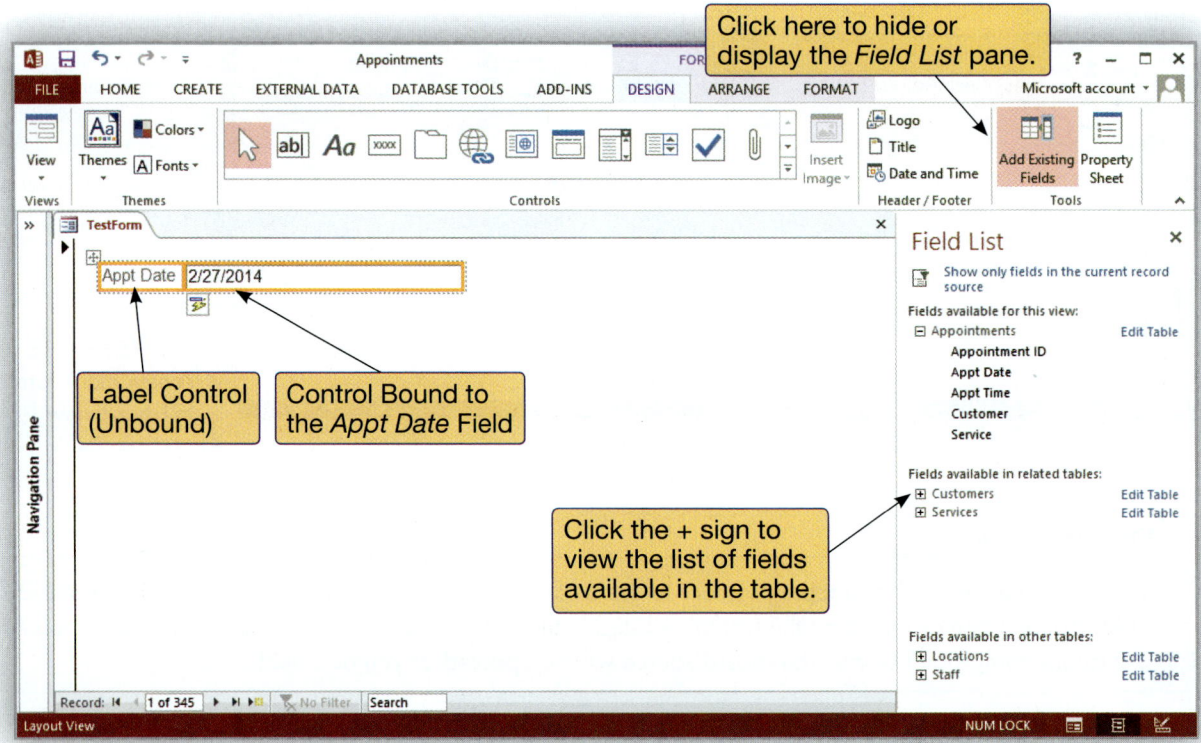

FIGURE AC 3.12

5. To add a second column to the stacked layout, click a field name in the *Field List,* and drag it to the right of the field you just added. Access displays an I-bar shape to indicate where the controls will be placed.

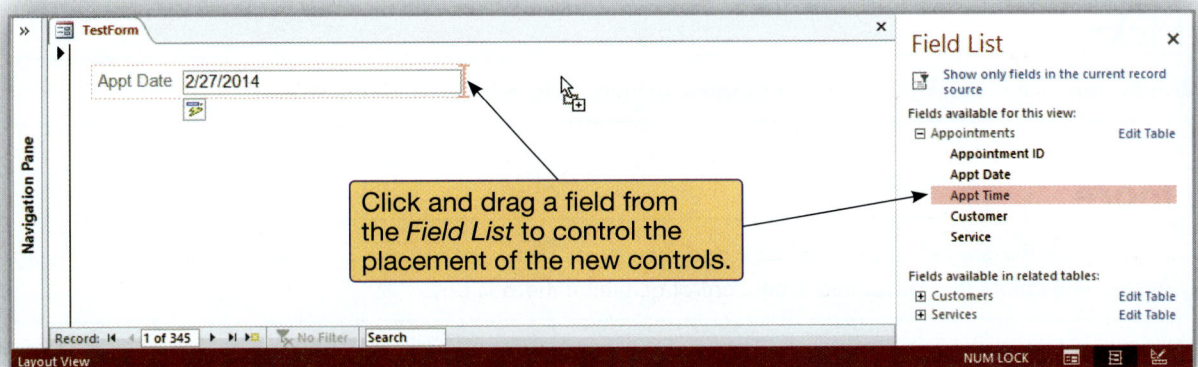

FIGURE AC 3.13

If you double-click the field name instead of dragging it, Access will maintain the single column stacked layout and add the new controls below the currently selected control.

6. Continue adding fields and editing labels until your form is complete. You can add fields to any space in the layout grid using the click-and-drag method. If you look closely, you can see the dotted lines outlining the grid. Use these lines as a guide when you are dragging fields to the layout.

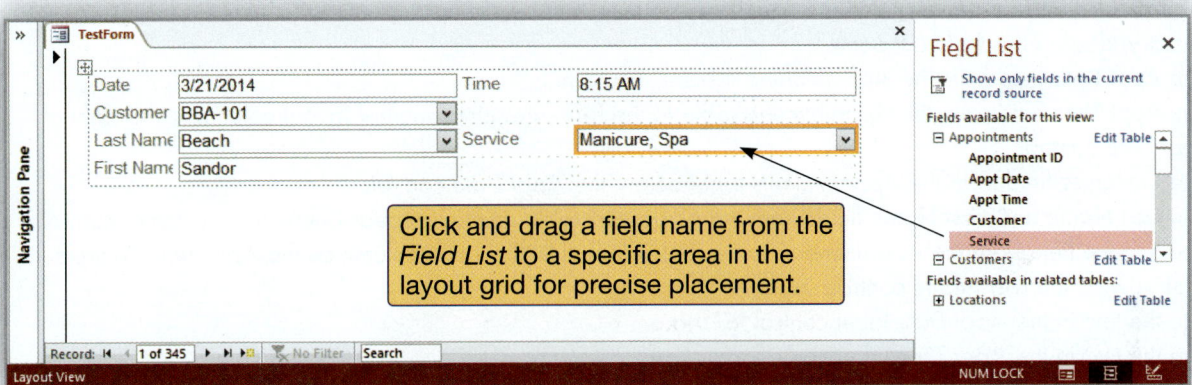

FIGURE AC 3.14

7. Save the form, and then switch to Form view to verify that it looks and behaves as you expect.

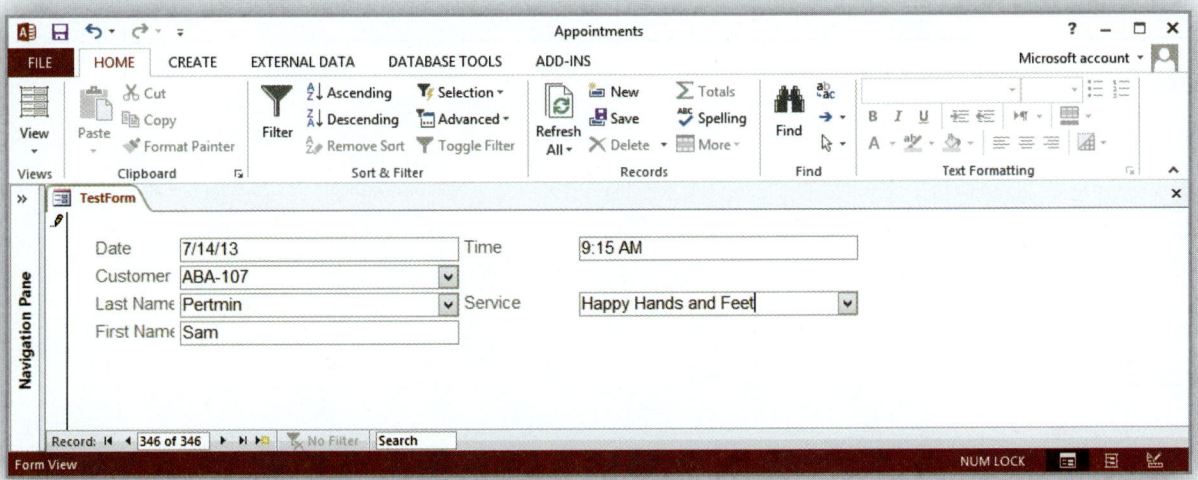

FIGURE AC 3.15
The final form in Form view

skill 3.6 Adding Fields to a Form in Layout View

tips & tricks

You don't have to start with a blank form. Use these same techniques to add fields to any form.

tell me more

To delete a control, click the control once to select it and then press `Delete` or `← Backspace`. If you delete a bound text box control, Access will delete the associated label control as well if there is one.

another method

If you prefer working in Design view, you can add fields using the same procedures as described for working in Layout view.

let me try

If the database is not already open, open the data file **AC3-Appointments** and try this skill on your own:

1. If necessary, open the *TestForm* form in Layout view. If your database does not include this form, create a new blank form in Layout view and save it as: `TestForm`
2. If necessary, display the *Field List* pane.
3. Add the **Appt Date** field from the *Appointments* table to the form.
4. Add the **Appt Time** field from the *Appointments* table to the form, creating another layout column to the right of the *Appt Time* control.
5. Add the **Customer** field from the *Appointments* table below the *Appt Date* controls.
6. Add the **Last Name** and **First Name** fields from the *Customers* table so they appear below the *Customer* controls.
7. Add the **Service** field from the *Appointments* table so it appears in the same column as the *Appt Time* controls in the same row as the *Last Name* controls.
8. Change the text in the *Appt Date* label control to: `Date`
9. Change the text in the *Appt Time* label control to: `Time`
10. Save the form.
11. Switch to Form view and try adding a new appointment in the form. Notice that when you select a different customer from the *Customer* drop-down list, the values in the *Last Name* and *First Name* bound text box controls update. This is because the *Customer* field in the *Appointments* table is a look-up field referencing the *Customer* table.
12. Close the form.

Skill 3.7 Creating a Basic Report Based on a Table or Query

A report displays data from a table or query in a format suitable for printing. Like forms, reports depend on a record source for their data. Unlike forms, you cannot enter new data into a report. The easiest way to create a new report is to use the *Report* button.

To create a basic report based on a table or query:

1. In the Navigation Pane, select the table or query record source for your report.
2. On the *Create* tab, in the *Reports* group, click the **Report** button.
3. When you save the report, notice that the default name in the *Report Name* box is the same as the name of the table or query that you based the report on. Type a new name if you want to use something else.

   In addition to the report title at the upper left side of the report header, the report includes the date and time in the upper-right corner of the header and the page number centered in the page footer.

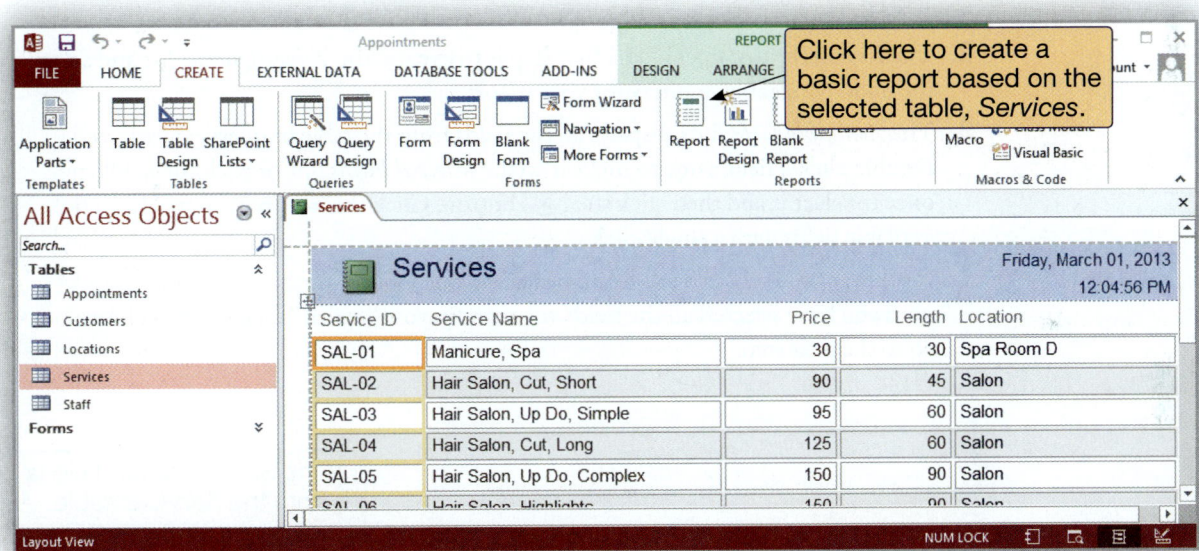

FIGURE AC 3.16
A basic report based on the selected table, *Services*

tips & tricks

The basic report layout is a simple grid with each record displayed as a new row similar to the Multiple Items form. If your report has many columns, this format may not fit on a single page.

let me try

If the database is not already open, open the data file **AC3-Appointments** and try this skill on your own:
1. Create a basic report from the **Services** table.
2. Save the report as: `ServicesReport`
3. Close the report.

skill 3.7 Creating a Basic Report Based on a Table or Query

Skill 3.8 Creating a Report Using the Report Wizard

The **Report Wizard** walks you step by step through the process of creating a report. The *Report Wizard* allows you to combine fields from more than one table or query and gives you more layout and design options than using the basic *Report* button from the *Create* tab.

To create a report using the *Report Wizard*:

1. On the *Create* tab, in the *Reports* group, click the **Report Wizard** button.

FIGURE AC 3.17

2. The *Report Wizard* opens. The first step is to expand the *Tables/Queries* list and select the underlying table or query for your report.

3. The *Available Fields* box displays all the fields from the table or query you selected. Double-click a field name to move it to the *Selected Fields* box or click the field name once to select it and then click the `>` button. Click the `>>` button to add all the available fields with a single click.

4. If you want to include fields from more than one table or query, repeat steps 2 and 3 until you have selected all the fields you want in your report. Click the **Next** button to go to the next step.

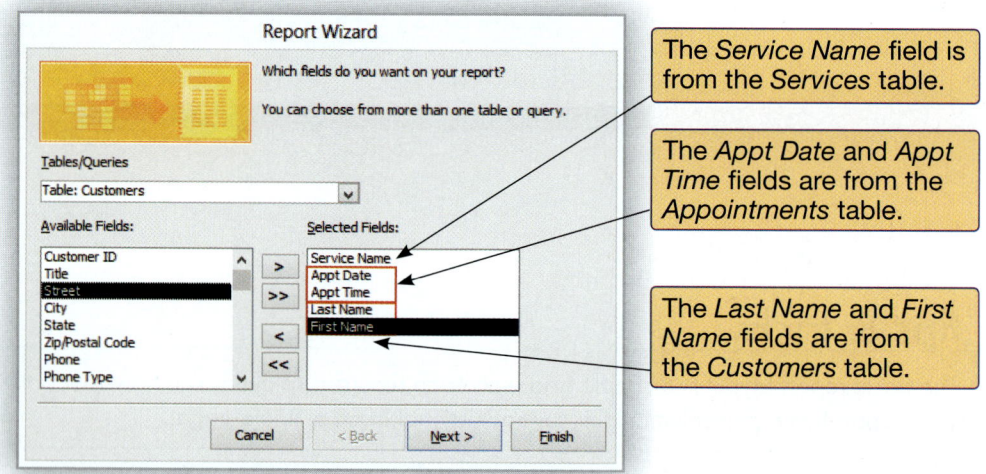

FIGURE AC 3.18

5. If you selected fields from related tables, the next step in the wizard asks how you want to organize the data in the report. Select the table that contains the field you want to use as the main grouping in the report, and then click **Next.** You will have the opportunity to add additional grouping levels in the next step.

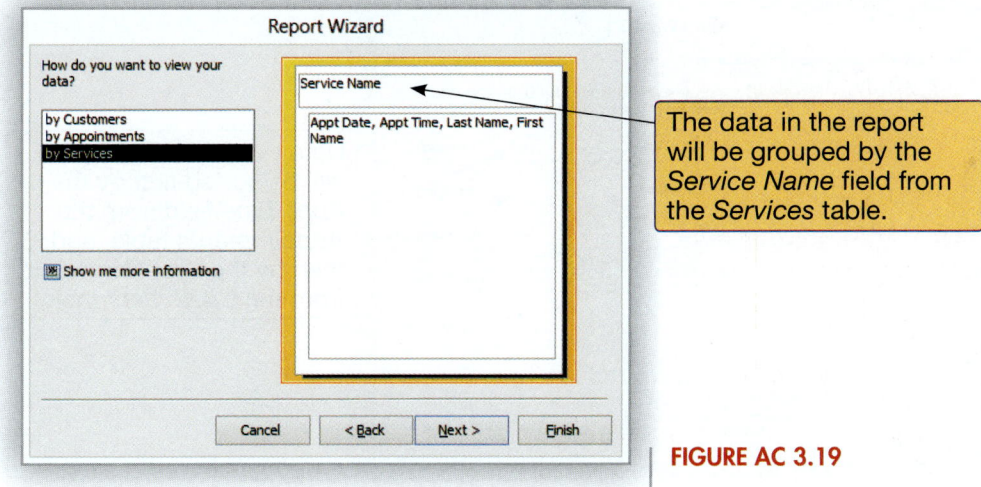

FIGURE AC 3.19

If you selected fields from only one table or query, you will not see this step.

6. Use grouping levels to organize the data into subgroups by the value of a specific field. Select the field you want to group by and then click the **>** button. You can add multiple grouping levels and reorder them if necessary using the *Priority* up and down arrows. When you are finished selecting grouping levels, click **Next**.

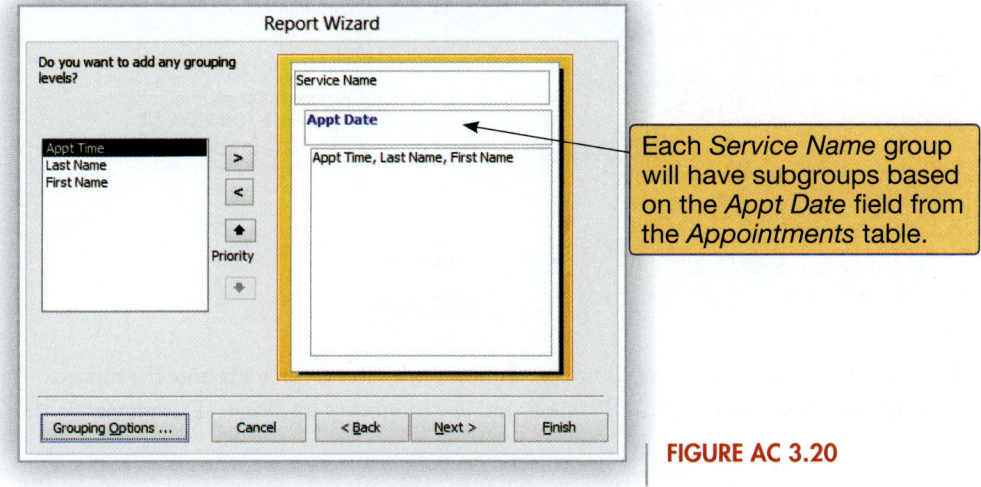

FIGURE AC 3.20

7. Next, specify how you want the data in each subgroup sorted. Expand the sort level list and select the field you want. You can include up to four fields to sort by. Click **Next**.

skill 3.8 Creating a Report Using the Report Wizard

FIGURE AC 3.21

8. Select the report layout, and select whether you want to print in **Portrait** or **Landscape** orientation. Click **Next**.

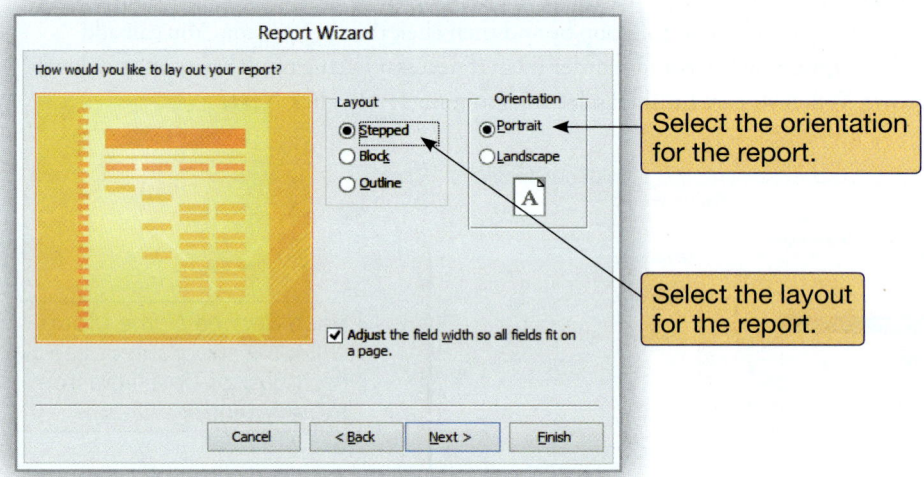

FIGURE AC 3.22

9. Give your report a meaningful title, and choose whether to preview how the report will look when printed (Print Preview view) or to modify its design (Design view).

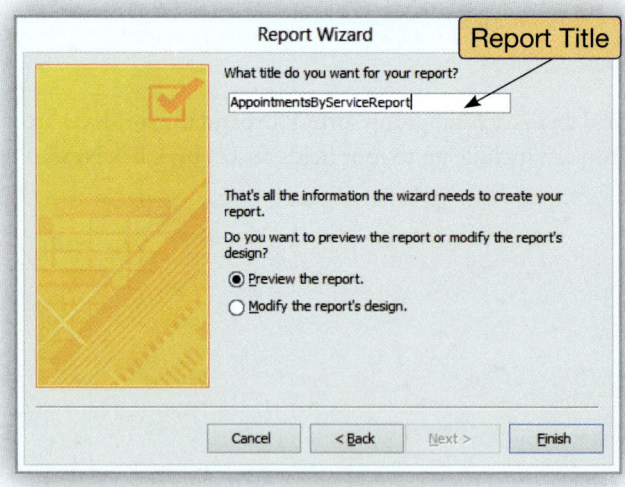

FIGURE AC 3.23

10. Click **Finish** to save the report.

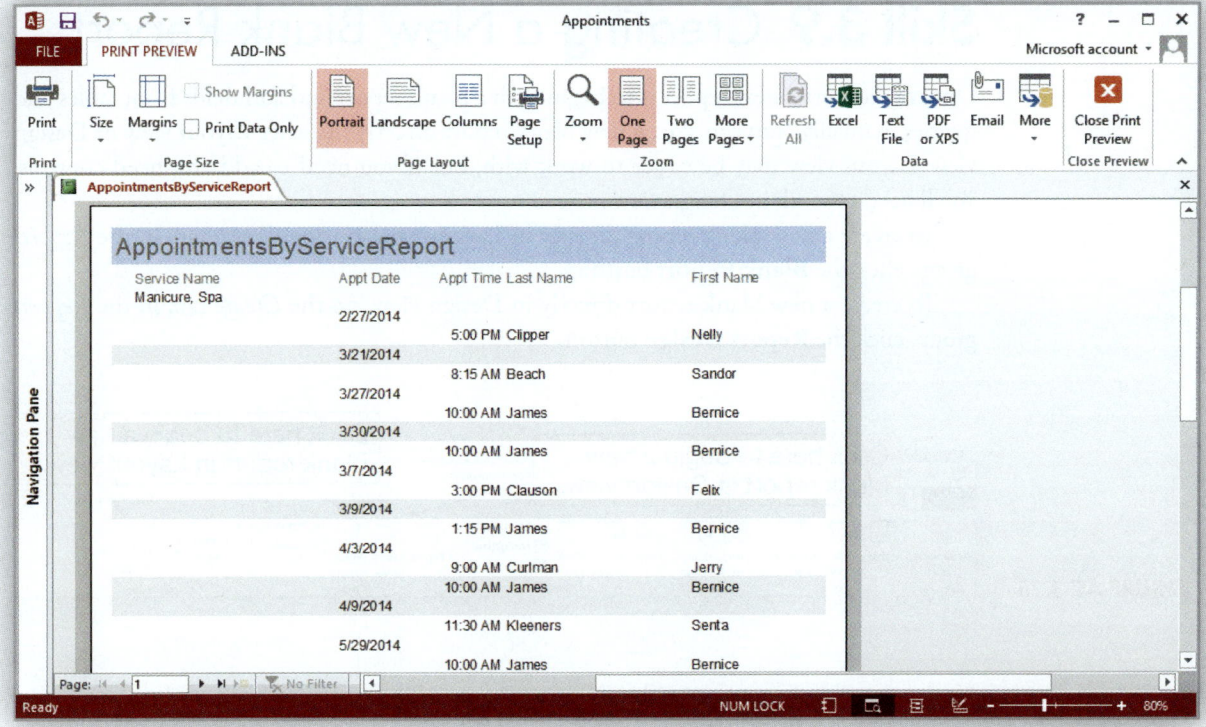

FIGURE AC 3.24
The new report in Print Preview view. Notice how the data are grouped in the report by service name and then by appointment date.

tips & tricks

Use Portrait orientation for reports with few columns; use Landscape orientation for reports with many columns.

tell me more

You can modify your grouping or sorting choices later by editing the report in *Layout* view.

let me try

If the database is not already open, open the data file **AC3-Appointments** and try this skill on your own:

1. Use the *Report Wizard* to create a new report. Include the **Service Name** field from the *Services* table, the **Appt Date** and **Appt Time** fields from the *Appointments* table, and the **Last Name** and **First Name** fields from the *Customers* table.
2. View the report data by the **Services** table.
3. Create subgroups by the **Appt Date** field.
4. Sort each subgroup first by **Appt Time,** and then by **Last Name.**
5. Use the **Stepped** layout and **Portrait** orientation for the report.
6. Name the report: `AppointmentsByServiceReport` and preview it in Print Preview view.
7. Close the report.

skill 3.8 Creating a Report Using the Report Wizard

Skill 3.9 Creating a New Blank Report

One way to start a new report is to begin with a blank report and add fields from tables and queries manually. You can start a new blank report directly in either Layout view or Design view. Layout view may be easier to work with, but if you need to add advanced controls, you'll need to work in Design view instead.

To create a new blank report directly in Layout view, on the *Create* tab, in the *Reports* group, click the **Blank Report** button.

To create a new blank report directly in Design view, on the *Create* tab, in the *Reports* group, click the **Report Design** button.

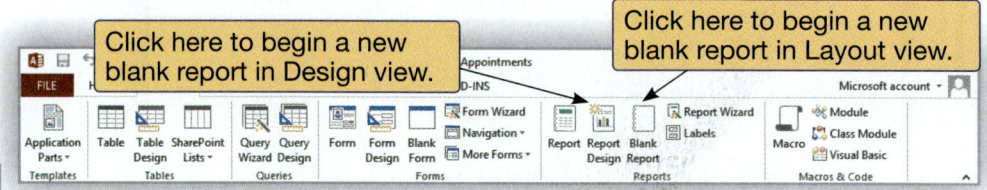

FIGURE AC 3.25

Notice that there are no records in the new report. The new blank report does not have a record source defined. The report is an empty layout until you add controls.

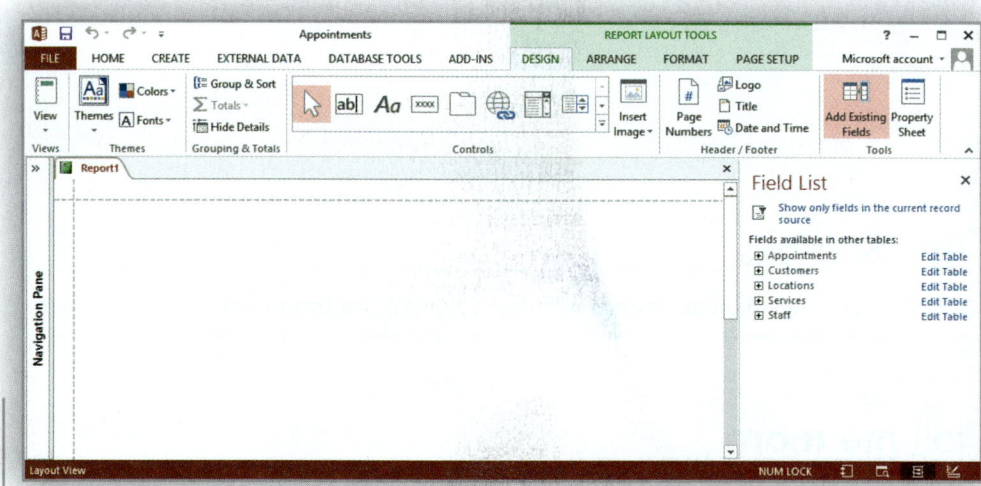

FIGURE AC 3.26
A new blank report in Layout view

tips & tricks

Access will sometimes select a table or query to use as the record source for the report based on the object selected in the Navigation Pane or based on the first table listed in the Navigation Pane. If this is not the record source you want to use for the report, don't worry. The record source will be updated as you add fields.

let me try

If the database is not already open, open the data file **AC3-Appointments** and try this skill on your own:
1. Create a new blank report so it opens directly in Design view.
2. Close the report without saving it.
3. Create a new blank report so it opens directly in Layout view.
4. Save the form as: **TestReport**

Skill 3.10 Adding Fields to a Report in Layout View

If you are starting with a blank report, you will need to add controls to display field data. By default, blank reports use a *tabular layout* in which the data are arranged similar to a table with the label controls at the top of each column.

To add fields to a report in Layout view:

1. If necessary, on the *Report Layout Tools Design* tab, in the *Tools* group, click the **Add Existing Fields** button to display the *Field List* pane.
2. In the *Field List* pane, click the + in front of the table or query that contains the field(s) you want to add.
3. Double-click a field name to add it. A new label control is automatically created at the top of the report with a bound text box control below it. In Layout view, Access displays values for multiple records in the column.
4. Continue double-clicking fields in the *Field List* to add them to the report.
5. When you are finished adding fields, save the report.

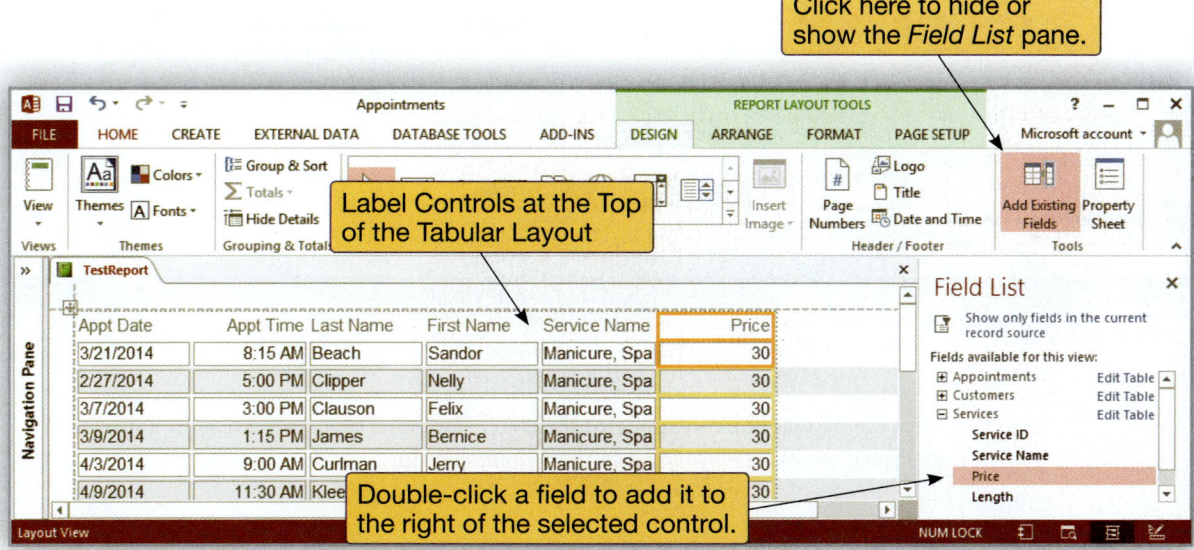

FIGURE AC 3.27

let me try

If the database is not already open, open the data file **AC3-Appointments** and try this skill on your own:

1. If necessary, open the *TestReport* report in Layout view. If your database does not include this report, create a new blank report in Layout view and save it as: `TestReport`
2. If necessary, display the *Field List* pane.
3. From the *Appointments* table, add the **Appt Date** field and then the **Appt Time** field.
4. From the *Customers* table, add the **Last Name** field and then the **First Name** field.
5. From the *Services* table, add the **Service Name** field and then the **Price** field.
6. Save the report.

Skill 3.11 Formatting Controls

Once you have created your form or report, it is easy to change formatting in Layout view. Click the control you want to change, and then make your formatting selections from the Ribbon. While these formatting techniques also work in Design view, in Layout view, you can immediately see the formatting change. The formatting options discussed in this skill are available for both forms and reports.

- For forms, these commands are found on the *Form Layout Tools Format* tab.
- For reports, these commands are found on the *Report Layout Tools Format* tab.

To apply the same formatting to multiple controls at the same time, press Ctrl as you click each control.

From the *Font* group, click the buttons to apply standard text formatting such as **bold,** *italic,* and underline, change the font, font size, or font color, and align text to the left, center, or right side of the control box. You can use *Format Painter* to copy the formatting from one control and apply it to another.

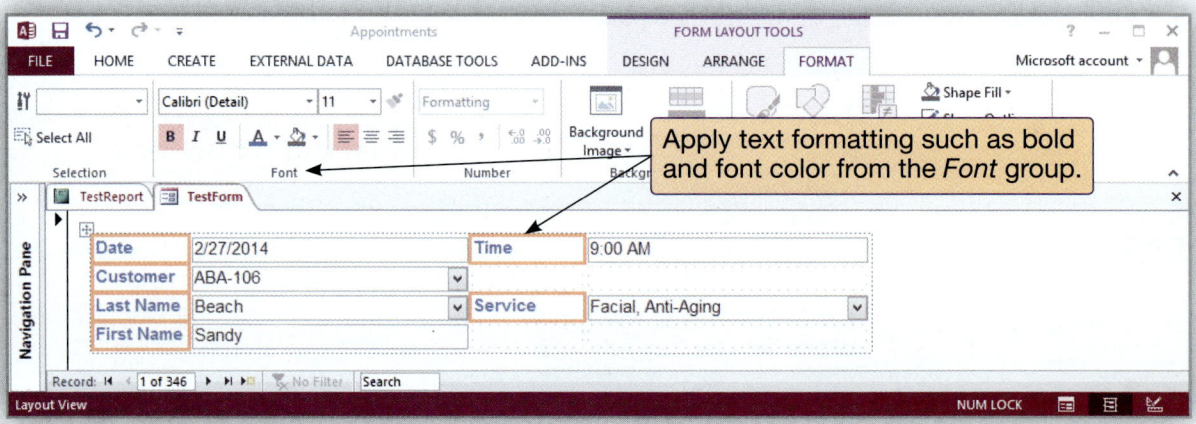

FIGURE AC 3.28

For bound text box controls with the Date/Time data type, you can apply a specific date/time format from the *Format* list in the *Number* group.

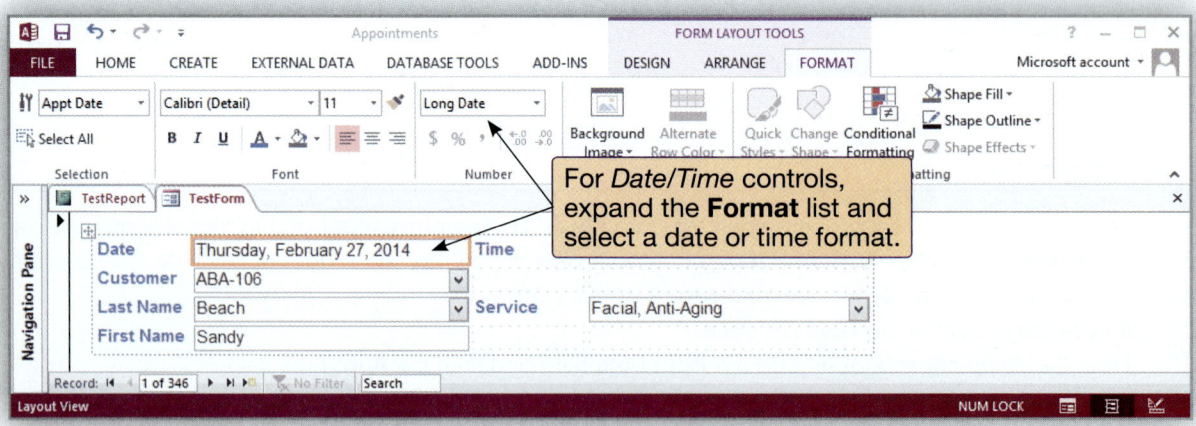

FIGURE AC 3.29

For bound text box controls with the *Number* or *Currency* data type, you can apply specific number formatting from the *Number* group, by clicking the **Apply Currency Format**, **Apply Percent Format**, or **Apply Comma Number Format** button. More number formats are available from the *Format* list.

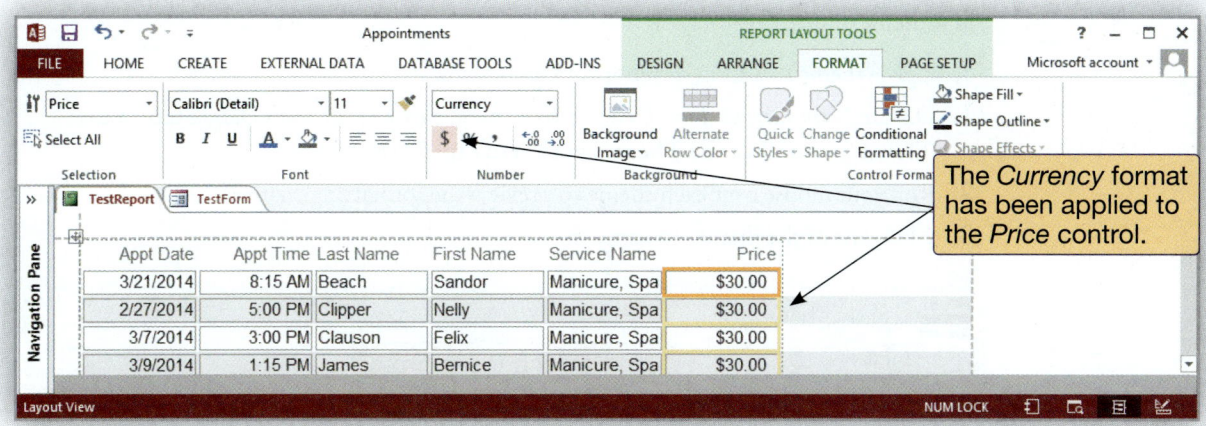

FIGURE AC 3.30

another **method**

Common keyboard shortcuts that you may be familiar with in other applications (e.g., Ctrl + B) also work in Access.

let me **try**

If the database is not already open, open the data file **AC3-Appointments** and try this skill on your own:

1. If necessary, open the *TestForm* form in Layout view. If your database does not include this form, create it following the steps in *Skill 3.5: Creating a New Blank Form* and *Skill 3.6: Adding Fields to a Form in Layout View*.
2. Select all the label controls in the form, **bold** them, and apply the **Blue, Accent 1** font color.
3. Apply the **Long Date** format to the **Appt Date** bound text box control.
4. Save the form.
5. If necessary, open the *TestReport* report in Layout view. If your database does not include this report, create it following the steps in *Skill 3.9: Creating a New Blank Report* and *Skill 3.10: Adding Fields to a Report in Layout View*.
6. Apply the **Currency** format to the **Price** bound text box control.
7. Save the report.

skill 3.11   Formatting Controls

Skill 3.12 Applying a Theme

A *theme* is a unified color and font scheme. When you apply a theme to a form or report, you update the look of all the database objects at once. A database can have only one theme applied at a time. Working with themes in Layout view allows you to see the effects of the new theme immediately.

To apply a theme to a form or report in Layout view:

1. On the *Form Layout Tools Design* tab or the *Report Layout Tools Design* tab, in the *Themes* group, click the **Themes** button to expand the gallery.
2. Roll your mouse over each theme to preview the formatting changes.
3. Click one of the themes to apply it.

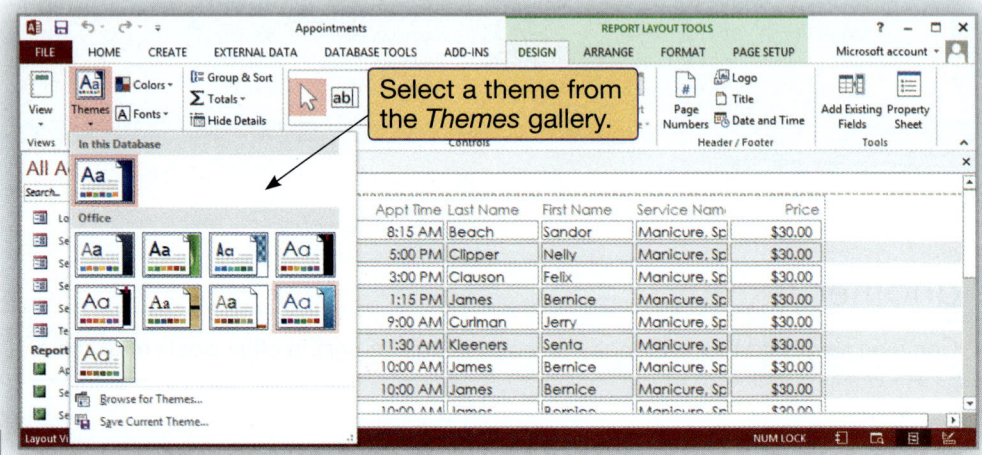

FIGURE AC 3.31

tips & tricks

If you change the theme, you may need to resize some controls to display the data completely.

tell me more

From the *Themes* group, you can apply specific aspects of a theme by making a selection from the *Theme Colors* or *Theme Fonts* gallery.

Theme Colors—Limits the colors available from the color palette for fonts, borders, and shading. Notice that when you change themes, the color palette changes for background colors, fills, outlines, and fonts.

Theme Fonts—Affects the fonts used for titles, label controls, bound controls, and other text in the form. Changing the theme fonts does not limit the fonts available to you from the *Font* list.

another method

Themes are also available from the *Form Design Tools Design* tab, *Themes* group, and the *Report Design Tools Design* tab, *Themes* group. However, you will not see the immediate impact of the theme as you do in Layout view.

let me try

If the database is not already open, open the data file **AC3-Appointments** and try this skill on your own:
1. If necessary, open the *TestReport* report in Layout view.
2. Apply the **Slice** theme.
3. Save the report.

Skill 3.13 Resizing Controls

When designing forms and reports, you should ensure that the controls are sized to fit the data properly. You can change the width and height of controls as necessary. When the control is part of a layout, changing the height of a single control affects all the controls in the row, and changing the width of a single control affects all the controls in the column. For example, in a tabular layout, changing the width of any control in the column will change the width of the entire column.

To change the width of a control in either Layout view or Design view, move the cursor to the right or left edge of the control, and when the cursor changes to ↔ click and drag to the right to make the control wider or to the left to make it smaller. Use the same technique to make rows taller or shorter.

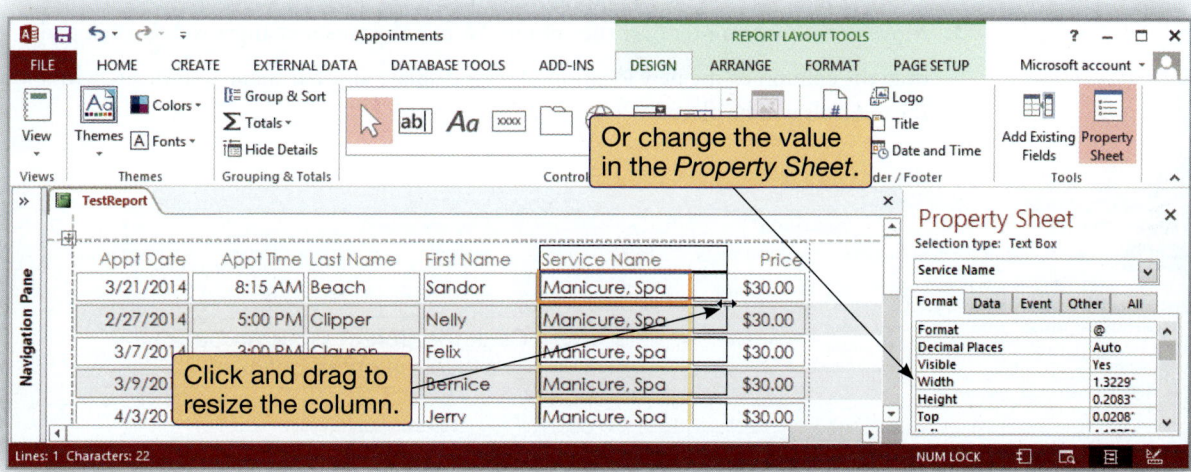

FIGURE AC 3.32

Clicking and dragging to resize controls can be imprecise. Use the *Property Sheet* if you need to specify an exact width or height:

1. On the *Form Layout Tools Design* tab or the *Report Layout Tools Design* tab, in the *Tools* group, click the **Property Sheet** button.
2. Ensure that the correct control is selected from the drop-down list at the top of the *Property Sheet*.
3. If necessary, click the *Property Sheet* **Format** tab.
4. Type the value you want (in inches) in the *Width* and *Height* boxes. Press **Enter** to apply the change.

let me try

If the database is not already open, open the data file **AC3-Appointments** and try this skill on your own:
1. If necessary, open the *TestReport* report in Layout view.
2. Modify the width of the **Service Name** controls (both the label and the bound text box control) so most of the service names are visible on one line (approximately 2.25 inches).
3. Save the report.

Skill 3.14 Moving and Arranging Controls

By default, all controls in a form or a report are included in the control layout. The **control layout** restricts movement of controls to the layout rows and columns ensuring that controls align with one another. Having controls grouped into a control layout makes it easy to add rows and columns to the layout and resize entire layout sections at once.

To rearrange columns in a tabular layout:

1. Click anywhere in the column you want to move.
2. On the *Report Layout Tools Arrange* tab or the *Form Layout Tools Arrange* tab, in the *Rows & Columns* group, click the **Select Column** button. This ensures that you will move the label control along with the bound text box control.
3. Move the mouse pointer over the column. When the cursor changes to, click and drag the column to the new location. Access displays an I-bar shape to indicate where the controls will be placed.

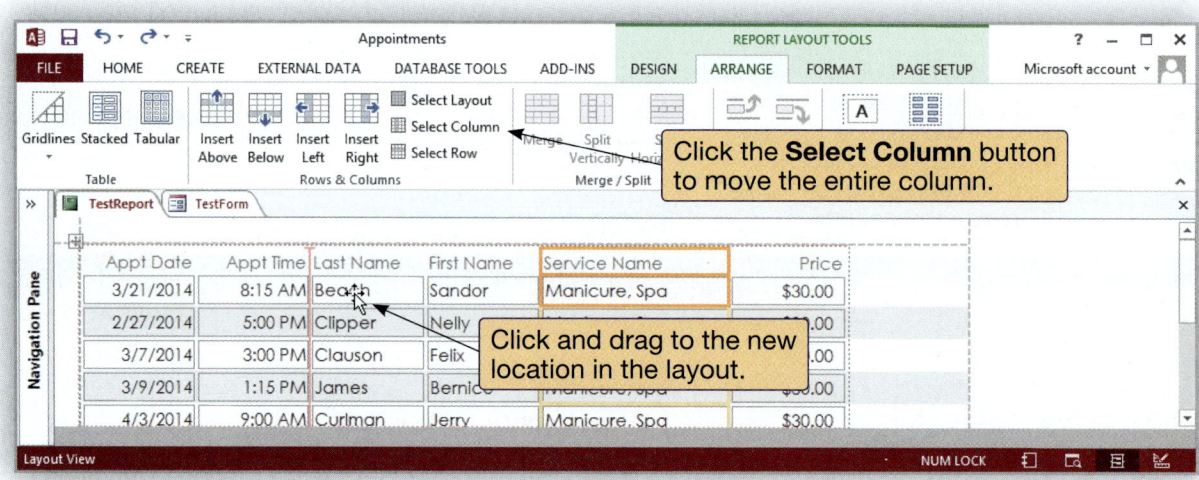

FIGURE AC 3.33
Moving controls in a report in Layout view

In a stacked layout, it is more common to move individual controls rather than an entire column.

1. Select the control or controls you want to move. To move both a bound control and its label control, select both controls by clicking one and pressing Ctrl as you click the other.
2. Move the mouse pointer over the selected controls. When the cursor changes to, click and drag to the new location. Access highlights the cell in the layout where the control will be placed. When you move multiple controls, Access maintains the relative layout of the controls.

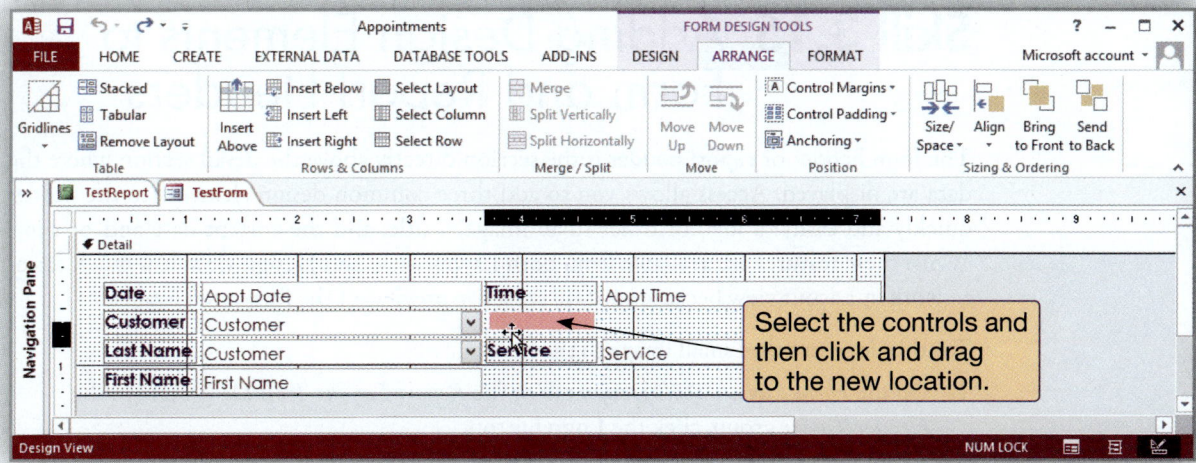

FIGURE AC 3.34
Moving controls in a form in Design view

To add a new empty row or column to the control layout, select a control in the layout, and then click the appropriate button in the *Rows & Columns* group: **Insert Above, Insert Below, Insert Left,** or **Insert Right.**

To remove a row or column from the control layout, right-click anywhere in the row or column, and select **Delete Row** or **Delete Column** from the right-click menu.

tell me more

There may be times you want to move a single control outside of the control layout. You must remove the control from the layout before you can manipulate it individually.

- In form or report Design view, click the control you want to remove from the control layout. On the *Form Design Tools Arrange* tab or the *Report Design Tools Arrange* tab, in the *Table* group, click the **Remove Layout** button to remove the control from the layout.
- The *Remove Layout* command is available in Layout view, but only from the right-click menu. Right-click the control you want to remove from the layout, point to **Layout,** and click **Remove Layout.**

let me try

If the database is not already open, open the data file **AC3-Appointments** and try this skill on your own:
1. If necessary, open the *TestReport* report in Layout view.
2. Move the **Service Name** column to place it between the *Appt Time* and *Last Name* columns.
3. Save the report.
4. If necessary, open the *TestForm* form in Layout view.
5. Move the **Service** control and its label control to the layout area directly below the *Appt Time* control and the *Time* label.
6. Save the form.

skill 3.14   Moving and Arranging Controls

Skill 3.15 Adding Design Elements to Form and Report Headers

The **form header** or **report header** is the section directly above the detail section where the data are displayed. Access allows you to add three common design elements to the header quickly and easily: a logo or other small image, a title, and the current date and/or time. While these features are available from both Layout view and Design view, it is much easier to work in Layout view because you will see a live preview of the formatted header.

To add a logo or other small image to the header:

1. On the *Form Layout Tools Design* tab or the *Report Layout Tools Design* tab, in the *Header/Footer* group, click the **Logo** button.
2. In the *Insert Picture* dialog, browse to find the image you want to use as the logo, select the file, and then click the **Open** button.
3. The image is added to the upper-left corner of the header.

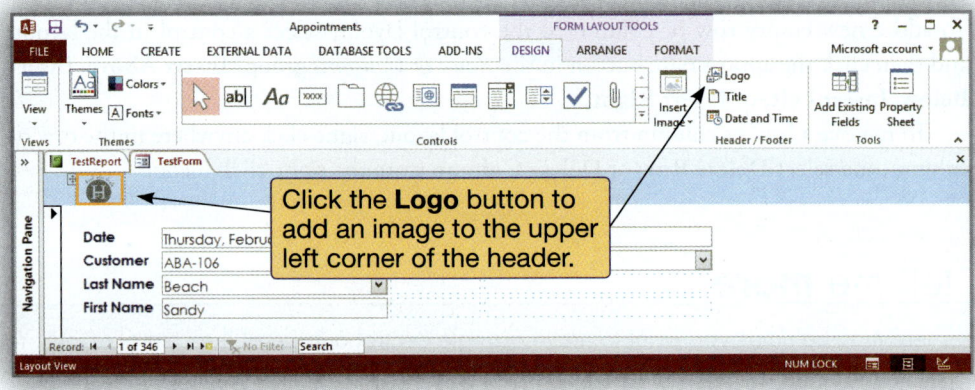

FIGURE AC 3.35

To add a title to the header:

1. On the *Form Layout Tools Design* tab or the *Report Layout Tools Design* tab, in the *Header/Footer* group, click the **Title** button.
2. An unbound text control with the name of the database object is added to the header, just to the right of the logo (if there is one).
3. To change the title, click in the box and modify the text.

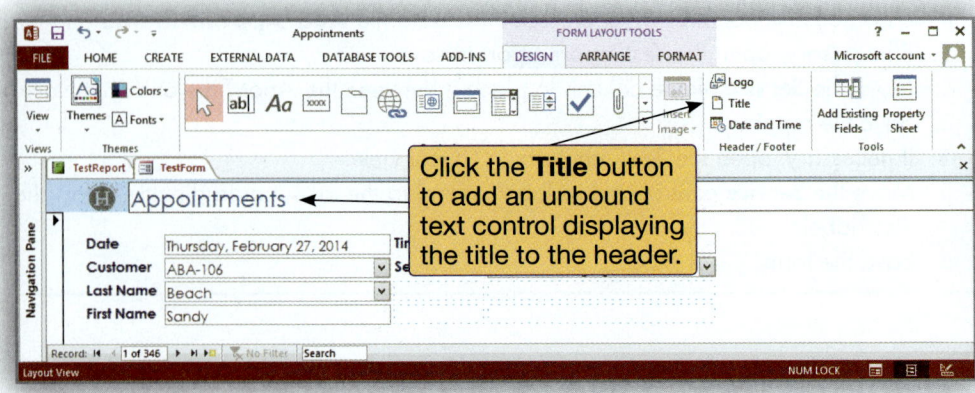

FIGURE AC 3.36

To add the date and/or time to the header:

1. On the *Form Layout Tools Design* tab or the *Report Layout Tools Design* tab, in the *Header/Footer* group, click the **Date and Time** button.
2. The *Date and Time* dialog opens. Check the boxes for the date and/or time formats you want.
3. Click **OK** to add the date and time options you selected to the upper-right corner of the header.

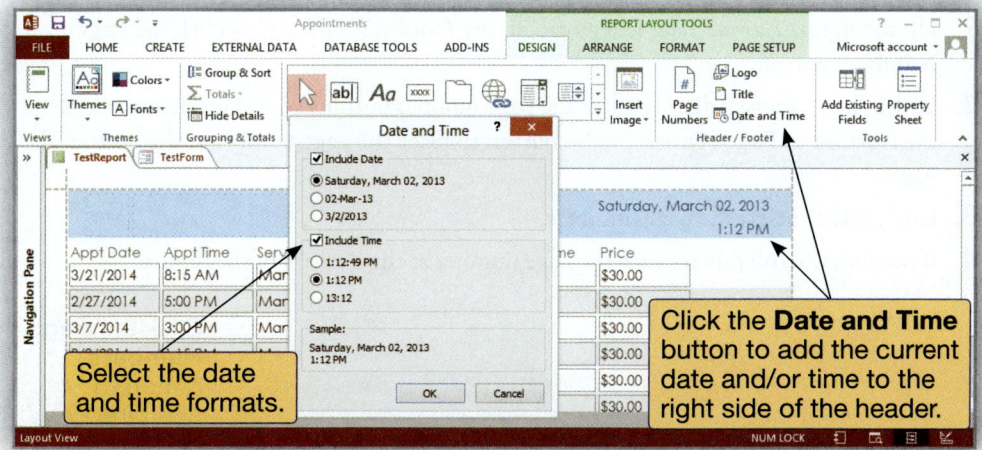

FIGURE AC 3.37

tell me more

In Design view, you will not see the actual date and time in the date and time controls. Instead, Design view displays the formulas used in the unbound text controls to calculate the current date and time: =Date( ) and =Time( )

let me try

If the database is not already open, open the data file **AC3-Appointments** and try this skill on your own:
1. If necessary, open the *TestForm* form in Layout view.
2. Add the image **SpaLogo** to the form header as a logo. The image file is located with the other data files for this book.
3. Add a title to the form header and change the text to: **Appointments**
4. Save and close the form.
5. If necessary, open the *TestReport* report in Layout view.
6. Add the date and time to the report header using the date format similar to **Saturday, March 02, 2013** and the time format similar to **1:12 PM.**
7. Save the report.

skill 3.15 Adding Design Elements to Form and Report Headers

Skill 3.16 Adding Page Numbers to Reports

Because reports are intended for printing, they include additional header and footer sections unavailable in forms. Data in the **page header section** and **page footer section** appear at the top and bottom of every printed page in the report; data in the **report header section** and **report footer section** appear only at the very beginning and the very end of the report.

To add page numbers to the page footer section:

1. On the *Report Layout Tools Design* tab, in the *Header/Footer* group, click the **Page Numbers** button.
2. In the *Page Numbers* dialog, select the page number options you want. Be sure to select the **Bottom of Page (Footer)** radio button to place the page number at the bottom the page.
3. Click **OK** to insert the page numbers.
4. If necessary, scroll down to see the page number at the bottom of the report.

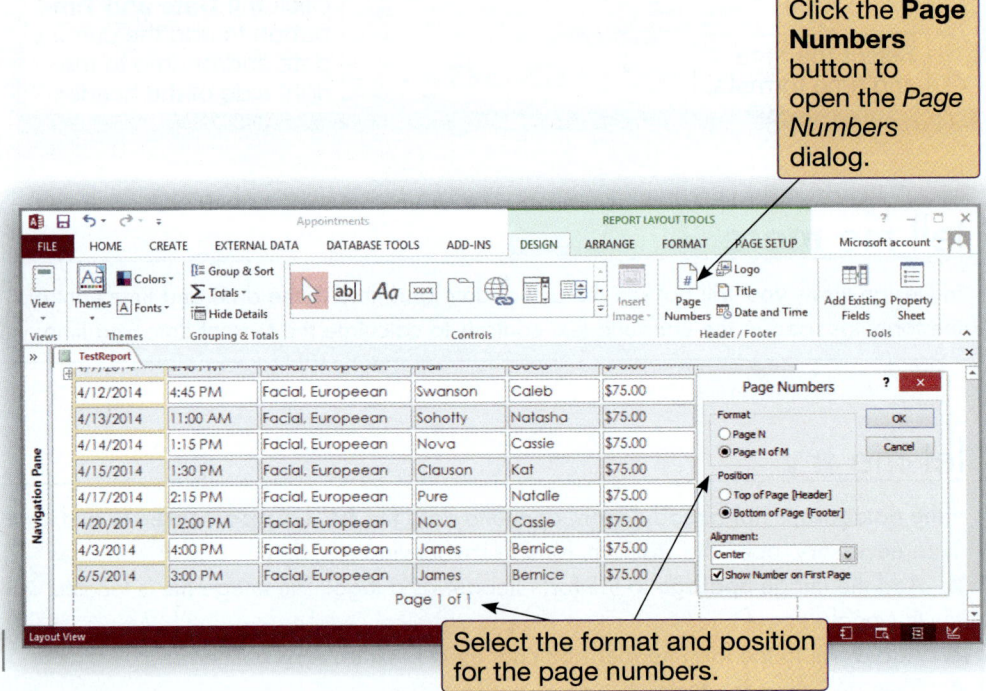

FIGURE AC 3.38

tips & tricks

If you use the page number format **Page N of M**, where *N* is the current page number and *M* is the total number of pages, you will always see Page 1 of 1 in Layout view. To test the page number format with the actual number of printed pages, switch to Print Preview view.

let me try

If the database is not already open, open the data file **AC3-Appointments** and try this skill on your own:

1. If necessary, open the *TestReport* report in Layout view.
2. Add automatic page numbers centered at the bottom of the page footer on every page. Use the format page **N of M.**
3. Save the report.

Skill 3.17 Grouping Records in a Report

If you have used the *Report Wizard* to create a report, you should already be somewhat familiar with the concept of grouping. Adding **grouping** organizes the report into sections (groups) by the value of a specific field. Grouping can make a long report much easier to follow. Grouping also allows you to add group-specific headers and footers where you can calculate totals for each group.

To add grouping to a report:

1. On the *Report Layout Tools Design* tab, in the *Grouping & Totals* group, click the **Group & Sort** button to display the *Group, Sort, and Total* pane at the bottom of the report window.
2. Click the **Add a group** button in the *Group, Sort, and Total* pane to display a list of available fields to group by. Click the field you want.
3. Access adds grouping to the report, including a group header for each group with a title. How the data are grouped depends on the type of field you selected. If you selected a date/time field, Access may group the data by year, quarter, month, week, or day. If you selected a text field, Access may group the data by specific text values. The data in Figure AC 3.39 are grouped by the *Appt Date* field by calendar quarter.

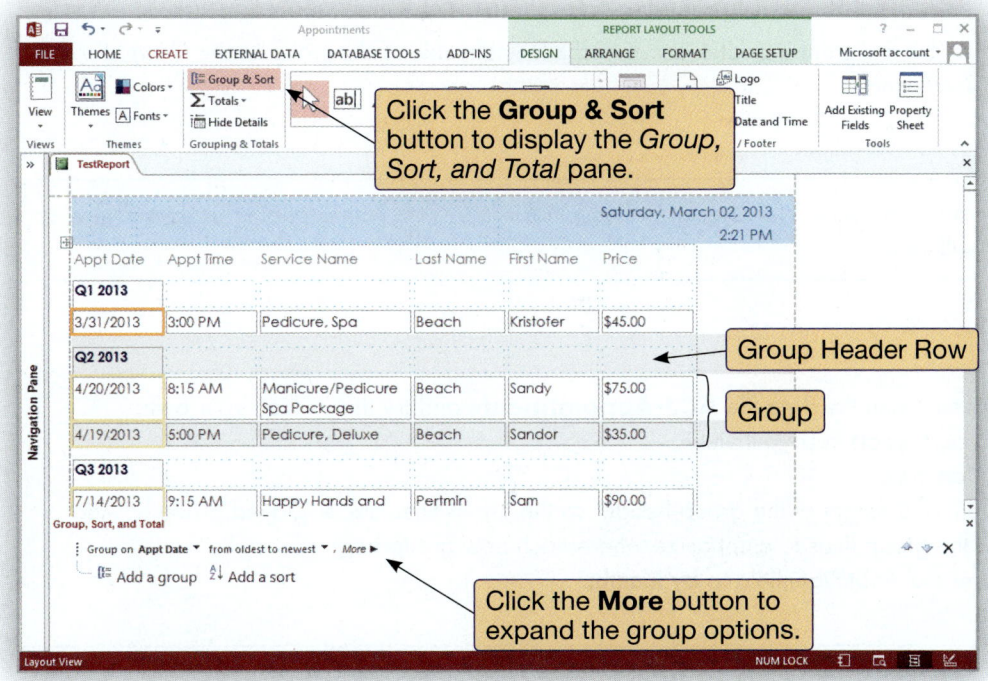

FIGURE AC 3.39

To change the grouping level Access selected:

1. Click the **More** button next to the group you want to change to expand the group options.
2. Click the arrow next to the grouping level description, and select a new option from the menu. In Figure AC 3.40, the grouping option has been changed from **by quarter** to **by month**.
3. To hide the options again, click the **Less** button.

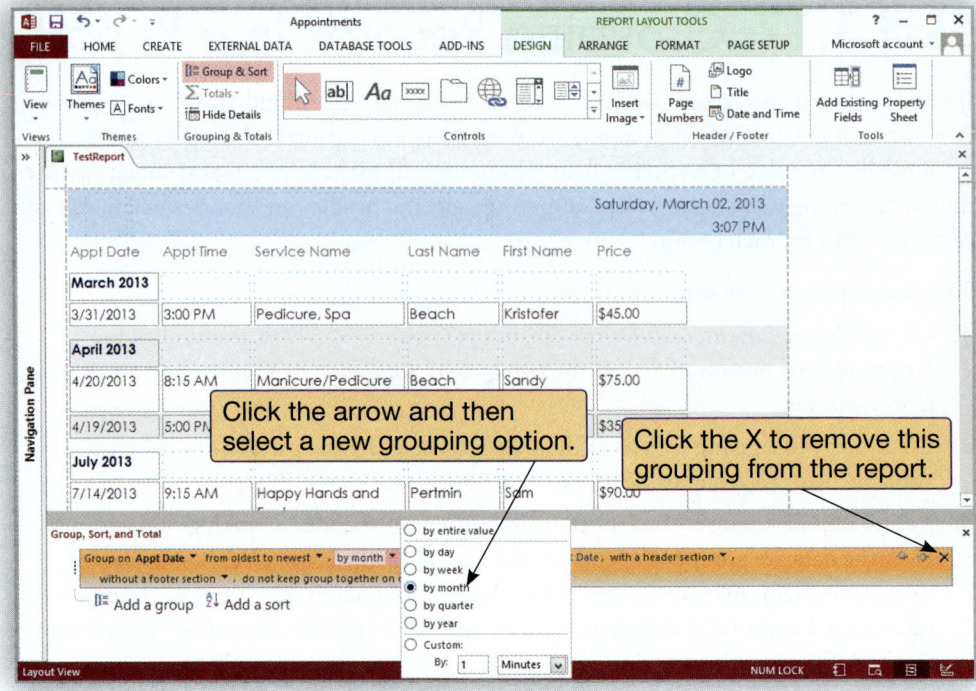

FIGURE AC 3.40

To delete a grouping, click the **X** at the far right side of the group in the *Group, Sort, and Total* pane.

tips & tricks

You can also add groupings from Design view. However, it's always easiest to work with grouping in Layout view so you can preview how the data will look.

let me try

If the database is not already open, open the data file **AC3-Appointments** and try this skill on your own:
1. If necessary, open the *TestReport* report in Layout view.
2. Add grouping by the **Appt Date** field.
3. If necessary, change the width and height of the group header so the group titles are displayed properly. Add formatting of your choice to the group titles to emphasize where each new group begins.
4. Change the grouping level for the *Appt Date* field to **by month.**
5. Save the report.

Skill 3.18 Adding Totals to a Report

Totals in a report display a calculation such as the sum or average of the values in a field or group. The formula to calculate the total is added to the report in a type of control called a **calculated control**—an unbound text box control that contains an expression (a formula). You do not need to know how to add a calculated control, however, in order to add totals to a report. Report Layout view provides a tool that adds totals for you.

To add totals to a report in Layout view:

1. Click any value in the control you want to add a total to.
2. On the *Report Layout Tools Design* tab, in the *Grouping & Totals* group, click the **Totals** button.
3. Select the function you want to use for the total.

Access automatically inserts the new calculated control into the report footer. The calculated control in the report footer calculates a grand total for all the values in the report. If the report includes grouping, Access also adds a calculated control in each group footer to calculate the total for records in that group.

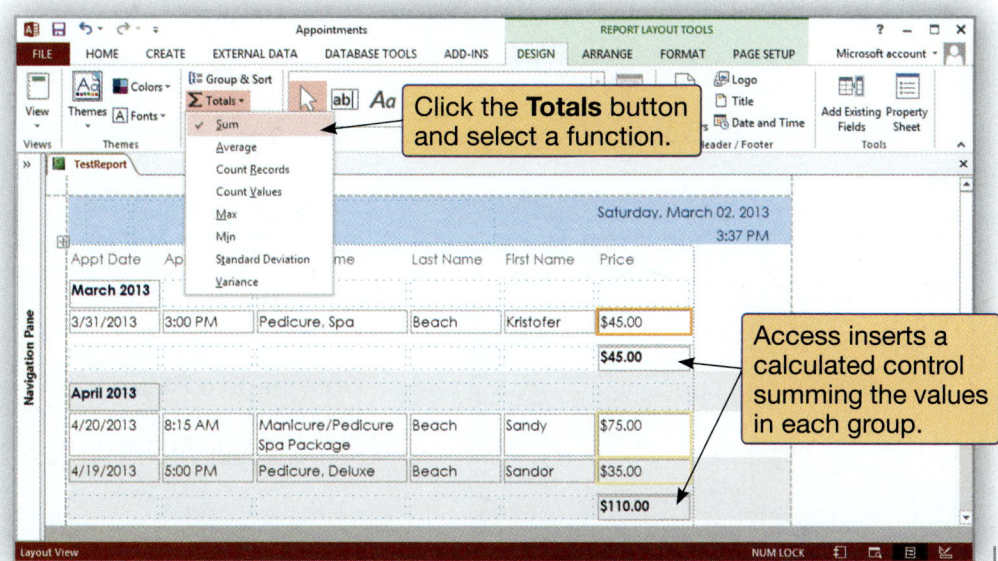

FIGURE AC 3.41

tips & tricks

The *Totals* button is also available on the *Report Design Tools Design* tab, in the *Grouping & Totals* group. However, in Design view, you will not see the total values. Instead, Design view displays the formulas used in the unbound text controls.

let me try

If the database is not already open, open the data file **AC3-Appointments** and try this skill on your own:

1. If necessary, open the *TestReport* report in Layout view.
2. Add totals to the *Price* column to calculate the sum of prices.
3. Adjust the height of the control in the group footer if necessary and bold it to emphasize the group totals.
4. Save the report.

Skill 3.19 Previewing and Printing a Report

Print Preview view shows you exactly how the report will look when it is printed. It is always a good idea to preview the report before printing. There are three main methods for switching to Print Preview view:

- Right-click the report tab, and select **Print Preview.**
- Click the **Print Preview** view button on the status bar.
- On the *Home* tab, in the *Views* group, click the **View** button, and select **Print Preview.**

If the printed report will result in blank pages, Access will display a warning message when you switch to Print Preview view. Click **OK** to dismiss the warning and continue to Print Preview view. You can use Print Preview view to adjust print settings as necessary.

If your report will print on more than one page, it is a good practice to preview the report in a multiple page layout. To preview more than one page at a time, in the *Zoom* group, click the **Two Pages** button or click the **More Pages** button and select an option to see **Four, Eight,** or **Twelve** pages at once.

In Figure AC 3.42, previewing the report two pages at a time shows that the report is just a little bit too wide, causing part of the header to spill over to a second page.

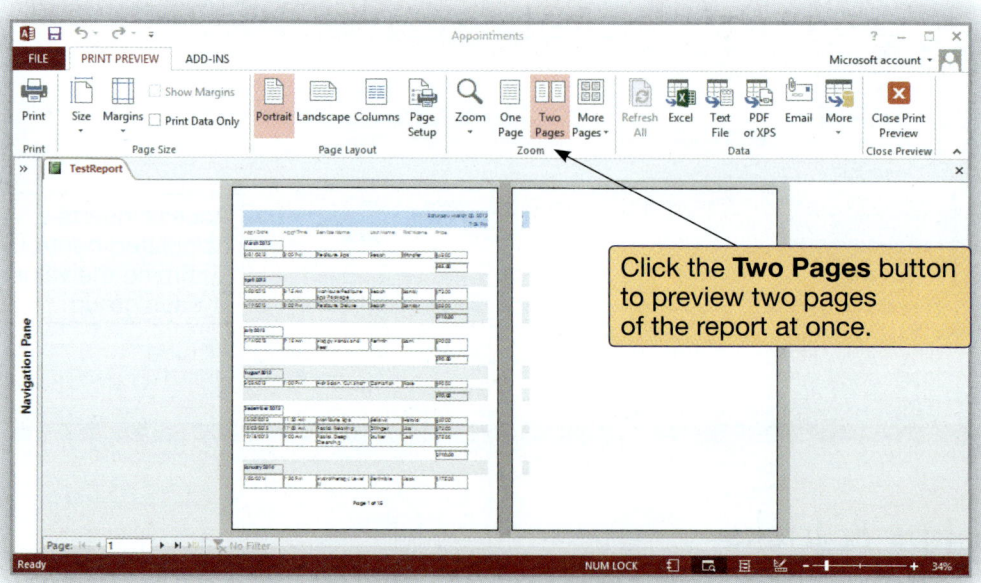

FIGURE AC 3.42

To print the report:

From Print Preview view, click the **Print** button at the far left side of the Ribbon to open the *Print* dialog. In the *Print* dialog you can specify which pages to print and how many copies to print. Click **OK** to send the report to the printer.

To close Print Preview view, click the **Close Print Preview** button at the far right side of the Ribbon.

another method

Print options are also available from Backstage.
1. With the report open in any view, click the **File** tab to open Backstage.
2. Click **Print.**
3. Select the print option you want.
   Quick Print sends the report to the printer without opening the *Print* dialog first.
   Print opens the *Print* dialog so you can check the printer settings before printing.
   Print Preview opens the report in Print Preview view.

let me try

If the database is not already open, open the data file **AC3-Appointments** and try this skill on your own:
1. If necessary, open the *TestReport* report.
2. Switch to Print Preview view. If you receive a warning that the section width is greater than the page width, click **OK** to dismiss the warning.
3. Change the view to show two pages at once.

from the perspective of . . .

LAWYER

I use Access to track time and billing for my law practice. I use forms to enter client information and to track time spent on each case, and I use reports to generate client invoices. I always check the invoice report in Print Preview view before printing. You never know when an adjustment to a column width will cause the report to spill over to a second page. When that happens, I can usually adjust the margins or switch the page orientation to keep the invoice to no more than one page wide.

skill 3.19 Previewing and Printing a Report

Skill 3.20 Controlling the Page Setup of a Report for Printing

When you create a new report from scratch, the default page orientation is **portrait**. This means the height of the page is greater than the width. You may want to change the page orientation to **landscape** to print sideways on the page if your report contains multiple columns of data.

Margins are the blank spaces at the top, bottom, left, and right of the printed page. If your report is just a little bit too wide to fit on one page, try adjusting the margins to a more narrow setting. This will give you more room on the page for printed data.

Use Print Preview view to adjust margins and page orientation for your reports before printing:

1. Switch to Print Preview view.
2. To change the page orientation, in the *Page Layout* group, click the **Portrait** or **Landscape** button.
3. To use a preset margin option, in the *Page Size* group, click the **Margins** button, and select an option: **Normal, Wide,** or **Narrow.**

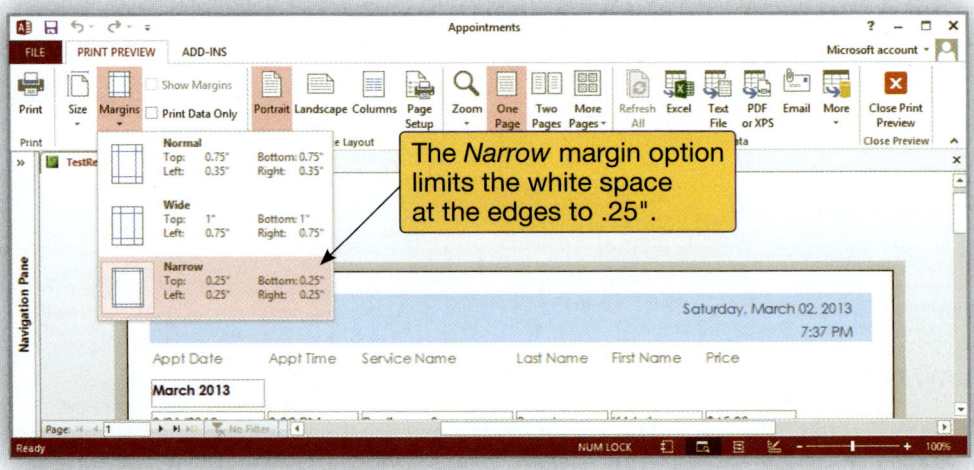

FIGURE AC 3.43

When you switch page orientation or margins, all the visible data in your report may fit on one page, but the report width may still be wider than the page. When that happens, Access will show a warning message that the report may print with blank pages.

FIGURE AC 3.44

To fix this problem:

1. Switch to Design view.
2. In Design view, you can clearly see that the report is wider than it needs to be.
3. Move the mouse pointer to the right side of the report detail section. When the cursor changes to the ↔ shape, click and drag the section boundary to the left to make it smaller. Access will not let you make the section so small that any controls are outside its border.

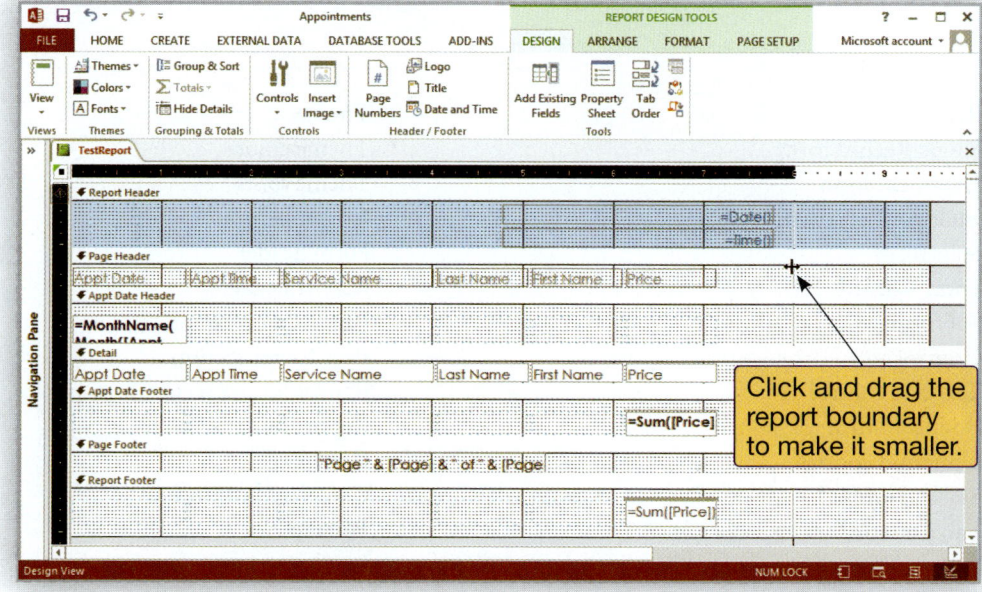

FIGURE AC 3.45

Another way to fix this problem is to allow Access to remove the excess space for you.

1. The green triangle in the report selector box at the upper left corner of the report indicates that there may be a problem. Click it to display the Smart Tag.
2. Hover the mouse pointer over the Smart Tag at the upper right corner of the report to see a description of the problem.
3. Click the **Smart Tag** to see the list of possible solutions.
4. Select **Remove Extra Report Space**.

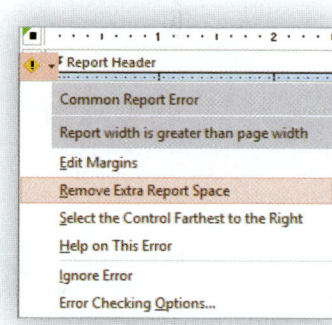

FIGURE AC 3.46

another method

The *Page Setup* tab is also available from Layout view and Design view, but it is best to adjust print settings from Print Preview view.

let me try

If the database is not already open, open the data file **AC3-Appointments** and try this skill on your own:

1. If necessary, open the *TestReport* report in Print Preview view.
2. Change the orientation so the report page is wider than it is tall.
3. Change back to **Portrait** orientation.
4. Change the margins setting to the **Narrow** option.
5. Save and close the report.

skill 3.20   Controlling the Page Setup of a Report for Printing

key terms

Record source
Single Record form
Datasheet form
Multiple Items form
Split form
Form Wizard
Subform
Control
Text box control
Bound control
Unbound control
Stacked layout
Label control
Report Wizard
Tabular layout

Theme
Theme colors
Theme fonts
Control layout
Form header
Report header
Page header section
Page footer section
Report header section
Report footer section
Grouping
Calculated control
Portrait
Landscape
Margins

concepts review

1. A _____ combines the convenience of a continuous Datasheet form with the usability of a Single Record form displaying one record at a time.
   a. Split form
   b. Datasheet form
   c. Multiple Items form
   d. Subform

2. A _____ is a form within a form that displays records related to the record in the main form.
   a. Split form
   b. Datasheet form
   c. Multiple Items form
   d. Subform

3. A _____ text control displays data from a field.
   a. label
   b. bound
   c. unbound
   d. calculated

4. Click and drag fields from the _____ to add controls to a blank report.
   a. *Property Sheet*
   b. *Field List* pane
   c. *Report Wizard*
   d. none of the above

5. Which of these design elements is not available in forms?
   a. Logo
   b. Date/Time
   c. Title
   d. Page Numbers
6. Page numbers can only be added to a footer section.
   a. True
   b. False
7. A stacked layout places labels across the top, with columns of data (similar to a datasheet or a spreadsheet).
   a. True
   b. False
8. An unbound text box control that contains an expression (formula) is called a(n) _____ control.
   a. calculated
   b. bound
   c. unbound
   d. label
9. Grand totals in a report are added to the _____.
   a. page footer section
   b. report footer section
   c. group footer section
   d. group header section
10. To change the direction a report prints on the page, change the page _____.
    a. margins
    b. orientation
    c. zoom
    d. layout

projects

Data files for projects can be found on
www.mhhe.com/office2013skills

skill review 3.1

In this project, you will continue to work with the Computer Science department database from the *Chapter 2, Skill Review 2.1*. It uses Access to manage employees and various items that are loaned to students and faculty. You will create a variety of forms for entering employee, loan, and item information.

Skills needed to complete this project:
- Creating a Single Record Form Based on a Table or Query (Skill 3.1)
- Creating a Multiple Items Form (Skill 3.2)
- Creating a Split Form (Skill 3.3)
- Creating a Form Using the Form Wizard (Skill 3.4)
- Applying a Theme (Skill 3.12)
- Creating a New Blank Form (Skill 3.5)
- Adding Fields to a Form in Layout View (Skill 3.6)
- Resizing Controls (Skill 3.13)
- Formatting Controls (Skill 3.11)
- Adding Design Elements to Form and Report Headers (Skill 3.15)

1. Open the start file **AC2013-SkillReview-3-1**.
2. If necessary, enable active content by clicking the **Enable Content** button in the Message Bar.
3. Save a copy of the file to work on named:
   `[your initials]AC-SkillReview-3-1`
4. If necessary, enable active content again.
5. Create a Single Record form using the *Employees* table as the record source.
   a. In the Navigation Pane, select the **Employees** table.
   b. On the **Create** tab, in the *Forms* group, click the **Form** button.
   c. Save the form with the name: `EmployeesForm`
   d. Close the form
6. Create a Multiple Items form using the *Employees* table as the record source.
   a. In the Navigation Pane, select the **Employees** table.
   b. On the **Create** tab, in the *Forms* group, click the **More Forms** button and select **Multiple Items** from the list.
   c. Save the form with the name: `EmployeesFormMulti`
   d. Close the form.
7. Create a Split form using the *Employees* table as the record source.
   a. In the Navigation Pane, select the **Employees** table.
   b. On the **Create** tab, in the *Forms* group, click the **More Forms** button and select **Split Form** from the list.

    c. Save the form with the name: `EmployeesFormSplit`

    d. Close the form.

8. Create a form using the *Form Wizard* to show items on loan to each employee.

    a. On the *Create* tab, in the *Forms* group, click the **Form Wizard** button.

    b. In the first step of the wizard, select **Table: Employees** from the *Tables/Queries* list box.

    c. Double-click the following fields to add them to the *Selected Fields* box in this order: **EmployeeID, LastName, FirstName**

    d. Expand the *Tables/Queries* list again and select **Table: Loans.**

    e. Double-click the following fields to add them to the *Selected Fields* box below the fields from the *Employees* table: **LoanID, ItemID, LoanDate.**

    f. Click the **Next** button.

    g. Verify that the form will be organized by data in the *Employees* table as a form with a subform. Click **Next.**

    h. Click the **Datasheet** radio button to use the Datasheet layout for the subform. Click **Next.**

    i. Enter the following title in the *Form* box: `EmployeeLoansForm`

    j. Enter the following title in the *Subform* box: `EmployeeLoansSubform`

    k. Verify that the **Open the form to view or enter information** radio button is selected.

    l. Click the **Finish** button. Do not close this form.

9. Apply a theme to the form.

    a. Switch to Layout view.

    b. Click the **Form Layout Tools Design** tab if it is not already selected.

    c. In the *Themes* group, click the **Themes** button. Select the **Wisp** theme.

10. Save and close the form.

11. Create a new blank form in Layout view.

    a. On the *Create* tab, in the *Forms* group, click the **Blank Form** button.

    b. Save the form with the name: `ItemsForm`

12. Add controls to the new *ItemsForm*.

    a. If necessary, display the *Field List* pane. On the *Form Layout Tools Design* tab, in the *Tools* group, click the **Add Existing Fields** button.

    b. If necessary, click the **Show All Tables** link in the *Field List* pane.

    c. Click the + in front of *Items*.

    d. Add the *ItemID* field to the form by double-clicking **ItemID** in the *Field List* pane.

    e. Click the **ItemName** field and drag it to the form to the right of the *ItemID* control. Pay close attention to the placement guide so you drop the new controls to the right of the *ItemID* control, not below it.

    f. Click and drag the **Cost** field to the form so it is placed directly below the *ItemName* field. Make sure the label controls line up in the same column.

    g. Click and drag the **Description** field to the form so it is placed directly below the *Cost* field. Make sure the label controls line up in the same column.

13. Modify the height of the *Description* control so the entire description is visible.

    a. If necessary, click the **Description** text box control to select it.

    b. Click and drag the bottom boundary of the control downward to make the control taller.

14. Apply a font color to all the labels in the form.
    a. Click the **ItemID** label control to select it. Press Ctrl and click each of the other label controls. All the label controls should be selected.
    b. On the *Form Layout Tools Format* tab, in the *Font* group, click the **Font Color** button arrow to view the color palette, and click the theme color **Olive Green, Accent 4**.
15. Add a title to the form header.
    a. On the *Form Layout Tools Design* tab, in the *Header/Footer* group, click the **Title** button.
    b. Change the title to: `Items`
16. Save and close the form.
17. Close the database and exit Access.

skill review 3.2

In this project you will continue working with the health insurance database from *Chapter 2, Skill Review 2.2*. You will create the following reports: a report to summarize physician member information by city, an order report summarizing orders by month including the physician and procedure, and a phone contact list for the physicians.

Skills needed to complete this project:
- Creating a Basic Report Based on a Table or Query (Skill 3.7)
- Resizing Controls (Skill 3.13)
- Moving and Arranging Controls (Skill 3.14)
- Grouping Records in a Report (Skill 3.17)
- Adding Totals to a Report (Skill 3.18)
- Formatting Controls (Skill 3.11)
- Applying a Theme (Skill 3.12)
- Previewing and Printing a Report (Skill 3.19)
- Controlling the Page Setup of a Report for Printing (Skill 3.20)
- Creating a Report Using the Report Wizard (Skill 3.8)
- Creating a New Blank Report (Skill 3.9)
- Adding Fields to a Report in Layout View (Skill 3.10)
- Adding Design Elements to Form and Report Headers (Skill 3.15)
- Adding Page Numbers to Reports (Skill 3.16)

1. Open the start file **AC2013-SkillReview-3-2**.
2. If necessary, enable active content by clicking the **Enable Content** button in the Message Bar.
3. Save a copy of the file to work on named:
   `[your initials]AC-SkillReview-3-2`
4. If necessary, enable active content again.
5. Create a basic report using the *Physicians* table as the data source.
   a. In the Navigation Pane, select the **Physicians** table.
   b. On the *Create* tab, in the *Reports* group, click the **Report** button.
   c. Save the report with the name: `PhysiciansReport`

6. Adjust the column widths to fit the data.
   a. The *PhysciansReport* should still be open in Layout view.
   b. Click anywhere in the **PhysicianID** column.
   c. Click and drag the right boundary of the control to the left to make the control smaller.
   d. Repeat this procedure with all the columns in the report. When you are finished, the page break should appear between the *City* and *ZipCode* fields. You should still be able to read the labels and all values in the table clearly.
7. Move the *City* column so it appears first in the report.
   a. Click the **City** label at the top of the column. On the *Report Layout Tools Arrange* tab, in the *Rows & Columns* group, click the **Select Column** button.
   b. Move the mouse pointer over the column. When the mouse pointer changes to the move shape, click and drag the entire column to the left. Release the mouse button when the I-bar move indicator appears at the very left side of the report.
8. Add grouping to the report by values in the *City* field.
   a. On the *Report Layout Tools Design* tab, in the *Grouping & Totals* group, click the **Group & Sort** button.
   b. In the *Group, Sort, & Total* pane at the bottom of the report, click **Add a Group,** and then click **City.**
9. Add totals to the report to calculate the total number of members. Calculate totals for each group as well as a grand total for the entire report.
   a. Click any **MemberCount** value.
   b. On the *Report Layout Tools Design* tab, in the *Grouping & Totals* group, click the **Totals** button, and click **Sum.**
10. Adjust the height of the controls displaying the totals.
    a. Click any of the controls displaying the total in one of the group footers.
    b. Drag the bottom boundary down so the entire number is visible.
    c. Scroll to the very bottom of the report.
    d. Click the grand total control immediately above the page number.
    e. Drag the bottom boundary down so the entire number is visible.
11. Apply bold formatting to all the total controls.
    a. Verify that the grand total control is still selected.
    b. Press `Ctrl` and click any of the group total controls.
    c. On the *Report Layout Tools Format* tab, in the *Font* group, click the **Bold** button.
12. Move the page number control so it is centered in the page footer section.
    a. If necessary, scroll to the bottom of the report so you can see the page number control in the page footer section.
    b. Click the control and drag it to the left so it is below the *Address* field. Be careful not to move the page number control out of the page footer section.
13. Apply a theme to the report. On the *Report Layout Tools Design* tab, in the *Themes* group, click the **Themes** button, and select **Integral.**
14. Adjust the layout settings so the report will print no more than one page wide.
    a. Switch to Print Preview view by right-clicking the report tab and selecting **Print Preview.**
    b. In the *Zoom* group, click the **More Pages** button and click **Four Pages** so you can preview the entire report at once.

c. Observe that in Portrait orientation, the report will print across two pages wide.

d. In the *Page Layout* group, click the **Landscape** button.

e. If the report is still more than one page wide, return to Layout view and repeat step 5 to further adjust the width of the columns until the entire report fits on two pages—one page wide and two pages tall.

f. If you receive a warning that the section width is greater than the page width and the report may print with blank pages, switch to Design view. Click the **Smart Tag** in the upper left corner of the report, and select **Remove Extra Report Space**. Switch back to Print Preview view and verify that this solved the problem.

15. Save and close the report.

16. Use the *Report Wizard* to create a report combining information from the *Orders, Physicians,* and *Procedures* tables.

    a. On the *Create* tab, in the *Reports* group, click the **Report Wizard.**

    b. Expand the **Tables/Queries** list, and select **Table: Orders.**

    c. Double-click the following fields to add them to the *Selected Fields* list in this order: **OrderID** and **OrderDate**

    d. Expand the **Tables/Queries** list again, and select **Table: Physicians.**

    e. Double-click the following fields to add them to the *Selected Fields* list in this order: **LastName** and **FirstName**

    f. Expand the **Tables/Queries** list, and select **Table: Procedures.**

    g. Double-click the **ProcedureName** field to add it to the *Selected Fields* list.

    h. Click the **Next** button to continue to the next step of the *Report Wizard.*

    i. Verify that **by Orders** is selected in the *How do you want to view your data?* box. Click **Next.**

    j. Add grouping by order date. Click **OrderDate** in the *Do you want any grouping levels?* box. Observe that Access will group the orders by month Click **Next.**

    k. Sort the records in the report by the procedure name. Next to the number **1,** click the arrow and select **ProcedureName** from the list of choices. Click **Next.**

    l. Verify that the report will use the **Stepped layout** with **Portrait orientation.** Click **Next.**

    m. Enter the following name in the *What title do you want for your report?* box: `OrderDetailsReport`

    n. If necessary, click the **Preview the report.** radio button so the report will open in Print Preview view.

    o. Click **Finish.**

17. Switch to Layout view so you can make changes to the report.

18. Edit the text in the **OrderDatebyMonth** label in the report header section. Click the label control and change the text to: `Month`

19. Adjust the control widths in the report so all values are visible.

    a. Click the **ProcedureName** label control. Press (Ctrl) and click any value in the column. Click and drag the **right** column border to the **left** to make the column slightly smaller.

    b. Click the **OrderID** label control. Press (Ctrl) and click any value in the column. Click and drag the **left** column border to the **left** to make the column slightly wider so the text in the label control is visible.

c. Click the **LastName** label control. Press Ctrl and click any value in the column. Click and drag the **left** column border to the **right** to make the column slightly smaller.

d. Click the **Order Date** label control. Press Ctrl and click any value in the column. Click and drag the **right** column border to the **right** to make the column slightly wider so the dates are visible.

20. Save and close the report.
21. Create a new blank report and add controls to it.
    a. On the *Create* tab, in the *Reports* group, click the **Blank Report** button.
    b. If necessary, on the *Report Layout Tools Design* tab, in the *Tools* group, click the **Add Existing Fields** button to display the *Field List* pane.
    c. In the *Field List* pane, if necessary, click the **Show all** tables link and then click the + button to expand the *Physicians* table.
    d. Double-click the following fields from the *Physicians* table in order to add them to the report in this order: **LastName, FirstName, Phone**
    e. Adjust column widths as necessary.
    f. Save the report with the name: `PhoneListReport`
22. Add a logo to the report header.
    a. On the *Report Layout Tools Design* tab, in the *Header/Footer* group, click the **Logo** button.
    b. In the *Insert Picture* dialog, navigate to the data files location for this project.
    c. Double-click the **CaduseusLogo** image file.
23. Add a title to the report header.
    a. On the *Report Layout Tools Design* tab, in the *Header/Footer* group, click the **Title** button.
    b. Type: `Phone List`
    c. Press Enter.
24. Add page numbers centered in the report page footer.
    a. On the *Report Layout Tools Design* tab, in the *Header/Footer* group, click the **Page Numbers** button.
    b. In the *Page Numbers* dialog, verify that the **Page N** radio button is selected.
    c. Click the **Bottom of Page [Footer]** radio button.
    d. Verify that **Center** is selected from the *Alignment* drop-down list.
    e. Verify that the **Show Number on First Page** check box is checked.
    f. Click **OK**.
25. Save and close the report.
26. Close the database and exit Access.

challenge yourself 3.3

In this project you will continue working with the greenhouse database from *Chapter 2, Challenge Yourself 2.3*. You will create a variety of forms for entering plant and maintenance information.

Skills needed to complete this project:
- Creating a Single Record Form Based on a Table or Query (Skill 3.1)
- Moving and Arranging Controls (Skill 3.14)
- Creating a Multiple Items Form (Skill 3.2)
- Creating a Split Form (Skill 3.3)
- Adding Fields to a Form in Layout View (Skill 3.6)
- Creating a Form Using the Form Wizard (Skill 3.4)
- Creating a New Blank Form (Skill 3.5)
- Resizing Controls (Skill 3.13)
- Applying a Theme (Skill 3.12)
- Formatting Controls (Skill 3.11)
- Adding Design Elements to Form and Report Headers (Skill 3.15)

1. Open the start file **AC2013-ChallengeYourself-3-3**.
2. If necessary, enable active content by clicking the **Enable Content** button in the Message Bar.
3. Save a copy of the file to work on named:
   `[your initials]AC-ChallengeYourself-3-3`
4. If necessary, enable active content again.
5. Create a **Single Record form** using the *Plants* table as the record source. Save the form with the name: `PlantsForm`
   a. Move the **DatePlanted** field so it is located directly above the *PurchasePrice* field.
   b. Save and close the form.
6. Create a **Multiple Items Form** using the *Plants* table as the record source. Save the form with the name `PlantsFormMulti` and close it.
7. Create a **Split Form** using the *MaintenanceLog* table as the record source. Save it with the name: `MaintenanceLogFormSplit`
   a. Add the **FirstName** field from the **Employees** table to just below the *EmployeeID* field in the form.
   b. Add the **LastName** field from the **Employees** table to just below the *FirstName* field in the form.
   c. Save and close the form.
8. Use the **Form Wizard** button to create a form showing employee information in the main form with a subform showing related maintenance records.
   a. Add the following fields to the form in this order:
      From the *Employees* table: **EmployeeID, LastName, FirstName, WeeklyHours**
      From the *MaintenanceLog* table: **Date_Time, PlantID, Watered, Inspected, Pruned**
   b. Organize the form by the *Employees* table with data from the *MaintenanceLog* table as a subform.

c. Format the subform as a Datasheet form.

   d. Name the main form: `EmployeeWorkLogForm`

   e. Name the subform: `WorkLogSubform`

   f. Review the form in Form view, and then close it.

9. Create a form from scratch.

   a. Start with a new blank form in Layout view. Save the form with the name: `MaintenanceTrackingForm`

   b. Add the following fields from the *MaintenanceLog* table to the form in this order: **Date_Time, EmployeeID, PlantID, Watered**

   c. Change the **Date_Time** label to: `Date`

   d. If necessary, adjust the width of the labels so all the text is visible.

   e. Add the **Inspected** field to the right of the *Watered* control.

   f. Add the **Pruned** field to the right of the *Inspected* control.

   g. Add the **LastName** field from the *Employees* table to the right of the *EmployeeID* control.

   h. Add the **FirstName** field from the *Employees* table to the right of the *LastName* control

   i. Add the **CommonName** field from the *Plants* table to the right of the *PlantID* field.

   j. If necessary, adjust the width of the labels so all the text is visible.

10. Format the form.

    a. Apply the **Facet** theme to the form.

    b. Change the font color for all the label controls to the theme color **Dark Green, Accent 2.**

    c. Modify the **Date_Time bound text box control** to use the **Long Date** format.

    d. Add the title `Maintenance Log` to the form header.

11. Save the form and close it.

12. Close the database and exit Access.

challenge yourself 3.4

In this project you will continue working with the vaccines database from *Chapter 2, Challenge Yourself 2.4.* You will create an inventory report and reports to summarize shipments by country and by target audience. Complete the steps below to create and modify these objects.

Skills needed to complete this project:

- Creating a Basic Report Based on a Table or Query (Skill 3.7)
- Resizing Controls (Skill 3.13)
- Moving and Arranging Controls (Skill 3.14)
- Adding Totals to a Report (Skill 3.18)
- Formatting Controls (Skill 3.11)
- Creating a Report Using the Report Wizard (Skill 3.8)
- Creating a New Blank Report (Skill 3.9)
- Adding Fields to a Report in Layout View (Skill 3.10)
- Grouping Records in a Report (Skill 3.17)

- Adding Design Elements to Form and Report Headers (Skill 3.15)
- Adding Page Numbers to Reports (Skill 3.16)
- Applying a Theme (Skill 3.12)
- Previewing and Printing a Report (Skill 3.19)

1. Open the start file **AC2013-ChallengeYourself-3-4**.
2. If necessary, enable active content by clicking the **Enable Content** button in the Message Bar.
3. Save a copy of the file to work on named:
   `[your initials]AC-ChallengeYourself-3-4`
4. If necessary, enable active content again.
5. Create a basic report using the *Vaccines* table as the data source.
   a. Save the report with the name: `InventoryReport`
   b. Adjust the width of the **VaccineID** column so it is just wide enough to display the column label.
   c. Move the page number control in the page footer section so it is centered below the *VaccineName* and *TargetAudience* columns. Be sure to keep the control in the page footer section.
   d. Add a total to the **Inventory** field to calculate the sum of the inventory on hand for all vaccines.
   e. Apply the **Comma** number format to the total control.
   f. If necessary, adjust the height of the total control so the number does not appear cut-off.
   g. Save and close the report.
6. Use the *Report Wizard* to create a report summarizing the vaccine shipments to each country.
   a. Include these fields in the report:
      From the *Shipments* table: **ShipmentID, DateShipped, Quantity**
      From the *Locations* table: **Country**
      From the *Vaccines* table: **VaccineName**
   b. Organize the report data by location.
   c. For each country, group the data by **DateShipped** by month.
   d. Sort the detail records first by **DateShipped,** and then by **VaccineName.**
   e. Use the **Stepped** layout and **Landscape** orientation.
   f. Name the report: `ShipmentsByCountryReport`
   g. Open the report in Print Preview view when the wizard is finished.
   h. Switch to Layout view.
   i. Move the **ShipmentID** column so it appears after the **DateShipped by Month** column.
   j. Modify the column widths so all the data are visible. Use any method you want. Ensure that the labels are completely visible.
   k. Save and close the report.
7. Create a new blank report in Layout view. Save the report with the name: `ShipmentsByAudience`
   a. Add the following controls in this order:
      From the *Vaccines* table: **TargetAudience, VaccineName**
      From the *Shipments* table: **ShipmentID, Quantity, Cost**

    b. Increase the width of the **TargetAudience** column so the data in the detail section do not wrap.

    c. Increase the width of the **VaccineName** column so the data in the detail section do not wrap.

    d. Add grouping by the **TargetAudience** field.

    e. Add totals to calculate the total quantity and cost for each group. Include a grand total at the end of the report in the report footer.

    f. Add bold formatting to the total controls. Don't forget to include the grand total in the report footer.

    g. Add a logo to the report header. Use the image file **GlobeLogo** included with the data files for this project.

    h. Add the title `Shipments by Target Audience` to the report header.

    i. Add the date to the report header. Use the format similar to **03-Mar-13**. Do not include the time.

    j. Add page numbers centered in the page footer. Use the format **Page N of M**. Ensure that the page number will be included on the first page of the report.

    k. Apply the **Ion** theme to the report.

    l. Preview the report and ensure that it will print on one page.

    m. Save and close the report.

8. Close the database and exit Access.

on your own 3.5

In this project, you will continue working with the movie database from *Chapter 2, On Your Own 2.5*. You will create forms to enter new movies and loans. You will also create reports to keep a printed record of current loans. Save your changes often as you work through the project.

Skills needed to complete this project:

- Creating a Single Record Form Based on a Table or Query (Skill 3.1)
- Creating a Multiple Items Form (Skill 3.2)
- Creating a Split Form (Skill 3.3)
- Creating a Form Using the Form Wizard (Skill 3.4)
- Creating a New Blank Form (Skill 3.5)
- Adding Fields to a Form in Layout View (Skill 3.6)
- Resizing Controls (Skill 3.13)
- Moving and Arranging Controls (Skill 3.14)
- Applying a Theme (Skill 3.12)
- Formatting Controls (Skill 3.11)
- Adding Design Elements to Form and Report Headers (Skill 3.15)
- Creating a Basic Report Based on a Table or Query (Skill 3.7)
- Creating a Report Using the Report Wizard (Skill 3.8)
- Creating a New Blank Report (Skill 3.9)
- Adding Fields to a Report in Layout View (Skill 3.10)
- Grouping Records in a Report (Skill 3.17)
- Adding Totals to a Report (Skill 3.18)
- Previewing and Printing a Report (Skill 3.19)
- Controlling the Page Setup of a Report for Printing (Skill 3.20)

1. Open the start file **AC2013-OnYourOwn-3-5**.
2. If necessary, enable active content by clicking the **Enable Content** button in the Message Bar.
3. Save a copy of the file to work on named:
   `[your initials]AC-OnYourOwn-3-5`
4. If necessary, enable active content again.
5. Create three forms: a Single Record form, a Multiple Items form, and a Split form. Use any table you want as the record source for each form.
6. Use the *Report Wizard* to create a form with all the fields from the *Movies* table and a subform displaying all the fields from the *Loans* table.
7. Create a new form in Layout view to use to enter new movie loans. Include any fields you want to create a form that will be easy to use. Resize controls as necessary. Apply a theme to the form. Apply formatting to the label controls so they stand out from the rest of the form. Be sure to add a form title.
8. Create a basic report using the *Borrowers* table as the record source.
9. Use the *Report Wizard* to create a report to summarize loans. At a minimum, include the movie title, borrower, date loaned, and date returned. Organize the report by borrower name. Resize and move controls as necessary. Preview how the report will look when printed and adjust the margins or orientation as you feel necessary.
10. Create another report starting from scratch in Layout view. Use this report to summarize the movie inventory by genre. Calculate the total value of the movies in each genre as well as the total value of all the movies in the collection. Resize controls as necessary. Add formatting to emphasize the labels for each group. Preview how the report will look when printed and adjust the margins or orientation as you feel necessary.
11. Close the database and exit Access.

fix it 3.6

In this project, you will continue working with the pet store database from *Chapter 2, Fix It 2.6*. Once again, the pet store employees tried to work with the database on their own, but their forms and reports need some help.

Skills needed to complete this project:

- Moving and Arranging Controls (Skill 3.14)
- Adding Fields to a Form in Layout View (Skill 3.6)
- Resizing Controls (Skill 3.13)
- Adding Design Elements to Form and Report Headers (Skill 3.15)
- Creating a Split Form (Skill 3.3)
- Adding Fields to a Report in Layout View (Skill 3.10)
- Grouping Records in a Report (Skill 3.17)
- Adding Totals to a Report (Skill 3.18)
- Formatting Controls (Skill 3.11)
- Adding Page Numbers to Reports (Skill 3.16)
- Previewing and Printing a Report (Skill 3.19)
- Controlling the Page Setup of a Report for Printing (Skill 3.20)
- Applying a Theme (Skill 3.12)

1. Open the start file **AC2013-FixIt-3-6**.
2. If necessary, enable active content by clicking the **Enable Content** button in the Message Bar.
3. Save a copy of the file to work on named: `[your initials]AC-FixIt-3-6`
4. If necessary, enable active content again.
5. Fix the *CustomersForm* as follows:
    a. Move the **LastName** controls to the right of the *FirstName* controls.
    b. Move the **ZipCode** controls to the right of the *City* controls.
    c. Move the **Phone** controls up so they are placed below the *City* controls.
    d. Add the **Newsletter** field to the form, right below the *Phone* control.
    e. Some of the label controls need to be wider. Fix them.
    f. The form is missing the store logo. Use the image file **PetShopLogo** located with the data files for this project.
    g. Save your changes.
6. Fix the *SalesForm* as follows:
    a. Move the **FirstName** controls to the right of the *SaleDate* controls, and then move the **LastName** controls so they appear below the *FirstName* controls.
    b. Move the **PhoneNumber** controls so they appear below the *LastName* controls.
    c. Add the **Breed, MainColor,** and **AgeInMonths** fields to below the *AnimalType* controls.
    d. Some of the label controls need to be wider. Fix them.
    e. The form is missing the store logo. Use the image file **PetShopLogo** located with the data files for this project.
    f. The form is also missing the title: `Sales`
    g. Save your changes.
7. The store owner would like another form for the *Sales* table—one that shows both a datasheet and a single record in one screen. Create this form for her. Name the form: `SalesFormSplit`
8. Fix the *PetsReport* as follows:
    a. The **PetID** field is missing from this report. Add it to the report so it is the first column.
    b. The report should be grouped by animal type with an average age for each group. Adjust the height of the total controls as necessary.
    c. All prices should be formatted using the **Currency** format.
    d. The report is missing the store logo. Use the image file **PetShopLogo** located with the data files for this project.
    e. The report is also missing the title: `Pet Inventory Report`
    f. The report is missing the page numbers. The page number should be centered in the page footer, and it should use the format **Page N**.
    g. Preview the report to make sure it will fit on no more than one page wide. If necessary, make the **MainColor** column narrow enough that the report will fit on one page wide without cutting off the information in the report.
    h. If necessary, switch to Design view and adjust the report width to remove the extra space.
    i. Save your changes.

9. Fix the *Sales* report as follows:
   a. Add the following fields in this order to the right of the *PetID* field.
      From the *Customers* table: **LastName, FirstName, Phone**
      From the *Pets* table: **AnimalType, Breed, Price**
   b. Adjust column widths as necessary so text does not wrap.
   c. The report should be grouped by sale date, by month.
   d. The report should include totals calculating the sum of the values in the **Price** field.
   e. The report is missing the store logo. Use the image file **PetShopLogo** located with the data files for this project.
   f. The report is also missing the title: `Detailed Sales Report`
   g. The report is missing the page numbers. The page number should be centered in the page footer, and it should use the format **Page N**.
   h. Check the report in Print Preview view. Be sure to view multiple pages at once.
   i. Switch to **Landscape** orientation so the report data fits on one page across.
   j. Now the report data fits, but the report is too wide. Switch to Design view and adjust the report width to remove the extra space.
   k. Switch back to Print Preview view to make sure you solved the problem.
   l. Save your changes.
10. The store owner would like all forms and reports to use the **Organic** theme. Apply the theme to all the forms and reports in the database. Save the changes as necessary.
11. Close any open database objects, close the database, and exit Access.

chapter 4

Using Queries and Organizing Information

In this chapter, you will learn the following skills:

- Create a simple query
- Add criteria to a query
- Organize the data in a query
- Create Unmatched and Find Duplicate queries
- Create a parameter query
- Filter and sort data in a datasheet

Skill **4.1** Using the Simple Query Wizard

Skill **4.2** Creating a Query in Design View

Skill **4.3** Adding Text Criteria to a Query

Skill **4.4** Adding Numeric and Date Criteria to a Query

Skill **4.5** Using AND and OR in a Query

Skill **4.6** Specifying the Sort Order in a Query

Skill **4.7** Hiding and Showing Fields in a Query

Skill **4.8** Adding a Calculated Field to a Query

Skill **4.9** Finding Unmatched Data Using a Query

Skill **4.10** Finding Duplicate Data Using a Query

Skill **4.11** Using a Parameter Query

Skill **4.12** Filtering Data Using AutoFilter

Skill **4.13** Filtering Data Using Filter by Selection

Skill **4.14** Sorting Records in a Datasheet

skills

introduction

This chapter shows you how to find information quickly by using queries, filters, and sorting in Access. You will learn to create a variety of select queries and add criteria. You will also use sorting and filtering techniques to organize data in Datasheet view. The *Let Me Try* exercises in this chapter use the AC4-Appointments database. You can keep the database open while you work in this chapter, opening and closing database objects as required for each *Let Me Try*.

Skill 4.1 Using the Simple Query Wizard

Queries allow you to display and manipulate a subset of data from a table. For example, a table of customer information may include many fields that you don't need on a daily basis. You can use a query to generate a more manageable list displaying just the customer first names, last names, and phone numbers.

Queries can also be used to combine data from related tables into a single database object. For example, if you want a list of appointments including the full customer name, use a query to show fields from both the *Appointments* and *Customers* tables. A query can combine data from both tables because there is a one-to-many relationship between the *Customer* field in the *Appointments* table (which stores the customer ID number) and the *Customer ID* field in the *Customers* table.

Use the Simple Query Wizard to create a simple select query. A **select query** displays data from one or more related tables or queries, based on the fields that you select.

To create a query using the *Simple Query Wizard*:

1. On the *Create* tab, in the *Queries* group, click the **Query Wizard** button.
2. In the *New Query* dialog, **Simple Query Wizard** is selected by default. Click **OK**.

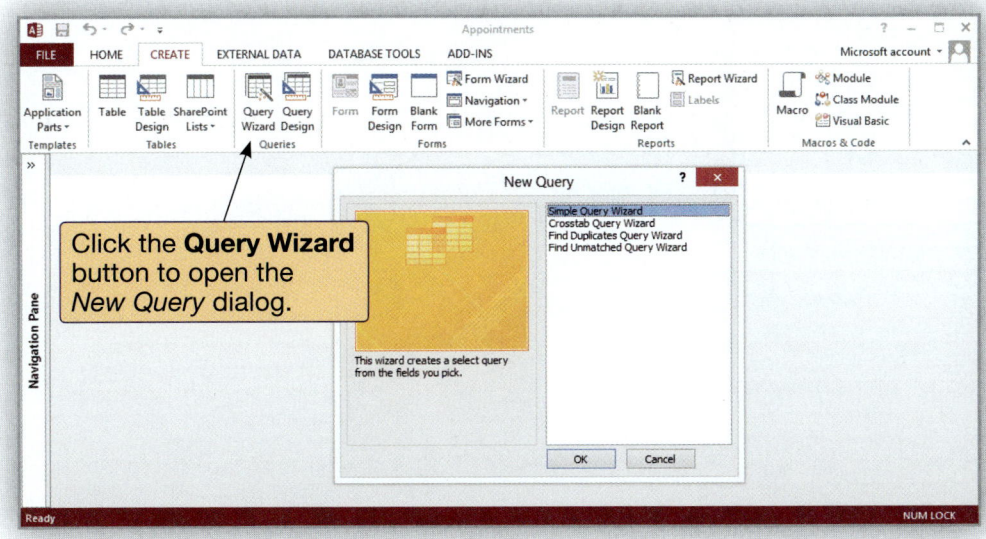

FIGURE AC 4.1

1. Click the **Tables/Queries** drop-down arrow. Click the first table or query that you want to select data from.
2. To add a field to the query, double-click the field name in the *Available Fields* list to add it to the *Selected Fields* list, or click the field name and then click the **>** button.

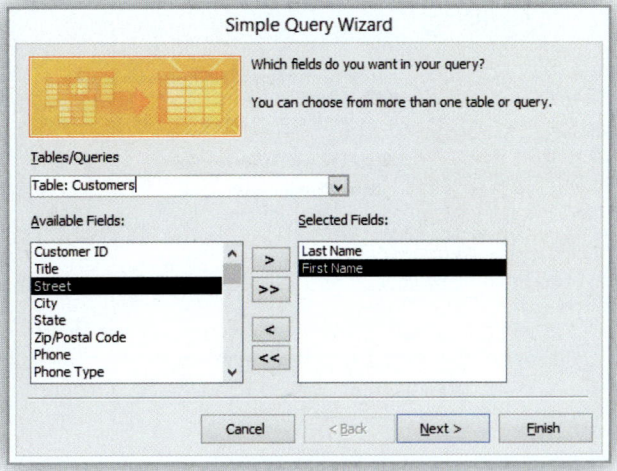

FIGURE AC 4.2

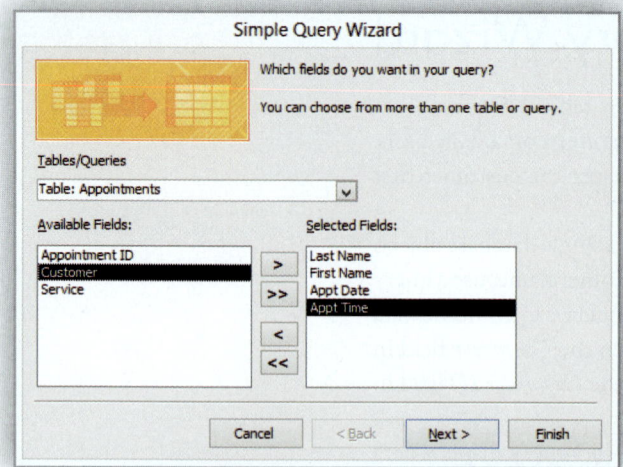

3. To add data fields from another table or query, click the **Tables/Queries** drop-down arrow again. Click the next table or query you want to select data from.
4. Add the field or fields you want to include in the query.
5. When you have added all the fields you want, click **Next**.

FIGURE AC 4.3

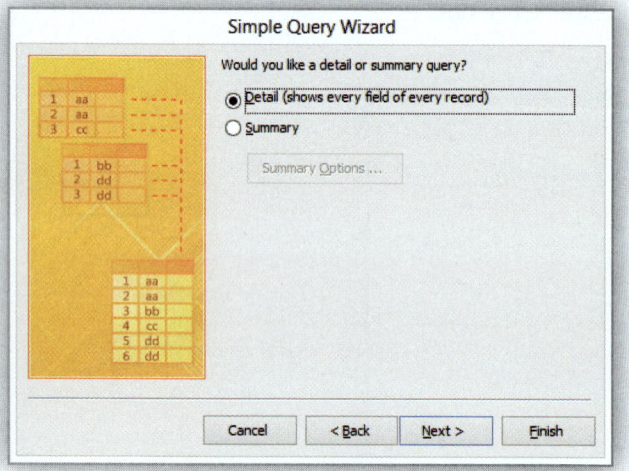

6. The radio button to create a detail query is selected by default. The detail query shows every field you selected for every record. Click **Next**.

FIGURE AC 4.4

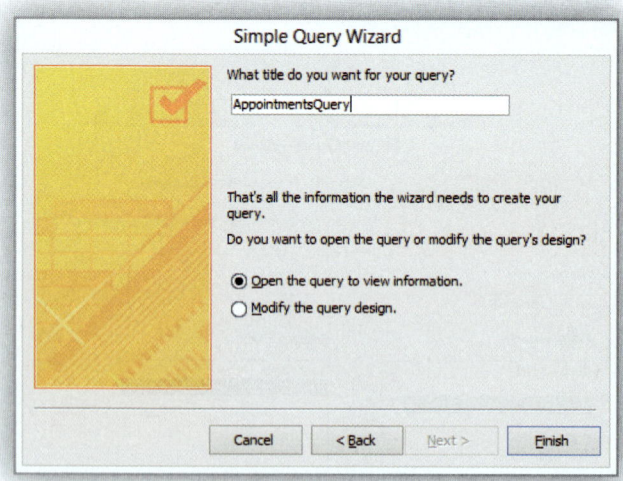

7. Give the query a meaningful title.
8. To see the results of the query immediately, verify that the **Open the query to view information.** radio button is selected.
9. Click **Finish**.

FIGURE AC 4.5

Notice that the query results datasheet looks like a table datasheet. It has the same navigation buttons at the bottom. However, the *Table Tools Fields* tab and the *Table Tools Table* tab are not available when you are viewing the query results datasheet. You cannot manipulate the structure of the underlying tables when you are viewing query results.

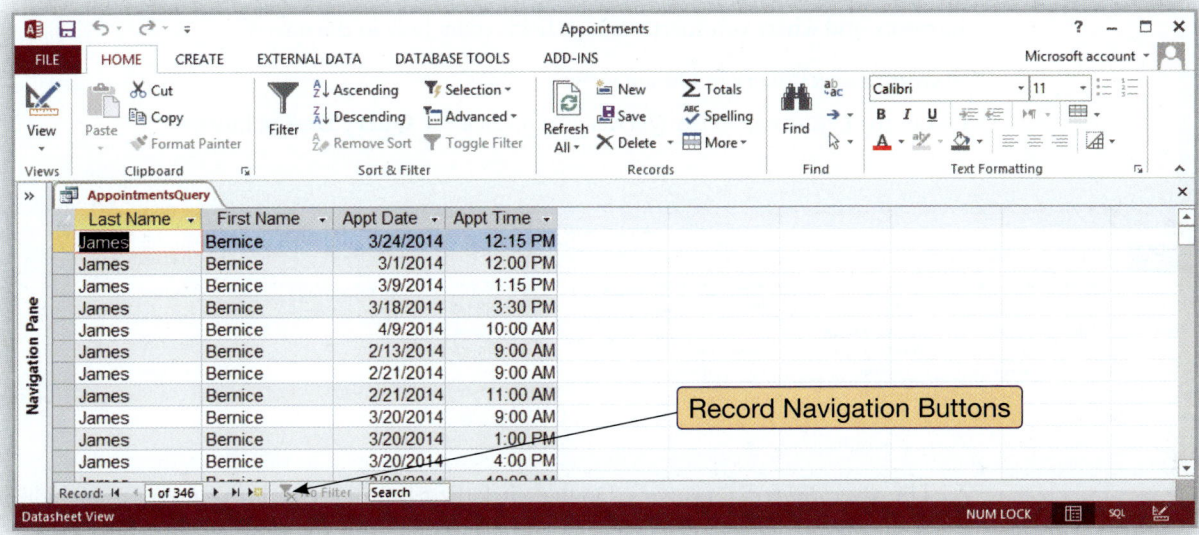

FIGURE AC 4.6
Query results

tips & tricks

You do not need to include the related primary key field and foreign key field(s) in the query.

let me try

If the database is not already open, open the data file **AC4-Appointments** and try this skill on your own:
1. Use the *Simple Query Wizard* to create a select query showing the details for every record in the results. Include these fields in this order: the **Last Name** and **First Name** fields from the *Customers* table and the **Appt Date** and **Appt Time** fields from the *Appointments* table. Select the option to open the query to view information. Use the query title: `AppointmentsQuery`
2. Review the query results, and then close the query.

skill 4.1   Using the Simple Query Wizard

Skill 4.2 Creating a Query in Design View

You can create a new query from scratch using Design view. The query Design window has two parts. The upper pane shows the tables referenced in the query. The lower pane shows the **query grid** where you specify which fields to include in the query.

To create a select query in Design view:

1. On the *Create* tab, in the *Queries* group, click the **Query Design** button.

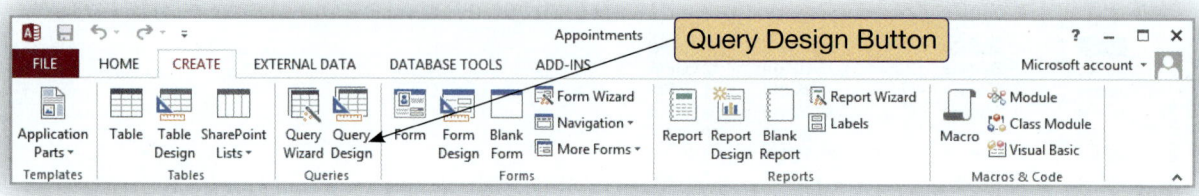

FIGURE AC 4.7

2. The *Show Table* dialog opens. Double-click the name of each table you want to include in the query (or click the table name once, and then click the **Add** button). Click the **Close** button when you have added the tables you want. You must close the *Show Table* dialog before continuing to build the query.

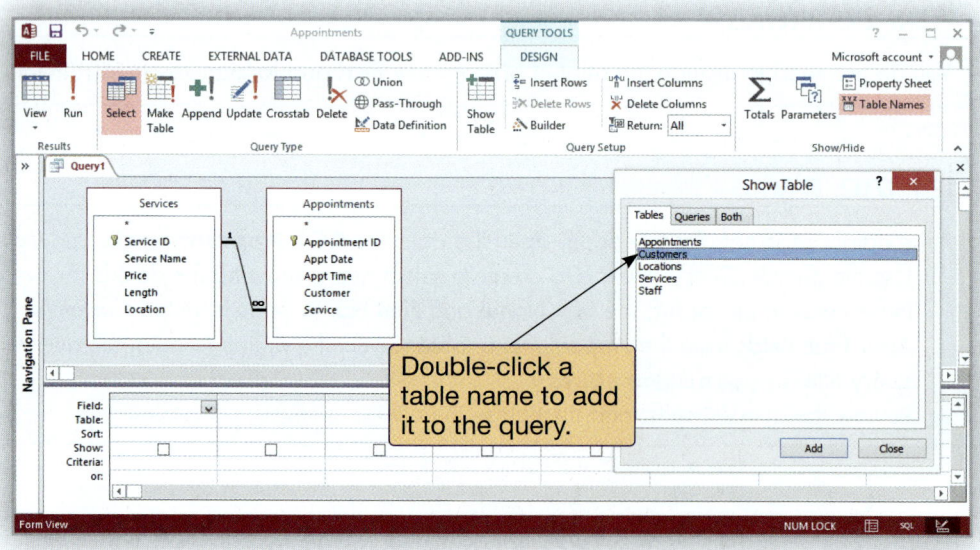

FIGURE AC 4.8

3. A complete field list for each table appears in the upper pane of the query Design window. When a relationship exists between two tables, a line connects the related fields.

    - You can adjust the relative size of the two panes in the query Design window by clicking and dragging the horizontal border just above the query grid.
    - You can adjust the size of a table box to see more fields by clicking and dragging the bottom boundary of the box downward.
    - You can rearrange the table boxes in the upper pane of the query Design window by clicking the box header and dragging the box to a new location (similar to rearranging tables in the Relationships window).

- To remove a table from the query Design window, right-click the table box header and select **Remove Table.**

4. Add fields to the query using one of these methods:
   - Double-click the field name in the field list.
   - Click the field name and drag it to the design grid.
   - Click in an empty cell in the *Field* row of the design grid, expand the list of available fields by clicking the arrow, and click the field name you want.

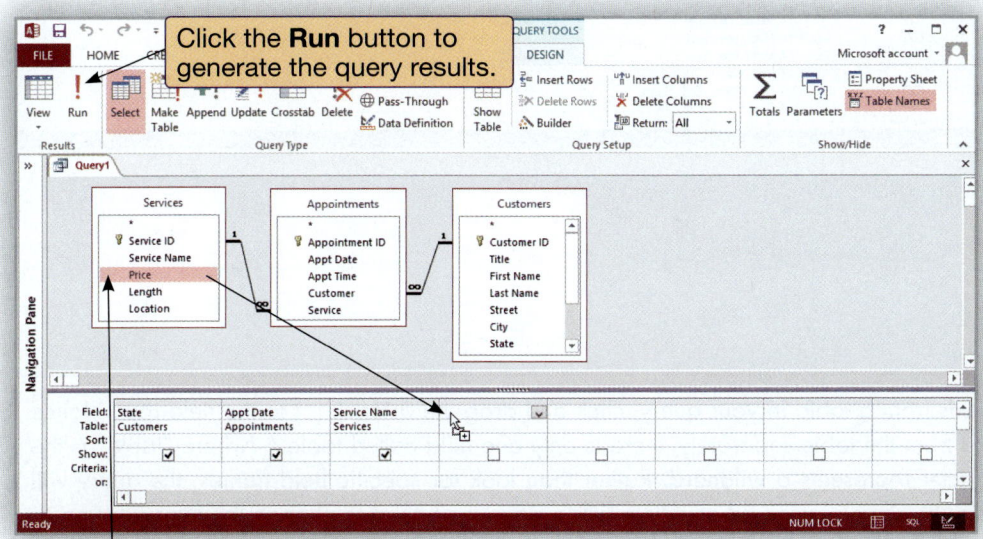

FIGURE AC 4.9

- To rearrange the order of fields in the query, move the mouse pointer to the top of the field column in the grid. When the mouse pointer changes to the ↓ shape, click to select the entire column, and then click and drag the column to the new position in the grid.
- To remove a field from the query grid, move the mouse pointer to the top of the field column in the grid. When the mouse pointer changes to the ↓ shape, click to select the entire column, and then press Delete.

5. When you have added all the fields you want, run the query by clicking the **Run** button near the left side of the Ribbon (on the *Query Tools Design* tab, in the *Results* group).

6. If you want to use the query again in the future, be sure to save the query, giving it a meaningful name.

skill 4.2   Creating a Query in Design View

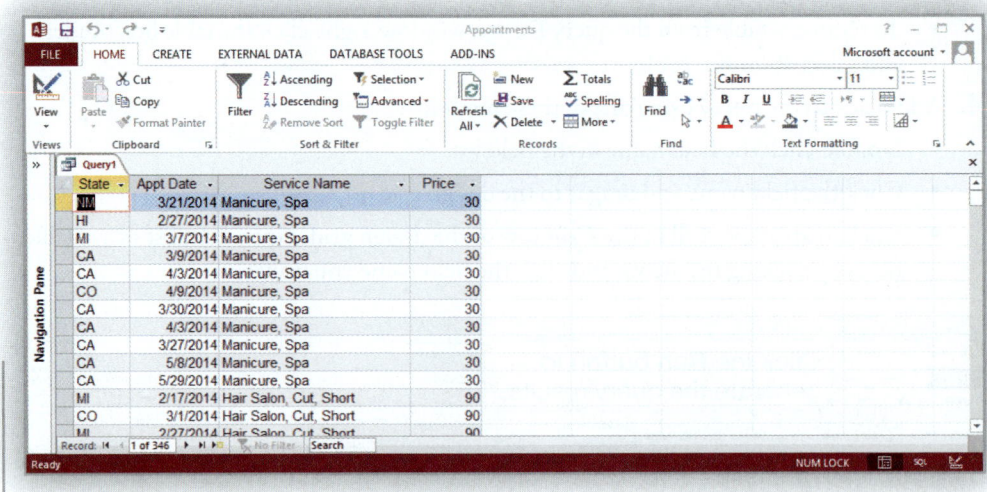

FIGURE AC 4.10
Query results showing fields from the *Customers*, *Appointments*, and *Services* tables

tips & tricks

If you want to include all the fields from a table in your query, click and drag the asterisk (*) to the field row. Notice that rather than listing each field from the table separately, there is only one field called table.* (where "table" is the name of the table). The * character represents a wildcard. Rather than look for specific field names, the query will look for all the fields in that table. So, if you later add or delete fields, you won't need to change the query design.

another method

You can also view the results of a query by switching to Datasheet view using one of these methods:
- On the *Query Tools Design* tab, in the *Results* group, click the **View** button.
- Click the **View** button arrow, and select **Datasheet View.**
- Right-click the query tab, and select **Datasheet View.**
- Click the **Datasheet View** button in the status bar.

tell me more

To display the *Show Table* dialog again to add other tables to the query, on the *Query Tools Design* tab, in the *Query Setup* group, click the **Show Table** button.

let me try

If the database is not already open, open the data file **AC4-Appointments** and try this skill on your own:
1. Begin a new query in Design view.
2. Add these tables: **Services, Appointments,** and **Customers.**
3. If necessary, adjust the size of the **Customers** table box so you can see the *State* field.
4. Add these fields to the query grid, in this order: **State** from the *Customers* table, **Appt Date** from the *Appointments* table, and **Service Name** and **Price** from the *Services* table.
5. Run the query.
6. Save the query with the name: `ServicesByStateQuery`

Skill 4.3 Adding Text Criteria to a Query

You can refine a select query in Design view so it shows only records that meet specific criteria. **Criteria** are conditions that the records must meet in order to be included in the query results. Each field data type takes a certain type of **criterion**. Text criteria are used for text and hyperlink fields.

To add text criteria to your query:

1. Open the query in Design view.
2. In the *Criteria* row, enter the text you want to match in the column for the appropriate field. For example, to include only records where the state is Colorado, enter the text criterion **"CO"** in the *Criteria* row under the *State* field. If you do not include the quotation marks when you enter text in the *Criteria* row, Access will place the text in quotation marks for you.
3. Run the query to see the results.

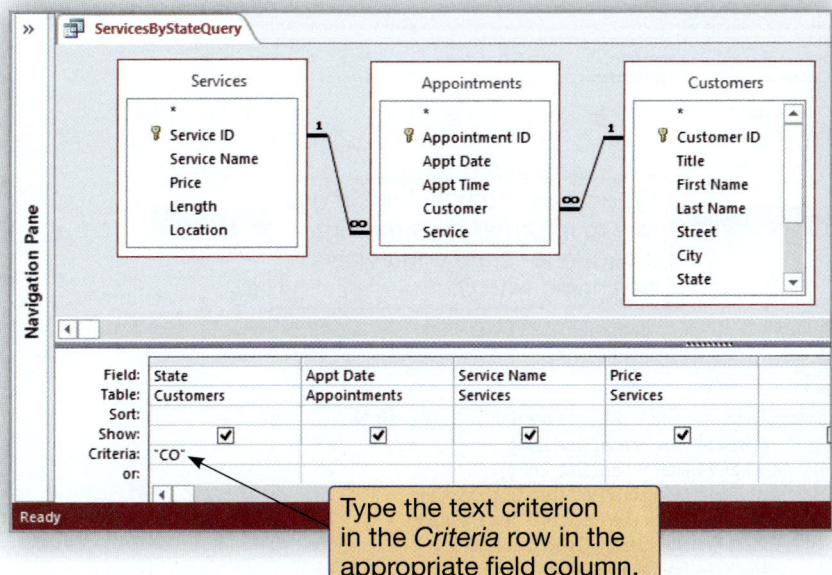

FIGURE AC 4.11

FIGURE AC 4.12

You can use the **wildcard** characters asterisk (*) and question mark (?) and the "like" construction in the query criteria to find inexact text matches. The * wildcard replaces any string of characters. The ? wildcard replaces a single character.

To include all records where the data in the *State* field begins with the letter C followed by one unknown letter, enter the criterion `Like "C?"`. The query in Figure AC 4.13 will return records for CA and CO. (There are no customers from CT in this database.)

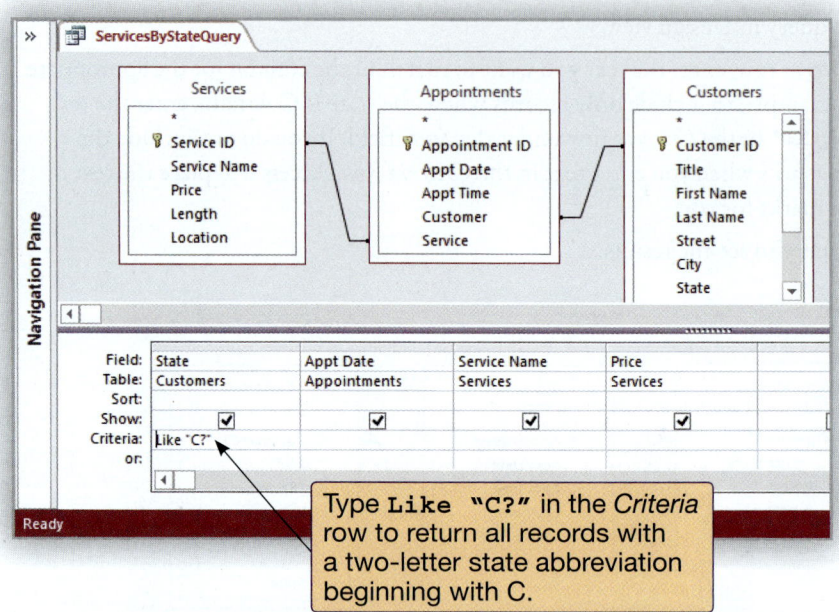

FIGURE AC 4.13

Type `Like "C?"` in the *Criteria* row to return all records with a two-letter state abbreviation beginning with C.

FIGURE AC 4.14

The query results now include records with both CO and CA in the *State* field.

Use the * wildcard instead of the ? wildcard if you're not sure of the exact number of characters you're looking for. The query in Figure AC 4.15 will return records where the data in the *State* field begins with the letter C—including CA, California, CO, and Colorado.

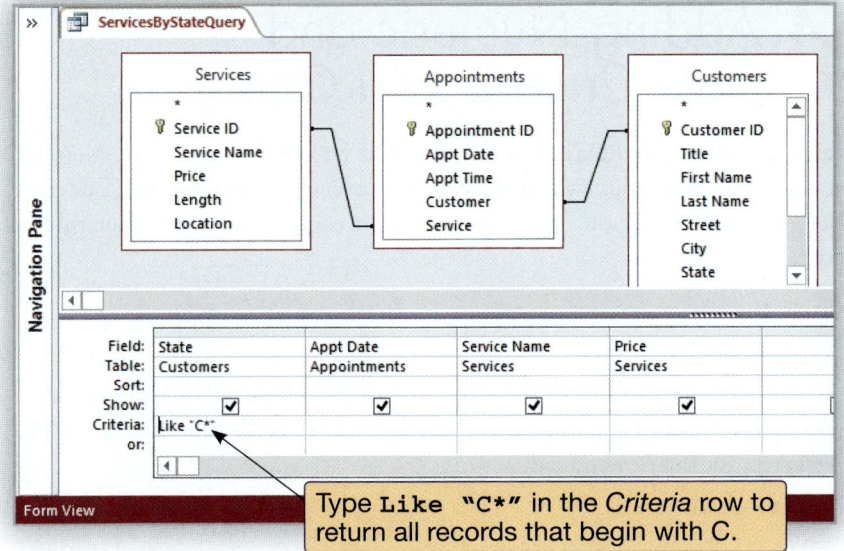

FIGURE AC 4.15

tips & tricks

When you begin typing in the criteria cell, Access may display a list of possible functions you could use if you were building an expression. This can be annoying if you're trying to enter text criteria instead. To prevent this, type the text criteria within quotation marks.

tell me more

Wildcard characters are not limited to the beginning of a text string. You can place them at the end or at both the beginning and end of the text.

- The criteria construction `Like "*Spa"` will find all records with data that end with the letters "Spa".
- The criteria construction `Like "*Spa*"` will find all records with the letters "Spa" anywhere within the data.
- The criteria construction `Not Like "*Spa*"` will find all records with data that do not include "Spa" anywhere within the text string.

let me try

If the database is not already open, open the data file **AC4-Appointments** and try this skill on your own:

1. If necessary, open the *ServicesByStateQuery* query in Design view. If your database does not include this query, create it following the steps in *Skill 4.2: Creating a Query in Design View*.
2. Add a criterion to the query so the results will include only records where the value of the *State* field is equal to the text CO.
3. Run the query and review the results.
4. Return to Design view and modify the query so the results will include any record where the value of the *State* field begins with the letter C.
5. Run the query and review the results.
6. Save and close the query.

skill 4.3 Adding Text Criteria to a Query

Skill 4.4 Adding Numeric and Date Criteria to a Query

Criteria are not limited to text fields. You can also add criteria to fields with Number, Currency, or Date/Time data types. When entering numeric or date criteria, you can enter values for exact matches, or you can enter an expression using comparison operators to broaden the criteria.

To add numeric or date criteria to your query:

1. Open the query in Design view.
2. In the *Criteria* row, enter the value or the expression in the column for the appropriate field. For example, to find all appointments that are longer than 75 minutes, enter **>75** in the *Criteria* row for the *Length* field.
3. Run the query to see the results.

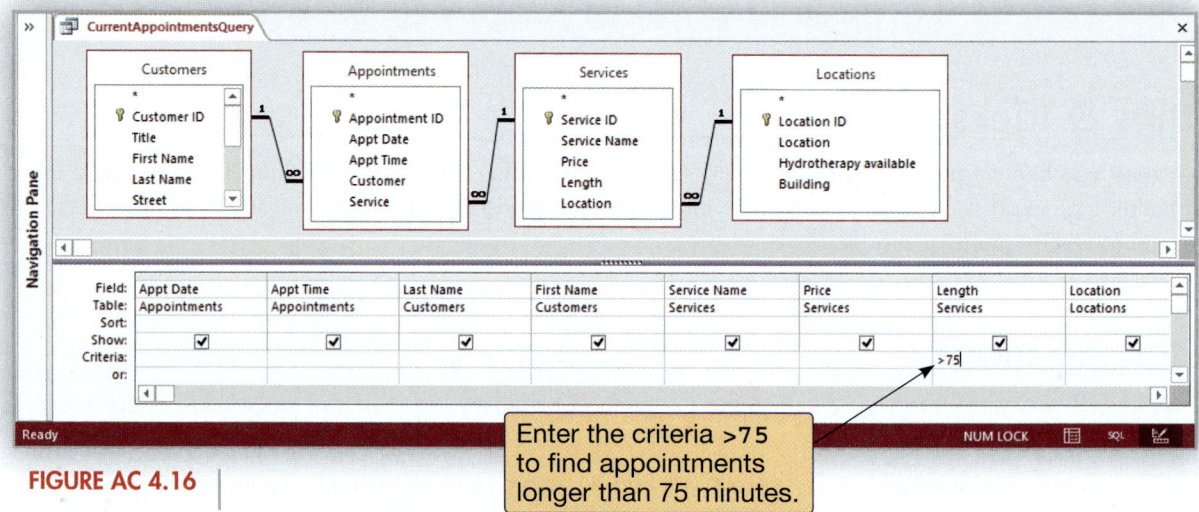

FIGURE AC 4.16

FIGURE AC 4.17

You can also use comparison operators with dates. To find all appointments that are scheduled for January 1, 2014 or later, enter the criterion **>=1/1/2014** in the *Criteria* row for the *Appt Date* field. When you enter dates in the *Criteria* row, Access places # symbols around the date. It is not necessary to type the # symbols yourself.

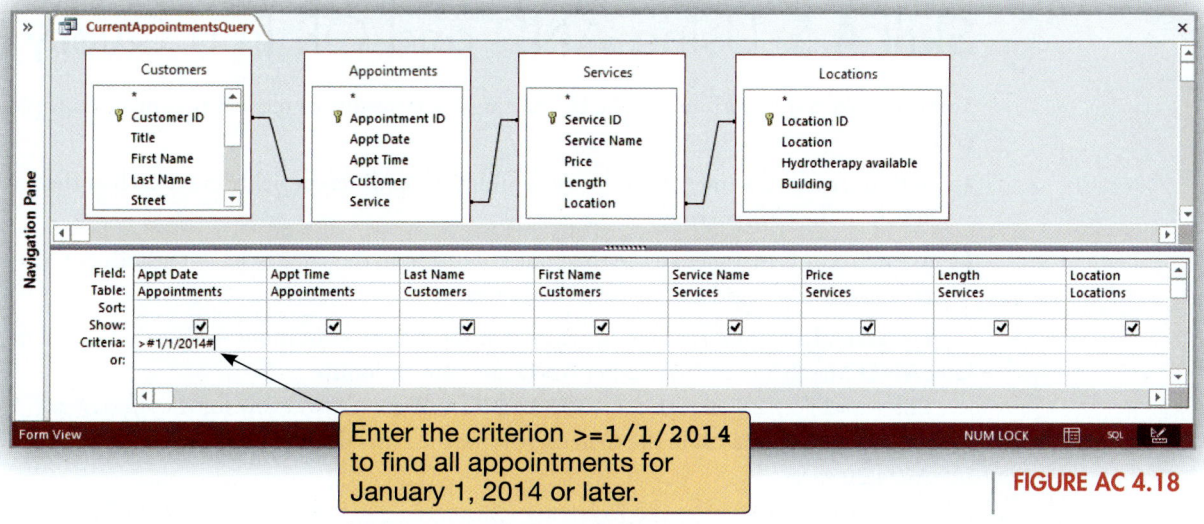

Enter the criterion >=1/1/2014 to find all appointments for January 1, 2014 or later.

FIGURE AC 4.18

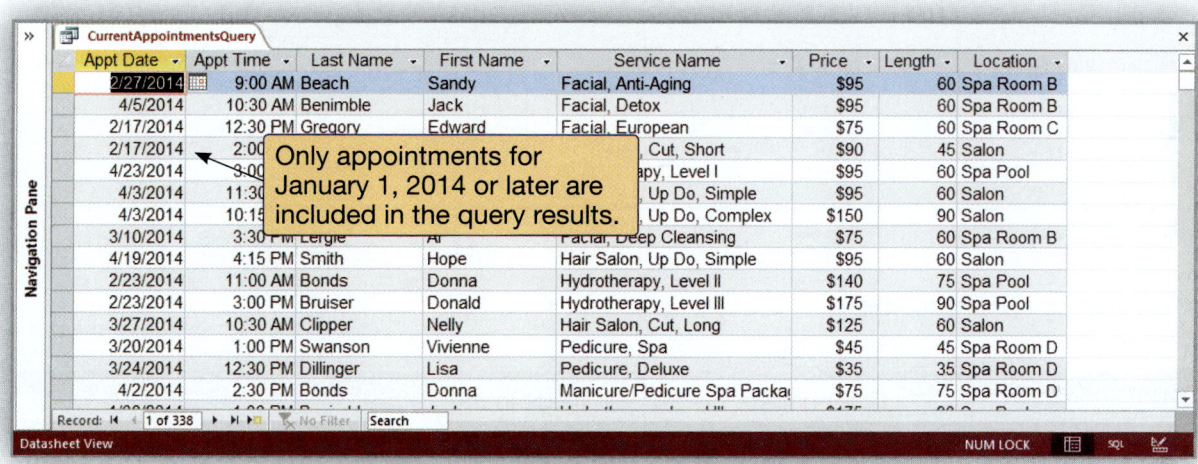

Only appointments for January 1, 2014 or later are included in the query results.

FIGURE AC 4.19

tips & tricks

Common comparison operators are:
- `>` greater than
- `<` less than
- `=` equal to
- `<>` not equal to
- `>=` greater than or equal to
- `<=` less than or equal to

let me try

If the database is not already open, open the data file **AC4-Appointments** and try this skill on your own:

1. If necessary, open the *CurrentAppointmentQuery* query in Design view.
2. Add criteria to limit the query to appointments longer than **75** minutes.
3. Run the query and review the results.
4. Return to Design view and add criteria to show appointments for **January 1, 2014** and later. Be sure to remove the criteria from the *Length* field first.
5. Run the query and review the results.
6. Save the query.

skill 4.4 Adding Numeric and Date Criteria to a Query

Skill 4.5 Using AND and OR in a Query

You can make a query more specific by limiting query results to records that meet multiple criteria:

- To find records that meet two or more conditions in different fields, enter each of the criteria in the *Criteria* row.
- To find records that meet more than one condition in the same field, enter both criteria separated by the word *and* in the *Criteria* row.

For example, to find all appointments that meet these conditions—January 1, 2014 or later **AND** March 31, 2014 or earlier **AND** last name is Smith:

Enter `>=1/1/2014 and <=3/31/2014` in the *Criteria* row for the *Appt Date* field and enter `Smith` in the *Criteria* row for the *Last Name* field as shown in Figure AC 4.20.

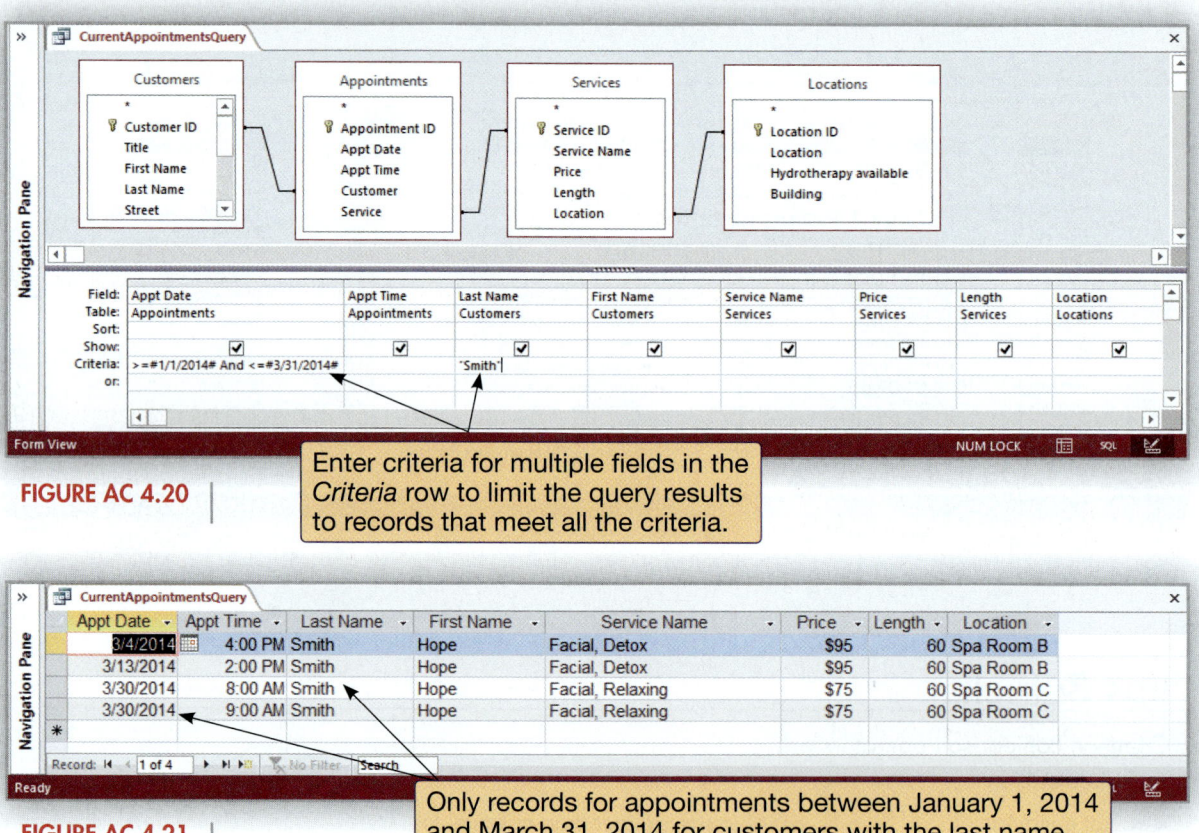

FIGURE AC 4.20 — Enter criteria for multiple fields in the *Criteria* row to limit the query results to records that meet all the criteria.

FIGURE AC 4.21 — Only records for appointments between January 1, 2014 and March 31, 2014 for customers with the last name Smith are included in the query results.

You can make a query broader by expanding the query results to records that meet any one of multiple criteria. To find records that meet any of the conditions, enter the criteria on separate rows in the query grid:

1. Enter the first criterion in the *Criteria* row.

2. Enter the second criterion in the *or* row (the row immediately below the *Criteria* row).

To find all appointments for customers with the last name Smith or Clauson, enter `Smith` in the *Criteria* row for the *Last Name* field, and then enter `Clauson` in the *or* row for the *Last Name* field as shown in Figure AC 4.22.

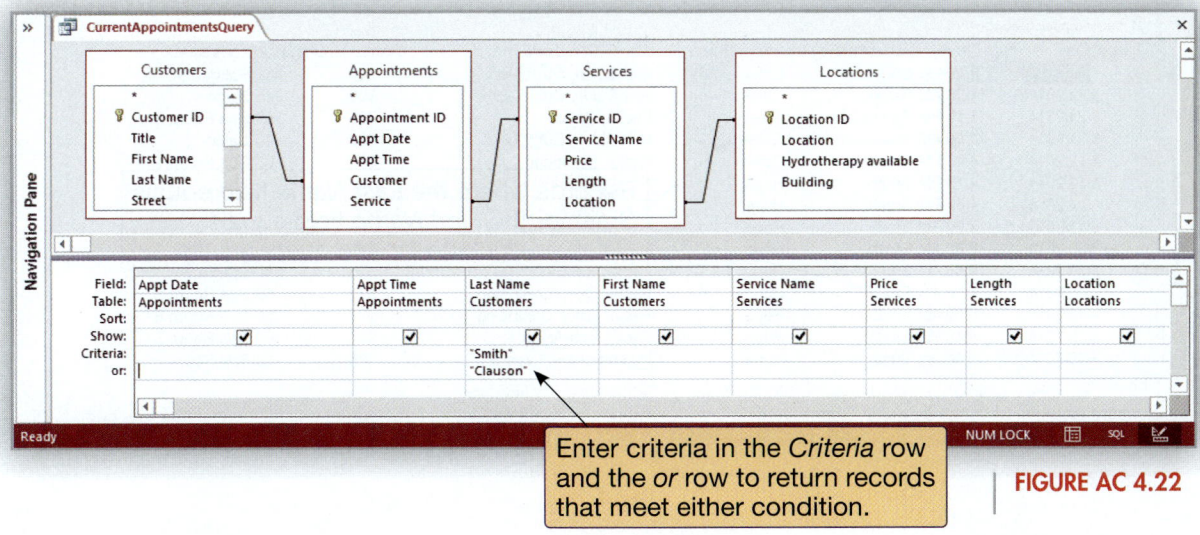

FIGURE AC 4.22

Enter criteria in the *Criteria* row and the *or* row to return records that meet either condition.

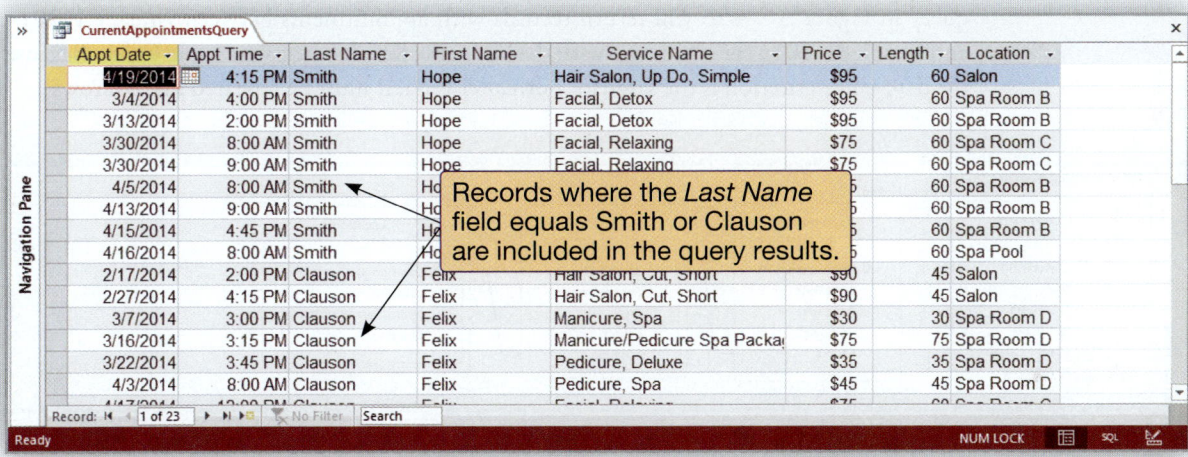

Records where the *Last Name* field equals Smith or Clauson are included in the query results.

FIGURE AC 4.23

Criteria do not need to be in the same field. When using an *or* construction with multiple fields, make sure that each criterion is on its own row. The query shown in Figure AC 4.24 will return records where the value of the *Last Name* field is Smith or the value of the *First Name* field is Caleb.

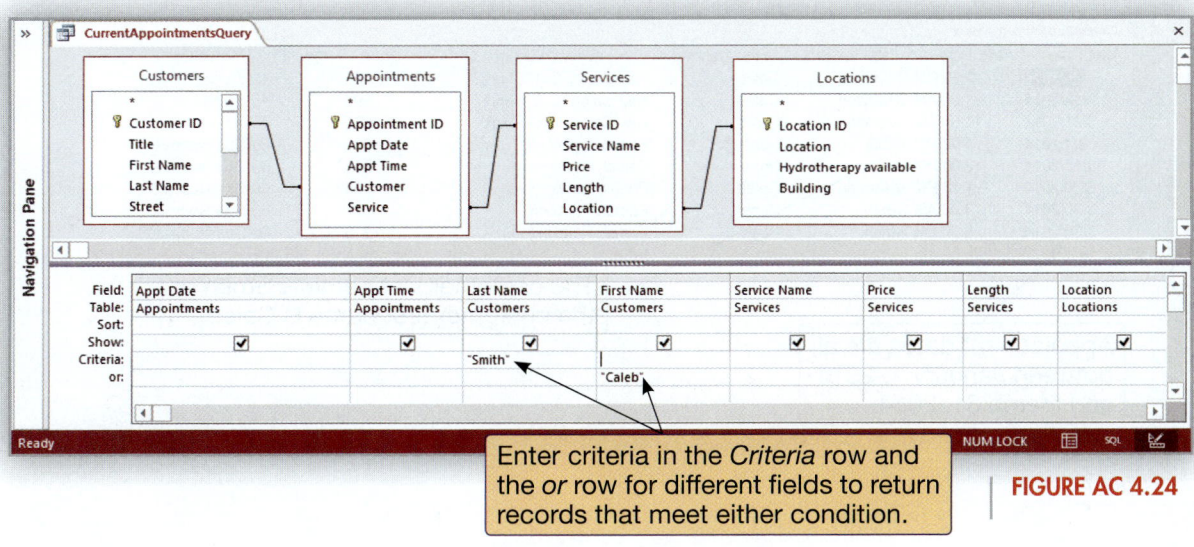

Enter criteria in the *Criteria* row and the *or* row for different fields to return records that meet either condition.

FIGURE AC 4.24

skill 4.5 Using AND and OR in a Query

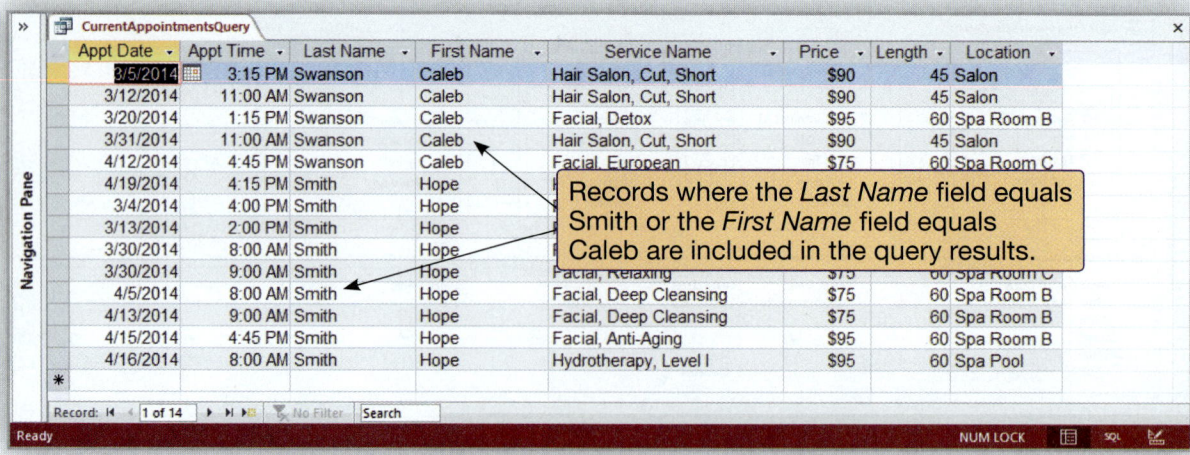

FIGURE AC 4.25

You can combine the *and* and *or* query constructions to create a very precise query. The query in Figure AC 4.26 will return records with appointments between January 1, 2014 and March 31, 2014 for customers with the last name Smith or the first name Caleb. Because the date range criterion is the same for both *or* criteria, it must be repeated in both rows.

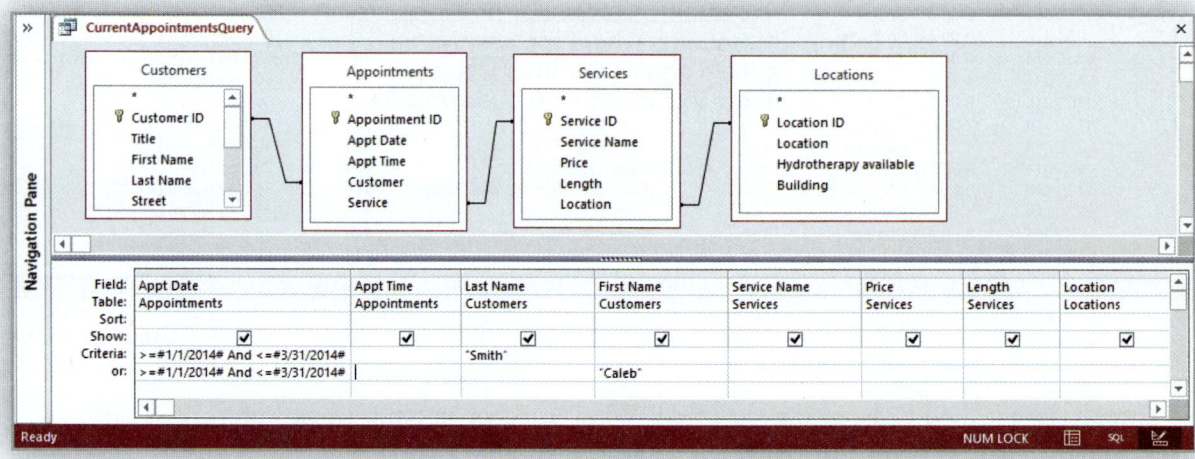

FIGURE AC 4.26

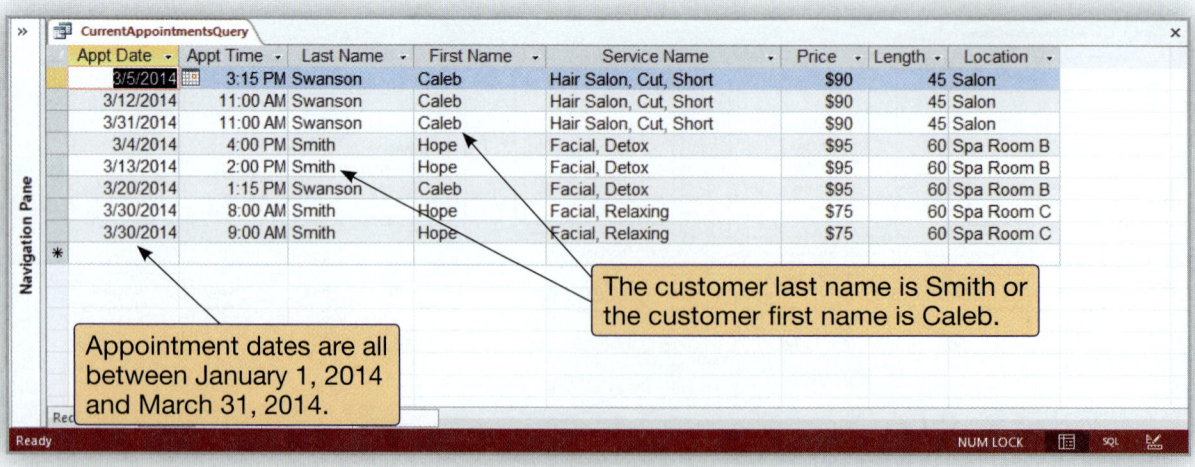

FIGURE AC 4.27

tips & tricks

If your query does not return the records you expect, check the placement of the criteria in the query grid.
- Criteria in the same row make the query more specific.
- Criteria in different rows make the query less specific.
- If you combine the *and* and *or* constructions, don't forget to include the *and* condition in every *or* row.

tell me more

You can add more *or* criteria by continuing to add criteria to the rows under the first *or* row.

let me try

If the database is not already open, open the data file **AC4-Appointments** and try this skill on your own:
1. If necessary, open the *CurrentAppointmentsQuery* query in Design view.
2. Remove any existing criteria.
3. Add criteria to find appointments between **January 1, 2014** and **March 31, 2014** (inclusive) for any customer with the last name **Smith**.
4. Run the query and review the results.
5. Return to Design view and delete the criteria for the *Appt Date* field.
6. Modify the query criteria to show all appointments for customers with the last name **Smith** or **Clauson**.
7. Run the Query and review the results.
8. Return to Design view and delete the *or* criterion for the *Last Name* field (Clauson).
9. Modify the query criteria to show all appointments for customers with the last name **Smith** or the first name **Caleb**.
10. Run the query and review the results.
11. Return to Design view and limit the query to include results between **January 1, 2014** and **March 31, 2014** (inclusive) for customers with the last name **Smith** or the first name **Caleb**.
12. Run the query and review the results.
13. Save and close the query.

skill 4.5   Using AND and OR in a Query

Skill 4.6 Specifying the Sort Order in a Query

Query results may display records in an unexpected order. If you want to control how records are displayed, set the sort order as part of the query design. The sort order will be applied every time the query is run.

To add a sort order to a query:

1. Open the query in Design view.
2. Click in the *Sort* row for the field you want to sort by. Click the arrow to expand the sort options list, and select **Ascending** or **Descending.**
3. Run the query.

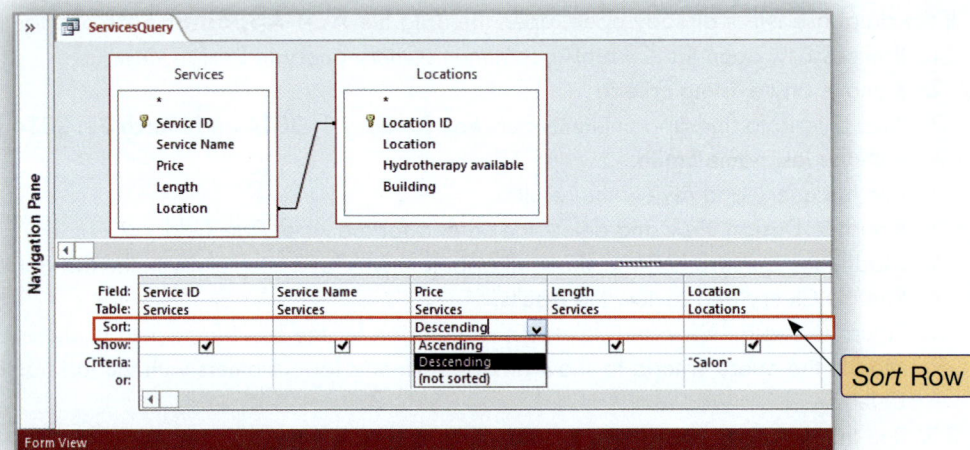

FIGURE AC 4.28

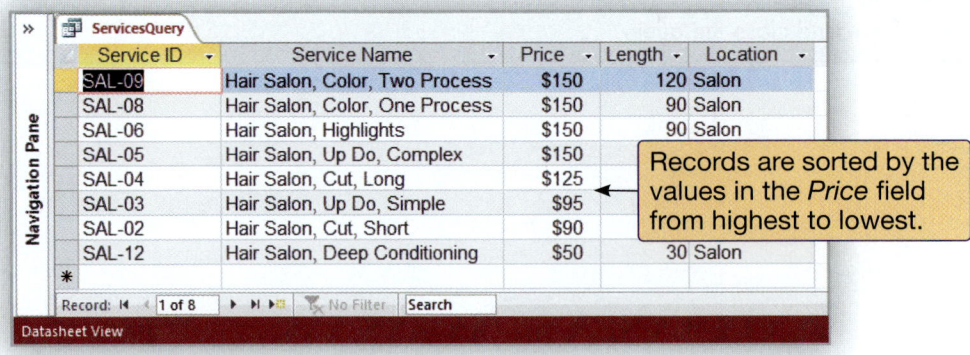

FIGURE AC 4.29

tell me more

For more information about sorting, refer to the skill *Sorting Records in a Table*.

let me try

If the database is not already open, open the data file **AC4-Appointments** and try this skill on your own:

1. Open the *ServicesQuery* query in Design view.
2. Set the sort order so the results will display records with the highest price first.
3. Run the query and review the results.
4. Save the query.

Skill 4.7 Hiding and Showing Fields in a Query

If you want to include a field in your query but do not want that field to show in Datasheet view, click the **Show** box to remove the checkmark. By hiding the field, you can use it to define criteria for the query without making the field visible in the final query results.

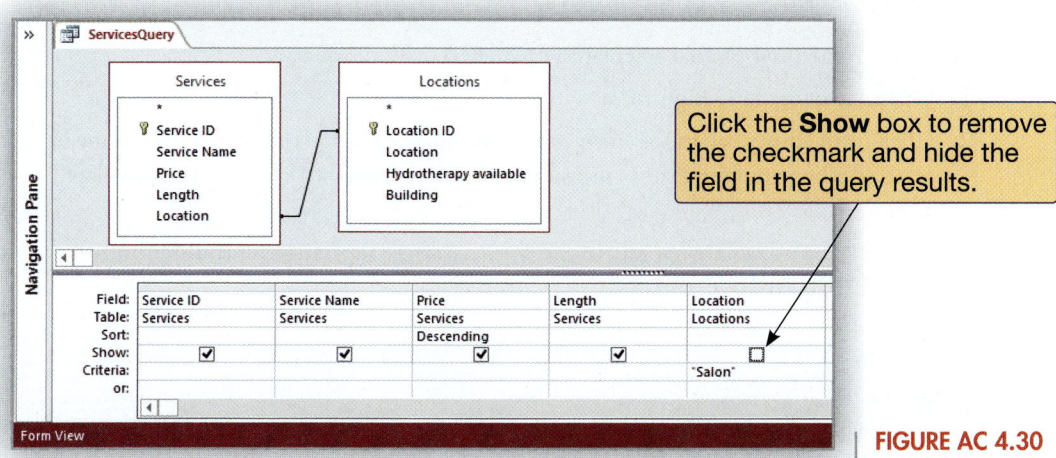
FIGURE AC 4.30

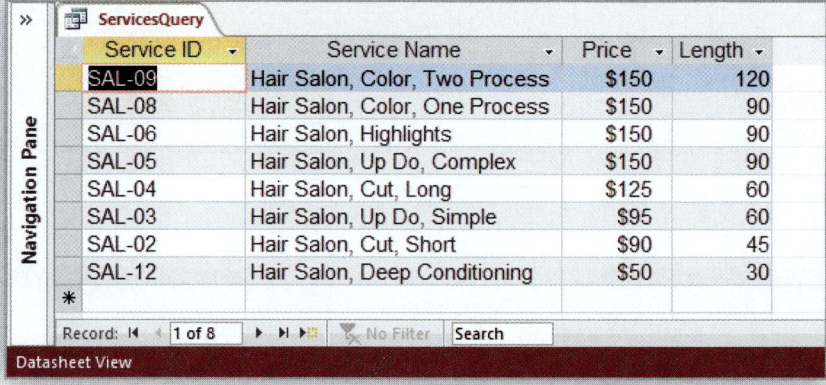
FIGURE AC 4.31
Query results with the *Location* field hidden

tips & tricks

Run the query to verify that it returns results as you expect before hiding the field.

let me try

If the database is not already open, open the data file **AC4-Appointments** and try this skill on your own:
1. If necessary, open the *ServicesQuery* query in Design view.
2. Notice that the criterion *Salon* is entered for the *Location* field.
3. Run the query and review the results.
4. Return to Design view and hide the **Location** field so it does not appear in the query results.
5. Run the query. Notice that the results are the same, but now the *Location* field is hidden. It was not necessary as every record in the result had the same value.
6. Save and close the query.

Skill 4.8 Adding a Calculated Field to a Query

Database fields generally display the data that are entered into them. However, a **calculated field** displays a value returned by an **expression** (a formula). Expressions can reference fields, mathematical operators, and functions. To create a calculated field using an expression, you can type the formula directly in the query grid or you can use the *Expression Builder* to build the formula.

To use the *Expression Builder* to create a calculated field in a query:

1. Open the query in Design view.
2. Click in an empty cell in the *Field* row in the query grid. If a cell with a field name is selected when you build the expression, you will replace the field with the calculated field.
3. On the *Query Tools Design* tab, in the *Query Setup* group, click the **Builder** button to open the *Expression Builder*.

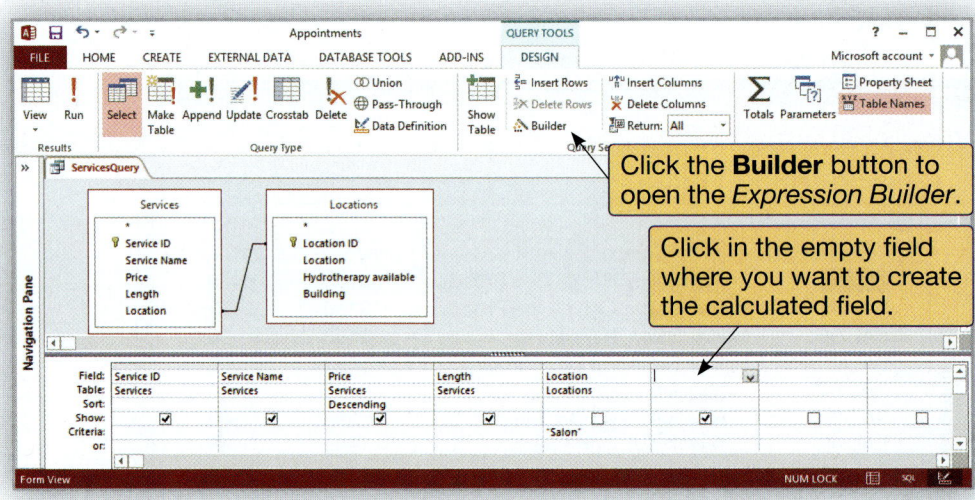

FIGURE AC 4.32

4. The center box in the *Expression Builder* lists fields in the query. In the *Expression Categories* box, double-click the field name to add it to the expression box at the top of the dialog. When referencing a field name in an expression, the field name is always enclosed in brackets.
5. Finish entering the expression. For example, to calculate a 15 percent increase, type *** 1.15** after the field name.

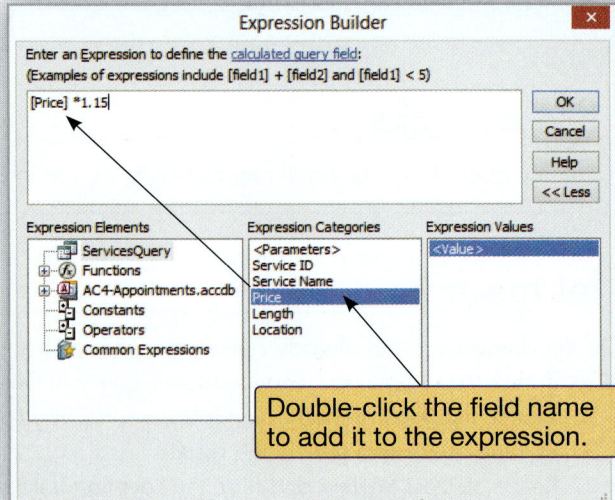

FIGURE AC 4.33

6. Click **OK** to add the expression to the query.
7. Notice that the new calculated field begins with *Expr1:*—this is the temporary name for the field. Click in the field and change **Expr1** to something more meaningful. Be careful not to delete the colon.

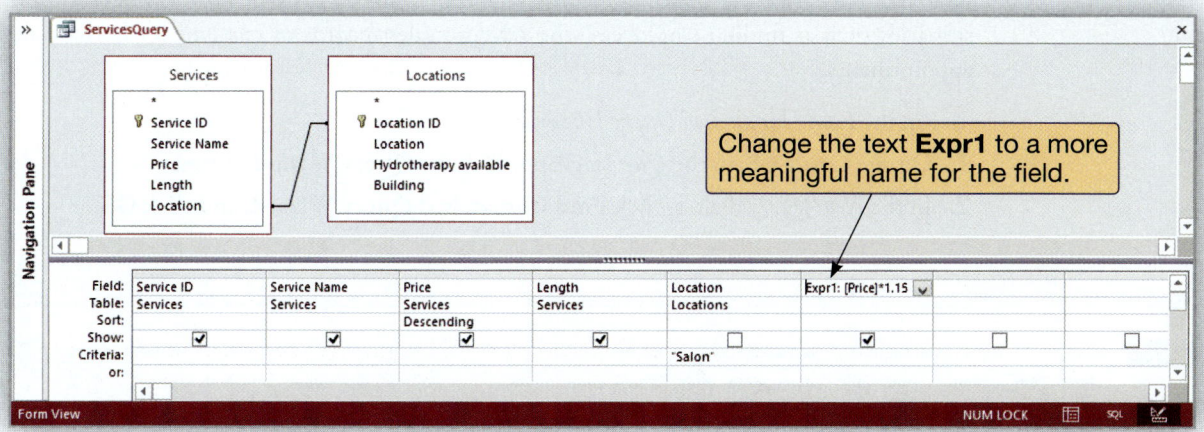

FIGURE AC 4.34

8. Run the query to see the results of the calculated field.

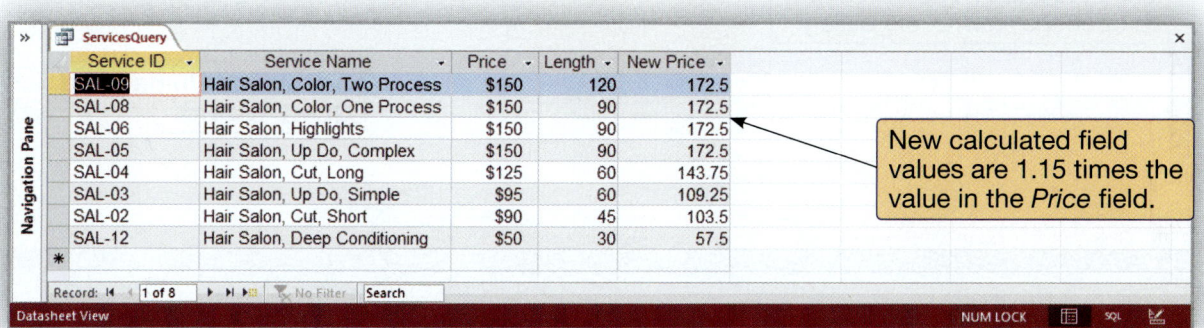

FIGURE AC 4.35

tips & tricks

When you add a calculated field to a query, the field can be used in forms and reports based on that query.

tell me more

The *Expression Builder* can be used to create complex expressions including functions similar to those in Excel. You use the *Expression Builder* to create calculated fields in tables and calculated controls in forms and reports.

let me try

If the database is not already open, open the data file **AC4-Appointments** and try this skill on your own:
1. If necessary, open the *ServicesQuery* query in Design view.
2. Add a new calculated field named **New Price** in the first empty column to the right of the *Length* field. The new field should calculate a value that is 1.15 times the value in the *Price* field.
3. Run the query and review the results.
4. Save and close the query.

skill 4.8 Adding a Calculated Field to a Query

Skill 4.9 Finding Unmatched Data Using a Query

Use the **Find Unmatched Query Wizard** to create a query that shows records from one table that have no corresponding records in another table. This type of query is useful for scenarios such as finding employees who have no sales records or customers who have no appointments.

To run the *Find Unmatched Query Wizard*:

1. On the *Create* tab, in the *Queries* group, click the **Query Wizard** button.
2. In the *New Query* dialog, click **Find Unmatched Query Wizard,** and click **OK**.

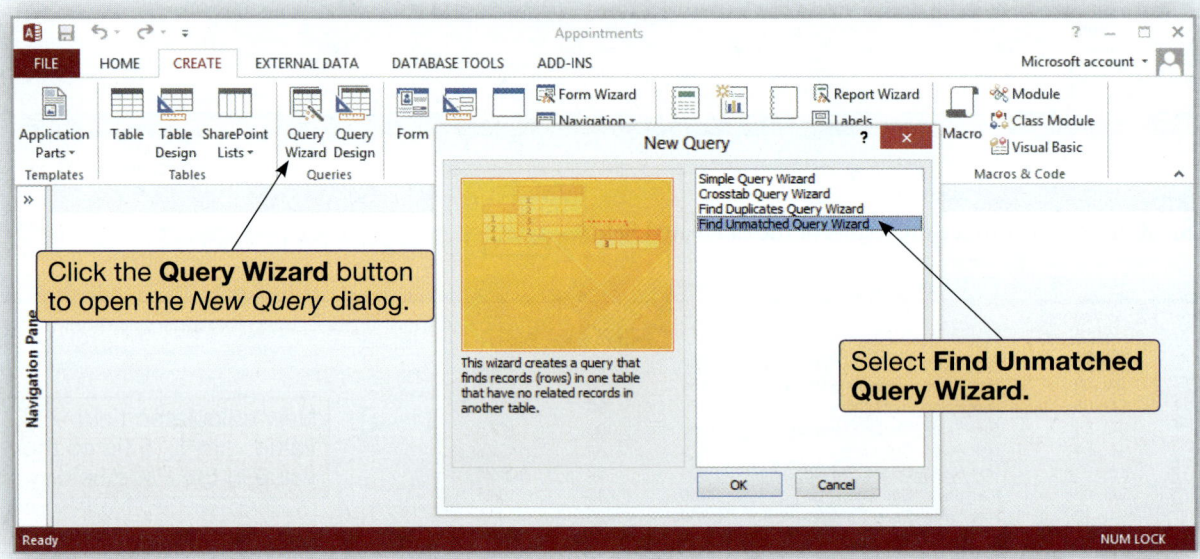

FIGURE AC 4.36

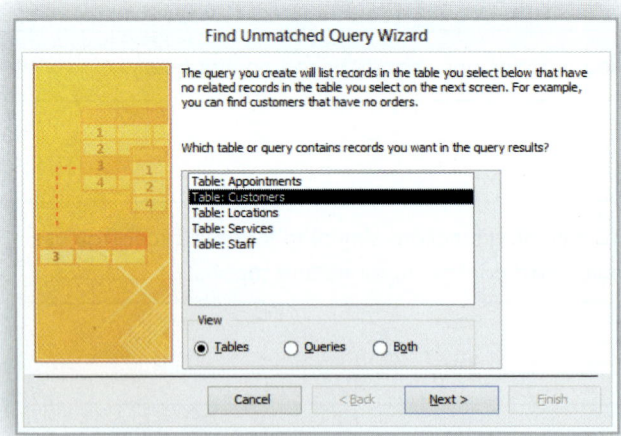

FIGURE AC 4.37

3. First, select the table or query that includes the records you want to match. Click **Next**.

4. Select the table or query that contains the related records. The query will return results from the first table that *do not* have corresponding records in this table. Click **Next**.

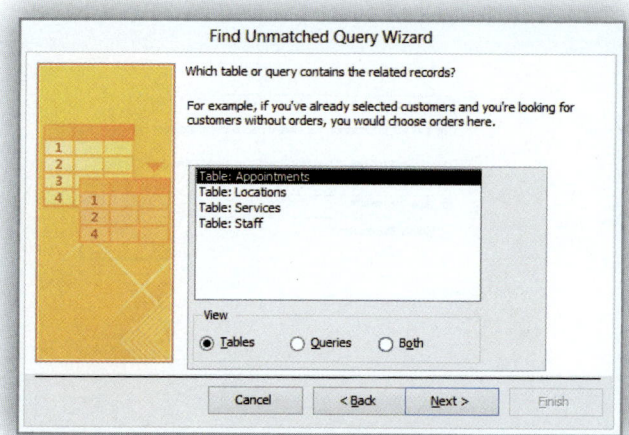

FIGURE AC 4.38

5. Now, find the fields in the two tables that might contain matches. If there is an obvious field (fields with the same name in both tables or fields with an established relationship), Access will automatically suggest it. Click **Next**.

FIGURE AC 4.39

6. Add additional fields that you want to include in the query results. Add the fields that will help identify how the field values are related or fields that you need to identify the records accurately. Click **Next**.

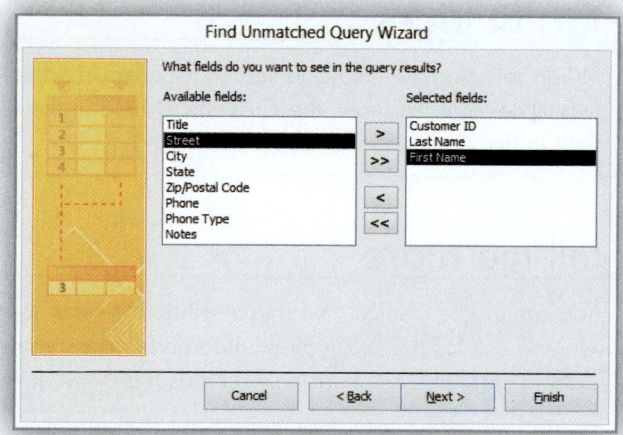

FIGURE AC 4.40

skill 4.9   Finding Unmatched Data Using a Query

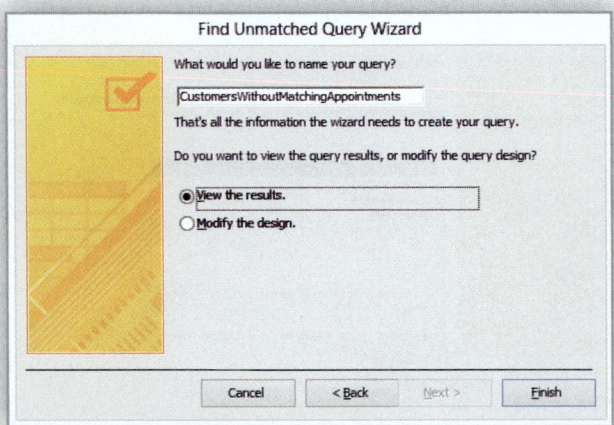

FIGURE AC 4.41

7. Give the query a title, and click **Finish** to view the results.

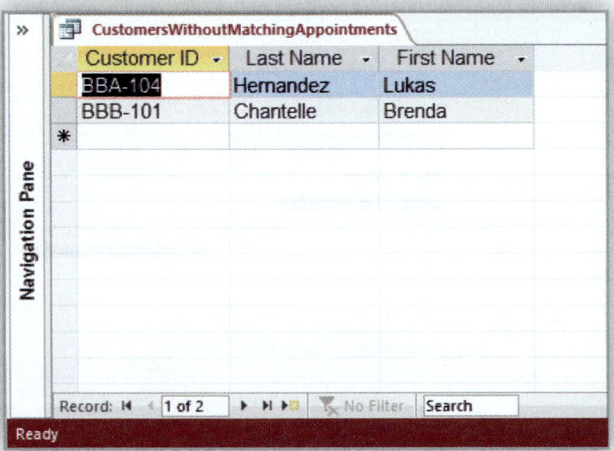

FIGURE AC 4.42

The results of the *Unmatched Query Wizard* display the specified fields from the first table for records that do not have corresponding records in the second table—in this case, the *Customer ID, Last Name,* and *First Name* fields from the *Customers* table where the customer does not have any matching records in the *Appointments* table.

tips & tricks

When selecting the field(s) to search for unmatched values, remember that the fields might be named differently in the two tables. For example, the *CustomerID* field in the *Customers* table might contain the same values as the *Customer* field in the *Appointments* table.

tell me more

You can create a select query yourself to find records that are missing data in a particular field. Type `Is Null` in the *Criteria* cell for the field you want to find. When you run the query, the results will show all records that are missing data in that field. To return only records that have data in the field, type `Is Not Null` in the *Criteria* cell instead.

let me try

If the database is not already open, open the data file **AC4-Appointments** and try this skill on your own:
1. Create a new query using the *Unmatched Query Wizard* to find records in the **Customers** table without corresponding records in the **Appointments** table. Include the **Customer ID, Last Name,** and **First Name** fields from the *Customers* table in that order. Name the query: `CustomersWithoutMatchingAppointments`
2. View the query results and then close the query.

Skill 4.10 Finding Duplicate Data Using a Query

You can create a query to find all the records that have duplicate values in one or more fields. A **Find Duplicates** query is useful for finding records that may have been entered more than once or for scenarios such as finding all employees who live in the same city (duplicates in the city field) or locating customers who may have duplicate appointments on the same day (duplicates in name and date fields).

To run the *Find Duplicates Query Wizard*:

1. On the *Create* tab, in the *Queries* group, click the **Query Wizard** button.
2. In the *New Query* dialog, click **Find Duplicates Query Wizard**. Click **OK**.

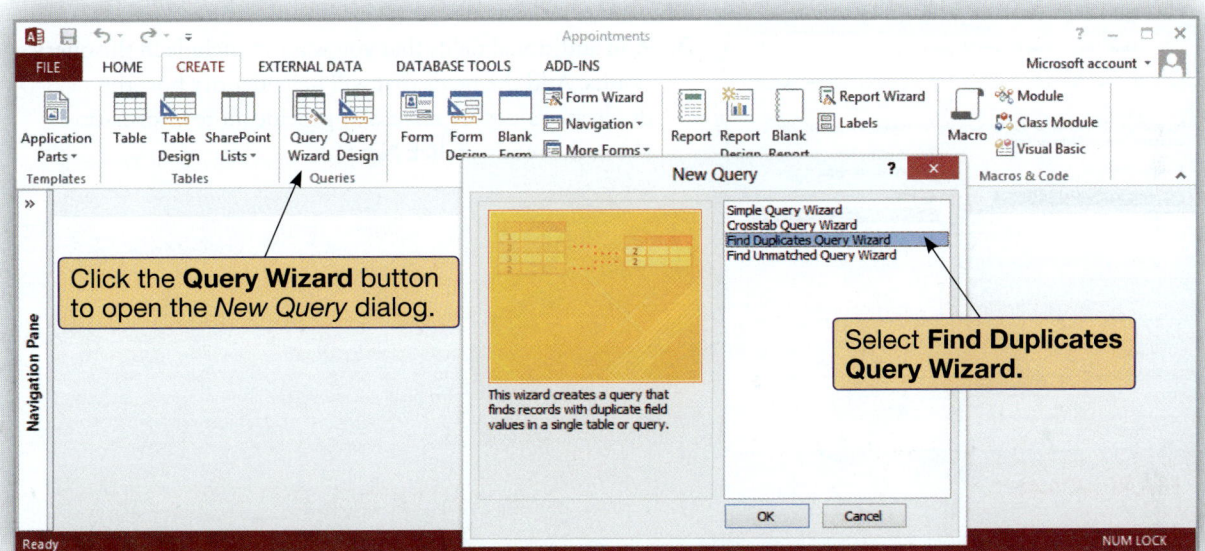

FIGURE AC 4.43

3. Select the table or query that you want to search for duplicate values. In Figure AC 4.44, we are selecting a query that includes fields from multiple tables. This allows us to include more useful information in the query results, such as the customer last name and first name. Click **Next**.

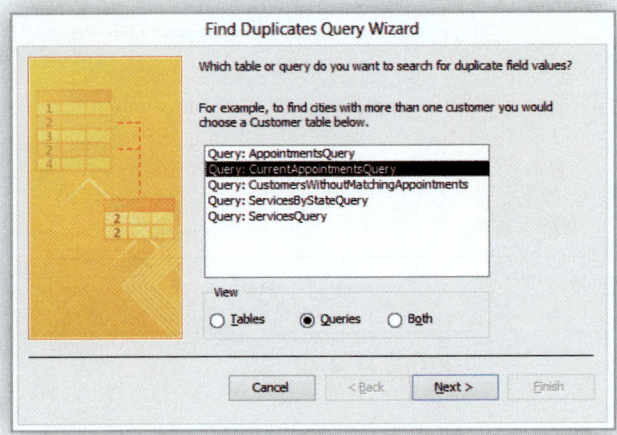

FIGURE AC 4.44

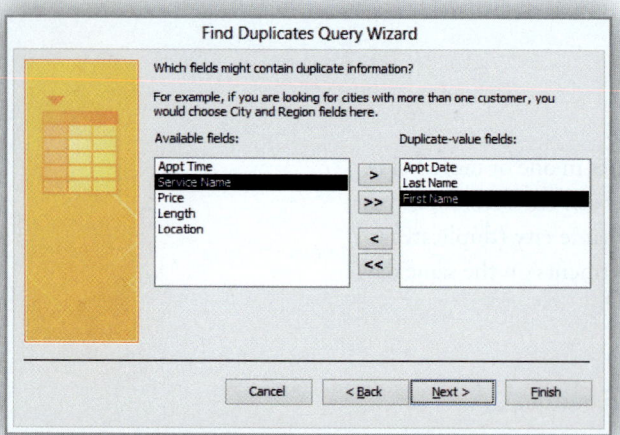

FIGURE AC 4.45

4. Add the field or fields that might contain duplicate values. Click **Next.**

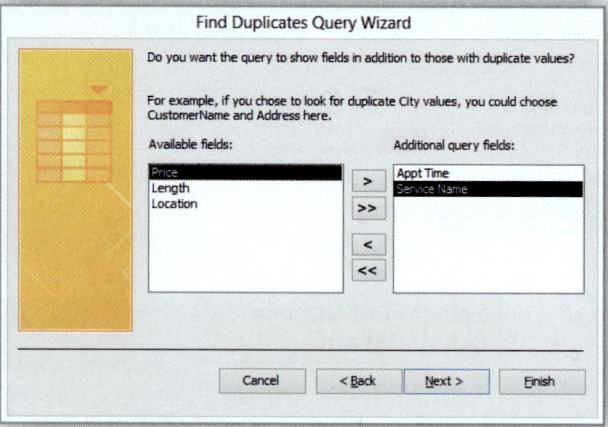

FIGURE AC 4.46

5. Add additional fields that you want to include in the query results. Add the fields that will help identify how the duplicate values are related or provide more information about the results. Click **Next.**

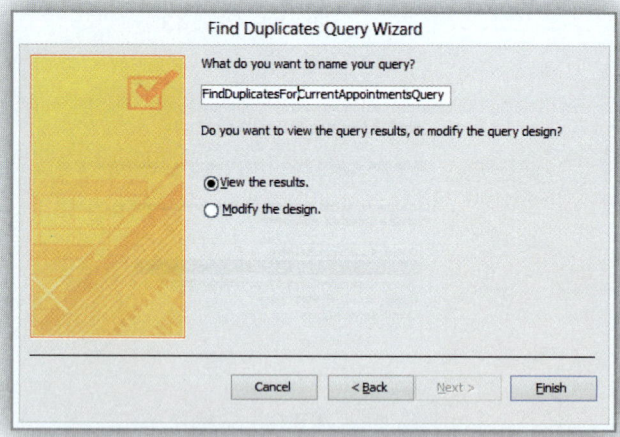

FIGURE AC 4.47

6. Give the query a title, and click **Finish** to view the results.

The results of the *Find Duplicates Query Wizard* display the specified fields from records with duplicate values in the specified fields—in this case, appointments with duplicate values in the *Appt Date, Last Name,* and *First Name* fields. The *Appt Time* and *Service Name* fields are included to provide more information about the possible duplicate appointments.

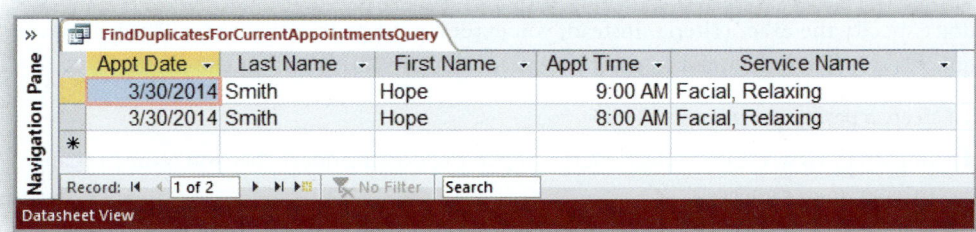

FIGURE AC 4.48

let me try

If the database is not already open, open the data file **AC4-Appointments** and try this skill on your own:

1. Create a query using the *Find Duplicates Query Wizard* to find appointments on the same day for the same customer. Use the **CurrentAppointmentsQuery.** Find duplicate values in the **Appt Date, Last Name,** and **First Name** fields. Include the **Appt Time** and **Service Name** fields to provide more information about the appointment. Name the query: `FindDuplicatesForCurrentAppointmentsQuery`
2. View the query results and then close the query.

from the perspective of . . .

PERSONAL TRAINER

I use Access to keep track of client appointments and billing. I use queries extensively as the basis for invoices and to create reports for specific clients. The *Unmatched Query Wizard* and the *Find Duplicates Query Wizard* help me create complex queries. As I work through the steps of a wizard, I think about the logic behind the query—considering which table or query contains the fields I want to apply criteria to and which fields I need to include in the results so I can make sense of them.

skill 4.10   Finding Duplicate Data Using a Query

Skill 4.11 Using a Parameter Query

A **parameter query** is a type of select query that allows the user to provide the criteria. When you create a parameter query, you specify the field or fields that the query will use to limit the records in the results just as you would if you were entering the criteria yourself, but you don't specify the exact criteria. Instead, you enter a prompt that the user will see when the query is run. Then the user can enter the exact value or values to use as the criteria.

To create a parameter query:

1. In Design view, create a select query or open the existing query that you want to change to a parameter query.

2. In the appropriate cell in the *Criteria* row, instead of entering specific criteria, type the prompt the user will see, enclosed in brackets. Ideally, the prompt will give the user direction as to what data to enter. For example, `[Enter Customer Last Name]` or `[Enter Appointment Date]`.

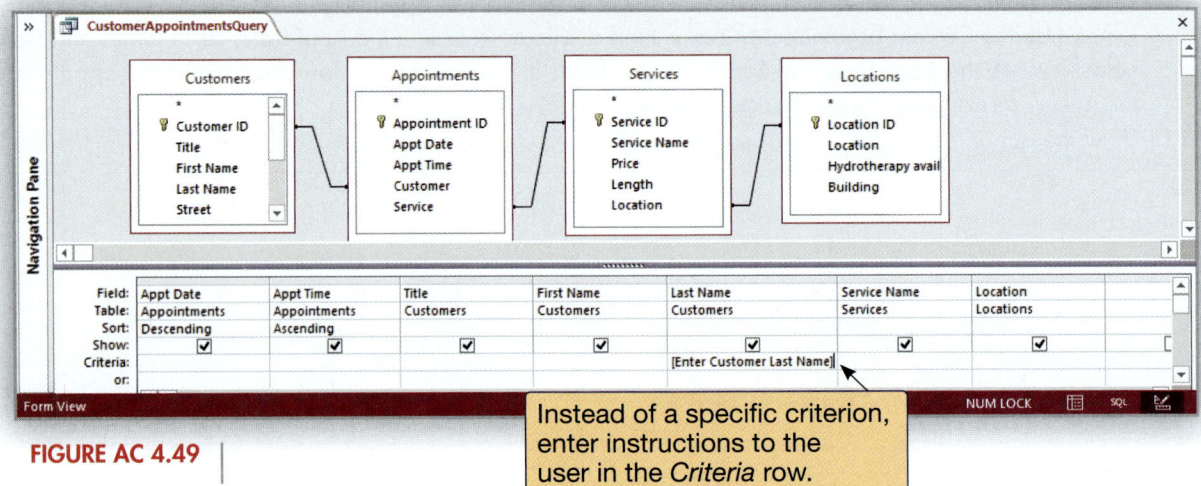

FIGURE AC 4.49

3. Run the query to test it. Notice that before results display, the *Enter Parameter Value* dialog appears with the prompt you created. Enter a value in the box, and then click **OK**.

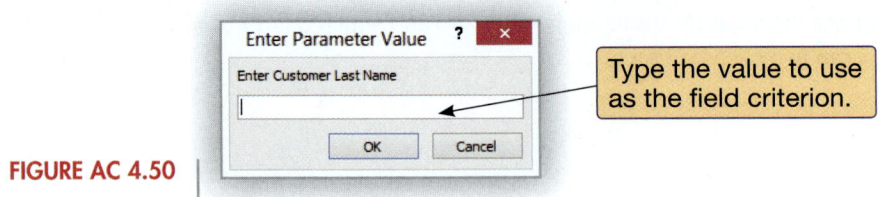

FIGURE AC 4.50

4. The results of the query display only records that match the value you typed in the *Enter Parameter Value* dialog.

In Figure AC 4.51, the query results are limited to records where the value in the *Last Name* field is *Swanson*. Typing **Swanson** in the *Enter Parameter Value* dialog has the same effect as typing **Swanson** in the *Criteria* row for the *Last Name* field.

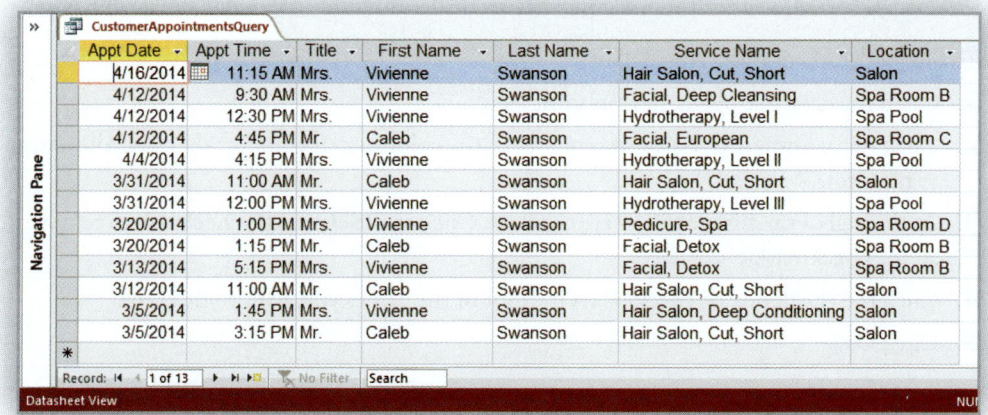

FIGURE AC 4.51

tell me more

You can prevent users from entering a parameter input in the wrong data type.

1. On the *Query Tools Design* tab, in the *Show/Hide* group, click the **Parameters** button.
2. The *Query Parameters* dialog opens.
3. In the *Parameter* column, enter the parameter prompt exactly as you entered it in the query grid.
4. In the *Data Type* column, select the appropriate data type.
5. Click **OK**.

Now if a user attempts to use a parameter value with the wrong data type, he or she will see an error message rather than incorrect query results.

let me try

If the database is not already open, open the data file **AC4-Appointments** and try this skill on your own:
1. Open the **CustomerAppointmentsQuery** query in Design view.
2. Create a parameter query where the user will enter a value to use as the criterion for the **Last Name** field. Use the prompt **Enter Customer Last Name.** Don't forget to enclose the prompt in brackets.
3. Test the parameter query using the last name **Swanson.**
4. Save and close the query.

Skill 4.12 Filtering Data Using AutoFilter

By applying a **filter** to a database object, you display a subset of records that meet the filter criteria. AutoFilter displays a list of all the unique values in the field. This feature is available for table, queries, and forms. If you have used Microsoft Excel, AutoFilter will be familiar to you.

To filter a datasheet using AutoFilter:

1. Open the database object in Datasheet view.
2. Click the arrow at the top of the column in the column that contains the data you want to filter for.
3. At first, all of the filter options are checked. Click the **(Select All)** check box to remove all the checkmarks.
4. Click the check box or check boxes in front of the values you want to filter for.
5. Click **OK**.

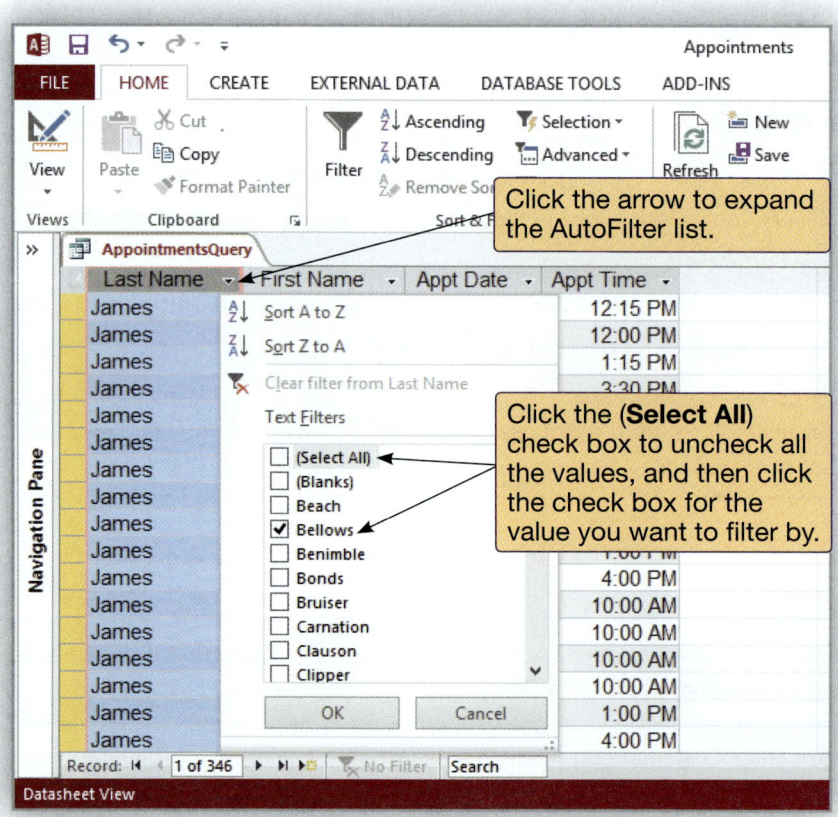

FIGURE AC 4.52

Access displays only the records that include the values you selected. The field that is filtered displays a filter icon next to the arrow in the field header.

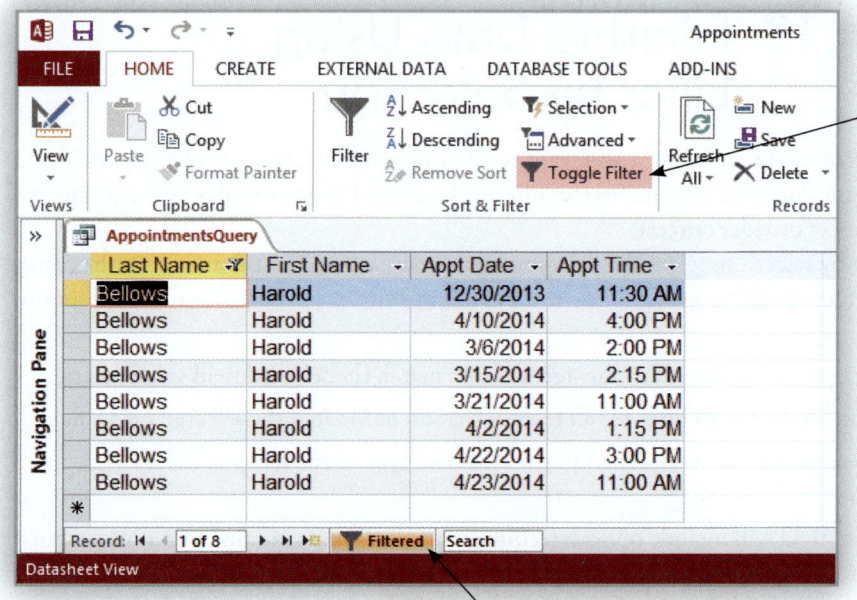

FIGURE AC 4.53

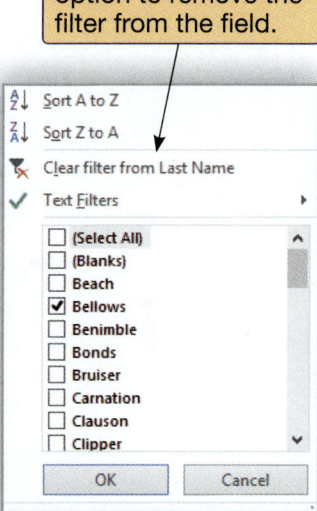

FIGURE AC 4.54

On the *Home* tab, in the *Sort & Filter* group, click the **Toggle Filter** button to clear the filter. Click the **Toggle Filter** button again to reapply the filter.

Notice that when the database object has a filter applied, the *Filtered* button is highlighted next to the navigation buttons at the bottom of the object. You can also click this button to toggle back and forth between the filtered view and the unfiltered view.

To remove the filter, display the AutoFilter list again, and select the **Clear filter** option. Once you use the *Clear filter* command, you cannot use the *Toggle Filter* or *Filtered* button to show the filter again. You have to recreate it.

tips & tricks

Filtering with AutoFilter is temporary. When you close the database object, the filter is not saved. If you want a more permanent filter applied to a query, add criteria in Design view instead.

another method

To display the AutoFilter list, on the *Home* tab, in the *Sort & Filter* group, click the **Filter** button.

let me try

If the database is not already open, open the data file **AC4-Appointments** and try this skill on your own:
1. If necessary, open the *AppointmentsQuery* query in Datasheet view. If your database does not include this query, create it following the steps in *Skill 4.1: Using the Simple Query Wizard*.
2. Use AutoFilter to filter the query results to show only records where the last name is **Bellows.**
3. Clear the filter from the field.

skill 4.12   Filtering Data Using AutoFilter

Skill 4.13 Filtering Data Using Filter by Selection

If a record that contains the data you want to filter for is visible, you can click the field and use the *Filter by Selection* feature. Besides filtering by matching exact values, you can filter for values that meet broader criteria.

To filter by selection, select the data you want to use as the filter criteria. On the *Home* tab, in the *Sort & Filter* group, click the **Selection** button to view the filtering options available.

> The first option is to filter for only records that match the selected field value exactly.

> The second option is to filter for all records that do not match the selected field value.

> The other options will vary depending on the data type of the selected field. For example:
> - A text field will include options to filter for records that contain or do not contain the text in the selected field.
> - A numeric field will include options to filter for records that are less than or greater than the selected field value.
> - A *Date/Time* field will include options to filter for records that include a date/time on or before or after the selected date.

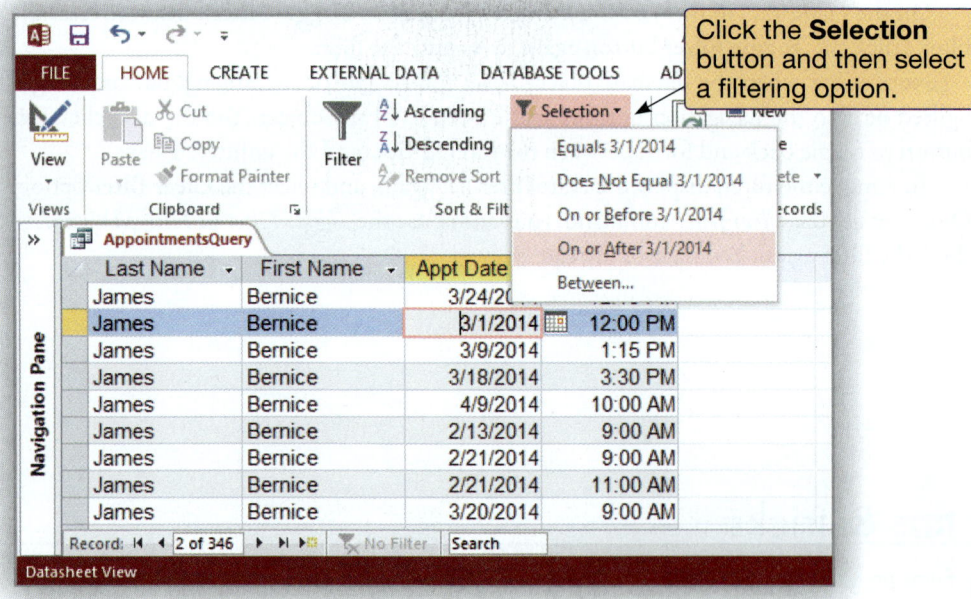

FIGURE AC 4.55

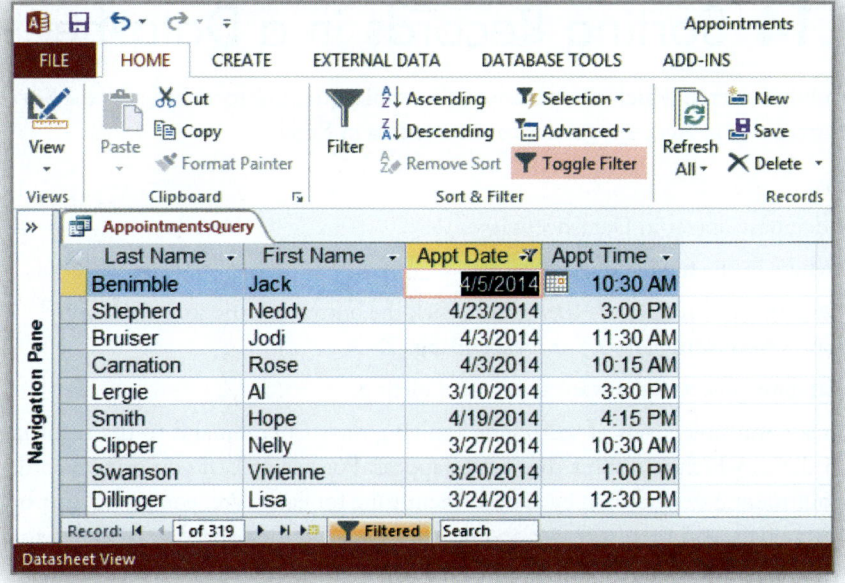

FIGURE AC 4.56
Query results filtered to show only records where the value in the *Appt Date* field is on or after 3/1/2014.

tell me more

You can apply filters to more than one field at a time.

To remove all filters from a database object, click the **Advanced Filter Options** button arrow and select **Clear All Filters.**

another method

The filter options available by right-clicking a value are more extensive than those available from the *Selection* button menu.

1. Right-click anywhere in the field you want to filter for.
2. Point to the **Filters** option and then click the filter option you want from the submenu. The *Filters* option will include the data type (for example, if the field is a text field, the right-click menu will include *Text Filters*; if it is a date/time field, the right-click menu will include *Date Filters*).
3. When you make a selection from the submenu, a dialog may open, allowing you to enter specific filter criteria.

let me try

If the database is not already open, open the data file **AC4-Appointments** and try this skill on your own:

1. If necessary, open the *AppointmentsQuery* query in Datasheet view. If your database does not include this query, create it following the steps in *Skill 4.1: Using the Simple Query Wizard*.
2. Clear any filters that may have been applied to the query results.
3. Filter the query results to show only appointment dates on or after **3/1/2014.** Hint: Use the *Appt Date* field for the second record in the dataset to filter by selection.
4. Clear the filter from the field.

skill 4.13   Filtering Data Using Filter by Selection

Skill 4.14 Sorting Records in a Datasheet

You can control the order in which records appear in a table, query, or form by using the **Sort** feature. Sorting records in Access is similar to sorting data in Excel.

To sort records:

1. Open the database object in Datasheet view.
2. Click anywhere in the field you want to sort.
3. On the *Home* tab, in the *Sort & Filter* group, click the button for the sort order you want to apply: **Ascending** (A–Z) or **Descending** (Z–A).
4. Save the database object if you want to save the sorting.

You can create multiple levels of sorting by applying the sort command to the fields in the *opposite* order in which you want the sort to appear. For example, if you want records sorted by appointment date and then by appointment time for each date, you would sort by appointment time first, and then sort by appointment date. The first sort level is called the outermost sort. The last sort level is called the innermost sort. When applying the sort commands, sort the innermost sort first and the outermost sort last. You can have as many sort levels as you want, but remember to begin with the innermost sort and work your way out.

In Figure AC 4.57, the query results are sorted first by dates in the *Appt Date* field, from newest to oldest. This is the outermost sort. The data are then sorted by the *Appt Time* field, from oldest to newest. This is the innermost sort. When creating the sort, we sorted on the *Appt Time* field first, and then applied the sort to the *Appt Date* field.

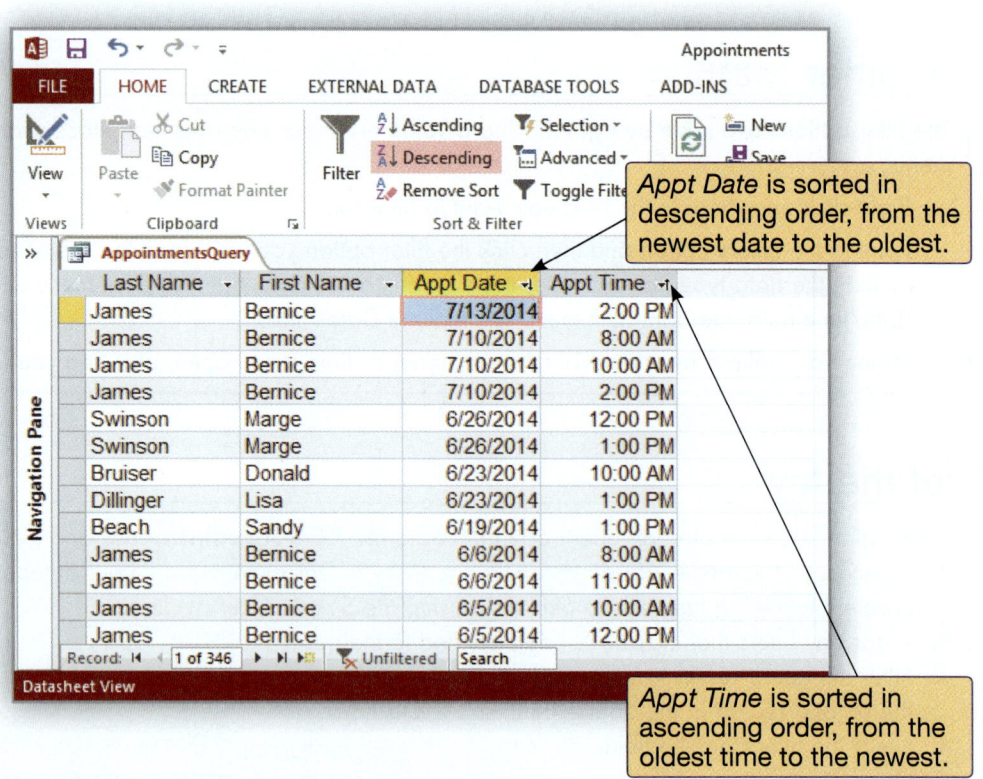

FIGURE AC 4.57

To clear all sorting from the database object, on the *Home* tab, in the *Sort & Filter* group, click the **Remove Sort** button.

tips & tricks

Unlike filters, the sort order you apply to a database object is saved when you save the object.

tell me more

The sort options will differ, depending on the data type of the field you are sorting:

- *Text* and *Hyperlink* fields sort alphabetically from *A–Z* or *Z–A*.
- *Number, Currency,* and *AutoNumber* fields sort on their numeric values from *Smallest to Largest* or *Largest to Smallest*.
- *Date/Time* fields sort by time from *Oldest to Newest* or *Newest to Oldest*. If you want to show the most recent records first, use the *Z–A* button (Newest to Oldest).
- *Yes/No* fields are often displayed as check boxes and sort from *Selected to Cleared* or *Cleared to Selected*. A checkmark or "yes" value is the "selected" state.

another method

- If the database object is in datasheet format, you can click the arrow at the top of the column you want to sort and select a sort option.
- You can also right-click a field and select a sort option.

let me try

If the database is not already open, open the data file **AC4-Appointments** and try this skill on your own:

1. If necessary, open the *AppointmentsQuery* query in Datasheet view. If your database does not include this query, create it following the steps in *Skill 4.1: Using the Simple Query Wizard*.
2. Clear any filters that may have been applied to the query results.
3. Sort the query results by last name, from A–Z.
4. Clear the sort.
5. Sort the query so the results are sorted by date, with the most recent date first, and then by time within each date, with the earliest time first.
6. Save and close the query.

key terms

Select query
Query grid
Criteria
Criterion
Wildcard
Calculated field
Expression

Find Unmatched query
Find Duplicates query
Parameter query
Filter
Outermost sort
Innermost sort

concepts review

1. A _____ displays data from one or more tables or queries, based on the fields that you select.
   a. crosstab query
   b. select query
   c. Find Unmatched query
   d. Find Duplicates query

2. The upper pane in query Design view shows the query grid where you specify which fields to include in the query.
   a. True
   b. False

3. _____ are conditions that the records must meet in order to be included in the query results.
   a. Data
   b. Fields
   c. Criteria
   d. Records

4. Entering < >80 as the criteria for a query will return results that are _____.
   a. greater than 80
   b. less than 80
   c. equal to 80
   d. not equal to 80

5. To limit query results to only records that meet all the criteria, enter criteria for multiple fields on the *Criteria* row, or enter multiple criteria for the same field separated by the word *And*.
   a. True
   b. False

6. A _____ displays a value returned by an expression.
   a. calculated field
   b. query
   c. formula
   d. parameter query

7. If you want to create a query that shows records from one table that have no corresponding records in another table, use a _____.

   a. parameter query
   b. select query
   c. Find Unmatched query
   d. Find Duplicates query

8. If you wanted to display records of all employees who live in the same city (from the City field in the table), you would use a _____.

   a. parameter query
   b. select query
   c. Find Unmatched query
   d. Find Duplicates query

9. When you create a _____, you specify the field or fields that the query will use, but you don't specify the exact criteria.

   a. parameter query
   b. select query
   c. Find Unmatched query
   d. Find Duplicates query

10. AutoFilter and Filter by Selection settings are saved with the database object.

   a. True
   b. False

projects

Data files for projects can be found on
www.mhhe.com/office2013skills

skill review 4.1

In this project, you will continue to work with the Computer Science department database from *Chapter 3, Skill Review 3.1*. You will add queries to the database to organize the *Employees* table and to manage equipment on loan. You will use sorting and filtering techniques to analyze the *Employees* and *Items* tables.

Skills needed to complete this project:
- Using the Simple Query Wizard (Skill 4.1)
- Adding Text Criteria to a Query (Skill 4.3)
- Specifying the Sort Order in a Query (Skill 4.6)
- Creating a Query in Design View (Skill 4.2)
- Adding Numeric and Date Criteria to a Query (Skill 4.4)
- Hiding and Showing Fields in a Query (Skill 4.7)
- Adding a Calculated Field to a Query (Skill 4.8)
- Finding Unmatched Data Using a Query (Skill 4.9)
- Finding Duplicate Data Using a Query (Skill 4.10)
- Filtering Data Using AutoFilter (Skill 4.12)
- Filtering Data Using Filter by Selection (Skill 4.13)
- Sorting Records in a Datasheet (Skill 4.14)

1. Open the start file **AC2013-SkillReview-4-1**.
2. If necessary, enable active content by clicking the **Enable Content** button in the Message Bar.
3. Save a copy of the file to work on named:
   `[your initials]AC-SkillReview-4-1`
4. Use the **Query Wizard** to create a select query from the *Employees* table.
   a. On the *Create* tab, in the *Queries* group, click the **Query Wizard** button. In the *New Query* dialog, verify that **Simple Query Wizard** is selected. Click **OK**.
   b. Verify that **Table: Employees** is selected in the *Tables/Queries* list. Click the >> button to add all the fields to the right. Use the < button to remove the *EmployeeID* field from the right side. Click **Next**.
   c. In this step, make sure that **Detail** is selected and click **Next**.
   d. In the last step, type `InstructorsByTenure` for the title. Select the radio button to **Modify the query design** and click **Finish**.
5. Add criteria to the query to return records where the value of the *Position* field is **Adjunct** or **Faculty**.
   a. Type `Adjunct` in the *Criteria* row under the *Position* field. Below that, in the *or* area, type: `Faculty`
   b. Click the drop-down arrow in the *Sort* row under the *LengthOfService* field. Select **Ascending**.

c. Click the **Run** button.

   d. Review the query results, and then save and close the query.

6. Create a query in Design view to return records from the *Items* table where the value of the *Category* field is **Software** and the value of the *Cost* field is **greater than or equal to 199.**

   a. On the *Create* tab, in the *Queries* group, click the **Query Design** button. In the *Show Table* dialog, double-click the **Items** table. Click the **Close** button.

   b. Notice the *Items* table in the upper pane of the query Design view window. Double-click each field name in the field list except *ItemID* in order to add them to your query.

   c. Type `Software` in the *Criteria* row under the *Category* field.

   d. Type `>=199` in the *Criteria* row under the *Cost* field.

   e. Uncheck the **Show** box under the *Category* field.

7. Create a calculated field to display a value that is 75% of the *Price* field value.

   a. Next to the *Cost* field, create a new calculated field by typing the following in the *Field* row: `OurCost: [Cost]*0.75`

   b. Click the **Run** button to check your work, and then return to Design view.

   c. On the *Query Tools Design* tab, in the *Query Setup* group, click the **Show Table** button. Double-click the **Loans** table and then click the **Close** button.

   d. Click the **Run** button and observe the new query results.

   e. Save the query with the name: `ExpensiveSoftwareOnLoan`

   f. Close the query.

8. Use the **Unmatched Query Wizard** to find items from the *Items* table that do not have corresponding records in the *Loans* table.

   a. On the *Create* tab, in the *Queries* group, click the **Query Wizard** button. In the *New Query* dialog, click **Find Unmatched Query Wizard** and click **OK**.

   b. Select **Table: Items.** Click **Next.**

   c. Select **Table: Loans.** Click **Next.**

   d. Confirm that Access has selected **ItemID** in both tables and then click **Next.**

   e. Add the following fields to the query by clicking the > button for each: **ItemName, Description, Category.** Click **Next.**

   f. Change the name to `ItemsNotOnLoan` and click **Finish.**

   g. Observe the query results and then close the query.

9. Use the **Find Duplicates Query Wizard** to find employees who have more than one entry in the *Loans* table.

   a. On the *Create* tab, in the *Queries* group, click the **Query Wizard** button. In the *New Query* dialog, click **Find Duplicates Query Wizard** and click **OK.**

   b. Select **Table: Loans.** Click **Next.**

   c. Select **EmployeeID** and add it to the right side by clicking the > button. Click **Next.**

   d. Add all fields by clicking the >> button. Click **Next.**

   e. Change the name to `EmployeeMultipleLoans` and click **Finish.**

   f. Observe the query results and then close the query.

10. Use AutoFilter to filter the *Employees* table to show only records where the value of the *Position* field is **Technician.**

    a. Open the **Employees** table in Datasheet view.

    b. Click the arrow in the **Position** field header. Use the check boxes to make sure that only the **Technician** option is checked. Click **OK** and observe the results.

11. Use *Filter by Selection* to filter the table further to include only employees where the length of service is 10 years or greater.
    a. Click in the *LengthOfService* field for any record where the value is **10**.
    b. On the *Home* tab, in the *Sort & Filter* group, click the **Selection** button.
    c. Click **Greater Than or Equal To 10.**
    d. Save and close the table.
12. Sort the *Items* table so records are organized alphabetically by category and then by cost from smallest to largest.
    a. Open the **Items** table in Datasheet view.
    b. Click anywhere inside the **Cost** field. On the *Home* tab, in the *Sort & Filter* group, click the **Ascending** button.
    c. Click anywhere inside the **Category** field. On the *Home* tab, in the *Sort & Filter* group, click the **Ascending** button.
    d. Save and close the table.
13. Close the database and exit Access.

skill review 4.2

In this project you will continue working with the health insurance database from *Chapter 3, Skill Review 3.2*. You will improve the functionality of the database by creating filters and queries for data most commonly searched for.

Skills needed to complete this project:
- Using the Simple Query Wizard (Skill 4.1)
- Adding Numeric and Date Criteria to a Query (Skill 4.4)
- Using AND and OR in a Query (Skill 4.5)
- Specifying the Sort Order in a Query (Skill 4.6)
- Creating a Query in Design View (Skill 4.2)
- Adding Text Criteria to a Query (Skill 4.3)
- Hiding and Showing Fields in a Query (Skill 4.7)
- Adding a Calculated Field to a Query (Skill 4.8)
- Finding Unmatched Data Using a Query (Skill 4.9)
- Finding Duplicate Data Using a Query (Skill 4.10)
- Using a Parameter Query (Skill 4.11)
- Filtering Data Using AutoFilter (Skill 4.12)
- Sorting Records in a Datasheet (Skill 4.14)

1. Open the start file **AC2013-SkillReview-4-2.**
2. If necessary, enable active content by clicking the **Enable Content** button in the Message Bar.
3. Save a copy of the file to work on named:
   `[your initials]AC-SkillReview-4-2`
4. Use the **Query Wizard** to create a select query from the *Physicians* table.
   a. On the *Create* tab, in the *Queries* group, click the **Query Wizard** button. In the *New Query* dialog, verify that **Simple Query Wizard** is selected. Click **OK**.

b. Click the **Tables/Queries** drop-down arrow. Select **Table: Physicians.** Click the **>>** button to add all the fields to the right. Use the **<** button to remove the *PhysicianID* field from the right side. Click **Next.**

c. In this step, make sure that **Detail** is selected and click **Next.**

d. In the last step, type `PhysiciansByZipCode` for the title. Select the radio button to **Modify the query design** and click **Finish.**

5. Add criteria to the query to limit the query to physicians with the zip code **33176** or **33186.**

   a. Type `33176` in the *Criteria* row under the *ZipCode* field.

   b. Below that, in the *or* row, type: `33186`

   c. Click the drop-down arrow in the **Sort** row under the *LastName* field. Select **Ascending.**

   d. Click the **Run** button and review the query results.

   e. Save and close the query.

6. Create a query in Design view:

   a. On the *Create* tab, in the *Queries* group, click the **Query Design** button. In the *Show Table* dialog, double-click the **Procedures** table. Click the **Close** button.

   b. Notice the *Procedures* table in the upper pane of the query Design view window. Double-click each field name in the field list except *ProcedureID* in order to add them to your query.

   c. Type `Yes` in the *Criteria* row under the *Covered* field.

   d. Type `<=30` in the *Criteria* row under the *ReimbursementAmt* field.

   e. Uncheck the **Show** box under the *Covered* field.

7. Add a calculated field to the query to display the result of a 5% increase in the reimbursement amount.

   a. Next to the *ReimbursementAmt* field, create a new calculated field by typing the following in the *Field* row: `5% Increase:[ReimbursementAmt]*1.05`

   b. Click the **Run** button to check your work and then return to Design view.

8. Add the *OrderDate* field from the *Orders* table to the query.

   a. On the *Query Tools Design* tab, in the *Query Setup* group, click the **Show Table** button. Double-click the **Orders** table and then click the **Close** button.

   b. Double-click the **OrderDate** field in the *Orders* table to add it to the query.

   c. Click the **Run** button and observe the new query results.

   d. Save the query with the name: `CheapCoveredProcedures`

   e. Close the query.

9. Use the **Unmatched Query Wizard** to find records in the *Procedures* table without corresponding records in the *Orders* table.

   a. On the *Create* tab, in the *Queries* group, click the **Query Wizard** button. In the *New Query* dialog, click **Find Unmatched Query Wizard** and click **OK.**

   b. Select **Table: Procedures.** Click **Next.**

   c. Select **Table: Orders.** Click **Next.**

   d. Confirm that Access has matched the **ProcedureID** field in the *Procedures* table and the **Procedure** field in the *Orders* table, and then click **Next.**

   e. Add all of the fields to the query by clicking the **>>** button. Click **Next.**

  f. Change the name to `ProceduresNotOrdered` and click **Finish**.

  g. Observe the query results and then close the query.

10. Use the **Find Duplicates Query Wizard** to find records in the *Orders* table with the same values in the *Physician* and *OrderDate* fields.

  a. On the *Create* tab, in the *Queries* group, click the **Query Wizard** button. In the *New Query* dialog, click **Find Duplicates Query Wizard** and click **OK**.

  b. Select **Table: Orders**. Click **Next**.

  c. Select **Physician** and add it to the right side by clicking the > button. Do the same for **OrderDate**. Click **Next**.

  d. Add all fields by clicking the >> button. Click **Next**.

  e. Change the name to `SameDateOrders` and click **Finish**.

  f. Observe the query results and then close the query.

11. Create a parameter query to allow database users to find records in the *Physicians* table by entering a city name.

  a. On the *Create* tab, in the *Queries* group, click the **Query Design** button. In the *Show Table* dialog, double-click the **Physicians** table. Click the **Close** button.

  b. Notice the *Physicians* table in the upper pane of the query Design view window. Double-click the following field names in order to add them to your query: **FirstName, LastName, City, Phone**

  c. Click the *Criteria* row under the *City* field and type the following:
`[Enter the city name]`

  d. Click the **Run** button. In the *Enter Parameter Value* dialog, type: `Miami` and then click **OK**. Observe the query results.

  e. Save the query with the name: `PhysiciansByCity`

  f. Close the query.

12. Filter the *Orders* table to display only records where the procedure is **flu vaccine** or **CBC**.

  a. Open the **Orders** table in Datasheet view.

  b. Click the arrow on the right side of the **Procedure** field header. Use the check boxes to make sure that only the **Flu Vaccine** and **CBC** options are checked. Click **OK** and observe the results.

  c. Save and close the table.

13. Sort the *Physicians* table so the records are sorted alphabetically by city and then by member count for each city.

  a. Open the **Physicians** table in Datasheet view.

  b. Click anywhere inside the **MemberCount** field. On the *Home* tab, in the *Sort & Filter* group, click the **Ascending** button.

  c. Click anywhere inside the **City** field. On the *Home* tab, in the *Sort & Filter* group, click the **Ascending** button.

  d. Save and close the table.

14. Close the database and exit Access.

challenge yourself 4.3

In this project you will continue working with the greenhouse database from *Chapter 3, Challenge Yourself 3.3*. Improve the functionality of this database by creating filters and queries for information that is commonly searched for.

Skills needed to complete this project:
- Using the Simple Query Wizard (Skill 4.1)
- Creating a Query in Design View (Skill 4.2)
- Adding Text Criteria to a Query (Skill 4.3)
- Adding Numeric and Date Criteria to a Query (Skill 4.4)
- Using AND and OR in a Query (Skill 4.5)
- Specifying the Sort Order in a Query (Skill 4.6)
- Hiding and Showing Fields in a Query (Skill 4.7)
- Adding a Calculated Field to a Query (Skill 4.8)
- Finding Unmatched Data Using a Query (Skill 4.9)
- Filtering Data Using AutoFilter (Skill 4.12)
- Filtering Data Using Filter by Selection (Skill 4.13)
- Sorting Records in a Datasheet (Skill 4.14)

1. Open the start file **AC2013-ChallengeYourself-4-3**.
2. If necessary, enable active content by clicking the **Enable Content** button in the Message Bar.
3. Save a copy of the file to work on named:
   `[your initials]AC-ChallengeYourself-4-3`
4. Create a new query named: `GreenhouseTechsFT`
   a. Add all the fields from the *Employees* table.
   b. The query should list all employees whose *Position* contains the word **greenhouse** and whose weekly hours are greater than or equal to **30**.
   c. Modify the query design so results are sorted alphabetically by last name.
   d. Add the *MaintenanceLog* table to this query and include the *Date_Time* field after the *WeeklyHours* field.
   e. Run the query to review the results.
   f. Save and close the query.
5. Create a new query named: `MediumSizePlants`.
   a. Add all the fields from the *Plants* table except *ScientificName*.
   b. The query should list all **white** or **yellow** colored plants whose *MaxHeightFeet* is at least **3** and not greater than **5**.
   c. Modify the query so results are sorted by *MaxHeightFeet* with the shortest plants listed first.
   d. Run the query to review the results.
   e. Save and close the query.
6. Create a new query named: `RedPlantSale`
   a. Add the following fields from the *Plants* table to the query: **CommonName, FlowerColor, PurchasePrice**.
   b. Select only those plants with a **red** color, but don't show this field in the query results.

c. Add a calculated field that displays a sale price that is 80 percent of the purchase price. Use the name **SalePrice** for the new field.

d. Run the query to review the results.

e. Save and close the query.

7. Use the **Find Unmatched Query Wizard** to create a new query that identifies the plants that have no entry in the *MaintenanceLog*.

   a. Include all fields from the *Plants* table except the *PlantID*.

   b. Name this query: **PlantsMissingMaintenance**

   c. Close the query.

8. Open the **MaintenanceLog** table. Apply a filter that shows only those plants that have been watered and pruned. Save and close the table.

9. Open the **Plants** table. Use sorting (in ascending order) so the records are sorted by flower color and then by the date planted for each color. Save and close the table.

10. Close the database and exit Access.

challenge yourself 4.4

In this project you will continue working with the vaccines database from *Chapter 3, Challenge Yourself 3.4*. Improve the functionality of this database by creating filters and queries for information that is commonly searched for.

Skills needed to complete this project:

- Using the Simple Query Wizard (Skill 4.1)
- Creating a Query in Design View (Skill 4.2)
- Adding Numeric and Date Criteria to a Query (Skill 4.4)
- Using AND and OR in a Query (Skill 4.5)
- Adding Text Criteria to a Query (Skill 4.3)
- Adding a Calculated Field to a Query (Skill 4.8)
- Specifying the Sort Order in a Query (Skill 4.6)
- Hiding and Showing Fields in a Query (Skill 4.7)
- Finding Unmatched Data Using a Query (Skill 4.9)
- Finding Duplicate Data Using a Query (Skill 4.10)
- Using a Parameter Query (Skill 4.11)
- Filtering Data Using AutoFilter (Skill 4.12)
- Filtering Data Using Filter by Selection (Skill 4.13)
- Sorting Records in a Datasheet (Skill 4.14)

1. Open the start file **AC2013-ChallengeYourself-4-4.**

2. If necessary, enable active content by clicking the **Enable Content** button in the Message Bar.

3. Save a copy of the file to work on named:
   [your initials]AC-ChallengeYourself-4-4

4. Create a new query named: **LargeJanShipments**

   a. Add all the fields from the *Shipments* table except *Cost*.

b. Configure the query so it returns only those orders from **1/1/14** to **1/31/14** (inclusive) that have a quantity greater than **75.**

   c. Run the query and review the results.

   d. Save and close the query.

5. Create a new query named: `YouthShipments`

   a. Add all the fields from the *Vaccines* table.

   b. The query should list the vaccines with a target audience of either children or teenagers.

   c. Add the *Shipments* table to this query and include the *DateShipped* field after the *TargetAudience* field.

   d. Run the query and review the results.

   e. Save and close the query.

6. Create a new query named: `PatientIncrease`

   a. Add all the fields from the *Locations* table.

   b. Add a calculated field named `PatientIncrease` to calculate a patient increase that is 20 percent higher than the current *PatientAvg*.

   c. Sort the query (descending) by this new calculated field.

   d. Hide the *PatientAvg* field from the query results.

   e. Run the query and review the results.

   f. Save and close the query.

7. Use the **Find Unmatched Query Wizard** to create a new query that identifies the vaccines in the *Vaccines* table that have no entry in the *Shipments* table.

   a. Include all fields from the *Vaccines* table except the *TargetAudience*.

   b. Name this query: `VaccinesNotShipped`

   c. Close the query.

8. Use the **Find Duplicates Query Wizard** to find out which Location IDs referenced in the *Shipments* table have received multiple shipments.

   a. Show all fields from the *Shipments* table.

   b. Name this query: `CountriesMultipleShipments`

   c. Close the query.

9. Create a new parameter query that displays all the fields from the *Locations* table. Configure the *Country* field so that it requests the name of the country from the user when the query is run.

   a. Use the user prompt: `Enter country name`

   b. Test the query and save it as: `CountrySearch`

   c. Close the query

10. Open the **Shipments** table. Apply a filter to show only those shipments that have a *VaccineID* of **Rabies.** Save and close the table.

11. Open the **Vaccines** table. Use sorting (in ascending order) so the records are sorted by the target audience and then by vaccine name. Save and close the table.

12. Close the database and exit Access.

on your own 4.5

In this project, you will continue working with the movie database from *Chapter 3, On Your Own 3.5*. Now that you have entered all of your movies, you will search for particular data using queries and filters.

Skills needed to complete this project:

- Finding Unmatched Data Using a Query (Skill 4.9)
- Finding Duplicate Data Using a Query (Skill 4.10)
- Using a Parameter Query (Skill 4.11)
- Using the Simple Query Wizard (Skill 4.1)
- Creating a Query in Design View (Skill 4.2)
- Adding Text Criteria to a Query (Skill 4.3)
- Adding Numeric and Date Criteria to a Query (Skill 4.4)
- Using AND and OR in a Query (Skill 4.5)
- Specifying the Sort Order in a Query (Skill 4.6)
- Hiding and Showing Fields in a Query (Skill 4.7)
- Adding a Calculated Field to a Query (Skill 4.8)
- Filtering Data Using AutoFilter (Skill 4.12)
- Filtering Data Using Filter by Selection (Skill 4.13)
- Sorting Records in a Datasheet (Skill 4.14)

1. Open the start file **AC2013-OnYourOwn-4-5.**
2. If necessary, enable active content by clicking the **Enable Content** button in the Message Bar.
3. Save a copy of the file to work on named: `[your initials]AC-OnYourOwn-4-5`
4. Create at least six queries. Of those six, you must have at least one parameter, one unmatched, and one duplicate query. For the other three select queries, you must demonstrate the use of the following features in a way that creates meaningful/useful queries:
   a. Apply text and numeric criteria, including using wildcards as well as *and* and *or* constructions.
   b. Creation of one calculated field.
   c. Hide a field in the query results
   d. Sort the query results
5. Apply a filter to one table.
6. Apply sorting to one table, demonstrating an understanding of proper use of innermost and outmost sorts.
7. Close the database and exit Access.

fix it 4.6

In this project, you will continue working with the pet store database from *Chapter 3, Fix It 3.6*. The store is currently having trouble with some queries. Find and fix their problems. Be sure to save the database objects after you make changes.

Skills needed to complete this project:

- Using a Parameter Query (Skill 4.11)
- Adding a Calculated Field to a Query (Skill 4.8)
- Hiding and Showing Fields in a Query (Skill 4.7)
- Adding Numeric and Date Criteria to a Query (Skill 4.4)
- Specifying the Sort Order in a Query (Skill 4.6)
- Adding Text Criteria to a Query (Skill 4.3)
- Using AND and OR in a Query (Skill 4.5)
- Sorting Records in a Datasheet (Skill 4.14)

1. Open the start file **AC2013-FixIt-4-6.**
2. If necessary, enable active content by clicking the **Enable Content** button in the Message Bar.
3. Save a copy of the file to work on named: `[your initials]AC-FixIt-4-6`
4. The **CustomersByPhone** query is not working properly. Fix it so when this query is run, it prompts the user to enter a phone number in order to find a particular customer. Use the prompt: `Enter customer phone number`
5. Fix the **PriceIncrease** query to correctly display a calculated field that increases the pet prices by 10 percent and hides the original pet price. Change the name of the calculated field to: `NewPrice`
6. The **OlderDogSales** query has several problems. Fix it so it correctly displays only dogs that are at least four months of age. Sort the results by pet age from the youngest to the oldest. Then, add the *Sales* table so only those dogs that have been sold are included in the query results. (Hint: Use the criterion `Is Not Null` to find records that are not blank.)
7. Fix the **Customers-W&B** query so only customers whose last names begin with a **W** or a **B** appear in the query results.
8. The *Pets* table is currently being sorted by *Price*. Remove this sort and change it so the data are sorted primarily by animal type, followed by the breeds within each animal type (both ascending).
9. Close the database and exit Access.

chapter 5

Exploring Advanced Tables

In this chapter, you will learn the following skills:

- Create new Access databases
- Import data from external sources
- Link to tables in other Access databases
- Add a calculated field to a table
- Customize field format and input mask properties
- Modify lookup field properties
- Apply validation rules to fields and tables
- Maintain data integrity through table relationships

Skill **5.1** Creating a Desktop Database from a Template
Skill **5.2** Creating a New Blank Database
Skill **5.3** Using Quick Start Application Parts
Skill **5.4** Importing Data from Excel
Skill **5.5** Importing Data from a Text File
Skill **5.6** Adding Records to a Table by Importing
Skill **5.7** Linking to a Table in Another Access Database
Skill **5.8** Adding a Calculated Field to a Table
Skill **5.9** Creating a Custom Text Field Format
Skill **5.10** Creating a Custom Input Mask
Skill **5.11** Modifying Lookup Field Properties
Skill **5.12** Creating Field Validation Rules
Skill **5.13** Creating Record Validation Rules
Skill **5.14** Enforcing Deletions and Updates in Relationships

introduction

This chapter expands on the basic table skills covered in Chapters 1 and 2. You will learn to create new databases from scratch using templates and Quick Start Application Parts and by importing data from a variety of source types. You will also learn to control data entry with custom text field formats, input masks, and lookup field properties. You will learn to manage data integrity by creating field and record validation rules and by enforcing cascading data changes between tables.

Skill 5.1 Creating a Desktop Database from a Template

A **template** is a file with predefined settings that you can use as a base to create a new database of your own. Using a template makes creating a fully formatted and designed database easy, saving you time and effort. Access templates include databases to manage contacts, track projects, and create a sales pipeline. When the database opens, you'll have an empty database structure complete with tables, forms, and reports, ready for you to enter data.

To create a new desktop database from a template:

1. If you already have a database open, click the **File** tab to open Backstage view, and click **New.**
2. The New page includes a few templates included when you installed Access. Most of these templates are for **Access web apps**—online databases that require a SharePoint server. To find templates for a **desktop database** (one that does not require SharePoint), type a keyword in the *Search for online templates* box or click one of the suggested terms listed below the search box.

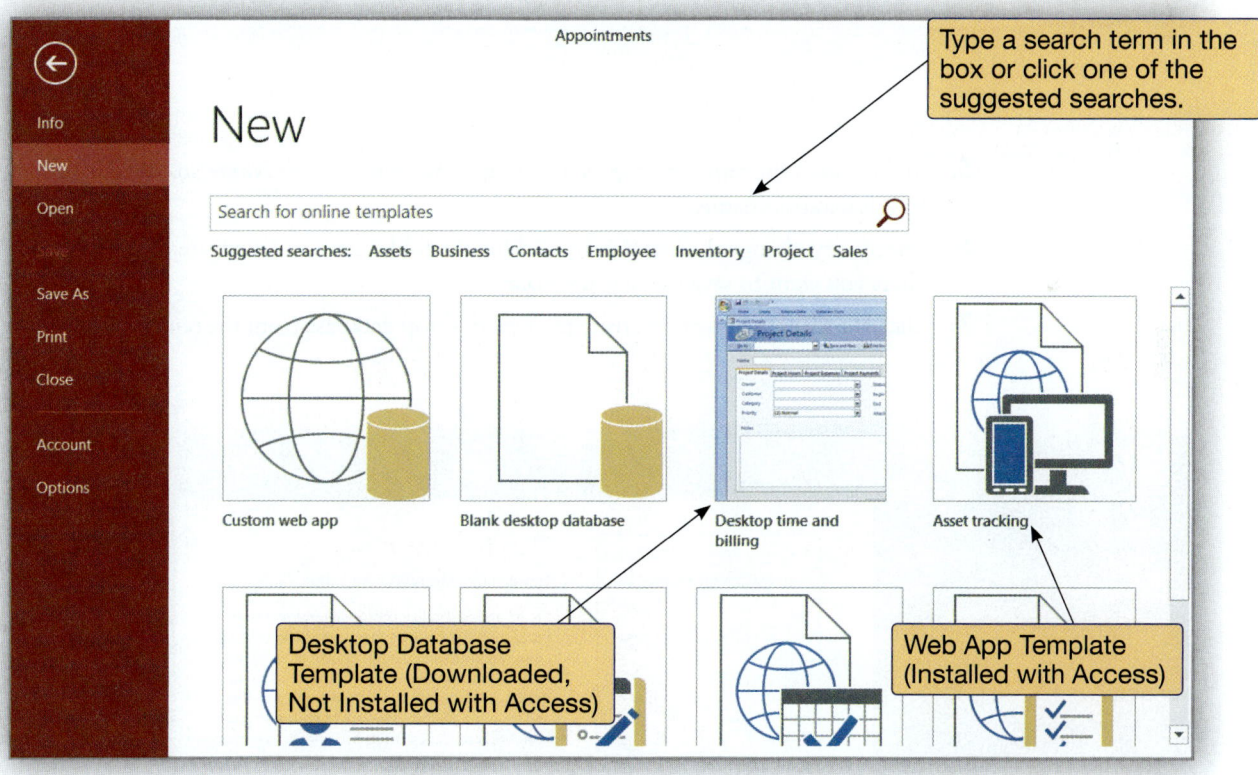

FIGURE AC 5.1

3. Access returns a list of templates that match the search. Note that desktop database templates usually include "desktop" in the template name. To search for a different template, type a new keyword in the search box, or select a category from the list at the right side of the page.
4. Click a template icon for a detailed description of the template. Notice that each description includes a star rating to let you know what other users thought of the template.

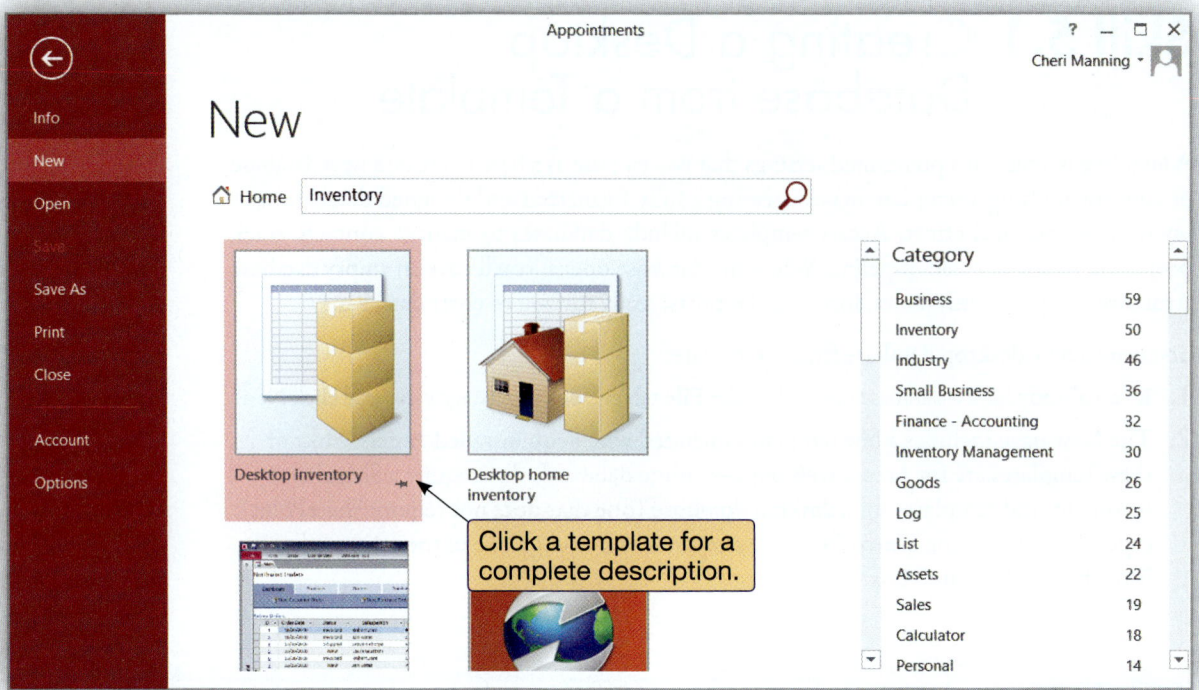

FIGURE AC 5.2

5. To download the template, type a meaningful name in the *File Name* box to replace the default database name.
6. If necessary, change the location by clicking the folder icon and navigate to the location where you want to save the new database.
7. Click the **Create** button to create the new desktop database from the template.

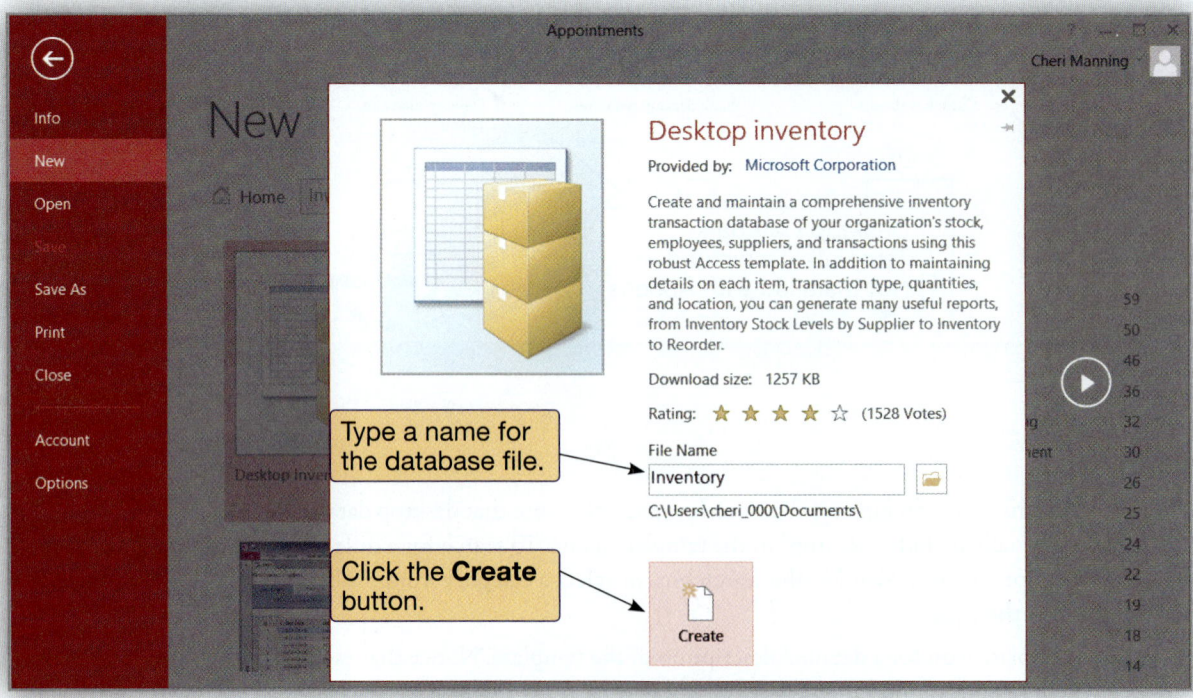

FIGURE AC 5.3

8. A new database opens, prepopulated with all the template objects.
9. If the database template you selected includes macros or other active content, the Message Bar will show a security warning. Click the **Enable Content** button to allow the active content to run.

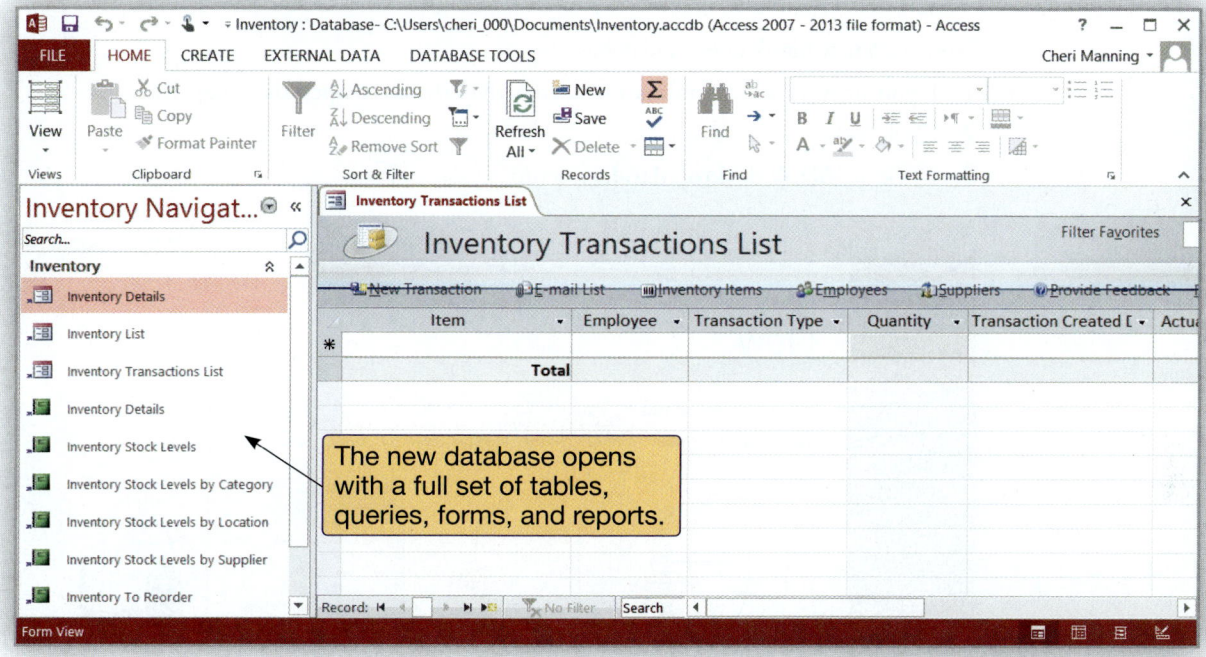

FIGURE AC 5.4

tips & tricks

Some of the database templates can be complicated, with many related tables. Before entering data, take some time to review the tables and table relationships. You should remove any unnecessary fields, but be careful not to remove a field that is part of a relationship.

another method

If you are opening the Access application directly, you begin at the Start page. Templates are listed at the right side of the page just as they are in the New page.

let me try

Open the data file **AC5-Working** and try this skill on your own:

1. Create a new desktop database from the **Desktop inventory** template. *Hint:* Search for the keyword *inventory* or use the **Inventory** link in the *Suggested searches* list.
2. Name the database: **Inventory**
3. Close the **Inventory** database.

skill 5.1 Creating a Desktop Database from a Template

Skill 5.2 Creating a New Blank Database

To begin a new Access database from scratch, you must first create the database file. You cannot begin creating tables, forms, and other database objects until the database has been saved.

To create a new blank desktop database:

1. If you already have a database open, click the **File** tab to open Backstage view.
2. Click **New**.
3. Click the **Blank desktop database** icon.

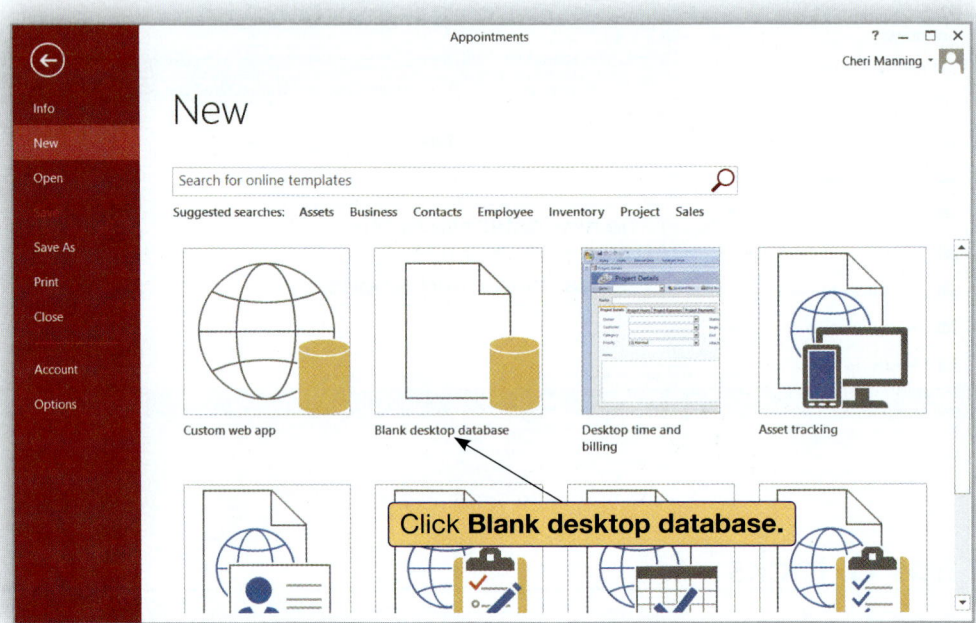

FIGURE AC 5.5

4. Enter a file name for the new database in the *File Name* box. If you want to create the file in a different location, click the folder icon and navigate to the location you want.
5. Click the **Create** button to create the new blank database.

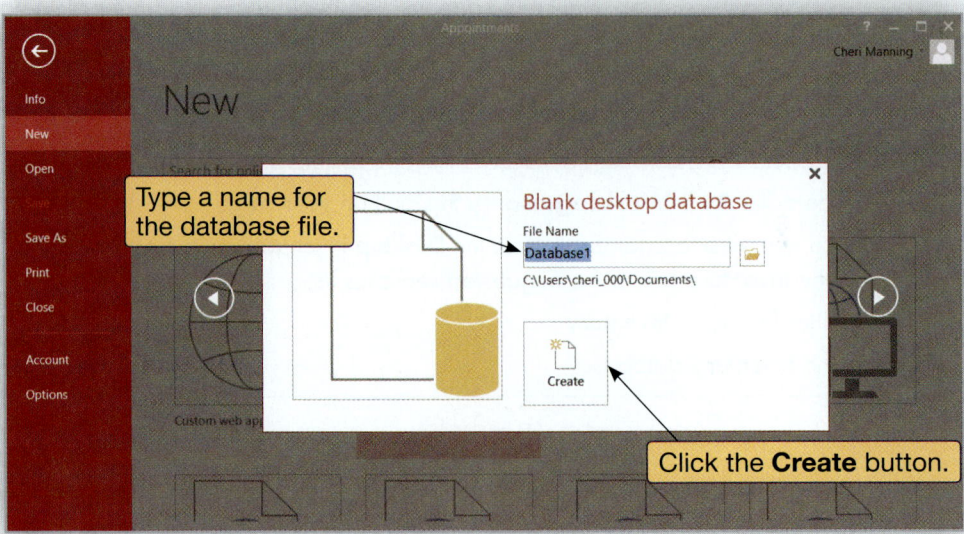

FIGURE AC 5.6

If you began with another database open, Access will close it and open the new blank database.

Access begins the new database with a temporary table, *Table1,* open in Datasheet view where you can begin adding data. As with any new table in Datasheet view, the first field is an AutoNumber field named *ID.* When you close the table, Access will prompt you to save the table with a new name. If you close the table and choose not to save it, Access will remove it from the Navigation Pane.

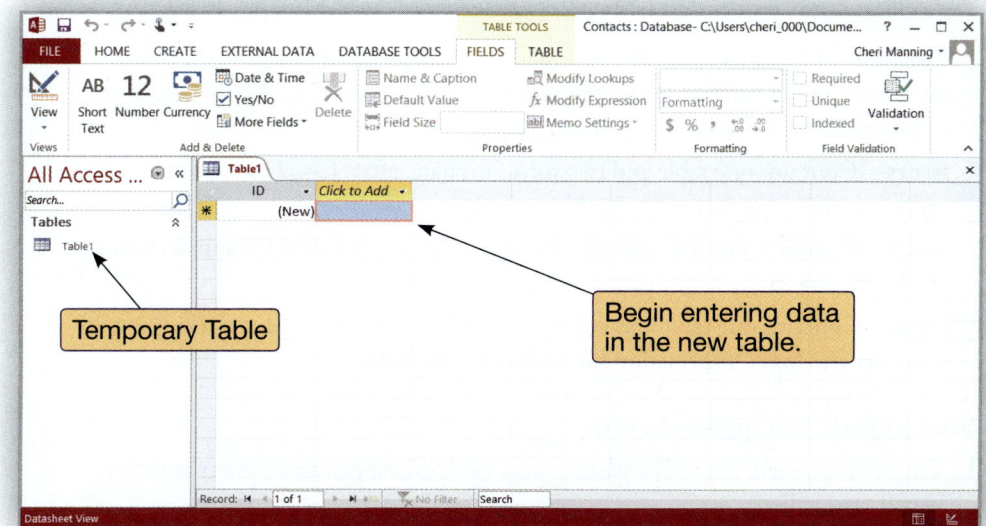

FIGURE AC 5.7

tips & tricks

Unlike other Microsoft Office applications, Access does not create a new blank database when you open the application. Instead, Access opens to Backstage view where you can select an existing database to open or begin a new one.

tell me more

For more information about working with new tables, refer to these skills:

- Creating and Saving a Table in Datasheet View
- Renaming Fields
- Adding Fields in Datasheet View
- Using Quick Start to Add Related Fields

let me try

Open the data file **AC5-Working** and try this skill on your own:

1. Create a new blank desktop database and name it: `Contacts`
2. Close the default table without saving it.
3. Keep the **Contacts** database open if you are moving on to the skill *Using Quick Start Application Parts* next; close it if you are finished working with these skills.

skill 5.2 Creating a New Blank Database

Skill 5.3 Using Quick Start Application Parts

Beginning a new blank database can be intimidating. **Quick Start application parts** provide a table template that you can use to start building a database. Most also include forms for data entry. There are five Quick Start application parts available:

Comments—Contains a single table. Good for maintaining a running list of changes to the database.

Contacts—Contains one table, one query, three forms, and four reports. Good for storing names, addresses, and phone numbers for customers, vendors, students, employees, or any similar group of people.

Issues—Contains one table and two forms for data entry. Good for tracking technical support issues or project-related problems.

Tasks—Contains one table and two forms for data entry. Good for a to-do list or parts of a larger project.

Users—Contains one table and two forms for data entry. Good for tracking e-mail addresses and login information for Web site or network users.

To use a Quick Start application part:

1. On the *Create* tab, in the *Templates* group, click the **Application Parts** button to expand the gallery.
2. In the *Quick Start* section, click the option you want to add.

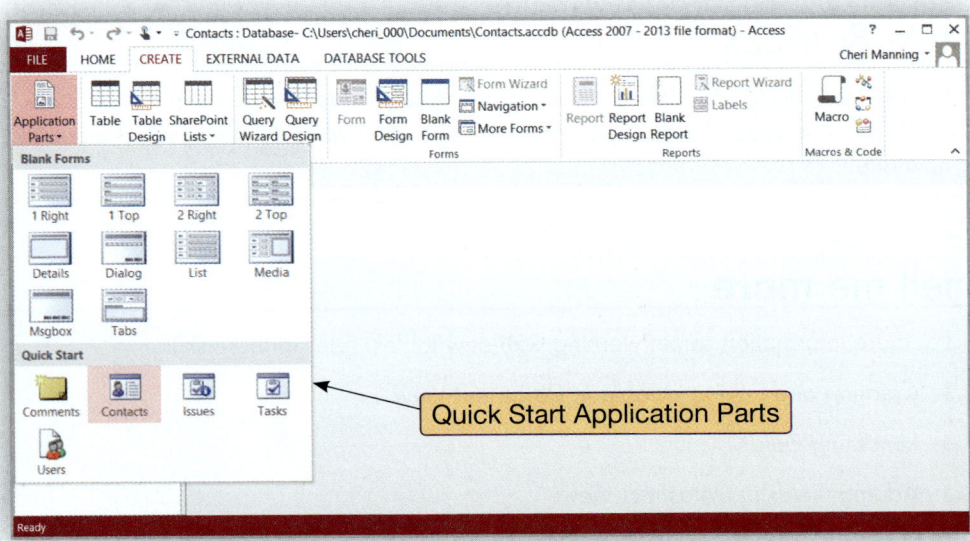

FIGURE AC 5.8

3. If you have any objects open, Access will ask to close them. Click **Yes.**
4. If your database has other tables, Access will ask if you want to establish a relationship between the new table added by the application part and another table in your database. To continue without adding any table relationships, select the **There is no relationship.** radio button. To create a one-to-many relationship between the tables, select the radio button for the relationship you want to create and then follow the prompts to create the new field for the "many" side of the relationship.
5. Access automatically adds the objects in the application part you selected to your database.

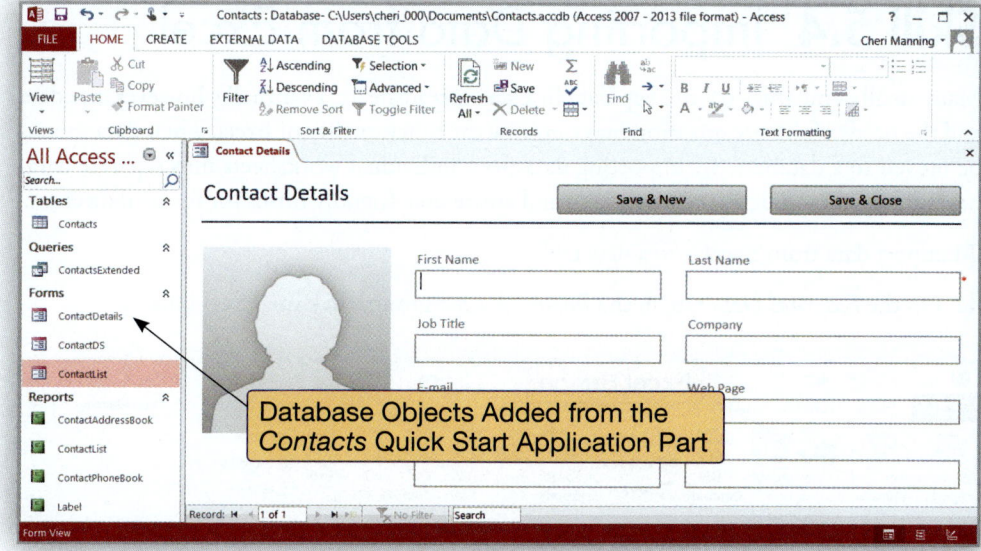

FIGURE AC 5.9

tell me more

If you have a table and related database objects that you use often, you can save the group as a custom application part.

1. Delete any database objects you don't want to include in the application part. (Be sure to make a copy of the database first!)
2. Click the **File** tab and then click **Save As.**
3. In the list of database file types, select **Template** and then click the **Save As** button.
4. In the *Create New Template from this Database* dialog, enter a name for the application part and a description.
5. Click the **Application Part** check box.
6. Click **OK**.

The new application part is now available from the *User Templates* section at the bottom of the *Application Parts* gallery.

let me try

If the Contacts databases is not already open, open the data file **Contacts** and try this skill on your own:

1. Add database objects from the **Contacts** Quick Start application part.
2. If Access displays the security warning, click the **Enable Content** button.
3. Open the **ContactDetails** form and enter information for a few records. Use the **Save & New** and **Save & Close** buttons.
4. Open the other database objects and observe how the database objects work together.
5. Close all open database objects without saving any changes you may have made and then close the database.

skill 5.3   Using Quick Start Application Parts

Skill 5.4 Importing Data from Excel

Many small companies try to keep data in Excel spreadsheets. Eventually, however, the data and the needs of the organization may outgrow the functionality of Excel. Their data should be moved to a database. By importing data from individual worksheets into separate database tables, you can define relationships and create user-friendly forms for future data entry.

To import data from Excel into a new table:

1. On the *External Data* tab, in the *Import & Link* group, click the **Excel** button.

FIGURE AC 5.10

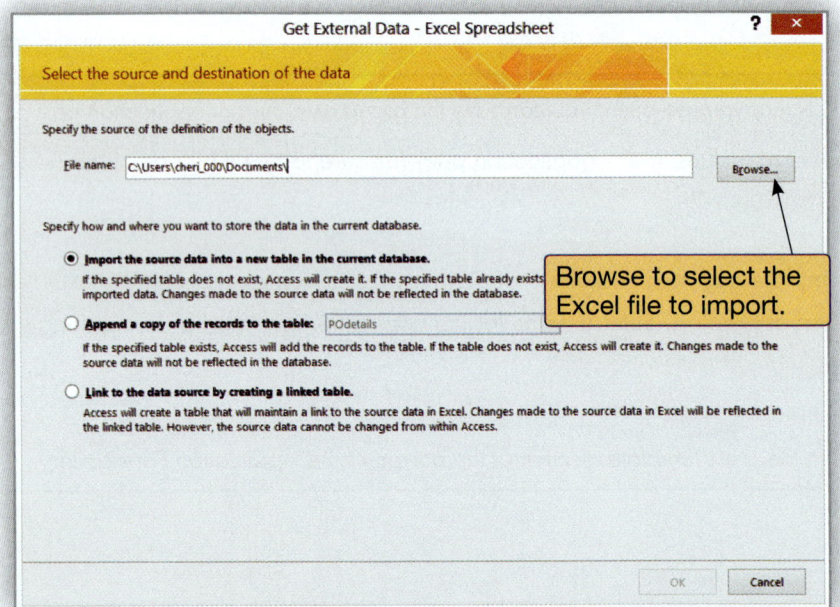

FIGURE AC 5.11

2. The *Get External Data - Excel Spreadsheet* dialog opens. Click the **Browse...** button and navigate to find the spreadsheet that contains the data you want to import.

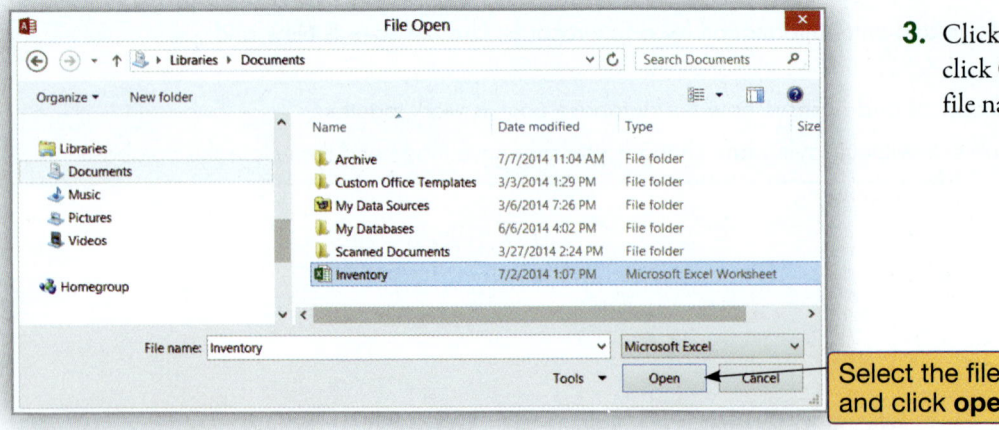

FIGURE AC 5.12

3. Click the file name and then click **Open,** or double-click the file name.

4. The option to import the source data into a new table is selected by default. Click **OK**.

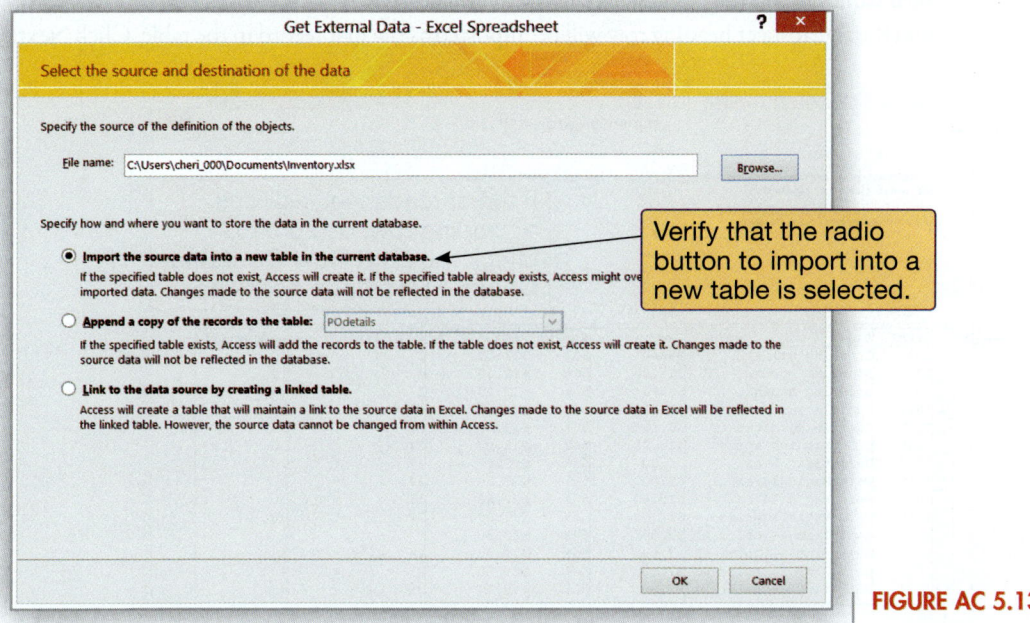

FIGURE AC 5.13

5. If your spreadsheet contains more than one worksheet, select the worksheet you want to import. If you want to import a specific named range instead of an entire worksheet, click the **Show Named Ranges** radio button and then select the named range you want to import. The preview box shows the columns in the worksheet you selected. Click **Next**.

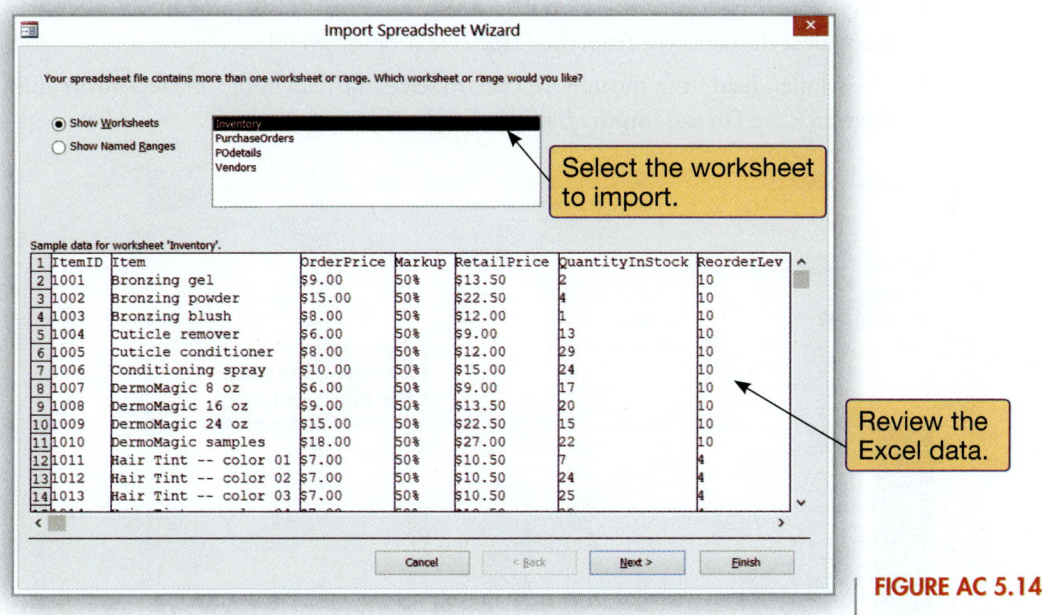

FIGURE AC 5.14

skill 5.4 Importing Data from Excel

6. If the first row of your spreadsheet corresponds to field names, click the **First Row Contains Column Headings** check box, and Access will automatically use the column headings as field names. If you forget to check this option, Access will name the fields *Field1, Field2*, etc., and the spreadsheet heading row will be imported as the first record in the table. Click **Next**.

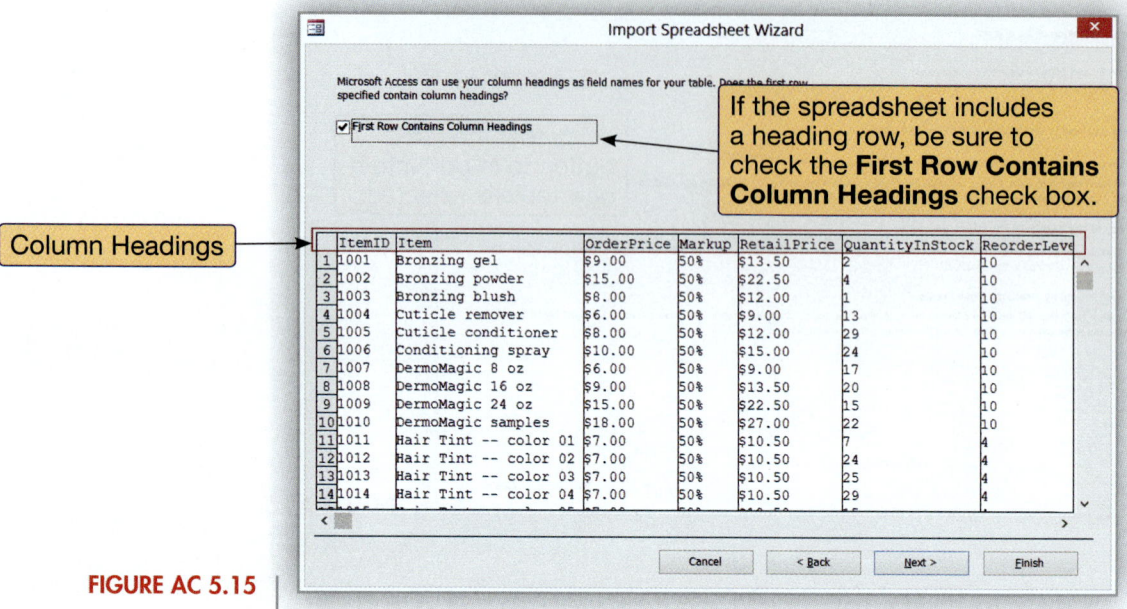

FIGURE AC 5.15

7. The next step allows you to specify properties for each of the fields. You can make changes here or modify field properties after the data import is complete. Click **Next** when you are finished modifying field properties.

   - To rename a field, click to select the field in the preview image and then type the new name in the *Field Name* box.
   - To specify a data type for a field, click to select the field in the preview image and then select the data type from the *Data Type* drop-down list.
   - To exclude a field from the import, click to select the field in the preview image and then click the **Do not import field (Skip)** check box.

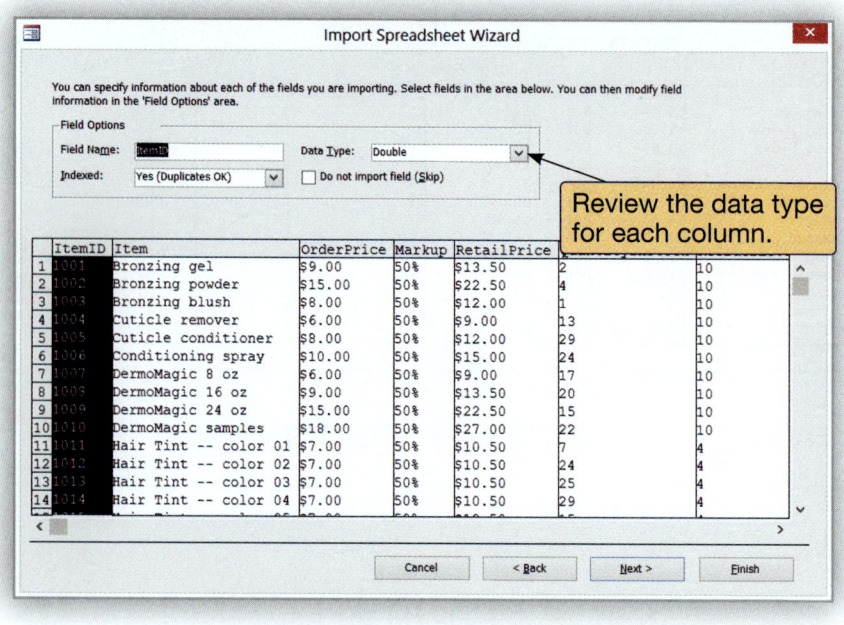

FIGURE AC 5.16

8. By default, Access will add a new AutoNumber field to the table to use as the primary key. If the worksheet already includes a column with a unique identifier for each record, click the **Choose my own primary key.** radio button and select the column name from the drop-down list. Click **Next** to finish the import.

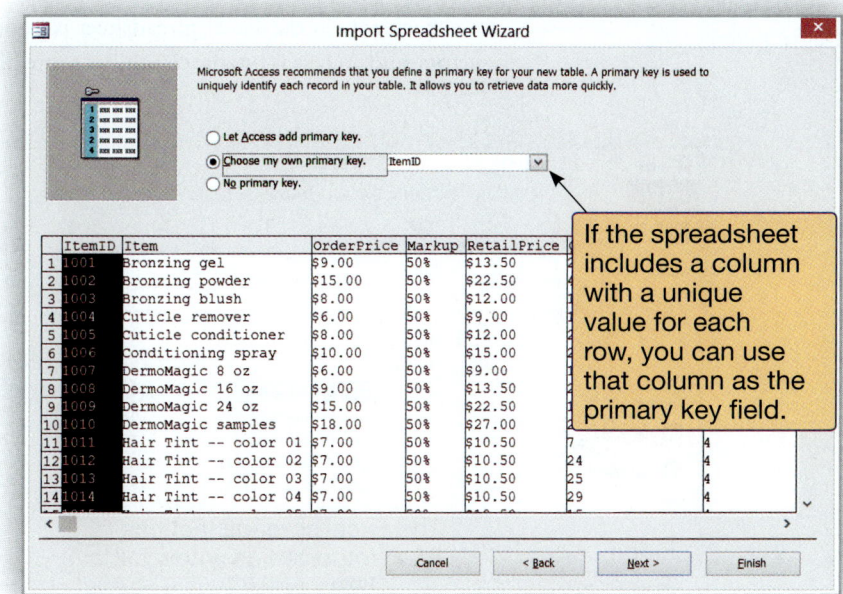

FIGURE AC 5.17

9. Access will suggest a name for the table using the Excel file name. You can modify the name or accept the suggestion. Click **Finish.**

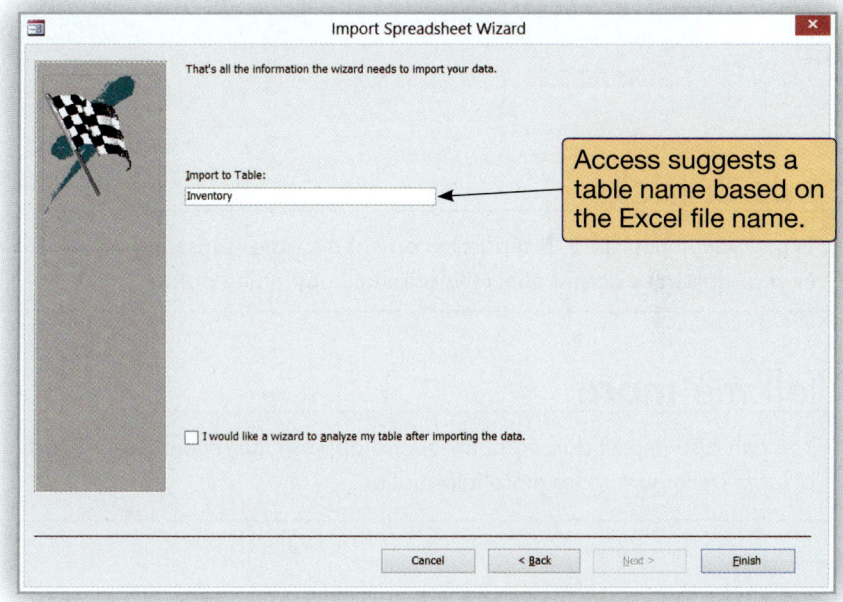

FIGURE AC 5.18

10. Click the **Close** button to close the wizard. If you want to save these import steps to repeat again later, be sure to check the **Save Import Steps** check box first.

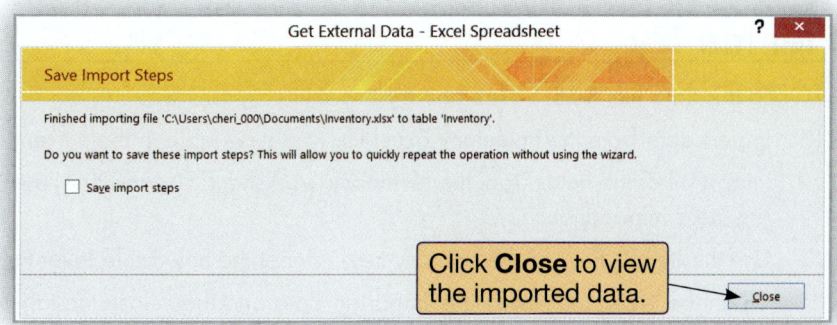

FIGURE AC 5.19

skill 5.4   Importing Data from Excel

Each row in the Excel spreadsheet is imported as a record in the new table. If there are errors, and Access is unable to import some of the data, you will see a warning message.

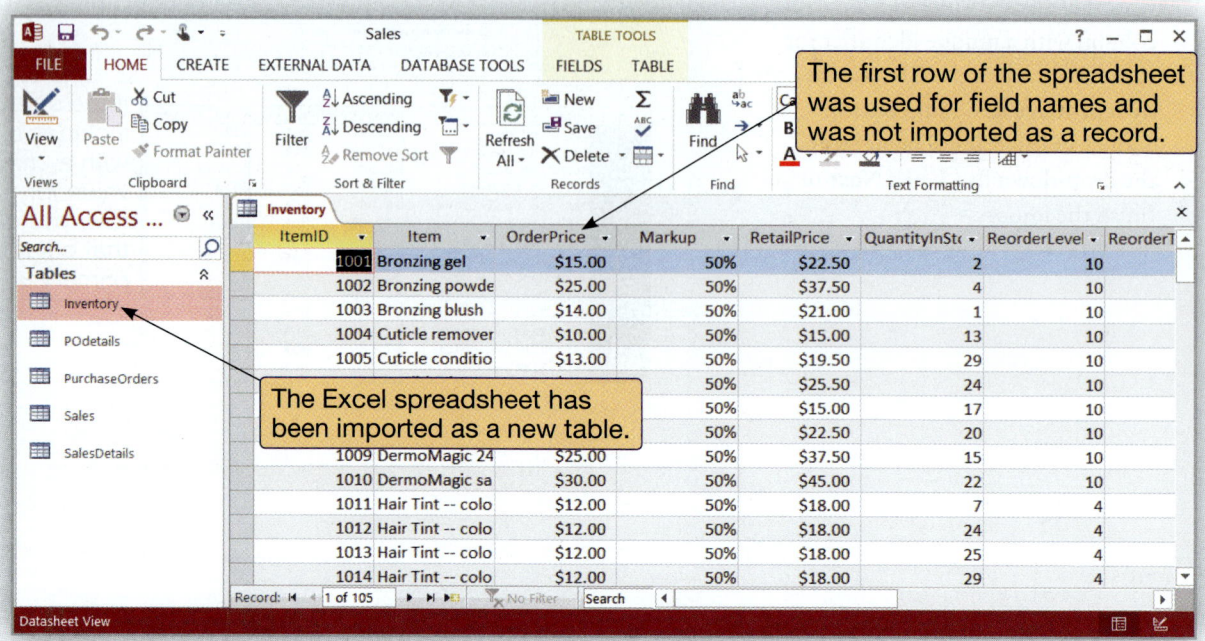

FIGURE AC 5.20

tips & tricks

When you **import** data, a separate copy of the data is inserted into your database. Changes you make to the records in your database do not affect the original copy of the data.

tell me more

You can also import data from Excel and append the records to an existing table. Refer to the skill *Adding Records to a Table by Importing* for more information.

another method

To import data from an Excel spreadsheet, right-click any table in the Navigation Pane, point to **Import,** and click **Excel.**

let me try

Open the data file **AC5-Sales** and try this skill on your own:

1. Import data from the **Inventory** Excel file to a new table in the current database.
2. Import all of the fields from the **Inventory** worksheet. Use the first row as column headings. Do not change any field information.
3. Use the **ItemID** field as the primary key. Accept the new table **Inventory.** Do not save the import.
4. Open the table and review the imported data and then close the table.

Skill 5.5 Importing Data from a Text File

Text files are a common format used when passing data between organizations because they can be read by many different application programs. A text file that includes multiple data fields may separate the fields with a specific character called a **delimiter**. Common delimiters are commas, tabs, semicolons, and spaces. Text files that use tabs, spaces, or semicolons as the delimiter are stored as text files with the .txt file extension. Text files that use a comma as the delimiter may be saved as a **CSV (comma-separated value)** file with the .csv extension.

To import data from a delimited text file into a new table:

1. On the *External Data* tab, in the *Import & Link* group, click the **Text File** button.

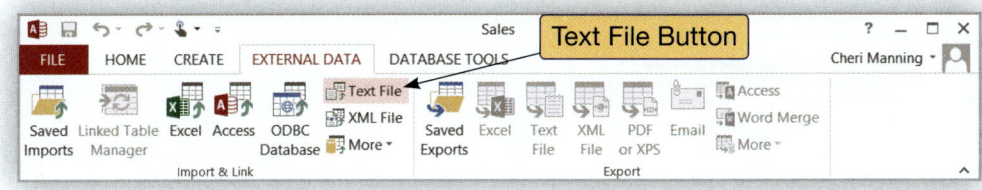

FIGURE AC 5.21

2. The *Get External Data - Text File* dialog opens. Click the **Browse...** button and navigate to find the text file that contains the data you want to import.

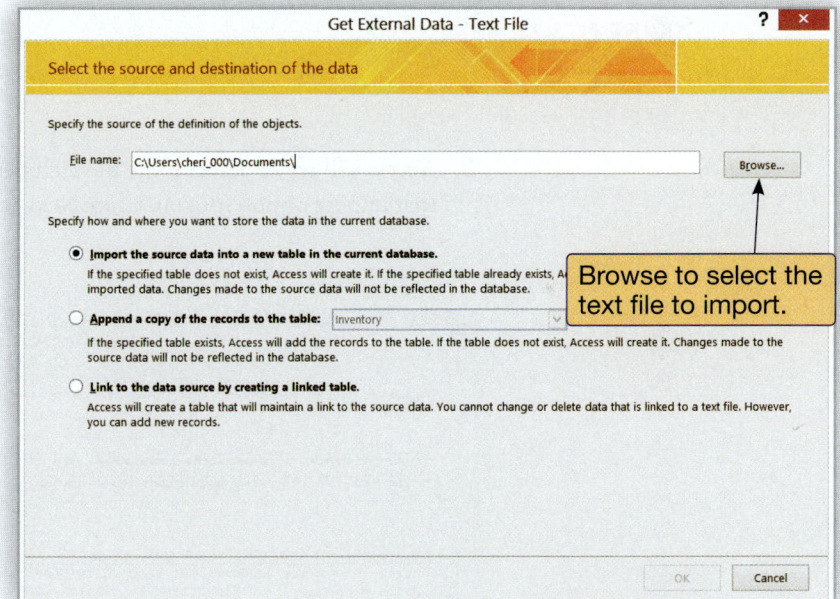

FIGURE AC 5.22

3. Click the file name and then click **Open**, or double-click the file name.

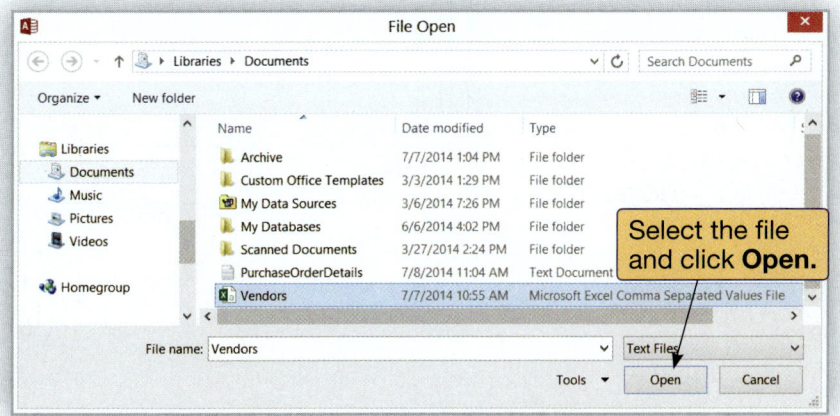

FIGURE AC 5.23

skill 5.5   Importing Data from a Text File

4. The option to import the source data into a new table is selected by default. Click **OK**.

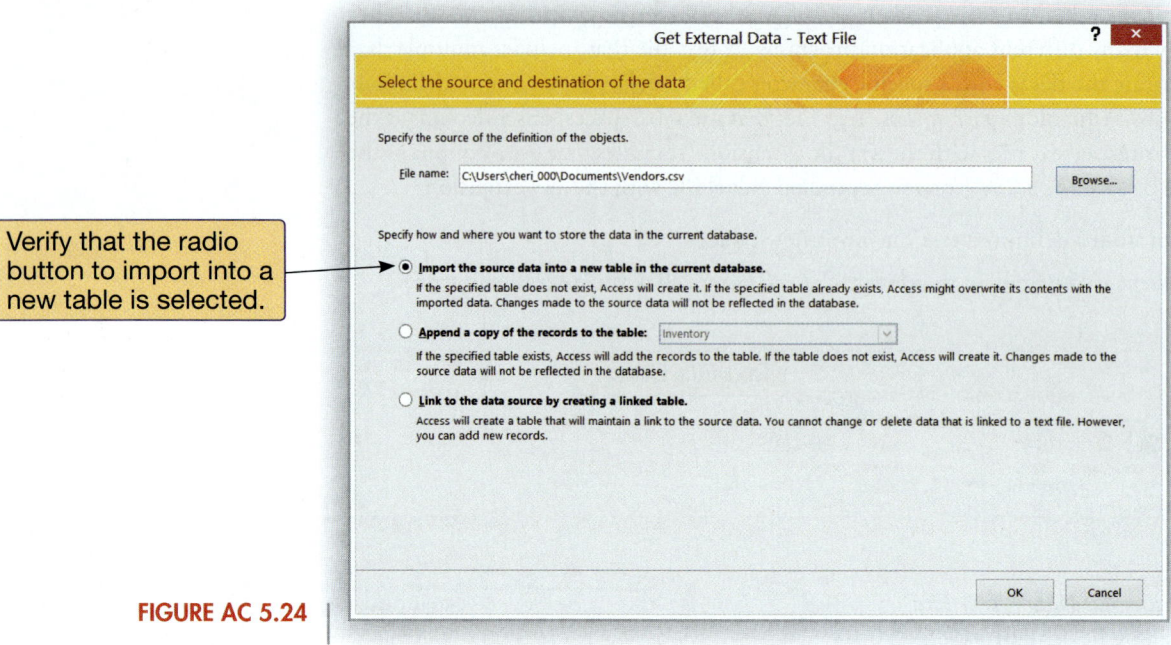

FIGURE AC 5.24

5. Access will try to detect if the file includes an obvious delimiter character and select that import option for you. Click **Next** to continue.

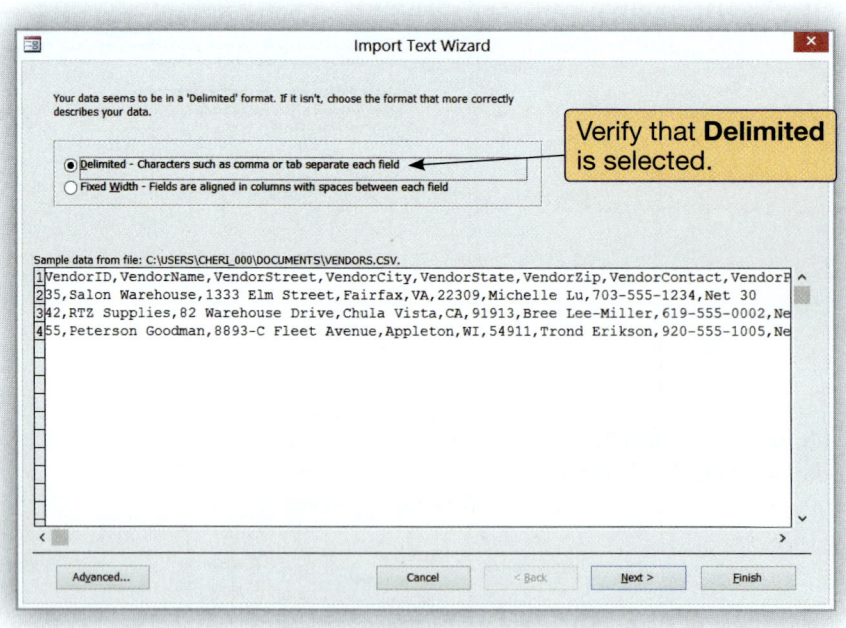

FIGURE AC 5.25

6. Click the radio button to select the delimiter character used in the file.
7. If the first row of the text file corresponds to field names, click the **First Row Contains Field Names** check box. Access will automatically use the column headings as field names. Review the import preview and then click **Next.**

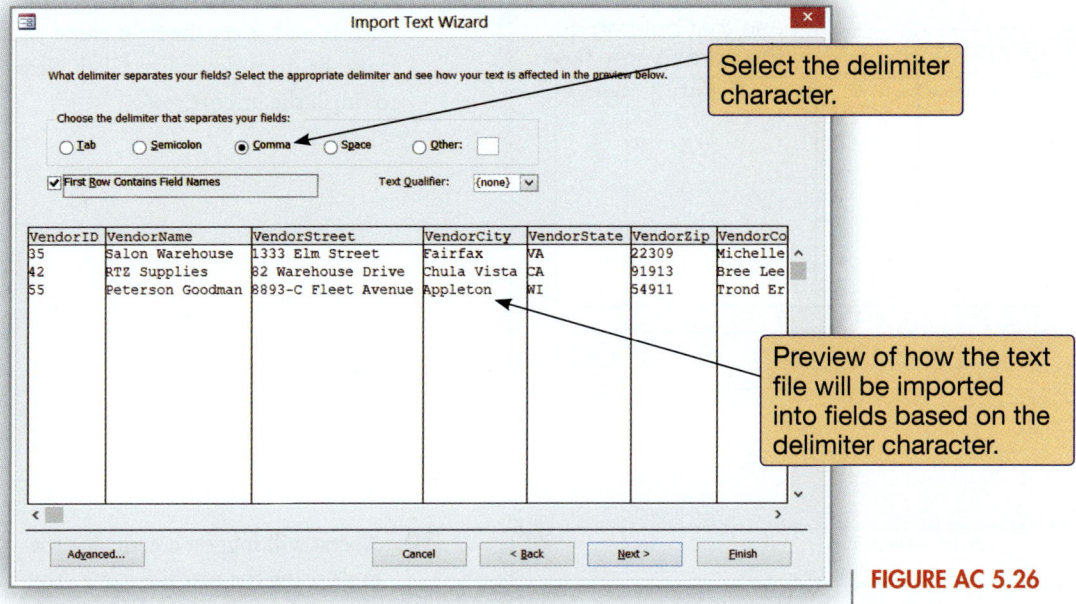

FIGURE AC 5.26

8. The next step allows you to specify properties for each of the fields. You can make changes here or modify field properties after the data import is complete. Click **Next** when you are finished modifying field properties.

- To rename a field, click to select the field in the preview image and then type the new name in the *Field Name* box.
- To specify a data type for a field, click to select the field in the preview image and then select the data type from the *Data Type* drop-down list.
- To exclude a field from the import, click to select the field in the preview image and then click the **Do not import field (Skip)** check box.

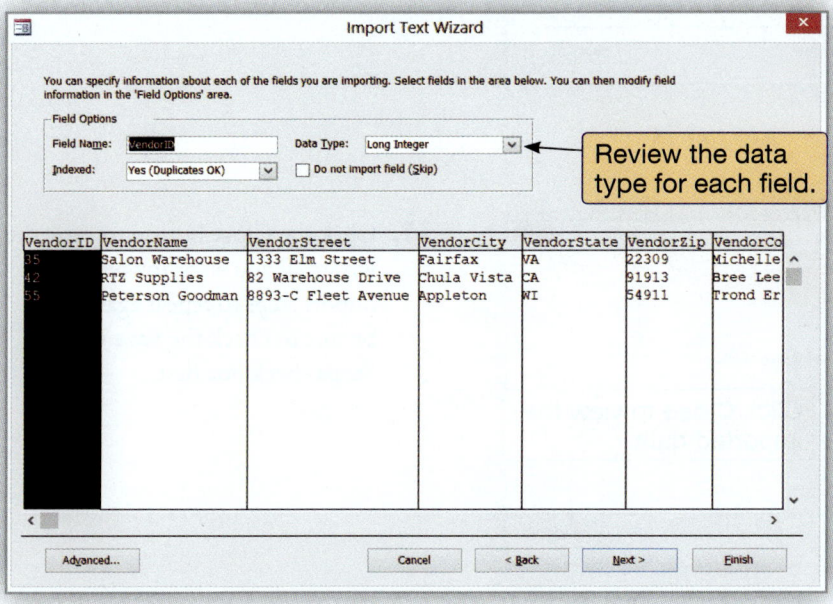

FIGURE AC 5.27

skill 5.5   Importing Data from a Text File

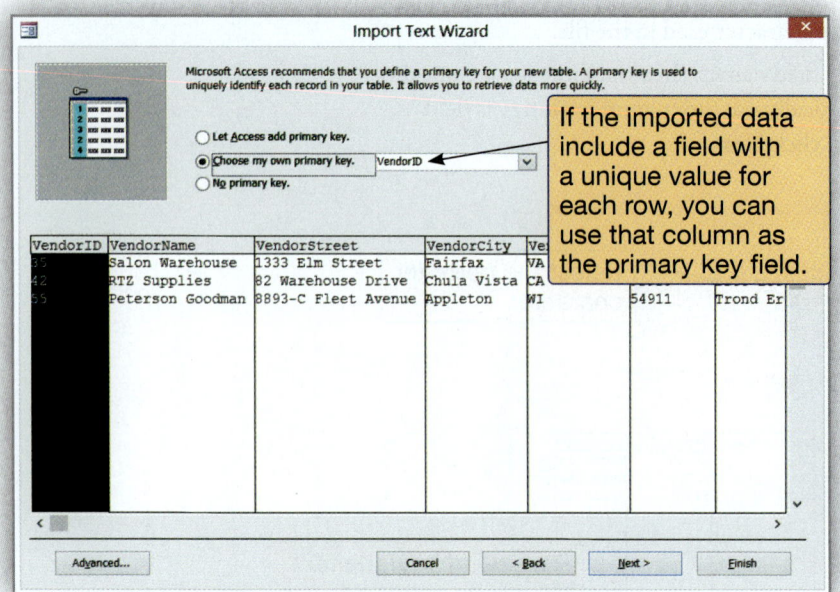

FIGURE AC 5.28

9. By default, Access will add a new AutoNumber field to the table to use as the primary key. If the file already includes a field with a unique identifier for each record, click the **Choose my own primary key.** radio button, and select the field name from the drop-down list. Click **Next** to finish the import.

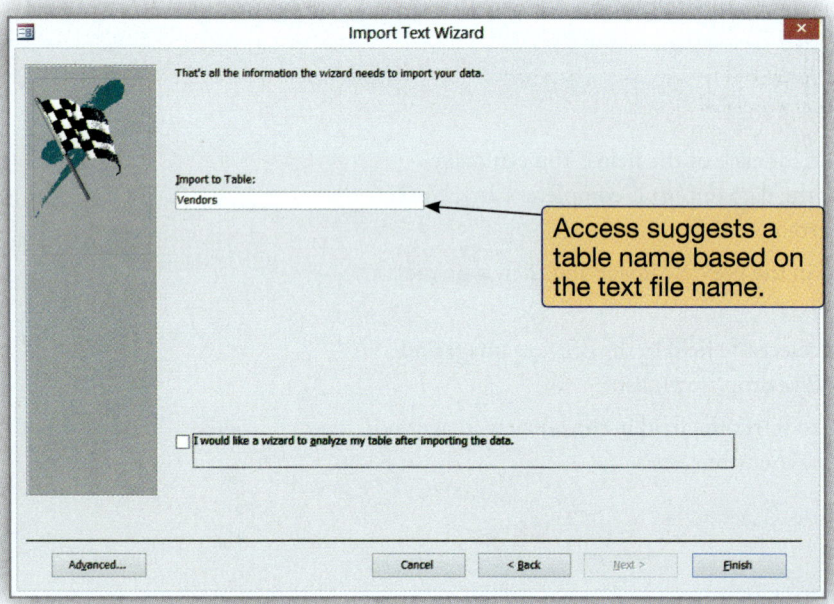

FIGURE AC 5.29

10. Access will suggest a name for the table using the text file name. You can modify the name or accept the suggestion. Click **Finish.**

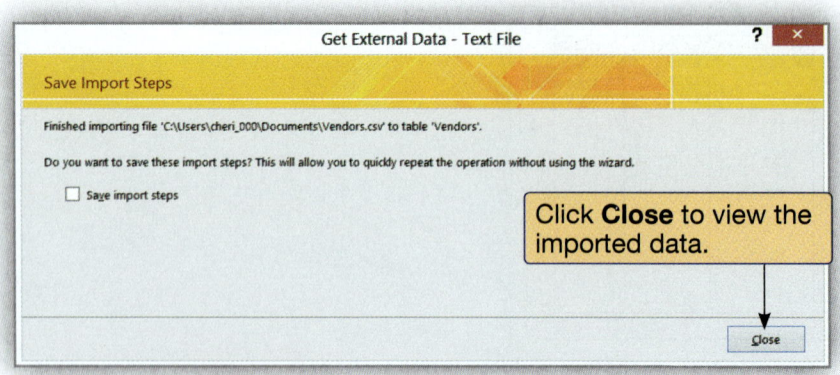

FIGURE AC 5.30

11. Click the **Close** button to close the wizard. If you want to save these import steps to repeat again later, be sure to check the **Save Import Steps** check box first.

Each line in the text file is imported as a record in the new table. If there are errors, and Access is unable to import some of the data, you will see a warning message.

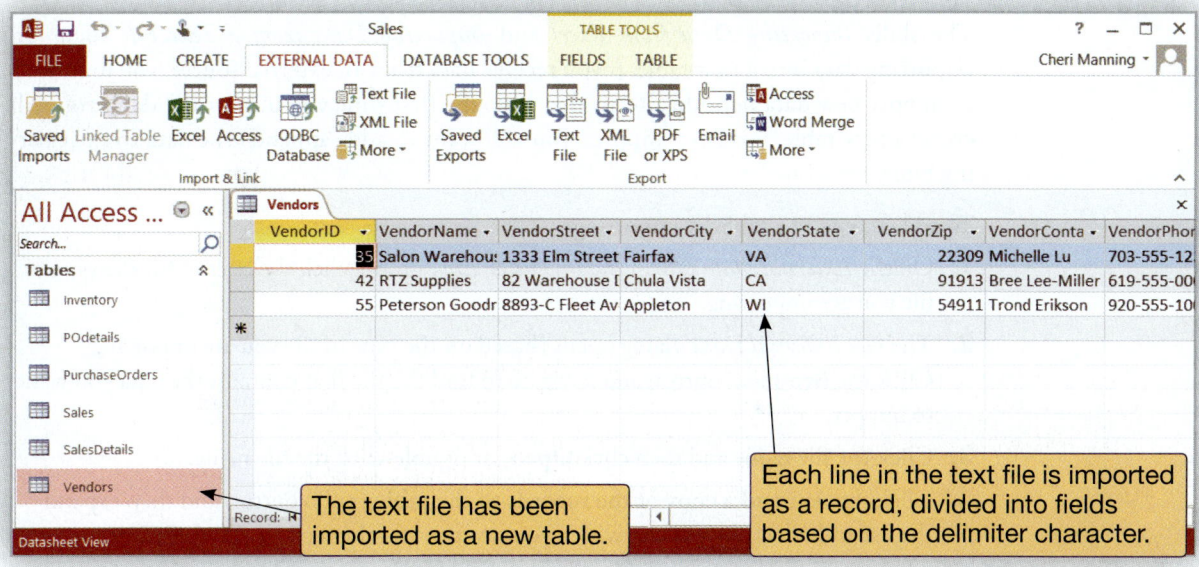

FIGURE AC 5.31

tips & tricks

When you import data, a separate copy of the data is inserted into your database. Changes you make to the records in your database do not affect the original copy of the data.

tell me more

You can also import data from a text file and append the records to an existing table. Refer to the skill *Adding Records to a Table by Importing* for more information.

another method

To import data from a text file, right-click any table in the Navigation Pane, point to **Import,** and click **Text File.**

let me try

If the database is not already open, open the data file **AC5-Sales** and try this skill on your own:

1. Import data from the **Vendors** comma-delimited text file to a new table in the current database.
2. Import all of the fields from the **Vendors** file. Use the first row as column headings. Do not change any field information.
3. Use the **VendorID** field as the primary key. Accept the new table **Vendors.** Do not save the import.
4. Open the table and review the imported data and then close the table.

skill 5.5   Importing Data from a Text File

Skill 5.6 Adding Records to a Table by Importing

The skills *Importing Data from Excel* and *Importing Data from a Text File* focus on importing data into a new table. If you receive data from an external source, you may need to import new data periodically. In that case, the first time you import the data, you will create a new table. For later imports, you will want to add (append) the data to the existing table.

To add records to a table by importing:

1. On the *External Data* tab, in the *Import & Link* group, click the button for the type of file you are importing.
2. The *Get External Data* dialog opens (based on the type of file you are importing). Click the **Browse...** button and navigate to find the file that contains the data you want to import.
3. Click the file name and then click **Open,** or double-click the file name.
4. Click the **Append a copy of the records to the table:** radio button and then expand the list and select the table to which you want to add the records. Click **OK.**

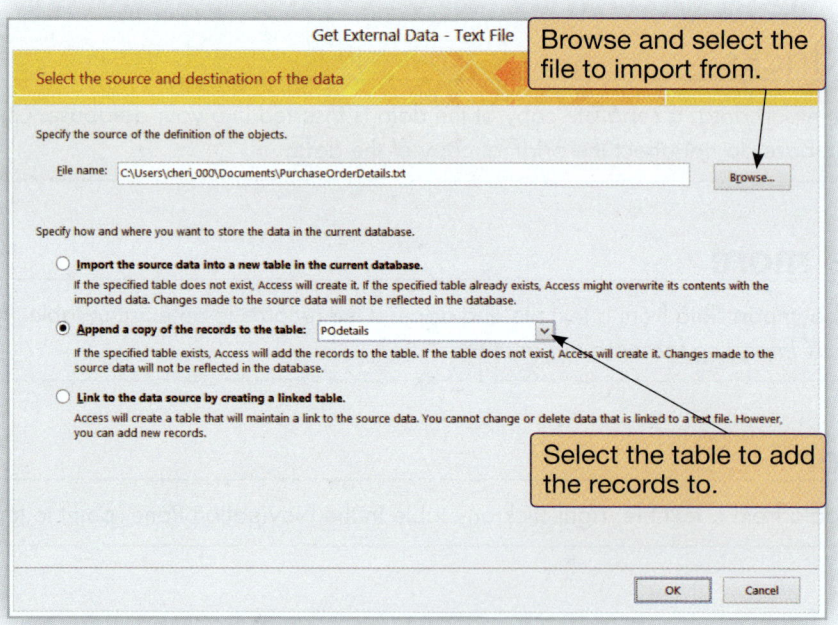

FIGURE AC 5.32

5. The next step is the same as if you were importing into a new table. If you are importing from Excel, select the worksheet or named range to import. If you are importing a text file, select whether the fields are separated by a delimiter character or by fixed width. Click **Next** to continue.
6. Again, the next step is the same as if you were importing into a new table. If the first row of the import corresponds to field names or column headings, click the check box.

If you are importing from a text file, select the delimiter character or set the column width in the preview box. Figure AC 5.33 shows the options for importing from a tab-delimited text file where the first row contains field names. Click **Next**.

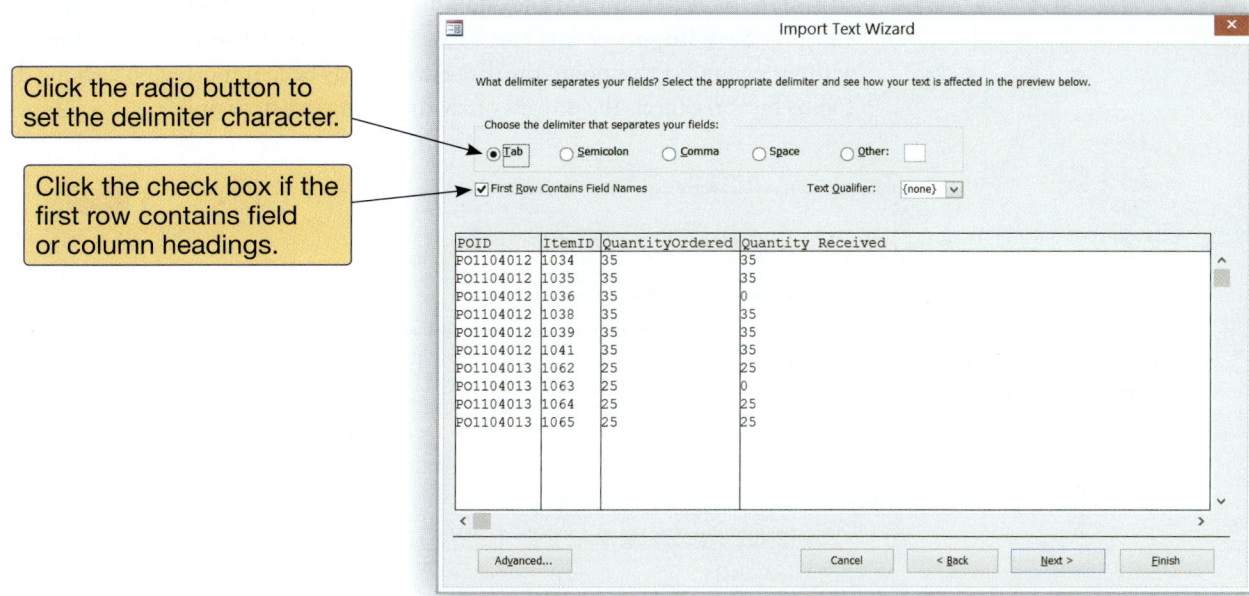

FIGURE AC 5.33

7. Because you are appending data to an existing table, you do not have the option to change the data type for any of the fields or to select a primary key. The final step is to click **Finish** to import the records and add them to the table.

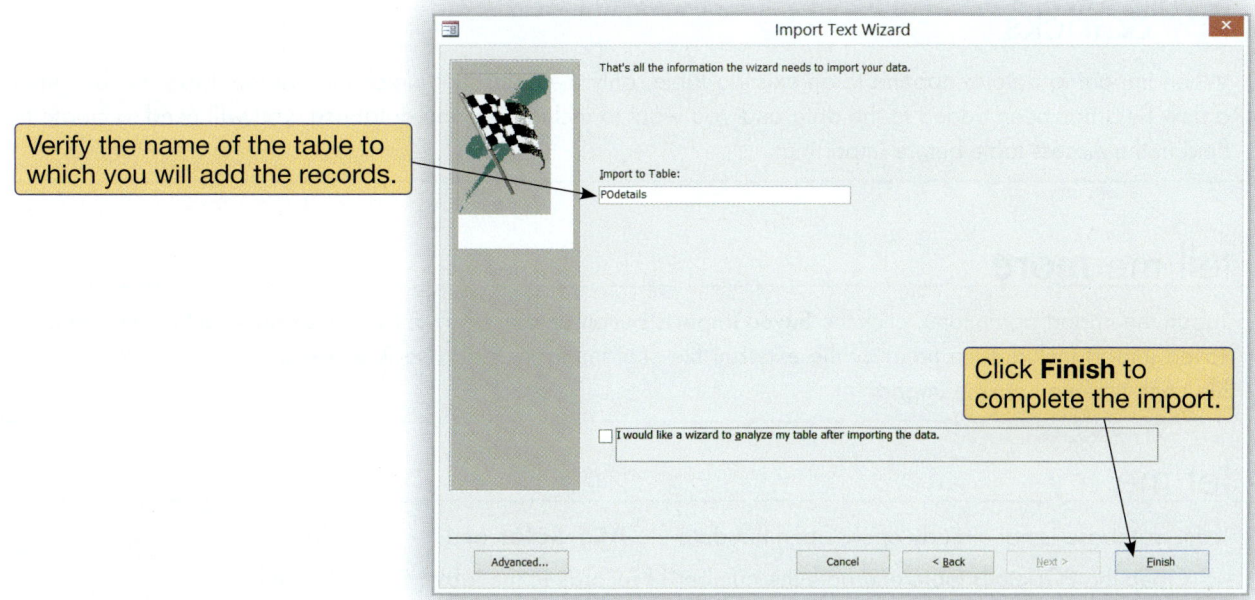

FIGURE AC 5.34

skill 5.6 Adding Records to a Table by Importing

8. To save these import steps to repeat again later, check the **Save Import Steps** check box. If not, click the **Close** button to close the *Get External Data* dialog.
9. When you click the *Save Import Steps* check box, the dialog updates to include details for the saved import. Verify the name for the saved import in the *Save as* box. You can change the name if you want and add a description of the import in the *Description* box. Click the **Save Import** button to save the import or click **Cancel** to close the dialog without saving. At this point, the data have already been imported, so clicking the *Cancel* button cancels the process of saving the import steps only.

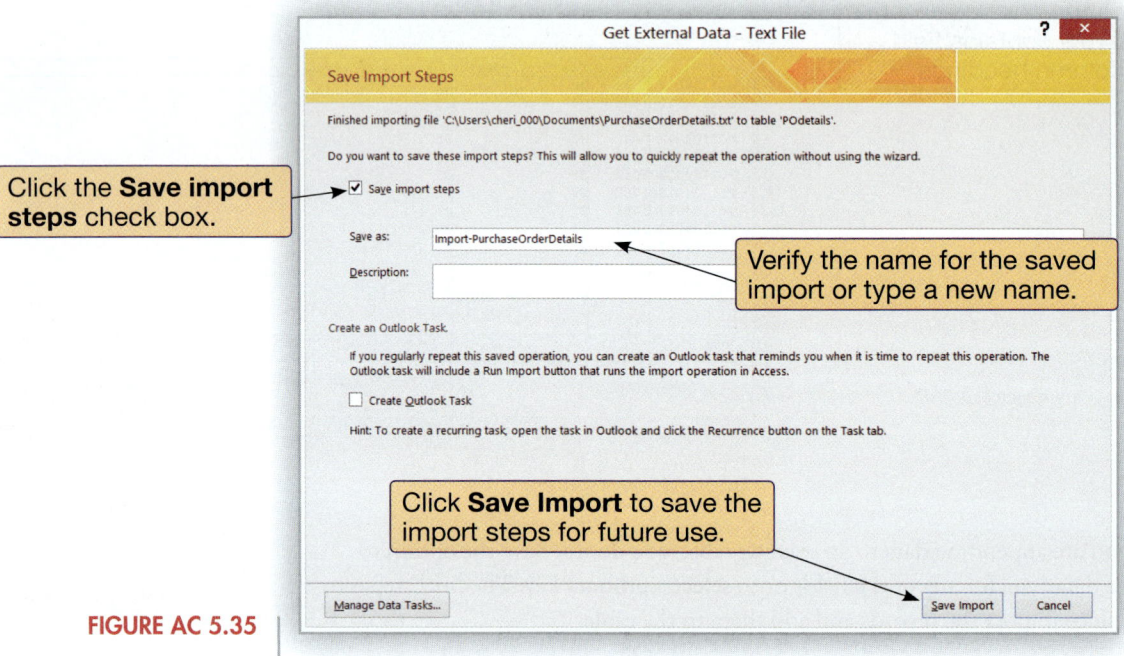

FIGURE AC 5.35

tips & tricks

When importing data to append to an existing table, only the fields that match the original table will be imported. If a new field has been added to the data and you want to include it in the database, you will need to create the new field in the Access table before importing.

tell me more

To run the import again later, click the **Saved Imports** button on the *External Data* tab and select the import to run. The saved import includes the name of the external file containing the data, so if necessary, be sure to rename the data file each time you run the import.

let me try

If the database is not already open, open the data file **AC5-Sales** and try this skill on your own:
1. Open the **PODetails** table and note the number of records in the table. Close the table.
2. Import data from the **PurchaseOrderDetails** text file and append the records to the **PODetails** table.
3. The data fields in the text file are separated by tabs. The first row in the text file is the header row.
4. Save the import steps. Use the default name suggested by Access.
5. Open the **PODetails** table and note the number of records. Close the table.

Skill 5.7 Linking to a Table in Another Access Database

When you import data, a separate copy of the data is inserted into your database. Changes you make to the records in your database do not affect the original copy of the data. However, keeping two independent versions of the data may not always be the best choice. If multiple databases share a common list of customers or employees, it makes more sense to maintain the data in one database and then create **linked tables** in the other databases.

When you link to a table in another Access database, the data remain in the original source file. You cannot change any properties in the linked table, including adding or removing a primary key, because all table properties are defined in the source file. However, any changes made to the record data in the current database will appear in the source file. Conversely, any changes made to the source database will appear in the linked table automatically, including both table property changes and additions, updates, and deletions to table record data.

To link to a table in another Access database:

1. On the *External Data* tab, in the *Import & Link* group, click the **Access** button.

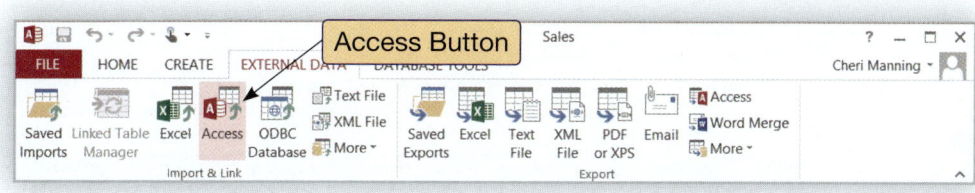

FIGURE AC 5.36

2. The *Get External Data – Access Database* dialog opens. Click the **Browse...** button. Navigate to find the Access database that includes the table you want to link to.
3. Select the file and click the **Open** button.
4. Click the **Link to the data source by creating a linked table.** radio button.
5. Click **OK**.

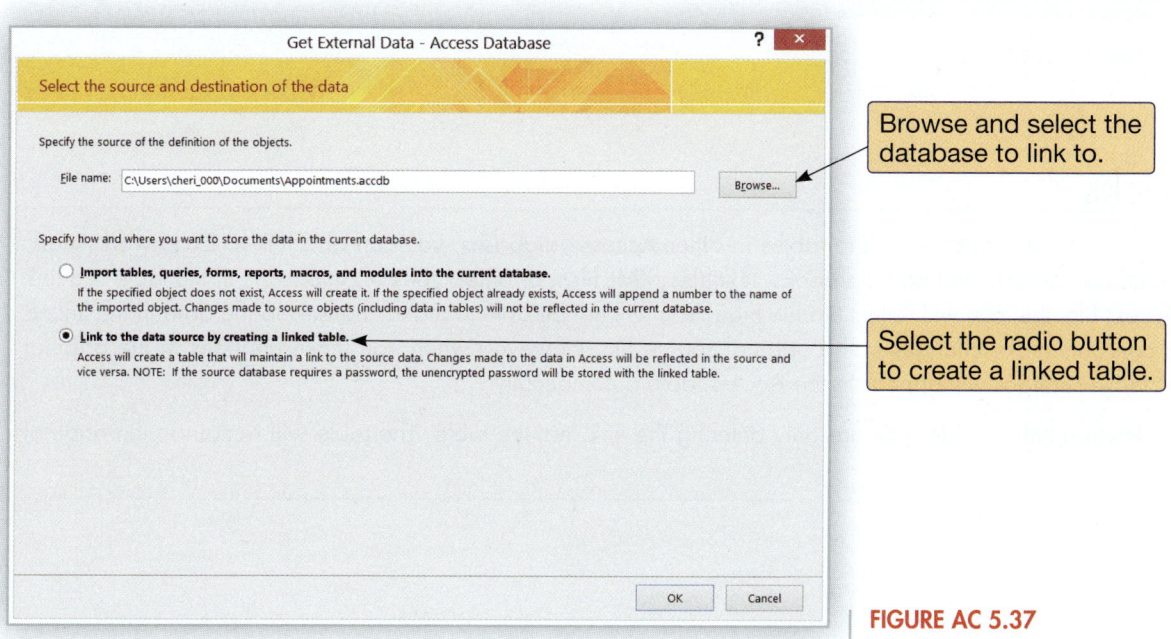

FIGURE AC 5.37

skill 5.7 Linking to a Table in Another Access Database

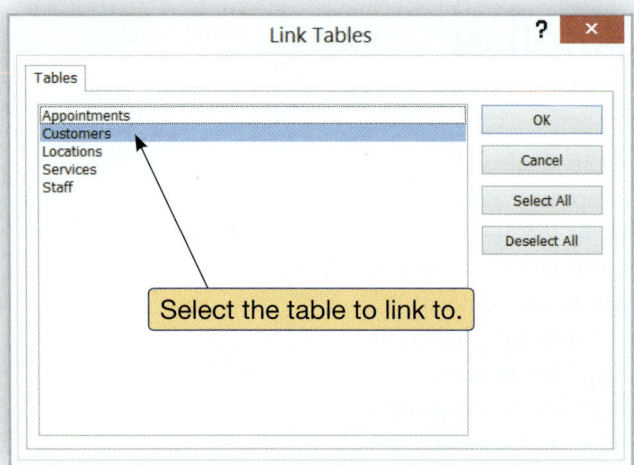

FIGURE AC 5.38

6. The *Link Tables* dialog appears. Click the table(s) you want to link to and then click **OK**.

The linked table now appears in your Access database with an arrow to the left of the icon in the Navigation Pane. When you add, edit, and delete records in the linked table, those changes will appear in the table in the original data source as well. However, you are very limited in the types of changes you can make. You cannot add or remove fields or change data types or formatting properties. You can modify the structure of the table only in the original source file.

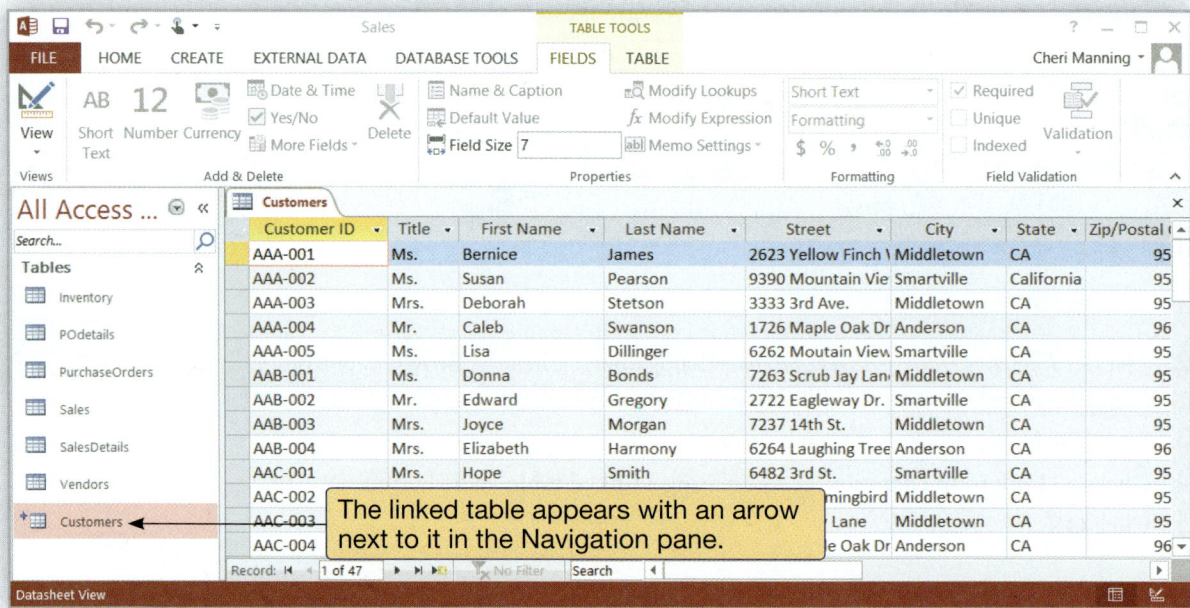

FIGURE AC 5.39

tips & tricks

- Although you will most commonly link to tables in other Access databases, you can also link to Excel worksheets, Microsoft Outlook contacts and address books, text files, XML files, or other types of databases. If the table is a link to a non-Access file, the icon will reflect the file type. You will not be able to make changes to the data in the linked table; you can only make changes in the original source file. However, when you make changes in the original source file, those changes will appear in the Access table automatically.

- When you delete a linked table, you are only deleting the link, not the table. The table will remain in the original source file.

tell me more

When you link to an external data source, Access stores the complete file path including the network name or drive letter. If you move the data source file, use the **Linked Table Manager** to update the file's location.

To update the location of a linked table:

1. On the *External Data* tab, in the *Import & Link* group, click the **Linked Table Manager** button.
2. Click the check boxes in front of the linked tables you want to update and then click **OK**.
3. If Access is unable to find and update the links, it will prompt you to select a new location. Navigate to the updated location, select the source file, and click **Open.**
4. Once Access is able to find and update the links successfully, it will display a message. Click **OK** to dismiss the message.
5. Click the **Close** button to close the Linked Table Manager.

another method

To import data from an Access database, right-click any table in the Navigation Pane, point to **Import,** and click **Access Database.**

let me try

If the database is not already open, open the data file **AC5-Sales** and try this skill on your own:

1. Create a linked table to link to the **Customers** table in the **Appointments** database.
2. Open the **Customers** table and add a new customer record.
3. Open the **Appointments** database. Open the **Customers** table and confirm that the new record appears in the *Customers* table in the *Appointments* database and then close the **Appointments** database.

from the perspective of . . .

SPORTING GOODS STORE PURCHASING MANAGER

Our store keeps inventory, purchasing, and sales in separate databases. We use a series of linked tables to keep tables up-to-date between database files. When I receive a shipment of goods from a purchase order, I import the information from the shipper (usually provided in a CSV file) into a linked table in my database. The original table in the inventory database is then updated automatically. A similar process happens with sales. When a sale is recorded in the sales database, the inventory database is updated automatically through the linked tables, which then updates the linked table in my database so I know when it's time to submit another purchase order. Without these links between databases, it would be a nightmare to keep track of inventory and to know when to order more.

skill 5.7 Linking to a Table in Another Access Database

Skill 5.8 Adding a Calculated Field to a Table

You can add a **calculated field** to a table to dynamically calculate text or numeric values. This is useful when values in one field are dependent on the value of another field or fields in the table. For example, the retail value of an inventory item can be calculated by multiplying the quantity in stock by the retail price. Each time the quantity in stock or the retail price is changed, the calculated field will update automatically.

A field with the *Calculated* data type uses an expression (similar to an Excel formula) to calculate a value. The expression is entered through the **Expression Builder**. Calculated fields can reference fields from the current table but not fields from other tables or queries in the database.

To add a calculated field to a table in Datasheet view using the Expression Builder:

1. Click the **Click to Add** column heading at the far right side of the table.
2. Point to **Calculated Field** and click the appropriate format for the new field (**Text, Number, Currency, Yes/No,** or **Date/Time**).

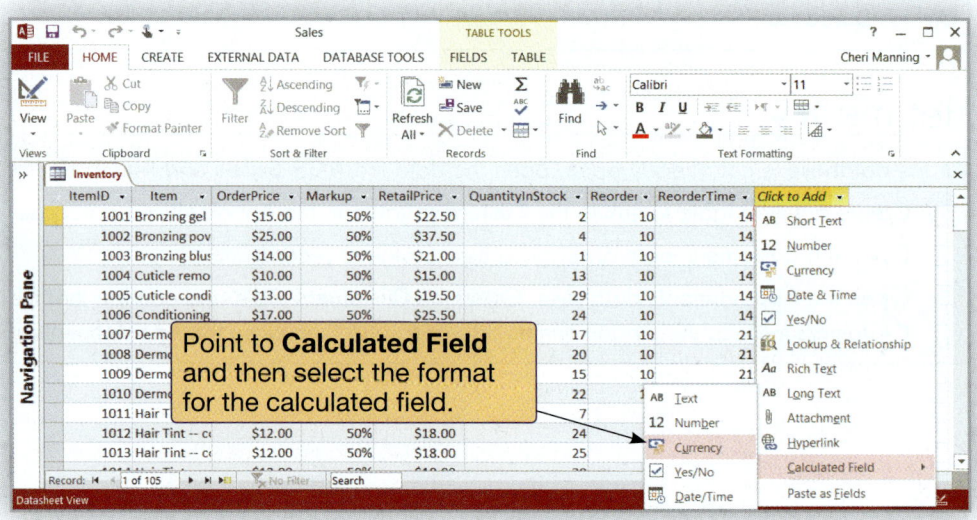

FIGURE AC 5.40

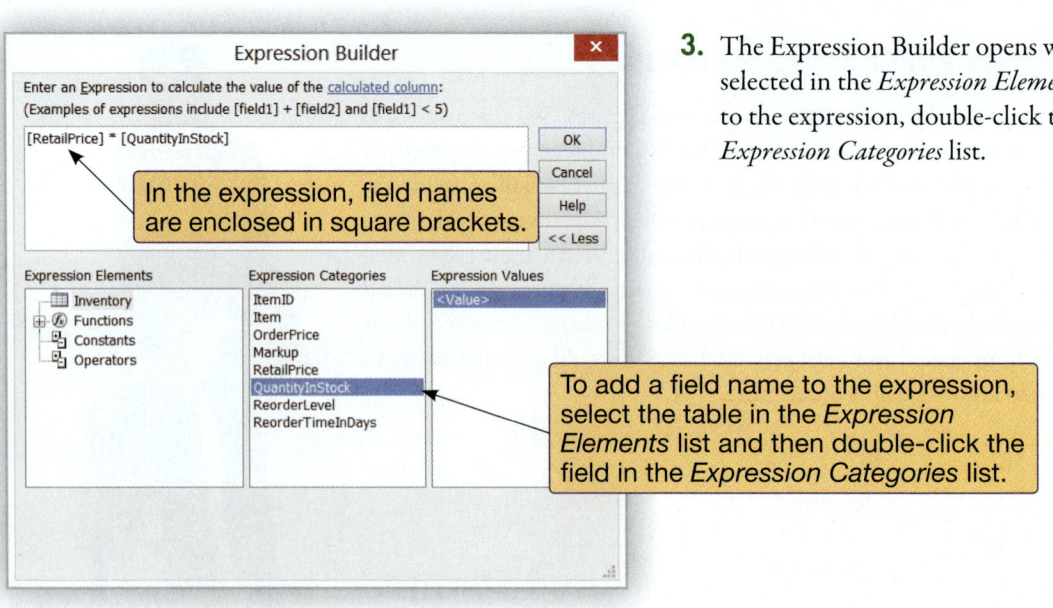

FIGURE AC 5.41

3. The Expression Builder opens with the current table selected in the *Expression Elements* list. To add a field to the expression, double-click the field name in the *Expression Categories* list.

4. To add a mathematical operator to the expression, you can type it directly in the expression, or if you're not sure what operators are available, click **Operators** in the *Expression Elements* list and then click a category in the *Expression Categories* list. Double-click an operator to add it to the expression.

5. Continue adding fields and operators as necessary. When you are finished building the expression, click **OK**.

6. The new temporary field name is highlighted. Type a new name for the field and press ⏎ Enter.

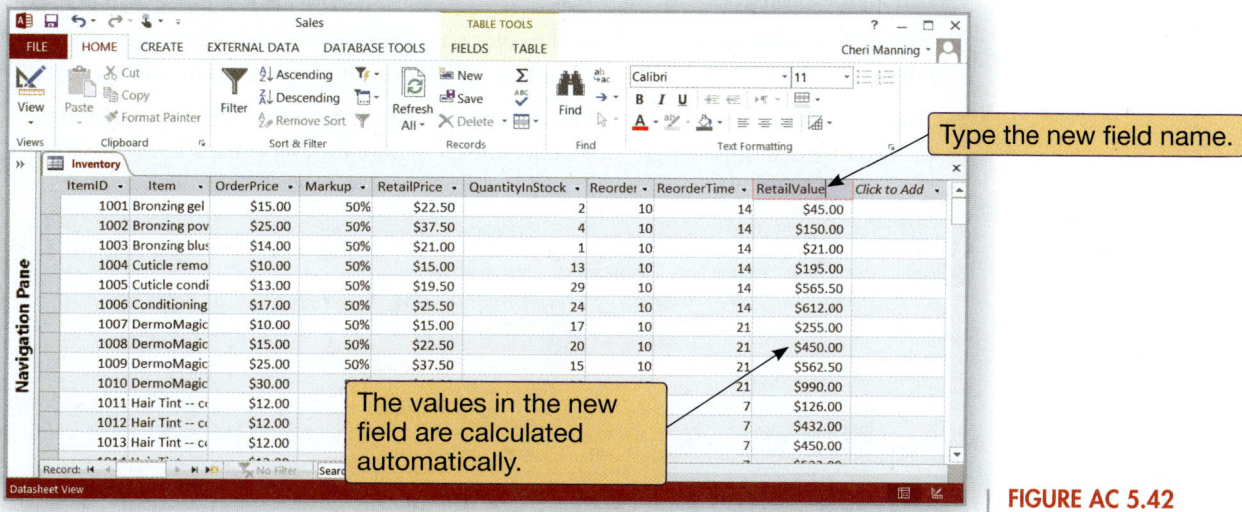

FIGURE AC 5.42

tell me more

To combine text fields together, click **String** in the *Expression Categories* list and then double-click **&** in the *Expression Values* list. To include spaces, enclose a space in quotation marks. To create a calculated field to display the value in the *FirstName* field followed by a space and the value in the *LastName* field: `[FirstName] & " " & [LastName]`

another method

› From Datasheet view, on the *Table Tools Fields* tab, in the *Add & Delete* group, click the **More Fields** button, point to **Calculated Field** at the bottom of the list, and click the field type you want to add.

› From Design view, add a new field, expand the **Data Type** list, and select **Calculated**. After you've created the expression in the Expression Builder, select the format for the calculated field through the Format property in the Field Properties pane.

let me try

If the database is not already open, open the data file **AC5-Sales** and try this skill on your own:

1. Open the **Inventory** table and add a new **Currency calculated field** to the far right of the table to calculate the retail value of the inventory stock for each item.
2. The expression should multiply the value of the **RetailPrice** field by the value of the **QuantityInStock** field.
3. Name the new field: `RetailValue`
4. Close the table when you are finished.

skill 5.8 Adding a Calculated Field to a Table

Skill 5.9 Creating a Custom Text Field Format

Database users cannot be relied on to enter data in a consistent format. To ensure that data appear uniform, apply a **Format property** to the field. In the skill *Formatting Fields,* you learned to apply a preset format to a field in Datasheet view. For fields with the *Short Text* or *Long Text* data type, you must enter a custom format through the Format property in Design view.

- To force all text to appear in the same case, type the > symbol for uppercase or the < symbol for lowercase.
- To specify a color for the text, type the color name enclosed in square brackets. The following colors are available: black, white, red, blue, yellow, green, cyan, and magenta.
- To display a minimum number of characters with spaces appearing before the text (so the text aligns along the right side), type one @ symbol for every character.

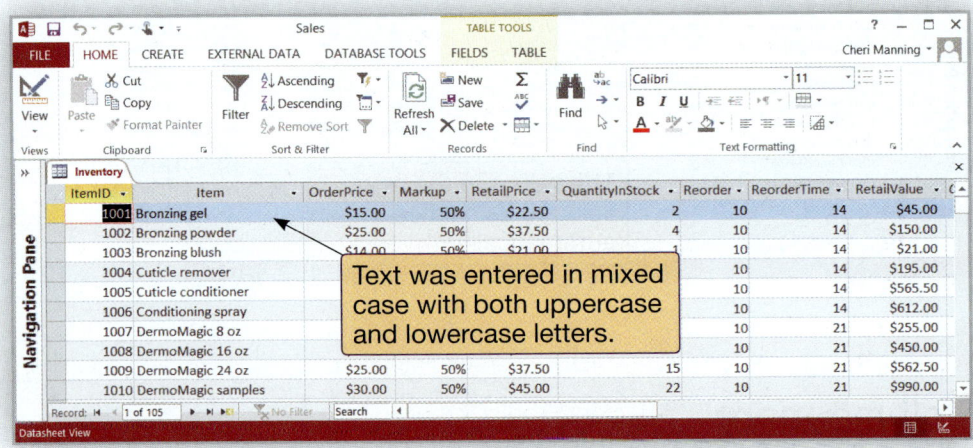

FIGURE AC 5.43

To create a custom field text format:

1. In Design view, select the field you want to modify.
2. Click the **Format** box on the *General* tab of the Field Properties pane.
3. Type the character(s) for the format you want. Press Enter.

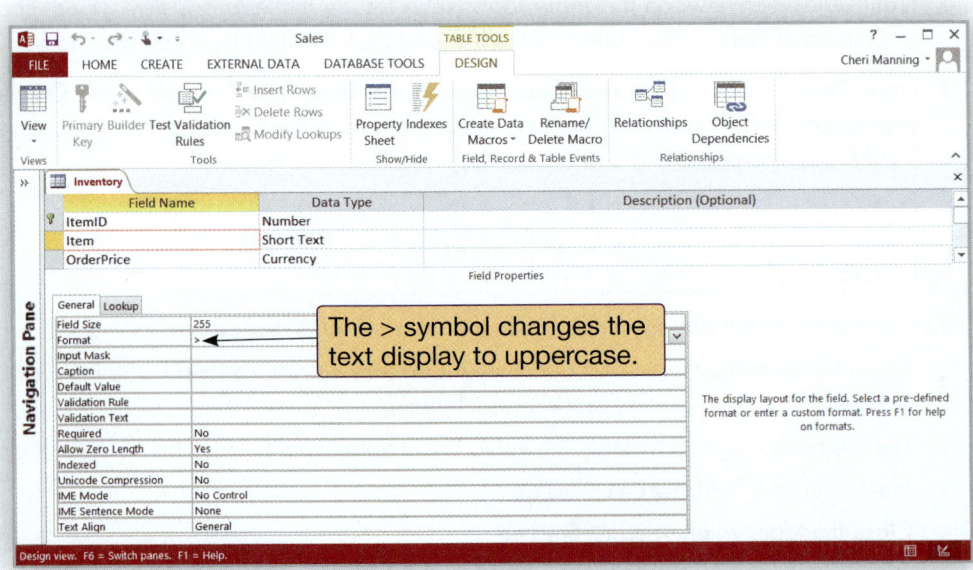

FIGURE AC 5.44

access 2013   chapter 5 Exploring Advanced Tables

4. Don't forget to save the changes to the table design before switching to Datasheet view.

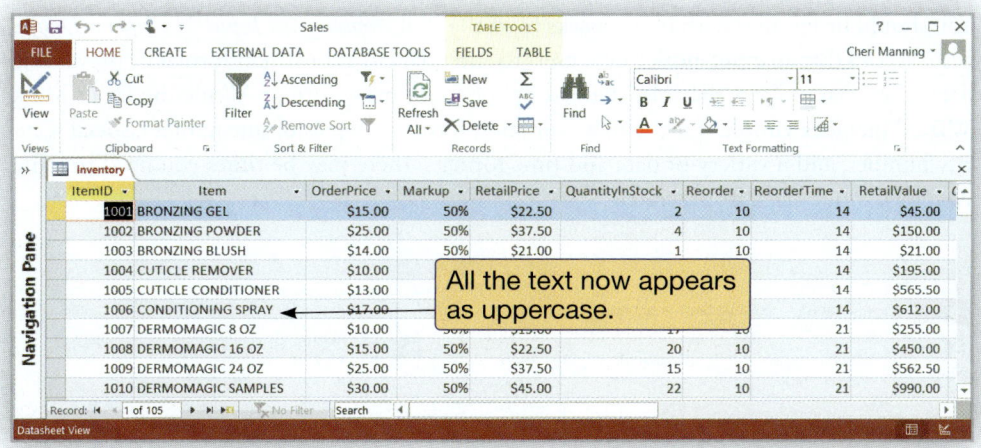

FIGURE AC 5.45

Remember, the Format property does not affect the data stored in the table; it only controls the way the data are displayed to the end user. However, the Format property applied to the field in the table *will* carry through to forms and reports. Applying the appropriate format to the field when designing the table can save you time when you design your forms and reports.

tips & tricks

When you import data into a *Short Text* field in a new table, Access automatically enters one @ symbol in the Format property. You can delete this symbol without affecting the underlying data.

tell me more

To limit the number of characters that can be entered in a text field, you must modify the **Size** property, not the Format property. Be careful when changing the Size property of a field that already contains data. Any characters beyond the limit of the Size property will be cut off. For more information about using the Size property, refer to the skill *Modifying Field Properties*.

let me try

If the database is not already open, open the data file **AC5-Sales** and try this skill on your own:

1. Open the **Inventory** table in Datasheet view and observe the text in the **Item** field.
2. Switch to Design view.
3. Add a custom format to the **Item** field to display text in all uppercase letters.
4. Save the table.
5. Switch to Datasheet view and observe the text in the **Item** field again. The item names should appear in all uppercase now.
6. Close the table.

skill 5.9   Creating a Custom Text Field Format

Skill 5.10 Creating a Custom Input Mask

You should be familiar with input masks from the skill *Applying an Input Mask from Design View*. Recall that an **input mask** forces users to enter data in a consistent format by preventing data entry that violates the rules defined by the input mask format. While the Input Mask Wizard includes samples for the most common formats such as phone number, social security number, and a variety of date and time formats, there may be times you need to write your own input mask from scratch.

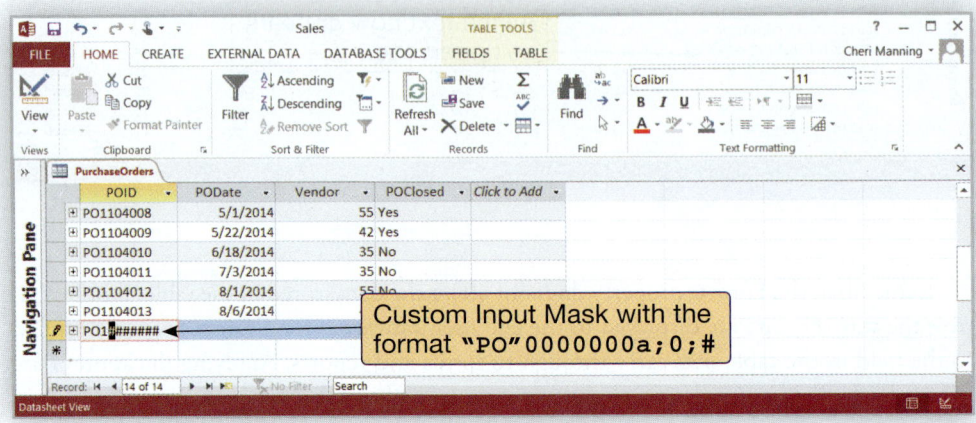

FIGURE AC 5.46

An input mask has three parts each separated by a semicolon. The *POID* field in Figure AC 5.46 uses the input mask `"PO"0000000a;0;#`.

The first part of the mask, `"PO"0000000a`, defines the data entry rules. In this example, `"PO"` is **literal text** included every time a record is entered. Note that literal text must be enclosed in quotation marks. The literal text, `PO`, is entered automatically during data entry. The user cannot delete or edit it. This ensures that every purchase order ID begins with the letters *PO* followed by the same number of digits with an optional letter at the end as defined by the remaining **placeholder characters** `0000000a`.

Use the following placeholder characters to define the data entry rules for the input mask:

0	Any digit (required)
9	Any digit (optional)
#	Any digit, space, plus (+), or minus (-) character (optional)
L	Letter (required)
?	Letter (optional)
A	Letter or digit (required)
a	Letter or digit (optional)
&	Any character including spaces (required)
C	Any character including spaces (optional)
>	All characters that follow are converted to uppercase
<	All characters that follow are converted to lowercase

The second part of the mask defines whether the data are stored with the literal characters or without the literal characters. In our sample, `0` determines that the literal text `PO` will be stored as part of the POID field for each record. When you only need to display the literal text and do not want to include it with the saved data, use `1` to save database space. If you omit this part of the input mask, Access assumes a value of `1`.

The third part of the mask defines the placeholder character that users will see during data entry. The default placeholder character is the underscore _, but you can use any character. In Figure AC 5.46, # is used as the placeholder character. This tells the user how many characters can be typed.

To create a custom input mask:

1. With the table open in Design view, click the field you want to apply the input mask to.
2. Click the **Input Mask** box on the *General* tab of the Field Properties pane.
3. Type the format for the input mask and then press Enter.
   a. Type the input mask format using literal text and placeholder characters followed by a semicolon.
   b. If you want the literal characters to be stored in the database, type a zero followed by a semicolon; if not, just type the semicolon.
   c. Finally, type the placeholder character users will see during data entry.
4. Save the table.

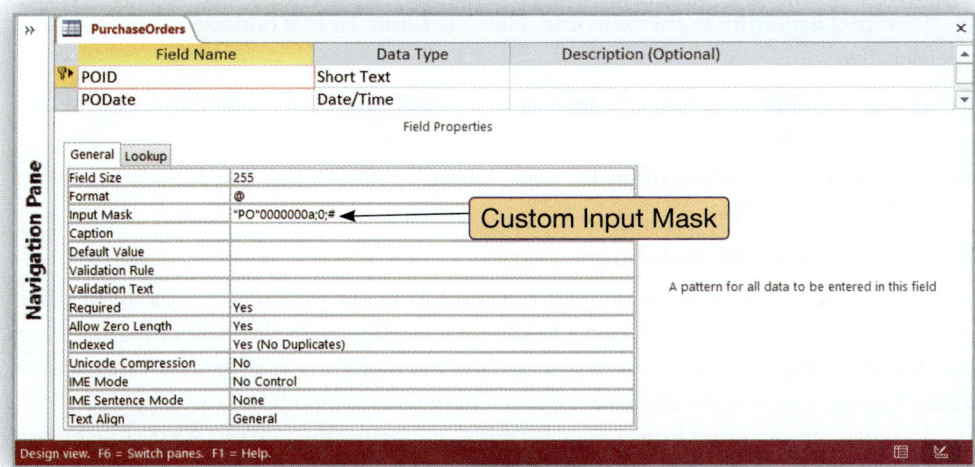

FIGURE AC 5.47

tips & tricks

If the custom input mask you want is similar to one of the built-in masks available through the Input Mask Wizard, you can use the wizard to modify the existing input mask. Any changes you make through the wizard apply only to the current table.

let me try

If the database is not already open, open the data file **AC5-Sales** and try this skill on your own:

1. Open the **PurchaseOrders** table in Design view.
2. Without using the Input Mask Wizard, create a custom input mask for the **POID** field to use the format PO1234567a where **PO** is literal text. The seven digits that follow are required. The last character in the input mask is an optional letter or digit. Store the literal text with the field data. Use the **#** symbol as the placeholder character.
3. Save the changes and then close the table.

skill 5.10   Creating a Custom Input Mask

Skill 5.11 Modifying Lookup Field Properties

The skills *Adding a Lookup Field from Another Table* and *Adding a Lookup Field from a List* introduced you to the concept of a lookup field. Once you establish a lookup field, you can continue to refine it—adding and removing list items, adjusting the number of columns that display, and controlling how users interact with the list. From Design view, you can modify the properties of a lookup field to control how it looks and behaves.

To modify the properties for a lookup field in Design view:

1. Select the field you want to modify.
2. In the Field Properties pane at the bottom of the screen, click the **Lookup** tab. The *Lookup* tab shows all the properties specific to the lookup field.
3. Adjust the width of the lookup list by changing the value in the *List Width* box.
4. If the lookup list includes more than one column, adjust the width of each column by changing the values in the *Column Widths* box.
5. To restrict data entry to list items only, click the **Limit To List** box, expand the list, and click **Yes**.
6. To allow multiple values for the field, click the **Allow Multiple Values** box, expand the list and click **Yes**.
7. To prevent editing of any of the list items, click the **Allow Value List Edits** box, expand the list, and click **No**.
8. Save the table to save your changes.

Recall that the values in a lookup list can come from one of two sources: a list of values that you enter yourself or values from a field in a table or query. In the Field Properties pane, the type of lookup is set in the *Row Source Type* box under the *Lookup* tab: **Value List** or **Table/Query**. The items in the list are defined in the *Row Source* box.

To add or remove items from a value list without opening the Lookup Wizard again, edit the text in the Row Source property box. Enclose each text item in quotation marks, and separate each list item with a semicolon: **"Cash";"Credit Card";"Gift Card"; "Store Credit"**

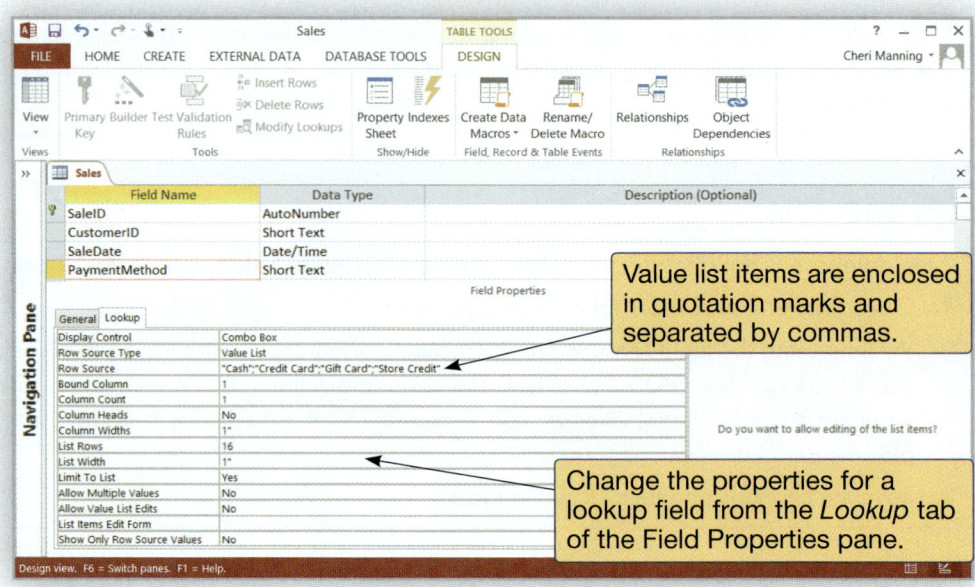

FIGURE AC 5.48

To modify the list items from a table or query, edit the SQL statement in the *Row Source* property box. The first part of the statement after SELECT defines the table and fields to display using the format [table].[field]. Both the table name and the field name are enclosed in square brackets. If the list displays more than one field, the fields are separated by commas.

`SELECT [Inventory].[ItemID], [Inventory].[Item] FROM Inventory ORDER BY [ItemID];`

The Column Count property controls how many columns are shown in list. If you add a field to the Row Source property, be sure to increase the value in the Column Count property so all the fields are visible when entering data in the table.

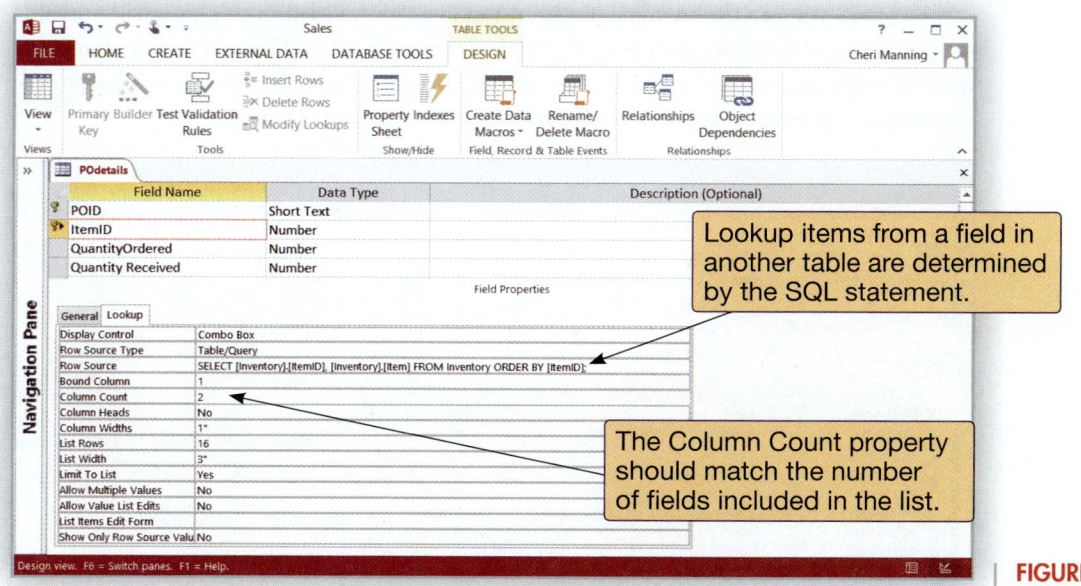

FIGURE AC 5.49

tips & tricks

To maintain consistent data, set the Limit to List property to **Yes** and the Allow Value List Edits property to **No**. Be sure to make any changes to the value list *before* you change the Allow Value List Edits property!

tell me more

For more information about using SQL, refer to the skill *Modifying a Query in SQL View*.

another method

To edit the items in a value list lookup field, click in the **Row Source** property box, and then click the **Build** button to open the *Edit List Items* dialog. Make changes to the list. Click **OK**.

let me try

If the database is not already open, open the data file **AC5-Sales** and try this skill on your own:

1. Open the **Sales** table in Datasheet view and observe the lookup list for the *PaymentMethod* field.
2. Switch to Design view and modify the lookup field properties so data entry is limited to items on the list.
3. Add a new item **Other** to the end of the lookup value list.
4. Save the table. Switch back to Datasheet view and observe the change to the lookup list.
5. Close the table.

skill 5.11 Modifying Lookup Field Properties

Skill 5.12 Creating Field Validation Rules

When you want to limit the content that can be entered in a field, but a value list lookup field would be too restrictive, try defining a **field validation rule**. When you enter an expression in the field's **Validation Rule property**, Access will judge the field value when the user leaves the field, and if the data violates the field validation rule, a message is displayed. In the field's **Validation Text property**, you can enter a message to tell the user in plain language why the entered value was rejected.

Although you can use any type of expression in a field validation rule, you will probably use comparison operators such as <, >, <=, and >= most often. Comparison operators are used to judge the value of a number or date. If you are using a date in the validation rule expression, you must enclose it in # characters similar to >=#1/1/2015#.

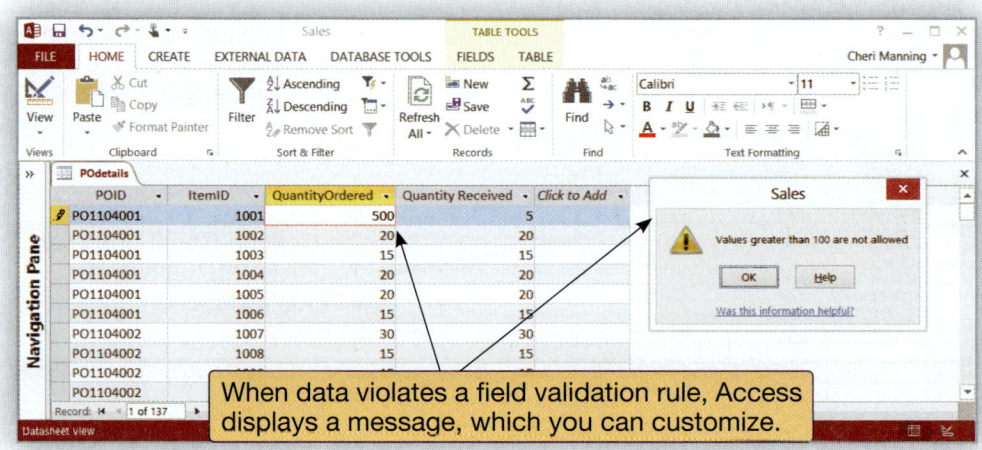

FIGURE AC 5.50

When data violates a field validation rule, Access displays a message, which you can customize.

In Figure AC 5.50, the expression <=100 is used in the Validation Rule property for the *QuantityOrdered* field. This prevents users from entering a value greater than 100. The error message `Values greater than 100 are not allowed` is defined in the Validation Text property.

To add a field validation rule from Design view:

1. Click the field you want to apply the validation rule to.

2. Click the **Validation Rule** box on the *General* tab of the Field Properties pane.

3. Type the validation rule expression. Press ⏎ Enter.

To add a custom message for the field validation rule from Design view:

1. Click the field you want to apply the validation text to.

2. Click the **Validation Text** box on the *General* tab of the Field Properties pane.

3. Type the message you want to appear when data entry violates the validation rule. Press ⏎ Enter.

Don't forget to save the table when you are finished.

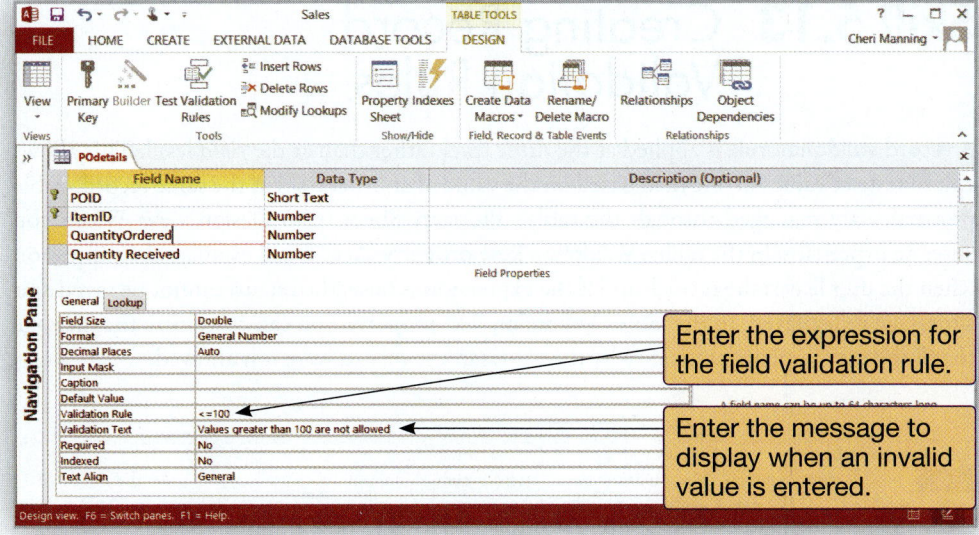

FIGURE AC 5.51

If the table contains data, Access will warn you that existing data may violate the new field validation rule. Click **Yes** to test the existing data against the new rule or click **No** to add the rule without testing the data.

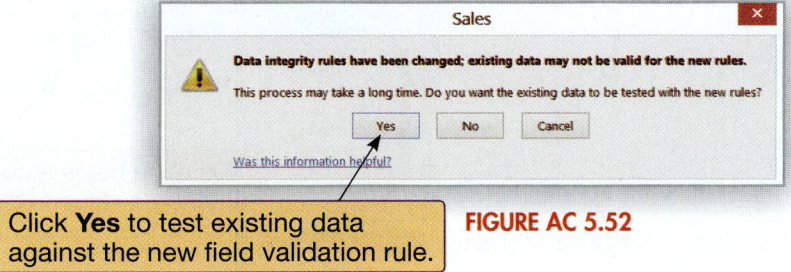

FIGURE AC 5.52

tips & tricks

While you can use field validation rules to limit text entries, in most cases, it is more efficient to use a lookup field with a list of the allowed values instead.

another method

- From Datasheet view, on the *Table Tools Fields* tab, in the *Validation* group, click the **Validation** button and select **Field Validation Rule** to open the Expression Builder and create the validation rule expression.
- From Datasheet view, on the *Table Tools Fields* tab, in the *Validation* group, click the **Validation** button and select **Field Validation Message** to open the *Enter Validation Message* dialog where you can type the validation message.

let me try

If the database is not already open, open the data file **AC5-Sales** and try this skill on your own:

1. Open the **POdetails** table in Design view.
2. Add a field validation rule to the **QuantityOrdered** field to require that values are **less than or equal to 100**.
3. Modify the field properties to display the message `Values greater than 100 are not allowed` when the field validation rule is violated.
4. Save the table.
5. Allow Access to test the existing data with the new rule.

skill 5.12   Creating Field Validation Rules

Skill 5.13 Creating Record Validation Rules

A **record validation rule** is applied at the *table* level rather than at the *field* level. This allows you to restrict values in one field based on the value of another field in the same record. Table properties are managed through the table's Property Sheet from Design view. When you enter an expression in the table's **Validation Rule property**, Access will evaluate the expression when the user leaves the record, and if the expression is false, the record cannot be saved and a message is displayed. In the table's **Validation Text property**, you can customize the message to tell the user in plain language why the values in the record were not allowed.

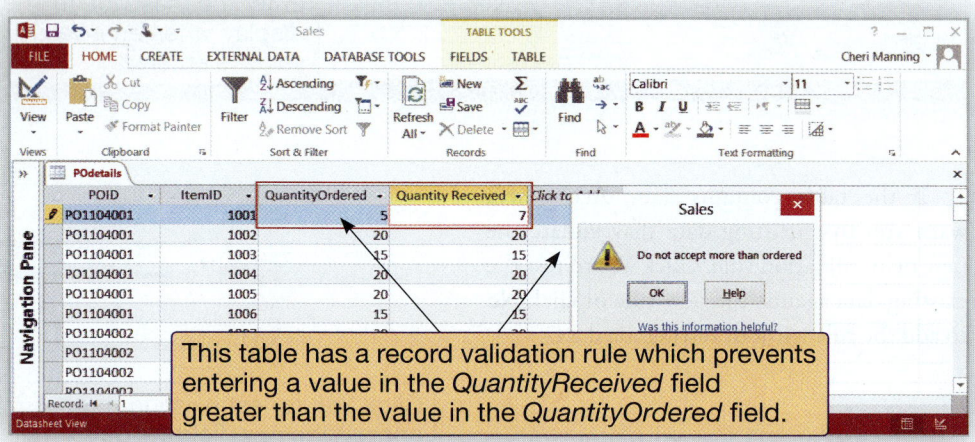

FIGURE AC 5.53

To add a record validation rule:

1. With the table open in Design view, on the *Design* tab, in the *Show/Hide* group, click the **Property Sheet** button to display the table properties.
2. In the *Validation Rule* box, type the validation rule. Be sure to enclose field names in square brackets. Press ⮐ Enter to move to the *Validation Text* box.
3. In the *Validation Text* box, type the message you want to appear when data entry violates the record validation rule.
4. Save the table.

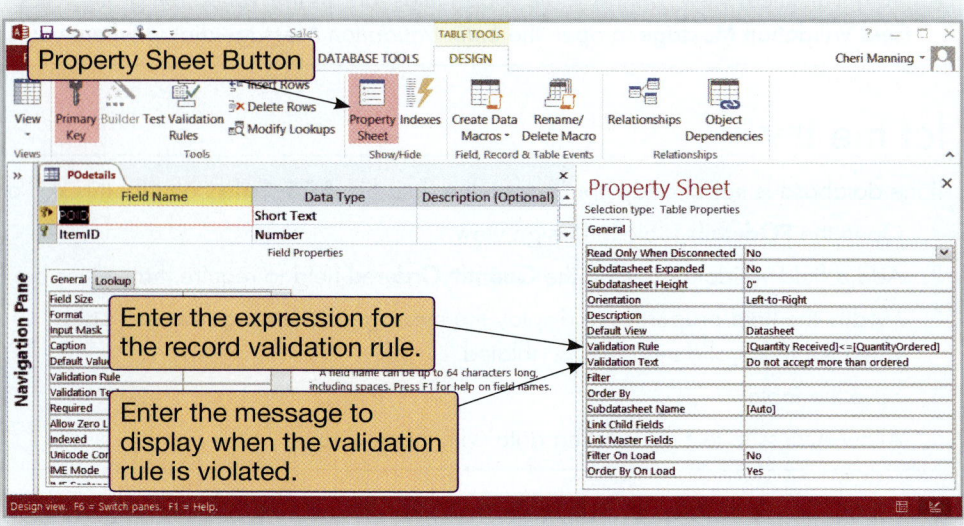

FIGURE AC 5.54

If the table contains data, Access will warn you that existing data may violate the new record validation rule. Click **Yes** to test the existing data against the new rule or click **No** to add the rule without testing the data.

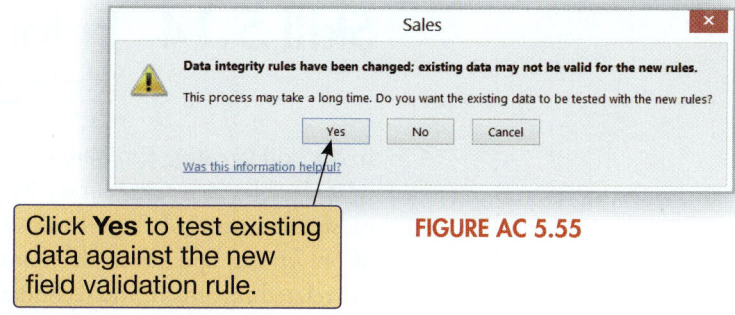

Click **Yes** to test existing data against the new field validation rule.

FIGURE AC 5.55

tips & tricks

You can test validation rules at any time. From Design view, on the *Design* tab, in the *Tools* group, click the **Test Validation Rules** button and follow the prompts.

tell me more

You can use the Expression Builder to build the record validation rule.
1. In the table Property Sheet, click in the **Validation Rule** box and then click the **Build** button.
2. The Expression Builder opens with the current table selected in the *Expression Elements* list. To add a field to the expression, double-click the field name in the *Expression Categories* list.
3. To add a mathematical operator to the expression, you can type it directly in the expression, or if you're not sure what operators are available, click **Operators** in the *Expression Elements* list and then click a category in the *Expression Categories* list. Double-click an operator to add it to the expression.
4. Continue adding fields and operators as necessary. When you are finished building the expression, click **OK**.

another method

> From Datasheet view, on the *Table Tools Fields* tab, in the *Validation* group, click the **Validation** button and select **Validation Rule** to open the Expression Builder and create the record validation rule expression.

> From Datasheet view, on the *Table Tools Fields* tab, in the *Validation* group, click the **Validation** button and select **Validation Message** to open the *Enter Validation Message* dialog where you can type the record validation message.

let me try

If the database is not already open, open the data file **AC5-Sales** and try this skill on your own:
1. If it is not already open, open the **POdetails** table in Design view.
2. Display the table properties.
3. Enter a validation rule for the table to require values in the **QuantityReceived** field to be **less than or equal to** the values in the **QuantityOrdered** field. Remember to enclose the field names in square brackets.
4. Modify the table properties to display the message `Do not accept more than ordered` when the record validation rule is violated.
5. Save the table.
6. Allow Access to test the existing data with the new rule.

skill 5.13   Creating Record Validation Rules

Skill 5.14 Enforcing Deletions and Updates in Relationships

In the skill *Creating Relationships,* you learned how enforcing referential integrity between related tables ensures accuracy by preventing deleting or updating of records that would cause a violation of the relationship between the primary and secondary tables. Instead of preventing updates or deletions, you can set relationship options to delete or update the related records in the secondary table. These options are known as **cascading options** because when they are enforced, an action on one table cascades to affect records in the related table.

Be careful when activating the *Cascade Delete* and *Cascade Update* options, as they may have unintended consequences. For example, deleting a customer from a table may also delete all related appointments linked to that customer name. Automatically removing future appointments may be desirable, but you probably wouldn't want to delete past appointments.

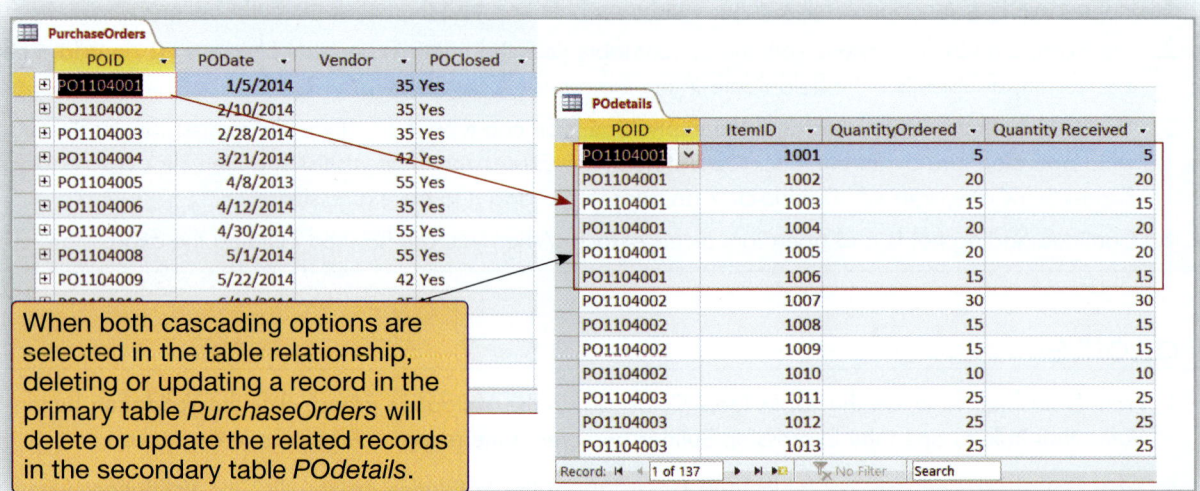

When both cascading options are selected in the table relationship, deleting or updating a record in the primary table *PurchaseOrders* will delete or update the related records in the secondary table *POdetails*.

FIGURE AC 5.56

To enforce cascading options between related tables:

1. On the *Database Tools* tab, in the *Relationships* group, click the **Relationships** button to open the Relationships window.

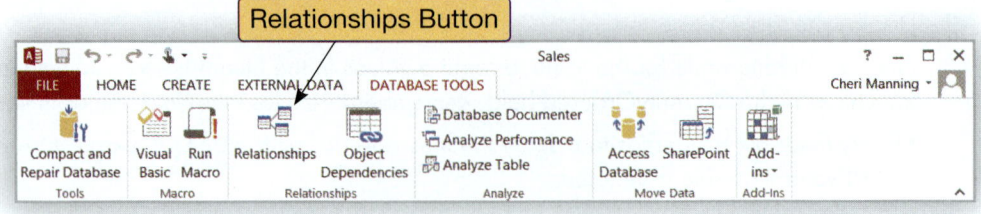

FIGURE AC 5.57

2. Double-click the line connecting the two related tables to open the *Edit Relationships* dialog.
3. To update related records in the "many" table when the "one" record is updated, click the **Cascade Update Related Fields** check box.

4. To delete records in the "many" table when the "one" record is deleted in the primary table, click the **Cascade Delete Related Records** check box.
5. Click **OK** to apply the changes and close the *Edit Relationships* dialog.

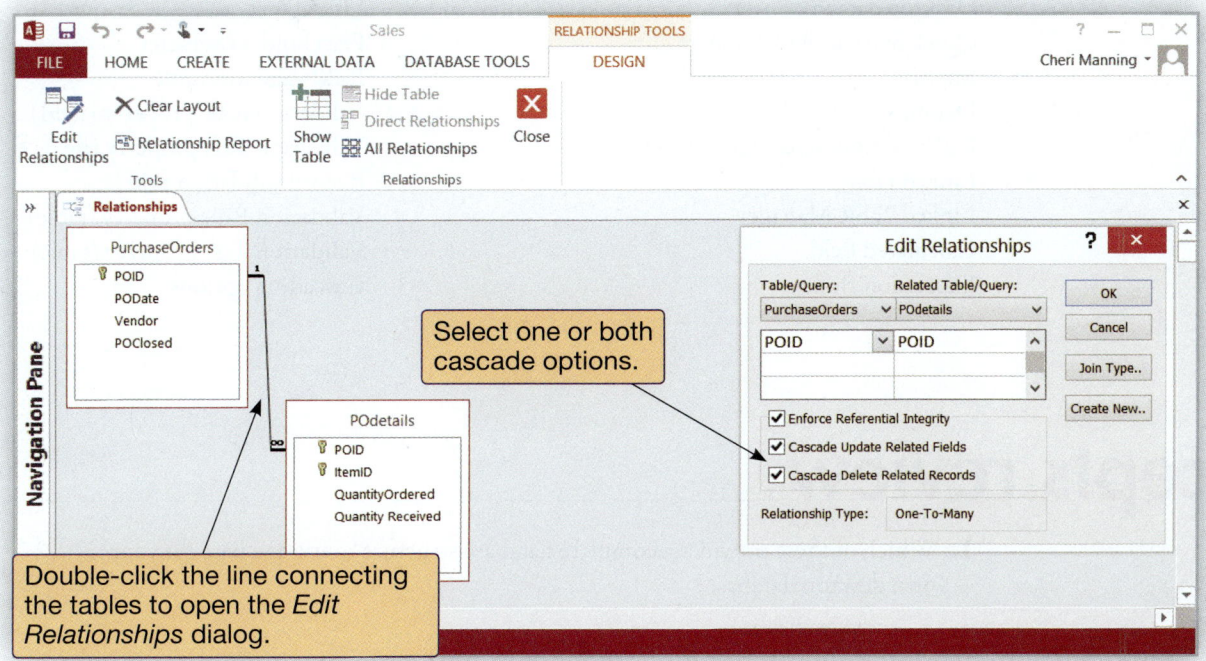

FIGURE AC 5.58

tips & tricks

If you have trouble double-clicking the line connecting the tables in the Relationships window, open the *Edit Relationships* dialog by clicking the **Edit Relationships** button on the *Relationship Tools Design* tab, in the *Tools* group.

another method

Right-click the line connecting the tables in the Relationships window and select **Edit Relationship...**

let me try

If the database is not already open, open the data file **AC5-Sales** and try this skill on your own:

1. Open the Relationships window.
2. Modify the relationship between the *PurchaseOrders* and *POdetails* tables so when a record in the *PurchaseOrders* table is deleted or updated, related records in the *POdeails* table will also be deleted or updated.
3. Close the Relationships window.

skill 5.14 Enforcing Deletions and Updates in Relationships

key terms

Template	Format property
Access web app	Input mask
Desktop database	Literal text
Quick Start application part	Placeholder character
Import	Field validation rule
Delimiter	Validation Rule property (field)
CSV (comma-separated values)	Validation Text property (field)
Linked table	Record validation rule
Linked Table Manager	Validation Rule property (table)
Calculated field	Validation Text property (table)
Expression Builder	Cascading options

concepts review

1. Which of these provides a complete database structure to use as a base for your own desktop database?
   a. Access web app
   b. Desktop database template
   c. Input mask
   d. Linked table

2. Before working with a new blank database, you must save it as a new file.
   a. True
   b. False

3. Which of these Quick Start application parts would be most useful in a database that manages customers?
   a. Contacts
   b. Issues
   c. Tasks
   d. Users

4. You *cannot* import data into Access from which of these file types?
   a. Access
   b. Excel
   c. Word
   d. Text file

5. When importing data into Access, you can identify a column or field from the imported data as the primary key.
   a. True
   b. False

6. A calculated field in a table can reference fields from any database object.
   a. True
   b. False

7. If you enter > in the field Format property, all text will appear in which format?
   a. *Short Text* data type
   b. *Long Text* data type
   c. Uppercase
   d. Lowercase
8. The input mask `"ID"00999;0;_` will store the literal text `"ID"` in the database.
   a. True
   b. False
9. If you require a value in a field to always be less than 25, which of the following you use?
   a. Format property
   b. Input mask
   c. Field validation rule
   d. Record validation rule
10. If you require the value in one field in a table to always be greater than the value of another field in the table, which of the following would you use?
    a. Format property
    b. Input mask
    c. Field validation rule
    d. Record validation rule

Data files for projects can be found on www.mhhe.com/office2013skills

projects

skill review 5.1

In this project you will import data into a college database. You will also create new database objects to manage users for the school's e-mail system. You will create a calculated field and implement a series of changes to the database tables to manage data entry.

Skills needed to complete this project:
- Importing Data from Excel (Skill 5.4)
- Adding Records to a Table by Importing (Skill 5.6)
- Linking to a Table in Another Access Database (Skill 5.7)
- Using Quick Start Application Parts (Skill 5.3)
- Adding a Calculated Field to a Table (Skill 5.8)
- Creating a Custom Text Field Format (Skill 5.9)
- Creating a Custom Input Mask (Skill 5.10)
- Creating Field Validation Rules (Skill 5.12)
- Enforcing Deletions and Updates in Relationships (Skill 5.14)

1. Open the start file **AC2013-SkillReview-5-1** and resave the file as: `[your initials]AC-SkillReview-5-1`
2. If necessary, enable active content by clicking the **Enable Content** button in the Message Bar.
3. Import data from the *Class* Excel file into a new table. The first row in the *Class* worksheet should be used as the field names. Use the *ClassCode* field as the primary key. You do not need to save the import steps.
    a. On the *External Data* tab, in the *Import & Link* group, click the **Excel** button.
    b. In the *Get External Data – Excel Spreadsheet* dialog, click the **Browse...** button.
    c. Navigate to the folder where the resource files for this project are stored and double-click the **Class** Excel file.
    d. Verify that the **Import the source data into a new table in the current database.** radio button is selected and click **OK**.
    e. In the Import Spreadsheet Wizard, verify that the **Class** worksheet is selected and click **Next**.
    f. Click the **First Row Contains Column Headings** checkbox. Click **Next**.
    g. Include all the fields in the import. You do not need to change any of the data types. Click **Next**.
    h. Click the **Choose my own primary key.** check box and verify that **ClassCode** is selected. Click **Next**.
    i. Verify the table name **Class** and click **Finish** to complete the import.
    j. Click **Close**.
4. Import the *IncomingFreshmanStudents* tab-delimited text file and append it to the *Student* table. The text file does not include column headings. Save the import steps with the suggested name.
    a. On the *External Data* tab, in the *Import & Link* group, click the **Text File** button.
    b. In the *Get External Data – Text File* dialog, click the **Browse...** button.
    c. Navigate to the folder where the resource files for this project are stored, and double-click the **IncomingFreshmanStudents** text file.
    d. Click the **Append a copy of the records to the table:** radio button and select **Student** from the drop-down list. Click **OK**.
    e. Verify that the **Delimited** radio button is selected. Click **Next**.
    f. Verify that the **Tab** radio button is selected. Click **Next**.
    g. Verify that **Student** is listed in the *Import to Table* box. Click **Finish**.
    h. Click the **Save import steps** check box.
    i. Click **Save Import**.
5. Create a linked table to link to the *Department* table in the *Department* database.
    a. On the *External Data* tab, in the *Import & Link* group, click the **Access** button.
    b. In the *Get External Data – Access Database* dialog, click the **Browse...** button.
    c. Navigate to the folder where the resource files for this project are stored and double-click the **Department** Access file.
    d. Click the **Link to the data source by creating a linked table.** radio button. Click **OK**.
    e. In the *Link Tables* dialog, click **Department**. Click **OK**.

6. Create a new table and two data entry forms from the *Users* Quick Start application part. There is no relationship to another table at this time.
   a. On the *Create* tab, in the *Templates* group, click the **Application Parts** button and then click **Users.**
   b. Click the **There is no relationship.** radio button.
   c. Click **Create.**
7. Create a calculated field named *RemainingHours* at the end of the *Student* table to calculate the remaining required credit hours for each student by subtracting the students' current credit hours from 160.
   a. Open the **Student** table in Datasheet view.
   b. Scroll to the far right of the table. Click **Click to Add,** point to **Calculated Field,** and click **Number.**
   c. In the Expression Builder, type: `160-`
   d. In the *Expression Categories* box at the bottom of the Expression Builder, double-click **Credits.**
   e. Click **OK.**
   f. Type `RemainingHours` and then press ⏎ Enter.
   g. Save the table, but don't close it yet.
8. Modify the format for the *Classification* field so the text appears in all uppercase letters.
   a. Switch to Design view.
   b. Select the **Classification** field.
   c. In the Field Properties pane, in the *Format* box, type: `>`
   d. Save the table.
   e. Switch to Datasheet view and review the change.
9. Add a field validation rule to the *GPA* field to prevent a GPA of greater than 4.0.
   a. Switch back to Design view.
   b. Select the **GPA** field.
   c. In the Field Properties pane, in the *Validation Rule* box, type: `<=4`
   d. In the *Validation Text* box, type: `GPA cannot be greater than 4.0`
   e. Save the table.
   f. Click **Yes** to test the data integrity against the new field validation rule.
   g. Close the table.
10. Open the *Course* table in Design view and create an input mask for the *CourseNumber* field to require that the field use the format AAA-123 where the first three characters are required letters, followed by a dash, which should be entered automatically, followed by three required numbers. You should not store the literal text in the database. Use the _ character as the placeholder.
    a. Open the **Course** table in Design view.
    b. Select the **CourseNumber** field.
    c. In the Input Mask box in the Field Properties pane, type: `LLL"-"000;;_`
    d. Save the table but do not close it yet.

11. Modify the format for the *CourseNumber* field so the text appears in all uppercase letters.
    a. Verify that the *CourseNumber* field is still selected.
    b. In the Field Properties pane, in the *Format* box, type: **>**
    c. Save the table.
    d. Switch to Datasheet view and review the change.
    e. Close the table.
12. Create a relationship between the *CourseNumber* field in the *Course* table and the *CourseNumber* field in the *Class* table. If a course is deleted or updated, the related classes should be deleted or updated as well.
    a. On the *Database Tools* tab, in the *Relationships* group, click the **Relationships** button to open the Relationships window.
    b. Display the **Class** table if it is not already visible in the Relationships window.
        i. On the *Relationship Tools Design* tab, in the *Relationships* group, click the **Show Table** button.
        ii. In the *Show Table* dialog, select **Class** and then click **Add.**
        iii. Click **Close** to close the *Show Table* dialog.
    c. Click the **CourseNumber** field in the **Course** table and drag it to the **CourseNumber** field in the **Class** table.
    d. Click the **Enforce Referential Integrity** check box.
    e. Click the **Cascade Update Related Fields** check box.
    f. Click the **Cascade Delete Related Records** check box.
    g. Click **Create.**
    h. Close the Relationships window.
13. Close the database and exit Access.

skill review 5.2

Seaside Rentals offers beachfront accommodations year-round. The database tracks guests, reservations, and units. In this project you will import new records from a text file and append them to an existing table. You will also import data from a text file into a new table and then work with that table to add a calculated field and modify fields to look up values in other tables. You will modify field properties and table relationships to ensure consistent data entry and maintain data integrity.

Skills needed to complete this project:
- Adding Records to a Table by Importing (Skill 5.6)
- Importing Data from a Text File (Skill 5.5)
- Adding a Calculated Field to a Table (Skill 5.8)
- Creating Field Validation Rules (Skill 5.12)
- Creating a Custom Text Field Format (Skill 5.9)
- Enforcing Deletions and Updates in Relationships (Skill 5.14)
- Creating a Custom Input Mask (Skill 5.10)
- Modifying Lookup Field Properties (Skill 5.11)

1. Open the start file **AC2013-SkillReview-5-2** and resave the file as:
   `[your initials]AC-SkillReview-5-2`
2. If necessary, enable active content by clicking the **Enable Content** button in the Message Bar.
3. Import records from the *NewGuest* CSV text file and append them to the *Guest* table. The first row ***does*** contain column headings. Save the import steps with the suggested name.
   a. On the *External Data* tab, in the *Import & Link* group, click the **Text File** button.
   b. In the *Get External Data – Text File* dialog, click the **Browse...** button.
   c. Navigate to the folder where the resource files for this project are stored and double-click the **NewGuest** CSV file.
   d. Click the **Append a copy of the records to the table:** radio button and verify that **Guest** is selected. Click **OK**.
   e. Verify that the **Delimited** radio button is selected. Click **Next**.
   f. Verify that the **Comma** radio button is selected. Click the **First Row Contains Field Names** check box. Click **Next**.
   g. Verify that **Guest** is listed in the *Import to Table:* box. Click **Finish**.
   h. Click the **Save import steps** check box.
   i. Click **Save Import**.
4. Import data from the *Reservation* comma-delimited text file into a new table. The first row in the *Reservation* file should be used as the field names. Use the *ReservationID* field as the primary key. You do not need to save the import steps.
   a. On the *External Data* tab, in the *Import & Link* group, click the **Text File** button.
   b. In the *Get External Data – Text File* dialog, click the **Browse...** button.
   c. Navigate to the folder where the resource files for this project are stored and double-click the **Reservation** text file.
   d. Verify that the **Import the source data into a new table in the current database.** radio button is selected and click **OK**.
   e. In the Import Text File Wizard, verify that the **Delimited** radio button is selected and click **Next**.
   f. Verify that the **Comma** radio button is selected. Click the **First Row Contains Field Names** checkbox. Click **Next**.
   g. Change the *Rate* field to use the *Currency* data type. Click in the **Rate** column. Expand the **Data Type** list and select **Currency**. Click **Next**.
   h. Click the **Choose my own primary key.** radio button and verify that **ReservationID** is selected. Click **Next**.
   i. Verify the table name **Reservation** and click **Finish** to complete the import.
   j. Click **Close**.
5. Add a calculated field to the new *Reservation* table to calculate the total price for the reservation by multiplying the number of nights by the rate. Insert the new field between the *Rate* field and the *Comment* field.
   a. Open the **Reservation** table in Datasheet view.
   b. Click anywhere in the **Rate** field.
   c. On the *Table Tools Fields* tab, in the *Add & Delete* group, click the **More Fields** button. Scroll to the bottom, point to **Calculated Field,** and select **Currency.**
   d. In the *Expression Categories* box at the bottom of the Expression Builder, double-click **Nights**.

e. In the Expression Builder box after [Nights], type: *

f. In the *Expression Categories* box at the bottom of the Expression Builder, double-click **Rate**.

g. Click **OK**.

h. Type `TotalPrice` and then press ⏎ Enter .

6. Add a validation rule to require all new reservation rates to be no less than $175. Add a message so users entering new reservations know that no rates less than $175 will be accepted.

    a. Select the **Rate** field.

    b. On the *Table Tools Fields* tab, in the *Field Validation* group, click the **Validation** button and select **Field Validation Rule**.

    c. Type `>=175` and click **OK**.

    d. Access should display a message that existing data violates the validation rule. Click **Yes** to continue testing.

    e. On the *Table Tools Fields* tab, in the *Field Validation* group, click the **Validation** button and select **Field Validation Message**.

    f. Type `The minimum rate for new reservations is $175.` and then click **OK**.

7. Modify the *Unit* field to lookup values from the *Unit* table. Include the *UnitID* and *UnitName* fields, but hide the *UnitID* field.

    a. Switch to Design view.

    b. Click in the **Data Type** column next to *Unit*, and select **Lookup Wizard...** from the list.

    c. Verify that the **I want the lookup field to get the values from another table or query.** radio button is selected. Click **Next**.

    d. Click **Table: Unit** and then click **Next**.

    e. In the *Available Fields* list, double-click **UnitID** and **UnitName**. Click **Next**.

    f. Sort the list by unit name. Expand the first sort box and select **UnitName**. Click **Next**.

    g. Verify that the **Hide the key column (recommended)** check box is checked. Click **Next**.

    h. Click **Finish**.

    i. Click **Yes** to save the table.

8. Modify the lookup field properties to allow multiple values.

    a. In the Field Properties pane, click the **Lookup** tab.

    b. Click in the **Allow Multiple Values** property box. Expand the list and select **Yes**.

    c. Click **Yes** to acknowledge that you cannot undo this change once you save the table.

    d. Save the table.

    e. Switch to Datasheet view and observe the changes to the *Unit* field.

9. Repeat steps 7–8 to use the Lookup Wizard to modify the **Guest** field to use values from the **Guest** table. Include the **GuestID, LastName,** and **FirstName** fields in that order. Sort the list by last name. Hide the **GuestID** field. When you have created the lookup field, modify the lookup field properties to allow multiple values. Switch to Datasheet view and observe the changes to the *Guest* field.

10. Change the width of the lookup list in the *Guest* field to 3 inches.

    a. Switch back to Design view and if necessary, select the **Guest** field and click the **Lookup** tab.

    b. Click in the *List Width* property box and type: **3**

c. Save the table.

   d. Switch to Datasheet view and observe the changes to the *Guest* field.

   e. Close the table.

11. In the *Guest* table, add a Format property to the *State* field so the state abbreviation always appears in uppercase letters.

    a. Open the **Guest** table in Design view.

    b. Select the **State** field.

    c. In the Field Properties pane, in the *Format* box, type: **>**

    d. Save the table.

    e. Switch to Datasheet view and review the change and then close the table.

12. Modify the relationship between the *Reservation* and *Unit* tables so changes to the *UnitID* field in the *Unit* table are allowed and will update the related field in the *Reservation* table.

    a. On the *Database Tools* tab, in the *Relationships* group, click the **Relationships** button to open the Relationships window.

    b. Double-click the line connecting the *Reservation* and *Unit* tables.

    c. Click the **Enforce Referential Integrity** check box.

    d. Click the **Cascade Update Related Fields** check box.

    e. Click **OK**.

    f. Close the Relationships window.

13. Open the **Unit** table in Datasheet view and observe the format of the unit IDs. They each begin with *Unit* followed by an underscore character before the unit number. Add a custom input mask to the *Unit* table to ensure that new units will follow this same pattern. Require one number after the literal text with an optional second number. Save the literal text in the database. Use # as the data entry placeholder character.

    a. Switch to Design view.

    b. Verify that the *UnitID* field is selected.

    c. In the Input Mask box in the Field Properties pane, type: `"Unit_"09;0;#`

    d. Save the table but do not close it yet.

14. Add a new item to the lookup list used for the *Beds* field and then restrict data entry to only values in the list.

    a. Select the *Beds* field.

    b. In the Field Properties pane, click the **Lookup** tab.

    c. Click in the **Row Source** property box. At the end of the list, type: `;"Bunk Beds"`

    d. Click in the **Limit to List** property box. Expand the list and select **Yes**.

    e. Save and close the table.

15. Close the database and exit Access.

challenge yourself 5.3

In this project you will work with a human resources database to ensure consistent data entry and prevent data errors. You will import new employee records from a text file. You will create links to tables in another Access database and modify a table to look up data from those tables. You will add a new table to track comments about the database. Finally, you will modify table relationships to allow cascade updates and deletes where appropriate.

Skills needed to complete this project:
- Creating a Custom Input Mask (Skill 5.10)
- Creating a Custom Text Field Format (Skill 5.9)
- Adding Records to a Table by Importing (Skill 5.6)
- Linking to a Table in Another Access Database (Skill 5.7)
- Modifying Lookup Field Properties (Skill 5.11)
- Creating Field Validation Rules (Skill 5.12)
- Creating Record Validation Rules (Skill 5.13)
- Using Quick Start Application Parts (Skill 5.3)
- Enforcing Deletions and Updates in Relationships (Skill 5.14)

1. Open the start file **AC2013-ChallengeYourself-5-3** and resave the file as: `[your initials]AC-ChallengeYourself-5-3`

2. If necessary, enable active content by clicking the **Enable Content** button in the Message Bar.

3. Open the **CityDepartment** table and make the following changes:
   a. Add an input mask to the **DeptCode** field to require three letters. Use # as the user input placeholder character.
   b. Modify the **DeptCode** field Format property to display the data in all uppercase letters.
   c. Save the table.
   d. Switch to Datasheet view and add a new record to check your work. You can use any department ID and department name you like.
   e. Close the table.

4. Import data from the **EmployeeTransers** tab-delimited text file and append the records to the **Employee** table. The first row of the text file includes field names. You do not need to save the import steps.

5. Import the **HealthPlan** and **DentalPlan** tables in the **InsurancePlans** database as linked tables.

6. Open the **Employee** table and make the following changes:
   a. Use the Lookup Wizard to modify the **HealthPlanCode** field to look up values in the **HealthPlan** table. Include the **HealthPlanCode** and **HealthPlan** fields. Sort by the **HealthPlanCode** field. Display both fields. Choose the **HealthPlanCode** field to store in the database. Allow Access to save the table.
   b. Use the Lookup Wizard to modify the **DentalPlanCode** field to look up values in the **DentalPlan** table. Include the **DentalPlanCode** and **DentalPlan** fields. Sort by the **DentalPlanCode** field. Display both fields. Choose the **DentalPlanCode** field to store in the database. Allow Access to save the table.
   c. Switch to Datasheet view and check the lookup fields. Switch back to Design view to modify the lookup field width properties.
      i. Change the Column Widths property so the first column is **.75"** and the second column is **1.75"**.
      ii. Change List Width property to **2.5"**.
      iii. Save the table. Switch back to Datasheet view and review the changes.
   d. Modify the **EmployeeID** field to use an input mask to require a four-digit number. Use # as the user input placeholder character.
   e. Modify the **DeptCode** field to set the lookup List Width property to **2"**.

f. Add a field validation rule to the **HourlyPay** field to require values to **be greater than or equal to 12.25**. Display the following message to the user when the field validation rule is violated: `Minimum wage is $12.25.`

g. Add a record validation rule to the table to require the termination date to be greater than the hire date. Display the following message to the user when the record validation rule is violated: `Termination date must be at least one day after the hire date.`

h. Save the table. Allow Access to test the new validation rules. There should be no data that violate these rules.

i. Close the table.

7. Add a new table to track comments. Use the **Comments** Quick Start application part. Do not create a relationship with any of the existing tables.

8. Close any open database objects and open the Relationships window.

   a. Modify the relationship between the **Employee** table and the **CityDepartment** table so, if a city department ID is updated, the related records in the *Employee* table will be updated as well.

   b. There is a one-to-one relationship between the **EmployeeID** field in the **Employee** table and the **EmployeeID** field in the **InsuranceElection** table. Modify the relationship so, if an employee record is deleted in the *Employee* table, the related records in the *InsuranceElection* table will be deleted as well.

9. Close the Relationships window.

10. Close the database and exit Access.

challenge yourself 5.4

In this project, you will track suspected cases of Influenza A, B, and C for the New England Flu database.

Skills needed to complete this project:
- Using Quick Start Application Parts (Skill 5.3)
- Adding a Calculated Field to a Table (Skill 5.8)
- Creating a Custom Input Mask (Skill 5.10)
- Modifying Lookup Field Properties (Skill 5.11)
- Creating Field Validation Rules (Skill 5.12)
- Creating Record Validation Rules (Skill 5.13)
- Enforcing Deletions and Updates in Relationships (Skill 5.14)
- Linking to a Table in Another Access Database (Skill 5.7)
- Importing Data from Excel (Skill 5.4)

1. Open the start file **AC2013-ChallengeYourself-5-4** and resave the file as: `[your initials]AC-ChallengeYourself-5-4`

2. If necessary, enable active content by clicking the **Enable Content** button in the Message Bar.

3. Add a new table and related forms to the table from the **Tasks** Quick Start application part. Do not establish a relationship at this time.

4. The **Locations** table lists the organization's locations around the world. Make the following changes:
   a. Add an input mask to the **LocationID** field to require three letters followed by one required number and two optional numbers. Use the _ character as the data entry placeholder character.
   b. Modify the lookup field properties for the **LocationType** field to limit data entry to values in the lookup list.
   c. Modify the lookup field properties for the **LocationType** field to allow multiple values.
   d. Save and close the table.
5. The **Shipments** table tracks shipments made to the organization's locations around the world. Open the **Shipments** table and make the following changes.
   a. Add a calculated field named **Loss** to the far right side of the **Shipments** table to calculate the number of units lost for each shipment. Use the expression: `[QuantityShipped]-[QuantityReceived]`
   b. Add a field validation rule to the **QuantityShipped** field to require the entry to be **greater than or equal to 10**. Enter the following validation text: `Shipments must contain at least 10 units.`
   c. Add a record validation rule to require the date in the **DateShipped** field to be before the date in the **DateReceived** field. Enter the following validation text: `Date received must be after date shipped.`
   d. Save and close the table.
6. Modify the table relationships to allow changes to the **VaccineID** field in the **Vaccines** table and automatically update related records in the **Shipments** table. Do not allow deletions when there are related records. Close the Relationships window when you are finished.
7. Add a linked table to the database to link to the **Diagnosis** table in the **Influenza** Access database. The file is located with the data files for this project.
8. Import data to a new *Volunteers* table from the **Volunteers** Excel file. The file is located with the data files for this project. The first row contains column headings. Use the **VolunteerID** field as the primary key.
9. Close the database and exit Access.

on your own 5.5

In this project, you will create your own database to track technical support issues for a tech company.

Skills needed to complete this project:
- Creating a New Blank Database (Skill 5.2)
- Linking to a Table in Another Access Database (Skill 5.7)
- Creating a Custom Input Mask (Skill 5.10)
- Using Quick Start Application Parts (Skill 5.3)
- Modifying Lookup Field Properties (Skill 5.11)
- Creating Field Validation Rules (Skill 5.12)

- Creating a Custom Text Field Format (Skill 5.9)
- Creating Record Validation Rules (Skill 5.13)
- Enforcing Deletions and Updates in Relationships (Skill 5.14)

1. Start a new blank desktop database and save the file as:
   `[your initials]AC-OnYourOwn-5-5`
2. Create a linked table in the database to track employee information, using a table in one of the other databases from this chapter. (*Hint:* You could use the *Employee* table from the database in *Challenge Yourself 5.3*)
3. Add a new table to the database to track projects.
   a. Include fields for a project ID, project name, and project manager.
   b. Do not use the *AutoNumber* data type for the project ID field. Instead, use the *Short Text* data type and apply a custom text input mask to the field to guide data entry.
   c. Use a *Lookup* field for the project manager name. The lookup list should display values from the linked table.
   d. Create a test record in the table.
   e. Close the table.
4. Add a table and data entry forms to the database from the **Issues** Quick Start application part. Do not create a relationship at this time.
5. Open the **Issues** table in Datasheet view and observe the lookup lists for these fields: *Status, Priority, Category, Project,* and *Resolution*.
6. Switch to Design view and observe the lookup properties for each of the lookup fields.

   The Row Source property for the **Status** field lists eight values. Because the Column Count property is 2, the values are divided into four rows in two columns like this:

1	1 - New
2	2 - Active
3	3 - Resolved
4	4 - Closed

   The Bound Column property tells Access which column's values to store with each record. The Column Widths property hides the first column during data entry by setting the width to 0".

   a. Modify the lookup list for the **Project** field to use values from the new project table you created. Display both the project ID and project name fields in the lookup list, but use the project ID field as the bound column. (*Hint:* While you could make these changes through the lookup field properties, it might be easier to use the Lookup Wizard.)
   b. Change the options available in the Row Source property for some of the other lookup fields. Be sure to change the generic category options in the Category field.
   c. Adjust the List Width properties as necessary.
   d. For each field you modified, review the Default Value property and update as necessary.
7. Review the field validation rules for the *OpenedDate* and *DueDate* fields and modify them as necessary.
   a. Change the **OpenedDate** field validation rule to require the issue open date to be no earlier than today's date and update the validation text to reflect the new date.
   b. Remove the field validation rule and validation text for the **DueDate** field.

8. Add a format to the **Keywords** field to display the values in all uppercase or all lowercase, whichever you prefer.
9. Review the Property Sheet for the **Issues** table and update the record validation rule.
   a. Add a record validation rule to prevent a due date before the issue was opened.
   b. Change the record validation text to something more appropriate to the new record validation rule.
   c. Switch to Datasheet view and enter a test record to test the record validation rule.
   d. Close the table.
10. Modify the relationship between the projects table you created and the *Issues* table so if a record in the projects table is updated or deleted, the related records in the *Issues* table will be update or deleted as well. (*Hint:* You will need to add the project table to the Relationships window.)
11. Close the database and exit Access.

fix it 5.6

Your clients from the pet store recommended your services to a pet rescue organization to help them fix their database. Don't forget to save the changes as you work through the project.

Skills needed to complete this project:
- Importing Data from Excel (Skill 5.4)
- Modifying Lookup Field Properties (Skill 5.11)
- Adding a Calculated Field to a Table (Skill 5.8)
- Creating a Custom Input Mask (Skill 5.10)
- Creating a Custom Text Field Format (Skill 5.9)
- Creating Field Validation Rules (Skill 5.12)

1. Open the start file **AC2013-FixIt-5-6** and resave the file as:
   `[your initials]AC-FixIt-5-6`
2. If necessary, enable active content by clicking the **Enable Content** button in the Message Bar.
3. A previous volunteer kept the employee list in an Excel spreadsheet. Import the data from the **Staff** Excel spreadsheet into a new table named: `Staff`. The Excel file is located with the data files for this project.
   a. The first row of the Excel file contains column headings.
   b. The **HourlyRate** field should be imported using the *Date/Time* data type.
   c. The table should use the **StaffID** field as the primary key.
   d. The imported table should be named: `Staff`
4. In the **Adoptions** table, the **PetID** field is a lookup field displaying values from the *Pets* table. Someone altered the lookup list to include additional fields from the *Pets* table but forgot to modify other lookup field properties.
   a. Change the **Column Count** property to display all three values.
   b. Change the **Column Widths** property so the first column is **.75"**, the second column is **.75"**, and the third column is **2"**. (*Hint:* Use a semicolon to separate the widths for each column.)

- c. Change the **List Width** property to **3.5"** so all three columns are visible in the lookup list without a horizontal scrollbar.
- d. Do not allow users to enter an adoption record for a pet unless that pet is listed in the lookup list.

5. The organization recently adopted a new policy to require a home visit within 30 days of the adoption. In the **Adoptions** table, add a new *Date/Time* calculated field named **HomeVisitDate** between the *AdoptionDate* and *HomeVisitCompleted* fields to calculate the date of the home visit. Use this expression to calculate the adoption date: `[AdoptionDate]+30`

6. In the **Friends** table, someone tried to use the field Format property and an input mask to ensure that the records are entered correctly. Please fix the mistakes:
   - a. In the **CustomerID** field, the input mask is set to allow two optional letters followed by two optional numbers. The format should *require* two letters followed by two numbers.
   - b. In the **City** field, the Format property is set to display the text in all uppercase. Please remove the format so the text will appear as entered.

7. In the **Pets** table, the **AnimalType** field uses a lookup list to limit data entry to "Cat" or "Dog." The list is missing some animal types, and database users should be able enter an animal type that is not on the list.
   - a. Add the following animal types to the list: **Bird, Guinea Pig,** and **Reptile.**
   - b. Modify the Limit to List property so users can enter animal types that are not on the list.

8. Pets are not available for adoption until they are 3 months old. Modify the **Pets** table to prevent entering a pet age less than 3.
   - a. Add a field validation rule to require that the pet age is at least 3 months. Use the expression: `>=3`
   - b. Add the validation text message: `We do not allow adoptions of animals less than 3 months old.`

9. Close the database and exit Access.

chapter 6

Exploring Advanced Forms

- Modify form properties using the Property Sheet
- Manage data entry through form and control properties
- Add list box, combo box, and command button controls
- Create subforms
- Add images to forms
- Create a navigation form
- Modify the tab order in a form

In this chapter, you will learn the following skills:

Skill **6.1** Creating a Blank Form from an Application Part

Skill **6.2** Working with a New Form in Design View

Skill **6.3** Setting the Sort Order in a Form

Skill **6.4** Controlling Data Entry in a Form

Skill **6.5** Controlling Data Entry for a Field in a Form

Skill **6.6** Disabling User Interface Elements in a Form

Skill **6.7** Adding a List Box Control to a Form

Skill **6.8** Adding a Command Button Control to a Form

Skill **6.9** Adding a Combo Box Control to a Form

Skill **6.10** Adding a Subform Based on a Table or Query

Skill **6.11** Adding a Subform Based on a Form

Skill **6.12** Modifying the Subform Properties

Skill **6.13** Displaying the Form Header and Footer

Skill **6.14** Adding Images to Forms

Skill **6.15** Creating a Navigation Form with Tabs

Skill **6.16** Defining the Tab Order of Controls

skills

introduction

This chapter expands on the basic form skills introduced in Chapter 3. Throughout this chapter, you will work primarily in Design view to create user-friendly forms by modifying the form and control properties. You will add new form controls to display list boxes, combo boxes, and command buttons to replace the record navigation buttons. You will learn to add subforms and images and to create a navigation form. Most of the skills you learn in this chapter can be completed in Layout view as well as Design view. The *Let Me Try* exercises in this chapter use the AC6-Sales database. You can keep the database open while you work in this chapter, opening and closing database objects as required for each *Let Me Try*.

Skill 6.1 Creating a Blank Form from an Application Part

One way to start a new form is to begin with a blank **form application part**. These application parts are essentially form templates. They provide a blank form with a preset layout and placeholders for labels and other controls.

To create a new form based on an application part:

1. On the *Create* tab, in the *Templates* group, click the **Application Parts** button.
2. In the *Blank Forms* section, click the form template you want.
3. Note the new form in the Navigation Pane.
4. Right-click the new form in the Navigation Pane and select **Rename**.
5. Type a new name for the form, and press ⏎ Enter.

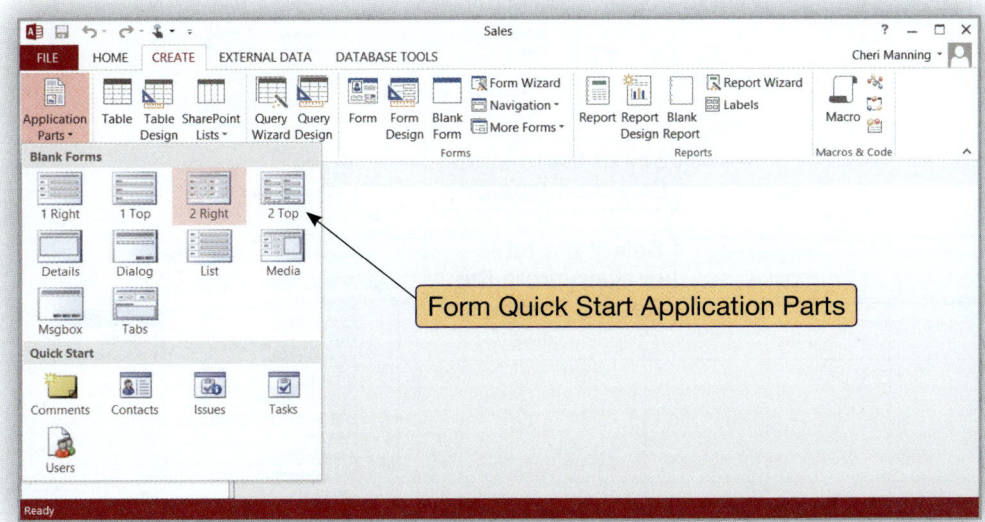

FIGURE AC 6.1

There are no records in the new form. The new blank form does not have a record source defined (an underlying table) and none of the controls in the form are bound to fields, so there are no records to display. The form is an empty layout until you modify it in Layout view or Design view and add bound controls.

let me try

Open the data file **AC6-Sales** and try this skill on your own:

1. Create a new form based on the **2 Right** form application part.
2. Rename the form: **InventoryForm**

skill 6.1 Creating a Blank Form from an Application Part

Skill 6.2 Working with a New Form in Design View

When you start a new blank form from scratch or from an application part, the first thing you should do is set a table or query as the **record source** for the form. The record source determines which fields can be included in the form. The form is not limited to fields in the record source, but fields selected from another table or query must have a relationship to one of the fields in the record source.

Use the **form Property Sheet** to set the record source and other form properties. Properties are grouped into four tabs: *Format, Data, Event,* and *Other.* The *All* tab displays all the properties in a single list.

To set the record source for a form from Design view:

1. On the *Form Design Tools Design* tab, in the *Tools* group, click the **Property Sheet** button to display the Property Sheet.

2. Verify that **Form** is selected in the *Selection type* box. If you have a control selected, the Property Sheet displays the properties for the selected control. To view and modify the properties of the form itself, expand the *Selection type* list at the top of the Property Sheet and select **Form.**

3. From the Property Sheet *Data* tab, click in the **Record Source** box, expand the list, and select the table or query you want.

4. Click the **X** in the upper right corner of the Property Sheet to close it.

5. Save the form.

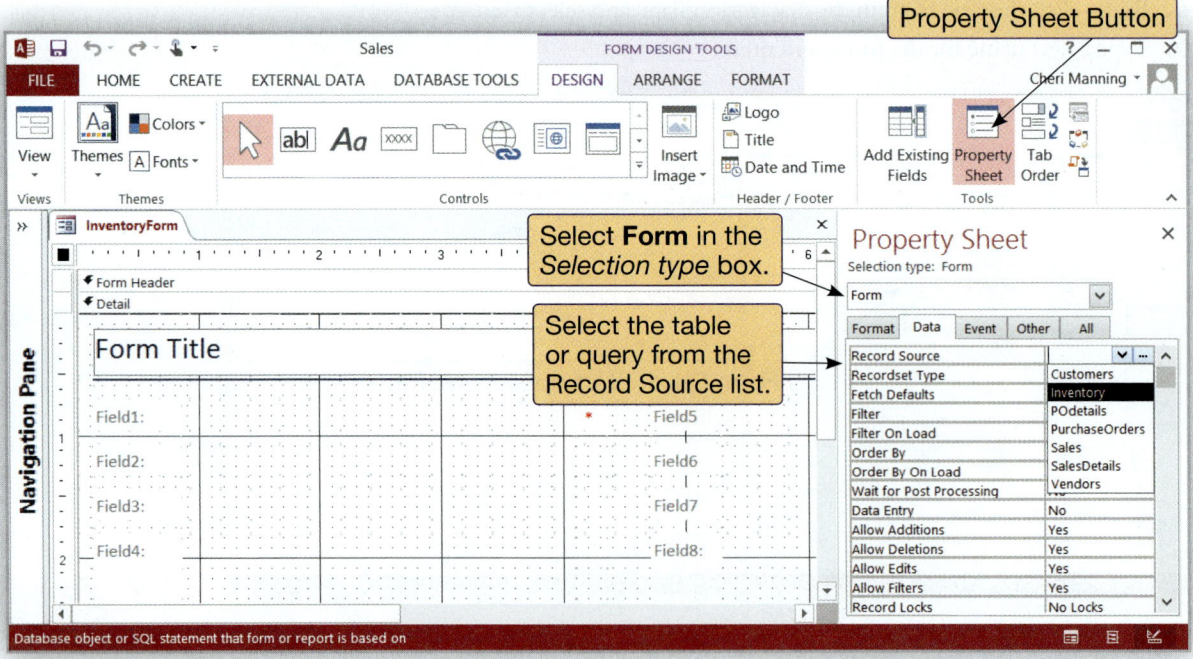

FIGURE AC 6.2

If you are working with a form created from an application part, it may include placeholder labels as part of the form design. Recall that when you add a field to a form, Access automatically adds a bound text control to display values from the field and a label control that displays the name of the field. You can prevent Access from including the label control by holding down the Ctrl key as you drag the field from the Field List pane.

Once you have set the record source from the form, add fields to the form using the Field List pane.

1. On the *Form Design Tools Design* tab, in the *Tools* group, click the **Add Existing Fields** button.
2. Click and drag fields from the Field List to the form. To prevent Access from including the label control, hold down the Ctrl key as you drag the field.

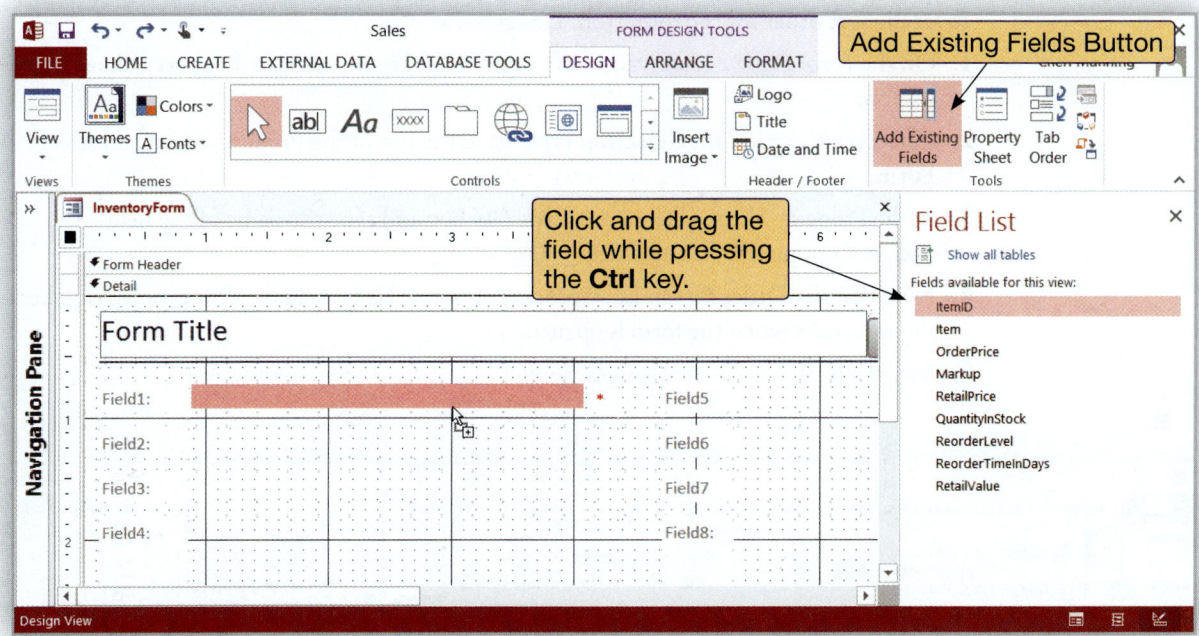

FIGURE AC 6.3

tips & tricks

If you do not set the record source for the form, Access will create an embedded query as the record source as you add fields to the form. The **embedded query** is a query created specifically for the form. In the Record Source box, it appears as an SQL statement. For more information about SQL statements, refer to the skill *Modifying a Query in SQL View*.

another method

- To open the form Property Sheet using a keyboard shortcut, press F4 or press Alt + Enter.
- To select the form, click the square at the upper left corner of the form, just below the form tab, to the left of the ruler. The *Selection type* box in the Property Sheet will update automatically.

let me try

If the database is not already open, open the data file **AC6-Sales** and try this skill on your own:

1. Open the **InventoryForm** form in Design view.
2. Set the **Inventory** table as the form's record source.
3. Add the **ItemID** field to the right of the **Field1:** label. Add the bound text control without the label control.
4. Save and close the form.

skill 6.2 Working with a New Form in Design View

Skill 6.3 Setting the Sort Order in a Form

If you want the records in the form to appear in a certain order, you can set the sort order through the Property Sheet. Access will use the ascending sort order. Text fields will be sorted from A to Z; number fields will be sorted from smallest to largest; and date fields will be sorted from oldest to newest. This skill focuses on using the Property Sheet in Design view. The same technique can be used in Layout view.

To set the sort order for the form from Design view:

1. On the *Form Design Tools Design* tab, in the *Tools* group, click the **Property Sheet** button.
2. If necessary, expand the **Selection type** list at the top of the Property Sheet and select **Form**.
3. In the Property Sheet, click in the **Order By** box and type the name of the field enclosed in square brackets. Press Enter.
4. Note that the Order By On Load property is set to *Yes* by default. This property applies the sort order when the form is opened.
5. Save the form to save the changes.

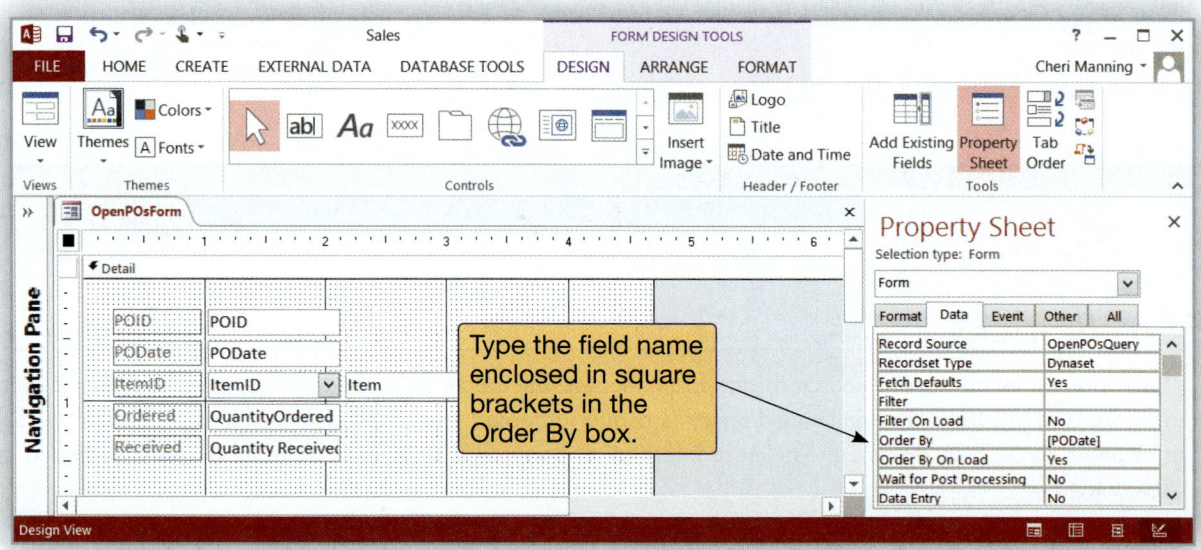

FIGURE AC 6.4

tips & tricks

If your form is based on a query, setting the sort order in the form will override any sort settings in the query.

let me try

If the database is not already open, open the data file **AC6-Sales** and try this skill on your own:

1. Open the **OpenPOsForm** form in Design view.
2. Modify the form properties so records in the form will be sorted by values in the **PODate** field.
3. Save and close the form.

Skill 6.4 Controlling Data Entry in a Form

When you create a new form, by default, all the records are visible in the form, and users can add new records, edit existing records, and delete records. The only constraints on user actions are edits or deletions that would violate table relationships. Through the form Property Sheet, you can change the default settings and control which data entry actions are available. This skill focuses on using the Property Sheet in Design view. The same techniques can be used in Layout view.

One of the most useful forms is a **data entry form** where the only action available to a user is adding a new record. The existing records in the table are not visible. Database users do not need to know how to add a new record to a form, because the form opens with a new, blank record ready for data entry.

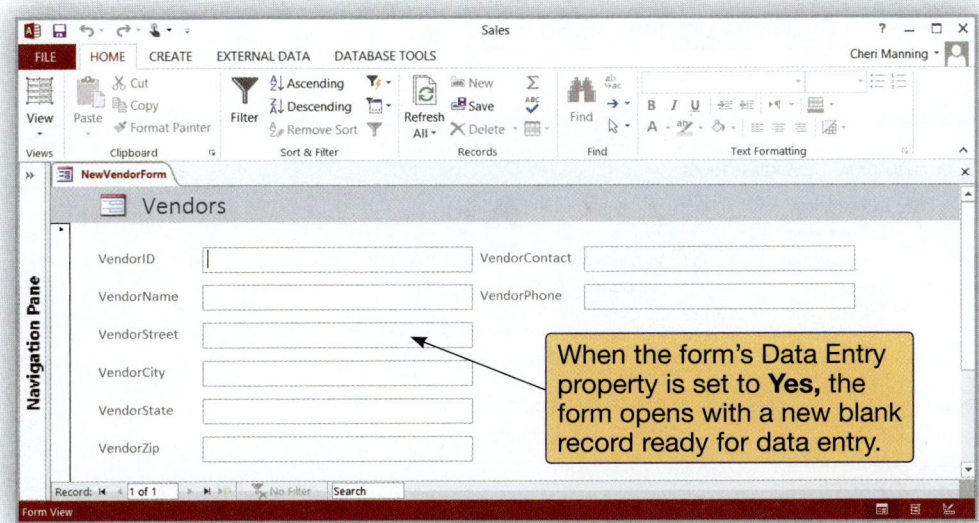

FIGURE AC 6.5

To restrict form data entry to new records only:

1. On the *Form Design Tools Design* tab, in the *Tools* group, click the **Property Sheet** button.
2. If necessary, expand the **Selection type** list at the top of the Property Sheet and select **Form**.
3. Click in the **Data Entry** property box, expand the list, and select **Yes**. Verify that the Allow Additions property is set to **Yes** as well.

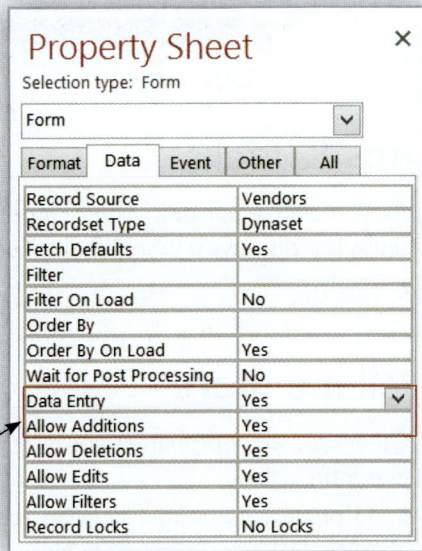

FIGURE AC 6.6

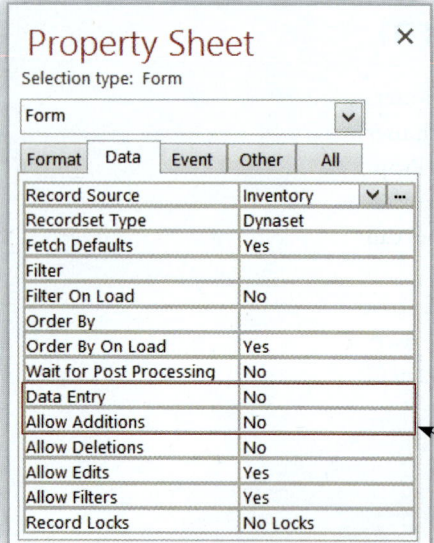

If you want the opposite of a data entry form, where users *cannot* enter new records, leave the Data Entry property set to **No,** and modify the Allow Additions property instead.

To prevent users from adding new records to a form:

1. From Design view, on the *Design Layout Tools Design* tab, in the *Tools* group, click the **Property Sheet** button.

2. If necessary, expand the **Selection type** list at the top of the Property Sheet and select **Form.**

3. On the Property Sheet *Data* tab, click in the **Allow Additions** box, expand the list, and select **No.** Verify that the Data Entry property is also set to **No.**

To prevent users from adding new records, set the Allow Additions property to **No.**

FIGURE AC 6.7

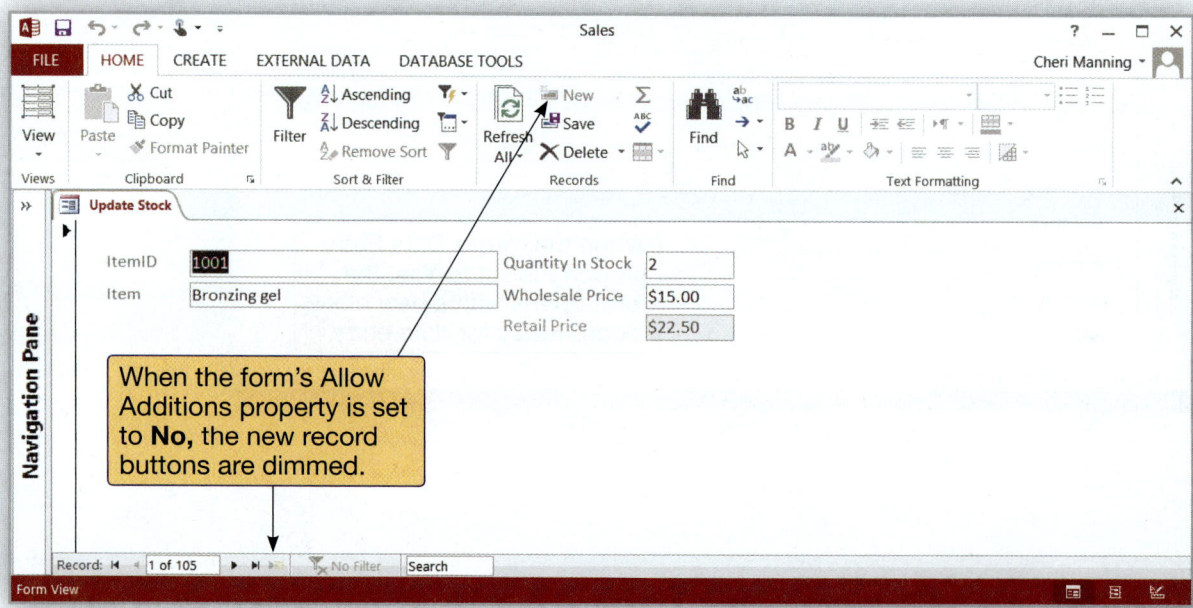

When the form's Allow Additions property is set to **No,** the new record buttons are dimmed.

FIGURE AC 6.8

tips & tricks

As you click each box in the Property Sheet, the status bar displays a user-friendly description of the property.

tell me more

Other data entry properties you may want to apply to a form include:

- To prevent users from deleting records, set the Allow Deletions property to **No.**
- To prevent users from changing data, set the Allow Edits property to **No.**

let me try

If the database is not already open, open the data file **AC6-Sales** and try this skill on your own:

1. Open the **NewVendorsForm** form in Form view and review the form.
2. Switch to Design view and modify the form's property to restrict data entry to new records only.
3. Switch back to Form view and observe the changes.
4. Save and close the form.
5. Open the **UpdateStockForm** form in Design view.
6. Modify the form's properties to *not* allow new records.
7. Switch to Form view and observe the changes.
8. Save the form.

Skill 6.5 Controlling Data Entry for a Field in a Form

If you want users to be able to edit some of the data in a form, but not all, you can restrict data entry for a specific field. Select the bound text control for the field first, and then use the **control Property Sheet** to disable it. Changing the Enabled property to **No** will dim the control, and when users tab through the controls in the form, the disabled control will be skipped. This skill focuses on using the Property Sheet in Design view. The same techniques can be used in Layout view.

To prevent data entry in a specific field in a form:

1. On the *Form Design Tools Design* tab, in the *Tools* group, click the **Property Sheet** button.
2. Click the control in the form, or expand the **Selection type** list at the top of the Property Sheet and select the control you want to modify.
3. On the Property Sheet *Data* tab, click in the **Enabled** box, expand the list, and select **No.**

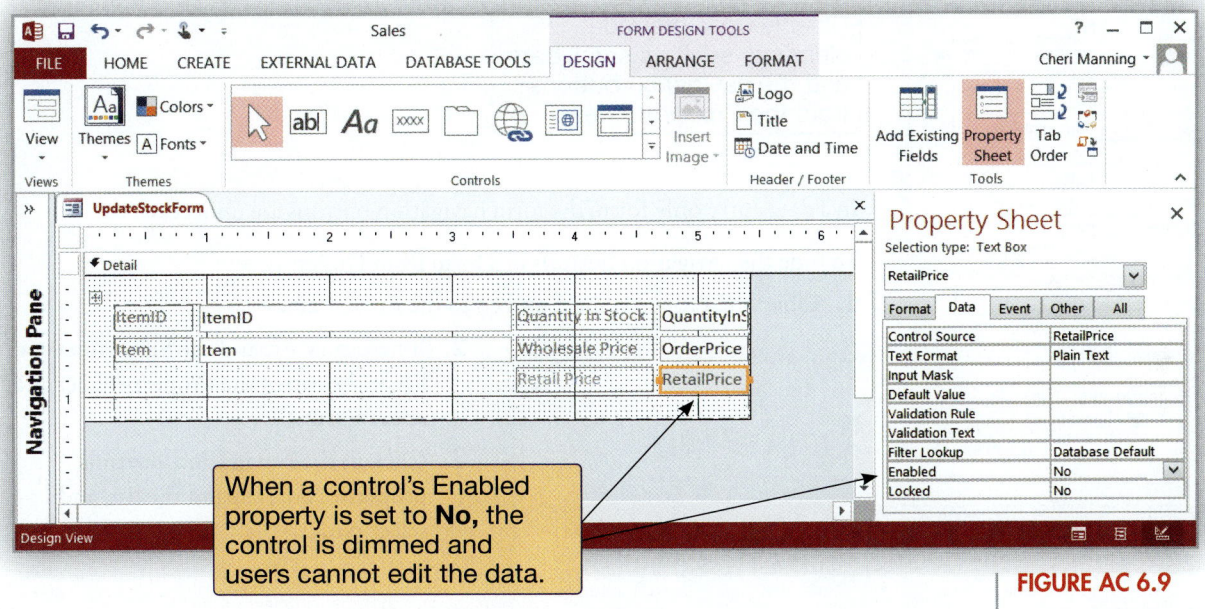

When a control's Enabled property is set to **No,** the control is dimmed and users cannot edit the data.

FIGURE AC 6.9

tips & tricks

The Locked property is similar to the Enabled property. When a control is locked, users cannot edit the data, but they can still select the control and it is included in the tab order. Using the Enabled property has the same effect, but it is more user-friendly as the disabled state shows that the control is unavailable for data entry.

let me try

If the database is not already open, open the data file **AC6-Sales** and try this skill on your own:

1. If the form is not already open, open the **UpdateStockForm** form in Design view.
2. Disable the **RetailPrice** bound text control so users cannot edit data in the field.
3. Switch to Form view and observe the changes.
4. Save and close the form.

Skill 6.6 Disabling User Interface Elements in a Form

Often, a form will include a vertical or horizontal scroll bar when it is not really necessary. Rather than changing the size of the Detail section and possibly having to modify the layout of the form, try hiding the scroll bar. This skill focuses on using the Property Sheet in Design view. The same techniques can be used in Layout view.

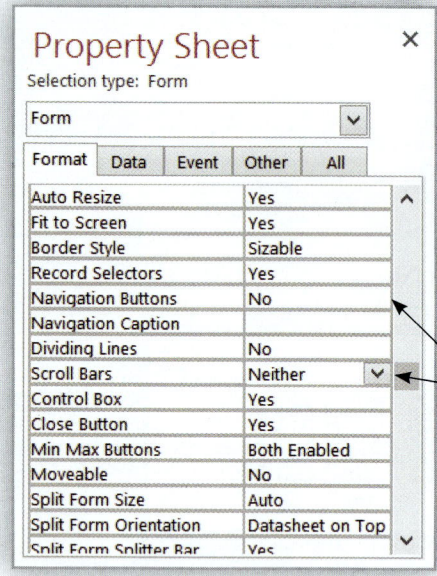

FIGURE AC 6.10

To hide both the vertical and horizontal scroll bars in a form from Design view:

1. On the *Form Design Tools Design* tab, in the *Tools* group, click the **Property Sheet** button.
2. If necessary, expand the **Selection type** list at the top of the Property Sheet and select **Form.**
3. From the Property Sheet *Format* tab, click in the **Scroll Bars** property box, expand the list, and select **Neither.**

Disable user interface elements such as scroll bars and the navigation buttons from the Property Sheet.

In a data entry only form, the form navigation buttons are unnecessary.

To hide the navigation buttons in a form from Design view:

1. Open the Property Sheet and go to the *Format* tab.
2. If necessary, expand the **Selection type** list at the top of the Property Sheet and select **Form.**
3. Click in the **Navigation Buttons** properties box, expand the list, and select **No.**

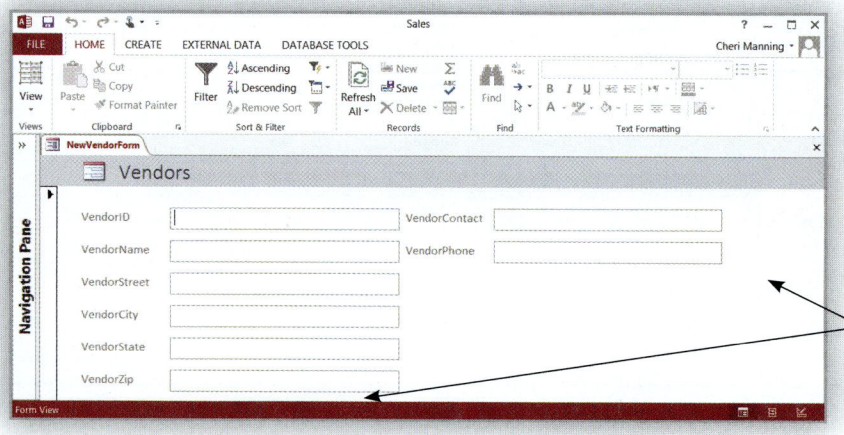

FIGURE AC 6.11

Both the navigation buttons at the bottom of the form and the vertical scroll bar at the right of the form are hidden.

let me try

If the database is not already open, open the data file **AC6-Sales** and try this skill on your own:

1. Open the **NewVendorForm** form in Design view.
2. Disable both the vertical and horizontal scroll bars.
3. Hide the form navigation buttons.
4. Switch to Form view and review the form.
5. Save the form.

Skill 6.7 Adding a List Box Control to a Form

A **list box control** presents users with a list of options to choose from. It can display values from a table or query, but usually you'll want the control to display values you enter yourself. By providing database users with a list of values to choose from, you can make data entry easier and prevent errors. Use a list box control when the list of values to choose from is short and all the values can be shown without scroll bars in the box.

New controls can be added to the form from Layout view or Design view. This skill focuses on using Design view where you have more control over the placement of the control.

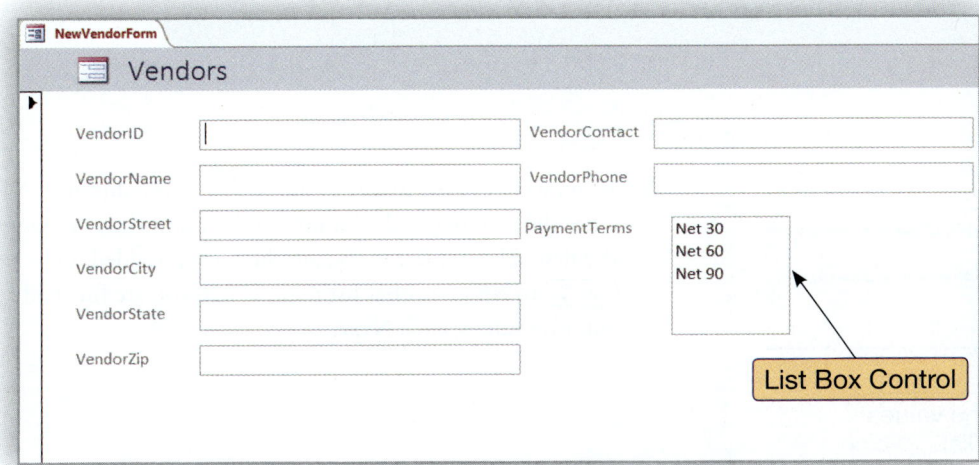

FIGURE AC 6.12

To add a list box control in Design view to display values from a list you enter yourself:

1. On the *Form Design Tools Design* tab, in the *Controls* group, expand the *Controls* gallery by clicking the **More** button, and verify that *Use Control Wizards* is enabled (the icon will appear highlighted). *Use Control Wizards* must be enabled to display the List Box Wizard.

2. In the *Controls* gallery, click the **List Box** button. You may need to click the **More** button to expand the *Controls* gallery to find the *List Box* button.

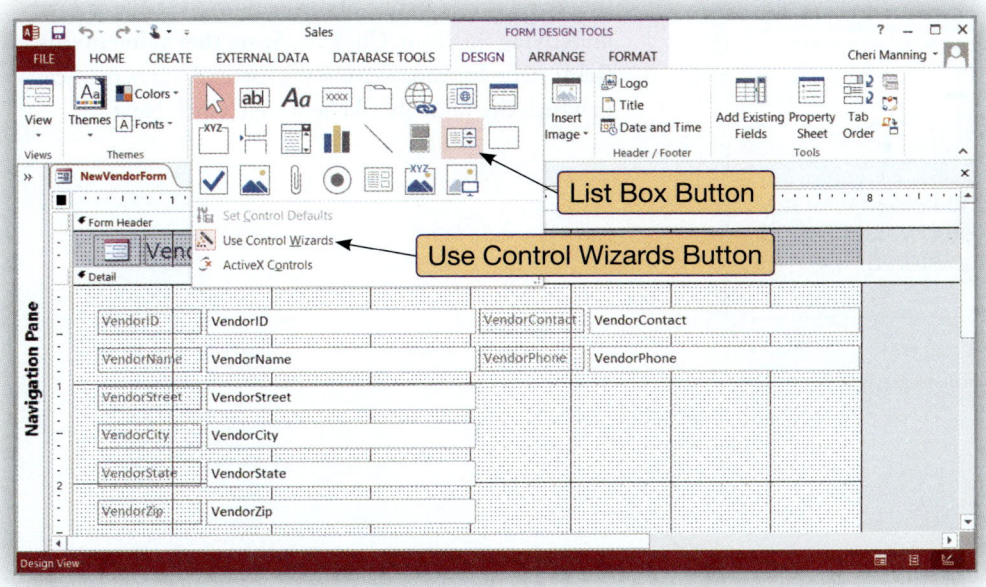

FIGURE AC 6.13

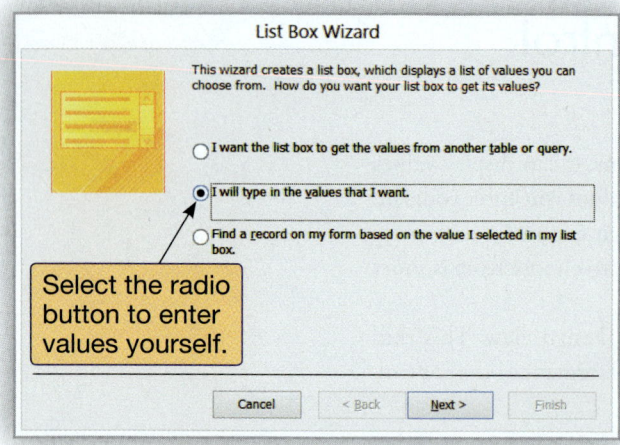

FIGURE AC 6.14

3. Click the area of the form where you want the list box. The List Box Wizard opens when you click the form.
4. In the first step of the wizard, select the **I will type in the values that I want.** radio button. click **Next**.

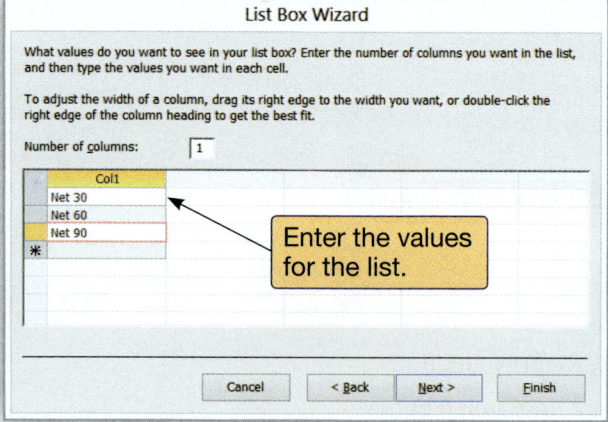

FIGURE AC 6.15

5. If you want the list to display more than one column, enter the number in the **Number of columns** box. Type the first value for the list box in the form provided. Press Tab to enter another list item. When you are finished entering values, click **Next.**

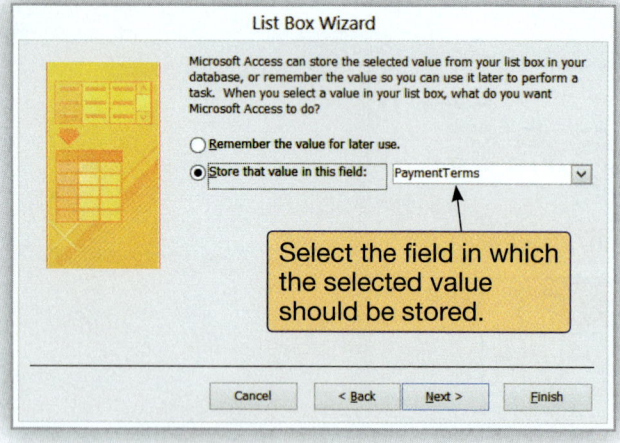

FIGURE AC 6.16

6. When using a list box for data entry, the selected value should be stored in one of the fields in the table or query underlying the form. Click the **Store that value in this field:** radio button. Expand the list, and select the field in which the value should be stored. Click **Next.**

7. Type the text for the label control that will appear with the list box. Click **Finish.**

FIGURE AC 6.17

8. Adjust the size and position of the list box control as necessary.

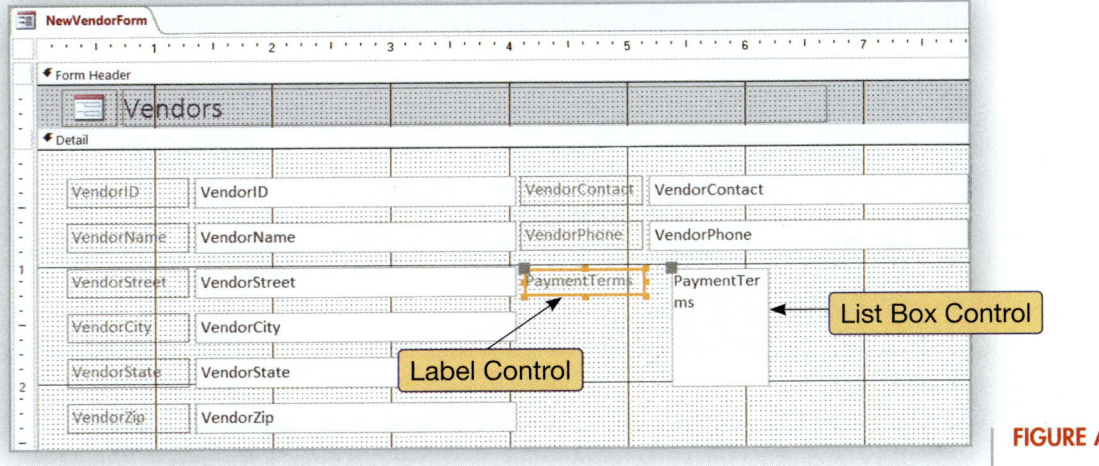

FIGURE AC 6.18

9. Switch to Form view to test the control and then save the form.

tips & tricks

When you use a field from a table or query as the source for a list box control, the list will include **every** value in the field. If the field uses a list value lookup list in the table, the list box control will display **every** value in the field, including duplicates. Instead of referencing values in the table field, you should enter the values yourself, using the same values you used in the lookup list.

tell me more

You can edit the list items from the control's Property Sheet. On the Property Sheet *Data* tab, click in the **Row Source** property box, and click the ⋯ button to open the *Edit List Items* dialog. Edit the list items and then click **OK**.

To prevent users from editing the list, on the control's Property Sheet *Data* tab, click in the **Allow Value List Edits** property box, expand the list, and select **No**.

let me try

If the database is not already open, open the data file **AC6-Sales** and try this skill on your own:

1. If the form is not already open, open the **NewVendorForm** form in Design view.
2. Add a list box control to the form below the **VendorPhone** text box control. Verify that **Use Control Wizards** is enabled.
3. The list box control should display fields the following values in this order:

   `Net 30`
   `Net 60`
   `Net 90`

4. Store the selected value in the **PaymentTerms** field.
5. The label should display: `PaymentTerms`
6. Adjust the size and position of the list box control as necessary.
7. Switch to Form view to test the control, then save the form.

skill 6.7   Adding a List Box Control to a Form

Skill 6.8 Adding a Command Button Control to a Form

A **command button control** provides a user-friendly way to interact with the form. Buttons can provide a variety of actions including navigation; add, delete, and save records; open or close a form or record; and exit the application. A command button control can be added to the form from Layout view or Design view. This skill focuses on using Design view where you have more control over the placement of the control.

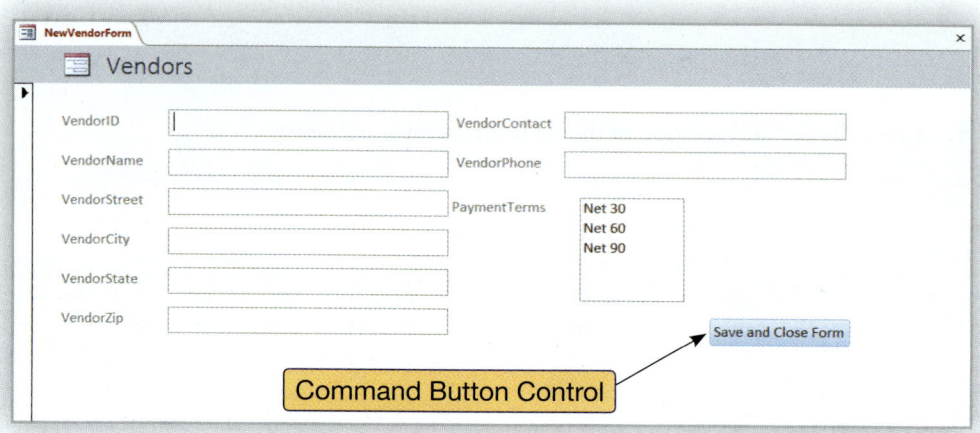

FIGURE AC 6.19

To add a command button control to a form in Design view using the Command Button Wizard:

1. On the *Form Design Tools Design* tab, in the *Controls* group, expand the *Controls* gallery by clicking the **More** button, and verify that *Use Control Wizards* is enabled (the icon will appear highlighted). *Use Control Wizards* must be enabled to display the Command Button Wizard.
2. In the *Controls* gallery, click the **Button** button. It should be visible in the Ribbon without expanding the gallery.
3. Click the area of the form where you want to place the button.

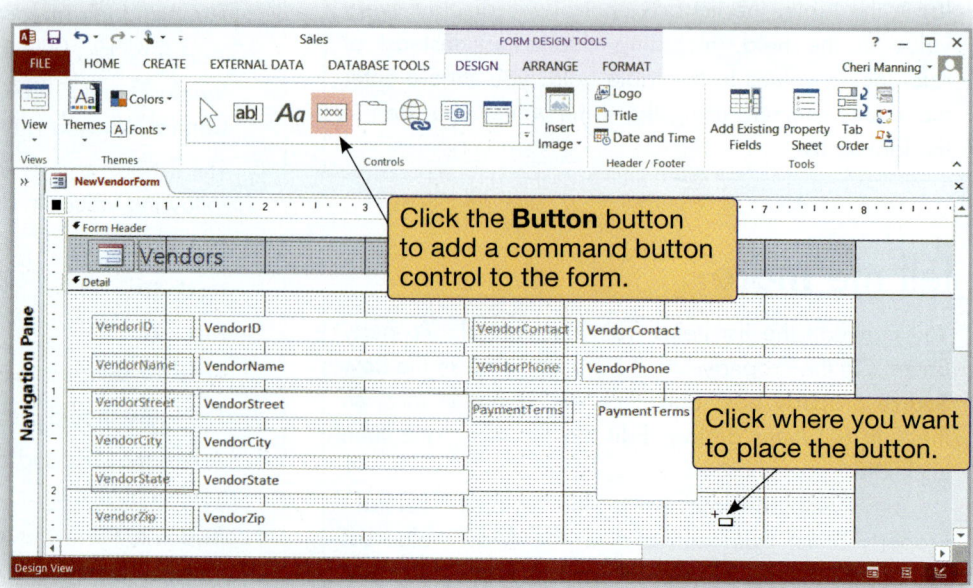

FIGURE AC 6.20

4. The Command Button Wizard opens.
5. The first step in the wizard allows you to define the action that will happen when the button is clicked. Click each category in the *Categories* list to see the list of actions available. Click an action in the *Actions* list to select it. Click **Next**.

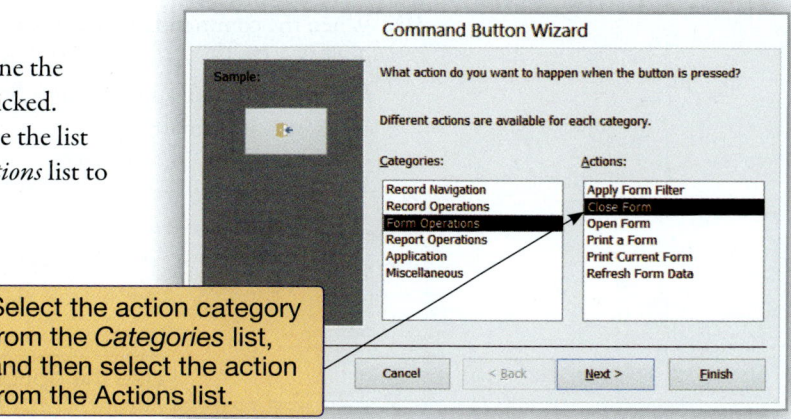

Select the action category from the *Categories* list, and then select the action from the Actions list.

FIGURE AC 6.21

6. The button can display text or an image. If you select the *Picture* radio button, Access will suggest standard button images to use. If you select text, you can edit the text. When using a close or new record action after data entry, consider changing to button text to include *Save* so your users understand that the new record will be saved when the current record is closed. Make your selection and click **Next**.

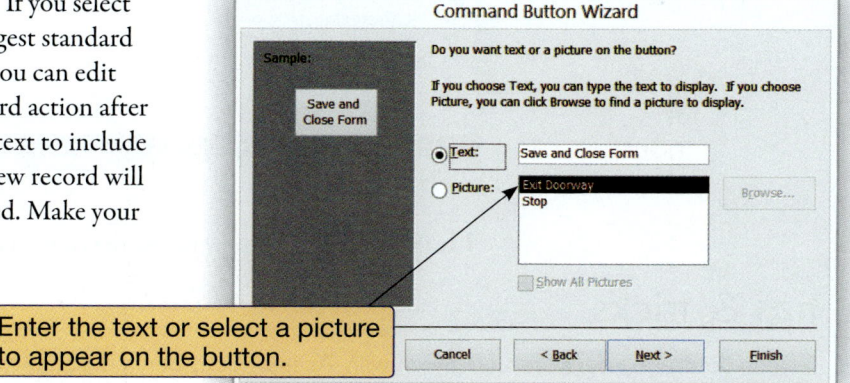

Enter the text or select a picture to appear on the button.

FIGURE AC 6.22

7. By default, Access names the button *Command##* (where ## is the next number in the number of controls you've created in the database). Type a more meaningful name in the box provided. Standard practice is for button names to begin with *cmd* or *btn* followed by a word or two describing what the button does (with no spaces).
8. Click **Finish**.

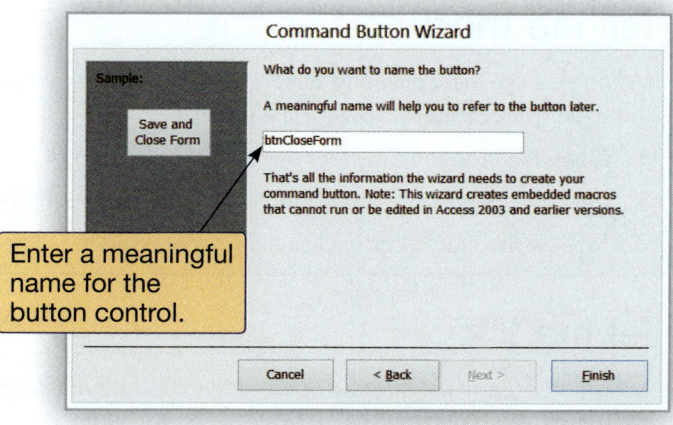

Enter a meaningful name for the button control.

FIGURE AC 6.23

9. Adjust the size and position of the command button control as necessary.

skill 6.8 Adding a Command Button Control to a Form

10. When the command button is selected in Design view, you can use the options on the *Form Design Tools Format* tab to change the look of the button. From the *Control Formatting* group, apply a Quick Style or change the button shape, outline color, fill color, or text formatting.

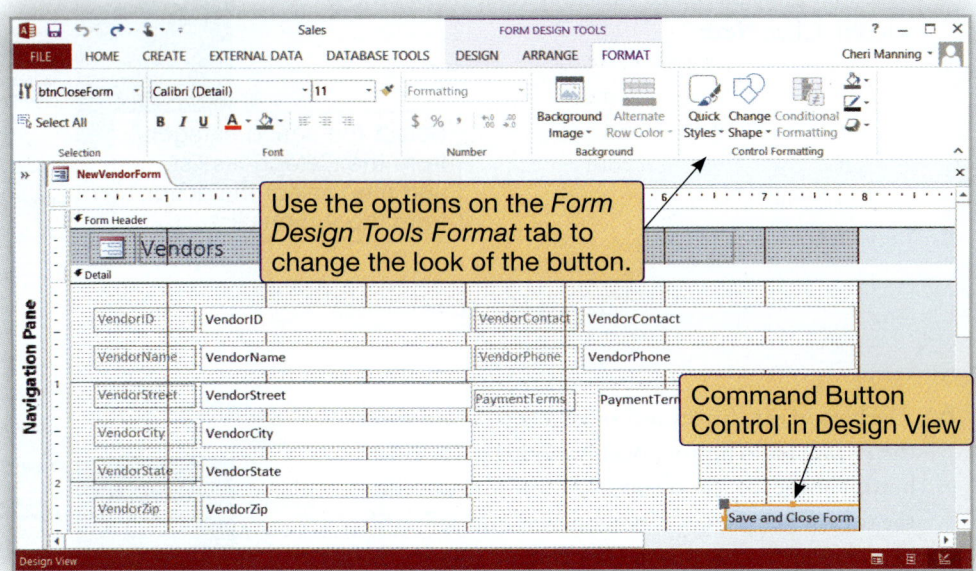

FIGURE AC 6.24

11. Switch to Form view to test the control and then save the form.

tips & tricks

If your database users are unfamiliar with Access, consider hiding the navigation buttons in your form and using command buttons instead. Notice that the command button in Figure AC 6.19 displays the caption *Save and Close Form*. Novice Access users may not realize that closing the form automatically saves the record they have just entered. The additional text on the button helps users understand the data entry process.

tell me more

When you use the Command Button Wizard, Access writes a macro for you, and embeds the macro code in the button's *On Click* property. To view the code:

1. Open the Property Sheet for the command button.
2. Click the **Event** tab. Notice that the *On Click* property box displays ...
3. To view the macro code, click the ... icon button.

let me try

If the database is not already open, open the data file **AC6-Sales** and try this skill on your own:

1. If the form is not already open, open the **NewVendorForm** form in Design view.
2. Add a command button control to the lower right corner of the form. Verify that **Use Control Wizards** is enabled.
3. Use the **Close Form** action from the *Form Operations* category.
4. Display this text on the button: `Save and Close Form`
5. Name the button control: `btnCloseForm`
6. Review the button in Form view and then save and close the form.

Skill 6.9 Adding a Combo Box Control to a Form

A **combo box control** provides users with a combination data entry control—users can type the data in the text box at the top of the control or they can expand the list and select a value. When you add a lookup field to a form, Access automatically creates a combo box control to mimic the list in table Datasheet view. You don't usually need to create the combo box yourself.

A combo box can also be used as a navigation device. When the user makes a selection, the form navigates to the first record with that value. Use a combo box when the list of values is very long or when a user might want to type the value to find instead of scrolling through the list of values.

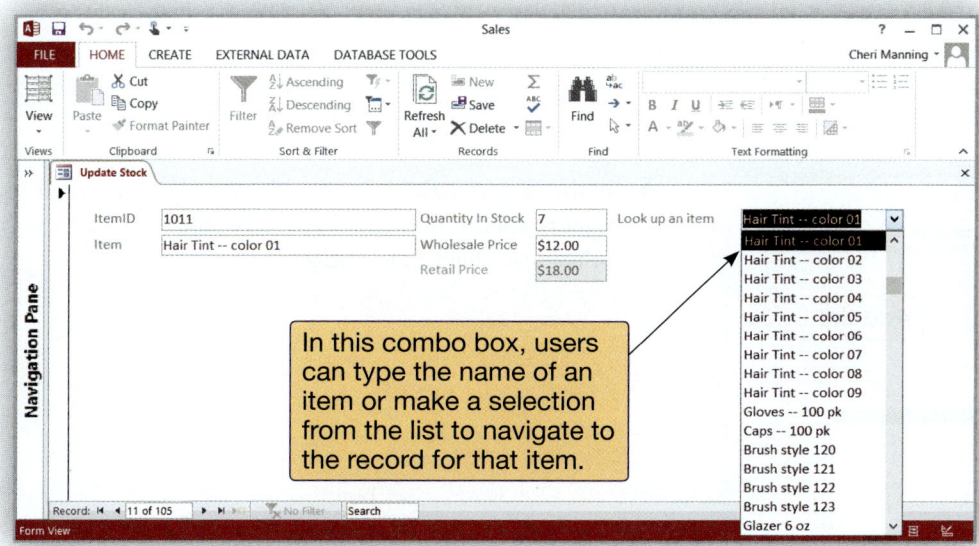

FIGURE AC 6.25

To create a combo box to use as a navigation device:

1. From the *Form Design Tools Design* tab, expand the *Controls* gallery by clicking the **More** button, and verify that *Use Control Wizards* is enabled (the icon will appear highlighted). *Use Control Wizards* must be enabled to display the Combo Box Wizard.

2. In the *Controls* gallery, click the **Combo Box** button. You may need to click the **More** button to expand the *Controls* gallery to find the *Combo Box* button.

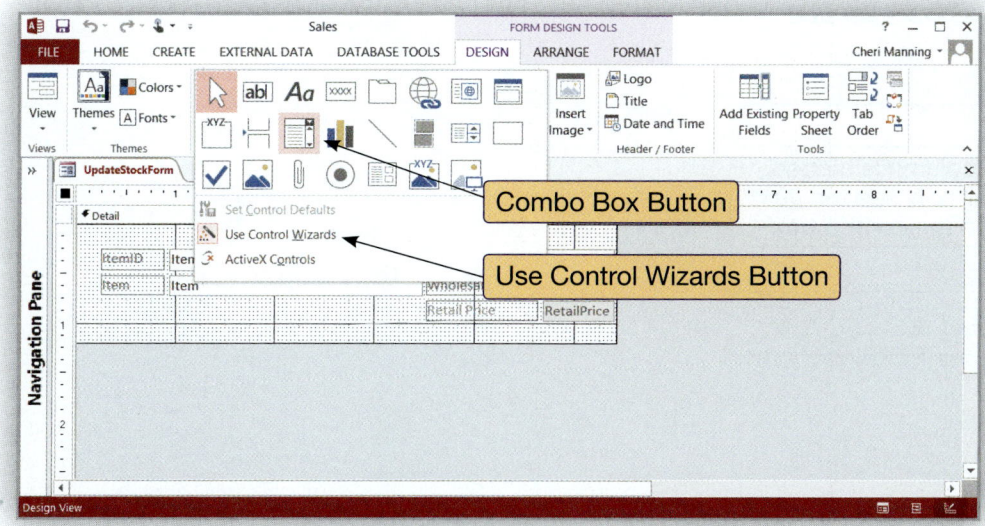

FIGURE AC 6.26

skill 6.9 Adding a Combo Box Control to a Form

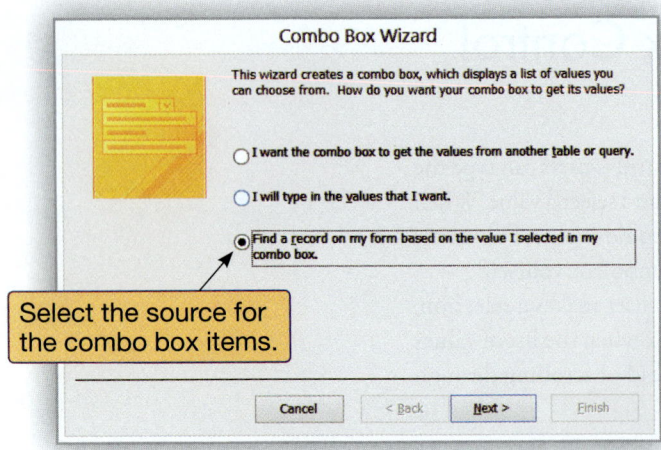

FIGURE AC 6.27

3. Click the area of the form where you want the combo box. The Combo Box Wizard opens when you click the form.

4. In the first step of the wizard, click the **Find a record on my form based on the value I selected in my combo box.** radio button. Click **Next**.

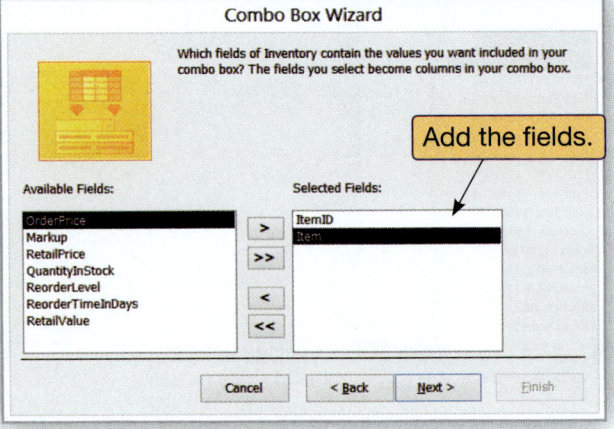

FIGURE AC 6.28

5. In the *Available Fields* list, double-click the field(s) you want to appear in the combo box. Be sure to include the primary key field. Click **Next**.

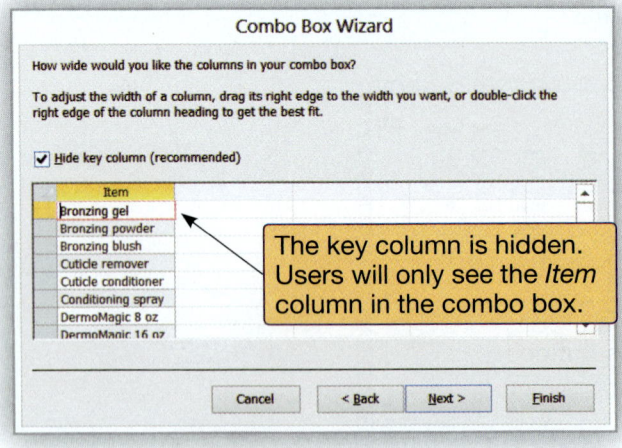

FIGURE AC 6.29

6. The primary key field is hidden by default. If necessary, resize the list so all items appear completely. Click **Next**.

7. Type the text for the label control that will appear with the combo box. Click **Finish**.

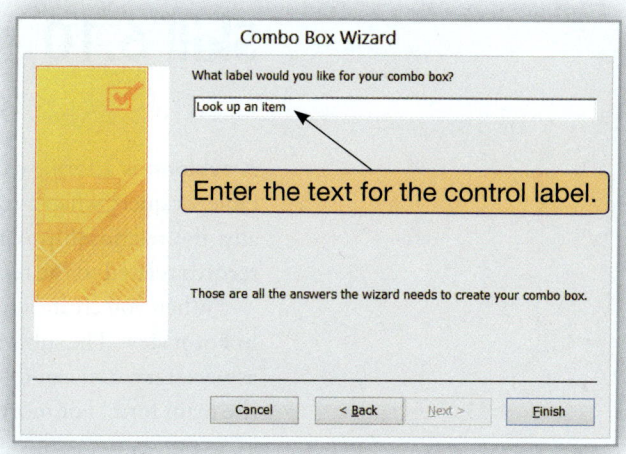

FIGURE AC 6.30

8. Adjust the size and position of the control as necessary.
9. Switch to Form view to test the control and then save the form.

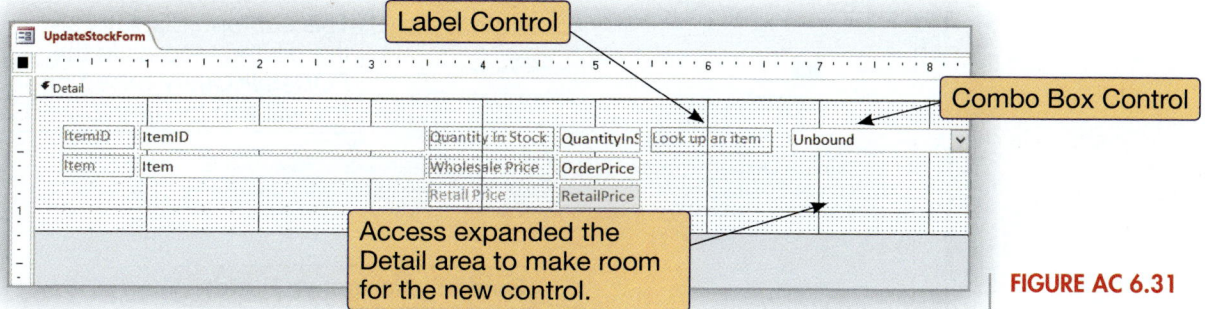

FIGURE AC 6.31

A combo box can be added to the form from Layout view or Design view. This skill focuses on using Design view where you have more control over the placement of the control. Notice that in Design view, when you add a control outside the form Detail area, Access expands the area automatically to make room for the new control.

tips & tricks

If you are using the combo box for navigation, use the control label to tell your users its purpose.

You may also want to modify the format of the combo box to make it stand out from the other controls on the form. Select the control, and then change the shape fill color or shape outline color or width from the options in the *Control Formatting* group on the *Form Design Tools Format* tab.

tell me more

You can control the height of the combo box drop-down list by setting the number of list items that appear. Open the control's Property Sheet. On the *Format* tab, change the value in the List Rows property box.

let me try

If the database is not already open, open the data file **AC6-Sales** and try this skill on your own:

1. Open the **UpdateStockForm** form in Design view.
2. Add a combo box control to the right of the *QuantityInStock* control. Access will expand the form Detail area for you.
3. Create a combo box that can be used as a navigation tool based on the value selected.
4. Use the **Inventory** table as the source for the combo box.
5. Add the **ItemID** and the **Item** fields to the combo box.
6. Allow Access to hide the key column.
7. Use this text for the label: `Look up an item`
8. Switch to Form view and text the combo box.
9. Save the form.

skill 6.9 Adding a Combo Box Control to a Form

Skill 6.10 Adding a Subform Based on a Table or Query

A **subform** is a form within a form. The subform can display records from another form, table, or query when a relationship exists between data in the main form and subform. Usually, the relationship is a one-to-many relationship, where the subform displays the many records related to the record in the main form.

When you create a subform based on a table or query, it is displayed as a Datasheet form in Form view. The subform includes its own set of navigation buttons and its own scroll bars as necessary. You can disable these from the subform's Property Sheet just as you would for the main form. For more information, refer to the skill *Modifying the Subform Properties*.

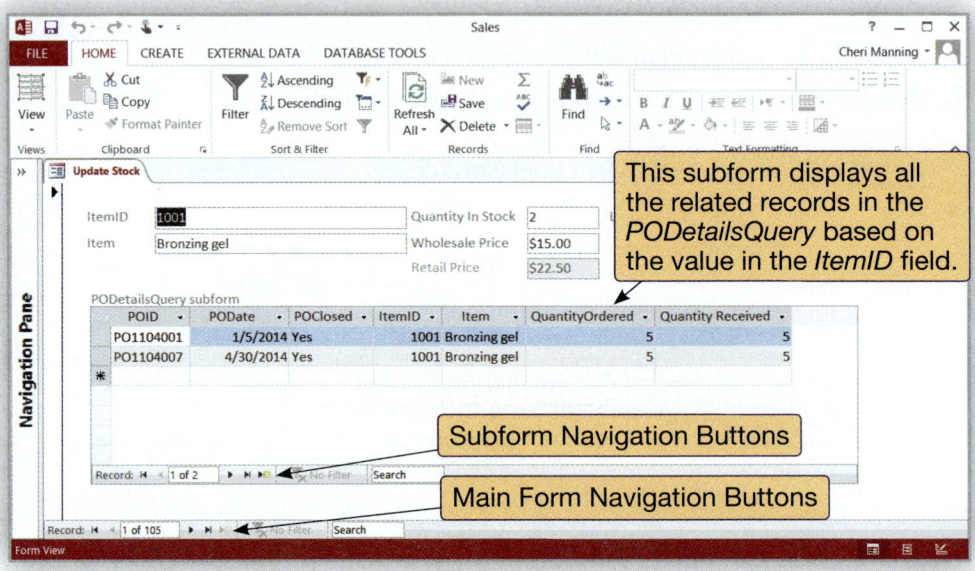

FIGURE AC 6.32

To use the SubForm Wizard to create a subform based on a table or query:

1. With the main form open in Design view, on the *Form Design Tools Design* tab, expand the *Controls* gallery by clicking the **More** button, and verify that *Use Control Wizards* is enabled (the icon will appear highlighted). *Use Control Wizards* must be enabled to display the SubForm Wizard.

2. In the *Controls* gallery, click the **Subform/Subreport** button. You will probably need to click the **More** button to expand the *Controls* gallery to find the *Subform/Subreport* button.

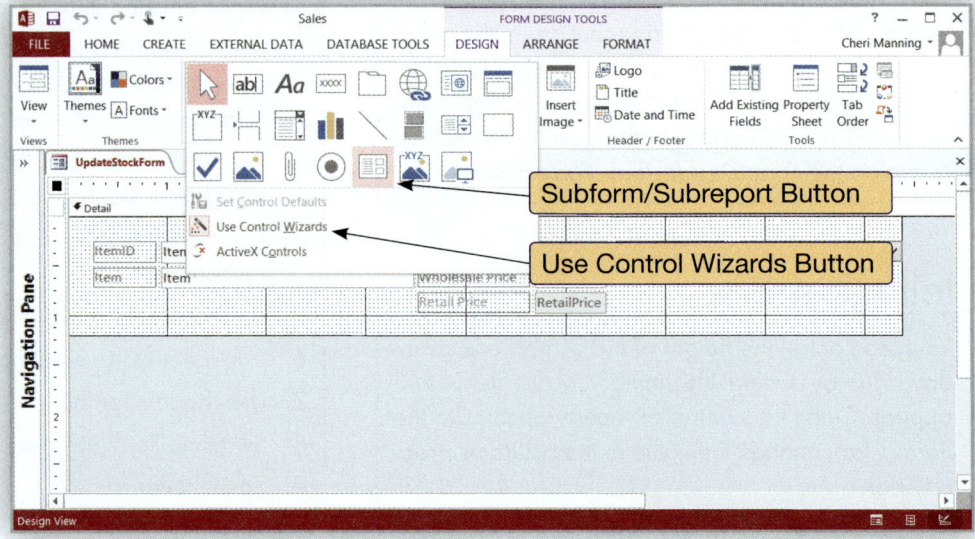

FIGURE AC 6.33

3. Click in the form where you want the subform to appear. The SubForm Wizard opens automatically when you click the form.
4. In the first step of the Subform Wizard, **Use existing Tables and Queries** is selected by default. Click **Next** to go to the next step.

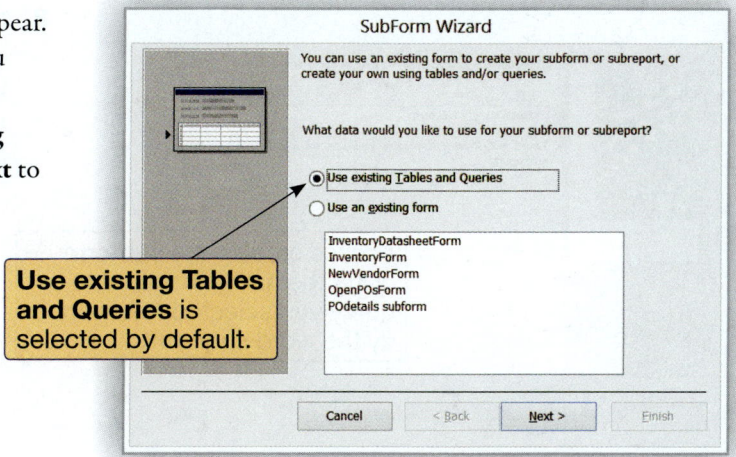

FIGURE AC 6.34

5. Expand the **Tables/Queries** list, and select the table or query that contains the fields you want to show in the subform.
6. In the *Available Fields* list, double-click the field(s) you want to appear in the subform. Click the >> button to add all the fields at once. Click **Next.**

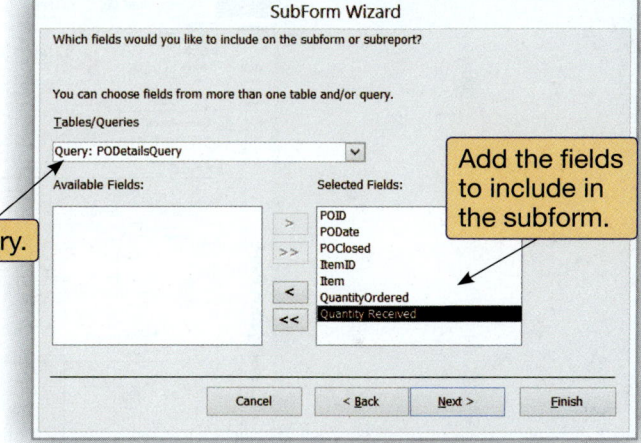

FIGURE AC 6.35

7. If one or more relationships exists between the main form and subform, Access will suggest the fields to link. If you want to display all records in the subform, select **None.** Select the relationship option you want to use, and click **Next.**

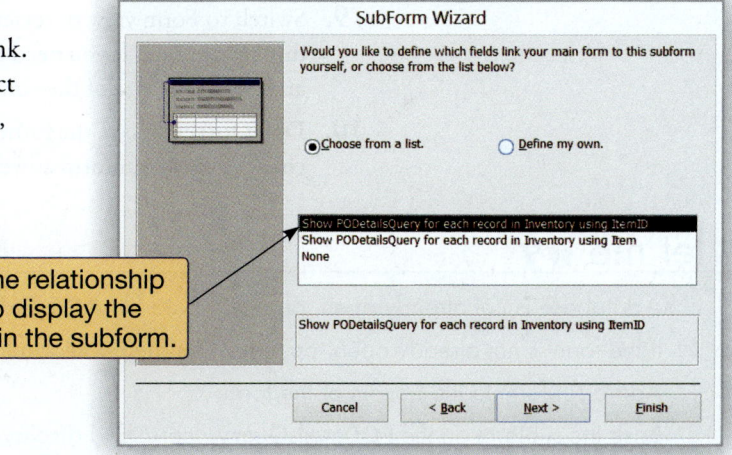

FIGURE AC 6.36

skill 6.10 Adding a Subform Based on a Table or Query

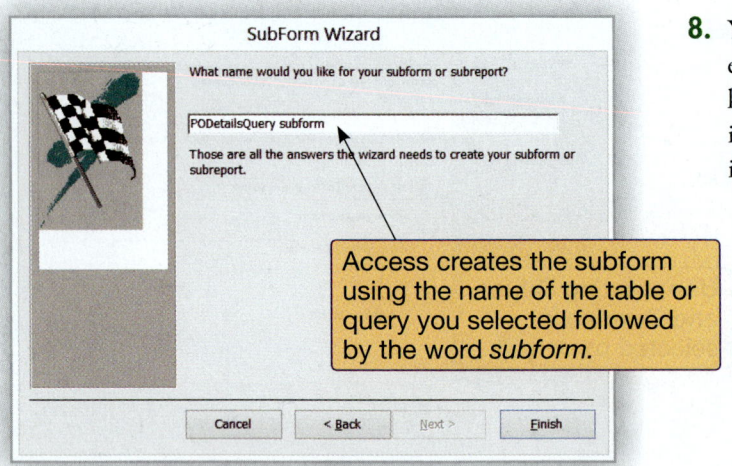

8. You can accept the suggested name for the subform or enter a different name in the box. It is a good practice to keep the word *subform* in the name to identify the form in the Navigation Pane, so you don't accidentally delete it. Click **Finish** to create the subform.

Access creates the subform using the name of the table or query you selected followed by the word *subform*.

FIGURE AC 6.37

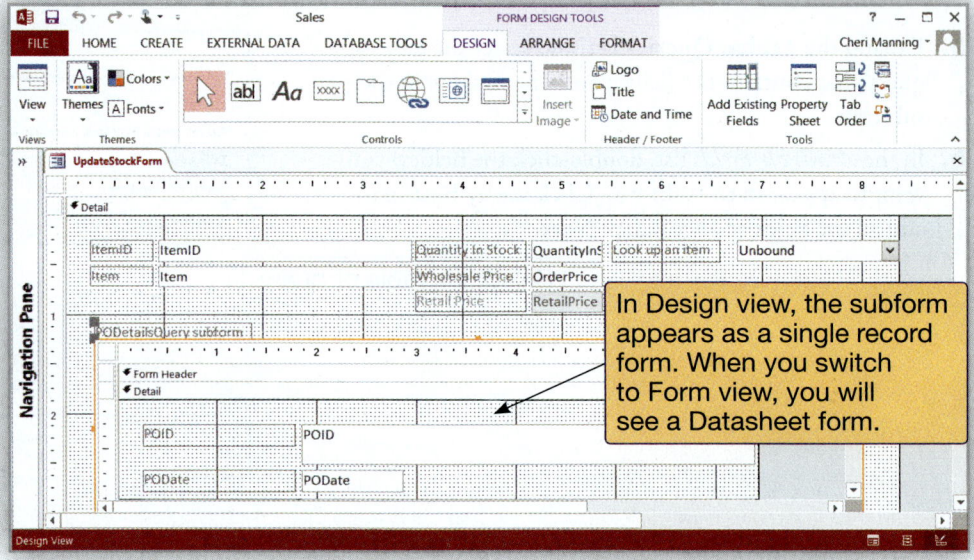

In Design view, the subform appears as a single record form. When you switch to Form view, you will see a Datasheet form.

FIGURE AC 6.38

9. Switch to Form view to review the subform. Adjust the column widths as necessary to display the data. If you need to make the subform wider, switch back to Design view and adjust the size of the control.

10. Don't forget to save the form. When necessary, Access will prompt you to save any changes to the subform as well.

let me try

If the database is not already open, open the data file **AC6-Sales** and try this skill on your own:

1. If the form is not already open, open the **UpdateStockForm** form in Design view.
2. Add a subform to the bottom of the form.
3. Base the subform on the **PODetailsQuery** query, and display all of the fields from the query.
4. Use the first form-subform relationship suggested by Access.
5. Accept the suggested name for the subform.
6. Review the form and subform in Form view. Make any adjustments necessary to view all the fields in the subform.
7. Save and close the form.

Skill 6.11 Adding a Subform Based on a Form

If a form already exists with the fields and formatting you want in the subform, base the subform on the existing form instead of creating a new subform from a table or query. An advantage to using a Datasheet form rather than basing the subform on a table or query is that you can reuse the Datasheet form as a subform in multiple forms without having to recreate it each time. Any changes made to the original form on which the subform is based will also appear in the subform.

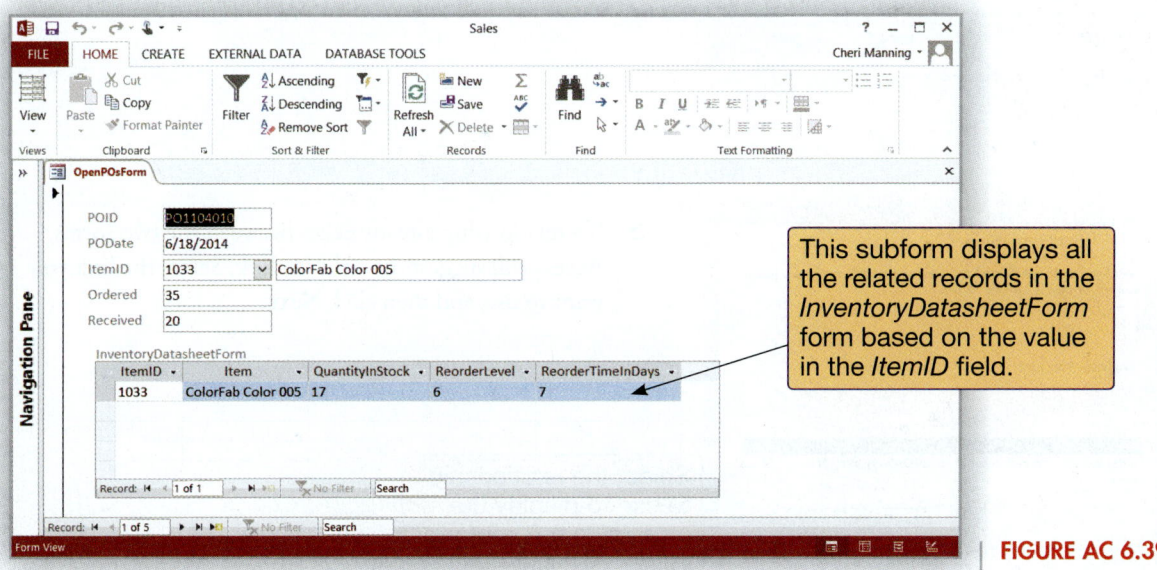

FIGURE AC 6.39

To add a subform based on another form:

1. With the main form open in Design view, on the *Form Design Tools Design* tab, in the *Controls* group, expand the *Controls* gallery by clicking the **More** button, and verify that *Use Control Wizards* is enabled (the icon will appear highlighted). *Use Control Wizards* must be enabled to display the SubForm Wizard.
2. Expand the *Controls* gallery and click the **Subform/Subreport** button.

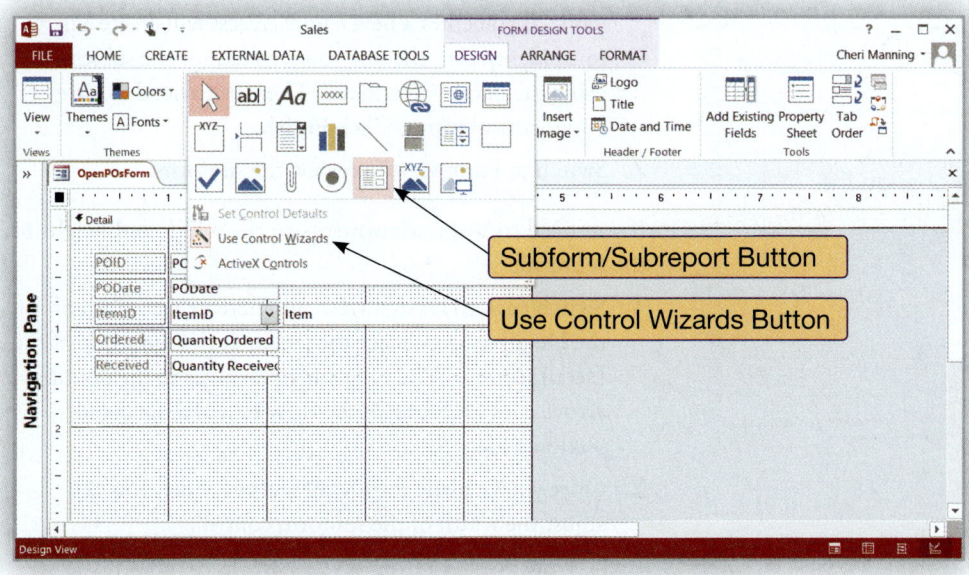

FIGURE AC 6.40

skill 6.11   Adding a Subform Based on a Form

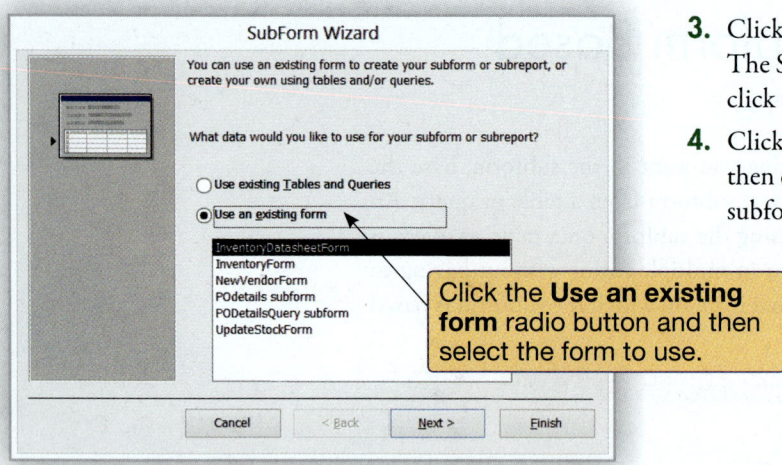

FIGURE AC 6.41

3. Click in the form where you want the subform to appear. The SubForm Wizard opens automatically when you click the form.
4. Click the **Use an existing form** radio button and then click the name of the form you want to use as the subform. Click **Next**.

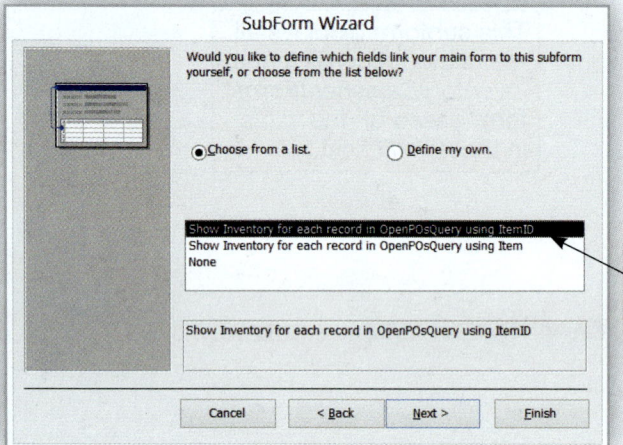

FIGURE AC 6.42

5. If a relationship already exists between the two forms, Access will suggest the fields to link. Select the link you want to use, and then click **Next.**

FIGURE AC 6.43

6. In the last step of the wizard, do not change the form name. If you enter a new name, Access will create a new form identical to the one you selected for the subform using the name you entered. There is no need to have two identical forms. Click **Finish.**
7. Switch to Form view to review the subform.

If you need to make adjustments to the width and height of the subform:

1. Switch back to Design view and increase the width of the Detail section. Place the cursor at the right side of the Detail section. When the cursor changes to the double arrow, click and drag to the right to make the detail section wider.
2. Once you've made the Detail section wider, you can adjust the width of the subform control.

3. Use the same technique to adjust the height of the subform. You may need to extend the bottom border of the Detail section to find the bottom of the subform.
4. Switch back to Form view again to review the changes.
5. When you close the form, Access will prompt you to save changes to both the main form and the subform form.

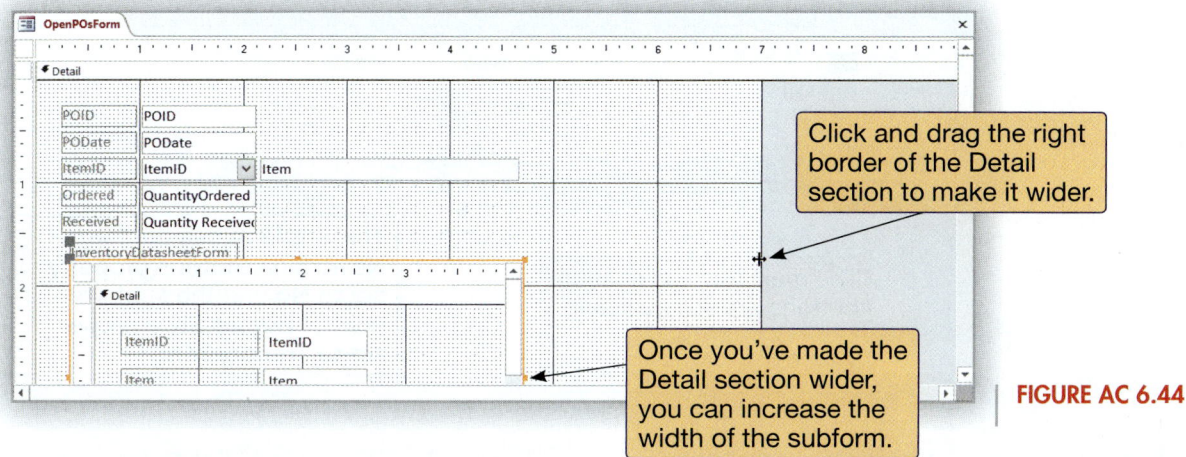

FIGURE AC 6.44

tell me more

If you find you need to modify the source for the subform or the fields that create the relationship between the main form and subform, you can do so through the subform properties.

1. With the main form open in Design view, on the *Form Design Tools Design* tab, in the *Tools* group, click the **Property Sheet** button.
2. Expand the box at the top of the Property Sheet and select the subform/subreport control.
3. On the Property Sheet *Data* tab, click in the **Source Object** property box. Expand the list and make a new selection to change the form, query, or table the subform is based on.
4. Click in the **Link Master Fields** property box, expand the list, and make a new selection to change the field in the main form that forms the relationship with the subform.
5. Click in the **Link Child Fields** property box, expand the list, and make a new selection to change the related field in the subform.
6. Save the form to save the changes.

let me try

If the database is not already open, open the data file **AC6-Sales** and try this skill on your own:

1. Open the **OpenPOForm** form in Design view.
2. Add a subform to the bottom of the form.
3. Base the subform on the **InventoryDatasheetForm** form.
4. Accept the first suggested link between the main form and subform.
5. Review the subform in Form view.
6. If necessary, adjust the widths of the main Form Detail section and the subform.
7. Save your changes.

skill 6.11 Adding a Subform Based on a Form

Skill 6.12 Modifying the Subform Properties

When working with the subform properties, it is important to distinguish between the subform *form* properties and the subform *control* properties.

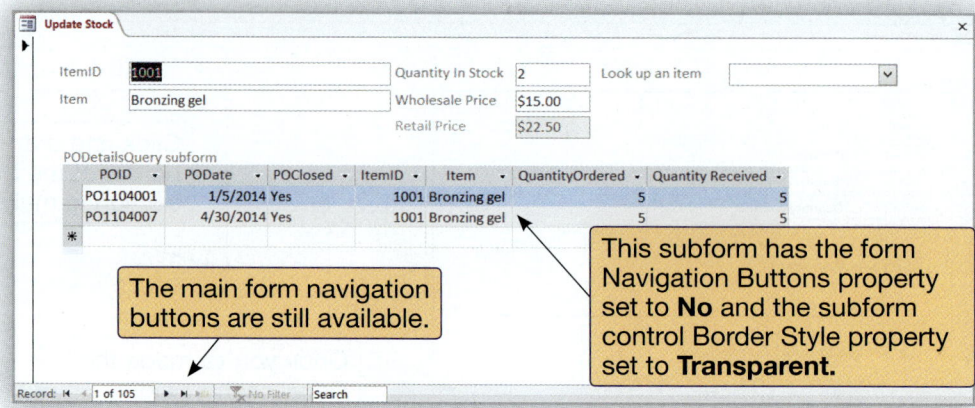

FIGURE AC 6.45

You may be familiar with form properties from the skills *Setting the Sort Order in a Form, Controlling Data Entry in a Form*, and *Disabling User Interface Elements in a Form*. These properties affect the way records are displayed in the form and how users can interact with the form. To modify these properties for a subform, you must first select the subform form by clicking the subform form selector button. Once you have selected the subform form, the Property Sheet can display the form properties for the subform.

Often the subform will display only a few records. If the subform is based on a table, query, or a Datasheet form, the record navigation buttons are unnecessary. To hide the navigation buttons in the subform, modify the Navigation Buttons property for the subform form.

To hide the navigation buttons in the subform:

1. With the main form open in Design view, display the Property Sheet. On the *Form Design Tools Design* tab, in the *Tools* group, click the **Property Sheet** button. Note that the Property Sheet displays the form properties for the *main* form.

2. To display the form properties for the subform, click the subform form selector button at the upper left corner of the subform once to select the subform control and then again to select the subform form. Be careful to select the subform, not the main form.

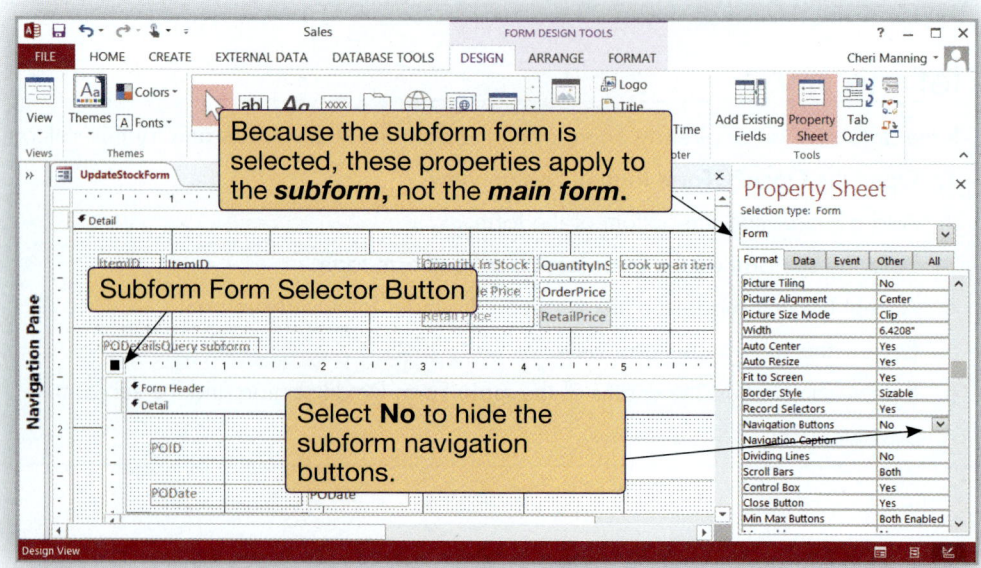

FIGURE AC 6.46

3. On the Property Sheet *Format* tab, scroll down the list to find the Navigation Buttons property. Click in the box, expand the list, and select **No.**

Other subform properties you may want to modify affect the way the subform *control* appears. One subform control property to consider changing is the Border Style property. Setting the border style to *Transparent* can improve the overall look of the form.

To hide the subform control border:

1. If the Property Sheet displays the form properties for the subform, click in the Detail section of the main form to select the main form instead.
2. Expand the **Selection type** box at the top of the Property Sheet and select the subform control.
3. On the Property Sheet *Format* tab, click in the **Border Style** box, expand the list, and select **Transparent.**

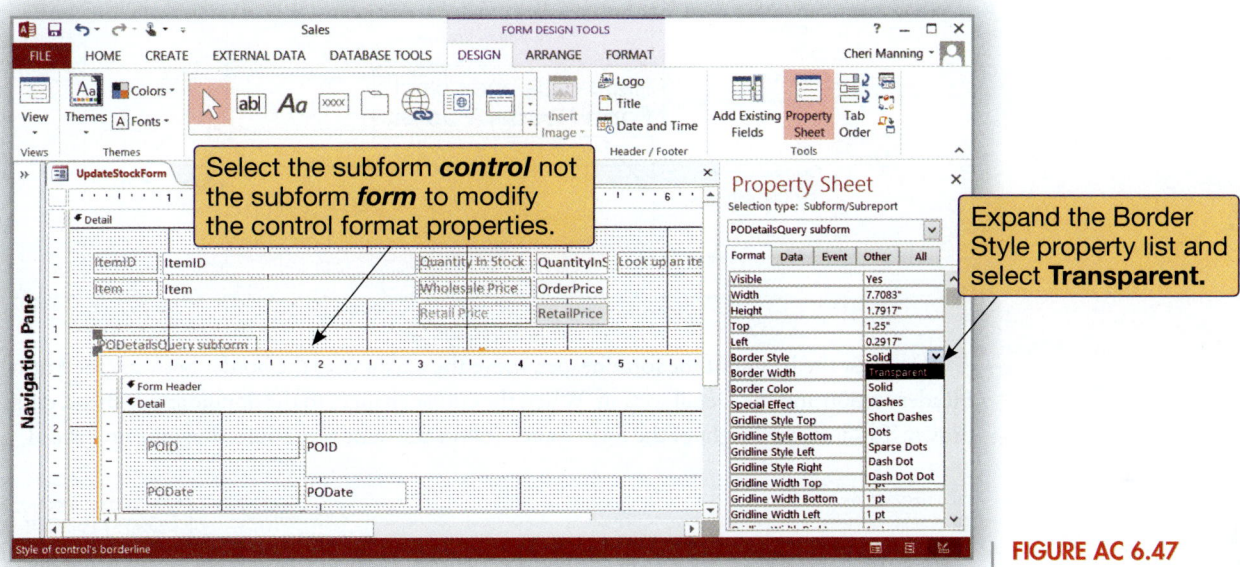

FIGURE AC 6.47

Review the subform in Form view. Switch back to Design view to adjust its height and width. When you close the form, Access will prompt you to save changes to the main form and the subform form.

let me try

If the database is not already open, open the data file **AC6-Sales** and try this skill on your own:

1. Open the **UpdateStockForm** form in Design view. If this form does not include a subform, first complete the *Let Me Try* in the skill *Adding a Subform Based on a Table or Query.*
2. Display the Property Sheet.
3. Select the subform so you can modify its form properties.
4. Hide the navigation buttons for the subform.
5. Change the **Border Style** property for the subform control to **Transparent.**
6. Review the form in Form view, and then switch back to Design view to modify the height and width of the subform as necessary.
7. Save and close the form.

skill 6.12   Modifying the Subform Properties

Skill 6.13 Displaying the Form Header and Footer

The **Form Header section** appears at the top of the form, and the **Form Footer section** appears at the bottom of the form. The form header is used to display the form title, an image, and other information you want to appear at the top of every record in the form. When you create a form from scratch in Design view, only the Detail section is visible. If you want to add controls to the form header, you must first display the Form Header section. To display the form header and footer, right-click an empty area of the Detail section or the Detail section bar, and select **Form Header/Footer.**

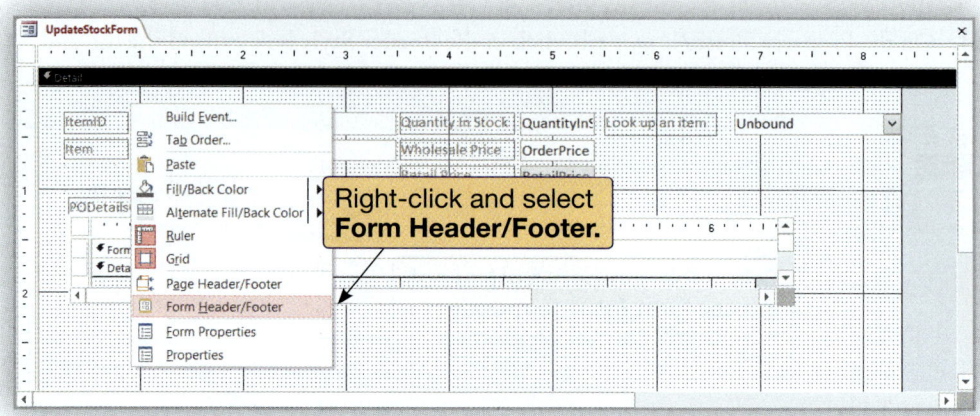

FIGURE AC 6.48

To adjust the height of the form header, move the cursor over the border between the Form Header section and the Detail section. When the cursor changes to the double arrow shape, drag drown. To adjust the height of the form footer, follow the same procedure, dragging up instead.

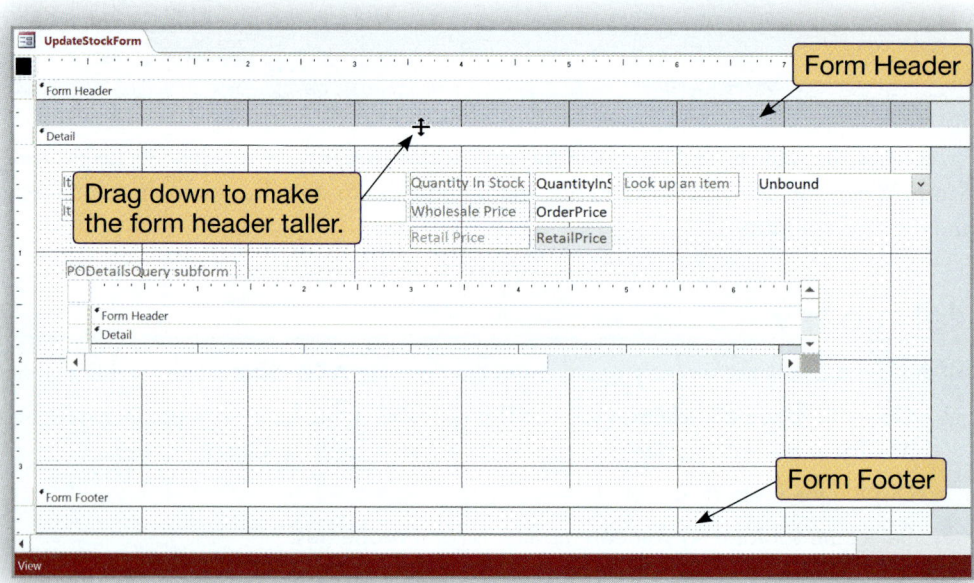

FIGURE AC 6.49

tell me more

The form can also include a page header and a page footer. These sections do not appear in Form view. When the form is printed, these sections can display the results of a calculation such as sum of the values in all the form records. Refer to the skill *Adding Calculated Controls to a Report* for more information.

let me try

If the database is not already open, open the data file **AC6-Sales** and try this skill on your own:

1. Open the **UpdateStockForm** form in Design view.
2. Display the Form Header and Form Footer sections.
3. Save the form.

Skill 6.14 Adding Images to Forms

When you add a photograph or illustration to a form, the image is stored in an **image control**. You may want to add an image to the Detail section of the form to add visual interest or add a logo to the form header. Although you can insert image controls from Layout view, it is often easier to work in Design view where you can resize and position the image independently of a row or column layout.

FIGURE AC 6.50

To add an image control to a form from Design view:

1. On the *Form Design Tools Design* tab, in the *Controls* group, expand the **Controls** gallery by clicking the **More** button. Click the **Image** button.

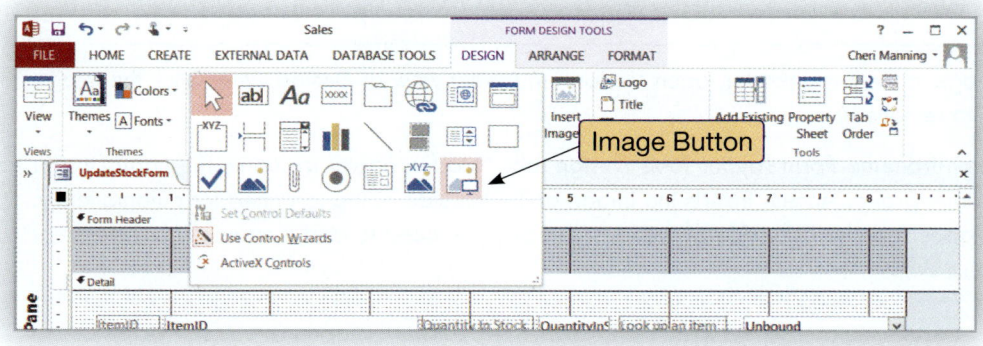

FIGURE AC 6.51

2. Click in the form where you want the image to appear. If you want to specify the size for the image, click and drag to create the size you want.
3. The *Insert Picture* dialog opens. Navigate to find the image you want. Click the file, and then click the **OK** button.
4. Adjust the size and position of the image as necessary.

Every time you add a new image to a form, it adds to the database file size. If you plan to use the same image multiple times, add it to the **Image Gallery**. Images are stored once in the database's Image Gallery and can be reused in multiple forms and reports without affecting the overall size of the database file. Note that when you add an image using an image control, it is not added to the Image Gallery.

To add a new image and add it to the Image Gallery:

1. On the *Form Design Tools Design* tab, in the *Controls* group, click the **Insert Image** button to open the Image Gallery. Click **Browse…**
2. The *Insert Picture* dialog opens. Navigate to find the image you want. Click the file and then click the **OK** button.

3. Click in the form to add the image.

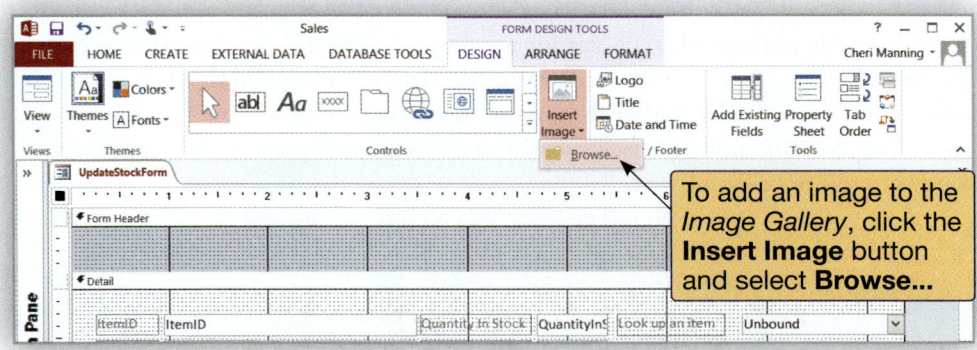

FIGURE AC 6.52

Once an image has been stored in the Image Gallery, you can insert it by expanding the Image Gallery, clicking the image you want, and then clicking in the form.

To remove an image from the Image Gallery:

1. On the *Form Design Tools Design* tab, in the *Controls* group, click the **Insert Image** button to open the Image Gallery.
2. Right-click the image and select **Delete**.

If you've used the image in a form or report, removing it from the Image Gallery will not affect the database objects in which it appears. Each individual instance of the image will be saved with the database, increasing the database file size.

tips & tricks

- To delete the default form image in the form header, open the form in Layout view or Design view. Click the image to select it, and press ⟦Delete⟧ to remove it.

- When you use the *Logo* button from the *Form Layout Tools Design* tab, *Header/Footer* group or the *Form Design Tools Design* tab, *Header/Footer* group, Access inserts the image at the left side of the form header automatically. If you want the form logo to appear at the right side of the form header, you need to add it manually using one of the techniques discussed in this skill.

tell me more

You can add an image as the form background from Layout view or Design view from the *Format* tab, *Background* group. Click the **Background Image** button and select an image from the gallery or click **Browse...** to add a new image.

Background images can be overwhelming and should be used sparingly.

let me try

If the database is not already open, open the data file **AC6-Sales** and try this skill on your own:

1. If it is not already open, open the **UpdateStockForm** form in Design view.
2. Add the **Stock** image file in an image control to the form Detail section just below the *Look up an item* label.
3. Add the **SpaLogo** image file to the right side of the form header, adding the image to the Image Gallery at the same time.
4. Save and close the form.

Skill 6.15 Creating a Navigation Form with Tabs

A **navigation form** allows you to group together all the forms and reports a user might need within a single form object. Users navigate between database objects in the navigation form by clicking tabs. Simple navigation forms have a single row of tabs along the top or left or right side of the form. Each tab displays a different database object.

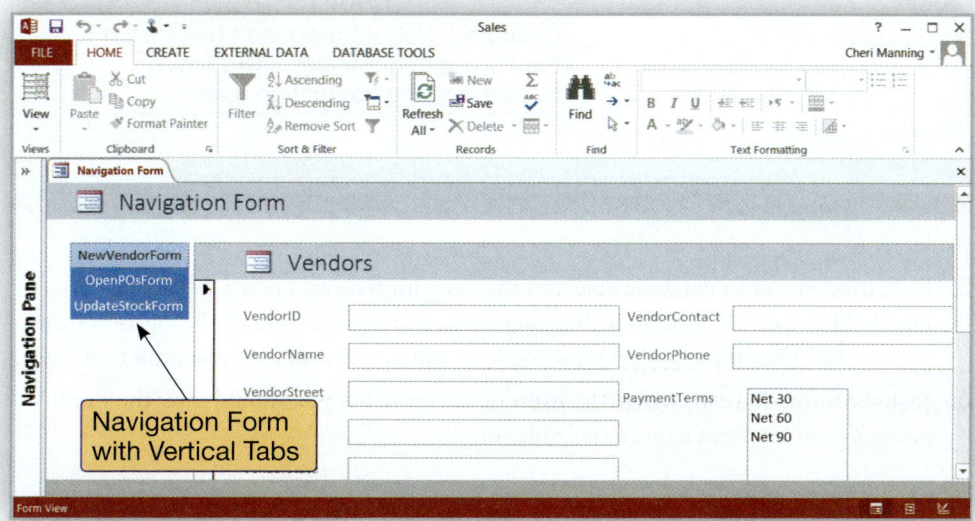

FIGURE AC 6.53

To create a navigation form:

1. On the *Create* tab, in the *Forms* group, click the **Navigation** button to expand the list of navigation forms, and then click the form layout you want. The first three forms in the list are simple single-level navigation forms.

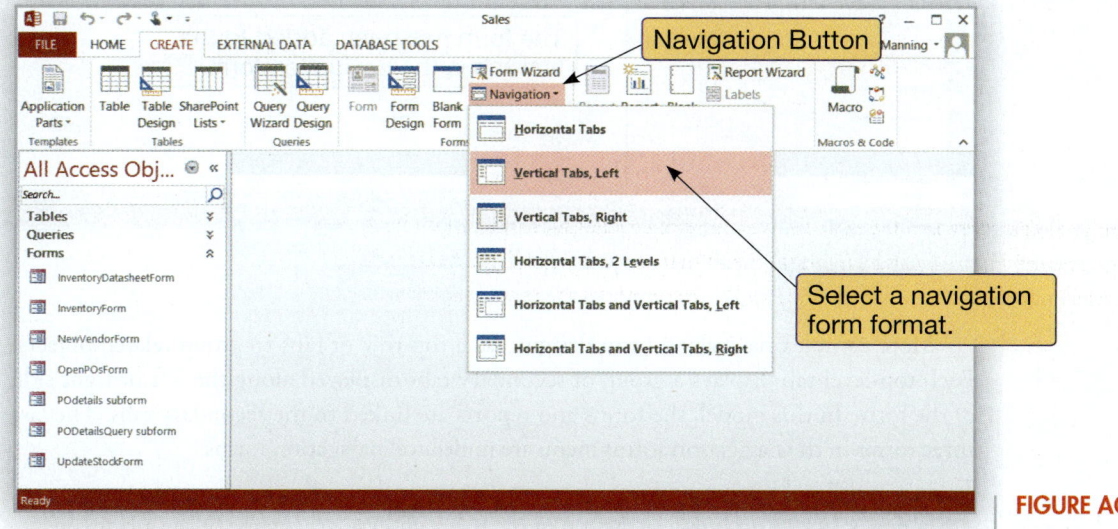

FIGURE AC 6.54

2. The Field List opens automatically. You don't need the Field List to create the navigation form, so you can close it if you want to.
3. The navigation form opens in Layout view with an *[Add New]* placeholder for the first tab.
4. Click and drag a form or report from the Navigation Pane to the tab placeholder to add it to the navigation form.

skill 6.15 Creating a Navigation Form with Tabs

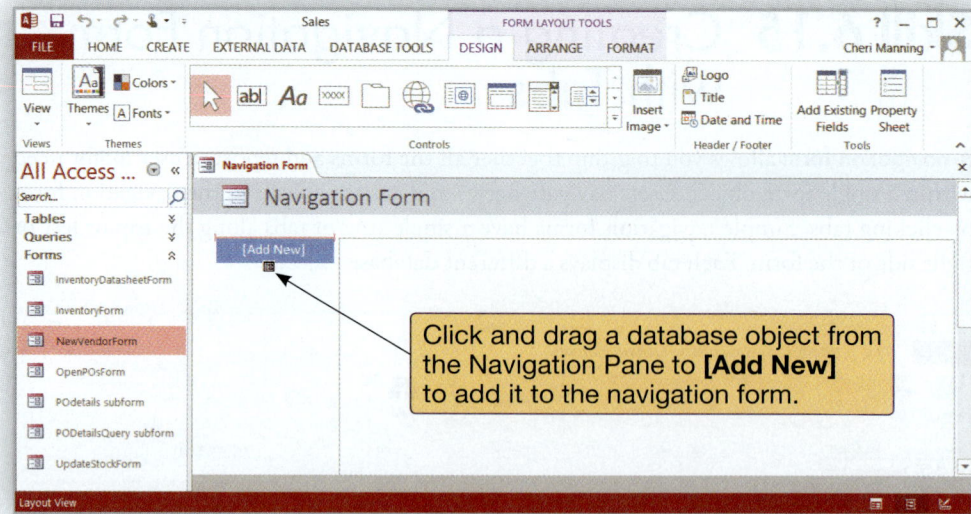

FIGURE AC 6.55

5. Each time you add a database object to the navigation form, a new *[Add New]* placeholder is added. Continue dragging forms and reports from the Navigation Pane to the *[Add New]* placeholders until you have added all the objects you want to include.

6. Save the form. You can change the name of the form, but you should leave the word *navigation* in the form name to help identify it.

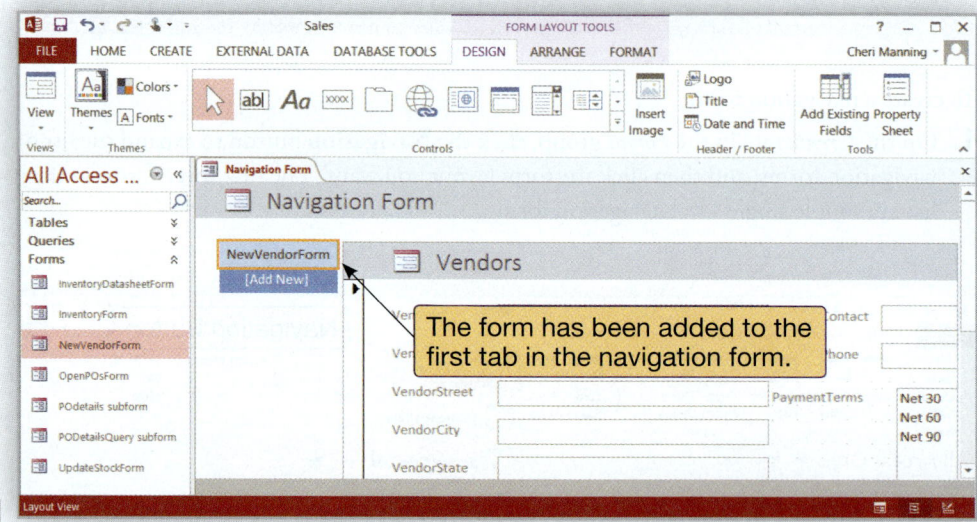

FIGURE AC 6.56

More complex navigation form designs use a top row of tabs to group related objects. Each top-level tab displays a group of secondary tabs displayed along the left or right side of the form. In this model, the forms and reports are linked to the secondary tabs. The last three forms in the navigation forms menu are multilevel navigation forms.

1. In a multilevel navigation form, use the top row of tabs to display category or group names. Click **[Add New]** at the top of the form, and type the name of the tab as you would like it to appear. Press (← Enter).

2. Click the top-level tab to select it, and then click **[Add New]** for the secondary tab. Add a form or report to the secondary tab by typing the object's name or dragging the object from the Navigation Pane.

tips & tricks

- Notice that the default title for the form is *Navigation Form*. You should change the title to something more meaningful to your users.
- The form caption (the title that appears on the object tab) is also *Navigation Form*. Use the form Property Sheet to change the Caption property to something more meaningful.

tell me more

- To delete a tab from the navigation form, open the navigation form in Layout view or Design view, and then right-click the tab and select **Delete.**
- If you type a name for a top-level tab and there is a form or report with that name, Access will display the database object. If you do not want the database object to appear (if you want the tab used only to group other tabs), click the tab to select it, and then open the Property Sheet. Under the *Property Sheet Data* tab, delete the object name in the *Navigation Target Name* property box.

another method

Double-click the **[Add New]** tab placeholder, and type the name of the object you want the tab to display. Press ⟵Enter. Access automatically adds the database object as the *Navigation Target Name* property and will display that object when the tab is clicked.

let me try

If the database is not already open, open the data file **AC6-Sales** and try this skill on your own:

1. Create a new navigation form using a single-level navigation layout with vertical tabs on the left.
2. Add the **NewVendorForm** form to the first placeholder in the navigation form.
3. Save the form. Keep the suggested name **Navigation Form.**

from the perspective of . . .

NON-PROFIT VOLUNTEER ORGANIZER

Our organization uses volunteers to enter information in the donations database. Most of the volunteers have never seen Access before and have no time for training, so I created a navigation form and set the database properties to open that form automatically. I've disabled the navigation buttons in all the forms and replaced them with command buttons. I also double-checked the tab order of controls to make sure users can tab through the forms in a logical order. Our volunteers no longer struggle with trying to learn a new application. Now they can open the database and get started entering data right away.

skill 6.15   Creating a Navigation Form with Tabs

Skill 6.16 Defining the Tab Order of Controls

When entering data in a form, you can press [Tab] to move from control to control. **Tab order** refers to the order in which controls are activated by pressing the [Tab] key. When you first add controls to the form, the tab order is set in the order in which the controls were added. However, if you modify your form, adding and removing controls, you may need to adjust the tab order. Always keep in mind how your users will work with the form, and verify that the tab order is a natural progression.

To set the tab order in a form:

1. From Design view, on the *Form Design Tools Design* tab, in the *Tools* group, click the **Tab Order** button.

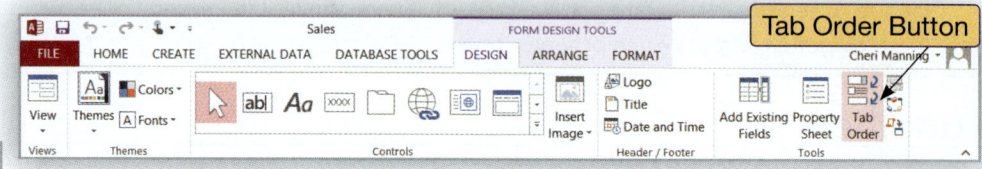

FIGURE AC 6.57

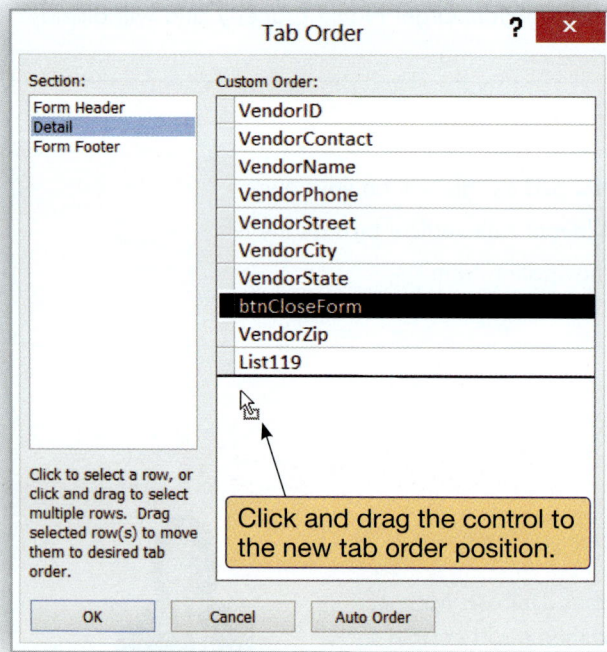

FIGURE AC 6.58

2. The left side of the *Tab Order* dialog shows the sections in the form. The right side shows the controls available in that section. If necessary, click the section you want. The *Detail* section is the main body of the form. This is the section you will most likely work with.

3. Click the **row selector** next to the control you want to reorder. Click again, and, holding down the mouse button, drag the control to the place in the tab order where you want it and then release the mouse button.

4. Click **OK** to save your changes and close the *Tab Order* dialog.

tips & tricks

When working with the *Tab Order* dialog, remember to click the row selector next to the control name, not the control name itself. You can only click and drag from the row selector.

tell me more

To set the tab order to move from left to right and then down, open the *Tab Order* dialog and click the **Auto Order** button.

let me try

If the database is not already open, open the data file **AC6-Sales** and try this skill on your own:

1. Open the **NewVendorForm** form in Design view.
2. Modify the tab order for the form so the **btnCloseForm** control is between the *VendorState* and *VendorZip* controls. Switch to Form view and test the change.
3. Switch back to Design view and modify the tab order again so the **btnCloseForm** control is last. Switch to Form view and test the change.
4. Save and close the form.

key terms

Form application part
Record source
Form Property Sheet
Embedded query
Data entry form
Control Property Sheet
List box control
Command button control
Combo box control
Subform
Form Header section
Form Footer section
Image control
Image Gallery
Navigation form
Tab order

concepts review

1. To set the underlying table or query for a new form, use which form property?
   a. Form Source
   b. Record Source
   c. Data Entry
   d. Allow Additions

2. To add a field to a form without adding the automatic label control, press which keyboard key while dragging the field from the Field List?
   a. Alt
   b. Shift
   c. Ctrl
   d. Shift + Ctrl

3. If you want the form to be used for entering new records only,
   a. Set the Allow Additions property to **No**.
   b. Set the Enabled property to **Yes**.
   c. Set the Data Entry property to **Yes**.
   d. Set the Allow Edits property to **No**.

4. To dim a single field in a form so users cannot select it or edit its content,
   a. Set the Allow Additions property to **No**.
   b. Set the Enabled property to **No**.
   c. Set the Data Entry property to **No**.
   d. Set the Allow Edits property to **No**.

5. Which control should you use to display a short list of values that users can choose from?
   a. Combo Box control
   b. Subform control
   c. Form application part
   d. List Box control

6. Which control should you use to display a long list of values where users can type the data in the text box at the top of the control or expand the list and select a value?
   a. Combo Box control
   b. Subform control
   c. Form application part
   d. List Box control

7. A subform displays records from another database object when a relationship exists between data in the main form and subform.
   a. True
   b. False

8. A subform can display records from which type of database object?
   a. Form
   b. Table
   c. Query
   d. All of the above

9. When you create a new blank form from scratch, the form header and form footer are visible.
   a. True
   b. False

10. When you add an image to a form using an Image control, the image is added to the database Image Gallery.
    a. True
    b. False

projects

Data files for projects can be found on www.mhhe.com/office2013skills

skill review 6.1

In this project, you will work with the database for Quality Foods, a food distributor that sells food stock to local convenience stores. You will create a navigation form and modify the design of other forms in the database to include a combo box, a list box, a subform, a button control, and an image control. You will modify form and control properties. Finally, you will create a new data entry only form.

Skills needed to complete this project:

- Creating a Navigation Form with Tabs (Skill 6.15)
- Adding a Combo Box Control to a Form (Skill 6.9)
- Adding a List Box Control to a Form (Skill 6.7)
- Adding a Subform Based on a Table or Query (Skill 6.10)
- Modifying the Subform Properties (Skill 6.12)
- Setting the Sort Order in a Form (Skill 6.3)

- Controlling Data Entry for a Field in a Form (Skill 6.5)
- Adding a Command Button Control to a Form (Skill 6.8)
- Adding Images to Forms (Skill 6.14)
- Disabling User Interface Elements in a Form (Skill 6.6)
- Defining the Tab Order of Controls (Skill 6.16)
- Controlling Data Entry in a Form (Skill 6.4)

1. Open the start file **AC2013-SkillReview-6-1** and resave the file as: `[your initials]AC-SkillReview-6-1`
2. If necessary, enable active content by clicking the **Enable Content** button in the Message Bar.
3. Create a navigation form.
    a. On the *Create* tab, in the *Forms* group, click the **Navigation** button.
    b. Select **Horizontal Tabs.**
    c. On the right side of the screen, close the Field List.
    d. Open the Navigation Pane if necessary.
    e. Click and drag the **Products** form from the Navigation Pane to [**Add New**] in the navigation form.
    f. Double-click the new [**Add New**] tab, and type `Suppliers` and press ⎯Enter.
    g. Double-click **Navigation Form** in the form header and change the navigation form title to: `Quality Foods Navigation`
    h. Save the form as `QualityFoodsNavigationForm`
    i. Switch to form view to test the navigation form and then close it.
4. Add a category combo box to the *Products* form.
    a. Open the **Products** form in Design view.
    b. Click the **CategoryID** text box control and press Delete to delete the *CategoryID* text box control and label.
    c. On the *Form Design Tools Design* tab, in the *Controls* group, click the **More** button to expand the *Controls* gallery.
    d. Verify **Use Control Wizards** is on.
    e. In the *Controls* gallery, click the **Combo Box** button.
    f. At the top of the form, across from *ProductCode,* click at the **6-inch** mark on the horizontal ruler.
    g. The Combo Box Wizard opens.
    h. Verify **I want the combo box to get the values from another table or query.** is selected. Click **Next**.
    i. Select **Table: ProductCategories.** Click **Next**.
    j. Click >> to add both fields to the *Selected Fields* list. Click **Next**.
    k. Click the drop-down sort arrow and select **Category.** Click **Next**.
    l. Double-click the right border of the *Category* column to autofit the column width to the data. Click **Next**.
    m. Select **Store that value in this field:** and select **CategoryID** from the drop-down list. Click **Next**.
    n. Type `Category` for the label of the combo box. Click **Finish**.
    o. Widen the *Category* combo box so it is **2** inches wide.
    p. Save the form and switch to Form view to test the combo box.

5. Add a supplier list box to the *Products* form.
   a. Switch to back to Design view.
   b. Click the **SupplierID** text box control and press Delete to delete the *SupplierID* text box control and label.
   c. On the *Form Design Tools Design* tab, in the *Controls* group, click the **List Box** button. Click the **More** button to expand the *Controls* gallery if the *List Box* button is not visible on the Ribbon.
   d. At the top of the form, across from *ProductName,* click under the *CategoryID* combo box.
   e. The List Box Wizard displays.
   f. Verify **I want the list box to get the values from another table or query.** is selected. Click **Next**.
   g. Select **Table: Suppliers.** Click **Next**.
   h. In the *Available Fields* list, double-click **SupplierID.**
   i. In the *Available Fields* list, double-click **Company.** Click **Next**.
   j. Click the drop-down sort arrow and select **Company.** Click **Next**.
   k. Double-click the right border of the **Company** column to autofit the column width to the data. Click **Next**.
   l. Select **Store that value in this field:** and then select **SupplierID** from the drop-down list. Click **Next**.
   m. Type `Supplier` as the label for the list box. Click **Finish**.
   n. Make the **Supplier** list box **2** inches wide.
   o. Save the form and switch to Form view to test the list box.
   p. Close the form.

6. Add the *Products* table as a subform to the *Suppliers* form.
   a. Open the **Suppliers** form in Design view.
   b. Place the pointer on the top edge of the Form Footer section bar, and drag the section bar down **1** inch to make the Detail section taller.
   c. On the *Form Design Tools Design* tab, in the *Controls* group, if necessary, click the **More** button to expand the *Controls* gallery, and then click the **Subform/Subreport** button.
   d. Click under *Zip*.
   e. The SubForm Wizard displays.
   f. Verify **Use existing Tables and Queries** is selected. Click **Next**.
   g. From the *Tables/Queries* drop-down list, select **Table: Products.**
   h. Click >> to add all available fields to the *Selected Fields* list. Click **Next**.
   i. Verify **Choose from a list** is selected. Verify **Show Products for each record in Suppliers using SupplierID** is selected. Click **Next**.
   j. Change the name to: `ProductsSubform`. Click **Finish**.
   k. Drag the right edge of the subform to widen the subform to **8** inches.
   l. Delete the **ProductsSubform** label.
   m. Save the form and switch to Layout view.
   n. Resize the subform columns to best fit by double-clicking the right border of each column header.
   o. Save the form.

7. Hide the navigation buttons in the subform.
   a. Switch to Design view.
   b. On the *Form Design Tools Design* tab, in the *Tools* group, click the **Property Sheet** button.
   c. Click the subform control once to select it. Note the box at the top of the Property Sheet displays *ProductsSubform*.
   d. Click the form selector at the top left corner of the subform next to the ruler.
   e. Verify that the box at the top of the Property Sheet now displays *Form*.
   f. Click the Property Sheet **Format** tab.
   g. Click in the **Navigation Buttons** property and select **No**.
   h. Close the Property Sheet.
   i. Save the form.
   j. Switch to Form view to review the changes.
8. Add a command button to the *Suppliers* form to add a new record.
   a. Switch to Design view.
   b. On the *Form Design Tools Design* tab, in the *Controls* group, if necessary, click the **More** button to expand the *Controls* gallery, and then click the **Button** button.
   c. Click across from **SupplierID** at the **6-inch** mark on the horizontal ruler. The Command Button Wizard displays.
   d. Click **Record Operations**.
   e. Verify that **Add New Record** is selected. Click **Next**.
   f. Click the **Text:** radio button. Type: `Add New Supplier` as the button text. Click **Next**.
   g. Type `btnAddNewRecord` for the button name. Click **Finish**.
   h. Save the form and switch to Form view to test the button.
9. Add an image to the *Suppliers* form header. Store the image in the Image Gallery for use in other forms.
   a. Switch to Design view.
   b. On the *Form Design Tools Design* tab, in the *Controls* group, click the **Insert Image** button, and click **Browse...**
   c. Navigate to the folder that contains the data files for this book. Select the **QualityFoodsLogo** image file and click **OK**.
   d. Click on the right side of the form header near the **6.5-inch** mark and drag to create a **1-inch by 1-inch** square.
   e. Save the form and switch to Form view.
   f. Close the form.
10. Change the form properties of the *Products* form to hide the record selectors and the scroll bars.
    a. Open the **Products** form in Design view.
    b. On the *Form Design Tools Design* tab, in the *Tools* group, click the **Property Sheet** button.
    c. In the Property Sheet, verify that *Form* is selected at the top of the Property Sheet.
    d. If necessary, click the Property Sheet **Format** tab.
    e. Click in the **Record Selectors** property and select **No**.
    f. Click in the **Scroll Bars** property and select **Neither**.

11. Set a sort order for the *Products* form so records will display in alphabetical order by product name.
    a. Click the Property Sheet **Data** tab.
    b. In the **Order By** property box, type: `[ProductName]`
12. Disable the *ProductCode* field so users cannot edit data in the field.
    a. Click the **ProductCode** text control to select it.
    b. Verify that the box at the top of the Property Sheet displays *ProductCode*.
    c. On the Property Sheet *Data* tab, click in the **Enabled** property box, and select **No**.
    d. Close the Property Sheet.
    e. Save the form and switch to Form view.
13. Press **Tab** to advance from one field to the next. Notice that the product code is skipped in the tab order because the control is disabled. You will change the tab order to move from left to right beginning with the *Category* combo box.
    a. Switch to Design view.
    b. On the *Form Design Tools Design* tab, in the *Tools* group, click the **Tab Order** button. The *Tab Order* dialog opens.
    c. In the *Section* box, verify that the **Detail** section is selected.
    d. Click the **Auto Order** button. Click **OK**.
    e. Save the form and switch to Form view.
    f. Press **Tab** to advance from one field to the next. Close the form.
14. Make a copy of the *Products* form to use as a data entry only form.
    a. In the Navigation Pane, right-click the **Products** form and select **Copy**.
    b. Press Ctrl + V to paste the copy of the form. Name the form: `NewProduct`
    c. Open the **NewProduct** form in Design view.
    d. On the *Form Design Tools Design* tab, in the *Tools* group, click the **Property Sheet** button.
    e. In the Property Sheet, verify that *Form* is selected at the top of the Property Sheet.
    f. Click the Property Sheet **Data** tab.
    g. Click in the **Data Entry** property and select **Yes**.
    h. Switch to Form view to view the new data entry form.
15. Add a command button to the *NewProduct* form to close the form.
    a. Switch to Design view.
    b. On the *Form Design Tools Design* tab, in the *Controls* group, if necessary, click the **More** button to expand the *Controls* gallery, and then click the **Button** button.
    c. Click below the **SupplierID** list box control. The Command Button Wizard displays.
    d. Click **Form Operations**.
    e. Click **Close Form** is selected. Click **Next**.
    f. Click the **Text:** radio button. Type: `Save and Close` as the button text. Click **Next**.
    g. Type `btnCloseForm` for the button name. Click **Finish**.
    h. Save and close the form.
16. Close the database and exit Access.

skill review 6.2

In this project you will work with a university database that keeps track of professors, students, departments, courses, classes offered, and enrollment in the classes. You will use a form application part to create a data entry form for adding new professors to the database. You will hide the navigation buttons in the new form and add a command button to allow the user to start a new record. Next, you will modify the *Class* form to add combo box and list box controls, a subform, and an image. You will need to modify the tab order for the form. Finally, you will create a navigation form to display the new form you created and the modified *Class* form.

Skills needed to complete this project:
- Creating a Blank Form from an Application Part (Skill 6.1)
- Working with a New Form in Design View (Skill 6.2)
- Controlling Data Entry in a Form (Skill 6.4)
- Disabling User Interface Elements in a Form (Skill 6.6)
- Adding a Command Button Control to a Form (Skill 6.8)
- Adding a Combo Box Control to a Form (Skill 6.9)
- Adding a List Box Control to a Form (Skill 6.7)
- Adding a Subform Based on a Form (Skill 6.11)
- Modifying the Subform Properties (Skill 6.12)
- Adding Images to Forms (Skill 6.14)
- Displaying the Form Header and Footer (Skill 6.13)
- Defining the Tab Order of Controls (Skill 6.16)
- Creating a Navigation Form with Tabs (Skill 6.15)

1. Open the start file **AC2013-SkillReview-6-2** and resave the file as:
   `[your initials]AC-SkillReview-6-2`
2. If necessary, enable active content by clicking the **Enable Content** button in the Message Bar.
3. Create a new blank form from an application part to use as a data entry form for adding new professors.
   a. On the *Create* tab, in the *Templates* group, click the **Application Parts** button.
   b. Select the **1 Right** template in the *Blank Forms* section.
   c. In the Navigation Pane, right-click **SingleOneColumnRightLabels** and select **Rename.**
   d. Type `NewProfessor` and press ⏎ Enter.
4. Assign a record source to the *NewProfessor* form and add fields.
   a. In the Navigation Pane, right-click the **NewProfessor** form and select **Design View.**
   b. On the *Form Design Tools Design* tab, in the *Tools* group, click the **Property Sheet** button.
   c. Verify that *Form* is selected in the box at the top of the Property Sheet.
   d. Click the arrow in the **Record Source** box and select **Professor.**
   e. Close the Property Sheet.
   f. On the *Form Design Tools Design* tab, in the *Tools* group, click the **Add Existing Fields** button.

g. In the Field List, click the **EmployeeID** field. Press the Ctrl key and drag the **EmployeeID** field to the placeholder to the right of the **Field1:** label to add the text box control without its label. If you accidentally add the label control, press Ctrl + Z to undo the action and try again, remembering to hold down the Ctrl key while you drag the field to the form.

h. Click the **Field1:** label control and change the text to: `ID:`

i. Add the remaining fields without their labels. Add the fields in this order: **LastName, FirstName,** and **DeptCode.**

j. Change the remaining label controls to: `Last Name:`, `First Name:`, and `Dept Code:`

k. Close the Field List.

l. Change the text in the form title label control at the top of the form header to: `New Professor`

5. Set the *NewProfessor* form to allow data entry only.

    a. Open the Property Sheet again, and select **Form** in the box at the top of the Property Sheet.

    b. On the Property Sheet *Data* tab, click in the **Data Entry** property box, and select **Yes.**

6. Hide the form navigation buttons.

    a. Click the Property Sheet **Format** tab.

    b. Click in the **Navigation Buttons** property box, and select **No.**

    c. Save the form.

7. Add a button to save the record and open a new record.

    a. In the Detail section of the form, remove the *Save* button that was included with the form application part. Click the **Save** button control and press Delete.

    b. On the *Form Design Tools Design* tab, in the *Controls* group, click the **More** button to expand the *Controls* gallery. Verify *Use Control Wizards* is enabled.

    c. In the *Controls* gallery, click the **Button** button.

    d. Click on the form next to the *Save & Close* button at the **3.5-inch** mark on the horizontal ruler.

    e. In the first step of the Command Button Wizard, click **Record Operations** in the *Categories* list. Verify that **Add New Record** is selected in the *Actions* list. Click **Next.**

    f. Click the **Text** radio button. Enter the text: `Save && New` (*Hint:* You must type two `&&` characters to display `&` in the button text.)

    g. Click **Next.**

    h. Enter `cmdSaveNew` as the command name. Click **Finish.**

8. Change the format of the buttons.

    a. Click the **Save & New** button. Press Ctrl and click the **Save & Close** button.

    b. On the *Form Design Tools Format* tab, in the *Control Formatting* group, click the **Quick Styles** button to expand the gallery, and select **Intense Effect - Blue, Accent 1.**

    c. Click anywhere in the form to deselect the buttons, and then click the **Save & Close** button to select it.

    d. In the Property Sheet, *Format* tab, click in the **Height** property box and copy the value.

- e. Click the **Save & New** button to select it. In the Property Sheet, *Format* tab, click in the **Height** property box and paste the value you just copied.
- f. If necessary move the **Save & New** button so it is immediately to the left of the **Save & Close** button. (*Hint:* This form includes control placeholders, so the button may snap into place in a location you don't want it. If that happens, move the control again and it should snap into place to the left of the *Save & New* button.)
- g. Switch to Form view to check your work, and then save and close the form.

9. Add a combo box to the *Class* form.
   - a. Open the **Class** form in Design view.
   - b. On the *Form Design Tools Design* tab, in the *Controls* group, click the **Combo Box** button. If the button is not available on the Ribbon, click the **More** button to expand the *Controls* gallery.
   - c. Click at the top of the form across from **ClassCode** at the **4.5-inch** mark on the horizontal ruler to open the Combo Box Wizard.
   - d. Verify **I want the combo box to get the values from another table or query.** is selected. Click **Next**.
   - e. Select **Table: Professor.** Click **Next**.
   - f. Double-click **EmployeeID, LastName,** and **FirstName** to add the three fields to the *Selected Fields* list. Click **Next**.
   - g. Click the drop-down sort arrow and select **LastName**. Click **Next**.
   - h. Verify that the **Hide key column (recommended)** check box is checked. Click **Next**.
   - i. Select **Store that value in this field:** and then select **Professor** from the drop-down list. Click **Next**.
   - j. Type `Professor` for the label of the combo box. Click **Finish**.
   - k. Save the form and switch to Form view to test the combo box.

10. Add a list box control to the *Class* form.
    - a. Switch back to Design view.
    - b. On the *Form Design Tools Design* tab, in the *Controls* group, click the **List Box** button. If the button is not available on the Ribbon, click the **More** button to expand the *Controls* gallery.
    - c. Click across from **CourseNumber** below the *Professor* combo box control to open the List Box Wizard.
    - d. Click the **I will type in the values that I want.** radio button. Click **Next**.
    - e. Click in the first empty cell and type: `1`
    - f. Press `Tab` and type: `2`
    - g. Press `Tab` and type: `3`
    - h. Click **Next**.
    - i. Select **Store that value in this field:** and select **Section** from the drop-down list. Click **Next**.
    - j. Type `Section` for the label of the list box. Click **Finish**.
    - k. Click the bottom of the **Section** list box control and drag up to shorten it until the bottom of the control is even with the bottom of the *Time* control.
    - l. Save the form and switch to Form view to test the list box.

11. Add the *ClassEnrollment* form as a subform to the *Class* form.
    a. Switch back to Design view.
    b. On the *Form Design Tools Design* tab, in the *Controls* group, click the **More** button to expand the *Controls* gallery, and click the **Subform/subreport** button.
    c. Click under the *Time* label at the bottom of the form.
    d. Click the **Use an existing form** radio button and verify that **ClassEnrollment** is selected. Click **Next**.
    e. Verify **Show ClassEnrollment for each record in Class using ClassCode** is selected. Click **Next**.
    f. Change the name to: `EnrollmentSubform` and then click **Finish**.
    g. Save the form and switch to Form view to see the new subform.

12. Hide the navigation buttons in the subform.
    a. Switch back to Design view.
    b. If the Property Sheet is not open, open it.
    c. Click the subform control once to select it. Note the box at the top of the Property Sheet displays *EnrollmentSubform*.
    d. Click the form selector at the top left corner of the subform next to the ruler.
    e. Verify that the box at the top of the Property Sheet now displays *Form*.
    f. On the Property Sheet *Format* tab, click in the **Navigation Buttons** property and select **No**.
    g. Close the Property Sheet.
    h. Save the form.
    i. Switch to Form view to review the changes.

13. Add an image in an image control to the *Class* form Detail section. Do not add the image to the Image Gallery.
    a. Switch to back to Design view.
    b. On the *Form Design Tools Design* tab, in the *Controls* group, click the **More** button to expand the *Controls* gallery, and then click the **Image** button.
    c. Click in the form Detail section across from the *Professor* combo box control at the **6.5-inch** mark on the horizontal ruler. Do not draw a box to insert the image control; instead, just click the form to allow Access to insert the image at its actual size.
    d. Navigate to the folder that contains the data files for this book. Select the **Notebook** image and click **OK**.
    e. Save the form and switch to Form view to see the changes.

14. Hide the Form Header section.
    a. Switch to back to Design view.
    b. Right-click the Detail section bar or a blank area of the Detail section. Select **Form Header/Footer** to disable the section.
    c. Click **Yes** to allow Access to remove any controls in the Header/Footer sections.
    d. Save the form and switch to Form view to see the changes.

15. Press `Tab` to advance from one field to the next in the form. You will need to change the tab order so the *Time* control is before the *Room* control.
    a. Switch to Design view.
    b. On the *Form Design Tools Design* tab, in the *Tools* group, click the **Tab Order** button to open the *Tab Order* dialog.

c. Click the record selector next to **Room** once to select it, and then click again and drag to the new tab order position before **Time.**

   d. Click **OK.**

   e. Save the form and switch to Form view to test the new tab order.

   f. Close the *Class* form.

16. Create a navigation form with tabs at the left side.

    a. On the *Create* tab, in the *Forms* group, click the **Navigation** button, and select **Vertical Tabs, Left.**

    b. Close the Field List on the right side of the screen.

    c. Double-click the new [**Add New**] tab, type `Class` and press `← Enter`.

    d. Click and drag the **NewProfessor** form from the Navigation Pane to [**Add New**] in the navigation form.

    e. Save the form as: `UniversityNavigationForm`

    f. Switch to Form view to test the navigation form and then close it.

17. Close the database and exit Access.

challenge yourself 6.3

In this project you will modify a form to make it a data entry only form. You will add a command button and an image to the form. You will add a combo box control to another form, modify the tab order, and display the form header. In a third form, you will add a subform and modify the subform properties. Finally, you will create a navigation form to organize the important forms in the database.

Be sure to save the forms often as you make changes throughout this project.

Skills needed to complete this project:

- Controlling Data Entry in a Form (Skill 6.4)
- Disabling User Interface Elements in a Form (Skill 6.6)
- Adding a Command Button Control to a Form (Skill 6.8)
- Adding Images to Forms (Skill 6.14)
- Adding a Combo Box Control to a Form (Skill 6.9)
- Defining the Tab Order of Controls (Skill 6.16)
- Displaying the Form Header and Footer (Skill 6.13)
- Adding a Subform Based on a Table or Query (Skill 6.10)
- Modifying the Subform Properties (Skill 6.12)
- Creating a Navigation Form with Tabs (Skill 6.15)

1. Open the start file **AC2013-ChallengeYourself-6-3** and resave the file as: `[your initials]AC-ChallengeYourself-6-3`

2. If necessary, enable active content by clicking the **Enable Content** button in the Message Bar.

3. Modify the **NewProduct** form to make it a data entry form.

   a. Make the **NewProduct** form a data entry only form.

   b. Hide the form navigation buttons.

   c. Add a command button to the lower right corner of the form Detail section to add a **new record.** The button should display the text: `Save and New`. Name the button control: `btnNewRecord`

d. Add the **CoffeeCup** image to the right side of the form at the **4.5-inch** mark on the horizontal ruler at the very top of the Detail section. Do not add the image to the Image Gallery. Allow Access to insert the image at its true size. The *CoffeeCup* image is included with the data files for this book.

e. Change the form title in the form header to: `New Product`

f. Save and close the form.

4. Add a combo box control to the **Employees** form.
   a. Create a **combo box** to display values from the **EmployeeJobTitles** table. Place the combo box next to the **FirstName** control at the **6-inch** mark on the horizontal rule.
   b. Include **all** the fields from the *EmployeeJobTitles* table.
   c. Sort the values in ascending order by **EmployeeJobTitle**.
   d. If necessary, modify the column width to fit the data. Allow Access to hide the primary key field.
   e. Store the value in the existing field **EmployeeJobTitleID**.
   f. Label the combo box: `Job Title`
   g. Make the combo box control wide enough to display all the job titles by extending the control to the left to the **5.5-inch** mark on the horizontal ruler.
   h. Save and close the form.

5. Modify the tab order on the **Employees** form so the **JobTitle** combo box comes after the **FirstName** control in the tab order. (*Hint:* In the *Tab Order* dialog, the combo box control will be named *Combo##*, where ## is the sequential control number assigned by Access.)

6. Display the form header/footer in the **Employees** form.
   a. Extend the height of the form header to the **.25-inch** mark on the vertical ruler.
   b. Add a label control to the form header at the **2.5-inch** mark on the horizontal ruler and enter the form title: `Employees`
   c. Modify the title text using the options on the *Format* tab. Use any formats you like. Be sure to increase the size of the label control as necessary after formatting the title.
   d. Save and close the form.

7. Add the **Suppliers** table as a subform to the bottom of the **Products** form.
   a. Add the fields **SupplierID, Company, ContactFirstName, ContactLastName,** and **Phone** in that order.
   b. Show records in the *Suppliers* table for each record in the *Products* table using the field **SupplierID**.
   c. Name the subform: `SuppliersSubform`
   d. Extend the form Detail section to the **7.5-inch** mark on the horizontal ruler, and then extend the subform control to the same width.
   e. Switch to Layout view and adjust the width of each of the columns in the subform to autofit the content.

8. Modify the subform properties to hide the navigation buttons.

9. Save and close any open database objects.

10. Create a navigation form to organize the database forms.
    a. Use the navigation form format **Vertical Tabs, Left.**
    b. Add these forms to the navigation form in this order: **Products, NewProduct, Suppliers, Customers, Employees.** (*Hint:* Remember to use Layout view to add forms to the navigation form tabs.)
    c. Save and close the navigation form. Name the form: `NavigationForm`

11. Close the database and exit Access.

challenge yourself 6.4

In this project, you will work with another university database to create forms to display students and professors and their class schedules. You will use both a query and a form in the subforms. You will create a new form using an application part and set the record source and add fields. You will also add combo box and list box controls to another form. Finally, you will create a navigation form to display the two forms you worked on.

Skills needed to complete this project:

- Creating a Blank Form from an Application Part (Skill 6.1)
- Working with a New Form in Design View (Skill 6.2)
- Adding a Subform Based on a Table or Query (Skill 6.10)
- Modifying the Subform Properties (Skill 6.12)
- Controlling Data Entry in a Form (Skill 6.4)
- Adding a Combo Box Control to a Form (Skill 6.9)
- Adding a List Box Control to a Form (Skill 6.7)
- Adding a Subform Based on a Form (Skill 6.11)
- Displaying the Form Header and Footer (Skill 6.13)
- Adding Images to Forms (Skill 6.14)
- Adding a Command Button Control to a Form (Skill 6.8)
- Creating a Navigation Form with Tabs (Skill 6.15)

1. Open the start file **AC2013-ChallengeYourself-6-4** and resave the file as: `[your initials]AC-ChallengeYourself-6-4`
2. If necessary, enable active content by clicking the **Enable Content** button in the Message Bar.
3. Create a new form from an application part.
   a. Use the **2 Right** application part to create the form.
   b. Rename the new form: `Professors`
   (*Hint:* The application part creates a form named **SingleTwoColumnRightLabels.**)
   c. Add the **Professors** table as the record source for the form.
   d. Include these fields in the form *without* their automatic labels. Change the text in the placeholder labels instead of allowing Access to place the automatic labels.
      i. Add the **EmployeeID** field to the placeholder to the right of the **Field1:** placeholder label. Change the label to: `ID`
      ii. Add the **LastName** field to the placeholder to the right of the **Field6:** placeholder label. Change the label to: `Last Name`
      iii. Add the **FirstName** field to the placeholder to the right of the **Field5:** placeholder label. Change the label to: `First Name`
      iv. Delete the following placeholder labels and the placeholders next to them: **Field2:, Field3:, Field4:, Field7:,** and **Field8.**
   e. In the Detail section, change the title to: `Professor Schedules`
4. Add a subform to the bottom of the form to display the **ProfessorSchedule** query.
   a. Place the subform below the **EmployeeID** controls at the **1.5-inch** mark on the horizontal ruler.
   b. Add all the fields from the **ProfessorSchedule** query in order.

c. In the subform, show records in the **ProfessorSchedule** query for each record in the **Professors** form using the **EmployeeID** field.

d. Name the subform: `ProfessorScheduleSubform`

e. Save and close the form.

5. Modify the properties of the **ProfessorScheduleSubform** as follows:

    a. Do not allow additions.

    b. Do not allow deletions.

    c. Hide the navigation buttons.

    d. Save and close the form.

6. Add a combo box control to the **Students** form to display selections for the student advisors.

    a. Place the combo box control to the right of the **StudentID** control at the **5-inch** mark on the horizontal ruler.

    b. Get the values for the combo box from the **Professor** table.

    c. Add these fields in this order: **EmployeeID, LastName,** and **FirstName.**

    d. Sort values in the combo box in ascending order by **LastName.**

    e. Allow Access to hide the primary key field.

    f. Store the value in the **Advisor** field.

    g. Label the combo box: `Advisor`

7. Add a list box control to the Students form to display selections for the student classification. You will enter the list box values yourself.

    a. Place the list box control to the right of the **FirstName** control at the **5-inch** mark on the horizontal ruler.

    b. Enter these four values for the list box: `FR, SO, JR, SR`

    c. Store the value in the **Classification** field.

    d. Label the list box: `Year`

8. Add the **StudentSchedule** form as a subform at the bottom of the form.

    a. Place the subform control below the **GPA** label at the **2.5-inch** mark on the vertical ruler.

    b. Use the **StudentSchedule** form as the source for the subform.

    c. Accept the link suggested by Access.

    d. Do not change the name of the subform.

9. Add an image to the Image Gallery and then add it to the form header.

    a. Display the form header and footer.

    b. Add the image **UniversityLogo** to the Image Gallery and add it to the left side of the form header at the **.5-inch** mark on the horizontal ruler. The *UniversityLogo* file is included with the data files for this project.

10. Add a command button to close the form.

    a. Place the command button to the right of the **Advisor** control at the **7-inch** mark on the horizontal ruler.

    b. Use the default button picture.

    c. Name the button: `btnCloseForm`

    d. Save and close the form.

11. Save and close any open database objects.
12. Create a navigation form to organize the database forms.
    a. Use the navigation form format **Horizontal Tabs.**
    b. Add these forms to the navigation form in this order: **Students** and **Professors.**
       (*Hint:* Remember to use Layout view to add forms to the navigation form tabs.)
    c. Save and close the navigation form. Name the form: `SchedulesNavigation`
13. Close the database and exit Access.

on your own 6.5

In this project you will continue working with the technical support database you created on your own in Chapter 5. You may work with the sample database provided or continue working with your solution file from the *On Your Own Project 5.5*. In the sample file, we have replaced the linked table with a regular table in the database.

Skills needed to complete this project:
- Creating a Blank Form from an Application Part (Skill 6.1)
- Working with a New Form in Design View (Skill 6.2)
- Adding a Combo Box Control to a Form (Skill 6.9)
- Adding a Subform Based on a Table or Query (Skill 6.10)
- Adding a Subform Based on a Form (Skill 6.11)
- Modifying the Subform Properties (Skill 6.12)
- Controlling Data Entry in a Form (Skill 6.4)
- Disabling User Interface Elements in a Form (Skill 6.6)
- Defining the Tab Order of Controls (Skill 6.16)

1. Open the start file **AC2013-OnYourOwn-6-5** or open your solution file from the Chapter 5 *On Your Own* project and resave the file as:
   `[your initials]AC-OnYourOwn-6-5`
2. If necessary, enable active content by clicking the **Enable Content** button in the Message Bar.
3. Create a new form using the **Projects** table as the record source. You can create the form from scratch or try using an application part.
4. Add a **combo box** control to display the project managers. The combo box should display the first name and last name of employees from the **Staff** table. You can place the combo box wherever you want, but be sure to position it and adjust its size so it does not overlap any other controls.
5. Add a subform to the form. The subform can use a table or a form as the source, but make sure there is relationship between the main form and the records in the subform so Access can determine what to show in the subform.
6. Add an image to the form. You can use any image you want. We have included an image file, **TechSupportImage,** with the data files for this project. You can add the image wherever you like on the form. Resize the image as necessary.

7. The sample database includes a **NewIssue** form. Modify the form properties so users can only add new records. Hide the navigation buttons. If your database does not include this form, create your own data entry form appropriate to the content in your database. If you hide the navigation buttons, be sure to add command buttons to allow the user to add a new record.
8. Check the tab order in the forms in your database. If the tab order in a form seems unnatural, adjust it using the *Tab Order* dialog.
9. Save and close any open database objects.
10. Close the database and exit Access.

fix it 6.6

In this project, you will continue helping the animal rescue organization from Chapter 5. They are trying to set up forms in their database to make it easier for volunteers to enter data without making mistakes. You will make two of the forms data entry forms and add command buttons so volunteers don't need to know how to use the form navigation buttons. You will also make the database more efficient by replacing the image controls in each form header with the logo image you will add to the Image Gallery. Finally, you will help them finish the navigation form they started.

Test your work as you go and save often!

Skills needed to complete this project:
- Controlling Data Entry in a Form (Skill 6.4)
- Disabling User Interface Elements in a Form (Skill 6.6)
- Adding a Command Button Control to a Form (Skill 6.8)
- Adding Images to Forms (Skill 6.14)
- Defining the Tab Order of Controls (Skill 6.16)
- Creating a Navigation Form with Tabs (Skill 6.15)
- Displaying the Form Header and Footer (Skill 6.13)

1. Open the start file **AC2013-FixIt-6-6** and resave the file as: `[your initials]AC-FixIt-6-6`
2. If necessary, enable active content by clicking the **Enable Content** button in the Message Bar.
3. Begin by fixing the "new" forms to make them data entry only.
   a. Modify the **NewAdoptionForm** form so it allows data entry only.
   b. Hide the navigation buttons in the form.
   c. Add a command button to close the form. The button should be located in the empty area of the form. The button should display the text: `Save and Close`. Name the control: `btnCloseForm`
   d. Add another command button to allow users to start another blank record. Position the button to the right of the first button. This button should display the text: `Save and New`. Name the control: `btnNewRecord`
   e. Adjust the position of the buttons as needed.
   f. Repeat steps a–e in the **NewFriendForm** form. Location the buttons in the empty area of the form below the zip code controls.

4. Notice the forms have the same logo image in the form header. Unfortunately, whoever created the form used an image control each time he added the image. It would be more efficient to add the image once to the database Image Gallery and then add the image from the Image Gallery to each form header. In each of the forms in this database, except the Navigation Form, delete the image control in the form header and replace it with the **PetRescueLogo** from the Image Gallery. The first time you replace the image, you will need to add it to the Image Gallery so you can use it in the other forms. Place the new image file at the **6.5-inch** mark on the horizontal ruler.

5. Check the tab order in the *NewAdoptionForm* and *NewFriendForm* forms. In the **NewAdoptionForm** form, fix the tab order so the **Phone** control comes before the **PetID** control.

6. Complete the navigation form by adding the **NewAdoptionForm** form to the first tab and the **NewFriendForm** form to the second tab. (*Hint:* Remember to use Layout view to add forms to the navigation form tabs.)

7. Hide the form header and footer in the navigation form. Allow Access to delete the controls in the header.

8. Save and close all open database objects.

9. Close the database and exit Access.

chapter 7

Exploring Advanced Reports

- Add a record source to a report
- Add and arrange controls
- Create calculated controls in Design view
- Work with report groups in Design view
- Add subreports to reports
- Apply conditional formatting to a report

In this chapter, you will learn the following skills:

Skill **7.1** Working with a Report in Design View

Skill **7.2** Understanding Report Sections

Skill **7.3** Arranging Controls in a Report

Skill **7.4** Adding Calculated Controls to a Report

Skill **7.5** Adding Report Grouping in Design View

Skill **7.6** Working with Group Headers and Footers

Skill **7.7** Hiding Repeated Values in a Report

Skill **7.8** Adding a Subreport Based on a Report

Skill **7.9** Displaying the Subreport Page Header

Skill **7.10** Adding a Subreport Based on a Table or Query

Skill **7.11** Applying Conditional Formatting to a Report

skills

introduction

This chapter expands on the basic report skills introduced in Chapter 3. Throughout this chapter, you will work primarily in Design view—changing the report record source, adding and arranging controls, creating calculated controls, and organizing records with grouping. You will also work with subreports both from another report and from a table or query. Most of the skills you learn in this chapter can be completed in Layout view as well as Design view. In the final skill in the chapter, you will work in Layout view where you can immediately see the effects of applying conditional formatting rules. The *Let Me Try* exercises in this chapter use the AC7-Sales database. You can keep the database open while you work in this chapter, opening and closing database objects as required for each *Let Me Try*.

Skill 7.1 Working with a Report in Design View

When you start a new blank report from scratch, the first thing you should do is set a table or query as the **record source** for the report. You can also change the record source for a report after you've created it. The record source determines which fields can be included in the report, so be sure to use a table or query that includes the fields in your report. The report is not limited to fields in the record source, but fields selected from another table or query must have a relationship to one of the fields in the record source.

Use the **report Property Sheet** to set the record source and other report properties. Properties are grouped into four tabs: *Format, Data, Event,* and *Other.* The *All* tab displays all the properties in a single list.

To set the record source for a report from Design view:

1. On the *Report Design Tools Design* tab, in the *Tools* group, click the **Property Sheet** button to display the Property Sheet.
2. Verify that **Report** is selected in the *Selection type* box. If you have a control selected, the Property Sheet displays the properties for the selected control. To view and modify the properties of the report itself, expand the *Selection type* list at the top of the Property Sheet and select **Report**.
3. From the Property Sheet *Data* tab, click in the **Record Source** box, expand the list, and select the table or query you want.
4. Click the **X** in the upper right corner of the Property Sheet to close it.
5. Save the report.

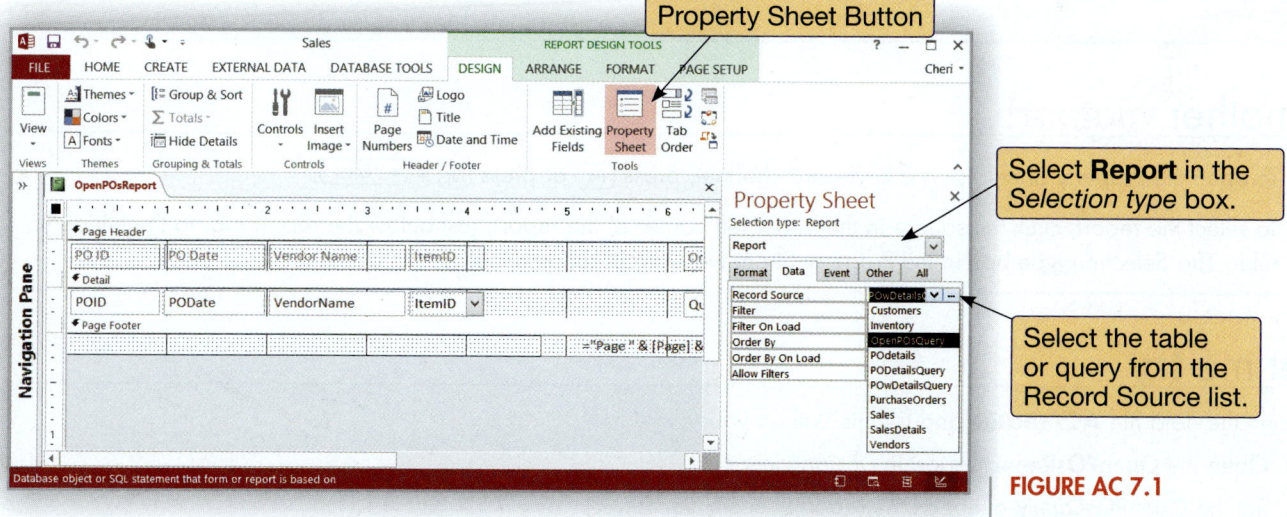

FIGURE AC 7.1

Recall that when you add a field to a report, Access automatically adds a label control to the left of the bound text control. You can prevent Access from including the label control when you insert a new bound text control by holding down the (Ctrl) key as you drag the field from the Field List pane.

Once you have set the record source from the report, add fields to the report using the Field List pane.

1. On the *Report Design Tools Design* tab, in the *Tools* group, click the **Add Existing Fields** button.
2. Click and drag fields from the Field List to the report. To prevent Access from including the label control, hold down the Ctrl key as you drag the field.

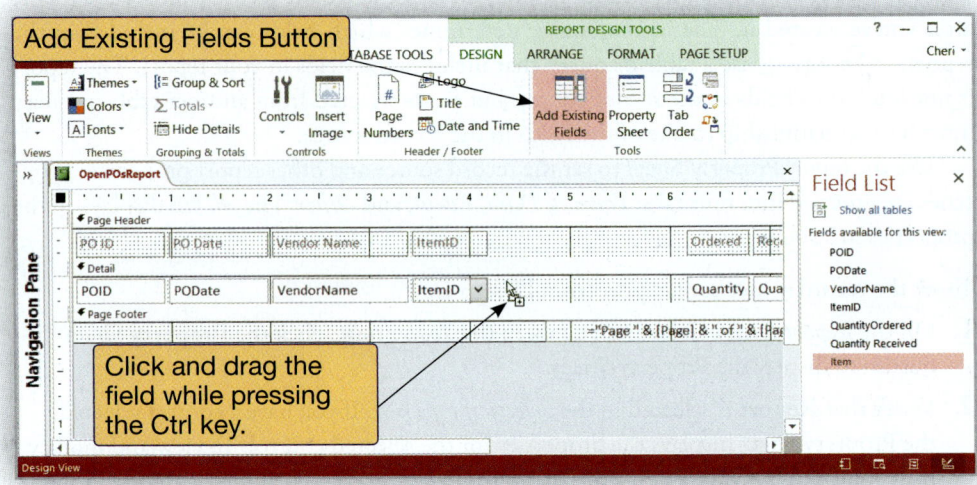

FIGURE AC 7.2

tips & tricks

If you do not set the record source for the report, Access will create an embedded query as the record source as you add fields to the report. The **embedded query** is a query created specifically for the report. In the *Record Source* box, it appears as an SQL statement. For more information about SQL statements, refer to the skill *Modifying a Query in SQL View*.

another method

- To open the Property Sheet using a keyboard shortcut, press F4 or press Alt + Enter.
- To select the report, click the square in the upper left corner of the report, just below the report tab, to the left of the ruler. The *Selection type* box in the Property Sheet will update automatically.

let me try

Open the data file **AC7-Sales** and try this skill on your own:

1. Open the **OpenPOsReport** report in Design view.
2. Set the **OpenPOsQuery** query as the report's record source.
3. Add the **Item** field to the right of the **ItemID** control. Add the bound text control without the label control.
4. Review the report in Report view, and then switch to Layout view and adjust the width of the **Item** control so you can see the full item name.
5. Save the report.

Skill 7.2 Understanding Report Sections

When you create a report from scratch in Design view, the Details, Page Header, and Page Footer sections are visible. The **report Detail section** includes the controls for the report data. The **report Page Header section** appears above the Detail section, and the **report Page Footer section** appears below the Detail section. These sections are used to display information included on every page of the report when it is printed or viewed in Print Preview view. The Page Footer section usually includes the control to display page numbers. For information about adding page numbers to reports, refer to the skill *Adding Page Numbers to Reports*.

Reports that use a tabular layout with columns include the label controls in the Page Header section so the column titles appear at the top of every printed page. In this type of report layout, the Detail section is narrow, containing only a single row of bound controls.

To add a label control to the report Page Header section:

1. On the *Report Design Tools Design* tab, in the *Controls* group, click the **Label** control. If the *Controls* gallery is not visible on the Ribbon, click the **Controls** button to display it.
2. Click in the report Page Header section above the bound control that you want to label.
3. Type the text for the label and press ⏎ Enter.

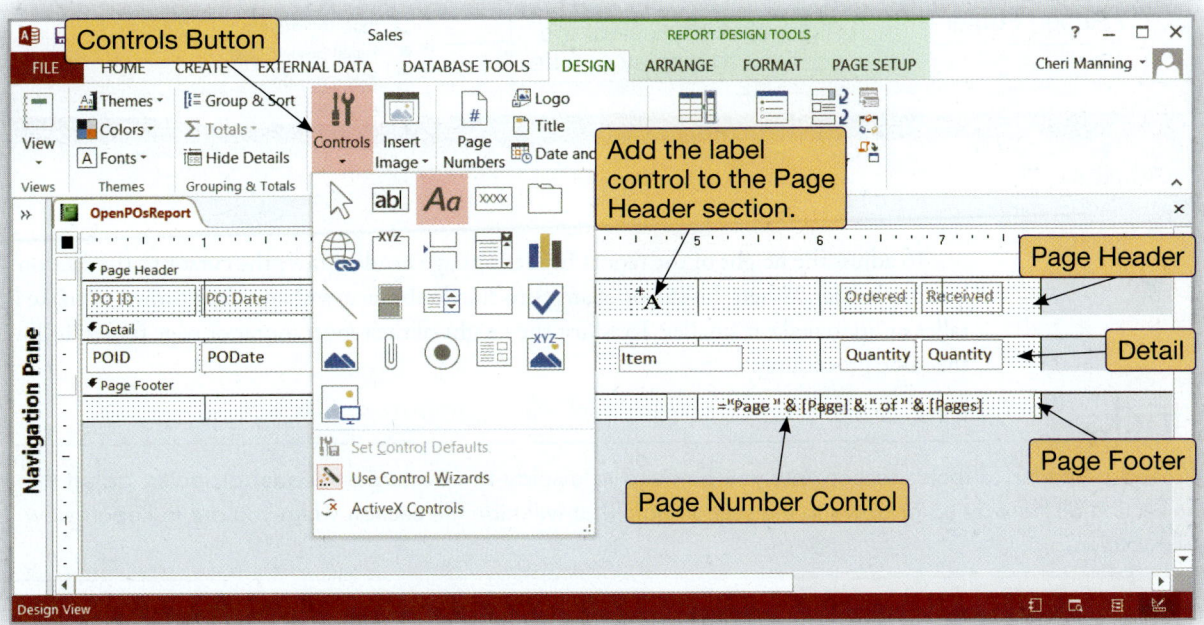

FIGURE AC 7.3

The **Report Header section** appears at the top of the report, and the **Report Footer section** appears at the bottom of the report. The Report Header section is used to display the report title, a company logo, and other information you want to appear only once at the beginning or end of the report. These sections are also used to display calculated controls to summarize values in the Detail section of the report. You will learn about creating calculated controls in the Report Footer section in the skill *Adding Calculated Controls to a Report*.

When you create a report from scratch in Design view, the Page Header/Footer sections are visible, but the Report Header/Footer sections are not. If you want to add controls to those sections you must first display them. Right-click an empty area of the report or one of the section bars, and select **Report Header/Footer.** You must be in Design view to hide or display report sections.

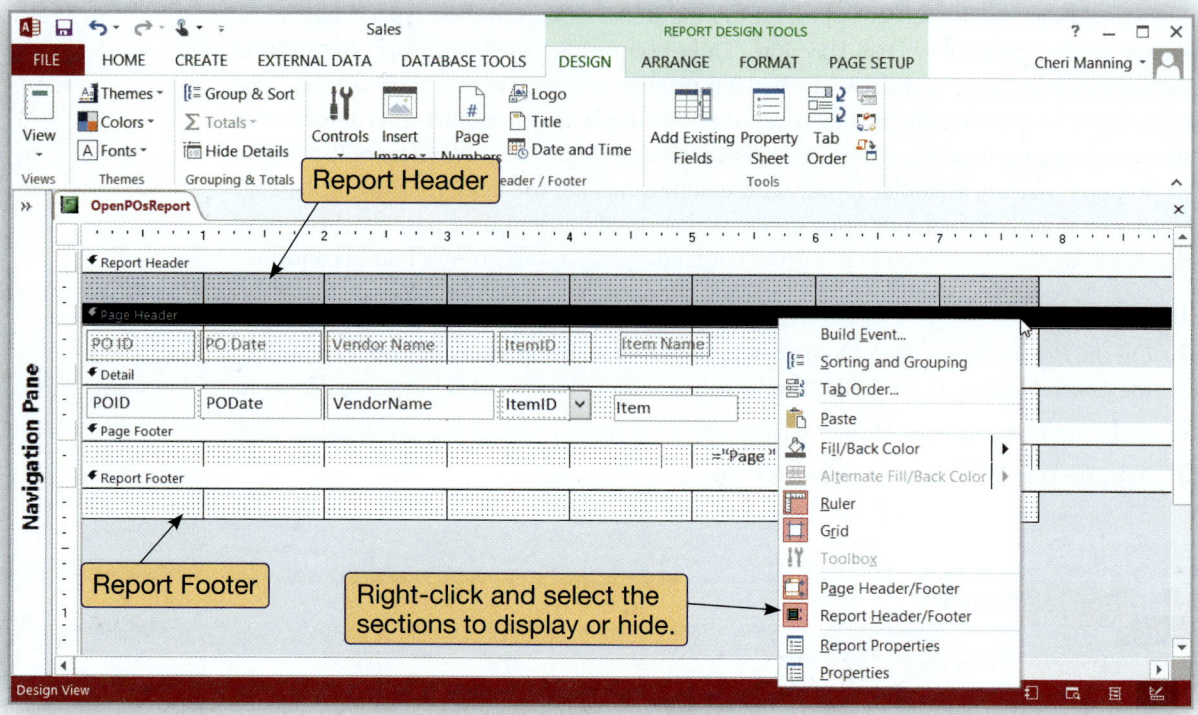

FIGURE AC 7.4

To adjust the height of the report header or page header, move the cursor to the section's bottom border. When the cursor changes to the double arrow shape, drag down to make it taller or up to make it smaller. To adjust the height of the report footer or page footer, follow the same procedures.

tips & tricks

If you don't need a header or footer section, but you do need to display its counterpart header or footer, adjust the height of the section all the way up or down to the section bar. That will hide the section when you are in Report view or Print Preview view.

tell me more

When you add grouping to a report, each group includes its own group header and group footer section. Refer to the skill *Working with Group Headers and Footers* for more information.

let me try

If the database is not already open, open the data file **AC7-Sales** and try this skill on your own:

1. If it is not already open, the **OpenPOsReport** report in Design view.
2. Add a new text control to the Page Header section above the **Item** control. Change the label text to: `Item Name`
3. Display the **Report Header/Footer** sections.
4. Review the changes in Report view or Print Preview view.
5. Save the report.

Skill 7.3 Arranging Controls in a Report

In a report with a tabular format, labels are located above the bound controls that display the report data. Labels should line up with their bound controls along the right or left side. The labels should align with each other at the top, as should the row of bound controls in the Detail section. Controls should also have a consistent height. All the options you need to arrange controls are found on the *Report Design Tools Arrange* tab in the *Sizing & Ordering* group.

To align controls in a report from Design view:

1. Select the controls you want to align. To select multiple controls, press Ctrl or Shift while clicking each control.
2. On the *Report Design Tools Arrange* tab, in the *Sizing & Ordering* group, click the **Align** button and select the alignment option you want.

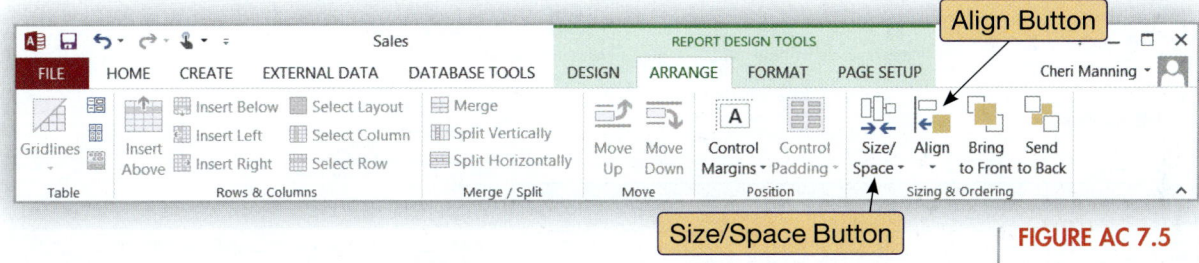

FIGURE AC 7.5

Often when you add a new control to a report, the default height will not match the other controls. To adjust the height of controls in a report from Design view:

1. Select the control you want to change and another control with the height or width you want to match.
2. On the *Report Design Tools Arrange* tab, in the *Sizing & Ordering* group, click the **Size/Space** button and select the option you want.

tips & tricks

These techniques taught in this skill work in Design view or Layout view for both forms and reports.

let me try

If the database is not already open, open the data file **AC7-Sales** and try this skill on your own:

1. If it is not already open, open the **OpenPOsReport** report in Design view.
2. Align the controls in the report Detail section at the top.
3. Modify the **Item** control so it is the same size as the tallest control in the report Detail section. (*Hint:* All the other controls in the Detail section are the same height, so you can select any or all of the controls along with the *Item* control.)
4. Align the controls in the report Page Header section along the top.
5. Modify the **Item Name** label so it is the same height as the tallest control in the report Page Header section. (*Hint:* All the other controls in the report Page Header section are the same height, so you can select any or all of the labels along with the *Item Name* label.)
6. Left-alight the **Item** control in the Detail section and its label in the report Page Header section.
7. Save the report.

Skill 7.4 Adding Calculated Controls to a Report

A **calculated control** is an unbound text control that contains an **expression** (formula). The skill *Adding Totals to a Report* covers how to use the *Totals* button to add calculated controls to the Report Footer section from Layout view. You can also create a calculated control by adding an unbound text control to the report, and then adding the expression to be calculated to the text control Control Source property. Using this technique, you are not limited to the aggregate functions available from the *Totals* button.

The part of the report to which you add the calculated control determines which records Access will use in the calculation.

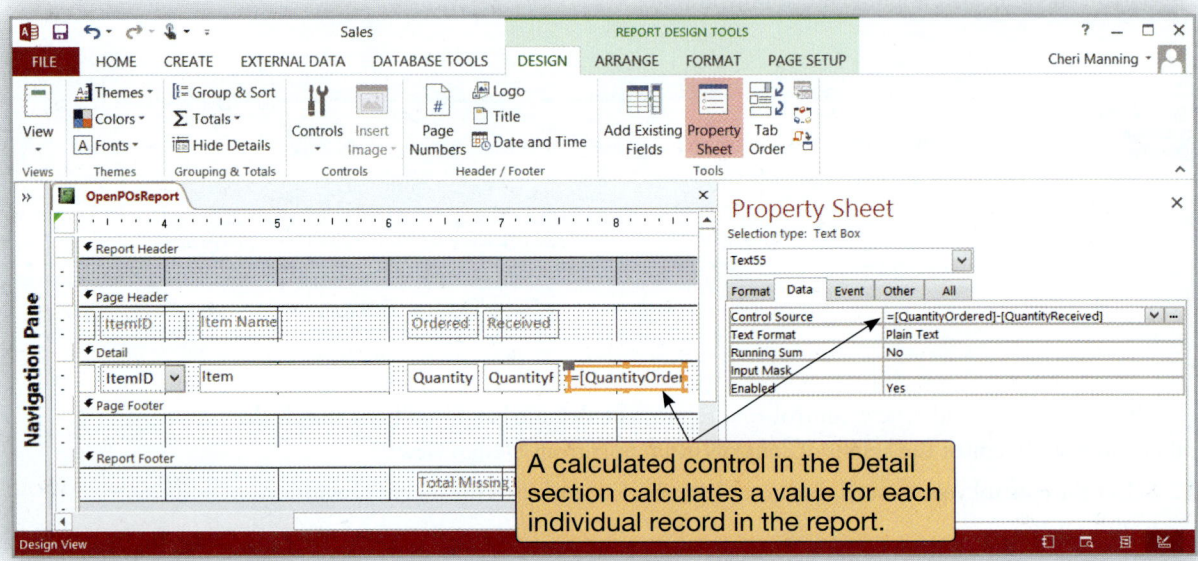

FIGURE AC 7.6

When you place a calculated control in the Detail section, as shown in Figure AC 7.6, the calculation uses the values from the individual record only. The calculated control will appear with each record in the report. Be sure to enclose field names in square brackets:

`=[QuantityOrdered]-[QuantityReceived]`

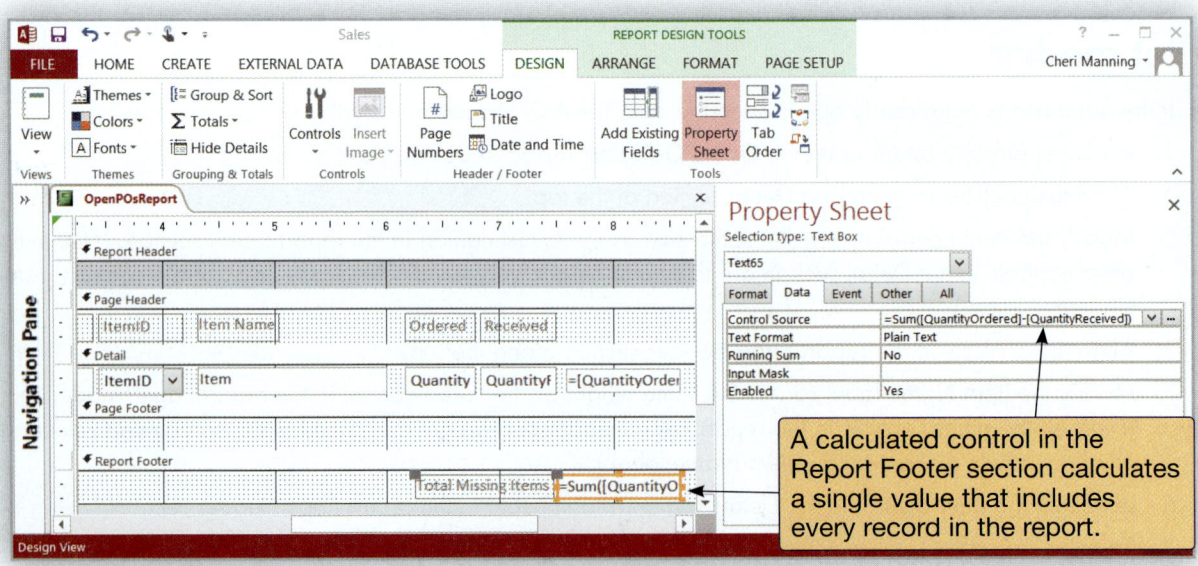

FIGURE AC 7.7

When you place a calculated control in the Report Header or Report Footer section, as shown in Figure AC 7.7, the calculation uses all the values from every record in the report in the calculation. Calculated controls in the Report Header or Report Footer section use aggregate functions such as SUM or COUNT. The expression following the function name must be enclosed in parentheses: `=SUM([QuantityOrdered]-[QuantityReceived])`

To add a calculated control to a report from Design view.

1. On the *Report Design Tools Design* tab, in the *Controls* group, click the **Text Box** button. If the *Controls* gallery is not visible on the Ribbon, click the **Controls** button to display it.
2. Click in the report where you want the new control to appear. If you do not want to include the label control, press Ctrl when you click in the report.
3. On the *Report Design Tools Design* tab, in the *Tools* group, click the **Property Sheet** button to open the Property Sheet for the new unbound text control.
4. On the Property Sheet *Data* tab, type the expression in **Control Source** property box. Start the expression with = and then type the formula you want to calculate. Enclose field names in square brackets. If you are using an aggregate function such as SUM or COUNT surround the expression in parentheses. Press Enter when you are finished typing the expression.

Switch to Report view or Layout view to see the results of the new calculated control.

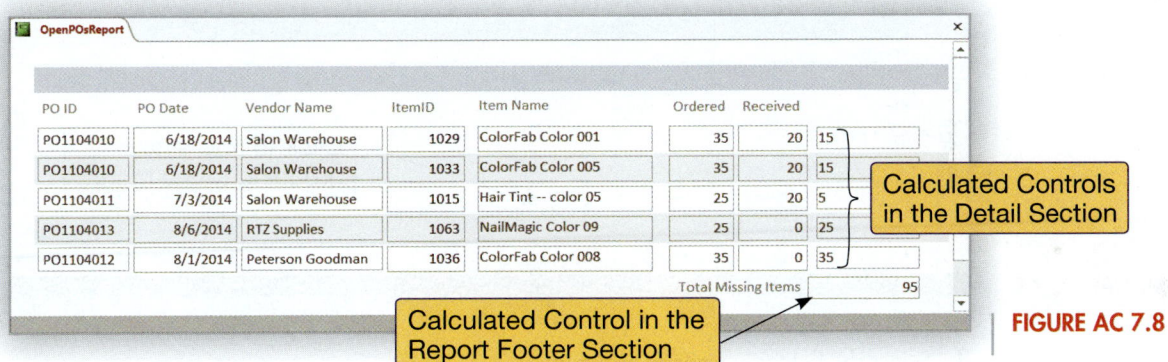

FIGURE AC 7.8

tips & tricks

The expression **=COUNT(*)** in a calculated control in the Report Header or Report Footer section counts all records in the report. In this expression, the COUNT function is not linked to a specific field.

another method

To create a calculated control, you can also type the expression in the unbound text control.

let me try

If the database is not already open, open the data file **AC7-Sales** and try this skill on your own:

1. If it is not already open, open the **OpenPOsReport** report in Design view.
2. Add a calculated control without a label to the right of the *QuantityReceived* control in the Detail section to calculate the value of the **QuantityOrdered** field – the **QuantityReceived** field for each individual record.
3. Add a calculated control with a label to the right side of the Report Footer section to calculate the **sum** of the **QuantityOrdered** field – the **QuantityReceived** field for the entire report.
4. Change the label text to: `Total Missing Items`
5. Review the report in Report view, and then save and close the report.

skill 7.4 Adding Calculated Controls to a Report

Skill 7.5 Adding Report Grouping in Design View

Adding **grouping** organizes the report into sections (groups) by the value of a specific field. Grouping can make a long report much easier to follow. Grouping also allows you to add group-specific footer sections where you can display totals for each group. The skills *Grouping Records in a Report* and *Adding Totals to a Report* cover the basics of adding grouping from Layout view. In this skill, you will learn to add grouping from Design view.

To add grouping to a report in Design view:

1. On the *Report Design Tools Design* tab, in the *Grouping & Totals* group, click the **Group & Sort** button to display the *Group, Sort, and Total* pane at the bottom of the report window.
2. Click the **Add a group** button in the *Group, Sort, and Total* pane.

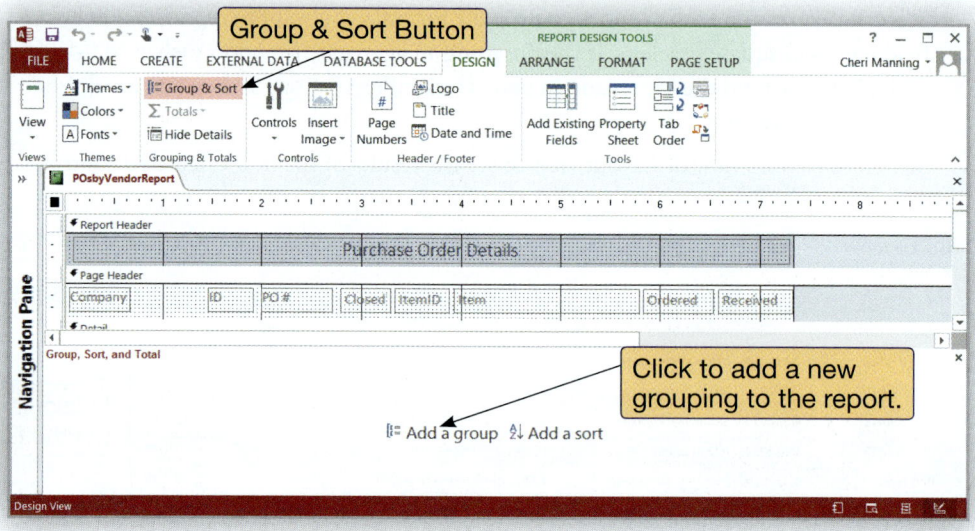

FIGURE AC 7.9

3. Select the field you want to group by.

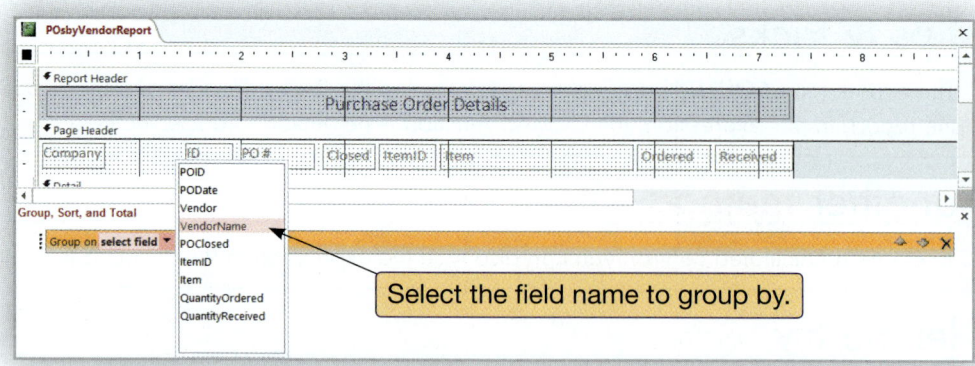

FIGURE AC 7.10

4. Access rearranges the report into groups by the field you selected.

let me try

If the database is not already open, open the data file **AC7-Sales** and try this skill on your own:

1. Open the **POsbyVendorReport** report in Design view.
2. Group the records in the report by values in the **VendorName** field.
3. Switch to Report view and scroll through the report to review the groups.
4. Save the report.

Skill 7.6 Working with Group Headers and Footers

When you add grouping to a report, Access automatically displays the **Group Header section**. The Group Header section is repeated above each group in the report. If you are not going to use the group header, you can hide it.

To hide the Group Header section:

1. In the *Group, Sort, and Total* pane, click the **More** button More ▶ for the group.
2. Click the arrow next to *with a header section* and select **without a header section** instead.

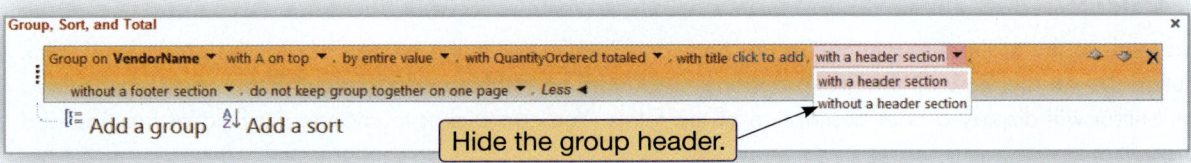

FIGURE AC 7.11

Group totals appear in the **Group Footer section** below each group in the report. The group footer is not displayed automatically unless you add totals to the groups using the *Totals* option. The skill *Adding Totals to a Report* discusses using the *Totals* button to add totals to each group.

If you have a calculated control in the Report Footer section that you created yourself, you can display the same calculation for each group, but you must first display the group footer manually:

1. In the *Group, Sort, and Total* pane, click the More button More ▶ for the group.
2. Click the arrow next to *without a footer section* and select **with a footer section** instead.

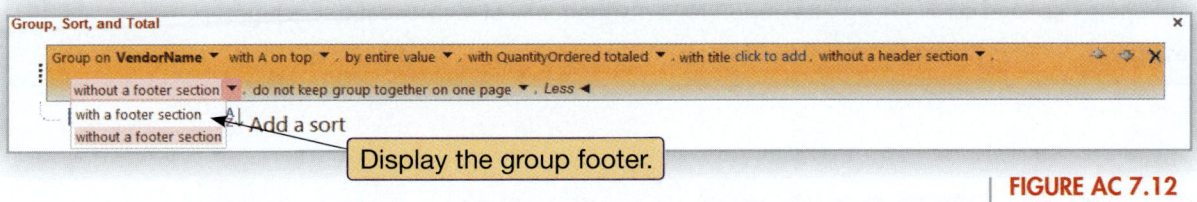

FIGURE AC 7.12

Once the group footer is visible, you can copy the calculated controls in the report footer and paste them into the group footer. You can use the **Copy** and **Paste** buttons on the *Home* tab, *Clipboard* group or the keyboard shortcuts Ctrl + C and Ctrl + V.

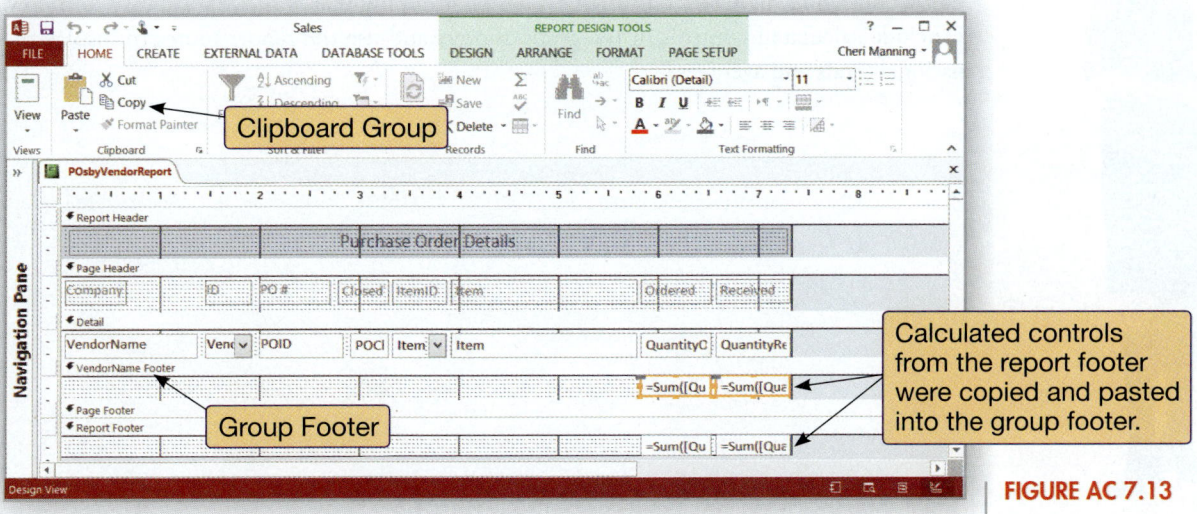

FIGURE AC 7.13

When you are finished setting up the grouping, hide the *Group, Sort, & Total* pane by clicking the **Group & Sort** button on the Ribbon. The *Group & Sort* button toggles the *Group, Sort, and Total* pane on and off. Hiding the *Group, Sort, and Total* pane does not remove the group.

tips & tricks

If you grouped by a *Date/Time* field, Access will add a title to the group header to indicate the time period for each group. You should keep the group header visible. If you grouped by values in a *Short Text* or *Number* field, the group header is not necessary, because the same value is repeated in every row of the group.

tell me more

You can add totals to the group through the *Group, Sort, and Total* pane. In the orange bar for the group level, click the **More** button `More ▶` to view all the group options. Click **with no totals** to add totals. If totals have been added already, this button will display a brief description of the totals. You can click it to change the field or function and other totaling options.

let me try

If the database is not already open, open the data file **AC7-Sales** and try this skill on your own:

1. If it is not already open, open the **POsbyVendorReport** report in Design view.
2. Hide the group header.
3. Display the group footer.
4. Copy the calculated controls from the report footer and paste them into the group footer.
5. Move the calculated controls to the right side of the group footer so they align with the controls in the report footer.
6. Switch to Report view and scroll through the report to verify the totals at the bottom of each group.
7. Save the report.

from the perspective of . . .

NATIONAL SALES MANAGER

An important part of my job is to generate reports every month to analyze sales for each of our product lines by district and region. Using grouping makes the reports easy to follow. I include calculated controls in the group footers and use the report footer to display the national totals and averages.

Skill 7.7 Hiding Repeated Values in a Report

When you review a report that has grouping, you'll see that the value you grouped by is repeated in every row. Once the records have been grouped together, repeating the value is not necessary.

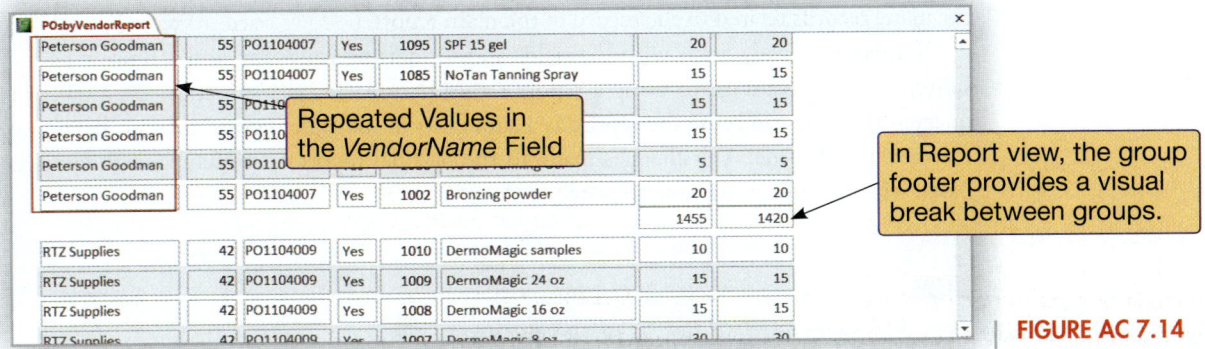

FIGURE AC 7.14

To hide repeated values in a report from Design view:

1. In the report Detail section, click the field you grouped by.
2. On the *Report Design Tools Design* tab, in the *Tools* group, click the **Property Sheet** button to open the Property Sheet for the selected control.
3. On the Property Sheet *Format* tab, click in the **Hide Duplicates** property box and change the selection to **Yes**. The Hide Duplicates property is near the bottom of the Property Sheet.

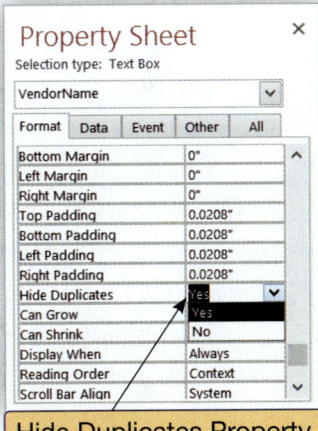

FIGURE AC 7.15

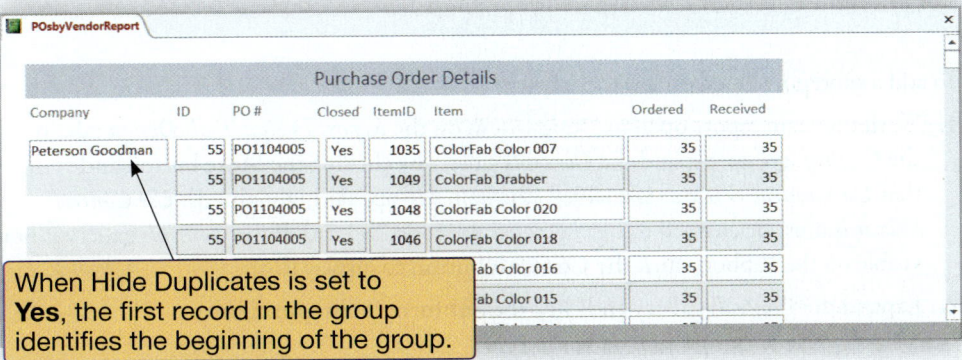

FIGURE AC 7.16

tips & tricks

If records in the table are sorted by values in the first field, you can hide duplicates for that field to make the report look as if grouping had been applied.

let me try

If the database is not already open, open the data file **AC7-Sales** and try this skill on your own:

1. If it is not already open, open the **POsbyVendorReport** report in Design view.
2. Review the report in Report view and note the repeated vendor names in each record in the group.
3. Switch to Design view and hide the duplicate values in the **VendorName** field.
4. Switch back to Report view and observe the change.
5. Save and close the report.

Skill 7.8 Adding a Subreport Based on a Report

A **subreport** is a report within a report. The subreport can display records from another report, table, or query when a relationship exists between data in the main report and subreport. Usually, the relationship is a one-to-many relationship, where the subreport displays the many records related to the record in the main report.

If a report already exists with the fields and formatting you want, you can use it as the subreport. An advantage to using a report rather than basing the subreport on a table or query is that you can reuse the report as a subreport in multiple reports without having to recreate it each time. Any changes made to the original report on which the subreport is based will also appear in the subreport.

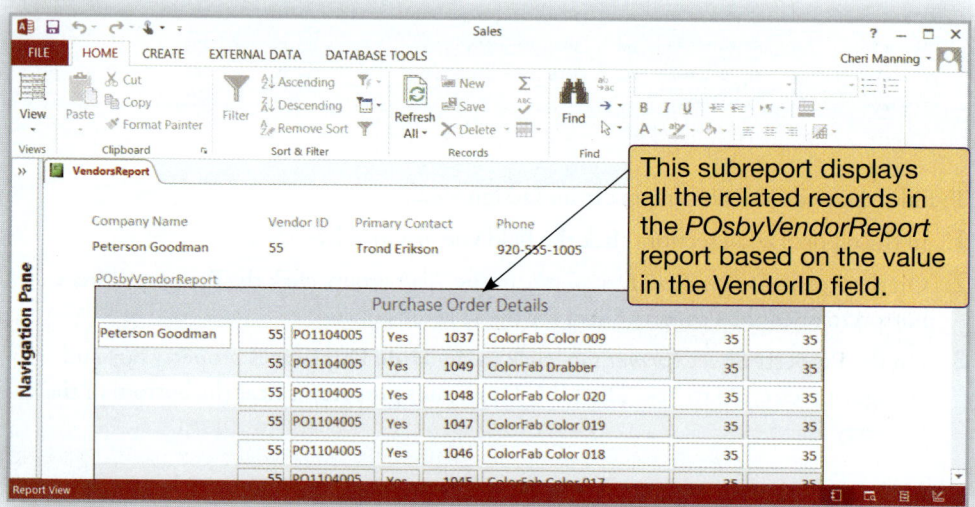

FIGURE AC 7.17

To add a subreport based on another report:

1. With the main report open in Design view, on the *Report Design Tools Design* tab, in the *Controls* group, expand the *Controls* gallery by clicking the **More** button and verify that *Use Control Wizards* is enabled (the icon will appear highlighted). *Use Control Wizards* must be enabled to display the SubReport Wizard. If the *Controls* gallery is not visible on the Ribbon, click the **Controls** button to display it.

2. Expand the *Controls* gallery and click the **Subform/Subreport** button.

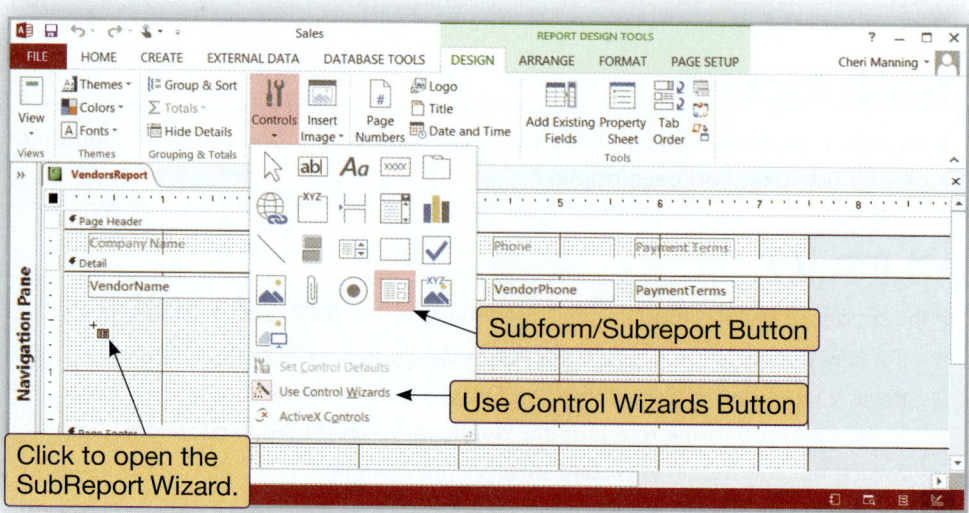

FIGURE AC 7.18

3. Click in the report where you want the subreport to appear. The SubReport Wizard opens automatically when you click the report.
4. Click the **Use an existing report or form** radio button, and then click the name of the report you want to use as the subreport. Click **Next**.

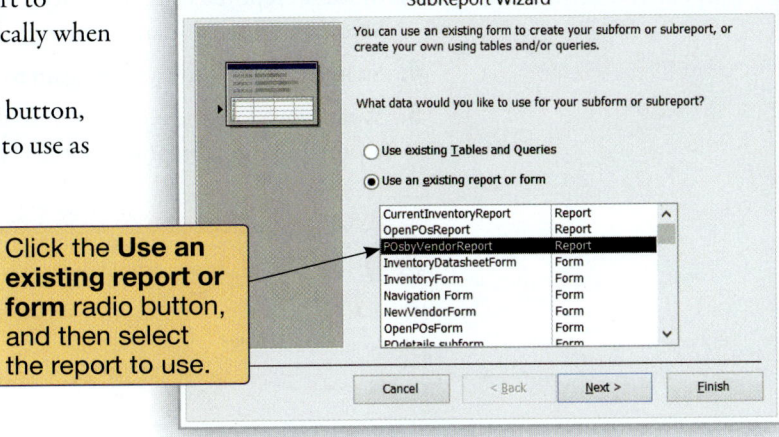

FIGURE AC 7.19

5. If a relationship already exists between the two reports, access will suggest the fields to link. Select the link you want to use and then click **Next**.

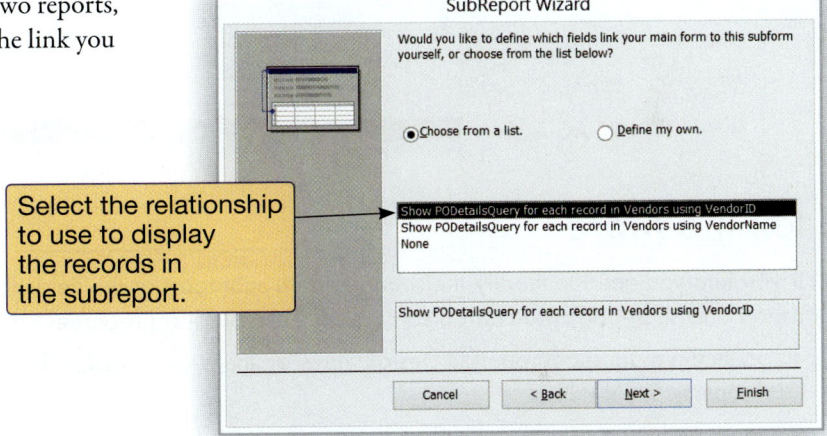

FIGURE AC 7.20

6. In the last step of the wizard, do not change the subreport name. Click **Finish**.
7. Switch to Report view to review the subreport.

If you need to make adjustments to the width and height of the subreport:

1. Switch back to Design view and increase the width of the Detail section. Place the cursor at the right side of the Detail section. When the cursor changes to the double arrow, click and drag to the right to make the detail section wider.
2. Once you've made the Detail section wider, you can adjust the width of the subreport control.

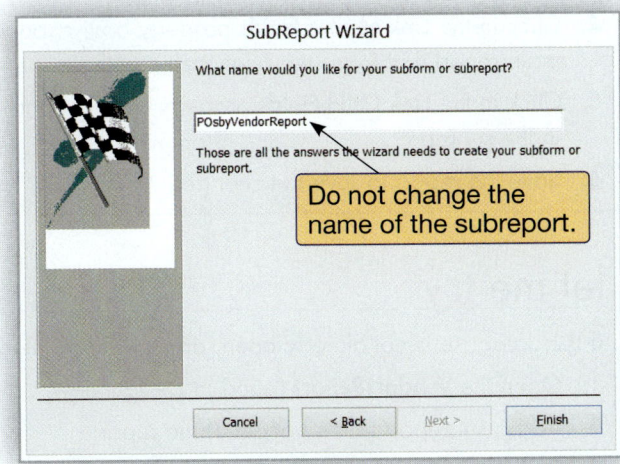

FIGURE AC 7.21

skill 7.8   Adding a Subreport Based on a Report

3. With subreports, you do not need to adjust the height. Access sizes the subreport automatically to display all the records.
4. Switch back to Report view again to review the changes.
5. When you close the report, Access will prompt you to save changes to both the main report and the subreport report.

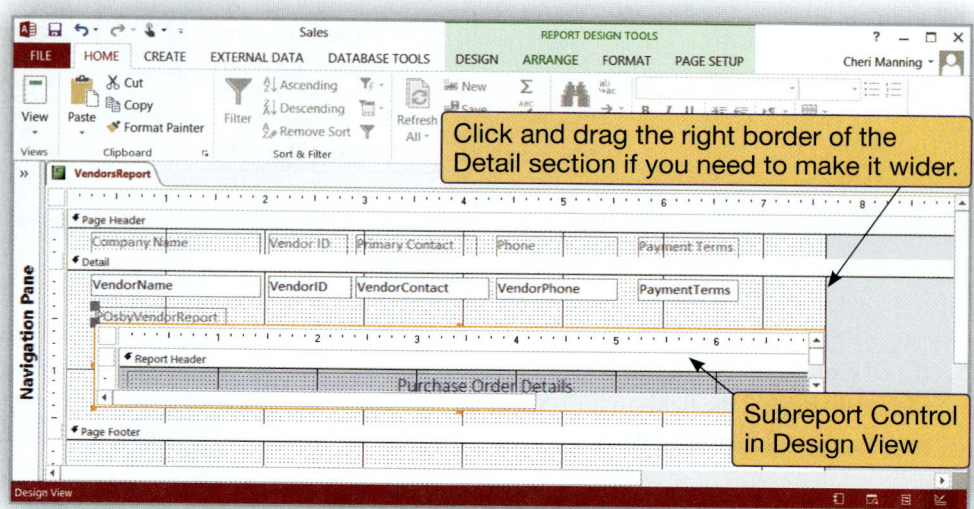

FIGURE AC 7.22

tell me more

If you find you need to modify the source for the subreport or the fields that create the relationship between the main report and subreport, you can do so through the subreport properties.

1. With the main report open in Design view, on the *Report Design Tools Design* tab, in the *Tools* group, click the **Property Sheet** button.
2. Expand the box at the top of the Property Sheet and select the subform/subreport control.
3. On the Property Sheet *Data* tab, click in the **Source Object** property box. Expand the list and make a new selection to change the report, query, or table the subreport is based on.
4. Click in the **Link Master Fields** property box, expand the list, and make a new selection to change the field in the main report that forms the relationship with the subreport.
5. Click in the **Link Child Fields** property box, expand the list, and make a new selection to change the related field in the subreport.
6. Save the report to save the changes.

let me try

If the database is not already open, open the data file **AC7-Sales** and try this skill on your own:

1. Open the **VendorsReport** report in Design view.
2. Add a subreport to the bottom of the report.
3. Base the subreport on the **POsbyVendorReport** report.
4. Use the **VendorID** field to link the report and subreport—the first suggested link between the report and subreport.
5. Review the subreport in Report view.
6. Save and close the report.

Skill 7.9 Displaying the Subreport Page Header

When you create a subreport based on another report, Access hides the Page Header and Page Footer section in the subreport control. If the subreport uses a column layout, the labels for the columns are located in the Page Header section and should be shown.

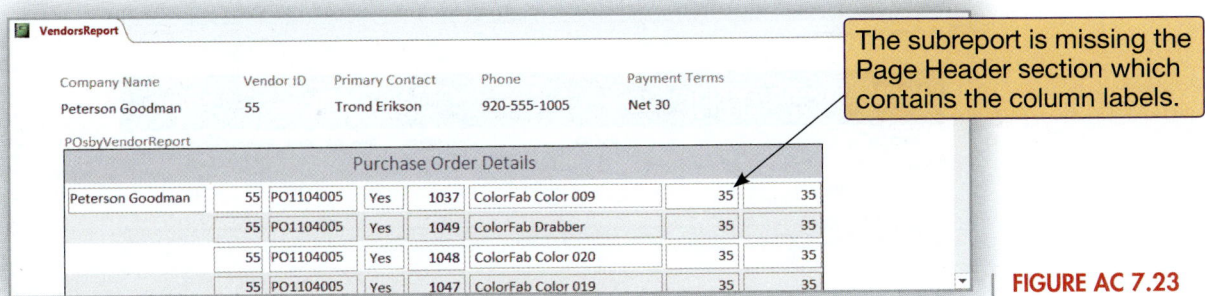

FIGURE AC 7.23

To display the Page Header section in a subreport:

1. With the main report open in Design view, display the Property Sheet. On the *Report Design Tools Design* tab, in the *Tools* group, click the **Property Sheet** button. Note that the Property Sheet displays the report properties for the *main* report.
2. To display the control properties for the subreport, click the subreport once to select it. The *Selection Type* box at the top of the Property Sheet should display the subreport name.
3. On the Property Sheet *Format* tab, scroll down to the bottom to find the Show Page Header and Page Footer property. Click in the box, expand the list, and select **Yes**.

FIGURE AC 7.24

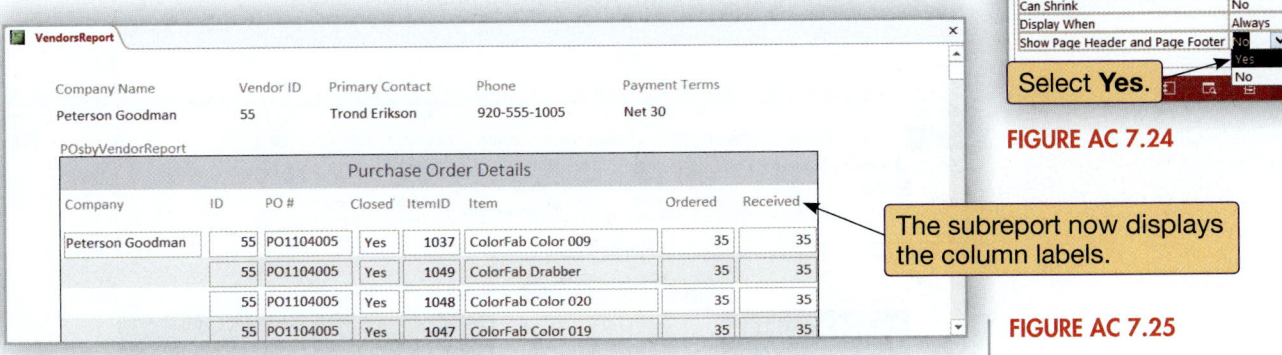

FIGURE AC 7.25

Switch to Layout view or Report view to review the Page Header labels.

let me try

If the database is not already open, open the data file **AC7-Sales** and try this skill on your own:

1. Open the **VendorsReport** report in Report view and observe the missing labels at the top of each column.
2. Switch to Design view, and modify the properties for the subreport control to display the Page Header and Page Footer sections.
3. Review the change in Report view again.
4. Save and close the report.

Skill 7.10 Adding a Subreport Based on a Table or Query

You can also create a subreport from a table or query if a relationship exists between the report record source and the table or query you want to use as the subreport. A subreport based on a table or query appears in tabular form, similar to a datasheet.

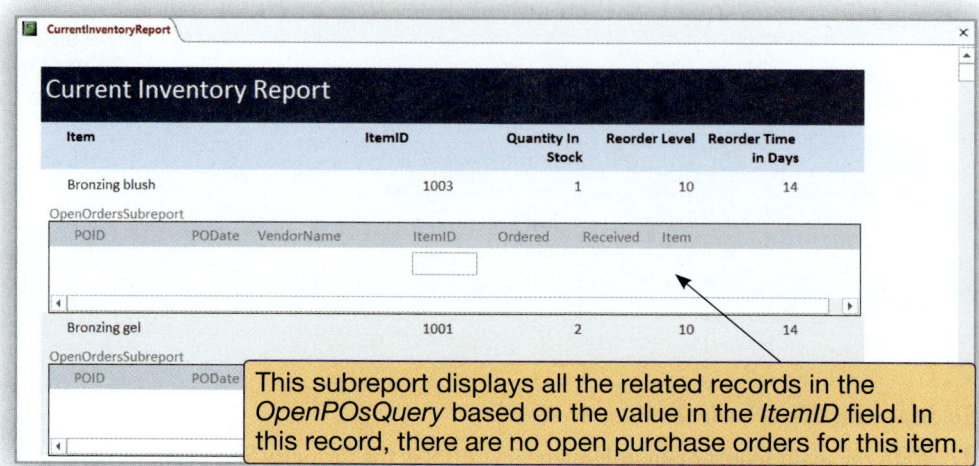

FIGURE AC 7.26

To use the SubReport Wizard to create a subreport based on a table or query:

1. With the main report open in Design view, on the *Report Design Tools Design* tab, in the *Controls* group, expand the *Controls* gallery, and verify that *Use Control Wizards* is enabled (the icon will appear highlighted). *Use Control Wizards* must be enabled to display the SubReport Wizard. If the *Controls* gallery is not visible on the Ribbon, click the **Controls** button to display it.

2. In the *Controls* gallery, click the **Subform/Subreport** button.

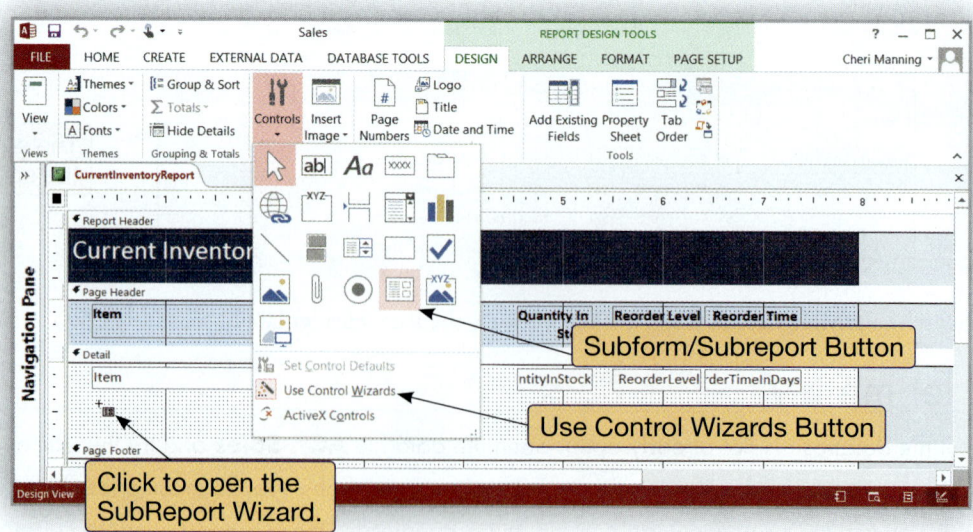

FIGURE AC 7.27

AC–314 | www.mhhe.com/simnet

access 2013 chapter 7 Exploring Advanced Reports

3. Click in the report where you want the subreport to appear. The SubReport Wizard opens automatically when you click the report.
4. In the first step of the SubReport Wizard, **Use existing Tables and Queries** is selected by default. Click **Next** to go to the next step.

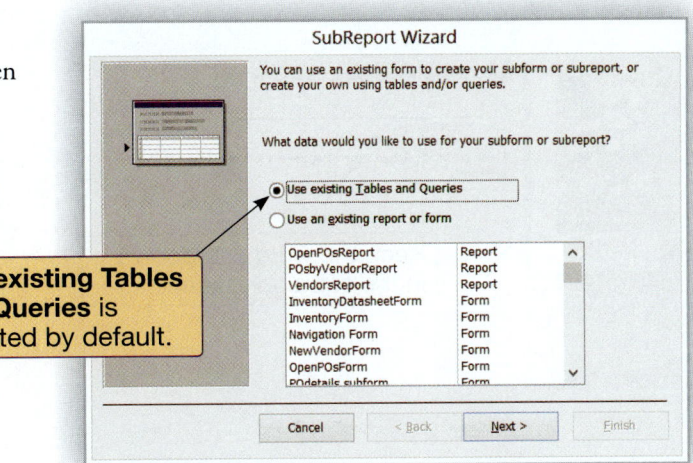

FIGURE AC 7.28

5. Expand the **Tables/Queries** list, and select the table or query that contains the fields you want to show in the subreport.
6. In the *Available Fields* list, double-click the field(s) you want to appear in the subreport. Click the >> button to add all the fields at once. Click **Next**.

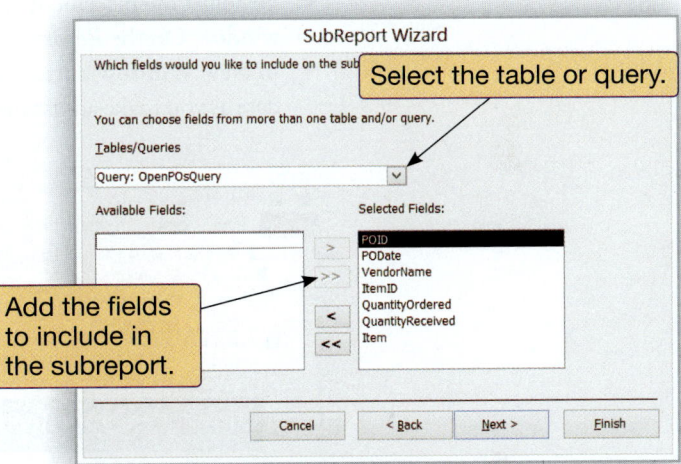

FIGURE AC 7.29

7. If one or more relationships exists between the main report and subreport, access will suggest the fields to link. If you want to display all records in the subreport, select **None**. Select the relationship option you want to use, and click **Next**.

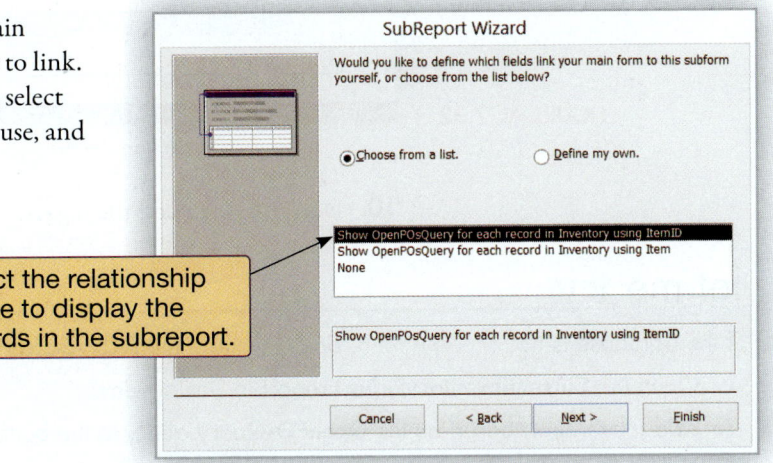

FIGURE AC 7.30

skill 7.10 Adding a Subreport Based on a Table or Query

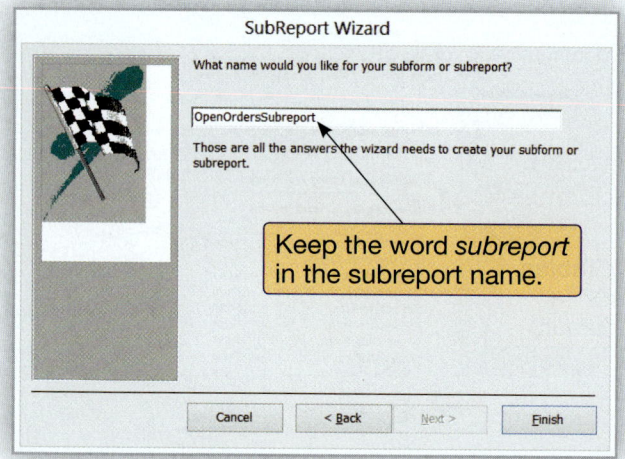

8. You can accept the suggested name for the subreport or enter a different name in the box. It is a good practice to keep the word *subreport* in the name to identify the report in the Navigation Pane, so you don't accidentally delete it. Click **Finish** to create the subreport.

FIGURE AC 7.31

9. To adjust the placement and size of controls in the subreport, try opening it in a new window. On the *Report Design Tools Design* tab, in the *Tools* group, click the **Subreport in New Window** button. You may want to use Layout view so you can see the report data as you make adjustments.

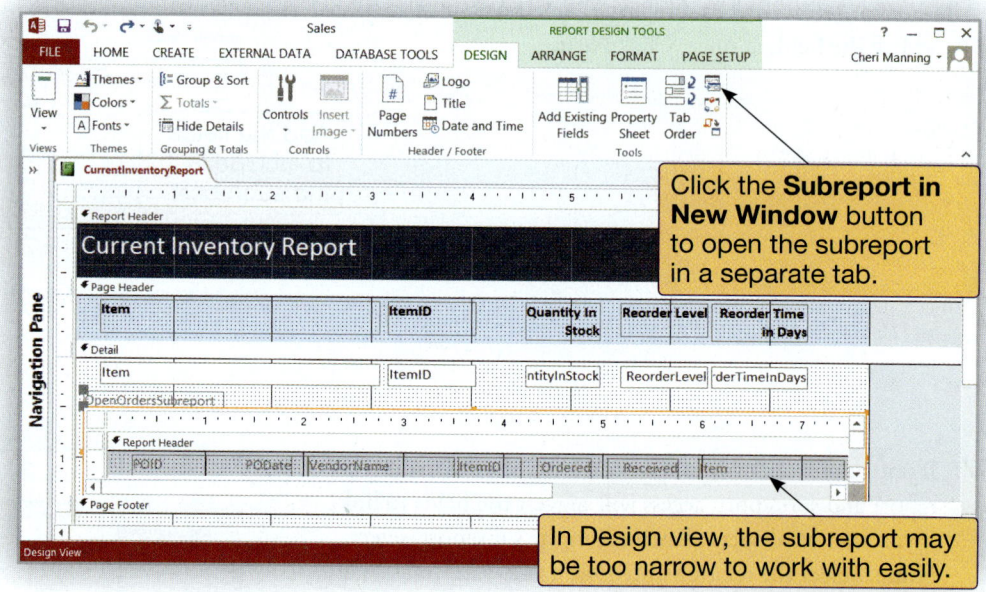

FIGURE AC 7.32

10. Don't forget to save the report.

let me try

If the database is not already open, open the data file **AC7-Sales** and try this skill on your own:

1. Open the **CurrentInventoryReport** report in Design view.
2. Add a subreport based on the **OpenPOsQuery** query to the bottom of the Detail section below the **Item** control.
3. Add all the fields in the query to the subreport.
4. Use the **ItemID** field to link the report and subreport—the first suggested link between the report and subreport.
5. Name the subreport: `OpenOrdersSubreport`
6. Switch to Layout view to review the subreport and make layout adjustments as necessary, and then save and close the report.

Skill 7.11 Applying Conditional Formatting to a Report

If you work with Microsoft Excel, you are probably familiar with conditional formatting. **Conditional formatting** applies formatting to data based on rules you define. In Access, there are two types of conditional formatting available. While you can create and apply conditional formatting rules in Design view, it is better to use Layout view so you can see the effect of the rule immediately.

The first type of conditional formatting applies a defined format to individual field values when certain conditions are met. The conditional formatting rule can compare the field to a specific value or compare the field to the value of another field.

To apply a conditional formatting rule that checks the field value:

1. From Layout view, click the control to which you want to apply conditional formatting.
2. On the *Report Layout Tools Format* tab, in the *Control Formatting* group, click the **Conditional Formatting** button to open the Conditional Formatting Rules Manager.

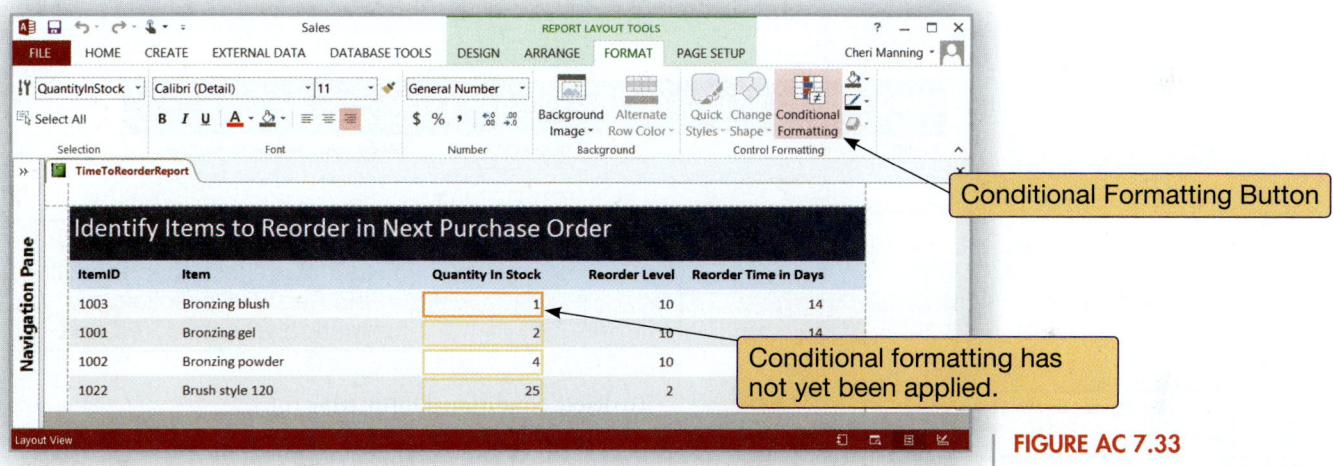

FIGURE AC 7.33

3. Confirm that the control to which you want to apply the formatting rule is selected in the *Show formatting rules for* box. Click **New Rule** to create a new conditional formatting rule.
4. The *New Formatting Rule* dialog opens. To create a rule based on the value of the field, verify that **Check values in the current record or use an expression** is selected.
5. In the *Format only cells where the:* section, leave the first box as *Field Value Is* to compare the value of the selected field to a specific value or the value of another field.
6. In the second box, expand the list and select the type of comparison you want to use.
7. In the third box, type the value or field name you want to evaluate against.

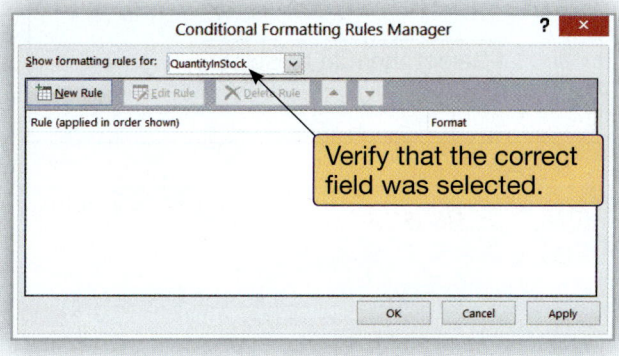

FIGURE AC 7.34

skill 7.11 Applying Conditional Formatting to a Report

8. Select the formatting options you want to apply if the condition is true.
9. Click **OK** to create the formatting rule.

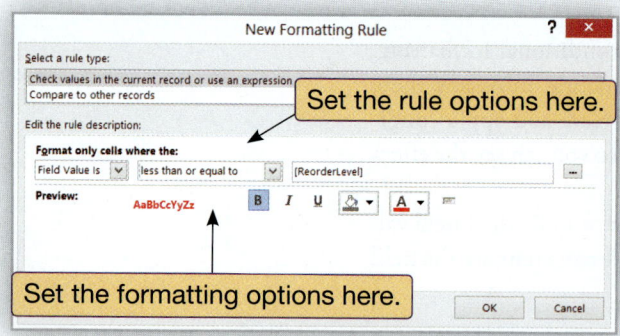

FIGURE AC 7.35

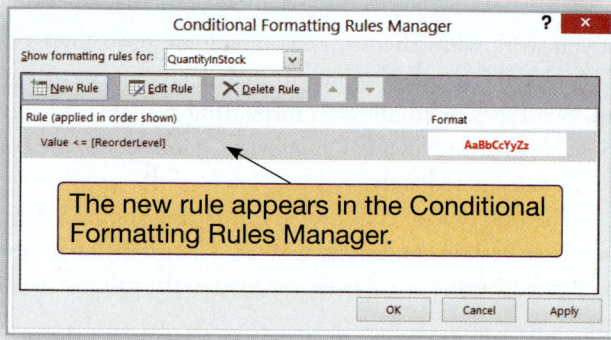

FIGURE AC 7.36

10. The new rule appears in the Conditional Formatting Rule Manager. Click **OK** again to close the Conditional Formatting Rules Manager.

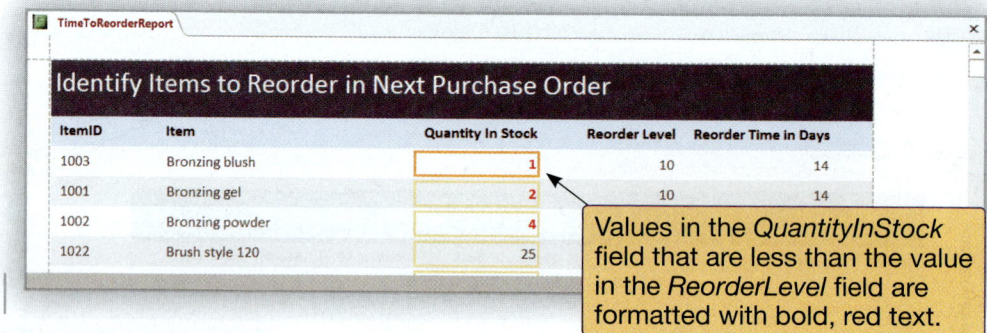

FIGURE AC 7.37

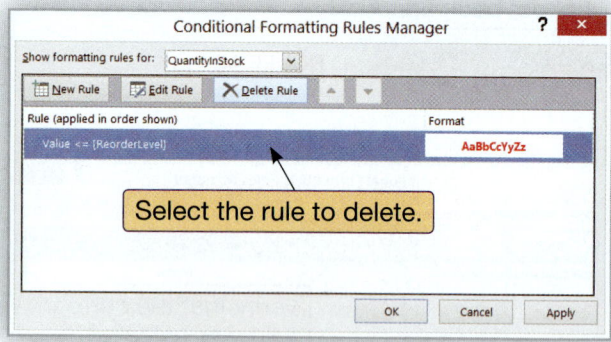

FIGURE AC 7.38

To delete conditional formatting rules:

1. In the Conditional Formatting Rules Manager, select the rule you want to delete, and then click the **Delete Rule** button.
2. Click **OK**.

The second type of conditional formatting displays a colored **data bar** representing the value of the record compared to other records. Generally, records with higher values have longer data bars. To add conditional formatting using data bars:

1. Open the Conditional Formatting Rules Manager. Verify that the control to which you want to apply conditional formatting is selected, and click the **New Rule** button.
2. In the *New Formatting Rule* dialog, click the **Compare to other records** option.
3. The default settings are to display a bright blue data bar with the shortest data bar for the lowest value and the longest data bar for the highest value. You can change these options if you want to create a custom data bar.

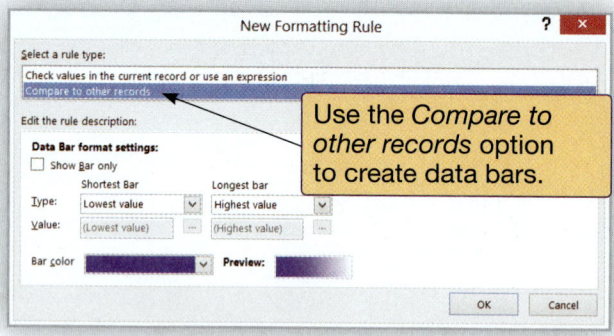

FIGURE AC 7.39

4. Click **OK** to close the *New Formatting Rule* dialog.
5. Click **OK** again to close the Conditional Formatting Rules Manager.

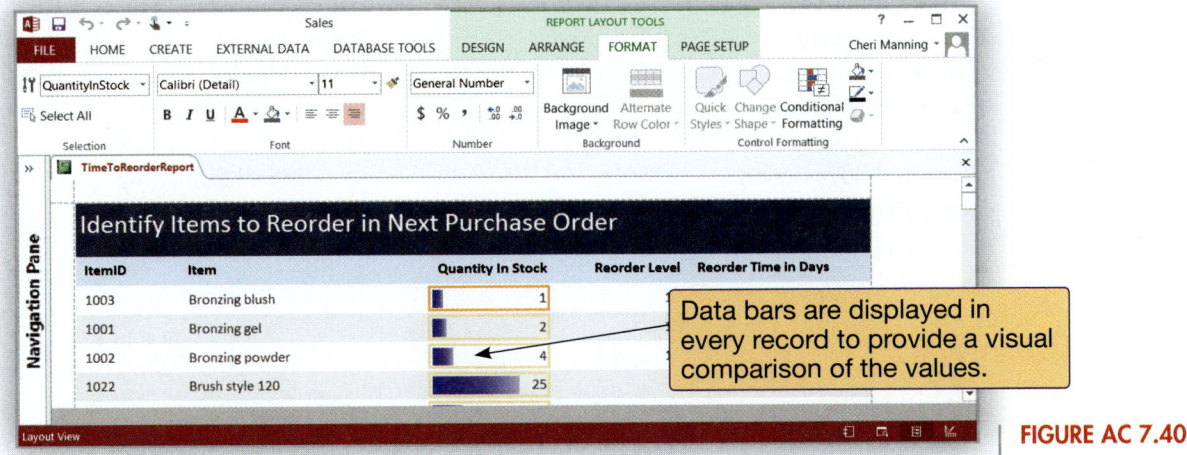

FIGURE AC 7.40

tell me more

To edit conditional formatting rules:

1. In the Conditional Formatting Rules Manager, select the rule you want to edit, and then click the **Edit Rule** button.
2. Make the changes you want in the *Edit Formatting Rule* dialog, and then click **OK**.
3. Click **OK** again to close the Conditional Formatting Rules Manager.

let me try

If the database is not already open, open the data file **AC7-Sales** and try this skill on your own:

1. Open the **TimeToOrderReport** report in Layout view.
2. Select the **QuantityInStock** control (below the *QuantityInStock* label).
3. Create a new conditional formatting rule to apply to the value if it is **less than or equal to** the value in the **ReorderLevel** field. Apply bold, red formatting. Red is the second color from the left in the last row of the color palette.
4. Observe the formatting change in Layout view, and then save the report and close it.
5. To try the data bars conditional formatting, first make a copy of the report. In the Navigation Pane, copy the **TimeToOrderReport** report and paste it with the new name: `DataBarsReport`. Open the new **DataBarsReport** report in Layout view.
6. Delete the conditional formatting rule applied to the **QuantityInStock** field.
7. Add a new conditional formatting rule to the **QuantityInStock** field to display data bars. Use the default data bars settings.
8. Save and close the report.

skill 7.11   Applying Conditional Formatting to a Report

key terms

Record source
Report Property Sheet
Embedded query
Report Detail section
Report Page Header section
Report Page Footer section
Report Header section
Report Footer section

Calculated control
Expression
Grouping
Group Header section
Group Footer section
Subreport
Conditional formatting
Data bars

concepts review

1. To set the underlying table or query for a new report, use which report property?
   a. Report Source
   b. Record Source
   c. Control Source
   d. Data Source

2. Reports that use a tabular layout with columns display the labels in which section?
   a. Detail
   b. Row Header
   c. Report Header
   d. Page Header

3. You must be in Design view to hide or show the Page Header/Footer and Report Header/Footer sections.
   a. True
   b. False

4. To add a field to a report without adding the automatic label control, press which keyboard key while dragging the field from the Field List?
   a. Alt
   b. Shift
   c. Ctrl
   d. Shift + Ctrl

5. To create a calculated control to appear with each record in the report, place it in which section?
   a. Detail
   b. Page Header
   c. Page Footer
   d. Report Footer

6. To create a calculated control to summarize values from every record in the report, place it in which section?
   a. Detail
   b. Page Header
   c. Page Footer
   d. Report Footer
7. When you add grouping to a report, the group footer is displayed automatically.
   a. True
   b. False
8. A subreport can display records from which type of database object?
   a. Report
   b. Form
   c. Query
   d. All of the above
9. To display the column labels in a subreport based on another report, you must change which property?
   a. Report Record Source
   b. Report Show Page Header and Page Footer
   c. Control Record Source
   d. Control Show Page Header and Page Footer
10. Which type of conditional formatting is available in Access?
    a. Data Bars
    b. Icon Sets
    c. Color Scales
    d. All of the above

projects

Data files for projects can be found on www.mhhe.com/office2013skills

skill review 7.1

In this project you will work with a database for Commonwealth Doctors Group, a clinic of specialists that accepts patients from all over the country. You will modify a patient visits report to change the record source to a query and then add controls and grouping. Next, you will work with the main *Patients* report to add calculated controls and conditional formatting. Finally, you will put it all together by adding the modified patient visits report as a subreport in the main patients report.

Skills needed to complete this project:

- Working with a Report in Design View (Skill 7.1)
- Understanding Report Sections (Skill 7.2)
- Arranging Controls in a Report (Skill 7.3)

- Adding Report Grouping in Design View (Skill 7.5)
- Working with Group Headers and Footers (Skill 7.6)
- Adding Calculated Controls to a Report (Skill 7.4)
- Applying Conditional Formatting to a Report (Skill 7.11)
- Hiding Repeated Values in a Report (Skill 7.7)
- Adding a Subreport Based on a Report (Skill 7.8)
- Displaying the Subreport Page Header (Skill 7.9)

1. Open the start file **AC2013-SkillReview-7-1** and resave the file as: `[your initials]AC-SkillReview-7-1`
2. If necessary, enable active content by clicking the **Enable Content** button in the Message Bar.
3. Change the record source for the *PatientVisitsAnalysis* report to the *PatientVisits* query.
   a. Open the **PatientVisitsAnalysis** report in Design view.
   b. On the *Report Design Tools Design* tab, in the *Tools* group, click the **Property Sheet** button to open the Property Sheet. Verify that **Report** is selected in the box at the top of the Property Sheet.
   c. On the Property Sheet *Data* tab, click the arrow in the Record Source property box to extend the list and select **PatientVisits.**
   d. Close the Property Sheet.
4. Add the fields *DateOfVisit* and *DoctorFullName* to the report without labels. Don't worry about exact placement or size. You will align and adjust the size of the controls later.
   a. On the *Report Design Tools Design* tab, in the *Tools* group, click the **Add Existing Fields** button to open the Field List.
   b. Press (Ctrl) and drag the **DateOfVisit** field from the Field List to the Detail section of the report to the right of the *PatientFirstName* control.
   c. Press (Ctrl) and drag the **DoctorFullName** field from the Field List to the Detail section of the report to the right of the *DateOfVisit* control.
   d. Close the Field List.
5. Add *DateOfVisit* and *DoctorFullName* labels to the Page Header section.
   a. On the *Report Design Tools Design* tab, in the *Controls* group, click the **Label** button in the *Controls* gallery. If the *Controls* gallery is not visible, click the **Controls** button.
   b. Click in the Page Header section to the right of the *PatientFirstName* label, above the *DateOfVisit* control.
   c. Type `DateOfVisit` and press (←Enter).
   d. On the *Report Design Tools Design* tab, in the *Controls* group, click the **Label** button in the *Controls* gallery. If the *Controls* gallery is not visible, click the **Controls** button.
   e. Click in the Page Header section to the right of the *DateOfVisit* label, above the *DoctorFullName* control.
   f. Type `DoctorFullName` and press (←Enter).
6. Align and size the labels with the other labels in the Page Header section.
   a. In the Page Header section, hold (↑Shift) and click the **DoctorFullName, DateOfVisit,** and **PatientFirstName** labels to select them.
   b. On the *Report Design Tools Arrange* tab, in the *Sizing & Ordering* group, click the **Align** button and select **Top.**
   c. On the *Report Design Tools Arrange* tab, in the *Sizing & Ordering* group, click the **Size/Space** button and select **To Tallest.**

7. Align and size the bound controls with the other controls in the Detail section.
   a. In the Detail section, hold [↑ Shift] and click the **DoctorFullName, DateOfVisit,** and **PatientFirstName** controls to select them.
   b. On the *Report Design Tools Arrange* tab, in the *Sizing & Ordering* group, click the **Align** button and select **Top.**
   c. On the *Report Design Tools Arrange* tab, in the *Sizing & Ordering* group, click the **Size/Space** button and select **To Tallest.**
8. Align the *DateOfVisit* and *DoctorFullName* controls with their labels.
   a. In the Page Header section, click the **DateOfVisit** label. Hold [↑ Shift] and click the **DateOfVisit** control in the Detail section.
   b. On the *Report Design Tools Arrange* tab, in the *Sizing & Ordering* group, click the **Align** button and select **Right.**
   c. In the Detail section, click the **DoctorFullName** control. Hold [↑ Shift] and click the **DoctorFullName** label in the Page Header section.
   d. On the *Report Design Tools Arrange* tab, in the *Sizing & Ordering* group, click the **Align** button and select **Left.**
9. Hide the borders around the *DateOfVisit* and *DoctorFullName* controls.
   a. In the Detail section, click the **DateOfVisit** control. Hold [↑ Shift] and click the **DoctorFullName** control.
   b. On the *Report Design Tools Format* tab, in the *Control Formatting* group, click the **Shape Outline** button and select **Transparent.**
   c. Save the report and check your work in Report view.
10. Add grouping to the report to group records by the patient's ID.
    a. Switch back to Design view.
    b. On the *Report Design Tools Design* tab, in the *Grouping & Totals* group, click the **Group & Sort** button.
    c. In the *Group, Sort, and Total* pane, click **Add a Group,** and then click **PatientID.**
11. Hide the Group Header section for each group.
    a. In the *Group, Sort, and Total* pane, click the **More** button.
    b. Click **with a header section,** and select **without a header section.**
12. Add a calculated control to the group footer for each group to calculate the number of visits for each patient.
    a. In the *Group, Sort, and Total* pane, click **without a footer section** and select **with a footer section.**
    b. Hide the *Group, Sort, and Total* pane by clicking the **Group & Sort** button again.
    c. On the *Report Design Tools Design* tab, in the *Controls* group, click the **Text Box** button in the *Controls* gallery. If the *Controls* gallery is not visible, click the **Controls** button.
    d. Click in the **PatientID Footer** section below the *PatientState* control at the far right side of the report.
    e. Click in the new unbound text control and type: **=COUNT([DateOfVisit])**
    f. Click in the label control and type: **Visits:**
13. Change the caption for the calculated control so you can identify it easily.
    a. Click the unbound text control you used for the calculated control.
    b. On the *Report Design Tools Design* tab, in the *Tools* group, click the **Property Sheet** button to open the Property Sheet.

c. On the Property Sheet *Other* tab, click in the **Name** property box, and replace the default control name with: `CountVisits`

d. Save the report and switch to Report view to check your work.

14. Use conditional formatting to highlight users who have visited the clinic at least five times.

    a. Switch to Layout view.

    b. Click any box that displays the number of visits calculation in the Group Footer sections.

    c. On the *Report Layout Tools Format* tab, in the *Control Formatting* group, click the **Conditional Formatting** button.

    d. Verify that **CountVisits** is selected in the *Show formatting rules for:* box at the top of the Conditional Formatting Rules Manager.

    e. Click the **New Rule** button.

    f. Verify that **Check values in the current record or use an expression** is selected.

    g. In the *Format cells only where the:* section, verify that **Field Value Is:** is selected in the first box.

    h. Expand the second box and select **greater than or equal to**.

    i. In the third box, type: **5**

    j. In the *Preview* section, click the **Bold** button.

    k. Expand the **Font Color** palette, and click **Red** (the second color from the left in the last row).

    l. Click **OK**.

    m. Click **OK** again to close the Conditional Formatting Rules Manager.

    n. Review the highlighted values, and then save the report.

15. Hide the repeated values in the **PatientID** field.

    a. Switch back to Design view.

    b. Display the Property Sheet if you closed it previously.

    c. Expand the list at the top of the Property Sheet and select **PatientID**.

    d. On the Property Sheet *Format* tab, scroll to the bottom and find the **Hide Duplicates** property. Click in the box, and then expand the list and select **Yes**.

    e. Save the report.

    f. Switch to Report view to check your work, and then close the *PatientVisitsAnalysis* report.

16. Add the *PatientVisitsAnalysis* report as a subreport in the *Patient* Report.

    a. Open the **Patient** report in Design view.

    b. Increase the height of the **Detail** section by clicking the bottom border of the section and dragging down to the first **1-inch** mark on the vertical ruler.

    c. On the *Report Design Tools Design* tab, in the *Controls* group, expand the *Controls* gallery and click the **Subform/Subreport** button. If the *Controls* gallery is not visible, click the **Controls** button.

    d. Click in the Detail section below the *PatientID* control at the **.5-inch** mark on the vertical ruler.

    e. In the SubReport Wizard, click the **Use an existing report or form** radio button and verify that the **PatientVisitsAnalysis** report is selected. Click **Next**.

    f. To link the reports using the *PatientID* field, verify that **Show PatientVisits for each record in Patient using PatientID** is selected. Click **Next**.

    g. Click **Finish**.

    h. Save the report.

    i. Switch to report view to check your work. Notice that the subreport is missing the column labels.

17. Display the subreport Page Header section.

    a. Switch back to Design view.

    b. If necessary, click the subreport control to select it.

    c. On the *Report Design Tools Design* tab, in the *Tools* group, click the **Property Sheet** button to open the Property Sheet.

    d. Verify that **PatientVisitsAnalysis** is selected in the box at the top of the Property Sheet.

    e. On the Property Sheet *Format* tab, find the **Show Page Header and Page Footer** property at the end of the properties list. Click in the box, and then expand the list and select **Yes**.

    f. Close the Property Sheet, and then switch to Report view to check your work.

    g. Save and close the report.

18. Close the database and exit Access.

skill review 7.2

In this project you will work with the database for eMusic Sales, which sells digital music online. You will create a report from scratch in Design view to analyze music sales by genre, including adding calculated controls, grouping, conditional formatting, and a subreport from a query.

Skills needed to complete this project:
- Working with a Report in Design View (Skill 7.1)
- Understanding Report Sections (Skill 7.2)
- Arranging Controls in a Report (Skill 7.3)
- Adding Calculated Controls to a Report (Skill 7.4)
- Adding Report Grouping in Design View (Skill 7.5)
- Working with Group Headers and Footers (Skill 7.6)
- Hiding Repeated Values in a Report (Skill 7.7)
- Adding a Subreport Based on a Table or Query (Skill 7.10)
- Applying Conditional Formatting to a Report (Skill 7.11)

1. Open the start file **AC2013-SkillReview-7-2** and resave the file as:
   `[your initials]AC-SkillReview-7-2`

2. If necessary, enable active content by clicking the **Enable Content** button in the Message Bar.

3. Create a new blank report in Design view.

    a. On the *Create* tab, in the *Reports* group, click the *Report Design* button.

    b. Save the report as: `MusicCatalog`

4. Add the *MusicCatalog* query as the report record source.
   a. On the *Report Design Tools Design* tab, in the *Tools* group, click the **Property Sheet** button to open the Property Sheet. Verify that *Report* is selected in the box at the top of the Property Sheet.
   b. On the Property Sheet *Data* tab, in the Record Source property box, click the arrow to extend the list, and select **MusicCatalog.**
   c. Close the Property Sheet.
5. Add labels to the Detail section.
   a. On the *Report Design Tools Design* tab, in the *Controls* group, click the **Label** button in the *Controls* gallery. If the *Controls* gallery is not visible, click the **Controls** button.
   b. Click in the Detail section at the **.5-inch** mark on the horizontal ruler. The label should be placed as close to the top of the Detail section as possible.
   c. Type `Genre Description` and press [←Enter].
   d. Place another label in the Detail section at the **2-inch** mark on the horizontal ruler. The label should be placed as close to the top of the Detail section as possible.
   e. Type `Item Number` and press [←Enter].
   f. Add a third label to the Detail section to the right of the *Item Number* label at the **3.5-inch** mark on the horizontal ruler. Type `Title` and press [←Enter].
6. Add fields to the report below their labels. Don't worry about exact placement or size. You will align and adjust the size of the controls later. Add the fields without labels—the labels already exist in the report.
   a. On the *Report Design Tools Design* tab, in the *Tools* group, click the **Add Existing Fields** button to open the Field List.
   b. Press [Ctrl] and drag the **GenreDescription** field from the Field List to the far left side of the Detail section, below the *Genre Description* label.
   c. Press [Ctrl] and drag the **ItemNumber** field from the Field List to the Detail section of the report below the *Item Number* label.
   d. Press [Ctrl] and drag the **Title** field from the Field List to the Detail section of the report below the *Title* label.
   e. Close the Field List.
7. Align the labels along the top.
   a. Click the **Genre Description** label, and then hold [↑Shift] and click the other labels to select them.
   b. On the *Report Design Tools Arrange* tab, in the *Sizing & Ordering* group, click the **Align** button and select **Top**.
8. Align the bound controls.
   a. Click the **GenreDescription** bound text control, and then hold [↑Shift] and click the other bound text controls to select them.
   b. On the *Report Design Tools Arrange* tab, in the *Sizing & Ordering* group, click the **Align** button and select **Top**.
9. Align the bound text controls with their labels.
   a. Click the **Genre Description** label. Hold [↑Shift] and click the **GenreDescription** bound text control. On the *Report Design Tools Arrange* tab, in the *Sizing & Ordering* group, click the **Align** button, and select **Left**.
   b. Click the **Item Number** label. Hold [↑Shift] and click the **Item Number** bound text control. On the *Report Design Tools Arrange* tab, in the *Sizing & Ordering* group, click the **Align** button and select **Left**.

- c. Click the **Title** label. Hold ⇧Shift and click the **Title** bound text control. On the *Report Design Tools Arrange* tab, in the *Sizing & Ordering* group, click the **Align** button and select **Left.**
- d. Switch to Layout view to check your work.

10. From Layout view, increase the width of the **Title** control so the entire title *Shoo Fly, Don't Bother Me* is visible.
    - a. Click the bound text control below the *Title* label. Only part of the title should be visible.
    - b. Move the cursor to the right side of the control, and, when it changes to the double arrow, click and drag to the right until the entire title is visible.
    - c. Switch back to Design view and observe how Access changed the height of the Detail section to just fit the controls.

11. Display the Report Header and Report Footer sections and add a calculated control to count the number of titles.
    - a. First, hide the Page Header/Footer as you are not using those sections. Right-click in an empty area of the Detail section, and select **Page Header/Footer** to remove the highlight.
    - b. Right-click in an empty area of the Detail section and select **Report Header/Footer.**
    - c. On the *Report Design Tools Design* tab, in the *Controls* group, click the **Text Box** button in the *Controls* gallery. If the *Controls* gallery is not visible, click the **Controls** button.
    - d. Click in the **Report Footer** section below the *Title* control.
    - e. Click in the new unbound text control and type: `=COUNT([Title])`
    - f. Click in the label control and change the default text to: `Titles:`

12. Align the calculated control with the *Title* control.
    - a. In the Detail section, click the **Title** control. Hold ⇧Shift and click the **calculated control** in the Report Footer section.
    - b. On the *Report Design Tools Arrange* tab, in the *Sizing & Ordering* group, click the **Align** button and select **Right.**

13. Adjust the size of the *Titles:* label so it lines up under the *Title* control.
    - a. Click the **Titles:** label in the report footer to select it.
    - b. Move the cursor to the right side of the label. When the cursor changes to the double arrow, click and drag to the right all the way to the calculated control.
    - c. Move the cursor to the left side of the label. When the cursor changes to the double arrow, click and drag to the right to the **3.5-inch** mark on the horizontal ruler.
    - d. Check your work in Report view. Scroll to the bottom of the report to view the calculated control.
    - e. If the *Title* label, *Title* control, and *Titles:* label do not appear aligned, switch back to Design view, select all three controls and left-align them.

14. Add grouping to the report by genre.
    - a. Switch back to Design view.
    - b. On the *Report Design Tools Design* tab, in the *Grouping & Totals* group, click the **Group & Sort** button.
    - c. In the *Group, Sort, and Total* pane, click **Add a Group,** and then click **GenreDescription.**
    - d. Hide the *Group, Sort, and Total* pane by clicking the **Group & Sort** button again.

15. Copy the label and calculated control from the Report Footer section and paste them into the group header.
    a. In the Report Footer section, click the calculated control. Press Ctrl + C to copy it. When you copy the control, its label is also copied.
    b. Click in the **GenreDescription Header** section, and press Ctrl + V.
    c. Access automatically pastes the label and calculated control at the left side of the group footer.
    d. Click in the label for the calculated control, and change the text to:
       `# of titles in genre:`
    e. Right-align the calculated control in the group header with the **Item Number** bound text control in the Detail section.
16. Change the caption for the calculated control in the group header so you can identify it easily.
    a. Click any empty area of the report to deselect the controls. Click the calculated control in the GenreDescription Header section. Verify that this is the only control you have selected.
    b. On the *Report Design Tools Design* tab, in the *Tools* group, click the **Property Sheet** button to open the Property Sheet.
    c. On the Property Sheet *Other* tab, click in the Name property box, and replace the default control name with: `GrpHdrCalculation`
17. Hide the repeated values in the GenreDescription field.
    a. Expand the list at the top of the Property Sheet and select **GenreDescription**.
    b. On the Property Sheet *Format* tab, scroll to the bottom and find the **Hide Duplicates** property. Click in the box, and then expand the list and select **Yes**.
    c. Close the Property Sheet.
    d. Save the report.
    e. Switch to Report view to check your work.
18. Delete the Genre Description label.
    a. Switch back to Design view.
    b. Click the **Genre Description** label (not the bound text control), and press Delete.
19. Remove the banding from the report and change the background color of the group header to help the groups stand out in the report.
    a. Click any empty area in the **Detail** section. Be careful not to select an individual control.
    b. On the *Report Design Tools Format* tab, in the *Background* group, click the **Alternate Row Color** button and select **No Color.**
    c. Click any empty area in the **GenreDescription Header** section. Be careful not to select the label or calculated control.
    d. On the *Report Design Tools Format* tab, in the *Background* group, click the **Alternate Row Color** button and select **No Color.**
    e. On the *Report Design Tools Format* tab, in the *Control Formatting* group, click the **Shape Fill** button and select **Blue-Gray, Text 2, Lighter 40%.** It is the fourth color from the left in the fourth row of theme colors in the color palette.
    f. In the GenreDescription Header section, click the label control to select it.
    g. On the *Report Design Tools Format* tab, in the *Font* group, click the **Font Color** button and select **White, Background 1.** It is the first color at the left in the first row of theme colors in the color palette.
    h. Save the report. Switch to Report view to check your work.

20. Use conditional formatting to highlight genres with more than three titles.
    a. Switch to Layout view.
    b. Click any box that displays the number of titles calculation in the Group Header sections.
    c. On the *Report Layout Tools Format* tab, in the *Control Formatting* group, click the **Conditional Formatting** button.
    d. Verify that **GrpHdrCalculation** is selected in the *Show formatting rules for:* box at the top of the Conditional Formatting Rules Manager.
    e. Click the **New Rule** button.
    f. Verify that **Check values in the current record or use an expression** is selected.
    g. In the *Format cells only where the:* section, verify that **Field Value Is:** is selected in the first box.
    h. Expand the second box and select **greater than**.
    i. In the third box, type: **3**
    j. In the *Preview* section, click the **Bold** button.
    k. Expand the **Font Color** palette, and click **Green** (the sixth color from the left in the last row).
    l. Click **OK**.
    m. Click **OK** again to close the Conditional Formatting Rules Manager.
    n. Scroll through the report and review the highlighted values, and then save the report.

21. Add the *SalesDetails* query as a subreport.
    a. Switch back to Design view.
    b. Increase the height of the **Detail** section by clicking the bottom border of the section and dragging down so you have enough room to add the subreport.
    c. On the *Report Design Tools Design* tab, in the *Controls* group, expand the *Controls* gallery and click the **Subform/Subreport** button. If the *Controls* gallery is not visible, click the **Controls** button.
    d. Click in the Detail section below the *GenreDescription* control.
    e. In the SubReport Wizard, **Use existing tables and queries** is selected by default. Click **Next**.
    f. Expand the **Tables/Queries** list and select **Query: SalesDetails**.
    g. Click the **>>** button to add all the fields from the query. Click **Next**.
    h. To link the query and report using values in the *ItemNumber* field, verify that **Show SalesDetails for each record in MusicCatalog using ItemNumber** is selected. Click **Next**.
    i. Change the subreport name to: `SalesDetailsSubreport`
    j. Click **Finish**.
    k. Click the **SalesDetailsSubreport** label and press (Delete) to delete it.
    l. Save the report.
    m. Switch to Report view to check your work.

22. Adjust the size and width of the *Price* and *Quantity* controls.
    a. Switch back to Design view.
    b. Click the subreport control to select it. On the *Report Design Tools Design* tab, in the *Tools* group, click the **Subreport in New Window** button to open the subreport in a new tab.
    c. Click the **Price label** in the Report Header section. Press (↑ Shift) and click the **Price control** in the Detail section.

d. Move the cursor to the right side of the **Price label** control. When the cursor changes to the double arrow, click and drag to the left to the **7-inch** mark on the horizontal ruler.

e. Click the **Quantity label** in the Report Header section. Press (↑ Shift) and click the **Quantity control** in the Detail section.

f. Move the cursor to the left side of the **Quantity label** control. When the cursor changes to the double arrow, click and drag to the left until the **Quantity label** text is fully visible.

23. Add a calculated control to the subreport Report Footer section.

    a. Click the bottom border of the Report Footer section and drag down to the **.5-inch** mark on the vertical ruler to make the Report Footer section taller.

    b. On the *Report Design Tools Design* tab, in the *Controls* group, click the **Text Box** button in the *Controls* gallery. If the *Controls* gallery is not visible, click the **Controls** button.

    c. Click in the **Report Footer** section at the **7-inch** mark on the horizontal ruler.

    d. Click in the new unbound text control and type: `=SUM([Price]*[Quantity])`

    e. Click in the label control and replace the default text with: `Total Sales:`

    f. Switch to Report view and scroll to the bottom to see the calculated control. (*Hint:* If you see an error, you probably placed the calculated control in the Page Footer section instead of the Report Footer section.)

    g. Save and close the subreport.

    h. Switch to Report view to see the results of the subreport changes in the main report. Observe that the subreport calculated control calculates the total price for each title in the report.

    i. Save and close the report.

24. Close the database and exit Access.

challenge yourself 7.3

In this project you will work with the billing database for Commonwealth Doctors Group. You will create a report showing unpaid balances for each patient. You will first create the *Unpaid-Invoices* report from scratch to calculate the total amount due for each patient. This report will include grouping, a calculated control in the group header, and conditional formatting with data bars. Then you will add this new report as a subreport in the *PatientBilling* report.

Review in Report view as you work through the project, and be sure to save often.

Skills needed to complete this project:

- Working with a Report in Design View (Skill 7.1)
- Understanding Report Sections (Skill 7.2)
- Arranging Controls in a Report (Skill 7.3)
- Applying Conditional Formatting to a Report (Skill 7.11)
- Adding Report Grouping in Design View (Skill 7.5)
- Hiding Repeated Values in a Report (Skill 7.7)
- Adding Calculated Controls to a Report (Skill 7.4)
- Adding a Subreport Based on a Report (Skill 7.8)
- Displaying the Subreport Page Header (Skill 7.9)

1. Open the start file **AC2013-Challenge-Yourself 7-3** and resave the file as: `[your initials]AC-ChallengeYourself-7-3`
2. If necessary, enable active content by clicking the **Enable Content** button in the Message Bar.
3. Create a new report from scratch in Design view. Name the report: `UnpaidInvoices`
4. Assign the **PatientUnpaidInvoices** query as the record source for the report.
5. Create the report with the bound text controls in the Detail section and labels in the Page Header section. The bound text controls should be placed at the top of the Detail section.
   a. Add a bound text control for the **PatientID** field in the Detail section at the **.5-inch** mark on the horizontal ruler.
   b. Add a label with the text `ID` in the Page Header section at the **.5-inch** mark on the horizontal ruler.
   c. Add a bound text control for the **DateOfVisit** field in the Detail section at the **2-inch** mark on the horizontal ruler.
   d. Add a label with the text `Date` in the Page Header section at the **2-inch** mark on the horizontal ruler.
   e. Add a bound text control for the **InvoiceAmount** field in the Detail section at the **3.5-inch** mark on the horizontal ruler.
   f. Add a label with the text `Amount Due` in the Page Header section at the **3.5-inch** mark on the horizontal ruler.
   g. Align the controls in each section at the **top**.
   h. Align each bound text control with its label at the **left**.
   i. Shorten the Detail section up to the **.5-inch** mark on the vertical ruler.
6. Add conditional formatting to compare the values in the **InvoiceAmount** field.
   a. Use the conditional formatting option that uses **data bars** to compare the values in each record.
   b. Change the default data bar color to **red**—the second color from the left in the last row of the color palette.
7. Group the report by the **PatientID** field.
8. Hide duplicate values in the **PatientID** field.
9. Add a calculated control to the group footer to calculate the total due for each patient.
   a. Hide the group header, and display the group footer.
   b. Place the calculated control at the very top of the group footer, flush against the top border.
   c. The calculated control should use this formula: `=SUM([InvoiceAmount])`
   d. Change the label to: `Total Due:`
   e. Left-align the calculated control with the **InvoiceAmount** control in the Detail section.
10. Save and close the **UnpaidInvoices** report.
11. Open the **PatientBilling** report in Design view and add the **UnpaidInvoices** report as a subreport.
    a. Place the subreport in the Detail section below the *PatientAddress* control at the **1-inch** mark on the vertical ruler.
    b. Use the **PatientID** field to link the main report and the subreport.
    c. Do not change the name of the subreport.
    d. Delete the subreport label.

12. Display the Page Header section in the subreport.
13. Review your work in Report view, and then save and close the **PatientBilling** report.
14. Close the database and exit Access.

challenge yourself 7.4

In this project you will create a report from scratch to track online auction sales. You will first create the main report to display the auction categories. Then you will add a subreport based on the *Item* table to display the items in each category. You will create a calculated control to calculate the profit or loss on each sale. You will apply conditional formatting to the calculated control to display losses in bold red text.

Skills needed to complete this project:

- Working with a Report in Design View (Skill 7.1)
- Understanding Report Sections (Skill 7.2)
- Arranging Controls in a Report (Skill 7.3)
- Adding a Subreport Based on a Table or Query (Skill 7.10)
- Adding Calculated Controls to a Report (Skill 7.4)
- Applying Conditional Formatting to a Report (Skill 7.11)

1. Open the start file **AC2013-ChallengeYourself-7-4** and resave the file as: `[your initials]AC-ChallengeYourself-7-4`
2. If necessary, enable active content by clicking the **Enable Content** button in the Message Bar.
3. Create a new report from scratch in Design view. Name the report: `CompletedSales`
4. Assign the **ItemCategory** table as the record source for the report.
5. Create the report with the bound text controls in the Detail section and labels in the Page Header section. The bound text controls should be placed at the top of the Detail section.
    a. Add a bound text control for the **ItemCategoryCode** field in the Detail section at the **.5-inch** mark on the horizontal ruler.
    b. Add a label with the text `Category Code` in the Page Header section at the **.5-inch** mark on the horizontal ruler.
    c. Add a bound text control for the **ItemCategoryDescription** field in the Detail section at the **2-inch** mark on the horizontal ruler.
    d. Add a label with the text `Category Description` in the Page Header section at the **2-inch** mark on the horizontal ruler.
    e. Align the controls in each section at the **top**.
    f. Align each bound text control with its label at the **left**.
    g. Shorten the Detail section up to the **.5-inch** mark on the vertical ruler.
6. Add a subreport to the **CompletedSales** report.
    a. Place the subreport in the Detail section just below the *ItemCategoryID* control.
    b. Include all the fields from the **Item** table.
    c. Use the **ItemCategoryCode** field to link the main report and the subreport.
    d. Name the subreport: `ItemSalesSubreport`
    e. Delete the subreport label.

7. Open the subreport in a new tab to work with its layout.
   a. Shorten the **ItemName** controls to end at the **3.5-inch** mark on the horizontal ruler.
   b. Move the **MyCost** controls to just next to the **ItemName** controls.
   c. Shorten the **MyCost** controls to end at the **4.5-inch** mark on the horizontal ruler.
   d. Move the **AuctionSellingPrice** controls to just next to the **MyCost** controls.
   e. Shorten the **AuctionSellingPrice** controls to end at the **5.75-inch** mark on the horizontal ruler.
   f. If you need to, realign the controls in each section along the top and realign the bound text controls with their labels along the left.
8. Add a calculated control to calculate the profit or loss for each sale.
   a. Add the calculated control without a label to the Detail section at the **6-inch** mark on the horizontal ruler.
   b. Use the formula: `=[AuctionSellingPrice]-[MyCost]`
   c. Add a label to the Report Header section at the **6-inch** mark on the horizontal ruler. Use the text: `Profit/Loss`
   d. Align the calculated control at the **top** with the other controls in the Detail section.
   e. Align the label at the **top** with the other labels in the Report Header section.
   f. Align the *Profit/Loss* label and the calculated control at the **left**.
9. Add conditional formatting to the calculated control to display any values **less than 0** in **bold, red** text. Red is the second color from the left in the last row of the color palette.
10. If you've opened the subreport in a new window, save the report, and close it.
11. Review the **CompletedSales** report in Report view, and then save and close the report.
12. Close the database and exit Access.

on your own 7.5

In this project you will continue working with the technical support database you created on your own in Chapters 5–6. You may work with the sample database provided or continue working with your solution file from the Chapter 5 or Chapter 6 *On Your Own* project. In the sample file, we have replaced the linked table from Chapter 5 with a regular table in the database. We have also added additional sample projects and issues.

Skills needed to complete this project:
- Working with a Report in Design View (Skill 7.1)
- Understanding Report Sections (Skill 7.2)
- Arranging Controls in a Report (Skill 7.3)
- Adding Calculated Controls to a Report (Skill 7.4)
- Adding Report Grouping in Design View (Skill 7.5)
- Working with Group Headers and Footers (Skill 7.6)
- Adding a Subreport Based on a Table or Query (Skill 7.10)
- Applying Conditional Formatting to a Report (Skill 7.11)

1. Open the start file **AC2013-OnYourOwn-7-5** or open your solution file from the Chapter 6 *On Your Own* project and resave the file as:
   `[your initials]AC-OnYourOwn-7-5`

2. If necessary, enable active content by clicking the **Enable Content** button in the Message Bar.
3. Create a new report from scratch using the **Projects** table as the record source.
4. Add the fields you want in the report. Be sure to include labels, either in the Detail section or in the Page Header section.
5. Align the controls.
6. Adjust the height of the Detail section as appropriate.
7. Add a subreport based on the *Issues* table or a query that you create to limit the records by criteria such as value in the *Status* field or date in the *DueDate* field.
8. Be sure to check in Report view or Layout view to make sure all the data are visible in the subreport. (*Hint:* If some of the fields in the report have long text descriptions, you can make the bound text control taller and the text will wrap to multiple lines when necessary.)
9. Modify the placement of controls in the subreport as necessary.
10. Add grouping to the subreport on *Status, Priority, Category,* or another field.
11. Add a calculated control to the group footer to count the number of issues in the group. (*Hint:* Use the COUNT function.)
12. Add conditional formatting to the subreport to identify issues that are overdue. (*Hint:* Use the *DueDate* field and compare to the function **Now()**—which returns today's date.)
13. When you are satisfied with the subreport, save and close it.
14. Review the subreport in the main report, and then save and close the main report.
15. Close the database and exit Access.

fix it 7.6

In this project, you will continue helping the animal rescue organization from Chapter 6. The organization's trusty volunteers have created a report to summarize all the pet adoptions, including a subreport to display the adoption details for each pet. As usual, they've made a few mistakes and need your help.

Test your work as you go, and save often!

Skills needed to complete this project:
- Working with a Report in Design View (Skill 7.1)
- Arranging Controls in a Report (Skill 7.3)
- Understanding Report Sections (Skill 7.2)
- Adding Calculated Controls to a Report (Skill 7.4)
- Working with Group Headers and Footers (Skill 7.6)
- Hiding Repeated Values in a Report (Skill 7.7)
- Applying Conditional Formatting to a Report (Skill 7.11)
- Adding a Subreport Based on a Table or Query (Skill 7.10)

1. Open the start file **AC2013-FixIt-7-6** and resave the file as:
   `[your initials]AC-FixIt-7-6`
2. If necessary, enable active content by clicking the **Enable Content** button in the Message Bar.

3. Open the **Adoptions** report in Report view and observe that it includes every pet in the database, not just those who have been adopted. The report currently uses the *Pets* table as the record source, but it should use the **AdoptedPets** query instead. Please fix it.
4. Fix the alignment and placement problems with the **Breed** and **AgeInMonths** controls and their labels.
5. In the *Adoptions* report, there is a calculated control to total the adoption fees, but it is in the wrong section and displays an error at the end of the report in Report view. Move the label and calculated control to the correct report section to sum all the adoption fees in the report.
6. Align the calculated control with the **AdoptionFee** control at the right side. (*Hint:* If you select both the label and the calculated control when you align the controls, the label will move with the calculated control.)
7. The rescue organization would also like the report to include the total adoption fees for each type of pet. They already added the correct grouping to the *Adoptions* report, but they don't understand why the calculated control doesn't appear in each group. Copy and paste the label and calculated control to the correct section to calculate the total for each group. Again, align the calculated control with the **AdoptionFee** control at the right side.
8. The group headers are not being used, so you should hide them.
9. They don't like the way Cat and Dog are repeated in every record in the groups. Fix the report so Cat and Dog appear only once, in the first record of each group.
10. Someone applied conditional formatting to the **AdoptionFee** control, but the organization doesn't like it. Delete the conditional formatting rule.
11. In the subreport, the **AdoptionDate** control is missing. Please add the bound text control (without a label), size it to match the width of the label, and align it properly. (*Hint:* Open the subreport in a new window to make it easier to work with.)
12. Review your changes in Report view, and then save and close all open database objects.
13. Close the database and exit Access.

chapter 8

Exploring Advanced Queries and Macros

In this chapter, you will learn the following skills:

- Create action queries (update, make table, delete, and append)
- Understand how join properties affect query results
- Use crosstab queries and total queries to summarize data
- Work in SQL view
- Create stand-alone macros

Skill 8.1 Understanding Action Queries
Skill 8.2 Updating Records through a Query
Skill 8.3 Creating a New Table through a Query
Skill 8.4 Deleting Records through a Query
Skill 8.5 Moving Records through a Query
Skill 8.6 Setting Join Properties in a Query
Skill 8.7 Adding Totals to a Query
Skill 8.8 Creating a Crosstab Query
Skill 8.9 Modifying a Query in SQL View
Skill 8.10 Creating a Stand-Alone Macro

introduction

This chapter expands on the basic query skills introduced in Chapter 4. You will create action queries including update, make table, delete, and append queries. You will control which records are included in the query results by manipulating the table join properties. You will create queries that summarize data. You will also learn about SQL—the language of queries. The chapter finishes with an overview of working with stand-alone macros. Most of the *Let Me Try* exercises in this chapter use the AC8-Appointments database. You can keep the database open while you work in this chapter, opening and closing database objects as required for each *Let Me Try*.

Skill 8.1 Understanding Action Queries

Recall that select queries display data from one or more related tables or queries. While select queries may be complex and include multiple criteria and calculated fields, they do not affect the data in the underlying table(s). However, there are special types of queries that *do* modify table data. **Action queries** perform an action on the records that meet the query specifications. There are four types of action queries:

- **Update** queries change (update) records that match the query criteria.
- **Make Table** queries create (make) a new table by copying records that meet the query criteria and pasting them into a new table.
- **Delete** queries remove (delete) records that match the query criteria.
- **Append** queries add (append) records to an existing table by copying records that meet the query criteria and pasting them into the specified table.

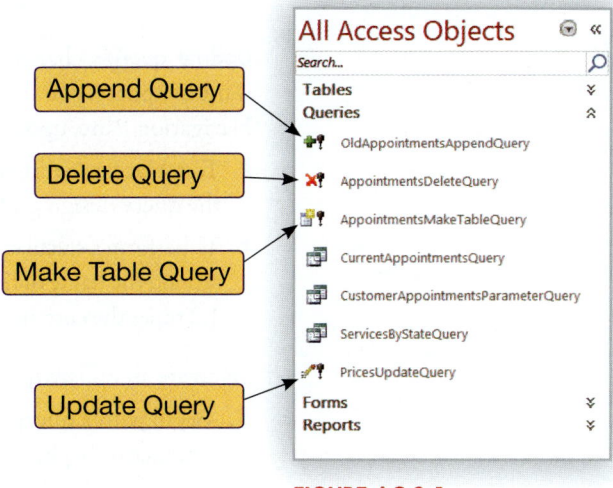

FIGURE AC 8.1

In the Navigation Pane, action queries are identified by special icons as shown in Figure AC 8.1.

Double-clicking an action query in the Navigation Pane will cause an irrevocable action to be taken. Access always warns you before running the query, though, so you have the opportunity to cancel if you did not intend to run the query but wanted to edit it instead.

To edit an action query, right-click the query in the Navigation Pane, and select **Design View**.

tips & tricks

When working with action queries, you should first create a select query and verify that the query returns the dataset you want. You cannot undo an action query once you run it.

let me try

Open the data file **AC8-AppointmentsCompleted** and try this skill on your own:

1. If necessary, expand the **Navigation Pane** and expand the **Queries** group.
2. Identify each action query in the Navigation Pane by its icon.
3. Open one of the action queries in Design view to edit it. Close the query without making any changes.
4. Close the database.

Skill 8.2 Updating Records through a Query

Update queries change (update) records that match the query criteria. For each field you want to update, you specify the text or expression to use when updating the field data. In the Navigation Pane, update queries are identified by this icon:

- To replace one text value with another, type the new text value in the *Update To* row in the query design grid.
- To perform a calculation based on the value of a field, type the expression, including brackets around the name of the field. For example, [Price]*1.2 would change the values in the field to 1.2 times the current value of the *Price* field (in other words, an increase of 20%).

To create an update query:

1. Begin with a query that includes only the records you want to update. It is a good practice to begin with a select query and verify that the query returns the records you want to update before creating and running the update query.

2. Change the query type to an update query. From Design view, on the *Query Tools Design* tab, in the *Query Type* group, click the **Update** button.

3. Notice that the query design grid now includes a new row, *Update To*. This is where you enter the update expression. You can enter a string to replace a text field or enter an expression to change the value of a current field.

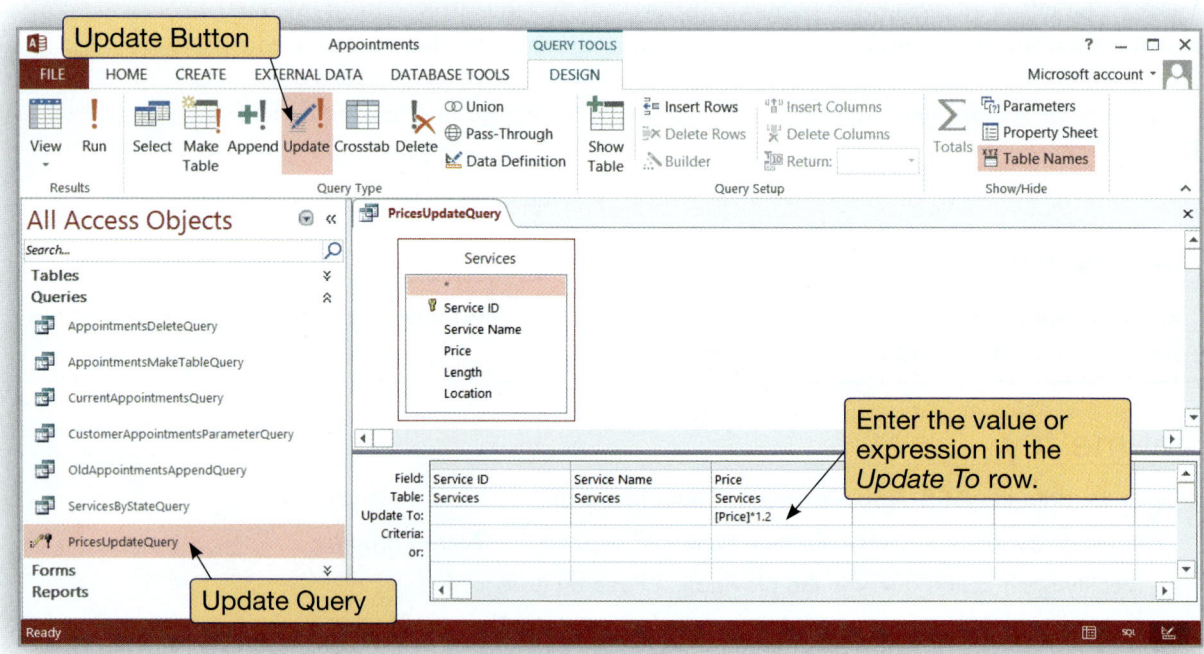

FIGURE AC 8.2

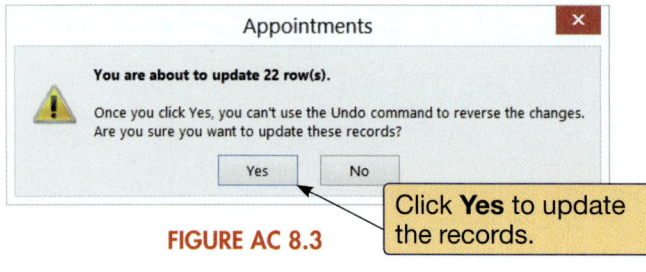

FIGURE AC 8.3

4. On the *Query Tools Design* tab, in the *Results* group, click the **Run** button.

5. Access will warn you that you are about to update records and that you cannot undo the changes. Click **Yes** to apply the update.

Once you change the query type to update, switching to Datasheet view shows you only the current values in the field that is about to be updated. Access will not actually update the values until you *run* the query. Figure AC 8.4 shows Datasheet view for the query results before and after running the update query.

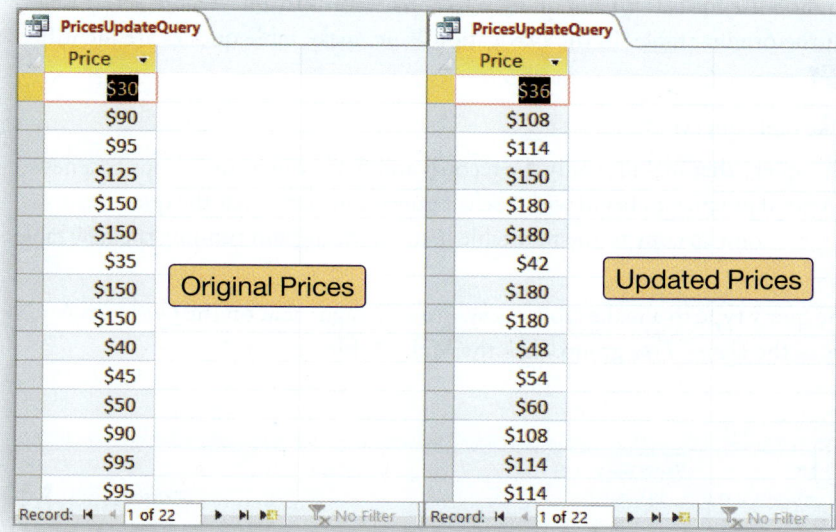

FIGURE AC 8.4

tips & tricks

Be careful! When you run an update query, you can't undo the action. The matching records will be changed permanently (even if you do not save the changes to the query). Consider making a backup copy of the table or using a make table query to create an archive of the records before you change them.

let me try

If the database is not already open, open the data file **AC8-Appointments** and try this skill on your own:

1. Open the **PricesUpdateQuery** query in Design view.
2. Change the query to an **update** query.
3. Update the value of the **Price** field by 20%. Use the expression: `[Price]*1.2`
4. Review the query results by switching to Datasheet view, and then switch back to Design view. Be careful not to run the query yet.
5. Now run the query. Access should warn you that you are about to update 22 records.
6. Switch to Datasheet view to review the query results. The first price in the list should have been updated to $36.
7. Save and close the query.

skill 8.2 Updating Records through a Query

Skill 8.3 Creating a New Table through a Query

Make table queries create (make) a new table by copying records that meet the query criteria and pasting them into a new table. Records are *copied* from the original table. No records are deleted. A common use for this type of query is to copy records to a new table before deleting them from the original table. In the Navigation Pane, make table queries are identified by this icon:

To create a make table query:

1. Begin with a query that includes only the records and fields you want to copy to a new table. It is a good practice to begin with a select query and verify that the query returns the records you want to copy to the new table before creating and running the new table query.

2. Change the query type to a make table query. From Design view, on the *Query Tools Design* tab, in the *Query Type* group, click the **Make Table** button.

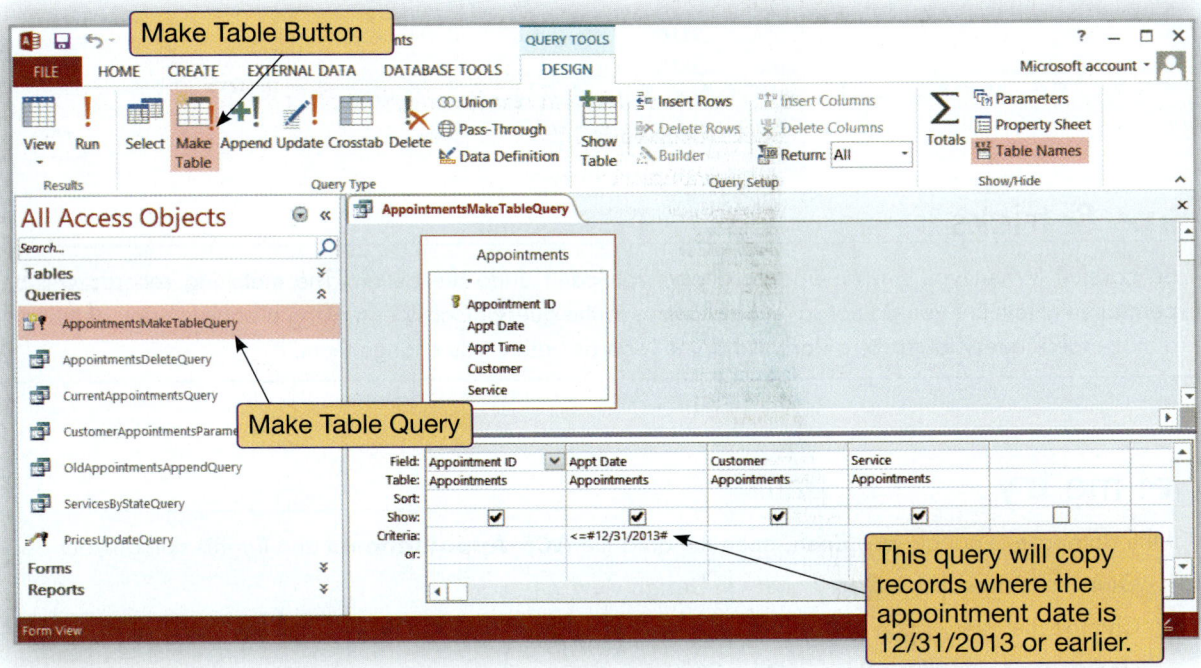

FIGURE AC 8.5

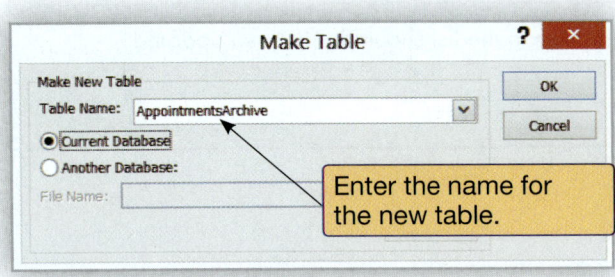

FIGURE AC 8.6

3. The *Make Table* dialog opens. Type a name for the new table. Click **OK**.

4. On the *Query Tools Design* tab, in the *Results* group, click the **Run** button. Switching to Datasheet view will show you the records that meet the query criteria, but it won't run the make table query.

5. Access will warn you that you are about to paste records into a new table and that you cannot undo the changes. Click **Yes** to complete the action.

Open the new table and verify the records were copied. The new table does not have a primary key or any relationships to other tables.

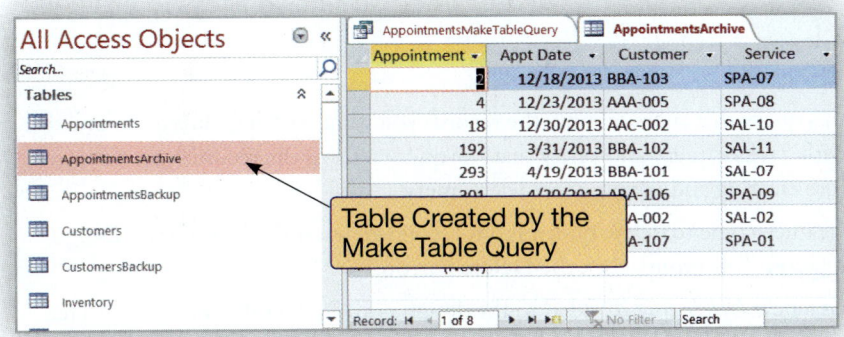

FIGURE AC 8.7

When you are finished copying the records to the new table, consider changing the query back to a select query before saving it. If you try to run the same query again as a make table query, Access will delete the table and replace it with the new table created by running the query again.

tips & tricks

If a field in the query is a lookup field displaying multiple fields from another table or query, the make table query includes only the foreign key field in the new table. To include all data in the new table, add fields to the query from the other tables. Make table queries can combine fields from multiple tables.

tell me more

To create the new table in another database:

1. In the *Make Table* dialog, select the **Another Database** radio button.
2. Click the **Browse** button and navigate to the database in which you want to create the new table.
3. Click **OK**.
4. Run the query. Click **Yes** when Access displays the warning that you will not be able to undo this action.

let me try

If the database is not already open, open the data file **AC8-Appointments** and try this skill on your own:

1. Open the **AppointmentsMakeTableQuery** query in Design view.
2. Note the criteria in the *Appt Date* field. Switch to Datasheet view to review the query results.
3. Switch back to Design view and change the query to a **make table** query.
4. Name the new table: `AppointmentsArchive`
5. Run the query. Access should warn you that you are about to paste 8 rows into a new table.
6. Save and close the query.
7. Open the new **AppointmentsArchive** table and review the records. (*Hint:* There should be eight records in the table.) Close the table.

skill 8.3 Creating a New Table through a Query

Skill 8.4 Deleting Records through a Query

Delete queries remove (delete) records that match the query criteria. This type of query can be useful for purging outdated records. In the Navigation Pane, delete queries are identified by this icon: ✖!

To create a delete query:

1. Begin with a query that includes only the records you want to delete. It is good practice to begin with a select query and verify that the query returns the records you want to delete before creating and running the delete query.

2. Change the query type to delete query. From Design view, on the *Query Tools Design* tab, in the *Query Type* group, click the **Delete** button.

3. Notice that a new *Delete* row is added to the design grid. By default, *Where* is selected for the field for which you have specified criteria. This means that Access will delete records *where* data in this field meet the criteria.

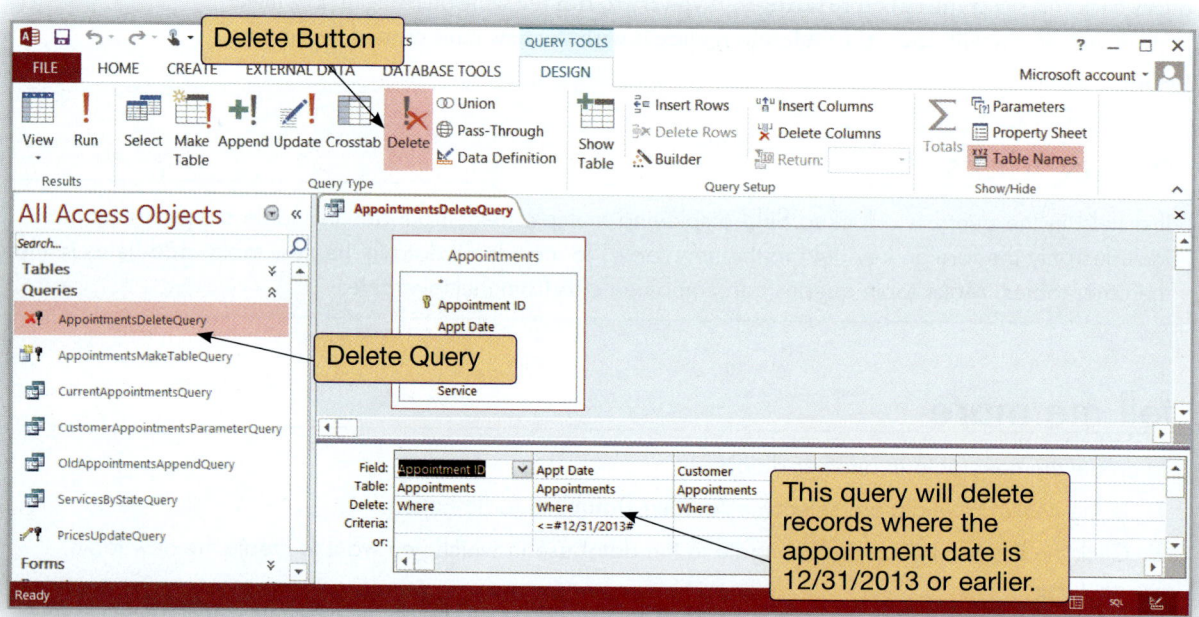

FIGURE AC 8.8

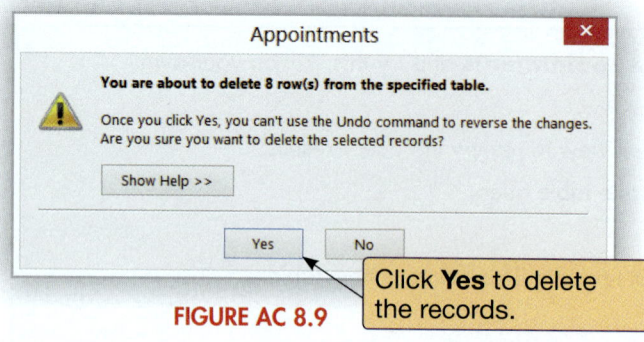

FIGURE AC 8.9

4. On the *Query Tools Design* tab, in the *Results* group, click the **Run** button.

5. Access will warn you that you are about to delete records and that you cannot undo the changes. Click **Yes** to complete the action.

5. On the *Query Tools Design* tab, in the *Results* group, click the **Run** button.
6. Access will warn you that you are about to append records and that you cannot undo the change. Click **Yes**.

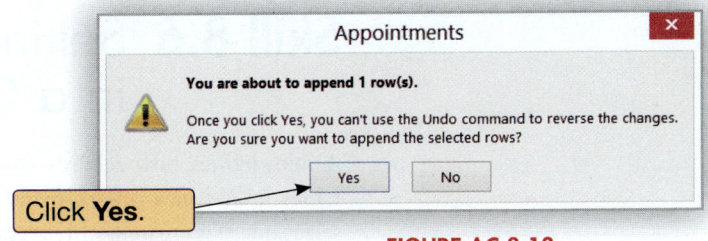

FIGURE AC 8.13

tell me more

To append data to a table in another database:
1. In the *Append* dialog, select the **Another Database** radio button.
2. Click the **Browse** button and navigate to the database that has the target table.
3. Click **OK**.
4. Run the query. Click **Yes** when Access displays the warning that you will not be able to undo this action.

let me try

If the database is not already open, open the data file **AC8-Appointments** and try this skill on your own:

1. Open the **OldAppointmentsAppendQuery** query in Design view.
2. Note the criteria in the *Appt Date* field. Switch to Datasheet view to review the query results. Enter the date **2/1/2014** when prompted. Observe that the query returns one record with the *Appointment ID* 19.
3. Switch back to Design view and change the query to an **append** query.
4. Select the **AppointmentsArchive** table to append the records to.
5. Run the query. Enter the date **2/1/2014** when prompted. Access should warn you that you are about to append 1 row.
6. Save and close the query.
7. Open the **AppointmentsArchive** table and verify that the new record with the *Appointment ID* 19 was copied to the table.
8. Close the table.

skill 8.5 Moving Records through a Query

Skill 8.6 Setting Join Properties in a Query

A **join** defines how records from two related tables are returned in a query. By default, tables linked in a one-to-many relationship have an **inner join**. This means that when a select query is created, only records that include matches in both tables will be displayed. In Figure AC 8.14, the query of customers and appointments includes only records from the *Customers* table with related records in the *Appointments* table.

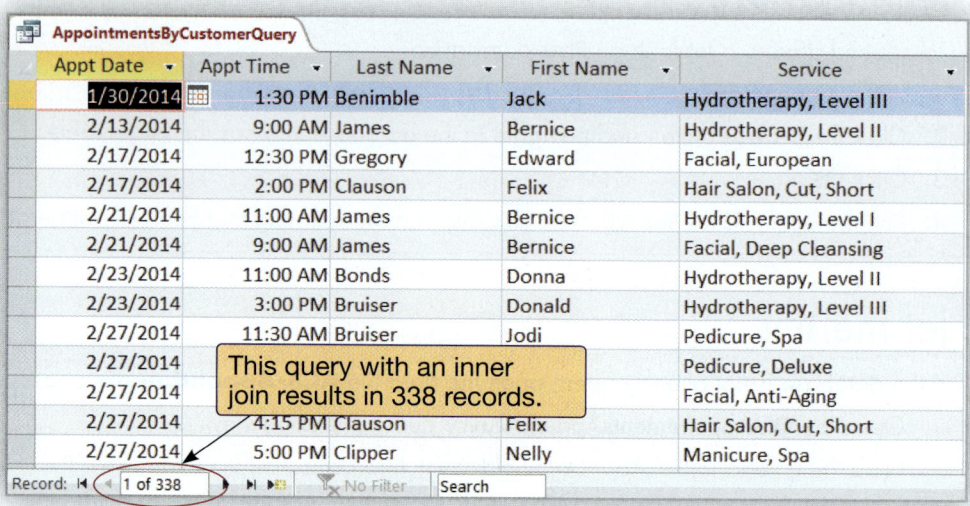

FIGURE AC 8.14

You can change the default join property between the two tables. If you edit the join property from the *Relationships* window, the change is a **global join** and it will apply throughout the database. If you edit the join property from Query Design view, the change is a **local join** (that is, it applies only to that query).

To modify local join properties between related tables from Query Design view:

1. Open the query in Design view.
2. Double-click the line connecting the two related tables to open the *Join Properties* dialog.
3. Click the radio button for the join type you want. Click **OK**.
   - By default, the first option is chosen. This is an inner join, which means that only records that include matches in both tables are included in query results.
   - The second choice represents a **left outer join**. This means that all records from the "one" side of the relationship will be included in the query, whether or not there is a corresponding match in the "many" table.
   - The third choice represents a **right outer join**. This means that all records from the "many" side of the relationship will be included in the query, whether or not there is a corresponding match in the "one" table.

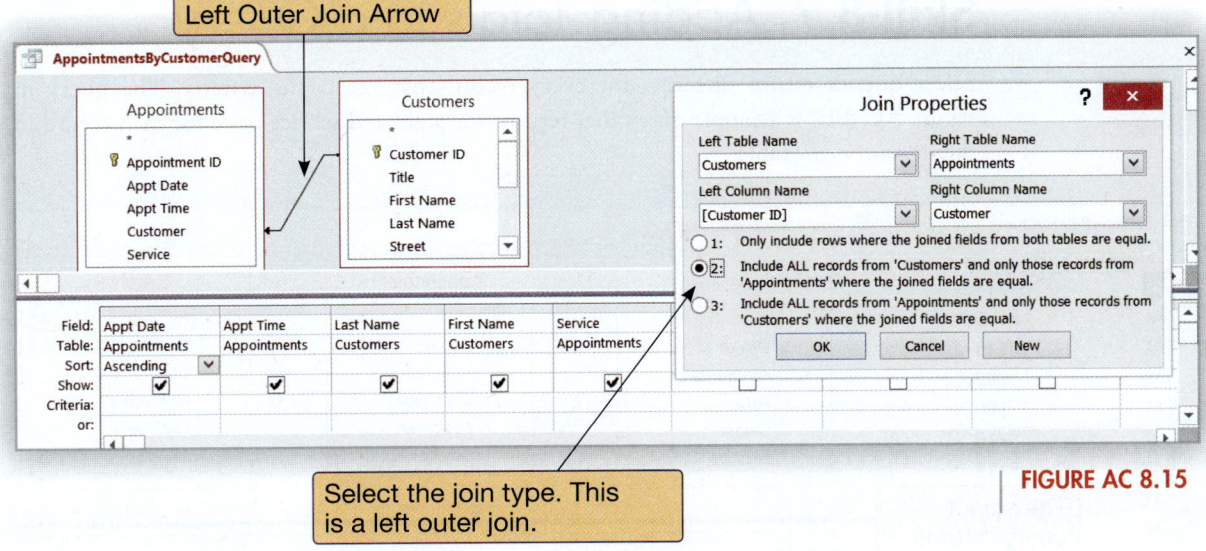

FIGURE AC 8.15

4. Notice the line linking the two tables changes to indicate the new join type.
5. Run the query again to see the new results.

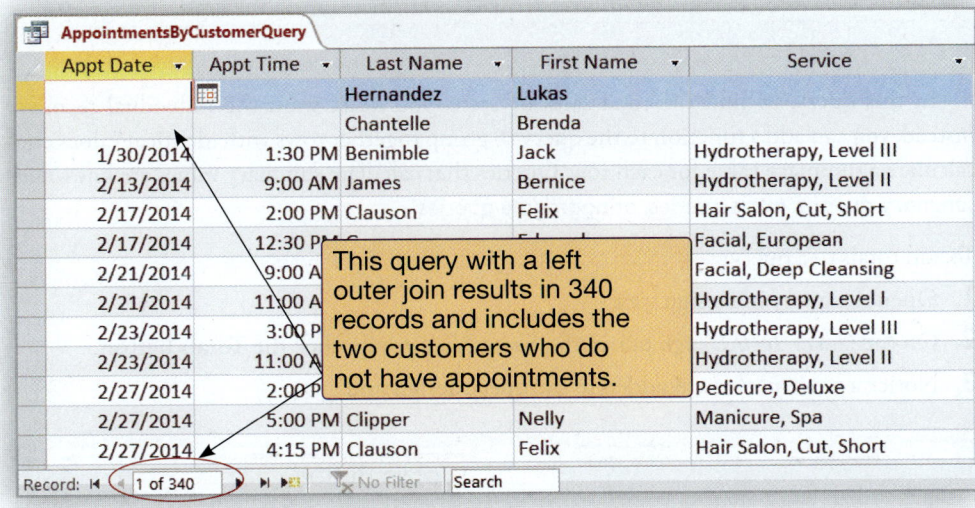

FIGURE AC 8.16

Remember, when you modify the join property through Query Design view, you are creating a local join, affecting only the open query. This change does not affect the default relationship between the two tables.

let me try

If the database is not already open, open the data file **AC8-Appointments** and try this skill on your own:

1. Open the **AppointmentsByCustomerQuery** query and review the query results. There should be 338 records in the results.
2. Switch to Design view.
3. Modify the relationship between the *Customers* and *Appointments* tables in this query only so the query results will include **all** customers (including customers who do not have any appointments). *Hint:* This requires a left outer join.
4. Run the query and review the results again. There should now be 340 records in the results.
5. Save and close the query.

skill 8.6 Setting Join Properties in a Query

Skill 8.7 Adding Totals to a Query

Select queries return one row for every record that meets the criteria. The query in Figure AC 8.17 is a simple query that returns the state and service price for each record in the *Appointments* table.

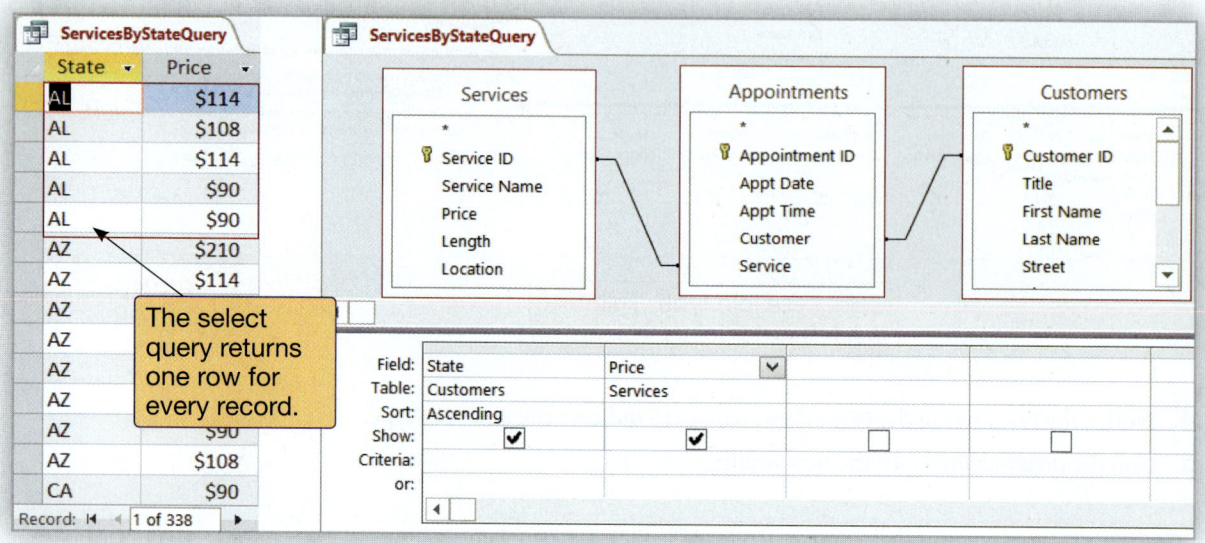

FIGURE AC 8.17

In this query, to find the total sales by state, you don't want the individual records. Instead, you can add a function to the query to group together rows with identical values and calculate a summary value for each row. Queries that calculate summary values are known as **summary queries**, **totals queries**, or **aggregate queries**.

To add totals to a query:

1. Open the query in Design view.
2. On the *Query Tools Design* tab, in the *Show/Hide* group, click the **Totals** button.
3. Notice a new *Total* row is added to the query design grid.

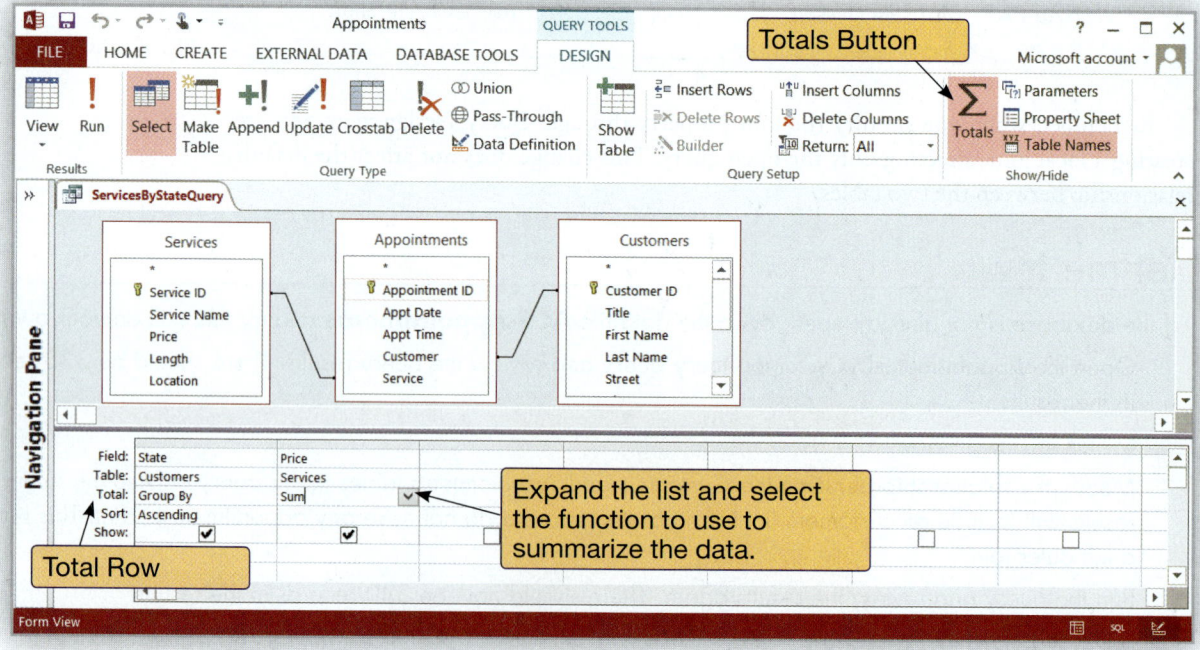

FIGURE AC 8.18

AC–348 | www.mhhe.com/simnet

access 2013 chapter 8 Exploring Advanced Queries and Macros

4. By default, the *Total* row lists *Group by* for each field in the query. For a concise summary query, include only the fields you want to group by or for which you want to calculate a summary value.

5. Expand the *Group by* list in the *Total* row for the field for which Access will calculate a summary value, and select the function you want to use. Select **Sum** to calculate a total, **Avg** to calculate the average, **Min** to find the smallest value, **Max** to find the largest value, or **Count** to count the number of records.

6. On the *Query Tools Design* tab, in the *Results* group, click the **Run** button.

As shown in Figure AC 8.19, the query now returns one row for every value in the *State* field and calculates the total of the values in the *Price* field for each row. Notice the field name in the results datasheet includes the function name.

ServicesByStateQuery

State	SumOfPrice
AL	$516.00
AZ	$1,026.00
CA	$17,286.00
CO	$1,674.00
DC	$2,076.00
FL	$264.00
GA	$990.00
HI	$1,494.00
KY	$702.00
MA	$744.00
MI	$1,278.00
MO	$1,386.00
NM	$2,508.00
NY	$732.00
OH	$588.00

The new field name includes the function name.

The query returns one row for each value in the *State* field and totals the values in the *Price* field for that state.

FIGURE AC 8.19

You can add multiple instances of a field to the query grid and select a different function for each instance. For example, select **Sum** for one instance and **Avg** for another to compare totals and averages or **Min** and **Max** to compare the minimum and maximum values for a group.

If you want to add criteria to one of the fields you are grouping by, you can add the criteria in the *Criteria* row as you would normally.

To narrow the query by criteria in a field you do not want included as a group:

1. Add the field to the query.
2. In the *Total* row, expand the **Group by** list, and select **Where.** When you select *Where,* Access unchecks the **Show** check box so the field is not included in the groupings in the query results.
3. Add the criteria in the *Criteria* row as you would normally.
4. Run the query.

Figure AC 8.20 shows the query narrowed further to restrict results to appointments on June 1, 2014, or later.

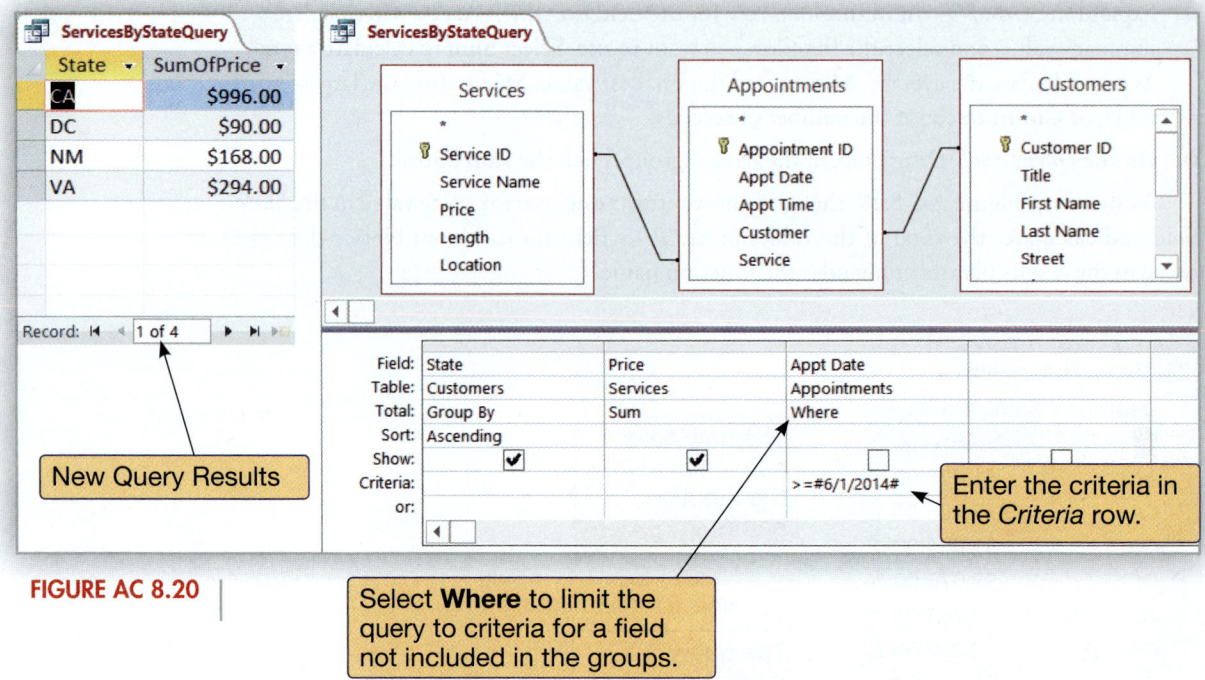

FIGURE AC 8.20

tips & tricks

Aggregate means to combine, total, or group. Sum, average, min, max, count, and similar functions are known as **aggregate functions** because they summarize data.

let me try

If the database is not already open, open the data file **AC8-Appointments** and try this skill on your own:

1. Open the **ServicesByStateQuery** query in Design view.
2. Display the *Total* row for the query.
3. Modify the query to group by values in the *State* field and calculate the **Sum** of the values in the *Price* field.
4. Run the query and review the results.
5. Return to Design view.
6. Add the **Appt Date** field from the *Appointments* field to the query.
7. Add criteria to limit the query results to records where the value in the **Appt Date** field is **greater than or equal to 6/1/2014**. Do not include the *Appt Date* field as a group.
8. Run the query and review the results.
9. Save and close the query.

Skill 8.8 Creating a Crosstab Query

A **crosstab query** summarizes data in a format similar to a spreadsheet. Values for one field are listed in the first column of the datasheet as row headings; values for another field are listed across the top row as column headings. A value is calculated at the intersection of each row and column.

Figure AC 8.21 shows the results of a crosstab query that calculates the total price by state for each service purchased.

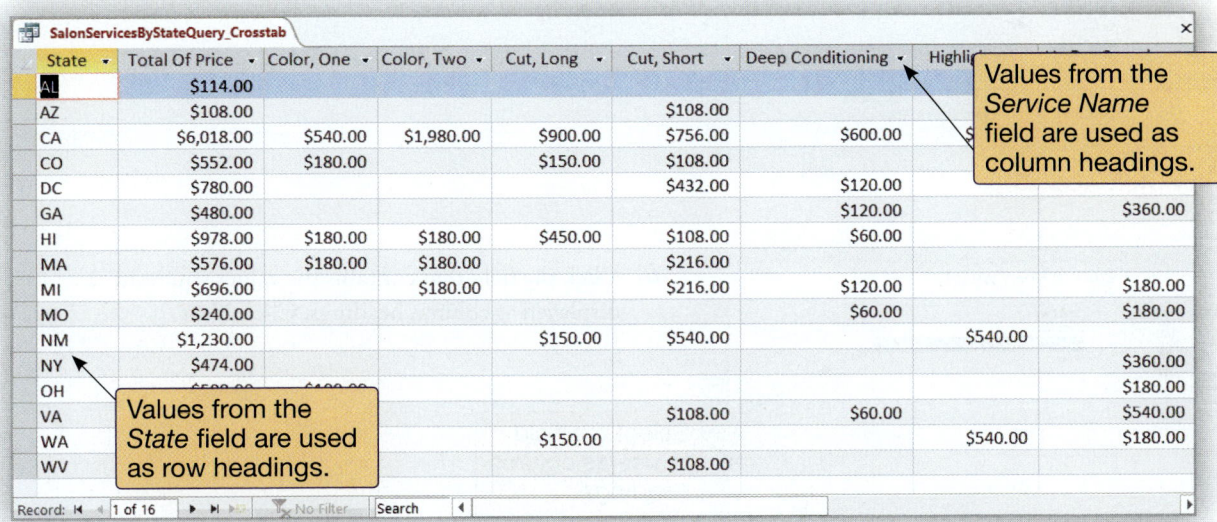

FIGURE AC 8.21

To create a crosstab query using the *Crosstab Query Wizard*:

1. On the *Create* tab, in the *Queries* group, click the **Query Wizard** button.
2. In the *New Query* dialog, click **Crosstab Query Wizard**. Click **OK**.
3. Select the table or query that contains the fields you want to include in the crosstab query. To display the list of queries, click the **Queries** radio button. Click **Next**.

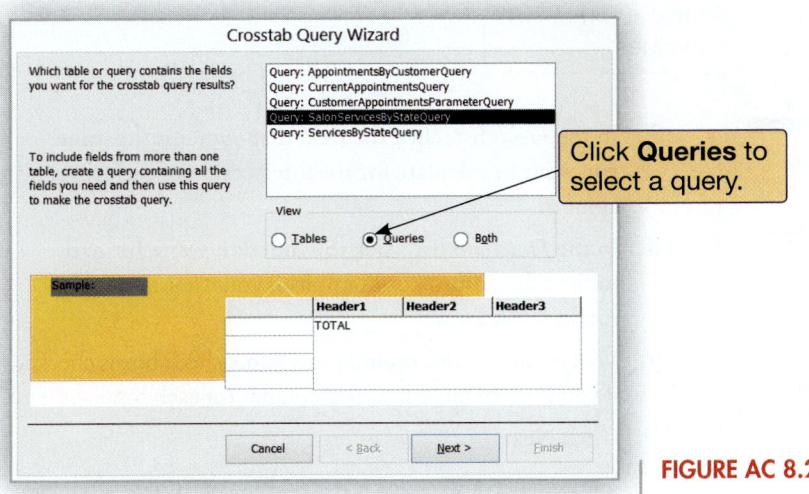

FIGURE AC 8.22

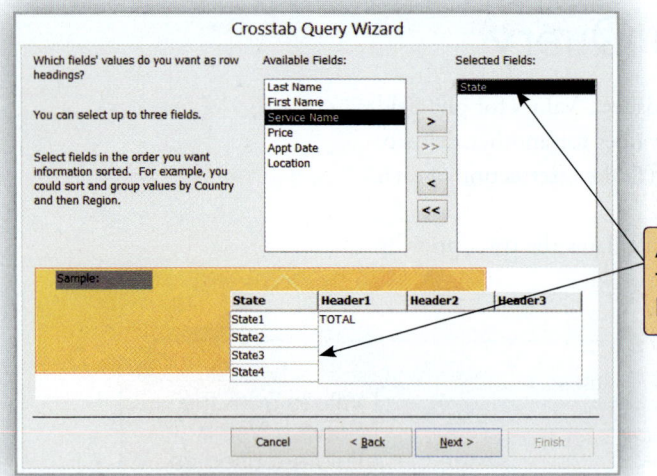

FIGURE AC 8.23

4. Double-click the field that contains the values you want displayed as row headings or click the field name once and then click the > button. You can include up to three fields as row headings.
5. Click **Next**.

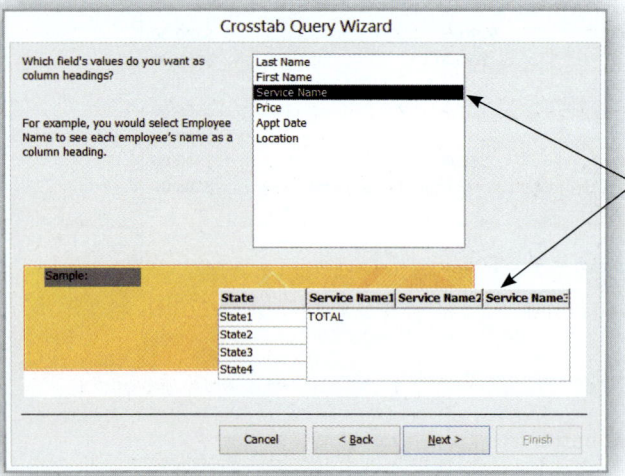

FIGURE AC 8.24

6. Click the field that contains the values you want displayed as column headings. Click **Next**.

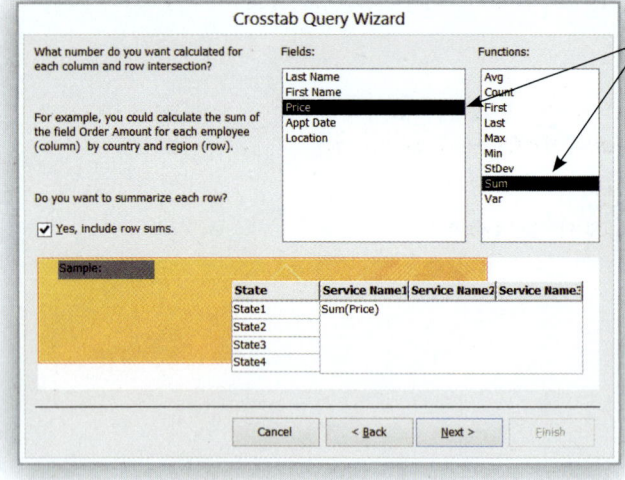

FIGURE AC 8.25

7. In the *Fields* list, click the field that contains the value you want to calculate for the intersection of each row and column.
8. In the *Functions* list, click the function you want to use in the calculation. For example, if you want to calculate totals, select **Sum**.
9. Verify that the **Yes, include row sums** check box is checked if you want to include a total column for each row.
10. Click **Next**.

11. If necessary, type a name for the query and select whether you want to view the query results or modify it in Design view.
12. Click **Finish**.

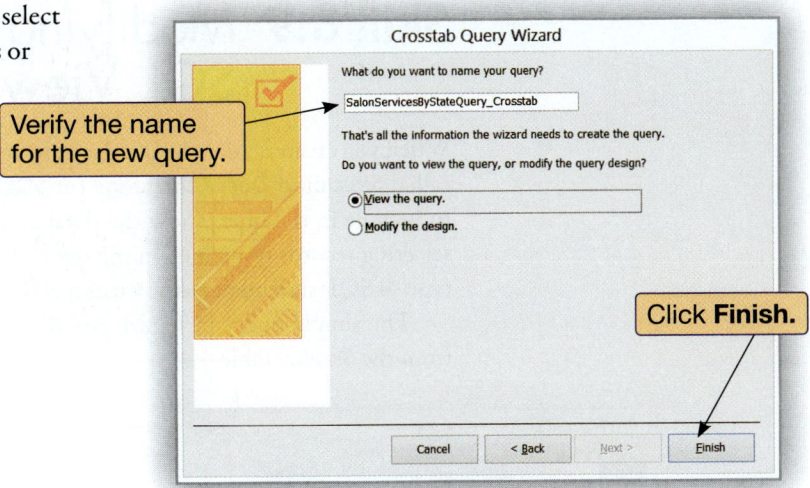

FIGURE AC 8.26

tell me more

To create a crosstab query in Design view:

1. Begin with a select query that includes the records you want to summarize in a crosstab query. Open the query in Design view.
2. Change the query to a crosstab query. On the *Query Tools Design* tab, in the *Query Type* group, click the **Crosstab** button.
3. Notice two new rows are added to the query design grid: *Total* and *Crosstab*.
4. Click in the *Crosstab* row for the field you want to use as row headings. Click the arrow to expand the list and select **Row Heading**.
5. Click in the *Crosstab* row for the field you want to use as column headings. Click the arrow to expand the list and select **Column Heading**.
6. Click in the *Crosstab* row for the field that contains the values you want to calculate. Click the arrow to expand the list and select **Value**. Expand the *Group by* list in the *Total* row and select the function you want to use.
7. On the *Query Tools Design* tab, in the *Results* group, click the **Run** button.

let me try

If the database is not already open, open the data file **AC8-Appointments** and try this skill on your own:

1. Use the *Crosstab Query Wizard* to create a new query.
2. The **SalonServicesByState** query contains the fields for the crosstab query results.
3. Select the **State** field as the row headings.
4. Select the **Service Name** field as the column headings.
5. Calculate the **sum** of the values in the **Price** field.
6. Accept the suggested name for the query.
7. Review the query results and then close the query.

skill 8.8 Creating a Crosstab Query

Skill 8.9 Modifying a Query in SQL View

When you create a query in Design view, you are generating programming code in a language called **Structured Query Language** (or **SQL**). The lines of SQL code tell Access which fields to include in the query, how the data are related for purposes of the query, any criteria for selecting records to include in the query, and how the query results should be ordered. This type of SQL statement is known as a **SELECT statement**.

The simple query in Figure AC 8.27 returns the list of service IDs and service names from the *Services* table.

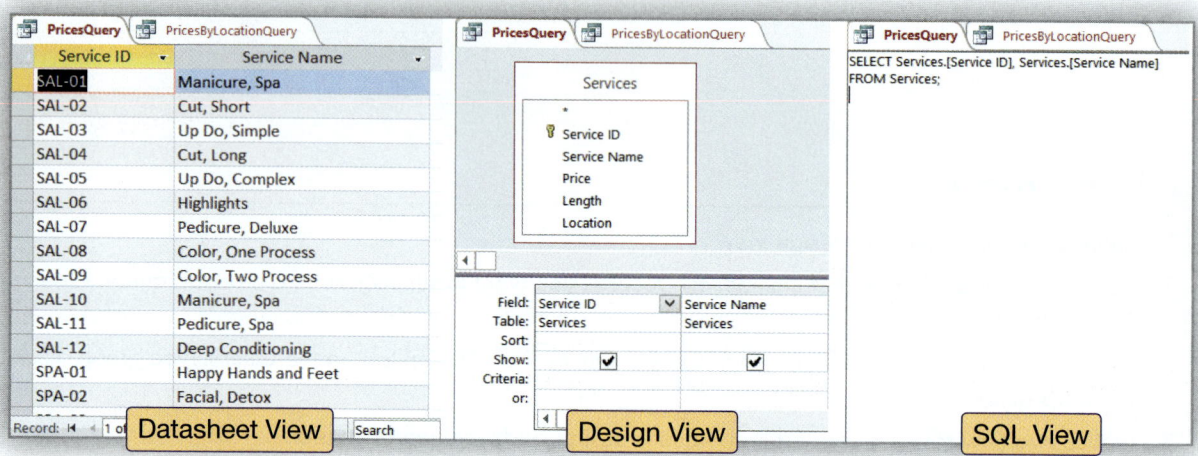

FIGURE AC 8.27

To review the SQL code behind a query, switch to SQL view:

On the *Query Tools Design* tab, in the *Results* group, click the **View** button arrow and select **SQL View**.

The SELECT statement is made up of a series of clauses. It ends with a semicolon either at the end of the last clause in the statement or on a line by itself at the end.

SELECT

The first clause in the SELECT statement is always the **SELECT clause**. This defines the fields included in the query. Each field name is separated by a comma. While not always necessary, it is good practice to include the table name with the field name using the format `Table.Field`.

- If the field name is used in more than one table in the database, you must include the table name.
- If the table or field name includes a space or other special character, you must enclose the name in square brackets.
- In the query results, the fields are displayed in the order in which they are listed in the SELECT clause.

```
SELECT [Service ID], [Service Name]
```
or
```
SELECT Services.[Service ID], Services.[Service Name]
```

To add another field to the query, place the cursor at the end of the SELECT clause, type a comma, space, and then type the new field identifier using the format `Table.Field`.

```
SELECT Services.[Service ID], Services.[Service Name], Services.Price
```

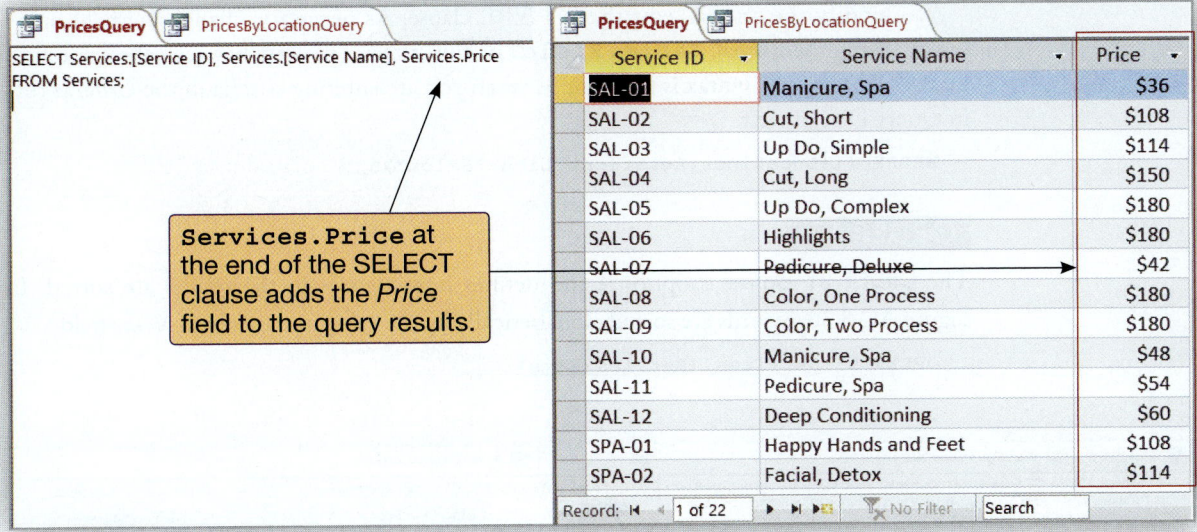

FIGURE AC 8.28

FROM

The second clause in the SELECT statement is the **FROM clause**. It defines how records are selected to include in the results. If the query includes only one table such as the one shown in Figure AC 8.28, this is simply the word **FROM** followed by a space and then the name of the table. If the table name includes spaces or other special characters, the table name must be enclosed in square brackets.

```
FROM Services
```

If there are multiple tables in the query, the FROM clause is more complicated and must define the relationship between the tables for purposes of including records in the query results. In Figure AC 8.29, the query includes records from both the *Services* and the *Locations* tables. Records from the *Locations* table are included only when there is a match between the *LocationID* field in the *Locations* table and the *Location* field in the *Services* table (an inner join).

```
FROM Locations INNER JOIN Services ON Locations.[Location ID] = Services.Location
```

WHERE

The **WHERE clause** is optional and defines the query criteria. In Figure AC 8.29, records are included only when the value in the *Location* field from the *Locations* table begins with *Spa*.

```
WHERE (((Locations.Location) Like "Spa*"))
```

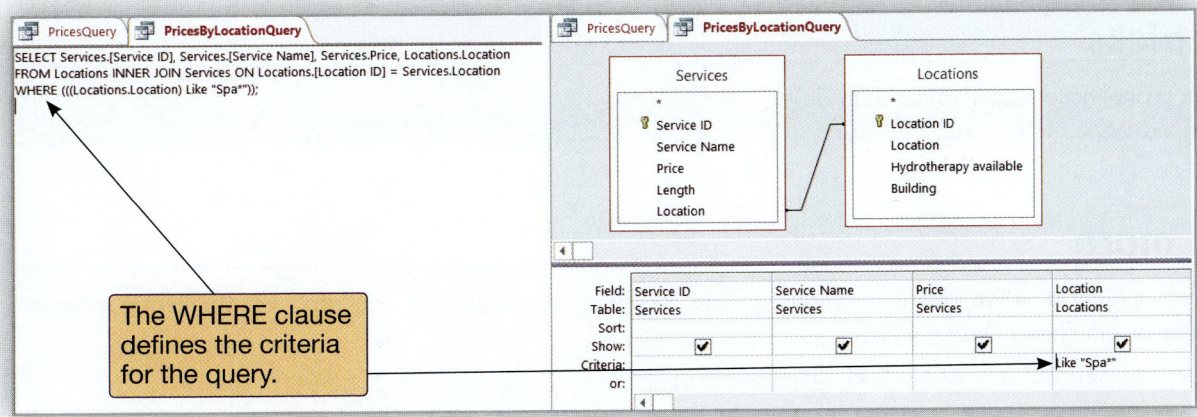

FIGURE AC 8.29

skill 8.9   Modifying a Query in SQL View

To modify the criteria, edit the WHERE clause. As necessary, change the field name (again, using the format `Table.Field`) or the criteria (the text between the quotation marks). The criteria syntax is the same as when you are entering criteria in the *Criteria* row in Query Design view.

```
WHERE (((Locations.Location) Like "Salon"))
```

ORDER BY

The **ORDER BY clause** is optional and defines how records in the results are sorted. In Figure AC 8.30, records are sorted alphabetically by the value in the *Service Name* field.

```
ORDER BY Services.[Service Name]
```

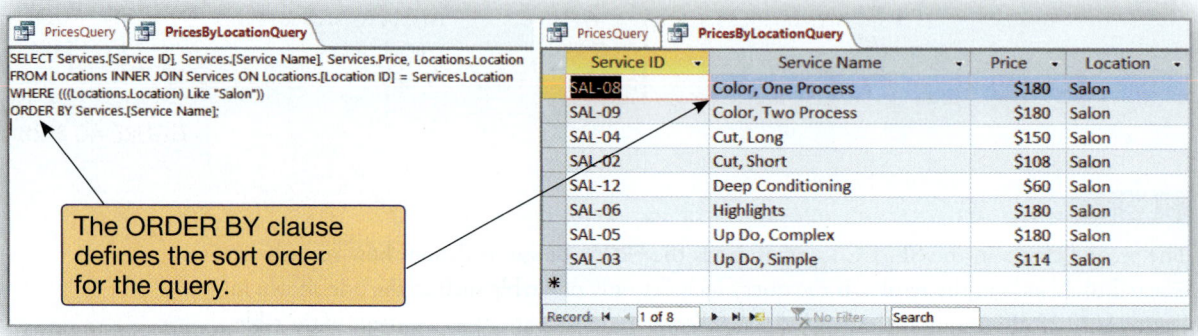

FIGURE AC 8.30

To add an ORDER BY clause to the SELECT statement:

1. Go to the last line in the statement and delete the semicolon.
2. Press `Enter` to start a new line.
3. Type `ORDER BY Table.Field` where `Table` is the name of the table and `Field` is the name of the field.
4. By default, the sort order is ascending (A–Z). If you want the sort order to be descending instead, add DESC to the end of the ORDER BY clause after the field name.

```
ORDER BY Services.[Service Name] DESC
```

5. Type a semicolon to end the SELECT statement. The semicolon can be on the same line as the ORDER BY clause or on its own line.

tips & tricks

SQL is often pronounced *sequel* rather than *S-Q-L*.

tell me more

You can use wildcards when defining criteria in the WHERE clause just as you can when entering criteria in the *Criteria* row in Query Design view.

- ***** matches any string of any length (including zero length).
- **?** matches a single character.
- **#** matches a single numeric digit.

AC-356 | www.mhhe.com/simnet

access 2013 | chapter 8 Exploring Advanced Queries and Macros

let me try

If the database is not already open, open the data file **AC8-Appointments** and try this skill on your own:

1. Open the **PricesQuery** query in Datasheet view. Switch to Design view and review the query design.
2. Switch to the view where you can edit the SQL code for the query.
3. Add the **Price** field from the **Services** table to the end of the SELECT clause, and then run the query to see the results.
4. Save and close the query.
5. Open the **PricesByLocationQuery** query in Datasheet view. Review the query results, and then switch to SQL view.
6. In SQL, modify the criteria to return only records where the value of the *Location* field in the *Locations* table is **Salon.** Run the query to see the results.
7. Switch back to SQL view.
8. Delete the semicolon at the end of the WHERE clause so you can add another clause to the SELECT statement.
9. Add a new clause to the end of the SELECT statement to sort the records alphabetically by values in the **Service Name** field from the **Services** table. Do not forget the square brackets around the field name.
10. Add a semicolon at the end of the new ORDER BY clause to end the SELECT statement.
11. Review the query results, and then save and close the query.

from the perspective of . . .

IT INTERN

Part of my job is to create the queries for the company's sales database. I'm not an Access expert, but as part of my computer science degree program, I studied SQL extensively. For me, it's easier to write the queries directly in SQL rather than learn the graphical user interface for Design view.

skill 8.9   Modifying a Query in SQL View

Skill 8.10 Creating a Stand-Alone Macro

Earlier, we introduced the idea of macros when we used the *Command Button Wizard* to add a command button to a form. A **macro** is a custom set of programming commands written in the Visual Basic for Applications (VBA) programming language. A command button macro is an **embedded macro**—that is, it is available only in the database object in which the button control was created.

A **stand-alone macro** exists independently of a specific database object. It can be run directly from the Navigation Pane, or it can be called from a control in a form or a report just like an embedded macro. Stand-alone macros are created using the Macro Builder. They are available from the Navigation Pane, under *Macros*. (The Navigation Pane will not include a *Macros* section until there are macros to display.)

To create a stand-alone macro using the Macro Builder:

1. On the *Create* tab, in the *Macros & Code* group, click the **Macro** button.

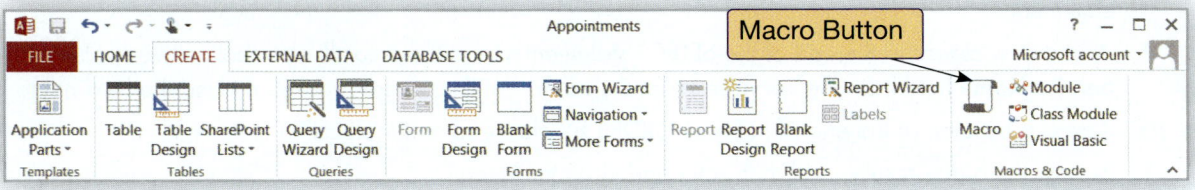

FIGURE AC 8.31

2. The Macro Builder opens.

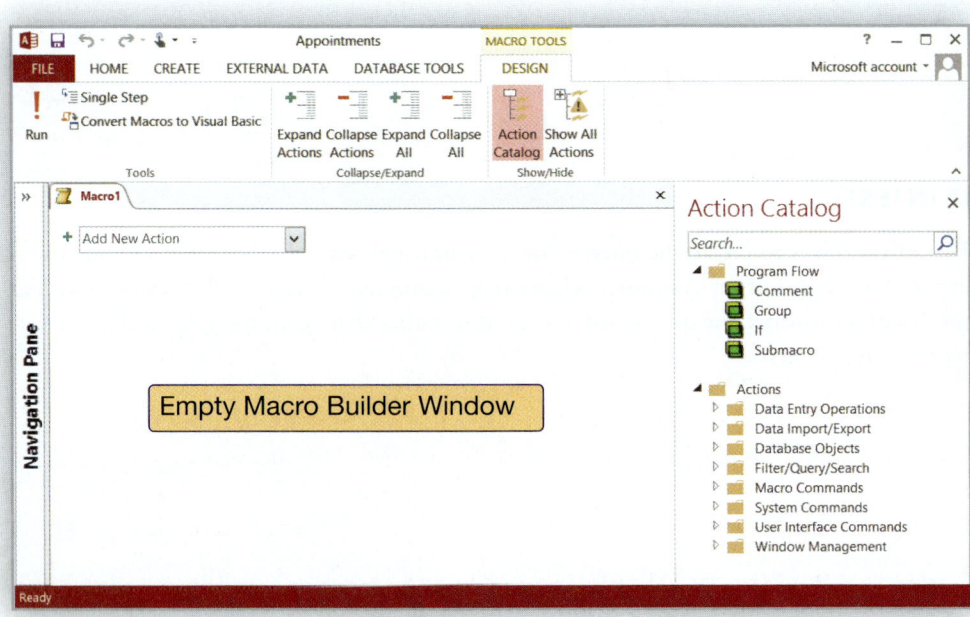

FIGURE AC 8.32

3. There are two ways to add an action to a macro in the Macro Builder:
   - Expand the *Add New Action* list and click the action you want.
   - In the *Action Catalog* pane at the right side of the Macro Builder, actions are grouped into folders. Under the *Actions* folder, click an arrow to expand a folder and then double-click the action you want.

4. The action block for the selected action opens. Fill in the arguments as necessary. For example, in Figure AC 8.33, the OpenForm action includes a drop-down list to select the name of the form to open when the macro is run.

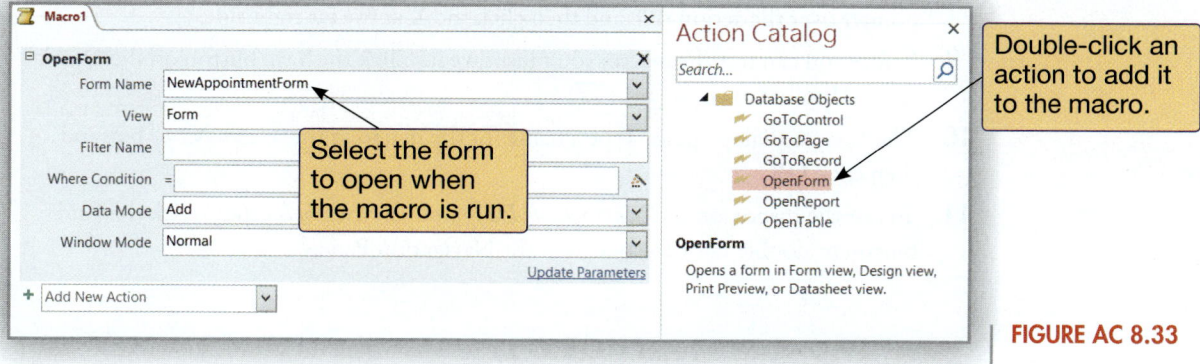

FIGURE AC 8.33

5. Continue adding actions to the macro. In Figure AC 8.34, we have added the OpenReport action block to the macro. Now when the macro is run, the *NewAppointmentForm* will open and then the *AppointmentsByMonthReport* will open.

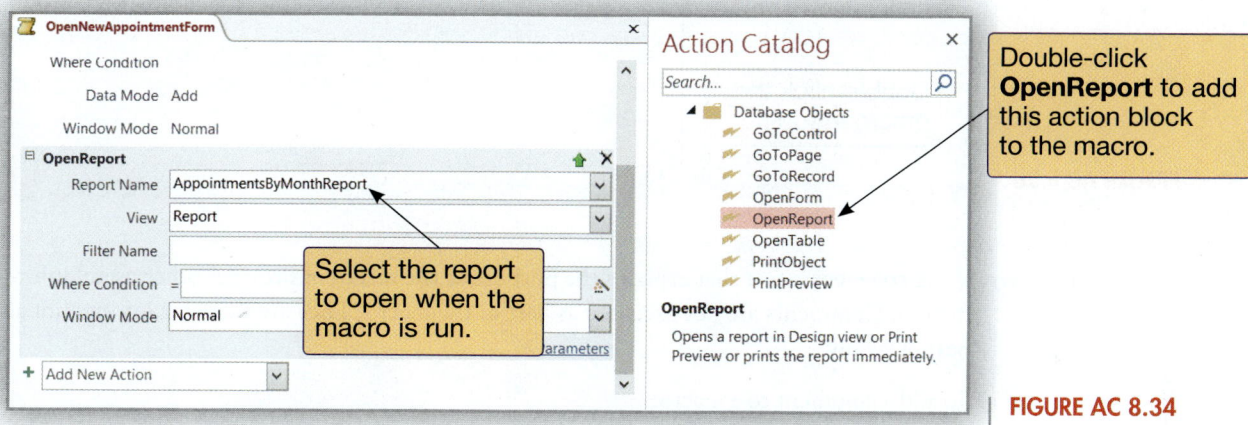

FIGURE AC 8.34

6. If you want more room to work in the Action Builder, collapse the action blocks as shown in Figure AC 8.35. On the *Macro Tools Design* tab, in the *Expand/Collapse* group, click the **Collapse Actions** button.

› To see the details for the action blocks again, click the **Expand Actions** button.
› To expand a single action block, move the mouse pointer over the action block, and then click the + that appears at the left side.

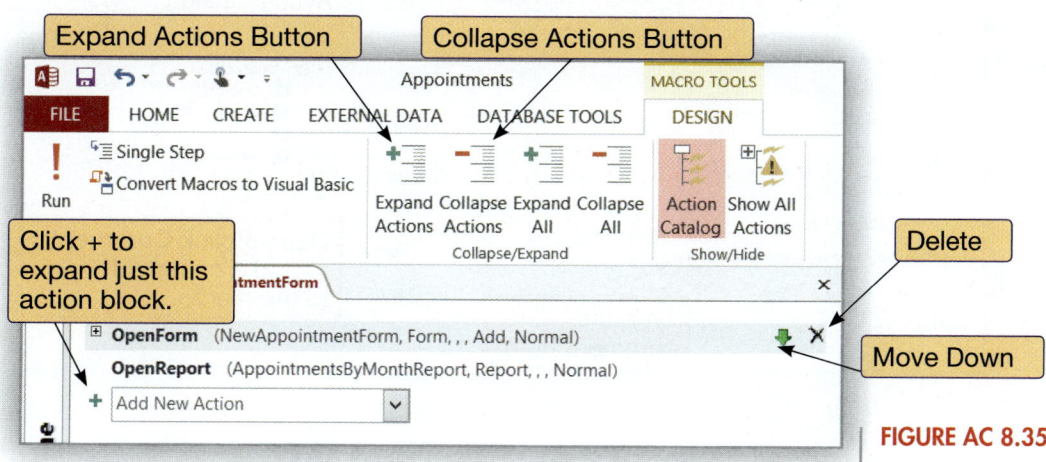

FIGURE AC 8.35

skill 8.10 Creating a Stand-Alone Macro

7. To change the order in which the action blocks are executed in the macro, click the action block to select it, or move the mouse pointer over the action title and then use the **Move up** or **Move down** arrow.
8. To delete an action from the macro, click the action to select it, or move the mouse pointer over the action title and then click the **X** at the far right side.
9. Before you can test the macro, you must save it. Click the **Save** button on the Quick Access Toolbar or press Ctrl + S.
10. The *Save As* dialog opens. Type a name for the macro in the *Macro Name* box and then click **OK**.
11. To test the macro, on the *Macro Tools Design* tab, in the *Tools* group, click the **Run** button or double-click the macro in the Navigation Pane.

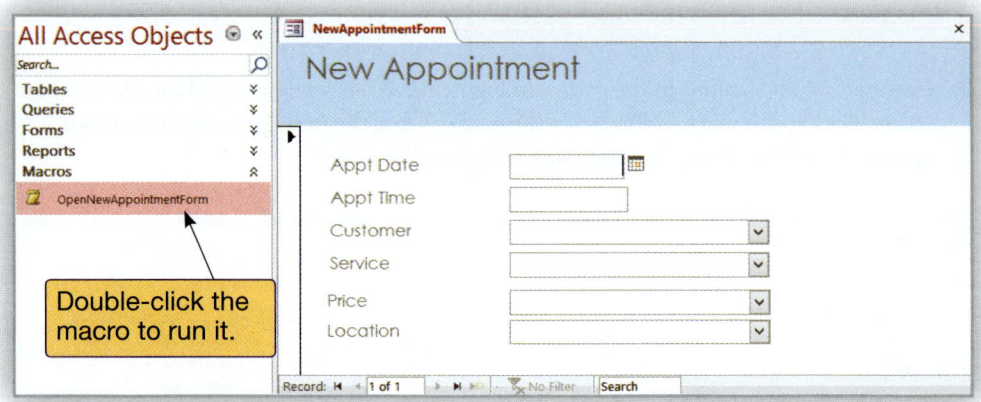

FIGURE AC 8.36

A **comment** is text that explains the purpose of the macro or provides other useful information. Comments are not executed as part of the macro. They are there for informational purposes only.

To add a comment to a macro:

1. Open the macro in the Macro Builder.
2. In the *Action Catalog,* double-click **Comment.** It is the first action in the *Program Flow* group at the top of the pane.
3. Type the comment in the box, and click anywhere outside the box when you are finished.

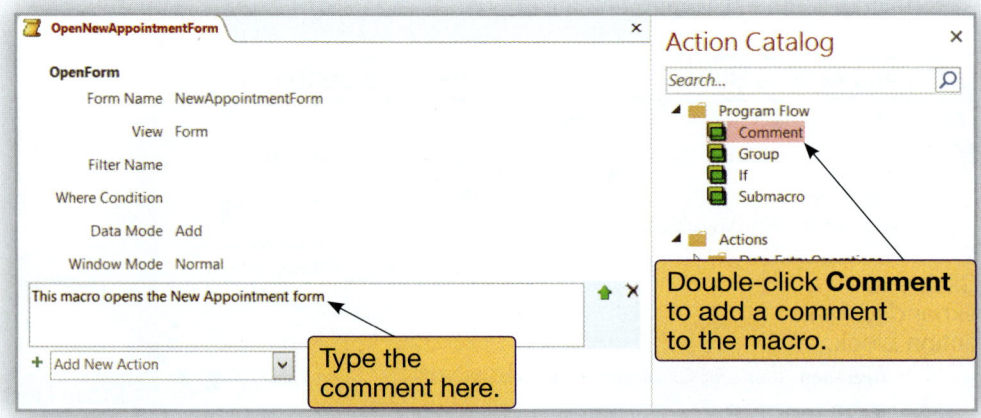

FIGURE AC 8.37

tips & tricks

If you have used macros in Microsoft Word or Microsoft Excel, you are probably familiar with the idea of recording a macro—that is, allowing the program to capture your mouse clicks or typing to create the macro and the underlying VBA code. Unfortunately, Access does not include a macro recorder.

tell me more

If you double-click a macro in the Navigation Pane, Access will run the macro. If you want to open the Macro Builder instead, right-click the macro name and select **Design View.**

another method

To run a macro directly from the *Database Tools* tab:

1. On the *Database Tools* tab, in the *Macro* group, click the **Run Macro** button.
2. In the *Run Macro* dialog, expand the list and select the macro you want to run.
3. Click **OK.**

let me try

If the database is not already open, open the data file **AC8-Appointments** and try this skill on your own:

1. Open the Macro Builder to create a new stand-alone macro.
2. Add the **OpenForm** action. It is located in the **Database Objects** folder.
3. Select **NewAppointmentForm** as the form to open when the macro is run.
4. Add the **OpenReport** action. It is located in the **Database Objects** folder.
5. Select **AppointmentsByMonthReport** as the report to open when the macro is run.
6. For the first macro you created (OpenForm), add a comment with the text: `This macro opens the New Appointment form`
7. Move the comment so it appears first.
8. Collapse the actions.
9. Delete the **OpenReport** action.
10. Save the macro with the name: `OpenNewAppointmentForm`
11. Run the **OpenNewAppointmentForm** macro.
12. Close all database objects.

skill 8.10 Creating a Stand-Alone Macro

key terms

Action query	Aggregate
Update query	Aggregate function
Make table query	Crosstab query
Delete query	Structured Query Language (SQL)
Append query	SELECT statement
Join	SELECT clause
Inner join	FROM clause
Global join	WHERE clause
Local join	ORDER BY clause
Left outer join	Macro
Right outer join	Embedded macro
Summary query	Stand-alone macro
Totals query	Comment
Aggregate query	

concepts review

1. Which of these queries is not an action query?
   a. Delete query
   b. Append query
   c. Select query
   d. Make table query

2. The actions performed by an action query can be undone.
   a. True
   b. False

3. Which of these queries changes the values in the records in the underlying table?
   a. Delete query
   b. Append query
   c. Select query
   d. Update query

4. Which of these queries copies records to an existing table?
   a. Delete query
   b. Append query
   c. Select query
   d. Update query

5. By default, tables linked in a one-to-many relationship have which type of join?
   a. Inner join
   b. Outer join
   c. Left outer join
   d. Right outer join

6. Queries that calculate summary values are known as
   a. Summary queries
   b. Totals queries
   c. Aggregate queries
   d. All of the above
7. Which of these queries summarizes data in a format similar to a spreadsheet?
   a. Select query
   b. Summary query
   c. Crosstab query
   d. Append query
8. To add another field to a query in SQL view, edit which clause?
   a. SELECT
   b. FROM
   c. WHERE
   d. ORDER BY
9. The SELECT statement ends with which character?
   a. .
   b. #
   c. ;
   d. !
10. Which type of macro exists independently of a specific database object?
    a. Embedded macro
    b. Stand-alone macro
    c. Comment
    d. None of the above

projects

Data files for projects can be found on www.mhhe.com/office2013skills

skill review 8.1

Middlesex University registrar's office is updating the *Student* table and preparing it for the fall semester. Using action queries, you will move out the graduating seniors, update the classifications for the new seniors, juniors, and sophomores, and move in the incoming freshmen. You will use a crosstab query to summarize the number of classes offered for each course. You will create and edit a stand-alone macro to open a table ready for data entry in a new record.

Skills needed to complete this project:

- Understanding Action Queries (Skill 8.1)
- Creating a New Table through a Query (Skill 8.3)

- Deleting Records through a Query (Skill 8.4)
- Updating Records through a Query (Skill 8.2)
- Moving Records through a Query (Skill 8.5)
- Creating a Crosstab Query (Skill 8.8)
- Modifying a Query in SQL View (Skill 8.9)
- Creating a Stand-Alone Macro (Skill 8.10)

1. Open the start file **AC2013-SkillReview-8-1** and resave the file as:
   `[your initials]AC-SkillReview-8-1`
2. If necessary, enable active content by clicking the **Enable Content** button in the Message Bar.
3. Create a make table query for all graduating seniors.
   a. Click the **Create** tab. In the *Queries* group, click the **Query Design** button.
   b. In the *Show Table* dialog, double-click **Student**. Click **Close**.
   c. Double-click the **Student** table title bar to select all fields. Click anywhere within the highlighted field list and drag the fields into the query design grid to add all the fields at once.
   d. Under the *Credits* field, in the query design grid, in the *Criteria* row, type:
      `>123`
   e. Under the *Classification* field, in the query design grid, in the *Criteria* row type:
      `Sr`
   f. Under the *GPA* field, in the query design grid, in the *Criteria* row type:
      `>=2.0`
   g. Switch to Datasheet view to check the query results. There should be 12 records in the results.
   h. Switch back to Design view.
   i. On the *Query Tools Design* tab, in the *Query Type* group, click the **Make Table** button.
   j. In the *Make Table* dialog, in the *Table Name* box, type **Alumni** and then click **OK**.
   k. On the *Query Tools Design* tab, in the *Results* group, click the **Run** button.
   l. Access should warn you that you are about to paste 12 rows into a new table. Click **Yes**.
   m. Save the query as: `MakeAlumni`
4. Change the *MakeAlumni* query to a delete query to remove graduating seniors from the *Student* table.
   a. Click the **File** tab. Click **Save As**. Click **Save Object As** and then click the **Save As** button. Type `DeleteGraduates` and then click **OK**.
   b. On the *Query Tools Design* tab, in the *Query Type* group, click the **Delete** button.
   c. On the *Query Tools Design* tab, in the *Results* group, click the **Run** button.
   d. Access should warn you that you are about to delete 12 rows. Click **Yes**.
   e. Save and close the query.
5. Create update queries to change *Jr* to *Sr*, *So* to *Jr*, and *Fr* to *So*.
   a. On the *Create* tab, in the *Queries* group, click the **Query Design** button.
   b. In the *Show Table* dialog, double-click **Student**. Click **Close**.
   c. In the *Student* table field list, double-click **Classification**.

d. On the *Query Tools Design* tab, in the *Query Type* group, click the **Update** button. An *Update To* row displays in the query grid.

e. Under the *Classification* field, in the *Update To* row, type: `Sr`

f. Under the *Classification* field, in the *Criteria* row, type: `Jr`

g. Switch to Datasheet view to check the query results. There should be 8 records in the results.

h. Switch back to Design view.

i. On the *Query Tools Design* tab, in the *Results* group, click the **Run** button.

j. Access should warn you that you are about to update 8 rows. Click **Yes**.

k. Save the query as: `UpdateJuniorToSenior`

6. Change *So* to *Jr*.
   a. Under the *Classification* field, in the *Update To* row, type: `Jr`
   b. Under the *Classification* field, in the *Criteria* row, type: `So`
   c. Switch to Datasheet view to check the query results. There should be 8 records in the results.
   d. Switch back to Design view.
   e. On the *Query Tools Design* tab, in the *Results* group, click the **Run** button.
   f. Access should warn you that you are about to update 8 rows. Click **Yes**.
   g. Click the **File** tab. Click **Save As**. Click **Save Object As** and then click the **Save As** button. Type `UpdateSophomoreToJunior` and then click **OK**.

7. Change *Fr* to *So*.
   a. Under the *Classification* field, in the *Update To* row, type: `So`
   b. Under the *Classification* field, click in the *Criteria* row, type: `Fr`
   c. Switch to Datasheet view to check the query results. There should be 4 records in the results.
   d. Switch back to Design view.
   e. On the *Query Tools Design* tab, in the *Results* group, click the **Run** button.
   f. Access should warn you that you are about to update 4 rows. Click **Yes**.
   g. Click the **File** tab. Click **Save As**. Click **Save Object As** and then click the **Save As** button. Type `UpdateFreshmanToSophomore` and then click **OK**.
   h. Close the query.

8. Create a query to append incoming freshmen to the *Student* table.
   a. On the *Create* tab, in the *Queries* group, click the **Query Design** button.
   b. In the *Show Table* dialog, double-click **IncomingFreshmanStudents**. Click **Close**.
   c. Double-click the **IncomingFreshmanStudents** table title bar to select all fields. Click within the highlighted field list and drag the fields into the query design grid to add all the fields at once.
   d. On the *Query Tools Design* tab, in the *Query Type* group, click the **Append** button.
   e. In the *Append* dialog, expand the **Table Name** box and select **Student**. Click **OK**.
   f. Switch to Datasheet view to check the query results. There should be 4 records in the results.
   g. Switch back to Design view.
   h. On the *Query Tools Design* tab, in the *Results* group, click the **Run** button.
   i. Access warns you that you are about to append 4 rows. Click **Yes**.
   j. Save the query as `AppendIncomingFreshman`. Close the query.

9. Use the Crosstab Query Wizard to create a crosstab query to total the number of classes per course. The existing query *CoursesByDept* contains the fields for the crosstab query results.

   a. On the *Create* tab, in the *Queries* group, click the **Query Wizard** button.

   b. In the *New Query* dialog, click **Crosstab Query Wizard.** Click **OK.**

   c. In the first step of the Crosstab Query Wizard, click the **Queries** radio button to display the list of available queries. Verify that **Query: CoursesByDept** is selected and click **Next.**

   d. Use the *CourseNumber* and *CourseDescription* fields as the row headings. In the *Available Fields* list, double-click **CourseNumber** and then double-click **CourseDescription.** Click **Next.**

   e. Use the *DeptName* field as the column headings. Verify that **DeptName** is selected and then click **Next.**

   f. To count the number of classes for each course number, verify that **ClassCode** is selected in the *Fields* list and **Count** is selected in the *Functions* list. Verify that the **Yes, include row sums** check box is checked. Click **Next.**

   g. Accept the suggested name **CoursesByDept_Crosstab.** Click **Finish** to view the query results.

   h. Close the query.

10. Modify the *FreshmanClassOfferings* query in SQL view to create a query to display sophomore course offerings.

    a. Open the **FreshmanClassOfferings** query in Datasheet view. Observe that there are 20 records in the results and each course number begins with the number 1 after the hyphen.

    b. On the *Home* tab, in the *Views* group, click the **View** drop-down arrow. Select **SQL View.**

    c. The following SQL code displays:

```
SELECT Class.ClassCode, Class.CourseNumber, Class.Section, Class.Time,
Class.Room, Class.Professor

FROM Class

WHERE (((Class.CourseNumber) Like "*-1*"))
```

    d. In the SQL window, in the WHERE clause, in the last line, change the **1** in `Like "*-1*"` to **2** to return records where the value in the *CourseNumber* field includes –2.

    e. On the *Query Tools Design* tab, in the *Results* group, click the **Run** button. Observe that there are now 15 records in the results and each course number begins with the number 2 after the hyphen.

    f. Click the **File** tab. Click **Save As.** Click **Save Object As** and then click the **Save As** button. Type `SophomoreClassOfferings` and then click **OK.**

    g. Close the query.

11. Create a macro to open the *Professor* table.

    a. On the *Create* tab, in the *Macros & Code* group, click the **Macro** button.

    b. Click the **Add New Action** drop-down arrow. Select **Group.**

    c. In the *Group* text box, type: `OpenTable`

    d. Click the **Add New Action** drop-down arrow. Select **OpenTable.**

    e. Click the **Table Name** drop-down arrow. Select **Professor.**

  f. Save the macro as: `OpenProfessorTable`
  g. On the *Macro Tools Design* tab, in the *Tools* group, click the **Run** button.
  h. Close the *Professor* table.
  i. Close the macro.
12. Modify the *OpenProfessorTable* macro so it not only opens the table but also begins a new record ready for data entry.
  a. In the Navigation Pane, in the *Macros* section, right-click **OpenProfessorTable** and select **Design View.**
  b. In the Action Catalog, expand the **Database Objects** section.
  c. Double-click **GoToRecord.**
  d. From the **Object Type** drop-down arrow, choose **Table.**
  e. From the **Object Name** drop-down arrow, choose **Professor.**
  f. From the **Record** drop-down arrow, choose **New.**
  g. Save and run the macro.
  h. Close the *Professor* table.
  i. Close the macro.
13. Close the database and exit Access.

skill review 8.2

Ocean View Rentals offers beachfront accommodations year-round. The database tracks guests, reservations, and units. You will create action queries to archive old reservations and to view and make changes to current reservations. You will create a macro to run two action queries in sequence.

Skills needed to complete this project:
- Understanding Action Queries (Skill 8.1)
- Creating a New Table through a Query (Skill 8.3)
- Moving Records through a Query (Skill 8.5)
- Deleting Records through a Query (Skill 8.4)
- Updating Records through a Query (Skill 8.2)
- Adding Totals to a Query (Skill 8.7)
- Setting Join Properties in a Query (Skill 8.6)
- Modifying a Query in SQL View (Skill 8.9)
- Creating a Stand-Alone Macro (Skill 8.10)

1. Open the start file **AC2013-SkillReview-8-2** and resave the file as: `[your initials]AC-SkillReview-8-2`
2. If necessary, enable active content by clicking the **Enable Content** button in the Message Bar.
3. Create a make table query to archive old 2013 reservations.
  a. On the *Create* tab, in the *Queries* group, click the **Query Design** button.
  b. In the *Show Table* dialog, double-click **Reservation.** Click **Close.**
  c. In the *Reservation* table field list, double-click these fields in this order: **ReservationID, UnitID, GuestID, CheckIn, Nights,** and **Rate**

d. Under the *CheckIn* field, in the *Criteria* row, type: `*2013`
e. On the *Query Tools Design* tab, in the *Query Type* group, click the **Make Table** button.
f. In the *Make Table* dialog, in the *Table Name* box type: `CompletedReservations`
g. Click **OK**.
h. Switch to Datasheet view to check the query results. There should be 50 records in the results.
i. Switch back to Design view.
j. On the *Query Tools Design* tab, in the *Results* group, click the **Run** button.
k. Access should warn you that you are about to paste 50 rows into a new table. Click **Yes**.
l. Save the query as: `MakeCompletedReservations`

4. Change the *MakeCompletedReservations* query to an append query to add January–March 2014 reservations to the *CompletedReservations* table.
   a. Click the **File** tab. Click **Save As**. Click **Save Object As** and then click the **Save As** button. Type `AppendJan-Mar` and then click **OK**.
   b. On the *Query Tools Design* tab, in the *Query Type* group, click the **Append** button.
   c. Verify that **CompletedReservations** is selected in the *Table Name* box, and then click **OK**.
   d. Under the *CheckIn* field, in the *Criteria* row, replace the existing criteria with: `Between 1/1/2014 And 3/31/2014`
   e. Switch to Datasheet view to check the query results. There should be 12 records in the results.
   f. Switch back to Design view.
   g. On the *Query Tools Design* tab, in the *Results* group, click the **Run** button.
   h. Access should warn you that you are about to append 12 rows. Click **Yes**.
   i. Save the query.

5. Change the *AppendJan-Mar* query to a delete query to delete all 2013 and January–March 2014 reservations from the *Reservation* table.
   a. Click the **File** tab. Click **Save As**. Click **Save Object As** and then click the **Save As** button. Type `Delete2013andJan-Mar` and then click **OK**.
   b. On the *Query Tools Design* tab, in the *Query Type* group, click the **Delete** button.
   c. Under the *CheckIn* field, in the *Criteria* row, replace the existing criteria with: `<4/1/2014`
   d. On the *Query Tools Design* tab, in the *Results* group, click the **Run** button.
   e. Access should warn you that you are about to delete 62 rows. Click **Yes**.
   f. Save and close the query.

6. Create an update query to add a comment to all reservations less than four nights.
   a. On the *Create* tab, in the *Queries* group, click the **Query Design** button.
   b. In the *Show Table* dialog, double-click **Reservation**. Click **Close**.
   c. In the *Reservation* table, double-click **Nights** and **Comments** in that order.
   d. On the *Query Tools Design* tab, in the *Query Type* group, click the **Update** button.
   e. Under the *Nights* field, in the *Criteria* row, type: `<4`
   f. Under the *Comments* field, in the *Update To* row, type: `Offer an additional night at a discounted rate.`

g. On the *Query Tools Design* tab, in the *Results* group, click the **Run** button.

h. A warning box displays. Click **Yes**.

i. Save the query as: `UpdateCommentsForShortRentals`

j. Close the query.

7. Create a query to calculate the number of nights that each unit is rented.

   a. On the *Create* tab, in the *Queries* group, click the **Query Design** button.

   b. In the *Show Table* dialog, double-click **Unit** and **Reservation**. Click **Close**.

   c. In the *Unit* table, double-click **UnitName**.

   d. In the *Reservation* table, double-click **Nights**.

   e. On the *Query Tools Design* tab, in the *Show/Hide* group, click the **Totals** button.

   f. Under the *Nights* field, in the *Total* row, change *Group by* to **Sum**.

   g. On the *Query Tools Design* tab, in the *Results* group, click the **Run** button.

   h. Save the query as: `RentalsByUnit`

8. Modify the *RentalsByUnit* query to include all records from the *Unit* table.

   a. In the top section of the Query Design window, double-click the line between the *Unit* and *Reservation* tables.

   b. In the *Join Properties* dialog, click the radio button in front of **2: Include ALL records from 'Unit' and only those records from 'Reservation' where the joined fields are equal.**

   c. Click **OK**.

   d. On the *Query Tools Design* tab, in the *Results* group, click the **Run** button.

   e. Save and close the query.

9. Modify the *JuneReservations* query in SQL view to display July reservations.

   a. Open the **JuneReservations** query in Design view.

   b. On the *Query Tools Design* tab, in the *Results* group, click the **View** drop-down arrow and select **SQL View**.

   c. The following SQL code displays:

   ```
   SELECT Reservation.CheckIn, Reservation.UnitID
   FROM Reservation
   WHERE (((Reservation.CheckIn) Like "6*"))
   ORDER BY Reservation.CheckIn, Reservation.UnitID;
   ```

   d. In the SQL window, in the WHERE clause, change the **6** in `Like "6*"` to **7**.

   e. On the *Query Tools Design* tab, in the *Results* group, click the **Run** button.

   f. Click the **File** tab. Click **Save As**. Click **Save Object As** and then click the **Save As** button. Type `JulyReservations` and then click **OK**.

   g. Close the query.

10. The *AppendApr-Jun* query and the *DeleteApr-Jun* query append reservations from April to June to the *CompletedReservations* table and delete them from the *Reservation* table. Create a macro to run both queries.

    a. On the *Create* tab, in the *Macros & Code* group, click the **Macro** button.

    b. Click the **Add New Action** drop-down arrow and select **Group**.

    c. In the *Group* text box, type: `RemoveApr-Jun`

    d. Click the **Add New Action** drop-down arrow and select **OpenQuery**.

    e. Click the **Query Name** drop-down arrow and select **AppendApr-Jun**.

f. In the Action Catalog, under the *Filter/Query/Search* folder, double-click **OpenQuery**.

g. Click the **Query Name** drop-down arrow and select **DeleteApr-Jun**.

h. On the *Macro Tools Design* tab, in the *Collapse/Expand* group, click the **Collapse Actions** button.

i. Save the macro as: `ArchiveApr-Jun`

j. On the *Macro Tools Design* tab, in the *Tools* group, click the **Run** button. Click **Yes** in response to all warnings. The macro actions should append 20 rows and then delete 20 rows.

k. Close the macro.

11. Close the database and exit Access.

challenge yourself 8.3

The Human Resources database contains employee and benefit information for city employees. Employees who work for the auditor's office and assessor's office are being transferred. You will create action queries to copy records into a new table and then delete them from the *Employee* table. You will create a query to select all family health plans and then update the cost of those plans. You will update a query directly in SQL view. Finally, you will create a stand-alone macro to display records from a form.

Skills needed to complete this project:
- Understanding Action Queries (Skill 8.1)
- Creating a New Table through a Query (Skill 8.3)
- Moving Records through a Query (Skill 8.5)
- Deleting Records through a Query (Skill 8.4)
- Updating Records through a Query (Skill 8.2)
- Creating a Crosstab Query (Skill 8.8)
- Modifying a Query in SQL View (Skill 8.9)
- Creating a Stand-Alone Macro (Skill 8.10)

1. Open the start file **AC2013-ChallengeYourself-8-3** and resave the file as: `[your initials]AC-ChallengeYourself-8-3`

2. If necessary, enable active content by clicking the **Enable Content** button in the Message Bar.

3. Create a make table query from the **Employee** table to add all employee data for employees who work for the auditor's department (**ADT**) to a new table named **TransferEmployee**. Add all fields to the query. The query should return records with **ADT** in the **DeptCode** field. Run the query. (*Hint:* The query should paste 8 rows into the new table.) Save the query as `MakeTransferEmployee`. Close the query.

4. Create an append query from the **Employee** table to append all employees who work for the assessor's department (**ASR**) to the **TransferEmployee** table. Add all fields to the query. The query should return records with **ASR** in the **DeptCode** field. Run the query. (*Hint:* The query should append 8 rows.) Save the query as `AppendASRtoTransferEmployee`. Close the query.

5. Create a delete query to delete **ADT** and **ASR** employees from the **Employee** table. Add all fields to the query. The query should return records with **ADT** or **ASR** in the **DeptCode** field. Run the query. (*Hint:* The query should delete 16 rows.) Save the query as `DeleteASRandADTfromEmployee`. Close the query.

6. Create an update query to update the cost of family health plans by 5% in the **HealthPlan** table. Use the criteria ***F** for the **HealthPlanCode** field to return only family plans. To update the **EmployeeWeeklyCost** of all family plans by 5%, in the *Update To* row use the following formula: `[EmployeeWeeklyCost]*1.05` Run the query. (*Hint:* The query should update 3 rows. The updated value in the *EmployeeWeeklyCost* field for the first record in the results should be $110.25.) Save the query as **IncreaseFamilyPlanEmployeeCostBy5%**. Close the query.

7. Create a crosstab query based on the **EmployeeHealthPlan** query. Use the **DeptName** field as row headings, the **HealthPlan** field as column headings, and **EmployeeID** as the value to be counted. Use the **Count** function. Run the query. Save the query as **EmployeeHealthPlan_Crosstab**. Close the query.

8. Modify the **HourlyPayByDepartment** query in SQL view to display only employees that have an hourly pay **greater than 20**. Insert `WHERE Employee.HourlyPay>20` before the ORDER BY clause. Run the query. (*Hint:* The query results should have 24 records.) Save the query as **HourlyPayGreaterThan20**.

9. Create a macro that will open the **Employee** form and display all the employee records using the **ShowAllRecords** action from the Action Catalog. Save the macro as **ShowAllEmployeeRecords**. Run the macro to test it. Close the form. Close the macro.

10. Close the database and exit Access.

challenge yourself 8.4

The New England Flu database is tracking suspected cases of Influenza A, B, and C. You will create action queries to modify the *Diagnosis* table and then create and run a stand-alone macro to open a form with a filter applied.

Skills needed to complete this project:
- Understanding Action Queries (Skill 8.1)
- Updating Records through a Query (Skill 8.2)
- Creating a New Table through a Query (Skill 8.3)
- Deleting Records through a Query (Skill 8.4)
- Adding Totals to a Query (Skill 8.7)
- Modifying a Query in SQL View (Skill 8.9)
- Creating a Stand-Alone Macro (Skill 8.10)

1. Open the start file **AC2013-ChallengeYourself-8-4** and resave the file as:
   `[your initials]AC-ChallengeYourself-8-4`

2. If necessary, enable active content by clicking the **Enable Content** button in the Message Bar.

3. Create an update query to update the **Comments** field in the **Diagnosis** table for all patients who have not had a flu shot. Add all fields from the **Diagnosis** table and use the criteria `false` for the **FluShot** field. Update the **Comments** field to: `Call patient to make appointment for flu shot.` Run the query. (*Hint:* The query should update 211 rows.) Save the query as **UpdateCommentsForFlushot**. Close the query.

4. Create a make table query from the **Diagnosis** table to add all records for patients with a negative diagnosis to a new table called **ResultsNegative**. Include the fields **DiagnosisID, PatientID, FluShot,** and **Diagnosis** in the query. Use the criteria `Negative` for the **Diagnosis** field. Run the query. (*Hint:* The query should paste 65 rows into the new table.) Save the query as **MakeTableResultsNegative**. Close the query.

5. Create a delete query to delete all records for patients with a negative diagnosis from the **Diagnosis** table. Add all fields to the query. Use the criteria `Negative` for the **Diagnosis** field. Run the query. (*Hint:* The query should delete 65 rows.) Save the query as **DeleteResultsNegative.** Close the query.

6. Create a query to summarize the number of patients for each diagnosis per state. From the **Patient** table, add the **State** field. From the **Diagnosis** table, add the **Diagnosis** and **Flushot** fields. Display the *Total* row, and then under the *FluShot* field, select **Count.** Run the query. Save the query as **FluShotByState.** Close the query.

7. Open the query **Under18.** Switch to SQL view. Modify the SQL code to display records for patients aged between 18 and 64 using this code:
   `WHERE (Patient.Age Between 18 and 64)`
   Run the query. (*Hint:* The query results should have 128 records.) Save the query as **Age18To64.** Do not close the query yet.

8. Switch back to SQL view. Modify the SQL to display cases for patients **over 64.** Run the query. (*Hint:* The query results should have 121 records.) Save the query as **AgeOver64.** Close the query.

9. Create a macro to open the **Age and Diagnosis** form and filter the results to show only records where the value of the **FluShot** field is false. Use a single action to open the **AgeAndDiagnosis** form. Use this expression in the *Where Condition* = box: `[Diagnosis]![FluShot] =False` Save the macro as **FilterForNoFluShot.** Run the macro. Close the form and the macro.

10. Close the database and exit Access.

on your own 8.5

The online store eTunes has decided to eliminate the sale of soundtracks and Broadway shows in the eTunes library and move them to another online specialized music sales site. In this project, you will create your own action queries to move and update data. You will also create a query to summarize sales data and create at least one stand-alone macro.

Skills needed to complete this project:
- Understanding Action Queries (Skill 8.1)
- Creating a New Table through a Query (Skill 8.3)
- Updating Records through a Query (Skill 8.2)
- Adding Totals to a Query (Skill 8.7)
- Creating a Crosstab Query (Skill 8.8)
- Creating a Stand-Alone Macro (Skill 8.10)

1. Open the start file **AC2013-OnYourOwn-8-5** and resave the file as:
   `[your initials]AC-OnYourOwn-8-5`

2. If necessary, enable active content by clicking the **Enable Content** button in the Message Bar.

3. Use an action query to copy all music with the genre code **BWY** or **SNT** from the **Music** table into a new table. (*Hint:* The query should paste 8 rows into the new table.) Name the new table: `Soundtracks`

4. Use an action query to increase the price of the music in the new table you created by **25%.**

5. Create a query to summarize the number of sales by genre. Include the **Music, Sales,** and **Genres** tables in the query. Include both the **GenreCode** and **GenreDescription**

fields from the **Genres** table. Include additional fields of your choice. You may want to create a query using totals, or you may want to create a crosstab query. Because this query requires fields from more than one table, if you want to use the Crosstab Query Wizard, you'll need to create a query first that includes all the fields, and then use that query as the base for the crosstab query.

6. Create at least one stand-alone macro to open one of the tables in this database.
7. Close all database objects.
8. Close the database and exit Access.

fix it 8.6

In this project, you will modify two select queries to make them action queries. You will also create a query to summarize data.

Skills needed to complete this project:
- Understanding Action Queries (Skill 8.1)
- Creating a New Table through a Query (Skill 8.3)
- Updating Records through a Query (Skill 8.2)
- Creating a Crosstab Query (Skill 8.8)

1. Open the start file **AC2013-FixIt-8-6** and resave the file as:
   `[your initials]AC-FixIt-8-6`
2. If necessary, enable active content by clicking the **Enable Content** button in the Message Bar.
3. Change the **MakeCollections** query to make a table, named **Collections**, of all unpaid invoices prior to 2014. Run the query. (*Hint:* The query should paste 11 rows into the new table.) Save and close the query.
4. A late fee of **10%** of the invoice amount is being added to all unpaid invoices with a date of visit from **January to May 2014.** Open the **UpdateJan-MayLateFee** query, and change it to an update query. In the *Update To* row in the **LateFee** field, enter a formula to calculate `.10*[InvoiceAmount]`. Run the query. (*Hint:* The query should update 30 rows. The updated value in the *InvoiceAmount* field in the first record should be $30.10.) Save and close the query.
5. Use the **TechnicianVisits** query as the base for a new query to summarize the data using **TechnicianLastName** as a row heading, **DepartmentName** as a column heading, and the count of **DateOfVisit** as a value. Do not include a summary for each row. Save the query as **TechnicianVisits_Crosstab.** View the results and then close the query.
6. Close the database and exit Access.

chapter 9

Finalizing the Database

- Find and eliminate redundant data
- Specify database startup options
- Specify database view and design options
- Create database back-end and front-end files
- Lock a front-end database
- Secure a database with a password
- Generate database documentation

In this chapter, you will learn the following skills:

Skill **9.1** Using the Table Analyzer
Skill **9.2** Using the Performance Analyzer
Skill **9.3** Viewing Dependencies
Skill **9.4** Customizing the Navigation Pane
Skill **9.5** Configuring Database Startup Options
Skill **9.6** Limiting Views and Design Options
Skill **9.7** Splitting a Database
Skill **9.8** Creating a Locked ACCDE File
Skill **9.9** Encrypting a Database with a Password
Skill **9.10** Using the Database Documenter
Skill **9.11** Printing the Relationship Report

skills

introduction

This chapter covers skills to finalize the database and prepare it for use by other users. You will learn how to use Access's tools to analyze the structure of the database to find and eliminate redundant data. You will also learn to set up the database for other users including configuring startup options, splitting the database into front-end and back-end components, creating a locked ACCDE file, and securing the database with a password. Finally, you will learn how to generate database documentation. You will use a variety of databases throughout this chapter. Be sure to use the correct data file for each *Let Me Try*.

Skill 9.1 Using the Table Analyzer

In a well-designed database, each independent set of data should be stored in its own table, rather than repeating the same information in multiple records. If you find the same data repeating in different records, that data should be pulled out of the table and stored in a separate table linked to the original table through a lookup field. If you have not yet created separate, related tables in your database, use the **Table Analyzer** tool to do it for you.

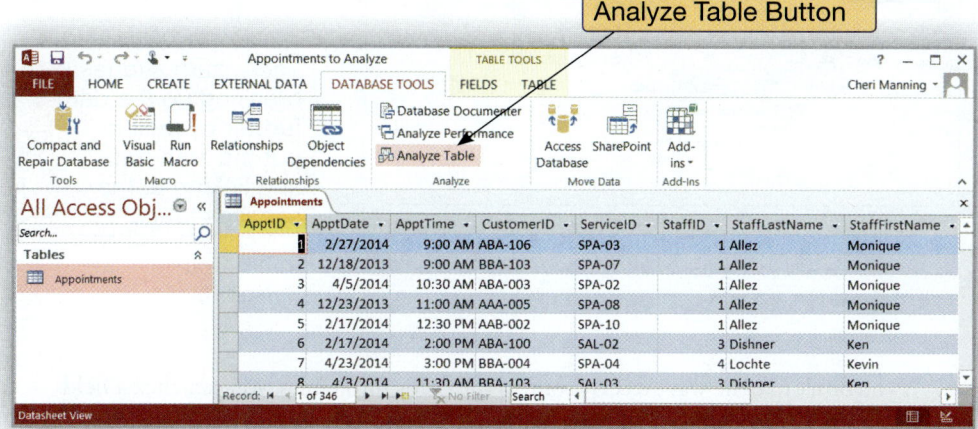

FIGURE AC 9.1

In Figure AC 9.1, each record in the *Appointments* table stores the information for a single appointment. However, the IDs in the *CustomerID* and *ServiceID* fields repeat as do the related information in the *StaffID, StaffLastName,* and *StaffFirstName* fields. The Table Analyzer will recognize these patterns and create the separate, related tables for you.

To run the Table Analyzer Wizard and accept the recommended changes:

1. If you have the table open, close it. On the *Database Tools* tab, in the *Analyze* group, click the **Analyze Table** button to open the Table Analyzer Wizard.
2. The first two steps in the wizard provide information about the Table Analyzer. When you have read the information carefully, click **Next** to continue.
   > To hide these steps in the future, in the third step of the wizard click the **Show Introductory Pages** check box to remove the checkmark.
3. Select the table to analyze. Click **Next**.
4. To allow Access to analyze the table and make suggestions, verify that the **Yes, let the wizard decide** radio button is selected. Click **Next**.

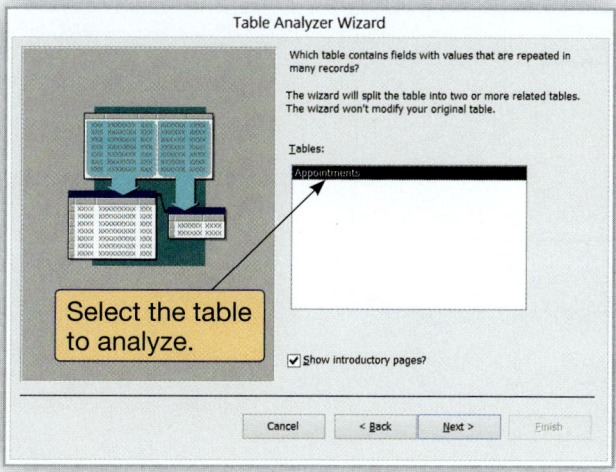

FIGURE AC 9.2

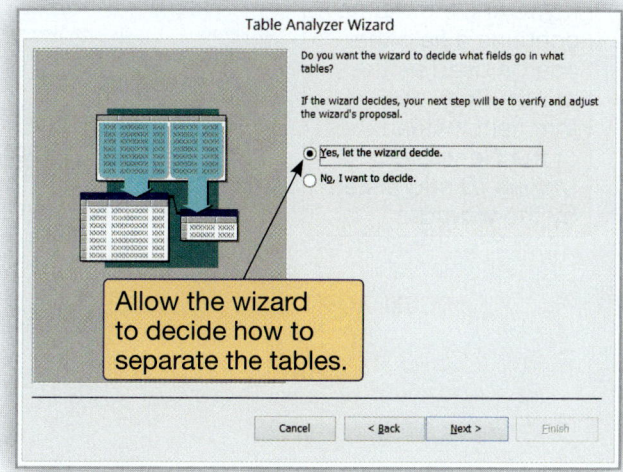

FIGURE AC 9.3

5. Access shows the suggestion for the new tables. Review the suggestions carefully.

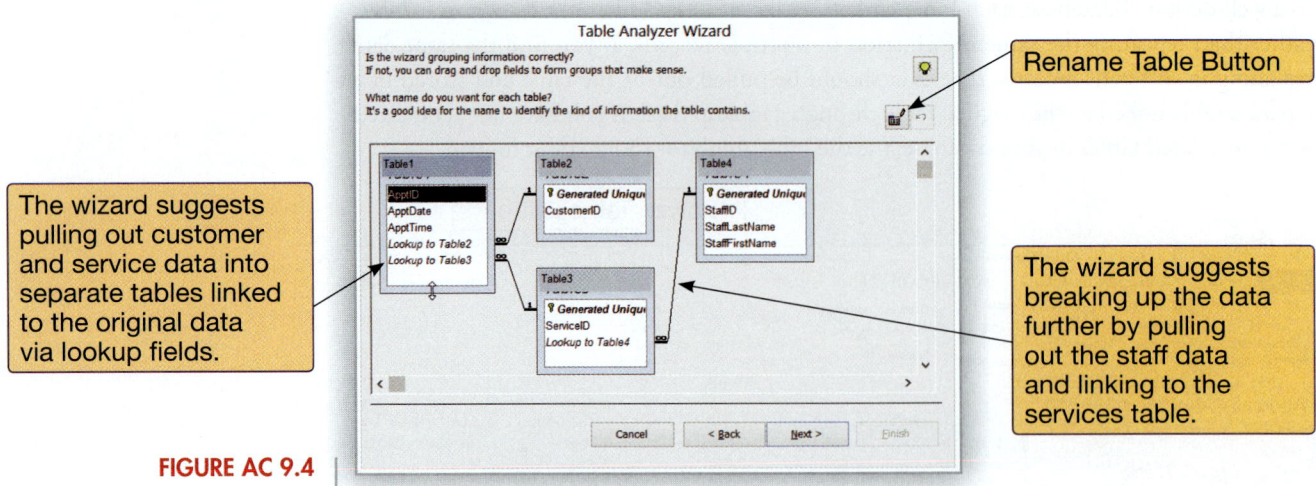

FIGURE AC 9.4

6. If you don't like the way Access grouped the fields into tables, you can click a field name and drag it to a different table or drag it to an empty area to create a new table. You can also click and drag to rearrange the order of fields within a table.
7. Each table is given a temporary name (*Table1, Table2,* and so forth). You should rename each table. Click the table you want to rename, and then click the **Rename Table** button. Type the table name in the *Table Name* box and click **OK**. (You can also double-click a table's title to rename it.)
8. Click **Next** to continue to the next step of the wizard.
9. Access makes a suggestion for a primary key for each new table. In some cases, if Access does not detect a unique field, it will suggest creating a *Generated Unique ID* (an AutoNumber primary key). You can define a primary key field yourself by clicking the field once to select it, and then clicking the **Set Unique Identifier** button.

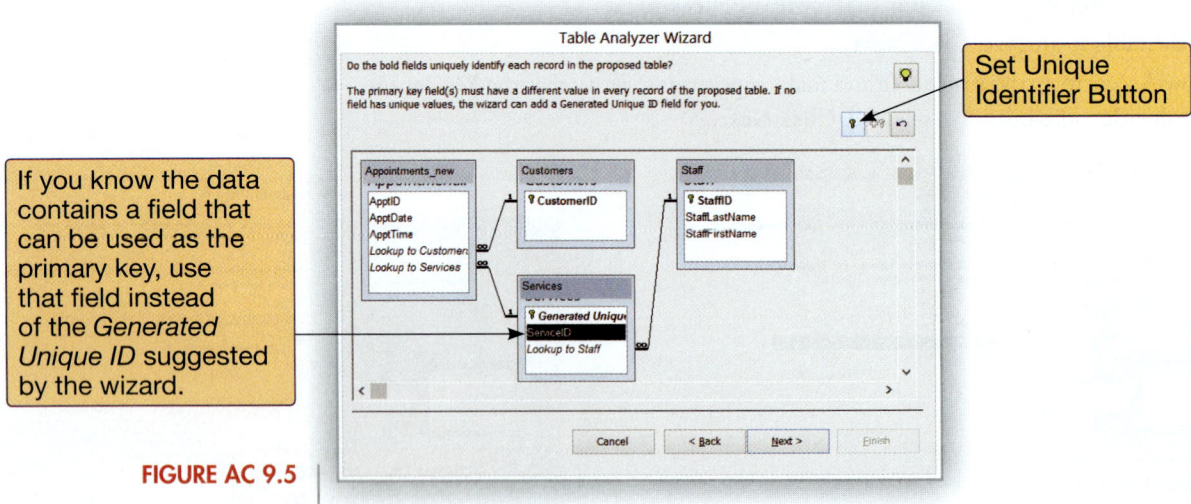

FIGURE AC 9.5

10. Click **Next** to continue.
11. Review any potential typographical errors detected by Access and make the appropriate choice for each. Access will skip this step of the wizard if there are no errors detected.
12. Click **Next** to continue to the last step of the wizard.

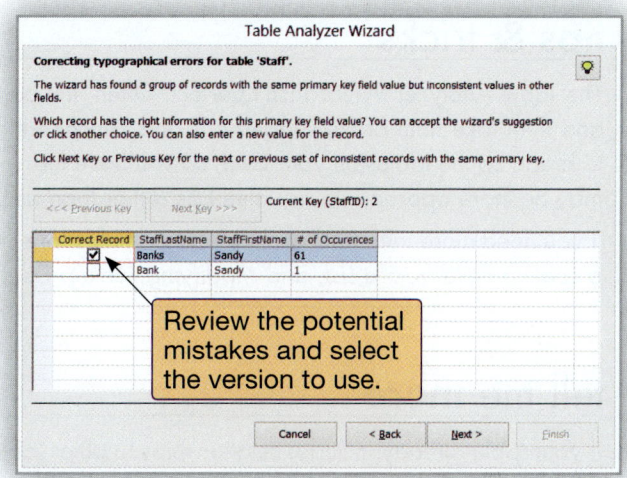

FIGURE AC 9.6

13. If your database does not include any forms or reports yet, it isn't necessary to create a query. On the last step of the Table Analyzer Wizard, select the **No, don't create the query.** radio button.
    - If you run the Table Analyzer after you've created forms and reports, allow Access to create a query for you based on the original table. This query will ensure that forms and reports based on the original table will still work.
14. Click **Finish** to create the new tables.

When the wizard is complete, Access opens the new tables. Notice the original table is still available. Once you have confirmed that the new tables work as you want, you can delete the original table (or create a backup), and rename *Table1* with the original table name.

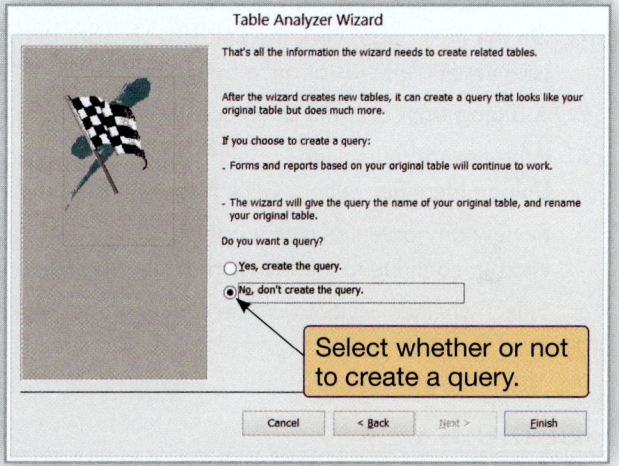

FIGURE AC 9.7

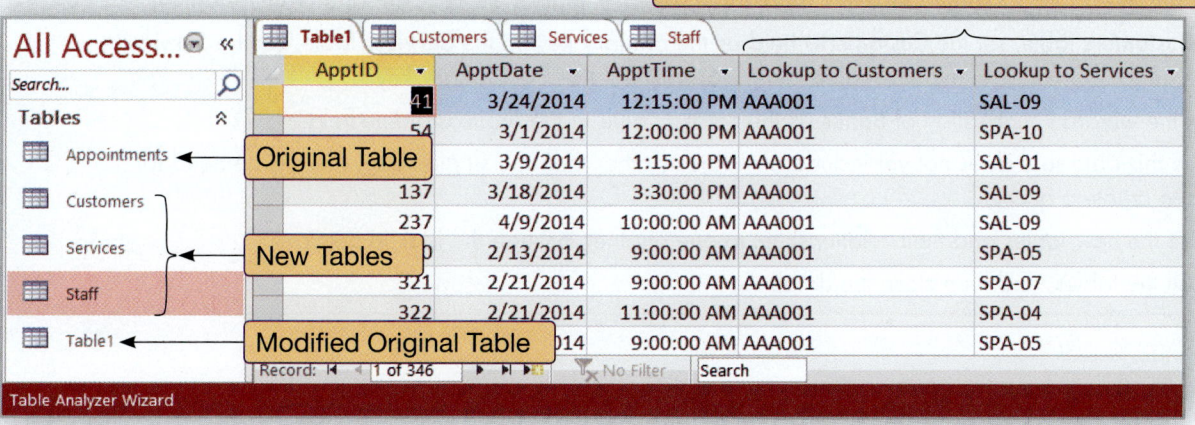

FIGURE AC 9.8

The process of splitting up a single table into separate, related tables is known as **normalization**. If you continue to study database design, you will learn about the rules of normalization and when to use each. For a typical Access user, it is enough to understand how to design an efficient database by relating tables to each other through lookup fields and enforcing referential integrity and cascading delete and update options.

skill 9.1 Using the Table Analyzer

tips & tricks

The Table Analyzer Wizard isn't perfect. Often, the best approach is to allow the Table Analyzer to make suggestions and then take note of the suggestions and cancel out of the wizard without implementing them. Use the suggestions to break up the tables on your own, so you have more control over how the tables relate to each other. Some lookups may be more appropriate as value lists rather than as their own separate tables.

If you need more information about lookup fields, refer to the skills *Adding a Lookup Field from Another Table*, *Adding a Lookup Field from a List*, and *Modifying Lookup Field Properties*.

tell me more

If your table already includes relationships to other tables through lookup fields, the Table Analyzer will not recognize this and will suggest new tables that you do not want. In this case, it is still worthwhile to review the suggestions that Access makes, but do not complete the wizard and make the changes. Instead, go back to the second step of the wizard after the two introductory steps and click the **No, I want to decide** radio button.

1. On the next page, click the field(s) you want to pull out into a separate table, and drag to a blank area. You can select multiple fields at once by holding ⇧Shift or Ctrl as you click.
2. A dialog appears with a temporary name for the table. Type a new name in the *Table Name* box and click **OK**.
3. If the new table includes a field that should be used as the primary key, click the field, and then click the **Set Unique Identifier** button. Click **Next**.
4. Review any potential typographical errors detected by Access and make the appropriate choice for each. Click **Next** to continue to the last step of the wizard.
5. Select whether or not to create a query, and then click **Finish** to create the new tables.

let me try

Open the data file **AC9-Appointments-Analyze** and try this skill on your own:

1. Open the **Table Analyzer** and analyze the structure of the **Appointments** table.
2. Allow the wizard to make recommendations.
3. Do not rename *Table1*. Rename **Table2:** `Customers`, rename **Table3:** `Services`, and rename **Table4:** `Staff`.
4. In the **Customers** table, set the **CustomerID** field as the primary key. In the **Services** table, set the **ServiceID** field as the primary key. In the **Staff** table, set the **StaffID** field as the primary key.
5. Accept the wizard's suggestion of **Banks** as the correct value in the *StaffLastName* field.
6. Because this database does not yet include any objects other than the single table, there is no need for Access to create a query.
7. Observe the new tables and their relationships to one another through the lookup fields.
8. Close all the tables, and then close the database.

Skill 9.2 Using the Performance Analyzer

A common performance optimization you may have missed while designing the database is to index the foreign key field in lookup relationships. Similar to a book index, the database **index** stores an internal pointer to the data to make it easier for the application to find it. Primary key fields are indexed automatically. To index a foreign key field, view the table in Design view and change the field's *Indexed* property to **Yes (Duplicates OK)**. The **Performance Analyzer** tool can do this for you and suggest other changes to optimize the database and speed up performance.

To use the Performance Analyzer:

1. On the *Database Tools* tab, in the *Analyze* group, click the **Analyze Performance** button.

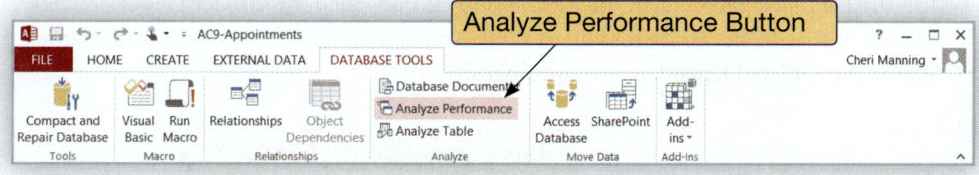

FIGURE AC 9.9

2. In the Performance Analyzer, click the tab for the type of database object you want to analyze or click the **All Object Types** tab to view all the database objects.
3. Click the check box for the specific object or click the **Select All** button to select all the objects.
4. Click **OK** to start the analysis.

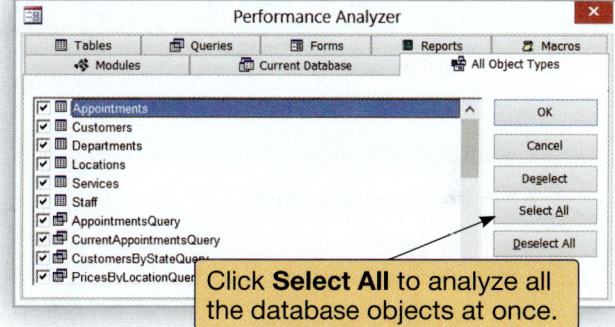

FIGURE AC 9.10

5. Click each result and review the description in the *Analysis Notes* section at the bottom of the dialog.
6. If there are any results with the type **Recommendation** or **Suggestion,** select the action in the *Analysis Results* box and click the **Optimize** button to allow Access to complete the action. You can select more than one action by holding the (↑ Shift) or (Ctrl) key as you click.
7. Once the action has been completed, the icon next to the result will change to a checkmark. Click the **Close** button to close the Performance Analyzer.

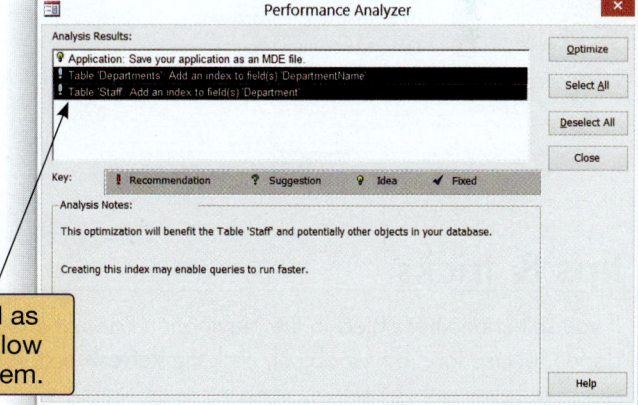

FIGURE AC 9.11

let me try

Open the data file **AC9-Appointments** and try this skill on your own:

1. Run the **Performance Analyzer** on all the database objects at once.
2. Access should have two **recommendations.** Select both recommendations and optimize the database.
3. Close the Performance Analyzer when you are finished.

Skill 9.3 Viewing Dependencies

Object dependencies are created when the data for a database object or a field come from another database object. A form or report is dependent upon the table or query used as its record source. A table that includes a lookup field to another table is dependent upon that table. Queries are dependent upon the tables from which they draw fields. In a complex database, dependencies are often nested—one object depends on another, which in turn depends on another database object. You can view object dependencies in the Object Dependencies pane.

To view the object dependencies in your database:

1. In the Navigation Pane, select the object for which you want to view dependencies.
2. On the *Database Tools* tab, in the *Relationships* group, click the **Object Dependencies** button. It may be necessary for you to allow Access to update dependency information before the Object Dependencies pane opens.

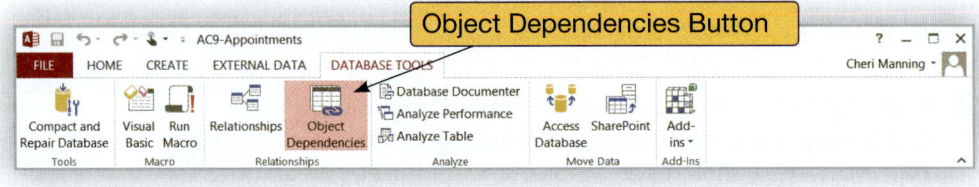

FIGURE AC 9.12

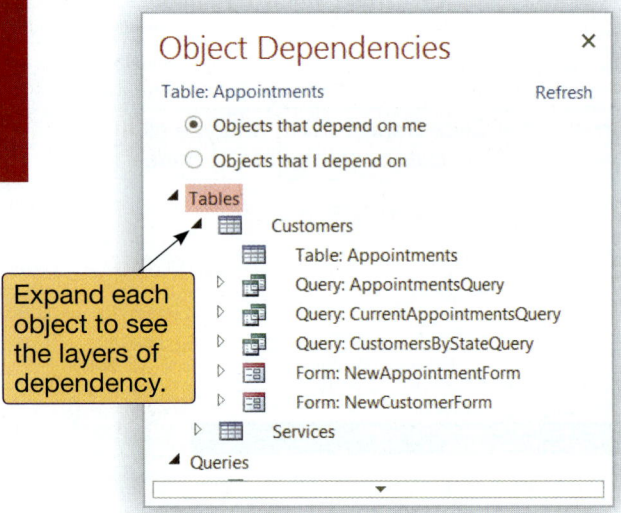

Expand each object to see the layers of dependency.

FIGURE AC 9.13

3. To view the objects that depend on the selected object, verify that the **Objects that depend on me** radio button is selected.
4. Click the arrow next to each database object to expand or collapse additional levels of dependency.
5. To view the objects used by the selected object, click the **Objects that I depend on** radio button.
6. To hide the Object Dependencies pane, click the **Object Dependencies** button again or click the **X** in the upper right corner of the pane.

tips & tricks

If you select another object in the Navigation Pane, the Object Dependencies pane will not update automatically. To see dependencies for the new object, click the **Refresh** button in the upper right corner of the Object Dependencies pane.

let me try

Open the data file **AC9-Appointments** and try this skill on your own:

1. View object dependencies for the **Appointments** table.
2. Expand the **Customers** table to view the objects that depend on it.
3. Switch the view in the Object Dependencies pane to see the objects on which the **Appointments** table is dependent.
4. Close the Object Dependencies pane when you are finished.

Skill 9.4 Customizing the Navigation Pane

In the skill *Organizing Objects in the Navigation Pane*, you learned to work with the standard Navigation Pane categories to organize database objects by object type, tables and related views, and date. You can also create your own custom categories and organize objects into groups within the custom category. Custom grouping is useful when you want to group together related forms and reports without showing the tables or queries.

To create a custom navigation category and groups:

1. Right-click the top of the Navigation Pane, and select **Navigation Options...** to open the *Navigation Options* dialog.
2. Click the **Add Item** button under the *Categories* list.
3. Type the name for the new category and press **Enter**.
4. To create a new group, verify that the new custom category is selected in the *Categories* list, and then click the **Add Group** button under the *Groups* list at the right side of the dialog.
5. Type the name for the new group and press **Enter**.
6. Create as many new groups as you want within the category. Note the default *Unassigned Objects* group. Do not delete it (yet). You need it to assign database objects to the custom group.
7. When you are finished creating custom categories and groups, click **OK**.

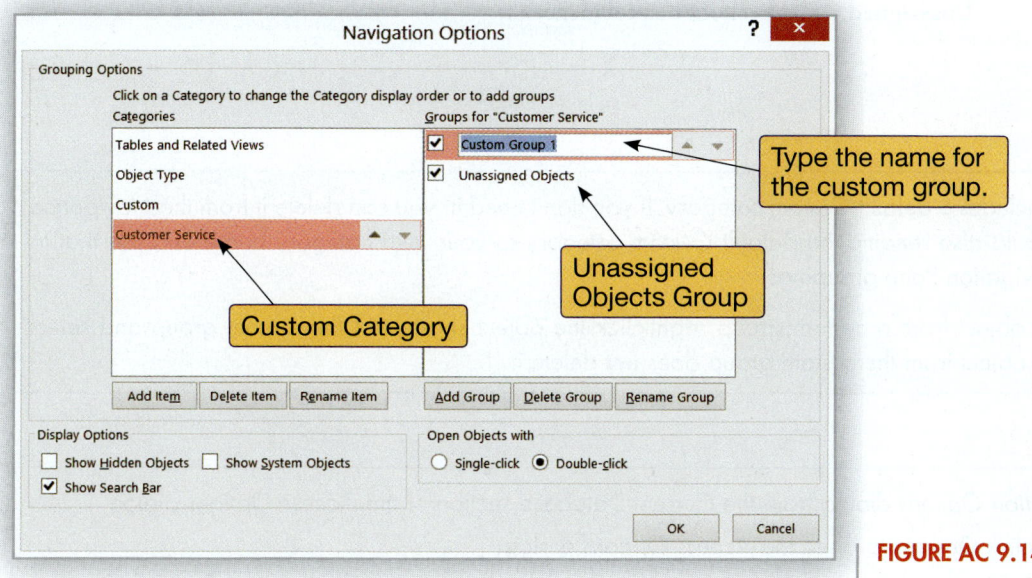

FIGURE AC 9.14

To add database objects to the new custom groups:

1. Click the arrow at the top of the Navigation Pane and select the custom category.
2. Until you add database objects to the custom groups, all database objects are included in the *Unassigned Objects* group within the custom category.
3. In the *Unassigned Objects* group, right-click a database object, point to **Add to Group...** and select the group you want to add it to. You can also click and drag an object from the **Unassigned Objects** group to the custom group where it belongs.

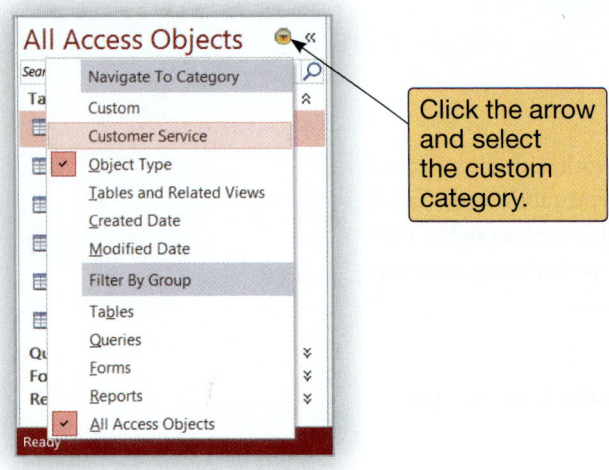

FIGURE AC 9.15

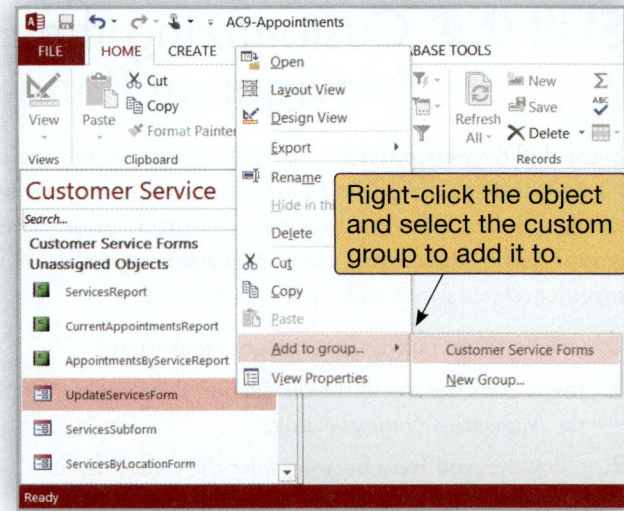

FIGURE AC 9.16

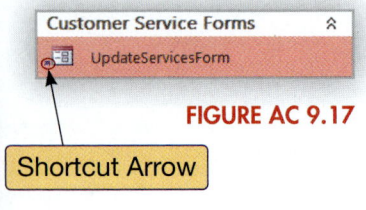

FIGURE AC 9.17

Observe that the database objects within the custom group have a small arrow next to the bottom left corner of the icon as shown in Figure AC 9.17.

This arrow indicates a shortcut to the actual database object. Database objects can have multiple shortcuts in different custom groups.

Once you have added all the database objects you want in your custom groups, you can hide the *Unassigned Objects* group in the custom category. In the *Navigation Options* dialog, select the custom category in the *Categories* list, and then in the *Groups* list, click the **Unassigned Objects** check box to uncheck it.

tips & tricks

- The Navigation Pane includes a default *Custom* category. If you don't need it, you can delete it from the *Navigation Options* dialog. You could also rename the default *Custom* category to your own category name and use that to create your custom Navigation Pane groupings.

- To remove a database object from a custom group, right-click the object shortcut in the custom group and select **Remove.** Removing the object from the custom group does not delete it.

another method

You can open the *Navigation Options* dialog from the Current Database section of the *Access Options* dialog.

1. Click the **File** tab and click **Options** to open the *Access Options* dialog.
2. Click **Current Database.**
3. Scroll down to the *Navigation* section, and click the **Navigation Options...** button.

let me try

Open the data file **AC9-Appointments** and try this skill on your own:

1. Create a new Navigation Pane category: `Customer Service`
2. Within the *Customer Service* category, create a new group: `Customer Service Forms`
3. Add the **UpdateServicesForm** form to the **Customer Service Forms** group.

Skill 9.5 Configuring Database Startup Options

Once you've completed the database design, optimized performance, and made your personal customizations, it's time to turn it over to the users who will enter data and run reports. If you are not the only person using the database, you can modify its appearance, so when less-experienced users open the file, they can focus on using the database rather than learning Access.

To identify the purpose of the database, add a database title. When you add a title to the database, the title appears in the window title bar instead of the file name. A title gives the database the appearance of a custom application.

If you've created a navigation form, you may want to set the database options to show the form automatically when the database is opened. Displaying a well-designed navigation form can eliminate the need for the Navigation Pane. Hiding the Navigation Pane can also prevent users from opening objects they shouldn't have access to.

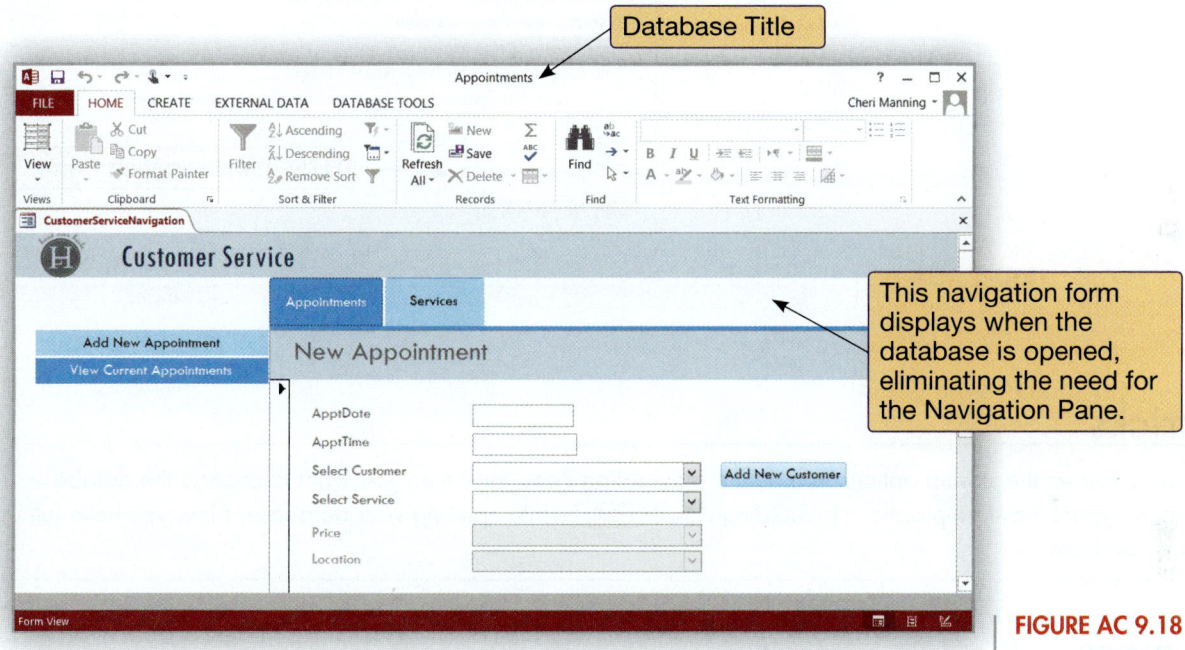

FIGURE AC 9.18

To set the database startup options from the *Access Options* dialog:

1. Click the **File** tab to open Backstage.
2. Click **Options** to open the *Access Options* dialog.
3. Click **Current Database** in the left-hand pane. Changing the options in the *Current Database* page affects only the open database.
4. Type a title for the database in the *Application Title* box.
5. In the *Navigation* section, click the **Display Navigation Pane** check box to remove the checkmark.
6. In the *Application Options* section, expand the **Display Form** list and select the form you want to use.
7. Click **OK** to accept the changes and close the *Access Options* dialog.
8. Depending on the options you changed, you may see a message that these changes will take effect next time you open the database. Click **OK** to dismiss the message box.

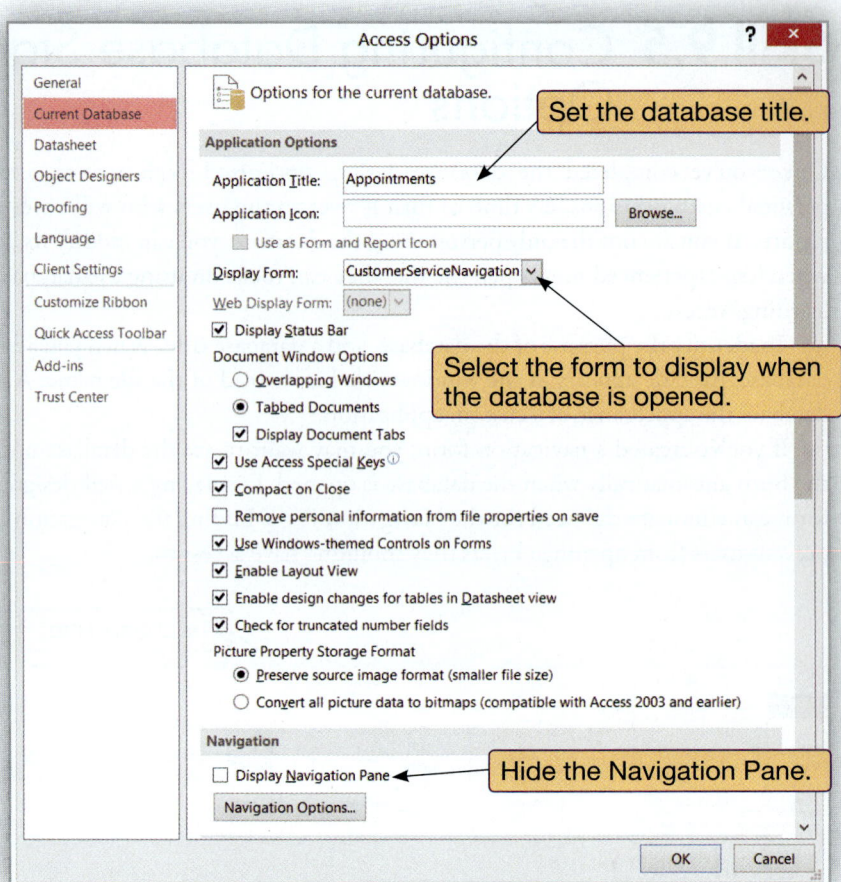

FIGURE AC 9.19

tips & tricks

What happens if you set the startup options to hide the Navigation Pane, and then you want to change the database design? You can bypass the startup options by holding down ⇧ Shift while opening your database. Now you have full access to your database.

tell me more

Other current database options are discussed in the skill *Limiting Views and Design Options*.

let me try

Open the data file **AC9-Appointments** and try this skill on your own:

1. Modify the database options to display **Appointments** in the title bar.
2. Set the **CustomerServiceNagivation** form to display at start up.
3. Hide the Navigation Pane.
4. Close the database and reopen it to observe the changes.

Skill 9.6 Limiting Views and Design Options

To discourage users from changing the database design, consider disabling Layout view for forms and reports. You can also disable design functionality for table Datasheet view. This option dims most of the buttons on the *Table Tools Fields* and *Tools* tabs. Finally, hide the status bar, so users aren't tempted to click the buttons at the lower right corner of the window to switch views.

To limit the view and design options available to database users:

1. Click the **File** tab to open Backstage.
2. Click **Options** to open the *Access Options* dialog.
3. Click **Current Database** in the left-hand pane.
4. To disable Layout view for forms and reports, click the **Enable Layout view** check box to remove the checkmark.
5. To disable the design options for tables in Datasheet view, click the **Enable design changes for tables in Datasheet view** check box to remove the checkmark.
6. To hide the status bar so users cannot easily switch to Design view, click the **Display Status Bar** check box to remove the checkmark.
7. Click **OK** to close the *Access Options* dialog and accept the changes.

Depending on the options you changed, you may see a message that these changes will take effect next time you open the database. Click **OK** to dismiss the message box.

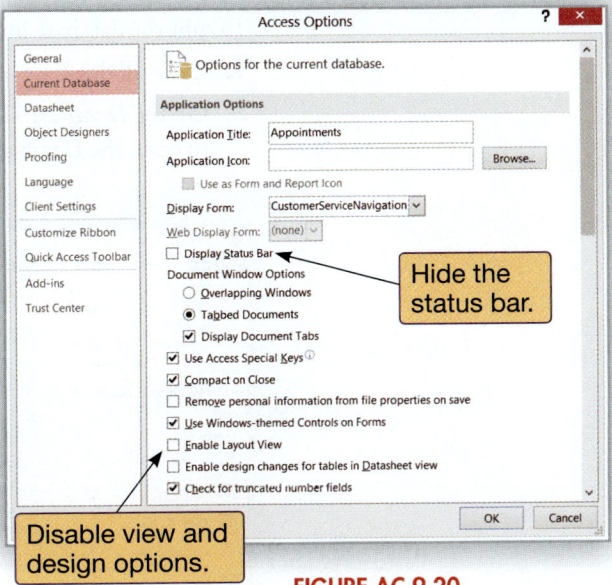

FIGURE AC 9.20

tell me more

If you want to really limit what users can do when they open the database, you can hide all the Ribbon tabs except the *Home* tab and limited options under the *File* tab. Open the *Access Options* dialog, in the *Current Database* page, scroll down to the *Ribbon and Toolbar Options* section, and click the **Allow Full Menus** check box to remove the checkmark.

If you need to open the database with the full Ribbon restored, press ⇧ Shift when you open the database file.

let me try

Open the data file **AC9-Appointments** and try this skill on your own:

1. Modify the database options to disable Layout view.
2. Modify the database options so users cannot make design changes to tables in Datasheet view.
3. Modify the database options to hide the status bar.
4. Close the database and reopen it to observe the changes.
5. Close the **AC9-Appointments** database.

Skill 9.7 Splitting a Database

The **Database Splitter** creates a database application with two separate files—a front end and a back end. The splitter copies all the tables from your database into a new Access file (the **back-end file**). Then the original tables are removed from the database and replaced with links to the new file. The original database file becomes the **front-end file**. This process allows you to keep the data tables in a secure location while giving other users access to the queries, forms, and reports via copies of the front end. Users can add, edit, and delete data through tables, queries, and forms in the front-end file, but they cannot change the structure of the underlying tables.

To split the database into separate front-end and back-end files:

1. Close all database objects.
2. On the *Database Tools* tab, in the *Move Data* group, click the **Access Database** button to open the Database Splitter Wizard.

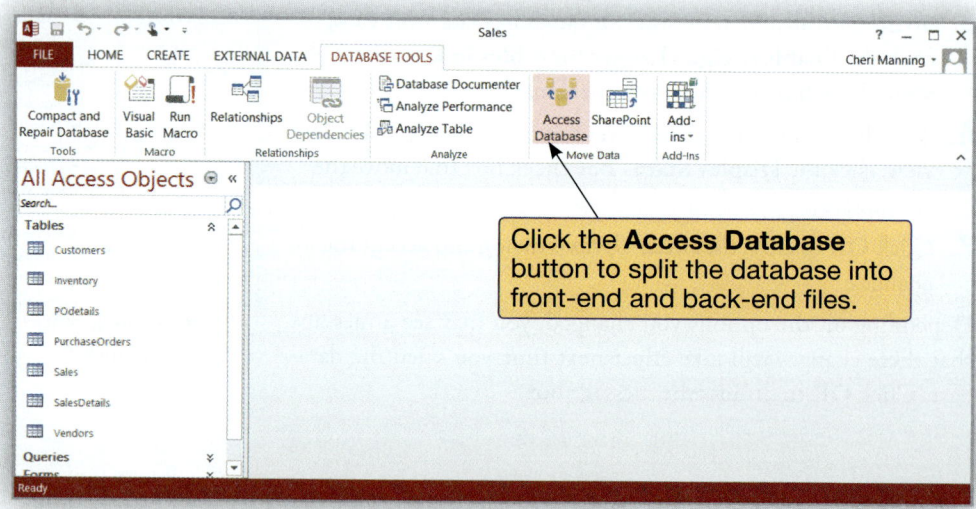

Click the **Access Database** button to split the database into front-end and back-end files.

FIGURE AC 9.21

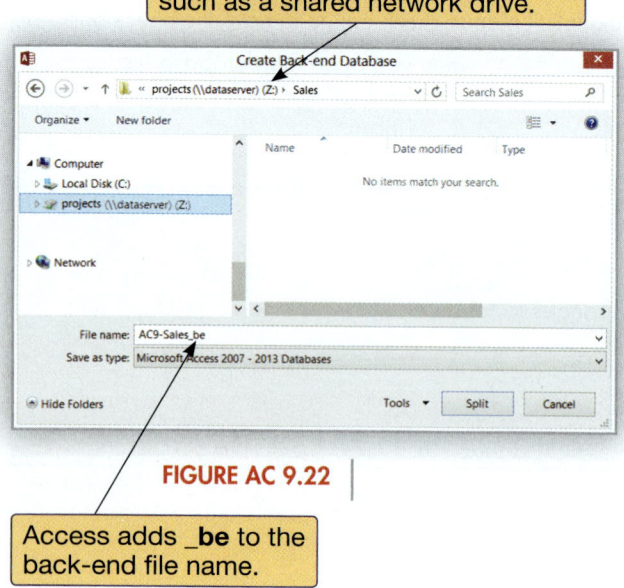

Save the back-end file in a location such as a shared network drive.

FIGURE AC 9.22

Access adds **_be** to the back-end file name.

3. The initial dialog explains what the Database Splitter does. Click the **Split Database** button to get started.
4. Navigate to the location for the back-end portion of the application. This is the database that contains the data tables. Because the various distributed copies of the front-end database use linked tables, the back-end database should be saved in a location available to all users such as a common network folder.
5. Review the file name in the *File name* box. By default, Access will suggest a name that is the same as the original database, followed by "**_be**".
6. Click the **Split** button.
7. When the process is finished, click the **OK** button to close the final dialog.

Notice when the splitting process is finished, the database you are working with is now the front end and the tables are linked to the back-end database you just created.

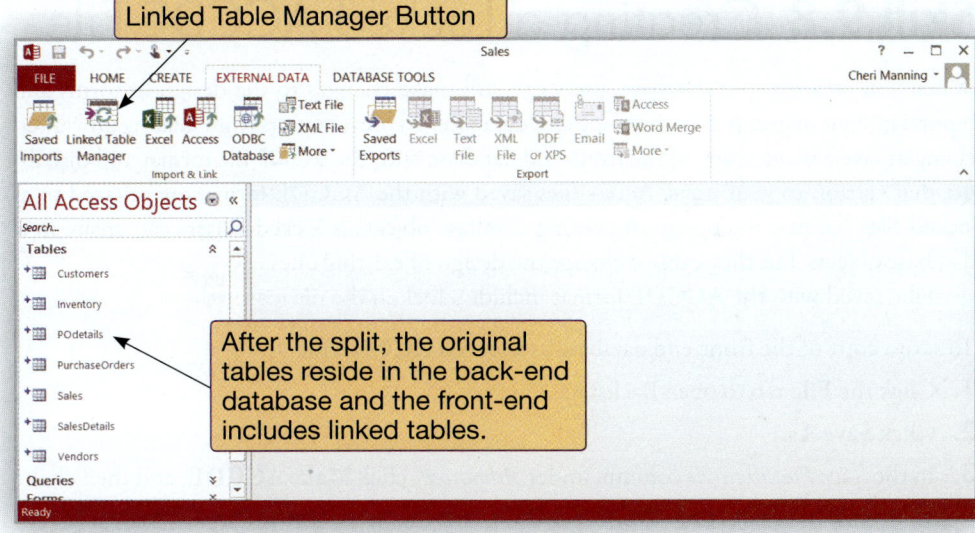

FIGURE AC 9.23

If you move the back-end database, use the Linked Table Manager in the front-end database to update the links.

To update the location of the back-end database:

1. On the *External Data* tab, in the *Import & Link* group, click the **Linked Table Manager** button.
2. Click the check boxes in front of the linked tables you want to update, and then click **OK**.
3. If Access is unable to find and update the links, it will prompt you to select a new location. Navigate to the updated location, select the back-end database file, and click **Open**.
4. Once Access is able to find and update the links successfully, it will display a message. Click **OK** to dismiss the message.
5. Click the **Close** button to close the Linked Table Manager.

tips & tricks

- Always make a backup or a copy of the database before splitting it.
- In the back-end version of the database, if you open multiple tables, they will open in cascading windows instead of tabs.

let me try

Make a copy of the data file **AC9-Sales** and try this skill on your own. Do not split the original **AC9-Sales** data file.

1. Split the database into separate front-end and back-end databases. Name the back-end database: `Sales_be`
2. Observe the change to the tables in the Navigation Pane.

skill 9.7 Splitting a Database

Skill 9.8 Creating a Locked ACCDE File

When you create a split database, users can still make changes to the design of forms and reports in their own copies of the front-end database. To prevent users from making unwanted changes, save a secure copy of the front-end database with the **ACCDE** file format and distribute that version to your users. Access files saved with the ACCDE format are referred to as **locked files** because the design of existing database objects is locked—users can create new database objects, but they cannot change the design of existing ones.

Files saved with the ACCDE format include a lock in the file icon:

To save a copy of the front-end database as a locked ACCDE file:

1. Click the **File** tab to open Backstage.
2. Click **Save As.**
3. In the *Save Database As* column, under *Advanced,* click **Make ACCDE,** and then click the **Save As** button.
4. In the *Save As* dialog, notice that the file extension in the *Save as type* box is *ACCDE File.*

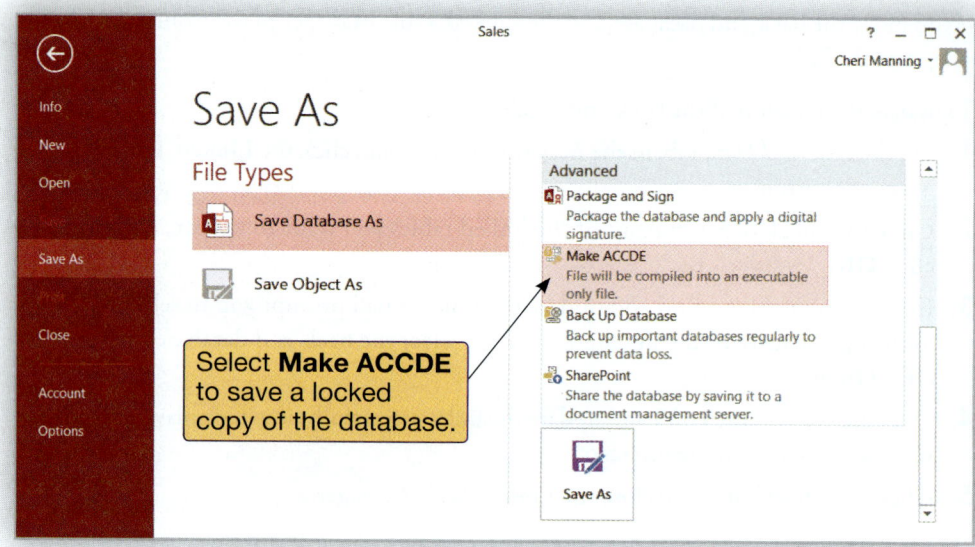

FIGURE AC 9.24

5. Enter a new name for the file in the *File name* box. Access does not change the file you're working on, it creates a copy. Use a different file name, so you can tell the difference easily!
6. Click **Save** to save a copy of the front-end database with the new file format.

tips & tricks

ACCDE files are sometimes referred to as "executables" because the "E" in ACCDE stands for "executable." That is slightly misleading, because users must still have Access installed to open and use the ACCDE file. However, if your end users do not have the Access application, you can package the ACCDE file with a free, run-time version of Access from Microsoft to create a true executable file: http://www.microsoft.com/en-us/download/details.aspx?id=39358

let me try

Continue working with the front-end database you created in the skill *Splitting a Database.*

1. Save a copy of the front-end file as an ACCDE file so users cannot change the design of forms and reports.
2. Name the file: `Sales_Locked`

Skill 9.9 Encrypting a Database with a Password

To secure your Access database, consider encrypting it by adding a password. Only users who know the password will be able to open the database. Before assigning a password, you'll need to open the database exclusively.

To open the database exclusively:

1. Click the **File** tab to open Backstage.
2. Click **Close** to close the current database.
3. Click the **Open Other Files** link at the bottom of the list of recent files. Be careful not to click a file name as that will open the file. You must open the file through the *Open* dialog in order to open it exclusively.
4. Click **Computer.** If the folder you want is listed, click it. If not, click the **Browse** button to navigate to the folder that contains the database.
5. In the *Open* dialog, click the file once to select it. Do not double-click it.
6. Click the arrow on the **Open** button and select **Open Exclusive.**

The database is now open for you exclusively.

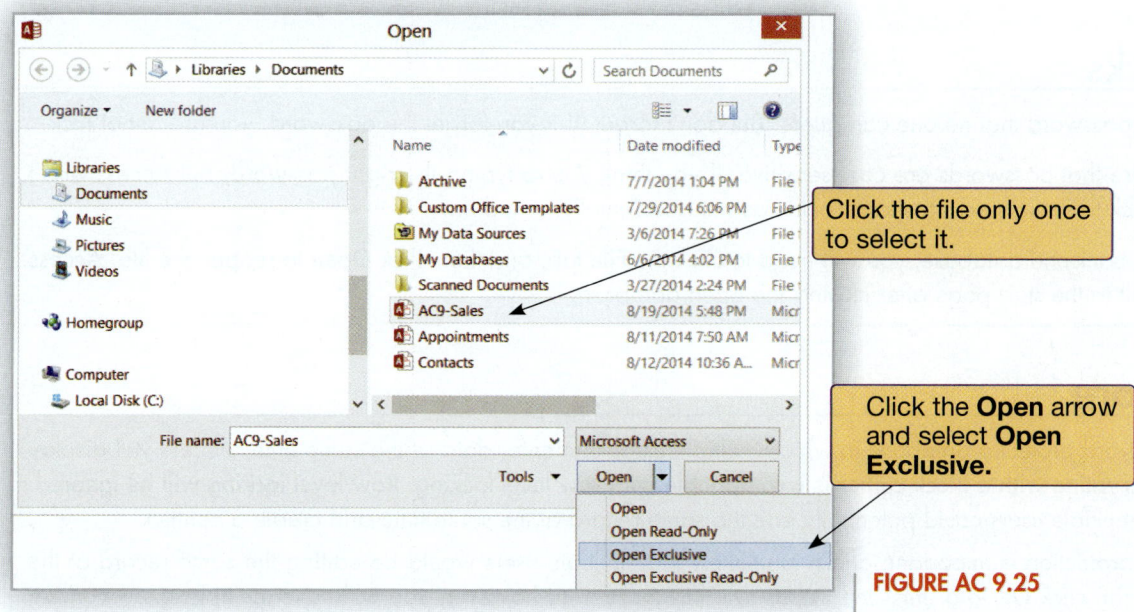

FIGURE AC 9.25

To set a password:

1. With the file opened exclusively, click the **File** tab. Click the **Encrypt with Password** button.

FIGURE AC 9.26

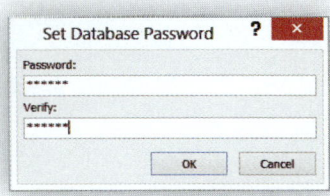

FIGURE AC 9.27

2. In the *Set Database Password* dialog, type the password in the *Password* box. Observe that Access displays * as you type.
3. Press **Tab** and type the password again in the *Verify* box.
4. Click **OK**.

Next time you or someone else opens the database, Access will ask for the password.

FIGURE AC 9.28

To remove the database password:

1. With the file opened exclusively, click the **File** tab. Click the **Decrypt Database** button.

FIGURE AC 9.29

2. In the *Unset Database Password* dialog, type the current password in the box. Access again displays * as you type.
3. Click **OK**.

The database is no longer password-protected.

tips & tricks

- Use a secure password that no one can guess. But don't forget it! If you forget the password, you are out of luck.
- Also, be aware that passwords are case-sensitive. If you think you're typing the right password, but Access won't accept it, check to make sure that Caps Lock was not accidentally turned on.
- If you close a back-end database, you will need to click the **File** tab, and then click **Open** to reopen the file. Access will not default to the start page after closing the open database.

tell me more

When you password protect a database in which multiple users can enter data at the same time, Access will display the message **Encrypting with a block cipher is incompatible with row level locking. Row level locking will be ignored.** This means that multiple users could potentially edit the same record at the same time and create a conflict.

If the password protection is important, and it is unlikely that multiple users would be editing the same record at the same time, you can click **OK** to dismiss the message and ignore it. If, however, you will have multiple users working on the same records at the same time, you might want to consider removing the password.

let me try

Open the data file **AC9-Sales** and try this skill on your own:

1. Make a backup copy of the database before adding the password.
2. Close the database without closing Access.
3. Reopen the database so you have exclusive access.
4. Add the password: `abc123`
5. Close the database, and then reopen it, again with exclusive access. Enter the password when prompted.
6. Remove the password.

Skill 9.10 Using the Database Documenter

The final step in developing your Access database is to document the database—including table relationships, field details, and macro code. Access provides a tool to generate the database documentation for you—the **Database Documenter**.

To create database documentation:

1. On the *Database Tools* tab, in the *Analyze* group, click the **Database Documenter** button.

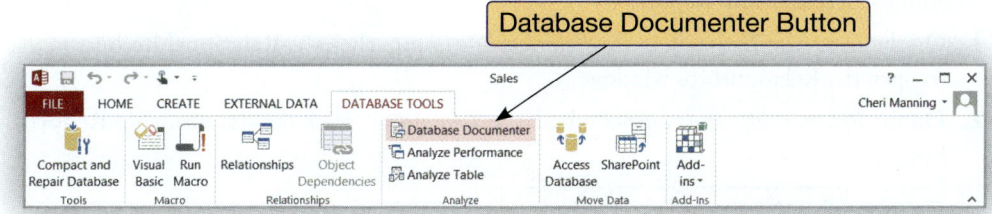

FIGURE AC 9.30

2. The *Documenter* dialog includes tabs for each type of database object. Click a tab and then click the check box in front of each object you want to include in the report.

3. You can specify the type of information to include by clicking the **Options...** button. Each type of database object has its own documentation options. Make your selections, and then click **OK** to return to the *Documenter* dialog.

4. When you are ready to generate the report, click **OK**.

5. The report opens in Print Preview view. To save the documentation, either save the report as a PDF or print it.

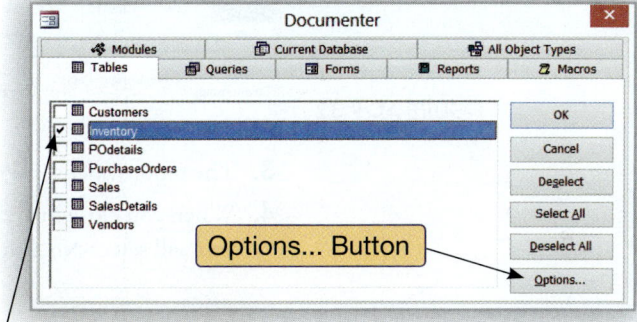

FIGURE AC 9.31

tips & tricks

If the documentation for a table is too long, consider turning off some of the field options in the *Print Table Definitions* dialog if you don't need them in the report.

let me try

Open the data file **AC9-Sales** and try this skill on your own:

1. Open the **Database Documenter.**
2. Generate documentation for the **Inventory** table. Review the options and verify that the documentation will include information about the table properties and relationships only and all the details for fields and indexes.
3. Review the documentation in Print Preview view. If necessary, click to zoom in so you can read the documentation. Use the navigation buttons at the bottom of the report to browse through all the pages.
4. When you are through, close Print Preview.

Skill 9.11 Printing the Relationship Report

When you are working with a complex database, it can be helpful to have a printed copy of the table relationships to help you understand the database structure. The **Relationship Report** prints the relationships exactly as they are displayed in the Relationships window. Rearrange tables in the Relationships window by clicking the title of each table box and dragging it to a new location. To make a table box taller, click the bottom border and drag down. Arrange the Relationships window exactly as you'd like it before generating the report.

To print the Relationship Report:

1. On the *Database Tools* tab, in the *Relationships* group, click the **Relationships** button to open the Relationships window.
2. On the *Relationship Tools Design* tab, in the *Tools* group, click the **Relationship Report** button.

FIGURE AC 9.32

3. The report opens in Print Preview. Print the report or save it as a PDF.
4. When you close Print Preview, Access will ask if you want to save the report. Usually, you will select **No** as it is easy to generate an up-to-date report at any time.

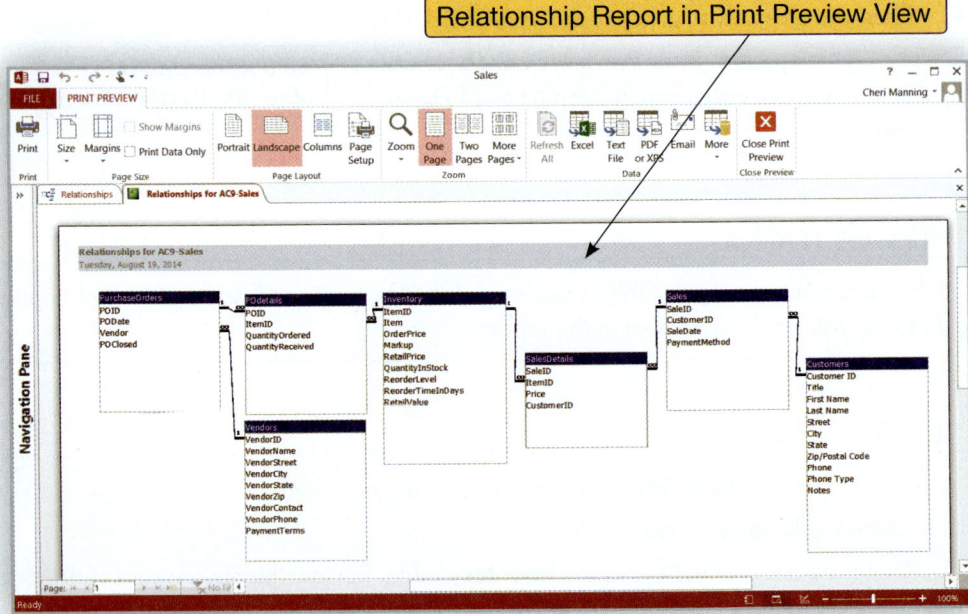

FIGURE AC 9.33

let me try

Open the data file **AC9-Sales** and try this skill on your own:

1. Open the **Relationships window** and modify the table layouts as necessary.
2. Open the **Relationship Report**.
3. Close Print Preview without saving the report, and then close the database.

key terms

Table Analyzer
Normalization
Index
Performance Analyzer
Object dependencies
Database Splitter
Back-end file
Front-end file
ACCDE
Locked file
Database Documenter
Relationship Report

concepts review

1. Which of these tools would you use to separate a table into multiple related tables?
   a. Table Analyzer
   b. Performance Analyzer
   c. Object Dependencies Pane
   d. Database Documenter

2. Which of these tools would you use to add indexes to tables to improve database performance?
   a. Table Analyzer
   b. Performance Analyzer
   c. Object Dependencies Pane
   d. Database Documenter

3. A form's record source is dependent upon the form.
   a. True
   b. False

4. Database objects can be added to only one custom group in the Navigation Pane.
   a. True
   b. False

5. To bypass the database startup options, press which key as you open the file?
   a. Ctrl
   b. Alt + Ctrl
   c. Shift
   d. Alt

6. The Database Splitter creates a locked ACCDE file.
   a. True
   b. False

7. In a split database, which part contains the linked tables?
   a. Front-end file
   b. Back-end file

8. In an ACCDE file, which actions are prevented?
   a. Creating new forms and reports
   b. Modifying the design of existing forms and reports
   c. Adding data to tables
   d. Deleting records

9. To add a password to a database, you must have it open in which mode?
   a. ACCDE
   b. Open exclusive
   c. Read only
   d. Encrypted
10. Which of these tools would you use to generate a PDF with information about a table's properties and relationships and details about fields and indexes?
    a. Table Analyzer
    b. Performance Analyzer
    c. Object Dependencies Pane
    d. Database Documenter

projects

Data files for projects can be found on www.mhhe.com/office2013skills

skill review 9.1

In this project, you will finalize a customer service database. You will use the Table Analyzer to split the *CustomerServiceCalls* table into related linked tables. You will review object dependencies and use the Performance Analyzer for optimization ideas. You will practice encrypting and decrypting the database with a password. You will prepare the database for other users by splitting it into back-end and front-end files and setting startup options in the front-end file. Finally, you will generate database documentation.

Skills needed to complete this project:
- Using the Table Analyzer (Skill 9.1)
- Viewing Dependencies (Skill 9.3)
- Using the Performance Analyzer (Skill 9.2)
- Encrypting a Database with a Password (Skill 9.9)
- Splitting a Database (Skill 9.7)
- Configuring Database Startup Options (Skill 9.5)
- Limiting Views and Design Options (Skill 9.6)
- Creating a Locked ACCDE File (Skill 9.8)
- Printing the Relationship Report (Skill 9.11)
- Using the Database Documenter (Skill 9.10)

1. Open the start file **AC2013-SkillReview-9-1** and resave the file as: `[your initials]AC-SkillReview-9-1`
2. If necessary, enable active content by clicking the **Enable Content** button in the Message Bar.

3. Use the Table Analyzer to check for and eliminate redundant data in the *CustomerServiceCalls* table.
   a. On the *Database Tools* tab, in the *Analyze* group, click the **Analyze Table** button.
   b. The Table Analyzer Wizard displays. Review the information in the first two steps. Click **Next** on each step to move forward.
   c. In the *Tables* list, verify that **CustomerServiceCalls** is selected. Click **Next**.
   d. Verify that the **Yes, let the wizard decide.** radio button is selected. Click **Next**.
   e. As necessary, click and drag the bottom of each table box down until all the fields are visible.
   f. Verify that the recommended **Table1** includes the following fields: *ServiceID, TechnicianID, DateOfVisit, InvoiceAmount, InvoicePaid, LateFee,* and *Lookup to Table2.*
   g. Verify that the recommended **Table2** includes the following fields: *CustomerID, LastName, FirstName, Address, City, State,* and *Zip.*
   h. Click the **Table1** title bar, and then click the **Rename Table** button. Type `ServiceCallsWithCustomerLookup` for the table name. Click **OK**.
   i. Double-click the **Table2** title bar. Type `Customer` for the table name. Click **OK**.
   j. Click **Next**.
   k. In the **Customer** table, verify that **CustomerID** is selected as the primary key. Click **Next**.
   l. Because this database includes other objects based on the original *CustomerServiceCalls* table, you should allow Access to create a query so you don't have to update the record source for those objects. Click the **Yes, create the query.** radio button.
   m. Click **Finish**.
   n. Observe that Access created a query named *CustomerServiceCalls* to mimic the original table. Review the query results and then close it.
   o. Observe that the original table has been renamed *CustomerServiceCalls_OLD*.
   p. Open the **MonthlyServiceCalls** report in Design view and observe the updated report record source in the Property Sheet *Data* tab, *Record Source* property box, and then close the report.
4. Review object dependencies for the new *CustomerServiceCalls* query.
   a. In the Navigation Pane, click the **CustomerServiceCalls** query once to select it.
   b. On the *Database Tools* tab, in the *Relationships* group, click the **Object Dependencies** button.
   c. Click **OK** to allow Access to update object dependencies in the database.
   d. Review the dependencies and then close the Object Dependencies pane by clicking the **Object Dependencies** button again.
5. Use the Performance Analyzer tool to optimize the database.
   a. On the *Database Tools* tab, in the *Analyze* group, click the **Analyze Performance** button.
   b. In the *Performance Analyzer* dialog, click the **All Object Types** tab.
   c. Click the **Select All** button.
   d. Click **OK**.
   e. Review the list of ideas. You will implement the idea to save an MDE file later in this project. "MDE" is the old file format for a locked database file. The new file format is ACCDE.
   f. Click the **Close** button.

6. Close the database without exiting Access and reopen it exclusively to add a password.
   a. On the **File** tab, select **Close.**
   b. Click the **Open Other Files** button at the bottom of the list of recent files.
   c. Click **Computer,** and then click the **Browse** button to open the *Open* dialog. Navigate to the folder that contains the data files for this book.
   d. Click your version of the **AC-SkillReview-9-1** database file *once* to select it. ***Do not double-click the file.***
   e. Click the **Open** button arrow and select **Open Exclusive.**
   f. Click the **File** tab. Click the **Encrypt with Password** button.
   g. In the *Password* box, type: `skillreview91`
   h. In the *Verify* box, type: `skillreview91`
   i. Click **OK.**
   j. Click **OK** on the informational message.
   k. On the *File* tab, select **Close** to close the database again without exiting Access.
7. Open the database exclusively and remove the password.
   a. Click the **Open Other Files** button at the bottom of the list of recent files.
   b. Click **Computer,** and then click the **Browse** button to open the *Open* dialog. Navigate to the folder that contains the data files for this book.
   c. Click your version of the **AC-SkillReview-9-1** database file *once* to select it. ***Do not double-click the file.***
   d. Click the **Open** button arrow, and select **Open Exclusive.**
   e. The database prompts you to enter a password. Type: `skillreview91`
   f. Click the **File** tab. Click the **Decrypt Database** button.
   g. In the *Unset Database Password* dialog, type: `skillreview91`
   h. Click **OK.**
8. Split the database.
   a. On the *Database Tools* tab, in the *Move Data* group, click the **Access Database** button.
   b. Read the information in the *Database Splitter* dialog, and then click the **Split Database** button.
   c. Navigate to the folder that contains the data files for this book Keep the suggested file name for the back-end database. Click the **Split** button.
   d. Click **OK.**
9. You are now working with the front-end database which retained the original file name. Observe the linked tables in the Navigation Pane.
10. Set the database application title.
    a. Click the **File** tab. Click **Options.**
    b. In the *Access Options* dialog, click **Current Database.**
    c. In the *Application Title* box, type: `Service Calls`
    d. Do not close the *Access Options* dialog yet.
11. Set a navigation form to display when the database is opened.
    a. In the *Access Options* dialog, expand the **Display Form** list.
    b. Select **ServiceCallsDashboard.**
    c. Do not close the *Access Options* dialog yet.

12. Hide the status bar and the Navigation Pane.
    a. In the *Access Options* dialog, click the **Display Status Bar** check box to remove the check box.
    b. Scroll down to the *Navigation* section.
    c. Click the **Display Navigation Pane** check box to remove the check box.
    d. Do not close the *Access Options* dialog yet.
13. Prevent design changes in table Datasheet view, and then close the *Access Options* dialog and accept the changes.
    a. Click the **Enable design changes for tables in Datasheet view** check box to remove the checkmark.
    b. Click **OK**.
    c. Access displays a message that you must close and reopen the database in order for the changes to take effect. Click **OK**.
    d. Close the database and reopen it.
    e. Observe the startup changes.
14. Save a locked copy of this database.
    a. Click the **File** tab.
    b. Click **Save As**.
    c. Under the *Advanced* section, click **Make ACCDE**.
    d. Click the **Save As** button.
    e. In the *Save As* dialog, in the *File name* box, type `[Your Initials]-ServiceCallsDatabase-Locked`
    f. Click **Save**.
15. View and save the Relationship Report.
    a. On the *Database Tools* tab, in the *Relationships* group, click the **Relationships** button.
    b. On the *Relationship Tools Design* tab, in the *Relationships* group, click the **All Relationships** button to display all the database relationships.
    c. Move and resize the table boxes in the Relationships window as necessary until all the tables and fields are visible in an attractive layout. To move a table box, click the title and drag it to a new location. To make a table box taller, click the bottom border and drag down.
    d. On the *Relationship Tools Design* tab, in the *Tools* group, click the **Relationship Report** button.
    e. View the report. If the right side of the report is not visible, click the **Landscape** button to change the report orientation. When you are finished reviewing the report, click the **Close Print Preview** button.
    f. Close the report. When you are prompted if you want to save the report, click **Yes**.
    g. Save the report as: `RelationshipReport`
    h. Click **OK**.
    i. Close the Relationships window.
16. Use the Database Documenter to create detailed documentation for the database tables.
    a. On the *Database Tools* tab, in the *Analyze* group, click the **Database Documenter** button.
    b. In the *Documenter* dialog, click the **Tables** tab. Click the **Select All** button.

c. Click **OK**. It may take a few seconds for the report to appear.

   d. Review the report in Print Preview view. Click the report to zoom in and use the navigation buttons at the bottom of the report to browse through all the pages.

   e. On the *Print Preview* tab, in the *Data* group, click the **PDF or XPS** button to save the report as a PDF if instructed to do so by your instructor.

   f. Click the **Close Print Preview** button to close Print Preview view.

17. Close the database and exit Access.

skill review 9.2

In this project, you will finalize a database for a small community bank. First, you will need to enter a password to open the file. Once the database is opened, you will close it and reopen it exclusively to remove the password. You will review object dependencies for the *CustomerLoans* table and then use the Table Analyzer to split it into related linked tables. You will run the Performance Analyzer for optimization ideas. You will prepare the database for other users by customizing the Navigation Pane and setting startup options. Finally, you will generate database documentation.

Skills needed to complete this project:
- Encrypting a Database with a Password (Skill 9.9)
- Viewing Dependencies (Skill 9.3)
- Using the Table Analyzer (Skill 9.1)
- Using the Performance Analyzer (Skill 9.2)
- Customizing the Navigation Pane (Skill 9.4)
- Configuring Database Startup Options (Skill 9.5)
- Limiting Views and Design Options (Skill 9.6)
- Printing the Relationship Report (Skill 9.11)
- Using the Database Documenter (Skill 9.10)

1. Open the start file **AC2013-SkillReview-9-2** (the password is **skillreview92**) and resave the file as: `[your initials]AC-SkillReview-9-2`

2. If necessary, enable active content by clicking the **Enable Content** button in the Message Bar.

3. Reopen the database exclusively and remove the password.

   a. On the **File** tab, select **Close** to close the database again without exiting Access.

   b. Click the **Open Other Files** button at the bottom of the list of recent files.

   c. Click **Computer,** and then click the **Browse** button to open the *Open* dialog. Navigate to the folder that contains the data files for this book.

   d. Click your version of the **AC-SkillReview-9-2** database file *once* to select it. ***Do not double-click the file.***

   e. Click the **Open** button arrow and select **Open Exclusive.**

   f. The database prompts you to enter a password. Type: `skillreview92`

   g. Click the **File** tab. Click the **Decrypt Database** button.

   h. In the *Unset Database Password* dialog, type: `skillreview92`

   i. Click **OK**.

4. Review object dependencies for the *CustomerLoans* table.
   a. In the Navigation Pane, click the **CustomerLoans** table once to select it.
   b. On the *Database Tools* tab, in the *Relationships* group, click the **Object Dependencies** button.
   c. Observe that no database objects are dependent on this table. Close the Object Dependencies pane by clicking the **Object Dependencies** button again.

5. Use the Table Analyzer to check for and eliminate redundant data in the *CustomerLoans* table.
   a. On the *Database Tools* tab, in the *Analyze* group, click the **Analyze Table** button.
   b. The Table Analyzer Wizard displays. Review the information in the first two steps. Click **Next** on each step to move forward.
   c. In the *Tables* list, verify that **CustomerLoans** is selected. Click **Next**.
   d. Verify that the **Yes, let the wizard decide.** radio button is selected. Click **Next**.
   e. As necessary, click and drag the bottom of each table box down until all the fields are visible.
   f. Verify that the recommended **Table1** includes the following fields: *LoanID, LoanDate, Amount, InterestRate, Term, Lookup to Table3,* and *Lookup to Table2*.
   g. Verify that the recommended **Table2** includes the following fields: *GeneratedUniqueID, FirstName, LastName, Address, City,* and *State*.
   h. Verify that the recommended **Table3** includes the following fields: *GeneratedUniqueID* and *Type*.
   i. Click the **Table1** title bar, and then click the **Rename Table** button. Type `LoanWithLookups` for the table name. Click **OK**.
   j. Double-click the **Table2** title bar. Type `Customer` for the table name. Click **OK**.
   k. Double-click the **Table3** title bar. Type `LoanType` for the table name. Click **OK**.
   l. Click **Next**.
   m. In the **LoanWithLookups** table, click the **LoanID** field and click the **Set Unique Identifier** button.
   n. In the **Customer** table, verify that **GeneratedUniqueID** is selected as the primary key.
   o. In the **LoanType** table, verify that **GeneratedUniqueID** is selected as the primary key.
   p. Click **Next**.
   q. As you determined by reviewing the Object Dependencies pane, there are no database objects dependent on the *CustomerLoans* table, so there is no need for a query. Click the **No, don't create the query.** radio button.
   r. Click **Finish**.
   s. Click **OK** to dismiss the informational message.
   t. Close the open tables.
   u. Delete the **CustomerLoans** table. It has been replaced by the new tables generated by the Table Analyzer.

6. Use the Performance Analyzer tool to optimize the database.
   a. On the *Database Tools* tab, in the *Analyze* group, click the **Analyze Performance** button.
   b. In the *Performance Analyzer* dialog, click the **All Object Types** tab.
   c. Click the **Select All** button.
   d. Click **OK**.

e. Review the list of ideas.

   f. Click the **Close** button.

7. Create a custom Navigation Pane category and custom group to organize the employee-related database objects.

   a. Right-click the top of the **Navigation Pane** and select **Navigation Options...**

   b. In the *Navigation Options* dialog, click the **Add Item** button and type: `Employee Data`

   c. Click the **Add Group** button and type: `Employee Dashboard Items`

   d. Click **OK**.

8. Add database objects to the new category and group.

   a. Click the arrow at the top of the Navigation Pane and select **Employee Data**.

   b. Click and drag each of the following items from the Unassigned Objects group to **Employee Dashboard Items** in the Navigation Pane: the *Employee* and *EmployeeVacationTime* tables, the *VacationAvailable* query, the *EmployeePortal* and *NewEmployee* forms, and the *VacationTime* report.

   c. If you are uncomfortable with clicking and dragging the objects, use the right-click method instead. Right-click the database object you want to move, point to **Add to group,** and click **Employee Dashboard Items**.

9. Remove the Unassigned Objects group from the *Employee Data* navigation category.

   a. Right-click the top of the **Navigation Pane** and select **Navigation Options...**

   b. In *Navigation Options* dialog, in the *Categories* list, click **Employee Data**.

   c. In the *Groups* list, click the **Unassigned Objects** check box to remove the checkmark.

   d. Click **OK**.

10. Set the database application title.

    a. Click the **File** tab. Click **Options**.

    b. In the *Access Options* dialog, click **Current Database**.

    c. In the *Application Title* box, type: `Company Database`

    d. Do not close the *Access Options* dialog yet.

11. Set a navigation form to display when the database is opened.

    a. In the *Access Options* dialog, expand the **Display Form** list.

    b. Select **EmployeePortal**.

    c. Do not close the *Access Options* dialog yet.

12. Disable Layout view for forms and reports.

    a. Click the **Enable Layout View** check box to remove the checkmark.

    b. Click **OK**.

    c. Access displays a message that you must close and reopen the database in order for the changes to take effect. Click **OK**.

    d. Close the database and reopen it.

    e. Observe the startup changes.

13. View and save the Relationship Report.

    a. On the *Database Tools* tab, in the *Relationships* group, click the **Relationships** button.

    b. On the *Relationship Tools Design* tab, in the *Relationships* group, click the **All Relationships** button to display all the database relationships.

c. Move and resize the table boxes in the Relationships window until all tables and fields are visible in an attractive layout. To move a table box, click the title and drag it to a new location. To make a table box taller, click the bottom border and drag down.

d. On the *Relationship Tools Design* tab, in the *Tools* group, click the **Relationship Report** button.

e. View the report. If the right side of the report is not visible, click the **Landscape** button to change the report orientation. When you are finished reviewing the report, click the **Close Print Preview** button.

f. Close the report. When you are prompted if you want to save the report, click **Yes**.

g. Save the report as: `RelationshipReport`

h. Click **OK**.

i. Close the Relationships window.

14. Use the Database Documenter to create detailed documentation for the database tables.

    a. On the *Database Tools* tab, in the *Analyze* group, click the **Database Documenter** button.

    b. In the *Documenter* dialog, click the **Tables** tab. Click the **Select All** button.

    c. Click **OK**. It may take a few seconds for the report to appear.

    d. Review the report in Print Preview view. Click the report to zoom in and use the navigation buttons at the bottom of the report to browse through all the pages.

    e. On the *Print Preview* tab, in the *Data* group, click the **PDF or XPS** button to save the report as a PDF if instructed to do so by your instructor.

    f. Click the **Close Print Preview** button to close Print Preview view.

15. Close the database and exit Access.

challenge yourself 9.3

In this project, you will finalize an events database for an advertising company. First, you will enter a password to open the file. Once the database is opened, you will close it and reopen it exclusively to remove the password. You will review object dependencies for the *AdsAndClients* table and then use the Table Analyzer to split it into related linked tables. You will use the Performance Analyzer for optimization ideas. You will prepare the database for other users by splitting it into back-end and front-end files and setting startup options in the front-end file. Finally, you will generate database documentation.

Skills needed to complete this project:

- Encrypting a Database with a Password (Skill 9.9)
- Viewing Dependencies (Skill 9.3)
- Using the Table Analyzer (Skill 9.1)
- Using the Performance Analyzer (Skill 9.2)
- Splitting a Database (Skill 9.7)
- Configuring Database Startup Options (Skill 9.5)
- Limiting Views and Design Options (Skill 9.6)
- Creating a Locked ACCDE File (Skill 9.8)
- Printing the Relationship Report (Skill 9.11)
- Using the Database Documenter (Skill 9.10)

1. Open the start file **AC2013-Challenge-Yourself 9-3** (the password is **challenge93**) and resave the file as: `[your initials]AC-ChallengeYourself-9-3`
2. If necessary, enable active content by clicking the **Enable Content** button in the Message Bar.
3. Open the database exclusively, and decrypt the database by removing the password **challenge93**.
4. Review object dependencies for the *AdsAndClients* table.
5. Use the Table Analyzer to check for and eliminate redundant data in the *AdsAndClients* table.
   a. Allow the wizard to split the table into three new tables.
   b. Name the tables: `AdsWithLookups`, `Clients`, and `AdTypes`
   c. The **AdsWithLookups** table includes a field that should be used as the primary key. Identify it and set it as the unique identifier.
   d. The other two tables should use a **Generated Unique ID** as the primary key as recommended by the wizard.
   e. Because this database includes other objects based on the original *AdsAndClients* table, you should allow Access to create a query so you don't have to update the record source for those objects.
   f. Review the new query results, and then close it.
6. Review object dependencies for the new *AdsAndClients* query.
7. Run the Performance Analyzer tool on all database objects at the same time. Review the results, but do not implement any of them.
8. Split the database. Save the back-end file in the folder that contains the data files for this book. Keep the suggested file name for the back-end database file.
9. You are now working with the front-end database.
10. Make the following changes to the startup appearance and functionality of the front-end database when it is opened:
    a. Set the database application title as: `Events Database`
    b. Display the **EventPortal** form when the database is opened.
    c. Hide the status bar.
    d. Hide the Navigation Pane.
    e. Prevent design changes in table Datasheet view.
    f. When you have made the changes, close the database. Reopen it and observe the startup changes.
11. Save a locked copy of this database with the file name: `[Your Initials]-EventsDatabase-Locked`
12. View and save the Relationship Report.
    a. On the *Relationship Tools Design* tab, in the *Relationships* group, click the **All Relationships** button to display all the database relationships.
    b. Move and resize the table boxes in the Relationships window until all tables and fields are visible in an attractive layout.
    c. View the Relationship Report. If the right side of the report is not visible, click the **Landscape** button to change the report orientation. When you are finished reviewing the report, click the **Close Print Preview** button.
    d. Close the report. When you are prompted if you want to save the report, click **Yes**.
    e. Save the report as: `RelationshipReport`

f. Click **OK**.

   g. Close the Relationships window.

13. Use the Database Documenter to create detailed documentation for all the database tables.

    a. Create documentation for all the tables.

    b. Review the report in Print Preview view. Click the report to zoom in and use the navigation buttons at the bottom of the report to browse through all the pages.

    c. On the *Print Preview* tab, in the *Data* group, click the **PDF or XPS** button to save the report as a PDF if instructed to do so by your instructor.

    d. Click the **Close Print Preview** button to close Print Preview view.

14. Close the database and exit Access.

challenge yourself 9.4

In this project, you will finalize a database for Small Town Investors. First, you will enter a password to open the file. Once the database is opened, you will close it and reopen it exclusively to remove the password. You will review object dependencies for the *FundClosingPrices* table and then use the Table Analyzer to split it into related linked tables. You will run the Performance Analyzer for optimization ideas. You will prepare the database for other users by customizing the Navigation Pane and setting startup options. Finally, you will generate database documentation.

Skills needed to complete this project:

- Encrypting a Database with a Password (Skill 9.9)
- Viewing Dependencies (Skill 9.3)
- Using the Table Analyzer (Skill 9.1)
- Using the Performance Analyzer (Skill 9.2)
- Customizing the Navigation Pane (Skill 9.4)
- Configuring Database Startup Options (Skill 9.5)
- Limiting Views and Design Options (Skill 9.6)
- Printing the Relationship Report (Skill 9.11)
- Using the Database Documenter (Skill 9.10)

1. Open the start file **AC2013-ChallengeYourself-9-4** (the password is **challenge94**) and resave the file as: `[your initials]AC-ChallengeYourself-9-4`

2. If necessary, enable active content by clicking the **Enable Content** button in the Message Bar.

3. Open the database exclusively, and decrypt the database by removing the password **challenge94**.

4. Review object dependencies for the *FundClosingPrices* table and observe that no database objects are dependent on this table.

5. Use the Table Analyzer to check for and eliminate redundant data in the *FundClosingPrices* table.

   a. Allow the wizard to split the table into three new tables.

   b. Name the tables: `ClosingPriceWithLookups`, `Fund`, and `FundType`

   c. The **ClosingPriceWithLookups** table includes a field that should be used as the primary key. Identify it and set it as the unique identifier.

d. The other two tables should use a **Generated Unique ID** as the primary key as recommended by the wizard.

e. As you determined by reviewing the Object Dependencies pane, there are no database objects dependent on the *CustomerLoans* table, so there is no need for a query.

f. Close the open tables.

g. Delete the original *FundClosingPrices* table. It has been replaced by the new tables generated by the Table Analyzer.

6. Run the Performance Analyzer tool on all database objects at the same time. Review the results, but do not implement any of them.

7. Create a custom Navigation Pane category named **AboutUs** with a custom group named **Basics** to organize the company database objects.

8. Add the following database objects to the new category and group: the *Advisor* and *InvestmentProducts* tables, the *AboutOurCompany* and *OurAdvisors* forms, and the *InvestmentProducts* report.

9. Modify the *AboutUs* navigation category and remove the Unassigned Objects group.

10. Make the following changes to the database startup options:

    a. Set the database application title to: `Small Town Investors`

    b. Display the **AboutOurCompany** navigation form when the database is opened.

    c. Disable Layout view for forms and reports.

11. When you have made the changes, close the database and reopen it. Observe the startup changes.

12. View and save the Relationship Report.

    a. On the *Relationship Tools Design* tab, in the *Relationships* group, click the **All Relationships** button to display all the database relationships.

    b. Move and resize the table boxes in the Relationships window as necessary until all the tables and fields are visible in an attractive layout.

    c. View the report. If the right side of the report is not visible, click the **Landscape** button to change the report orientation. When you are finished reviewing the report, click the **Close Print Preview** button.

    d. Close the report. When you are prompted if you want to save the report, click **Yes**.

    e. Save the report as: `RelationshipReport`

    f. Close the Relationships window.

13. Use the Database Documenter to create detailed documentation for all the database tables.

    a. Review the report in Print Preview view. Click the report to zoom in and use the navigation buttons at the bottom of the report to browse through all the pages.

    b. On the *Print Preview* tab, in the *Data* group, click the **PDF or XPS** button to save the report as a PDF if instructed to do so by your instructor.

    c. Click the **Close Print Preview** button to close Print Preview view.

14. Close the database and exit Access.

on your own 9.5

In this project, you will set up the database for a small physicians group. The database has a single table currently, but it does not follow database normalization standards. The office administrator would like the database to be secure so the front desk staff cannot change the design of the tables. They would also like the database to have a professional user-friendly appearance. Set startup options to achieve those goals.

- Using the Table Analyzer (Skill 9.1)
- Using the Performance Analyzer (Skill 9.2)
- Viewing Dependencies (Skill 9.3)
- Customizing the Navigation Pane (Skill 9.4)
- Configuring Database Startup Options (Skill 9.5)
- Limiting Views and Design Options (Skill 9.6)
- Splitting a Database (Skill 9.7)
- Creating a Locked ACCDE File (Skill 9.8)
- Encrypting a Database with a Password (Skill 9.9)
- Using the Database Documenter (Skill 9.10)
- Printing the Relationship Report (Skill 9.11)

1. Open the start file **AC2013-OnYourOwn-9-5** and resave the file as: `[your initials]AC-OnYourOwn-9-5`
2. If necessary, enable active content by clicking the **Enable Content** button in the Message Bar.
3. Use tools such as the Table Analyzer and Performance Analyzer to review the **PatientAppointments** table. Is a single table the best choice? If not, create new tables and relationships of your choice for an optimal database structure.
   a. If you use the Table Analyzer, be sure to review the table recommendations carefully. There may be one field that belongs in a table other than the one recommended by Access. Remember, in the Table Analyzer Wizard, you can click and drag fields from one table box to another.
   b. Pay close attention to the primary key fields for each table.
   c. If you split the original **PatientAppointments** table into new tables, be sure to delete the original table or rename it so users know it is for backup purposes only.
4. If you are comfortable with forms, consider creating data entry forms and a navigation form. Consider creating queries to use as the record source for your forms.
5. Consider separating the database into a front-end file and a back-end file.
6. If you've added forms or reports to the database, consider saving the front-end file in a locked file format.
7. If the front-end database will include the Navigation Pane, consider creating a custom category and organizing the database objects into custom groups.
8. Implement other security measures as appropriate. If you add a password, be sure to provide it to your instructor if you submit the file for grading!
9. Generate database documentation to provide to the office administrators.
10. Close the database and exit Access.

fix it 9.6

An employee who was about to be fired made some modification to a local plumbing company's database. They are in a panic because they don't know how to undo what he did. Can you help them?

Skills needed to complete this project:
- Configuring Database Startup Options (Skill 9.5)
- Encrypting a Database with a Password (Skill 9.9)
- Limiting Views and Design Options (Skill 9.6)
- Splitting a Database (Skill 9.7)
- Creating a Locked ACCDE File (Skill 9.8)
- Using the Database Documenter (Skill 9.10)
- Printing the Relationship Report (Skill 9.11)

1. Open the start file **AC2013-FixIt-9-6** (the password is **IQuit**) and resave the file as: `[your initials]AC-FixIt-9-6`
2. If necessary, enable active content by clicking the **Enable Content** button in the Message Bar.
3. "This company stinks" appears in the title bar every time the database is opened. Fix it so the title bar displays `The Best Plumbing Company in Town` instead.
4. The database requires the password **IQuit** to open it. They would like the password removed. (*Hint:* Remember, passwords are case sensitive.)
5. The **Billing Navigation** form no longer opens automatically when the database is opened.
6. The Navigation Pane is missing. When the database opens it looks like there's nothing there.
7. The status bar is missing.
8. The company realizes they are lucky that the disgruntled employee didn't mess with the data tables. They would like you to set up the database so the data tables are in a separate file that they can place on the network server, in a location where only administrators can open the file. They would like to distribute the front-end files to employees as a "locked" file—but they don't know how to create those files. **Please provide them with a back-end file and a locked front-end file for distribution.** (*Hint:* Close the *Billing Navigation* form before splitting the database.)
    a. Use the default file name for the back-end database file.
    b. Add `-Locked` to the end of the file name for the locked version of the front-end database file.
9. Finally, they need printed documentation (or at least a PDF) of the table relationship design and the details for all the tables and fields.
    a. Save the relationship documentation as a PDF named: `Relationships`
    b. Do not save the report generated by the relationship documentation.
    c. Save the tables documentation as a PDF named: `Tables`
10. Close the database and exit Access.

appendix A

Office 2013 Shortcuts

Office 2013 Keyboard Shortcuts

ACTION	KEYBOARD SHORTCUT
Display Open page in Backstage view	Ctrl + O
Create a new blank Word, Excel, or PowerPoint file (bypassing Backstage view)	Ctrl + N
Copy	Ctrl + C
Cut	Ctrl + X
Paste	Ctrl + V
Undo	Ctrl + Z
Redo	Ctrl + Y
Save	Ctrl + S
Select All	Ctrl + A
Help	F1
Bold	Ctrl + B
Italic	Ctrl + I
Underline	Ctrl + U
Close Start page or Backstage view	Esc
Close a file	Ctrl + W
Minimize the Ribbon	Ctrl + F1
Switch windows	Alt + Tab

www.mhhe.com/simnet ACA–1

Access 2013 Keyboard Shortcuts

ACTION	KEYBOARD SHORTCUT
Display New page in Backstage view	Ctrl + N
Display Open page in Backstage view	Ctrl + O
Go to the next field in the record	→
Go to the previous field in the record	←
Go to the next record	↓
Go to the previous record	↑
Go to the first record	Ctrl + ↑
Go to the last record	Ctrl + ↓
Navigate from field to field within a record	Tab
Navigate from the last field in the record to the first field in the next record	Tab
Create a new blank record from the last record in the dataset	Tab
Add a new blank record to a table or form	Ctrl + ↑ Shift + =
Cut	Ctrl + X
Copy	Ctrl + C
Paste	Ctrl + V
Undo	Ctrl + Z
Redo	Ctrl + Y
Delete a record	Delete or Ctrl + -
Open the *Spelling* dialog	F7
Open or close Navigation Pane	F11
Open selected object in Design view	Ctrl + Enter
Save a database object. If first time saving the object, opens the *Save As* dialog.	Ctrl + S
Open the *Save As* dialog	F12
Open shortcut menu for the selected object	↑ Shift + F10
Move to preceding cell in a table, query, or form	↑ Shift + Tab
Insert line break when entering data in a *Short Text* or *Long Text* field	Ctrl + Enter

ACTION	KEYBOARD SHORTCUT
Undo changes to current field and all changes if more than one field on current record has been changed	Esc
Switch between Edit mode (insertion point displayed) and Navigation mode	F2
Increase selection to add adjacent column to the right	Shift + →
Increase selection to add adjacent column to the left	Shift + ←
Open *Find and Replace* dialog	Ctrl + F
Open *Find and Replace* dialog with the Replace tab selected	Ctrl + H
Find next	Shift + F4
Open Expression Builder	Ctrl + F2
Open Zoom window	Shift + F2
Open or close the Property Sheet for the selected control	F4
Show or hide Field List	Alt + F8
Open *Page Setup* dialog from Print Preview view	S
Open *Print* dialog from Print Preview view	Ctrl + P
Switch to Form view from Design view	F5
Open the form Property Sheet	F4 or Alt + Enter

glossary of key terms

Office 2013 Overview

a

Account page: Page in Backstage view that lists information for the user currently logged in to Office. This account information comes from the Microsoft account you used when installing Office.

b

Backstage view: Tab that contains the commands for managing and protecting files, including *Save, Open, Close, New,* and *Print.*

c

Contextual tabs: Contain commands specific to the type of object selected and are visible only when the commands might be useful.

e

Enhanced ScreenTip: A ScreenTip that displays the name of the command, the keyboard shortcut (if there is one), and a short description of what the button does and when it is used.

f

File properties: Information about a file such as the location of the file, the size of file, when the file was created and when it was last modified, the title, and the author. File properties can be found on the Info page in Backstage view.

File **tab:** Tab located on the far left side of the Ribbon. Opens the Microsoft Office Backstage view.

g

Groups: Subsections of a tab on the Ribbon. They organize commands with similar functions together.

h

Home **tab:** Contains the most commonly used commands for each Office application.

k

Keyboard shortcuts: Keys or combinations of keys that, when pressed, execute a command.

l

Live Preview: Displays formatting changes in a file before actually committing to the change.

m

Metadata: All the information about a file that is listed under the Properties section of the Info page in Backstage view including the location of the file, the size of file, when the file was created and when it was last modified, the title, and the author.

Microsoft Access: A database program. Database applications allow you to organize and manipulate large amounts of data.

Microsoft Excel: A spreadsheet program. Originally, spreadsheet applications were viewed as electronic versions of an accountant's ledger. Today's spreadsheet applications can do much more than just calculate numbers; they include powerful charting and data analysis features.

Microsoft PowerPoint: A presentation program. Such applications enable you to create robust, multimedia presentations.

Microsoft Word: A word processing program. Word processing software allows you to create text-based documents. Word processing software also offers more powerful formatting and design tools, allowing you to create complex documents, including reports, résumés, brochures, and newsletters.

Mini toolbar: Provides access to common tools for working with text. When text is selected and then the mouse is rested over the text, the Mini toolbar fades in.

n

New **command:** Creates a new file in an Office application without exiting and reopening the program.

o

Office Help: System for searching topics specifically tailored for working with an application.

OneDrive: Microsoft's free cloud storage where you can save documents, workbooks, presentations, videos, pictures, and other files and access those files from any computer or share the files with others.

p

Protected View: Provides a read-only format that protects your computer from becoming infected by a virus or other malware.

q

Quick Access Toolbar: Toolbar located at the top of the application window above the *File* tab. The Quick Access Toolbar gives quick one-click access to common commands.

r

Ribbon: Located across the top of the application window and organizes common features and commands into tabs.

s

ScreenTip: A small information box that displays the name of the command when the mouse is rested over a button on the Ribbon.

Shortcut menus: Menus of commands that display when an area of the application window is right-clicked.

Start page: Displays when you first launch an application. The Start page gives you quick access to recently opened files and templates for creating new files in each of the applications.

t

Tab: Subsection of the Ribbon; organizes commands further into related groups.

Tags: Keywords used for grouping common files together or for searching.

Access 2013

a

ACCDE: File format that prevents users from making changes to the design of any database objects. Also referred to as locked files.

Access web app: Online database that requires a SharePoint server.

Action query: Query type that performs an action on the records that meet the query specifications. Action queries include delete queries, make table queries, update queries, and append queries.

Aggregate: To combine, total, or group.

Aggregate function: Function such as sum, average, min, max, and count which summarizes data.

Aggregate query: Query that calculates summary values. Also known as summary query or totals query.

Append query: Query that adds (or appends) records to an existing table by copying records that meet the query criteria and pasting them into the specified table. Records are *copied* from the original table. No records are deleted.

Attachment data type: Stores files as attachments to records. Attachments can be images, Word documents, or almost any other type of data file.

AutoNumber data type: Fields with this data type are automatically assigned their values by Access. Database users cannot edit or enter data in an AutoNumber field. AutoNumber fields are often used as a primary key if no other unique field exists in the table.

b

Back-end file: In a split database, the database file that contains the tables. The file name for the back-end database as recommended by Access ends in _be. A database can be split using the Database Splitter.

Bound control: Control that displays a value from a specific field.

c

Calculated control: An unbound text control in a form or report that contains an expression (formula).

Calculated field: A field with the Calculated Field data type which dynamically calculates text or numeric values.

Calculated Field (in a query): Displays a value returned by an expression (a formula). The field values are calculated each time the query is run.

Calculated Field data type: Table field that displays a value returned by an expression (a formula). The field values are calculated each time the table is opened.

Cascading options: Delete and update options that may be applied to relationships between tables. When they are enforced, actions on one table affect records in the related table.

Combo box control: A control type that provides users with a combination data entry control. Users can type the data in a text box or select from a list of items. The combo box can display values from another table or query or from a list of values that the user enters.

Comma Style format: Displays the comma symbol (,) within the number and two digits to the right of the decimal.

Command button control: A control type that provides a user-friendly way to interact with the form. Buttons can provide a variety of actions including navigation; add, delete, and save records; open or close a form or record; and exit the application.

Comment (macro): Text not executed as code in a macro. Used to describe the purpose of the macro and provide additional information to users.

Compact & Repair tool: Tool that eliminates hidden, temporary database objects that take up database space unnecessarily.

Conditional formatting: A rule that applies formatting to the control only if user defined criteria are met.

Control: Displays data or allows user to enter and edit data in a form or report. Controls can be bound, unbound, or calculated.

Control layout: Combines multiple controls in a database form or report into a single layout object in one of two formats: tabular or stacked.

Control Property Sheet: Displays the properties for the selected control in a form or report.

Copy: Command that places a duplicate of the selected text or object on the Clipboard without changing the file.

Criteria: Conditions that the records must meet in order to be included in the query results. Criteria is a plural word that refers to more than one criterion.

Criterion: Singular form of the word criteria.

Crosstab query: Query that summarizes data in a format similar to a spreadsheet. Values for one field are listed in the first column of the datasheet as row headings; values for another field are listed across the top row as column headings. A value is calculated at the intersection of each row and column.

CSV (comma-separated values): File format for saving text files that uses a comma as the delimiter. These files have a *.csv* file extension.

Currency data type: Fields with this data type store a numerical value with a high degree of accuracy (up to four decimal places). Access will not round the values stored in Currency fields, regardless of the format in which the value displays.

Currency format: Displays a dollar sign ($) before the number and two digits to the right of the decimal place.

Cut: Command that removes the selected text or object from the file and places it on the Office Clipboard for later use.

d

Data bars: A type of conditional formatting that displays a colored data bar representing the value of the record compared to other records. Records with higher values have longer data bars.

Data entry form: A form limited to new record entry only. Users cannot use the form to find, edit, or delete other records.

Database: A collection of data. An effective database allows you to enter, store, organize, and retrieve large amounts of related data.

Database Documenter: Tool that generates database documentation—information about table relationships, field details, and macro code.

Database Splitter: Tool that creates a database application with a front end and a back end. The splitter copies all the tables from a database into a new Access file (the "back end"). Then the original tables are removed from the database and replaced with links to the new file. The original file becomes the "front end" of the application.

Datasheet form: Form that reproduces the exact look and layout of the table datasheet.

Datasheet view, tables: View to use when entering data in a table or to sort and filter data. By default, tables open in Datasheet view.

Datasheets: Table data and query results displayed in Datasheet view.

Date/Time data type: Fields with this data type store a numerical value that is displayed as a date and time. The format in which the date and/or time displays is controlled by the Format property.

Default Value property: Adds a preset value to the field.

Delete query: Query that removes (or deletes) records that match the query criteria.

Delimiter: A specific character that separates the fields in a text file with multiple data fields. Common delimiters are commas, tabs, semicolons, and spaces.

Design view, tables: View where you establish the table primary key and table properties as well as specific properties or formatting for individual fields. Use Design view when you want to change the structure or properties of the table.

Desktop database: A database that does not require a SharePoint server.

e

Embedded macro: A macro available only in the database object in which the button control was created.

Embedded query: Query created as the record source for a form or report if the form or report does not have a table or query defined as its record source. In the *Record Source* property box, it appears as an SQL statement.

Expression: A formula used in a calculated field in a table or query or a calculated control in a form or report.

Expression Builder: Tool used to create formulas (expressions) for calculated fields and controls.

f

Field: Each column in a table.

Field Properties pane: Allows you to set field properties in table Design view.

Field Size property: Limits the number of characters that can be entered and stored in a text field.

Field validation rule: Expression or formula that governs what data can be entered in a field. If the data violates the field validation rule, a message is displayed and the data entry is rejected.

Filter: Limits the database records displayed to only those that meet specific criteria. Filters are temporary and are not saved with the database object unless they are defined in the object's properties.

Find Duplicates query: Query that finds duplicate records in a table.

Find Unmatched query: Query that finds records in one table that do not have matching records in another table.

Foreign key: In a one-to-many relationship, the field in the secondary table that relates to the primary key in the primary table.

Form: Allows database users to input data through a friendly interface.

Form application part: Blank form template with a preset layout and placeholders for labels and other controls.

Form Detail section: The main section of the form which includes the controls for the form data.

Form Footer section: The section immediately below the form Detail section. Used to display information you want to appear at the bottom of every record in the form.

Form Header section: The section immediately above the form Detail section. Used to display the form title, an image, and other information you want to appear at the top of every record in the form.

Form Property Sheet: Displays the properties for the form.

Form view: Provides a user-friendly interface for entering data in a database. From Form view, you cannot change the form layout or formatting.

Form Wizard: Wizard that walks you through the steps of creating a form, including selecting fields and a layout. You can use the Form Wizard to create a form combining fields from multiple related tables.

Format property: Field property that controls the way the data are displayed to the end user.

FROM clause: The part of the SQL statement that defines how records are selected to include in the query results.

Front-end file: In a split database, the database file that contains the forms, reports, queries, and links to the tables in the back-end database file.

g

Global join: The defined relationship between two tables in the Relationships window; it applies throughout the database unless specifically overwritten by a local join.

Group Footer section: Section repeated below each group in a report.

Group Header section: Section repeated above each group in a report.

Grouping: Feature that organizes records into distinct sections within an Access report.

h

Hyperlink data type: Fields with this data type store a Web address or e-mail address.

i

Image control: A control type that stores a graphic.

Image Gallery: Images are stored once in the database's Image Gallery and can be reused in multiple forms and reports without affecting the overall size of the database file.

Import: Adding a database object or record data from an external source.

Index: Similar to a book index, the database index stores an internal pointer to the data to make it easier for the application to find it. Primary key fields are indexed automatically. To index a foreign key field, view the table in Design view, and change the field's *Indexed* property to **Yes (Duplicates OK)**.

Inner join: Method in a simple query for displaying records that match in both tables.

Innermost sort: In a multilevel sort, the last field the data are sorted on.

Input mask: Field property that forces users to enter data in a consistent format by preventing data entry that violates the rules defined by the input mask format.

j

Join: Method for defining how records from two related tables are returned in a query. Join types include Left, Outer Join; Right, Outer Join; Global Join; and Local Join.

l

Label control: Unbound control that displays the field name or other text.

Landscape: Page orientation where the width of the page is greater than the height.

Layout view: View where you can modify some (but not all) structural elements in a form or report.

Left outer join: Join type in which all records from the "one" side of the relationship are included in the query, whether or not there is a corresponding match in the "many" table.

Linked table: A link to a table in another Access database. All of the data remain in the original source file. You cannot change any properties in the linked table, because all table properties are defined in the source file. However, any changes made to the record data in the current database will appear in the source file. Any changes made to the source database will appear in the linked table automatically, including both table property changes and changes to table data.

Linked Table Manager: Tool that allows you to update the connection to linked data.

List box control: A control type that presents users with a list of options to choose from. A list box control is differentiated from a combo box, as there is no text input option and the list is always visible on the form. Like a combo box control, a list box control can display values from another table or query or values that you enter yourself.

Literal text: In an input mask, the letters, numbers or symbols that display in the data format automatically, exactly as they are entered in the input mask, without the user having to type them. Common literal text includes periods, parentheses, and dashes.

Local join: The relationship defined between two tables for a specific query; it overrides the global join for that query only.

Locked file: Database file saved in the ACCDE format. The design of existing database objects is locked. Users can create new database objects, but they cannot change the design of existing ones.

Long Text data type: Holds text and numbers like a Short Text field, except you can enter up to 65,535 characters in a Long Text field. Text in Long Text fields can be formatted using Rich Text Formatting. In previous versions of Access, the Long Text data type was called the Memo data type.

Lookup field: Allows the user to select data from a list of items.

m

Macro: Programming instruction that can be run from within a file. Macros are used to automate data entry and formatting processes and to execute commands from buttons in database forms and reports.

Make table query: Query that creates (or makes) a new table by copying records that meet the query criteria and pasting them into a new table. Records are *copied* from the original table. No records are deleted.

Margins: The blank spaces at the top, bottom, left, and right of a page.

Message Bar: Displays a warning at the top of the window, below the Ribbon, when a database includes active content.

Multiple Items form: Displays multiple records at once. The layout and design of a Multiple Items form can be modified.

n

Navigation form: A form type that allows you to group together all the database objects a user might need within a single form object. Users navigate between database objects by clicking tabs.

Navigation Pane: Pane that organizes all the objects for a database. The Navigation Pane is docked on the left side of the screen.

Normalization: The process of removing repeated data from a table into separate, related tables.

Number data type: Fields with this data type hold a numerical value. The default number is described as a long integer, a number between –2,147,483,648 and 2,147,483,647.

o

Object dependencies: Relationships between database objects when the data for a database object or a field come from another database object.

OLE Object data type: Stores a graphic or file as part of the database. It is maintained in Access 2013 for backward compatibility with databases created prior to Access 2007.

One-to-many relationship: A relationship between two database tables where the primary table contains a primary key field that is included as a field (the foreign key) in the secondary table. Thus, one record in the first table can relate to many records in the second table.

ORDER BY clause: The part of the SQL statement that defines how records in the query results are sorted.

Outermost sort: In a multilevel sort, the first field the data are sorted on.

p

Page footer: Section that appears at the bottom of every printed page in a form or report.

Page header: Section that appears at the top of every printed page in a form or report.

Parameter query: A query with user-controlled criteria input. When the query is run, the user is prompted to enter a value for a specific field (the parameter input) that will be used as the criterion when generating results.

Paste: Command that is used to insert text or an object from the Clipboard into a file.

PDF (Portable Document Format): Type of file that can be read by anyone who has the Adobe Reader software installed.

Percent format: Displays the number as a percentage, so .05 displays as 5, and 5 displays as 500. It does not display the percent symbol (%) in the table.

Performance Analyzer: Tool that suggests changes to optimize the database and speed up performance.

Placeholder characters: In an input mask, the letters, numbers, or symbols that define the acceptable input characters. For example, in an input mask, using a 0 requires the user to enter a digit from 0 to 9. Using a 9 as a placeholder character instead of 0 makes the digit optional.

Portrait: Page orientation where the height of the page is greater than the width.

Primary key field: The field that contains data unique to each record in a table.

Print Preview: A specific report view that shows how the database report will appear when printed.

q

Query grid: The lower pane in query Design view where the fields and criteria for the query are defined.

Query: Extracts data from a table or multiple related tables.

Quick Start application part: A table template that you can use to start building a database. There are five Quick Start application parts to choose from: *Comments, Contacts, Issues, Tasks,* and *Users.* Most also include forms for data entry.

Quick Start field types: Provide an easy way to add address fields and other common field groups to your table.

r

Record: Each row in a table in a database.

Record source: The associated table or query for a database form or report.

Record validation rule: Rule applied at the table level to restrict values in one field based on the value of another field in the same record. When you enter an expression in the table's Validation Rule property, Access will evaluate the expression when the user leaves the record, and if the expression is false, the record cannot be saved and a message is displayed.

Redo: Reverses the *Undo* command and restores the file to its previous state.

Referential integrity: The policy that ensures that related database records remain accurate. If a relationship has referential integrity enforced, then no modification can be made to either table that would violate the relationship structure.

Relational database: A database that allows you to relate tables and databases to one another through common fields.

Relationship Report: Prints the table relationships exactly as they are displayed in the Relationships window.

Relationships window: Window that provides a visual representation of the table relationships in your database.

Report: Displays database information for printing or viewing on-screen.

Report Detail section: The main section of the report which includes the controls for the report data.

Report Footer section: Section below the report Detail section and the Report Page Footer section (if visible). Often used to display calculated controls to summarize values in the Detail section of the report.

Report Header section: Section above the report Detail section and the Report Page Header section (if visible). Used to display the report title, a company logo, and other information you want to appear only once at the beginning of the report.

Report Page Footer section: Section immediately below the report Detail section. Used to display information included on every page of the report when it is printed or viewed in Print Preview view. The Page Footer section usually includes the control to display page numbers.

Report Page Header section: Section immediately above the report Detail section. Used to display information included on every page of the report when it is printed or viewed in Print Preview view.

Report Property Sheet: Displays the properties for the report.

Report view: Shows a static view of the database report. You cannot change the layout or formatting of the report from Report view.

Report Wizard: Wizard that walks you step by step through the process of creating a report. The Report Wizard allows you to combine fields from more than one table or query and gives you more layout and design options than using the basic *Report* button from the *Create* tab.

Rich Text Format (RTF): Text format that can be used with any word processing program, not just Microsoft Word.

Right outer join: Join type in which all records from the "many" side of the relationship are included in the query, whether or not there is a corresponding match in the "one" table.

S

SELECT clause: The part of the SQL statement that defines the fields included in the query.

Select query: Displays data from one or more tables or queries, based on the fields that you select.

SELECT statement: The lines of SQL code that tell Access which fields to include in the query, how the data are related for purposes of the query, any criteria for selecting records to include in the query, and how the query results should be ordered.

Short Text data type: Can hold up to 255 characters. Short Text fields are used for short text data or numbers that should be treated as text.

Single Record form: Form that displays one record at a time.

Split form: Combines the convenience of a continuous datasheet form with the usability of a single form displaying one record at a time.

SQL view: Shows the code that Access uses to build a query.

Stacked layout: Places the form or report labels at the left side with data to the right (similar to many paper forms or reports).

Stand-alone macro: A macro that exists independently of a specific database object. It can be run directly from the Navigation Pane, or it can be called from a control in a form or a report just like an embedded macro.

Structured Query Language (SQL): Programming language used in Access and other relational database management systems to define queries.

Subform: A form within the form, displays the related records from the "many" table in a one-to-many relationship.

Subreport: A report within a report, displays the related records from the "many" table in a one-to-many relationship.

Summary query: Query that calculates summary values. Also known as aggregate query or totals query.

T

Tab order: The order in which controls are activated in a form by pressing Tab.

Table: Stores all the database data. Tables are the basic building blocks of the database.

Table Analyzer: Tool that finds repeated data in a table and pulls it out into separate related tables.

Tabular layout: Places the form or report labels across the top, with columns of data (similar to a datasheet or a spreadsheet).

Template: A file with predefined settings that you can use as a base to create a new database of your own.

Text box control: Control that displays text, numbers, dates, and similar data. Text box controls can be bound or unbound.

Theme: A unified font and color scheme applied to the entire database.

Theme colors: Aspect of the theme that limits the colors available from the color palette for fonts, borders, and shading.

Theme fonts: Aspect of the theme that controls which fonts are used for built-in text styles. Changing the theme fonts does not limit the fonts available from the *Font* group on the Ribbon.

Total row: A row that calculates an aggregate function, such as the sum or average, of all the values in the column. Total rows can be added to tables and queries in Datasheet view in Access.

Totals query: Query that calculates summary values. Also known as aggregate query or summary query.

U

Unbound control: A control that is not linked to a field.

Undo: Reverses the last action performed.

Update query: Query that changes (or updates) records that match the query criteria. For each field you want to update, you specify the text or expression to use when updating the field data.

V

Validation Rule property (field): Expression or formula that governs what data can be entered in a field. If the data violates the field validation rule, a message is displayed and the data entry is rejected.

Validation Rule property (table): Rule applied at the table level to restrict values in one field based on the value of another field in the same record. When you enter an expression in the table's Validation Rule property, Access will evaluate the expression when the user leaves the record, and if the expression is false, the record cannot be saved and a message is displayed.

Validation Text property (field): Field property through which you can customize the message to tell the user in plain language why the value in the field violates the field validation rule.

Validation Text property (table): Table property through which you can customize the message to tell the user in plain language why the value in the record violates the record validation rule.

W

WHERE clause: The part of the SQL statement that defines the query criteria.

Wildcard: Special characters used in criteria to substitute for any character. The * wildcard replaces any string of characters. The ? wildcard replaces a single character.

Y

Yes/No data type: Fields with this data type store a true/false value as a −1 for yes and 0 for no.

office index

a

Account information, changing, OF-15–OF-16
Account page, ACG-1
    changing account information on, OF-15–OF-16
    changing background and theme with, OF-17
Applications
    closing, OF-27
    in Microsoft Office 2013, OF-3–OF-5

b

Background, changing, OF-17
Backstage, ACG-1
    displaying Open page, OF-7
    enabling editing with, OF-18
    in user interface, OF-9
Blank files, creating, OF-20
Bookmark feature, OF-19

c

Changing
    account information, OF-15–OF-16
    background and theme, OF-17
Closing
    applications, OF-27
    files, OF-8
Contextual tabs, OF-9, ACG-1
Copy command, OF-10
Creating
    folders in OneDrive, OF-25
    new blank files, OF-20
Cut command, OF-10

d

Database programs, OF-4
Databases, relational, OF-4
Disabling
    Protected View, OF-18
    user interface features, OF-13

e

Editing, Protected View and, OF-18

Enabling
    editing from Protected View, OF-18
    user interface features, OF-13
Enhanced ScreenTips, OF-12, ACG-1

f

File format, OF-26
File Properties, OF-22, ACG-1
File tab, OF-9, OF-24, ACG-1
Files
    closing, OF-8
    creating blank, OF-20
    opening, OF-6–OF-7
    saving, OF-23–OF-26
Folders, creating, OF-25
Font formatting, OF-12
Formatting, OF-12
Forms, database, OF-4

g

Groups, OF-9, ACG-1

h

Help, OF-21
Help toolbar, OF-21
Home tab, OF-9, ACG-1

k

Keyboard shortcuts, OF-10, ACA-1, ACG-1
    for accessing Office Help system, OF-21
    for closing files, OF-8
    for creating new files, OF-20
    for displaying Open page, OF-7
    for saving to local drive, OF-24

l

Live Preview feature, OF-12, ACG-1
Local drive, saving files to, OF-23–OF-24

m

Metadata, OF-22, ACG-1
Microsoft Access 2013, OF-4, ACG-1

Microsoft Excel 2013, OF-3, OF-25, ACG-1
Microsoft Office, previous versions of, OF-26
Microsoft Office 365, OF-5
Microsoft Office 2013
    applications in, OF-3–OF-5
    busy parent on, OF-14
    changing look of, OF-17
    keyboard shortcuts, ACA-1
    Office 365 vs., OF-5
    trial version, OF-5
    user interface, OF-9–OF-13
Microsoft Office Backstage view; *see* Backstage view
Microsoft PowerPoint 2013, OF-4, OF-19, ACG-1
Microsoft Word 2013, OF-3, ACG-1
    bookmark feature, OF-19
    Home tab, OF-9
    sharing OneDrive documents, OF-25
Mini toolbar, OF-11, ACG-1
Minimizing Ribbon, OF-9
Modifying Quick Access Toolbar, OF-11

n

Names, new, OF-26
New command, OF-20, ACG-1

o

Office Help system, OF-21, ACG-1
OneDrive, OF-16, OF-25, ACG-1
Open command, OF-10
Opening files, OF-6–OF-7
Options dialog, OF-13

p

Paragraph formatting, OF-12
Parents, OF-14
Paste command, OF-10
Photo, user, OF-15–OF-16
Picture formatting, OF-12
Presentation programs, OF-4
Printer icon (Help toolbar), OF-21
Protected View, OF-18, ACG-2
Pushpin icon (Help toolbar), OF-21

q

Quick Access Toolbar, OF-11, ACG-2
Quick Print button, OF-11
Quick Styles, OF-12

r

Relational databases, OF-4
Reports, database, OF-4
Ribbon, OF-9, ACG-2

s

Save command, OF-10
Saving files, OF-23–OF-26
    and closing files, OF-8
    to local drive, OF-23–OF-24
    with new names, OF-26
    to OneDrive, OF-25
ScreenTips, OF-12, ACG-2
Searching in Office Help, OF-21
Security settings, OF-18
Shape styles, OF-12
Sharing OneDrive documents, OF-25
Shortcut menus, OF-10, ACG-2
SmartArt, OF-12
Spreadsheet applications, OF-3
Start page, OF-14, ACG-2

t

Tables, OF-4, OF-12
Tabs, OF-9, ACG-2; *see also specific tabs*
Tags, OF-22, ACG-2
Templates, OF-20
Themes, OF-17
Trust Center, OF-18

u

Undo command, OF-10
User interface, OF-9–OF-13
User photo, changing, OF-15–OF-16

v

View, Protected, OF-18

w

Windows 7, OF-5
Windows 8, OF-4
Word processing software, OF-3

access index

& (ampersand), AC-224
* (asterisk), AC-21, AC-158
@ (at symbol), AC-222
= (equal to operator), AC-161
> (greater than operator), AC-161, AC-222, AC-224
>= (greater than or equal to operator), AC-161
< (less than operator), AC-161, AC-222, AC-224
<= (less than or equal to operator), AC-161
9 (placeholder), AC-224
< > (not equal to operator), AC-161
(pound symbol), AC-224
? (question mark), AC-21, AC-158, AC-224
0 (placeholder), AC-224

a

A (placeholder), AC-224
a (placeholder), AC-224
ACCDE file format, AC-388, ACG-2
Access Options dialog, AC-383–AC-384
Access web apps, AC-197, ACG-2
Action queries, AC-337–AC-345, ACG-2
   creating new tables with, AC-340–AC-341
   deleting records with, AC-342–AC-343
   moving records with, AC-344–AC-345
   types of, AC-337
   updating records with, AC-338–AC-339
Actions, adding, to macros, AC-358–AC-359
Active content, enabling, AC-6
Adding
   actions to macros, AC-358–AC-359
   attachments, AC-70–AC-71
   blank records, AC-17, AC-19
   calculated controls, AC-304–AC-305
   calculated fields to tables, AC-220–AC-221
   combo box controls, AC-263–AC-265
   command button controls, AC-260–AC-262
   comments to macros, AC-360
   conditional formatting, AC-318–AC-319
   criteria to queries, AC-165
      numeric and date criteria, AC-160–AC-161
      text criteria, AC-157–AC-159
   default values, AC-66
   design elements to headers, AC-124–AC-125
   fields, AC-55–AC-56, AC-59
      calculated fields, AC-168–AC-169
      with Field List pace, AC-251
      to forms, AC-108–AC-110
      lookup fields, AC-73–AC-79
      to queries, AC-151–AC-152, AC-155, AC-156, AC-168–AC-169
      to reports, AC-117
   group totals, AC-308
   grouping, AC-127, AC-128, AC-306
   images, AC-275–AC-276
   label controls, AC-301
   list box controls, AC-257–AC-259
   ORDER BY clauses, AC-356
   page numbers, AC-126
   preventing addition of records by users, AC-254
   queries to SELECT clauses, AC-354
   rows or columns to control layout, AC-123
   subforms, AC-266–AC-271
   subreports, AC-310–AC-312, AC-314–AC-316
   tables to Relationship window, AC-8–AC-9
   titles, AC-383
   Total rows, AC-72
   totals, AC-129, AC-348–AC-350
   validation messages, AC-229, AC-231
   value list items, AC-226
Adjusting
   column widths, AC-57, AC-226
   control heights, AC-303
   margins and page orientation, AC-132
   subform height and width, AC-270–AC-271
   subreport controls, AC-316
   subreport height and width, AC-311–AC-312
Aggregate (term), AC-350, ACG-2
Aggregate functions, AC-350, ACG-2
Aggregate queries, AC-348–AC-350, ACG-2
Aligning controls, AC-303
All Relationships button, AC-9
Allow Multiples Values check box, AC-226
Allow Value List Edits check box, AC-226, AC-227
Ampersand (&), AC-224
AND, in queries, AC-162–AC-165
Append Only property, AC-67
Append queries, AC-337, AC-344–AC-345, ACG-2
Appending tables, importing data and, AC-208, AC-213
Application parts
   custom, AC-203
   form, AC-249, ACG-3
   Quick Start, AC-202–AC-203, ACG-5
Applying
   conditional report formatting, AC-317–AC-319
   filters, AC-180–AC-181
   input masks, AC-68–AC-69
   themes, AC-120
Arranging
   controls, AC-122–AC-123, AC-303
   Relationships Window, AC-392
Arrow keys, navigating records with, AC-14–AC-15
Asterisk (*), AC-21, AC-158
At symbol (@), AC-222
Attachment data type, AC-63, ACG-2
Attachment fields, AC-70–AC-71
Attachments, adding, AC-70–AC-71
AutoFilter, AC-178–AC-179
Automatic compacting, AC-32
AutoNumber data type, AC-62, ACG-2
AutoNumber fields, sorting, AC-183
AutoNumber format, AC-17
Average function, AC-72, AC-349

b

Back-end databases, AC-387, AC-390
Back-end files, AC-386, ACG-2
Background images, AC-276
Backstage view, AC-131, AC-201

Backups
    database, AC-33–AC-34
    table, AC-339
Blank databases, AC-200–AC-201
Blank forms
    adding fields to, AC-108–AC-110
    creating, AC-107, AC-249
Blank pages, warnings about, AC-130, AC-132–AC-133
Blank records, AC-17, AC-19
Blank reports, AC-116
Block cipher, AC-390
Borders, subform control, AC-273
Bound controls, AC-108, AC-118–AC-119, ACG-2
Bypassing startup options, AC-384

C

C (placeholder), AC-224
Calculated controls
    adding, AC-304–AC-305
    defined, AC-129, ACG-2
    in Group Footer section, AC-307
Calculated Field data type, AC-63, ACG-2
Calculated fields, ACG-2
    adding, to queries, AC-168–AC-169
    adding, to tables, AC-220–AC-221
Calculations, in update queries, AC-338
Cascading options, ACG-2
    and delete queries, AC-343
    enforcing updates in relationships with, AC-232–AC-233
Case-sensitive passwords, AC-390
Changing; *see also* Modifying
    data types, AC-62–AC-63
    Format field property, AC-64
    grouping level, AC-127–AC-128
    and preventing changes to records, AC-254
    records in linked tables, AC-218
Checking spelling, AC-25
Closing
    back-end databases, AC-390
    objects, AC-5
Code for macros, AC-262
Collapsing groups, AC-10
Color of text, specifying, AC-222
Column Count property, AC-227
Column Width dialog, AC-57
Columns
    adjusting width of, AC-57, AC-226
    in control layout, AC-123

Combining text fields, AC-221
Combo box controls, AC-263–AC-265, ACG-2
Comma-separated value (CSV) files, AC-209
Comma Style format, AC-64, ACG-2
Command button controls, AC-260–AC-262, ACG-2
Comments, AC-202, AC-360, ACG-2
Compact & Repair tool, AC-32, ACG-2
Comparison operators
    in field validation rules, AC-228
    in numeric/date criteria, AC-160–AC-161
Conditional formatting, AC-317–AC-319, ACG-2
Configuring startup options, AC-383–AC-384
Contacts (application part), AC-202
Control labels, AC-265
Control layout, AC-122–AC-123, ACG-3
Control Property Sheet, AC-255, AC-259, ACG-3
Controlling page setup, AC-132–AC-133
Controls, AC-253–AC-265, ACG-2
    adding
        combo box controls, AC-263–AC-265
        command button controls, AC-260–AC-262
        list box controls, AC-257–AC-259
    arranging, AC-303
    bound, AC-108, AC-118–AC-119, ACG-2
    calculated, AC-129, AC-304–AC-305, AC-307, ACG-2
    combo box, AC-263–AC-265, ACG-2
    command button, AC-260–AC-262, ACG-2
    controlling data entry in forms, AC-253–AC-255
    deleting, AC-110
    for forms, AC-108
    image, AC-275, ACG-4
    label, AC-108, AC-299, AC-301, ACG-4
    list box, AC-257–AC-259, ACG-4
    for reports, AC-303–AC-305
        adding calculated controls, AC-304–AC-305
        arranging, AC-122–AC-123, AC-303
        controlling page setup, AC-132–AC-133

    formatting, AC-118–AC-119
    moving, AC-122–AC-123
    resizing, AC-121
    for subreports, AC-316
    tab order of, AC-280
    text box, AC-108, ACG-6
    unbound, AC-108, AC-305, ACG-7
Copy command, AC-22, AC-307, ACG-3
Copying
    calculated controls, AC-307
    data, AC-22
    databases, AC-34
    records, AC-340–AC-341, AC-344–AC-345
Count function, AC-72, AC-349
=COUNT(*) expression, AC-305
Created Date grouping option, AC-11
Creating
    append queries, AC-344–AC-345
    blank databases, AC-200–AC-201
    calculated fields, AC-168–AC-169
    crosstab queries, AC-351–AC-353
    custom field text formats, AC-222–AC-223
    custom input masks, AC-224–AC-225
    delete queries, AC-342–AC-343
    desktop databases from templates, AC-197–AC-199
    field validation rules, AC-228–AC-229
    forms, AC-101–AC-107, AC-249
    locked ACCDE files, AC-388
    make table queries, AC-340–AC-341
    new records, AC-16–AC-19
    queries, AC-151–AC-156, AC-176
    record validation rules, AC-230–AC-231
    relationships between tables, AC-80–AC-81
    reports, AC-111–AC-116
    stand-alone macros, AC-358–AC-361
    tables, AC-53, AC-58, AC-340–AC-341
    update queries, AC-338–AC-339
Criteria
    defined, AC-157, ACG-3
    defining, AC-355
    modifying, AC-356
    for narrowing summary queries, AC-349
    numeric and date, AC-160–AC-161
    placement of, AC-165

text, AC-157–AC-159
using AND with, AC-162–AC-165
using OR with, AC-163–AC-165
and WHERE clause, AC-355–AC-356
Criterion, AC-157, ACG-3
Crosstab queries, AC-351–AC-353, ACG-3
CSV (comma-separated value) files, AC-209
Currency data type, AC-62, AC-119, ACG-3
Currency fields, AC-79, AC-183
Currency format, AC-64, ACG-3
Custom application parts, AC-203
Custom category, in Navigation Pane, AC-382
Custom field text formats, AC-222–AC-223
Custom grouping option, AC-11
Custom input masks, AC-224–AC-225
Cut command, AC-22, ACG-3

d

Data
 copying, AC-22
 cutting, AC-22
 entering, AC-16–AC-19
 exporting, AC-27–AC-29
 filtering, AC-178–AC-181
 finding, AC-20–AC-21, AC-170–AC-175
 pasting, AC-22
 repeated, AC-52
 replacing, AC-20–AC-21
 searching for, AC-20–AC-21
 storing data in tables, AC-51–AC-52
 testing validation rules against, AC-229, AC-231
Data bars, AC-318–AC-319, ACG-3
Data entry, controlling, AC-253–AC-255
Data entry forms, AC-253, AC-256, ACG-3
Data types, AC-62–AC-63, AC-177
Database Documenter, AC-391, ACG-3
Database objects; see Objects
Database programs, exporting data to, AC-28
Database Splitter, AC-386–AC-387, ACG-3
Databases; see also Finalizing databases
 appending data to tables in separate, AC-345
 back-end, AC-387, AC-390
 backups of, AC-33–AC-34
 creating new blank, AC-200–AC-201
 creating new tables in separate, AC-341
 defined, AC-3, ACG-3
 desktop, AC-197–AC-201, ACG-3
 front-end, AC-387, AC-388
 linking tables in, AC-217–AC-219
 opening, AC-389
 relational, AC-3, ACG-6
 replacing, with backup copies, AC-34
 splitting, AC-386–AC-387
Datasheet format, AC-183
Datasheet forms, AC-102, AC-103, ACG-3
Datasheet subforms, AC-101
Datasheet view, AC-53–AC-55, ACG-3
 adding calculated fields, AC-220–AC-221
 adding fields, AC-55, AC-70, AC-73
 adding validation messages, AC-229, AC-231
 adding validation rules, AC-229, AC-231
 adjusting column width, AC-57
 changing data types, AC-62–AC-63
 changing Format field property, AC-64
 creating and saving tables, AC-53
 as default view, AC-12
 deleting fields, AC-61
 deleting records, AC-24
 hiding/showing fields of queries, AC-167
 modifying Default Value property, AC-66
 modifying Field Size property, AC-67
 renaming fields, AC-54
 switching Design and, AC-156
 Undo command in, AC-23
Datasheets, AC-13, ACG-3
 adding Total rows, AC-72
 filtering, AC-178–AC-179
 sorting records, AC-182–AC-183
Date criteria, in queries, AC-160–AC-161
Date/Time data type, AC-62, AC-118, ACG-3
Date/Time fields
 filtering data in, AC-180
 grouping by, AC-308
 Input Mask property for, AC-69
 modifying, to use lookup lists, AC-79
 sorting of, AC-183
Dates, in headers, AC-125
Decrease Decimals button, AC-65
Default Value property, AC-66, ACG-3
Default values, AC-66
Delete key, AC-24
Delete queries, AC-337, AC-342–AC-343, ACG-3
Deleting
 conditional formatting rules, AC-318
 controls, AC-110
 default form image, AC-276
 fields, AC-61
 groupings of records, AC-128
 objects, AC-26
 preventing deletion of records by users, AC-254
 records, AC-24
 records via queries, AC-342–AC-343
 relationships between tables, AC-81
 table relationships, AC-232–AC-233
 tabs from navigation forms, AC-279
 value list items, AC-226
Delimited files, AC-209–AC-213
Delimiters, AC-209, ACG-3
Dependencies, object, AC-380, ACG-5
Design elements, in headers, AC-124–AC-125
Design options, limiting, AC-385
Design view, AC-12, ACG-3
 adding calculated controls, AC-305
 adding calculated fields, AC-221
 adding combo box controls, AC-265
 adding command button controls, AC-260–AC-262
 adding field validation rules, AC-228–AC-229
 adding fields to forms, AC-110
 adding grouping for reports, AC-127, AC-306
 adding image controls, AC-275
 adding list box controls, AC-257–AC-259
 adding lookup fields, AC-73
 adding totals in reports, AC-129
 aligning controls, AC-303
 applying input masks, AC-68–AC-69
 AutoFilter vs., AC-179
 changing data types, AC-63
 changing Format field property, AC-65

Design view—*Cont.*
  creating new blank forms, AC-107
  creating new blank reports, AC-116
  creating queries, AC-154–AC-156, AC-353
  creating tables, AC-58
  custom field text formats, AC-222–AC-223
  date and time, AC-125
  deleting fields, AC-61
  disabling user interface elements, AC-256
  displaying Report Header/Footer sections, AC-301–AC-302
  forms in, AC-107, AC-250–AC-251
  hiding repeated values, AC-309
  inserting fields, AC-59
  modifying Default Value property, AC-66
  modifying Field Size property, AC-67
  removing controls from layout, AC-123
  removing excess space in reports, AC-132
  reports in, AC-116, AC-299–AC-300
  resizing controls, AC-121
  setting primary key in, AC-60
  setting sort order, AC-252
  switching to Datasheet view from, AC-156
Designing tables, AC-51–AC-52
Desktop databases
  creating new blank, AC-200–AC-201
  defined, AC-197, ACG-3
  from templates, AC-197–AC-199
Disabling
  Layout view, AC-385
  user interface elements, AC-256
Displaying
  Group Footer section, AC-307
  headers and footers of forms, AC-274
  page headers of subreports, AC-313
  Report Header/Footer sections, AC-301–AC-302
  subform properties, AC-272
Dragging, resizing controls by, AC-121
Drop-down list, combo box, AC-265
Duplicate data, AC-173–AC-175

e

Edit Relationships dialog, AC-81, AC-233
Editing
  conditional formatting rules, AC-319
  list items, AC-259
  reports, AC-115
  value list items, AC-227
Embedded macros, AC-358, ACG-3
Embedded queries, AC-251, AC-300, ACG-3
Enable Data Integrity check box, AC-75
Enabled property, AC-255
Enabling active content, AC-6
Encrypting databases, AC-389–AC-390
Enforce Referential Integrity check box, AC-80
Enter key, AC-19
Entering data
  in forms, AC-18–AC-19
  in tables, AC-16–AC-17
Equal to operator (=), AC-161
Executables, AC-388
Existing data, testing validation rules against, AC-229, AC-231
Exporting data, AC-27–AC-29
Expression Builder
  adding calculated fields with, AC-168–AC-169, AC-220–AC-221
  defined, ACG-3
Expressions, AC-168, AC-304, ACG-3
External data sources, linking tables to, AC-219

f

Field List pane, AC-251
Field names
  importing data with, AC-206, AC-211
  queries for tables with different, AC-344
Field Properties pane, AC-58, ACG-3
Field size, AC-57
Field Size property, AC-67, ACG-3
Field validation rules, AC-228–AC-229, ACG-3
Field values, checking, AC-317–AC-318
Field width, AC-57

Fields, ACG-3
  adding
    with Field List pace, AC-251
    to forms, AC-108–AC-110
    to reports, AC-117, AC-299–AC-300
    to tables, AC-55–AC-56, AC-59
  applying filters to, AC-180–AC-181
  Attachment, AC-70–AC-71
  AutoNumber, AC-183
  calculated, AC-168–AC-169, AC-220–AC-221, ACG-2
  combining, AC-106
  controlling data entry in, AC-255
  Currency, AC-79, AC-183
  and database relationships, AC-7
  Date/Time, AC-183, AC-308
    filtering data in, AC-180
    Input Mask property for, AC-69
    modifying, to use lookup lists, AC-79
    sorting of, AC-183
  defined, AC-3
  deleting, AC-61
  FirstName, AC-221
  foreign key, AC-7, ACG-3
  formatting, AC-64–AC-65
  hyperlink, AC-183
  of imported data, AC-206, AC-211, AC-216
  LastName, AC-221
  lookup, ACG-4
    adding, AC-73–AC-79
    entering data in, AC-17
    from lists, AC-78–AC-79
    in make table queries, AC-341
    from other tables, AC-73–AC-77
  Memo, AC-63
  modifying, AC-73, AC-78–AC-79
  modifying properties of, AC-66–AC-67
  Number, AC-183, AC-308
  POID, AC-224
  primary key, AC-7, AC-60, ACG-5
  in queries
    adding, AC-151–AC-152, AC-155, AC-156
    calculated fields, AC-168–AC-169
    hiding and showing, AC-167
  Quick Start types, AC-56
  renaming, AC-54
  Short Text, AC-67, AC-69, AC-308
  Text, AC-63, AC-180, AC-183, AC-221–AC-223
  Yes/No, AC-183

Filter by Selection feature, AC-180–AC-181
Filtering data, AC-178–AC-181
Filters
   AutoFilter, AC-178–AC-179
   defined, AC-178, ACG-3
   for Navigation Pane, AC-11
Finalizing databases, AC-374–AC-392
   configuring startup options, AC-383–AC-384
   creating locked ACCDE files, AC-388
   customizing the Navigation Pane, AC-381–AC-382
   with Database Documenter, AC-391
   encrypting databases with passwords, AC-389–AC-390
   limiting views and design options, AC-385
   with Performance Analyzer, AC-379
   printing Relationship Reports, AC-392
   splitting databases, AC-386–AC-387
   with Table Analyzer, AC-375–AC-378
   viewing object dependencies, AC-380
Find and Replace dialog, AC-20, AC-21
Find command, AC-20
Find Duplicates query, AC-173–AC-175, ACG-3
Find Unmatched query, AC-170–AC-172, ACG-3
Finding data, AC-20–AC-21
   duplicate data, AC-173–AC-175
   unmatched data, AC-170–AC-172
First Record button, AC-14
FirstName field, AC-221
Footers
   form, AC-274, ACG-3
   group, AC-307–AC-308
   Group Footer section, AC-302, ACG-4
   Page Footer section, AC-126, AC-274, ACG-5
   Report Footer section, AC-126, AC-129, AC-301–AC-302, AC-305, ACG-6
   Report Page Footer section, AC-301, ACG-6
Foreign key fields, AC-7, ACG-3
Form application parts, AC-249, ACG-3
Form Detail section, ACG-3
Form footers, AC-274, ACG-3
Form headers, AC-124–AC-125, AC-274, ACG-4
Form Layout Tools Format tab, AC-118
Form Property Sheet, AC-250–AC-252, ACG-4
Form view, AC-12, AC-23, ACG-4
Form Wizard, AC-104–AC-106, ACG-4
Format field property
   creating custom text field formats with, AC-222–AC-223
   defined, ACG-4
   and input mask format, AC-69
   making changes to, AC-64–AC-65
Formatting
   conditional, AC-317–AC-319, ACG-2
   controls for reports, AC-118–AC-119
   fields, AC-64–AC-65
Forms, AC-3–AC-4, AC-101–AC-110, AC-248–AC-280
   adding
      design elements to headers, AC-124–AC-125
      fields, AC-108–AC-110
      images, AC-275–AC-276
      subforms, AC-269–AC-271
   applying themes to, AC-120
   attachments in, AC-71
   calculated fields in, AC-169
   controls, AC-253–AC-265
      adding combo box controls, AC-263–AC-265
      adding command button controls, AC-260–AC-262
      adding list box controls, AC-257–AC-259
      controlling data entry in forms, AC-253–AC-255
      defining tab order of, AC-280
      formatting, AC-118–AC-119
      moving and arranging, AC-122–AC-123
      resizing, AC-121
   creating, AC-101–AC-107
      from application parts, AC-249
      with Form Wizard, AC-104–AC-106
      Multiple Items forms, AC-102
      new blank forms, AC-107
      new records in forms, AC-18–AC-19
      Single Record forms, AC-101
      Split forms, AC-103
   custom text field formats in, AC-223
   Cut, Copy, and Paste commands in, AC-22
   data entry, AC-253, AC-256, ACG-3
   Datasheet, AC-102, AC-103, ACG-3
   defined, ACG-3
   deleting records in, AC-24
   in Design view, AC-250–AC-251
   disabling user interface elements in, AC-256
   Multiple Items, AC-102, ACG-5
   navigating records in, AC-14–AC-15
   navigation, AC-277–AC-279, AC-383, ACG-5
   setting sort order in, AC-252
   Single Record, AC-101, ACG-6
   Split, AC-103, ACG-6
   subforms, AC-266–AC-273, ACG-6
      adding, AC-266–AC-271
      automatic insertion of, AC-101
      creating, AC-104
      modifying subform properties, AC-272–AC-273
   with tabs, AC-277–AC-280
   views for, AC-12
FROM clause, AC-355, ACG-4
Front-end databases, AC-387, AC-388
Front-end files, AC-386, ACG-4

g

Global joins, AC-346, ACG-4
Greater than operator (>), AC-161, AC-222, AC-224
Greater than or equal to operator (>=), AC-161
Group, Sort, and Total pane, AC-308
Group Footer section, AC-302, AC-307–AC-308, ACG-4
Group Header section, AC-302, AC-307–AC-308, ACG-4
Group totals, AC-307
Grouping, AC-127–AC-128, AC-306–AC-308
   adding, AC-127, AC-306
   defined, AC-306, ACG-4
   hiding repeated values to simulate, AC-309
   using group headers and footers, AC-307–AC-308
Groups, AC-10–AC-11

h

Headers
    form, AC-124–AC-125, AC-274, ACG-4
    Group Header section, AC-302, AC-307–AC-308, ACG-4
    Page Header section, AC-126, AC-274, AC-313, ACG-5
    report, AC-124–AC-125, ACG-6
    Report Header section, AC-126, AC-301–AC-302, AC-305
    Report Page Header section, AC-301, ACG-6
    subreport, AC-313
Height
    combo box drop-down list, AC-265
    control, AC-303
    form header, AC-274
    report/page header, AC-302
    subform, AC-271
    subreport, AC-311, AC-312
Hide key column check box, AC-75
Hiding
    Group, Sort, and Total pane, AC-308
    Group Header section, AC-307
    horizontal and vertical scroll bars, AC-256
    navigation buttons, AC-256, AC-262, AC-272–AC-273
    primary keys, AC-264
    query fields, AC-167
    Relationships window, AC-9
    repeated values, AC-309
    Ribbon tabs, AC-385
    subform control borders, AC-273
Home tab
    creating new records, AC-17, AC-19
    navigating records, AC-15
Horizontal scroll bars, AC-256
Hyperlink data type, AC-63, ACG-4
Hyperlink fields, sorting, AC-183

i

Image controls, AC-275, ACG-4
Image Gallery, AC-275–AC-276, ACG-4
Images, AC-275–AC-276
Import Spreadsheet Wizard, AC-205–AC-207
Importing data, ACG-4
    adding records by, AC-214–AC-216
    from Excel, AC-204–AC-208
    from text files, AC-209–AC-213

Increase Decimals button, AC-65
Index, AC-379, ACG-4
Info page, active content from, AC-6
Inner joins, AC-346, ACG-4
Innermost sort, AC-182, ACG-4
Input masks
    applying, AC-68–AC-69
    creating custom, AC-224–AC-225
    defined, AC-224, ACG-4
    entering data with, AC-16–AC-17
    modifying, AC-225
Issues (application part), AC-202

j

Joins, AC-346–AC-347, ACG-4
    global, AC-346, ACG-4
    inner, AC-346, ACG-4
    left outer, AC-346, AC-347, ACG-4
    local, AC-346–AC-347, ACG-4
    right outer, AC-346, ACG-6

k

Keyboard shortcuts, ACA-2–ACA-3
    for adding blank records, AC-17, AC-19
    for Copy command, AC-22, AC-307
    for Cut command, AC-22
    for deleting records, AC-24
    in Microsoft Access 2013, AC-119
    for opening form Property Sheet, AC-251
    for opening Print dialog, AC-31
    for opening report Property Sheet, AC-300
    for opening Spelling dialog, AC-25
    for Paste command, AC-22, AC-307
    for saving objects, AC-53
    for Undo and Redo commands, AC-23

l

L (placeholder), AC-224
Label controls, AC-108, AC-299, AC-301, ACG-4
Landscape orientation, AC-115, AC-132, ACG-4
Last Record button, AC-14
LastName field, AC-221

Lawyers, AC-131
Layout
    control, AC-122–AC-123, ACG-3
    report, AC-111
    stacked, AC-108, AC-122–AC-123, ACG-6
    tabular, AC-117, AC-122, ACG-6
Layout view, AC-13, ACG-4
    adding fields to forms, AC-108–AC-110
    adding fields to reports, AC-117
    adding groupings to reports, AC-127
    adding totals to reports, AC-129
    applying themes, AC-120
    creating new blank forms, AC-107
    creating new blank reports, AC-116
    disabling, AC-385
    editing reports, AC-115
    formatting controls, AC-118–AC-119
    Remove Layout command, AC-123
    resizing controls, AC-121
Left outer joins, AC-346, AC-347, ACG-4
Less than operator (<), AC-161, AC-222, AC-224
Less than or equal to operator (<=), AC-161
Limit To List check box, AC-79, AC-226, AC-227
Linked Table Manager, AC-387, ACG-4
Linked tables, AC-217–AC-219, ACG-4
List box controls, AC-257–AC-259, ACG-4
Lists
    adding/deleting items on, AC-226
    editing items in, AC-227
    Look In, AC-20
    lookup, AC-73, AC-78–AC-79, AC-259
    Match, AC-20
    modifying items on, AC-227
    Search, AC-20
Literal text, AC-224, ACG-4
Local joins, AC-346–AC-347, ACG-4
Locked files, AC-388, ACG-4
Locked property, AC-255
Logo button (Form Layout Tools Design tab), AC-276
Logos, in headers, AC-124
Long Text data type
    defined, AC-62, ACG-4
    entering custom formats for, AC-222–AC-223
    in previous versions of Access, AC-63

Long Text fields, AC-67
Look In list, AC-20
Lookup fields, ACG-4
    adding, AC-73–AC-79
    entering data in, AC-17
    from lists, AC-78–AC-79
    make table queries with, AC-341
    modifying properties of, AC-226–AC-227
    from other tables, AC-73–AC-77
Lookup lists, AC-73, AC-78–AC-79, AC-259
Lookup Wizard, AC-74–AC-76

m

Macro Builder, AC-358–AC-361
Macros, AC-5, ACG-5
    creating, AC-358–AC-361
    defined, AC-358
    embedded, AC-358, ACG-3
    recording, AC-361
    running, AC-361
    stand-alone, AC-358–AC-361, ACG-6
    viewing code for, AC-262
Make table queries, AC-337, AC-340–AC-341, ACG-5
Margins, AC-132, ACG-5
Match Case check box, AC-20
Match list, AC-20
Mathematical operators, AC-221
Maximum function, AC-72, AC-349
Memo fields, AC-63
Memo Settings button, AC-67
Message Bar, AC-6, ACG-5
Microsoft Access 2013, AC-3
    exporting data from, AC-27–AC-29
    free, run-time version of, AC-388
    keyboard shortcuts in, AC-119, ACA-2–ACA-3
    lawyer on, AC-131
    national sales manager on, AC-308
    non-profit volunteer organizer on, AC-279
    objects in, AC-3–AC-5
    personal trainer on, AC-175
    project manager on, AC-15
    small business owner on, AC-77
    sporting goods store purchasing manager on, AC-219
    Undo command in, AC-23
Microsoft Excel
    importing data from, AC-204–AC-208
    linking tables to files in, AC-218
    recording macros in, AC-361

Microsoft Excel, exporting data to, AC-27–AC-28
Microsoft Outlook, linking tables to files in, AC-218
Microsoft Word
    exporting data to, AC-27–AC-28
    recording macros in, AC-361
Minimum function, AC-72, AC-349
Missing data, AC-172
Modified Date grouping option, AC-11
Modifying; *see also* Changing
    field properties, AC-66–AC-67
    fields and lookup lists, AC-73, AC-78–AC-79
    input masks, AC-225
    local join properties, AC-346–AC-347
    lookup field properties, AC-226–AC-227
    queries, AC-354–AC-357
    query criteria, AC-356
    Size property of text fields, AC-223
    subform properties, AC-271–AC-273
    subform sources, AC-271
    subreport sources, AC-312
    value list items, AC-227
Moving
    controls in reports, AC-122–AC-123
    records via queries, AC-344–AC-345
Multilevel navigation forms, AC-278
Multiple Items forms, AC-102, ACG-5
Multiple page layout, AC-130

n

Named ranges, importing data from, AC-205
Naming
    command button controls, AC-261
    navigation forms, AC-279
    subforms, AC-268, AC-270
    subreports, AC-316
    tables of imported data, AC-207, AC-212
National sales managers, AC-308
Navigating records, AC-14–AC-15, AC-263–AC-265
Navigation buttons, AC-256, AC-262, AC-272–AC-273
Navigation forms
    creating, AC-277–AC-279
    defined, ACG-5
    startup options for, AC-383

Navigation Options dialog, AC-382
Navigation Pane, AC-5, ACG-5
    action queries, AC-337
    Custom category of, AC-382
    customizing, AC-381–AC-382
    default object view, AC-12
    deleting tables and objects, AC-26
    exporting data, AC-28, AC-29
    importing data, AC-208, AC-213, AC-219
    organizing objects, AC-10–AC-11
New blank forms, AC-107
New blank reports, AC-116
New fields, importing data from, AC-216
New records
    preventing addition of, AC-254
    restricting data entry to, AC-253
New tables, queries for creating, AC-340–AC-341
Next Record button, AC-14
9 (placeholder), AC-224
Non-profit volunteer organizers, AC-279
Normalization, AC-377, ACG-5
Not equal to operator (< >), AC-161
Number data type, AC-62, AC-119, ACG-5
Number fields, AC-183, AC-308
Numeric criteria, AC-160–AC-161
Numeric fields, filtering in, AC-180

o

Object dependencies, AC-380, ACG-5
Object Type grouping option, AC-10–AC-11
Objects; *see also specific types*
    adding, to custom groups, AC-381–AC-382
    Compact & Repair tool for, AC-32
    deleting, AC-26
    exporting, to PDF files, AC-29
    in Microsoft Access 2013, AC-3–AC-5
    in Navigation Pane, AC-10–AC-11
    opening and closing, AC-5
    preventing automatic display of, AC-279
    previewing, AC-30–AC-31
    printing, AC-30–AC-31
    renaming, AC-26
    restoring, from backups, AC-34
    saving, AC-53
    switching views of, AC-12–AC-13

OLE Object data type, AC-63, ACG-5
One-to-many relationships, AC-7, AC-8, ACG-5
   and Datasheet subforms, AC-101
   and lookup fields, AC-77, AC-80
Opening
   databases, AC-389
   objects, AC-5
   Relationships window, AC-8
Operators, mathematical, AC-221
OR, in queries, AC-162–AC-165
ORDER BY clause, AC-356, ACG-5
Order By On Load property, AC-252
Orientation, AC-115, AC-132
Outermost sort, AC-182, ACG-5

p

Page footer section, AC-126, AC-274, ACG-5, ACG-6
Page Header section, AC-126, AC-274, AC-313, ACG-5, ACG-6
Page N of M format, AC-126
Page numbers, in reports, AC-126
Page orientation, AC-115, AC-132
Page setup, for reports, AC-132–AC-133
Page Setup tab, AC-133
Parameter queries, AC-176–AC-177, ACG-5
Parameter values, data type and, AC-177
Passwords, database, AC-389–AC-390
Paste command, AC-22, AC-307, ACG-5
PDF (Portable Document Format) files, AC-29, ACG-5
Percent format, AC-64, ACG-5
Performance Analyzer, AC-379, ACG-5
Personal trainers, AC-175
Placeholder characters, AC-224–AC-225, ACG-5
Placeholder labels, AC-250
Plain text, exporting data as, AC-28
POID field, input mask, AC-224
Portable Document Format (PDF) files, AC-29, ACG-5
Portrait orientation, AC-115, AC-132, ACG-5
Pound symbol (#), AC-224
Previewing; *see also* Print Preview view
   objects, AC-30–AC-31
   reports, AC-130
Previous Record button, AC-14

Primary key
   hiding, AC-264
   for imported Excel data, AC-207
   for imported text data, AC-212
   Table Analyzer suggestions of, AC-376
Primary key fields, AC-7, AC-60, ACG-5
Print dialog, AC-31
Print Preview, AC-13, ACG-5
Print Preview view, AC-30, AC-130, AC-132
Printing
   objects, AC-30–AC-31
   Relationship Reports, AC-392
   reports, AC-130–AC-133
Project managers, AC-15
Property Sheet, AC-121
   Control, AC-255, AC-259, ACG-3
   Form, AC-250–AC-252, ACG-4
   Report, AC-299, ACG-6
Purchasing managers, AC-219

q

Queries, AC-4, AC-151–AC-177, AC-336–AC-357, ACG-5
   AND in, AC-162–AC-165
   action, AC-337–AC-345, ACG-2
      creating new tables with, AC-340–AC-341
      deleting records with, AC-342–AC-343
      moving records with, AC-344–AC-345
      types of, AC-337
      updating records with, AC-338–AC-339
   adding
      calculated fields, AC-168–AC-169
      criteria, AC-157–AC-161
      subforms, AC-266–AC-268
      totals, AC-348–AC-350
   aggregate, AC-348–AC-350, ACG-2
   append, AC-337, AC-344–AC-345, ACG-2
   creating, AC-151–AC-156
   crosstab, AC-351–AC-353, ACG-3
   delete, AC-337, AC-342–AC-343, ACG-3
   for duplicate data, AC-173–AC-175
   embedded, AC-251, AC-300, ACG-3
   forms based on, AC-101
   functions of, AC-151

   hiding and showing fields in, AC-167
   make table, AC-337, AC-340–AC-341, ACG-5
   modifying, in SQL view, AC-354–AC-357
   navigating records in, AC-14–AC-15
   numeric and date criteria for, AC-160–AC-161
   OR in, AC-162–AC-165
   parameter, AC-176–AC-177, ACG-5
   reports based on, AC-111
   select, AC-151, AC-337, ACG-6
   setting join properties in, AC-346–AC-347
   and sort order, AC-166, AC-252
   subreports based on, AC-314–AC-316
   summary, AC-348–AC-350, ACG-6
   in Table Analyzer, AC-377
   text criteria for, AC-157–AC-159
   totals, AC-348–AC-350, ACG-6
   for unmatched data, AC-170–AC-172
   update, AC-337–AC-339, ACG-7
   views for, AC-13
Query Design view, AC-346–AC-347
Query grid, AC-154, ACG-5
Question mark (?), AC-21, AC-158, AC-224
Quick Print command, AC-31
Quick Start application parts, AC-202–AC-203, ACG-5
Quick Start field types, AC-56, ACG-5

r

Record source
   defined, AC-101, ACG-5
   selection of, AC-107, AC-116
   setting, AC-250, AC-299
Record validation rules, AC-230–AC-231, ACG-5
Records
   adding, by importing data, AC-214–AC-216
   creating new, AC-16–AC-19
   defined, AC-3, ACG-5
   deleting, AC-24, AC-342–AC-343
   grouping of, AC-127–AC-128
   moving, AC-344–AC-345
   navigating, AC-14–AC-15
   preventing addition/deletion of, AC-254

preventing changes to, AC-254
restricting data entry to, AC-253
sorting, AC-182–AC-183
updating, AC-338–AC-339
Redo command, AC-23, ACG-5
Referential integrity, AC-80, ACG-5–ACG-6
Relational databases, AC-3, ACG-6
Relationship Reports, AC-392, ACG-6
Relationships
of forms and subforms, AC-267, AC-270
of reports and subreports, AC-311, AC-315
of tables
creating, AC-80–AC-81
and delete queries, AC-343
enforcing updates and deletions in, AC-232–AC-233
establishing, AC-202
and fields from unrelated tables, AC-106
and join properties, AC-347
and lookup lists, AC-77
Table Analyzer's recognition of, AC-378
in templates, AC-199
understanding and viewing, AC-7–AC-9
Relationships Window, AC-7–AC-9, AC-392, ACG-6
Remove Layout command, AC-123
Removing
database passwords, AC-390
excess space in reports, AC-132–AC-133
filters, AC-179
images from Image Gallery, AC-276
rows/columns from control layout, AC-123
Renaming
fields, AC-54
objects, AC-26
Repeated data, AC-52
Repeated values, AC-309
Replacing
data, AC-20–AC-21
databases, AC-34
text values, AC-338
Report button, AC-111
Report Detail section, AC-301, AC-304, ACG-6
Report Footer section
adding page numbers in, AC-126
calculated controls in, AC-129, AC-305
defined, ACG-6
displaying, AC-301–AC-302

Report header, AC-124–AC-125
Report Header section
adding page numbers in, AC-126
calculated controls in, AC-305
defined, ACG-6
displaying, AC-301–AC-302
Report Layout Tools Format tab, AC-118
Report Page Footer section, AC-301, ACG-6
Report Page Header section, AC-301, ACG-6
Report Property Sheet, AC-299, ACG-6
Report view, AC-12, ACG-6
Report Wizard, AC-112–AC-115, ACG-6
Reports, AC-4–AC-5, AC-111–AC-133, AC-298–AC-319
adding
design elements to headers, AC-124–AC-125
fields, AC-117
grouping, AC-127–AC-128, AC-306
page numbers, AC-126
subreports, AC-310–AC-312, AC-314–AC-316
totals, AC-129
applying
conditional formatting, AC-317–AC-319
themes, AC-120
attachments in, AC-71
calculated fields in, AC-169
controls in, AC-303–AC-305
adding calculated controls, AC-304–AC-305
arranging controls, AC-122–AC-123, AC-303
controlling page setup, AC-132–AC-133
formatting controls, AC-118–AC-119
moving controls, AC-122–AC-123
resizing controls, AC-121
creating, AC-111–AC-116
custom text field formats in, AC-223
defined, ACG-6
in Design view, AC-299–AC-300
grouping in, AC-306–AC-308
adding grouping, AC-127–AC-128, AC-306
using group headers and footers, AC-307–AC-308

hiding repeated values in, AC-309
previewing, AC-130
printing, AC-130–AC-133
sections of, AC-301–AC-302
subreports, AC-310–AC-316
adding, AC-310–AC-312, AC-314–AC-316
based on reports, AC-310–AC-312
based on tables/queries, AC-314–AC-316
displaying page headers of, AC-313
views for, AC-12, AC-13
Resizing controls, for reports, AC-121
Restoring objects from backups, AC-34
Restrict Delete radio button, AC-76
Ribbon tabs, hiding, AC-385
Rich Text Format (RTF), AC-27, ACG-6
Rich Text Formatting property, AC-67
Right-click menu, Cut and Copy commands in, AC-22
Right outer joins, AC-346, ACG-6
Row level locking, AC-390
Row selector, changing tab order with, AC-280
Rows
in control layout, AC-123
Total, AC-72, ACG-6
RTF (Rich Text Format), AC-27, ACG-6

S

Saved Exports button, AC-28
Saving
data in Access, AC-19
database backups, AC-33–AC-34
import steps, AC-207, AC-212, AC-215–AC-216
locked ACCDE files, AC-388
objects, AC-53
tables, AC-53
Scroll bars, AC-256
Search list, AC-20
Searching for data, AC-20–AC-21
Sections, report, AC-301–AC-302
Security warnings, AC-6
SELECT clause, AC-354, ACG-6
Select queries, AC-151, AC-337, ACG-6
SELECT statements, AC-354–AC-356, ACG-6
Selection button, AC-180, AC-181
Setting primary key field, AC-60

Short Text data type
  defined, AC-62, ACG-6
  entering custom formats for, AC-222–AC-223
  in previous versions of Access, AC-63
Short Text fields, AC-67, AC-69, AC-308
Show Table dialog, AC-9
Showing fields, in queries, AC-167
Shutter Bar Open/Close button, AC-5
Simple Query Wizard, AC-151–AC-153
Single Record forms, AC-101, ACG-6
Size property, modifying, AC-223
Small business owners, AC-77
Smart Tags, AC-133
Sort
  innermost, AC-182, ACG-4
  order of, AC-166, AC-252
  outermost, AC-182, ACG-5
Sort feature, AC-182–AC-183
Sorting records
  in datasheets, AC-182–AC-183
  and ORDER BY clause, AC-356
Spelling command, AC-25
Spelling dialog, AC-25
Split forms, AC-103, ACG-6
Splitting databases, AC-386–AC-387
Sporting goods store purchasing managers, AC-219
Spreadsheet programs, exporting data to, AC-28
SQL (Structured Query Language), AC-354, ACG-6
SQL view, AC-13, AC-354–AC-357, ACG-6
Stacked layout, AC-108, AC-122–AC-123, ACG-6
Stand-alone macros, AC-358–AC-361, ACG-6
Standard Deviation function, AC-72
Start page, templates on, AC-199
Startup options, database, AC-383–AC-384
Status bar, switching views with, AC-12
Storing table data, AC-51–AC-52
Structured Query Language (SQL), AC-354, ACG-6
Subform control borders, AC-273
SubForm Wizard, AC-266–AC-271
Subforms, AC-266–AC-273
  adding subforms based on forms, AC-269–AC-271
  adding subforms based on tables/queries, AC-266–AC-268
  automatic insertion of, AC-101
  creating, AC-104
  defined, AC-104, AC-266, ACG-6
  modifying properties of, AC-272–AC-273
SubReport Wizard, AC-310–AC-311, AC-314–AC-316
Subreports, AC-310–AC-316
  adding, AC-310–AC-312, AC-314–AC-316
  based on reports, AC-310–AC-312
  based on tables/queries, AC-314–AC-316
  defined, ACG-6
  displaying page headers of, AC-313
  properties of, AC-312
Suggestions, Table Analyzer, AC-376–AC-378
Sum function, AC-72, AC-349
Summary queries, AC-348–AC-350, ACG-6
Switching views, AC-12–AC-13

T

Tab key, AC-19
Tab order, AC-280, ACG-6
Table Analyzer, AC-375–AC-378, ACG-6
Table Tools Fields tab, AC-55
Tables, AC-50–AC-81, AC-196–AC-233
  adding
    calculated fields, AC-220–AC-221
    fields, AC-55–AC-56, AC-59
    lookup fields, AC-73–AC-79
    records by importing data, AC-214–AC-216
    to Relationship window, AC-8–AC-9
    subforms, AC-266–AC-268
    Total rows, AC-72
  adjusting column widths, AC-57
  applying input masks, AC-68–AC-69
  Attachment fields, AC-70–AC-71
  attachments in, AC-71
  changing data types, AC-62–AC-63
  combining fields from unrelated, AC-106
  creating, AC-53, AC-58
    custom field text formats, AC-222–AC-223
    custom input masks, AC-224–AC-225
    desktop databases, AC-197–AC-199
    field validation rules, AC-228–AC-229
    new blank databases, AC-200–AC-201
    new records, AC-16–AC-17
    record validation rules, AC-230–AC-231
  Cut, Copy, and Paste commands in, AC-22
  in Datasheet view, AC-53–AC-55
  defined, AC-3, ACG-6
  deleting, AC-26
  deleting fields, AC-61
  in Design view, AC-58–AC-59
  designing, AC-51–AC-52
  enforcing relationship updates and deletions in, AC-232–AC-233
  formatting fields, AC-64–AC-65
  forms based on, AC-101
  importing data into, AC-204–AC-213
  linked, AC-217–AC-219, ACG-4
  modifying
    field properties, AC-66–AC-67
    lookup field properties, AC-226–AC-227
  navigating records in, AC-14–AC-15
  Quick Start application parts, AC-202–AC-203
  Quick Start field types, AC-56
  relationships between
    creating, AC-80–AC-81
    and delete queries, AC-343
    enforcing updates and deletions in, AC-232–AC-233
    establishing, AC-202
    and fields from unrelated tables, AC-106
    and join properties, AC-347
    and lookup lists, AC-77
    Table Analyzer's recognition of, AC-378
    in templates, AC-199
    understanding and viewing, AC-7–AC-9
  renaming fields, AC-54
  reports based on, AC-111
  saving, AC-53
  setting primary key field, AC-60
  subreports based on, AC-314–AC-316
  views for, AC-12, AC-13
Tables and Related Views category, AC-10
Tabs, forms with, AC-277–AC-280

Tabular layout, AC-117, AC-122, ACG-6
Tasks (application part), AC-202
Templates
    creating desktop databases from, AC-197–AC-199
    defined, AC-197, ACG-6
Testing
    of field validation rules, AC-229
    of record validation rules, AC-231
Text
    field validation rules for, AC-229
    literal, AC-224, ACG-4
Text box controls, AC-108, ACG-6
Text criteria, AC-157–AC-159
Text fields, AC-221–AC-223
    creating custom formats for, AC-222–AC-223
    defined, AC-63
    filtering in, AC-180
    modifying Size property of, AC-223
    sorting options with, AC-183
Text files, importing data from, AC-209–AC-213
Theme colors, AC-120, ACG-6
Theme fonts, AC-120, ACG-6
Themes, AC-120, ACG-6
Time, in headers, AC-125
Titles, AC-124, AC-383
Total rows, AC-72, ACG-6
Totals
    adding, to queries, AC-348–AC-350
    group, AC-307
    for groups, AC-308
    in reports, AC-129
Totals queries, AC-348–AC-350, ACG-6
Trust Center, AC-6
Typographical errors, AC-377

U

Unbound controls, AC-108, AC-305, ACG-7
Undo command, AC-23, ACG-7
Unmatched data, AC-170–AC-172
Update queries, AC-337–AC-339, ACG-7
Updating
    object dependencies, AC-380
    records via queries, AC-338–AC-339
    table relationships, AC-232–AC-233

User interface elements, disabling, AC-256
Users (application part), AC-202

V

Validation Rule property, AC-228, AC-229, ACG-7
Validation Text property, AC-228, AC-229, ACG-7
Variance function, AC-72
Vertical scroll bars, AC-256
Viewing relationships between tables, AC-80
Views
    Backstage, AC-131, AC-201
    Datasheet, AC-53–AC-55, AC-220–AC-221, ACG-3
        adding calculated fields, AC-220–AC-221
        adding fields, AC-55, AC-70, AC-73
        adding validation messages, AC-229, AC-231
        adding validation rules, AC-229, AC-231
        adjusting column width, AC-57
        changing data types, AC-62–AC-63
        changing Format field property, AC-64
        creating and saving tables, AC-53
        as default view, AC-12
        deleting fields, AC-61
        deleting records, AC-24
        hiding/showing fields of queries, AC-167
        modifying Default Value property, AC-66
        modifying Field Size property, AC-67
        renaming fields, AC-54
        switching Design and, AC-156
        Undo command in, AC-23
    Design, AC-12, AC-221, ACG-3
        adding calculated controls, AC-305
        adding calculated fields, AC-221
        adding combo box controls, AC-265
        adding command button controls, AC-260–AC-262
        adding field validation rules, AC-228–AC-229
        adding fields to forms in, AC-110

        adding groupings for reports, AC-127
        adding image controls, AC-275
        adding list box controls, AC-257–AC-259
        adding lookup fields, AC-73
        adding totals in reports, AC-129
        aligning controls, AC-303
        applying input masks, AC-68–AC-69
        AutoFilter vs., AC-179
        changing data types, AC-63
        changing Format field property, AC-65
        creating new blank forms, AC-107
        creating new blank reports, AC-116
        creating queries, AC-154–AC-156, AC-353
        creating tables, AC-58
        custom field text formats, AC-222–AC-223
        date and time, AC-125
        deleting fields, AC-61
        disabling user interface elements, AC-256
        displaying Report Header/Footer sections, AC-301–AC-302
        forms in, AC-250–AC-251
        hiding repeated values, AC-309
        inserting fields, AC-59
        modifying Default Value property, AC-66
        modifying Field Size property, AC-67
        removing controls from layout, AC-123
        removing excess space in reports, AC-132
        reports in, AC-299–AC-300
        resizing controls, AC-121
        setting primary key in, AC-60
        setting sort order, AC-252
        switching to Datasheet view from, AC-156
    Form, AC-12, AC-23, ACG-4
    Layout, AC-13, AC-385, ACG-4
        adding fields to forms in, AC-108–AC-110
        adding fields to reports in, AC-117
        adding groupings to reports in, AC-127
        adding totals to reports in, AC-129
        applying themes in, AC-120

Views—*Cont.*
    creating new blank form in, AC-107
    creating new blank report in, AC-116
    editing reports in, AC-115
    formatting controls in, AC-118–AC-119
    Remove Layout command, AC-123
    resizing controls in, AC-121
limiting, AC-385
Print Preview, AC-30, AC-130, AC-132
Query Design, AC-346–AC-347
Report, AC-12, ACG-6

SQL, AC-13, AC-354–AC-357, ACG-6
switching, AC-12–AC-13

W

Warnings
    blank page, AC-130, AC-132–AC-133
    imported data, AC-208, AC-213
    security, AC-6
Web apps, Access, AC-197, ACG-2
WHERE clause, AC-355–AC-356, ACG-7
Width
    column, AC-57, AC-226
    field, AC-57

subform, AC-270
subreport, AC-311
Wildcards, AC-21, ACG-7
    in query criteria, AC-158
    in text strings, AC-159
Worksheets, importing data from, AC-205

Y

Yes/No data type, AC-62–AC-63, ACG-7
Yes/No fields, AC-183

Z

0 (placeholder), AC-224

photo credits

Page OF–1: © Burazin/Photographer's Choice/Getty
Page OF–14: Stockbytey/Getty Images

Page AC–1: © Burazin/Photographer's Choice/Getty
Page AC–15: © Jose Luis Pelaez, Inc./Blend Images/Corbis
Page AC–77: Rubberball/Getty Images
Page AC–131: © Blend Images/Alamy

Page AC–175: Rubberball Productions
Page AC–219: © Stockbyte/Punchstock
Page AC–279: © Ryan McVay/Getty Images
Page AC–308: © Ryan McVay/Getty Images
Page AC–357: © Lane Oatey/Getty Images

Cover image: © Burazin/Photographer's Choice/Getty